Fodor's

BRAZIL

WELCOME TO BRAZIL

Whether you go during Carnival or not, Brazil is always a party. You can tan and mingle with the locals on the country's seemingly endless beaches, from Rio's glamorous Ipanema to the unspoiled treasures along the northeastern shores. In the vast interior, outdoor adventures thrill: take a spray-soaked boat ride into Iguaçu's raging waterfalls or spot exotic wildlife in the Pantanal. On rugged treks through the Amazon rain forest or on shopping expeditions in São Paulo's chic boutiques, you will plunge into a vibrant mix of colors, rhythms, and cultures.

TOP REASONS TO GO

★ **Cool Cities:** Brasília, Rio de Janeiro, São Paulo, Salvador, to name just a few.

★ **Beaches:** Glitzy or secluded, there's a strand here to suit every taste.

★ **Amazon Excursions:** Jungle lodges and river tours entice with adventures aplenty.

★ **Soccer:** Chanting with the fans at an iconic stadium is a truly memorable experience.

★ **Architecture:** From Salvador's baroque gems to Brasília's modernism, Brazil dazzles.

★ **Brazilian Beats:** Samba, bossa nova, and forró rhythms pulse through the country.

12
TOP EXPERIENCES

Brazil offers terrific experiences that should be on every traveler's list. Here are Fodor's top picks for a memorable trip.

1 Postcard-Perfect Beaches

Slip into your beachwear for a day of sunbathing and people-watching on Brazil's most beautiful beaches, including Copacabana (above), Ipanema, and Búzios. *(Ch. 2, 3, 5, 9, 10)*

2 Carnival

Brazilians can throw a party like no one else, and Carnival is the biggest party of the year—a raucous bacchanal of music, drink, and flesh. *(Ch. 2, 9)*

3 Brasília's Architecture

Built from scratch in less than five years in the late 1950s, Brasília, the country's planned capital, is an architecture buff's dream. *(Ch. 8)*

4 Brazilian Beats

Music is woven into the fabric of Brazilian life, and no trip here is complete without catching a live show, whether samba, bossa nova, axé, or forró. *(Ch. 1)*

5 Brazilian Wildlife

The biodiversity in Brazil is astonishing. With any luck, you'll spot capybaras and anteaters in the Pantanal, and toucans and pink dolphins in the Amazon. *(Ch. 8, 11)*

6 Food and Drink

From black bean stews to Amazonian fish dishes, Brazil's cuisines will delight your taste buds. Start your meal with a caipirinha, the national cocktail. *(Ch. 1)*

7 Iguaçu Falls

Iguaçu's raging, jungle-fringed waterfalls will leave you speechless, especially on a spray-soaked boat tour. *(Ch. 6)*

8 Christ the Redeemer

Don't leave Rio without making a trip to the statue of Christ the Redeemer, arms outstretched to embrace the city from its perch on Corcovado Mountain. *(Ch. 2)*

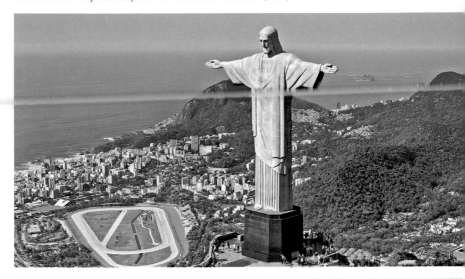

9 Ouro Preto

This former gold-rush town is nestled in the Minas Gerais mountains, with cobblestoned streets and red-roofed buildings that climb the hills. *(Ch. 7)*

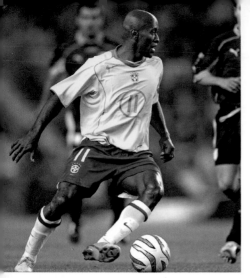

10 Soccer Matches

Soccer is a national passion and an art form in Brazil. It's a blast to sit among thousands of cheering, chanting fans in one of the country's iconic stadiums. *(Ch. 1)*

11 São Paulo Nightlife

São Paulo's nightlife options are seemingly endless, and the numerous bars and nightclubs prove worthy venues for even the feistiest nighthawk. *(Ch. 4)*

12 Jungle Lodges

There's no better way to explore the Amazon rain forest than by staying right in the middle of it in an all-inclusive riverside lodge. *(Ch. 11)*

CONTENTS

CONTENTS

MAPS

ABOUT THIS GUIDE

Fodor's Recommendations

Everything in this guide is worth doing—we don't cover what isn't—but exceptional sights, hotels, and restaurants are recognized with additional accolades. Fodor's Choice★ indicates our top recommendations. Care to nominate a new place? Visit Fodors.com/contact-us.

Trip Costs

We list prices wherever possible to help you budget well. Hotel and restaurant price categories from $ to $$$$ are noted alongside each recommendation. For hotels, we include the lowest cost of a standard double room in high season. For restaurants, we cite the average price of a main course at dinner or, if dinner isn't served, at lunch. For attractions, we always list adult admission fees; discounts are usually available for children, students, and senior citizens.

Hotels

Our local writers vet every hotel to recommend the best overnights in each price category, from budget to expensive. Unless otherwise specified, you can expect private bath, phone, and TV in your room. For expanded hotel reviews, facilities, and deals, visit Fodors.com.

Top Picks		Hotels &
★ Fodor's Choice		**Restaurants**
		🏨 Hotel
Listings		↪ Number of
✉ Address		rooms
🏠 Branch address		🍴 Meal plans
☎ Telephone		✕ Restaurant
🖷 Fax		⚓ Reservations
⊕ Website		👔 Dress code
✉ E-mail		▭ No credit cards
🎫 Admission fee		$ Price
🕓 Open/closed		
times		**Other**
Ⓜ Subway		⇨ See also
⊹ Directions or		☞ Take note
Map coordinates		🏌 Golf facilities

Restaurants

Unless we state otherwise, restaurants are open for lunch and dinner daily. We mention dress code only when there's a specific requirement and reservations only when they're essential or not accepted. To make restaurant reservations, visit Fodors.com.

Credit Cards

The hotels and restaurants in this guide typically accept credit cards. If not, we'll say so.

EUGENE FODOR

Hungarian-born Eugene Fodor (1905–91) began his travel career as an interpreter on a French cruise ship. The experience inspired him to write *On the Continent* (1936), the first guidebook to receive annual updates and discuss a country's way of life as well as its sights. Fodor later joined the U.S. Army and worked for the OSS in World War II. After the war, he kept up his intelligence work while expanding his guidebook series. During the Cold War, many guides were written by fellow agents who understood the value of insider information. Today's guides continue Fodor's legacy by providing travelers with timely coverage, insider tips, and cultural context.

EXPERIENCE
BRAZIL

BRAZIL TODAY

Brazil is immensely diverse—socially, culturally, racially, economically—and rife with profound contradictions that are not always evident at first. All this makes for a complex nation that eludes easy definitions—but is fascinating to discover.

Culture

Brazil's contrasts are everywhere. Take a look around when you land. Dense forests that are home to pint-sized monkeys and birds found nowhere else brush up against gleaming high-rises, which in turn border *favelas* (shantytowns). Juxtapositions of this sort can make any experience breathtaking and shocking at once.

Brazilians are known for their warmth, their tiny bikinis, their frequent public displays of affection—it's not uncommon to see couples kissing at length on a park bench or a beach blanket—and their riotous displays of joie de vivre in annual Carnival celebrations. But the country is also home to the world's largest Catholic population, and conservative sexual mores shape the culture more than visitors might imagine.

A stroll through any Brazilian town will show you this is one of the most racially mixed populations anywhere. The country was shaped not only by the Portuguese, who brought their religion and language, but also by millions of enslaved Africans, the native indigenous, and waves of European, Arabic, and Japanese immigrants. Most Brazilians include elements from several of these backgrounds in their cultural and ethnic heritage.

Brazil never had the institutionalized discrimination that marked the United States, yet it is far from being a color-blind society. In spite of the recent economic boom, blacks and the indigenous still face stiff discrimination and underrepresentation in government. They also far outweigh whites at the broad base of Brazil's economic pyramid.

Politics

Brazil's current president, Dilma Rouseff, is an example of how Brazil defies stereotypes. The fact that she is a woman—and twice divorced at that, currently living without a husband—was scarcely discussed during her 2010 and 2014 campaigns for president, even though this is a country were *machismo* (male chauvinism) still thrives.

Of far greater importance to voters during her first presidential campaign was that she is a member of the Partido dos Trabalhadores (PT) or Workers Party, and had the support of the immensely popular outgoing president, Luiz Inácio Lula da Silva, who had towered over the political landscape for the previous decade. Lula's story is fascinating. Born into poverty in the country's Northeast, he rose to prominence in São Paulo as a union leader while the country was still under the rule of a military dictatorship that had seized power in 1964. Buoyed by his charisma and his appeal to poor Brazilians, Lula was elected to the presidency twice. His popularity played a large part in securing victory for Rousseff in her initial election campaign.

During Rousseff's first term, the country slipped into recession, and many took to the streets to demand better public services. Rousseff has divided the country by keeping in place transfer-of-wealth policies that have helped alleviate poverty, but which many wealthier Brazilians see as spoon-feeding the poor in return for votes. She is widely popular in the North and Northeast, but has less support in São Paulo and the South.

Economy

After punishing years of economic instability and hyperinflation in the 1980s and '90s, Brazil's GDP began to grow along with prices and demand for the commodities that make up the base of its economy, including soybeans, sugar, iron ore, and oil.

The last decade of social progress has created real improvement in the quality of life for Brazil's new middle class. About 35 million Brazilians have hoisted themselves out of poverty in that time. More than half of the country's 194 million people now officially belong to the middle class. However, many still hover perilously close to the bottom, and many more live in neighborhoods that still don't have such services as trash collection, sewage treatment, and safety. Even though the improvements have been real and visible, there have been increasing protests recently over issues such as public health care and education.

Religion

Brazil has the world's largest Catholic population, although Roman Catholicism has been losing worshippers to Evangelical churches. These churches are booming, especially in poorer communities where it is not uncommon to see several modest storefront churches on a single street.

In religion, like in so many other aspects of Brazil, the reality is more complex than it first appears. The country's rich ethnic and cultural heritage means that the dominant Christianity is often blended with other sects and religions, creating fascinating local variants that are unique to Brazil.

The most widespread examples of this blending happen within Afro-Brazilian religious practices. Forbidden from worshipping the deities they brought with them from Africa, enslaved men and women established connections between their *orixas*, or gods, and saints from the Catholic faith of their masters. This way, they could pay homage to their own gods while keeping up appearances by seeming to pray to Catholic saints.

While freedom of religion is enshrined in the Constitution, Brazil's many contradictions surface in attitudes toward Afro-Brazilian faiths such as Candomble, the more orthodox of the variations, and Umbanda, an even more syncretic religion incorporating elements of French-based spiritualism. Although some Afro-Brazilian practices are popular, including wearing white on New Year's Eve and leaving gifts of flowers and fruit on the beach to honor Iemanja, the orixa of oceans and seas, serious practitioners can be frequent targets of discrimination.

Sports

Even before the 2014 FIFA World Cup, the world knew that soccer—or *futebol*—was king here. The country's mad about it, and there's good reason: Brazil has produced some of the world's best players, and it is the only nation to have won five World Cups. The displays of passion seen during major games make them worthy of a visit. Although there is criticism over the way soccer is run, love for the "jogo bonito," or beautiful game, is unabated.

Volleyball is also a favorite. Beaches are often settings for spectacular displays of beach volleyball, and of a Brazilian combination of the two: *futevolei*, where the players can use only their feet, chest, and head to touch the volleyball.

WHAT'S WHERE

The following numbers refer to chapters.

2 Rio de Janeiro. This verdant city cascades down dramatic mountains and out to beaches that line the metropolitan area. The breathtaking landscapes are glorious in all seasons.

3 Side trips from Rio. Inland from Rio de Janeiro are several historical towns in refreshing mountainous settings along with quieter beach destinations.

4 São Paulo. This huge metropolis is lined with skyscrapers and buzzes with fast-paced urban life. It also has some of the country's best restaurants, boutiques, theaters, and museums.

5 Side Trips from São Paulo. São Paulo's heartland includes mountainous regions with charming resort towns, and beautiful beaches that offer a range of water sports.

6 The South. The three southernmost states include charming European architecture, a subdued pace of life, and the mighty rushing waterfalls of Foz do Iguaçu.

7 Minas Gerais. This inland state is dotted with picturesque gold and mineral-spa towns all within a short drive of one another.

1

Cayenne
50°W
Macapá
Belém
São Luís
Caxias
Teresina
Maraba
BRAZIL
SERRA GERAL DO GOIAS
Alvorada
Barreiras
SERRA DO ESPINHAÇO
8
BRASÍLIA
Goiania
Uberlandia
BRAZILIAN HIGHLANDS
7
Belo Horizonte
SERRA DO MAR
Campinas
Sorocaba
Ponta Grossa
4
5 São Paulo
Curitiba
Florianopolis
Caxias do Sul
Porto Alegre
Pelotas
URUGUAY

40°W
Equator   0°
Fortaleza
Natal
10
Recife
Petrolina
Maceio
10°S
Feira de Santana
9
Salvador
Vitoria da Conquista
Montes Claros
20°S
Vila Velha
2
Rio de Janeiro
3
ATLANTIC OCEAN
30°S

8 **Brasília and the West.** Built from scratch in five years, Brasília has become a global model of urbanism. Farther west, the Pantanal is an untamable mosaic of swamp and forest teeming with wildlife.

9 **Salvador and the Bahia Coast.** The epicenter of Afro-Brazilian culture, Salvador teems with life, history, and flavor. Along Bahia's southern coast are some of Brazil's most beautiful beaches.

10 **The Northeast.** On Brazil's curvaceous Northeast coast are gorgeous colonial cities and beaches lapped by warm waters and cooling breezes.

11 **The Amazon.** Flowing for more than 4,000 miles, the gargantuan Amazon River is banked by a rain forest that houses the greatest variety of life on Earth.

NEED TO KNOW

BRAZIL

Brasília ✪

Atlantic Ocean

AT A GLANCE

Capital: Brasília

Population: 202,656,788

Currency: Real

Money: ATMs are common. Credit cards are accepted in big cities; carry cash for gas stations and rural areas.

Language: Portuguese

Country Code: 55

Emergencies: Police: 190; Ambulance: 192; Fire: 193.

Driving: On the right

Electricity: The current in Brazil isn't regulated, so it differs across the country.

Time: Brazil has 4 time zones, from 1 hour behind to 2 hours ahead of New York.

Documents: Tourist visas are valid for 90 days and must be obtained in advance from your local consulate.

WEBSITES

Visit Brazil (Brazilian Tourism Department): ⊕ www.visitbrasil.com

Brazil-Help: ⊕ www.brazil-help.com

GETTING AROUND

✈ **Air Travel:** The Guarulhos Airport in São Paulo is Brazil's busiest, followed by Galeão Airport in Rio and Brasília's Presidente Juscelino Kubitschek Airport.

🚌 **Bus Travel:** Brazil's *ônibus* (bus) network is affordable, comprehensive, and efficient. Every major city can be reached by bus, as can most small to medium-size communities.

🚗 **Car Travel:** Traveling by car is recommended if you're not pressed for time and you enjoy driving even in places you do not know well. It's also reasonably safe in most areas, especially if you avoid driving at night.

PLAN YOUR BUDGET

	HOTEL ROOM	MEAL	ATTRACTIONS
Low Budget	R$ 200	R$ 20	Imperial Museum ticket, R$8
Mid Budget	R$ 375	R$ 40	Christ the Redeemer statue, R$43
High Budget	R$ 500	R$ 60	Samba dinner show, R$330

WAYS TO SAVE

Stay in Pousadas. Cheaper than hotels, but with more privacy than hostels, *pousadas* are simple inns, often in historic houses. Some have cooking facilities.

Eat like a local. Choose eateries aimed at locals. Meals often consist simply of *feijão preto* (black beans) and *arroz* (rice) served with beef, chicken, or fish.

Take the bus. The cheapest way to get around the country is by bus. The quality of bus service is excellent and tickets are affordable and easy to purchase.

Focus on the free. Many of Brazil's attractions don't cost a single real. Churches, parks, libraries, and many of the museums in both Rio and São Paulo are free.

PLAN YOUR TIME

Hassle Factor	High. Brazil has good transportation, but it's a big country, so expect to travel long distances. U.S. citizens must obtain visas ahead of time through an arduous process.
3 days	Explore Rio de Janeiro, saving time for a side trip out to the hillside imperial city of Petrópolis, a short drive or bus ride from the city.
1 week	In seven days you'll have just enough time to get a taste for Rio de Janeiro and São Paulo, with a short jaunt to Iguaçu Falls.
2 weeks	If you're willing to do a bit of domestic air travel, you can check out the highlights of Rio, São Paulo, and Brasília, and still have time to visit the Amazon, Iguaçu Falls, and a few of the country's famous beaches.

WHEN TO GO

High Season: Mid-December through Carnival (February or early March) is when Brazil sees the most tourism; this time of year is not only the most festive, but also the warmest—expect crowds at popular beach resorts. Winter vacation is in July, and a lot of Brazilians use this month to take family holidays.

Low Season: March–April see fewer tourists than other times of year, partially because of the higher possibility of rain. November and the first half of December also tend to be less crowded.

Value Season: If you're looking for a bargain, stick to May–June and August–October. Rio and beach resorts, especially in the Northeast, sizzle with heat November–April, but in Rio the temperature can drop to uncomfortable levels for swimming June–August.

BIG EVENTS

February–March: Carnival is Brazil's best-known festival, and is fêted across the country with street parties and parades. The biggest celebration is in Rio.

June: John the Baptist is honored with parties and fanfare at Festa Junina (June Fest).

June: Two teams compete through performance-based storytelling about an ox at the Parintins Folklore Festival, the second-largest festival in the country.

October: Independent films from around the planet are showcased at the annual São Paulo International Film Festival. ⊕ www.37.mostra.org/en

READ THIS

■ *A Death in Brazil,* Peter Robb. A modern travelogue exploring Brazil through history, culture, and a good dose of personal anecdote.

■ *Futebol Nation* David Goldblatt. A look at Brazil's love of the "beautiful game" and how soccer shaped the nation.

■ *Running the Amazon,* Joe Kane. The story of the first group to travel the length of the Amazon.

WATCH THIS

■ *Favela Rising.* A documentary on life in a Brazilian slum.

■ *Elite Squad* Hit film based on the operations of Brazil's highly trained "Elite Squad" police unit.

■ *Black Orpheus.* A 1959 retelling of the Orpheus and Eurydice myth, set in a Rio *favela* (slum).

EAT THIS

■ *Pão de queijo*: Savory rolls of manioc flour and cheese, oven-baked.

■ *Açaí berry*: This tart berry is native to the Amazon.

■ *Feijoada*: A stew of beans, beef, and pork.

■ *Moqueca de Camarão*: Shrimp stew simmered in richly spiced coconut milk.

■ *Farofa*: A toasted cassava flour mixture.

FLAVORS OF BRAZIL

Food, for Brazilians, is a social affair—portions are often heaping and, rather than coming individually on one plate, arrive in a series of platters meant to be shared among diners.

Meat and Carbs

Perhaps the most well-known Brazilian staple is meat, especially those that come from *churrascarias* (grills): sizzling cuts of beef, some lined generously with fat, served on skewers by men in aprons and boots called *gaúchos*. (The name refers to the southern state of Rio Grande do Sul, with which the style is associated, though churrascarias are found throughout Brazil.) Brazilians also love their carbs. White rice is served with virtually every meal, often alongside potato fries or *aipim* (cassava), which is usually served fried or baked in butter.

Churrascarias also serve up sausages (*linguiça*), chicken (*frango*), and various types of fish. Expect little in the way of spice—just salt and garlic. The natural flavors of the meat are meant to carry the meal. In a rodízio-style churrascaria, you get all the meat and side dishes you can eat at a fixed price. *Rodízio* means "going around," which explains the *gaúchos* who constantly circle the restaurant, only resting their skewers to slice another strip of meat onto your plate.

Feijoada, black beans stewed with fatty pork parts, is a popular party food synonymous with carefree weekend afternoons spent digesting the heavy dish. The dish is often topped with *farofa* (toasted manioc root) and served with *couve* (collard greens) and rice. The dish is traditionally served with orange slices, which are said to aid digestion and stop cholesterol levels from soaring.

Native Fruits and Vegetables

Beyond the meat-and-carbs crowd-pleasers, Brazil's tropical expanse allows for a diversity of fruits and vegetables. Visitors will find these on display in colorful *feiras* (fresh food fairs) throughout the country. Tropical fruits include *maracujá* (passion fruit), *abacaxi* (pineapple), *mamão* (papaya), *caqui* (persimmon), and *acerola* a sour berry with vitamin C levels that are said to be 100 times higher than the orange. When in season, Brazilian fruits crop up as alternatives to lime in *caipirinhas*, Brazil's national drink made with *cachaça*, a sugarcane-based liquor.

Visitors should make a point to sample some of the unique flavors of the Amazon, such as *cupuaçú*, a fragrant yellow fruit, or *mangaba*, something of a cross between a honeydew and a durian. At *lanchonetes*, no-frills snack bars that consist of metal chairs lined along a bar, you'll often find bowls of a purple, sorbet-style concoction made with açaí, a purple Amazonian berry that is touted for its health benefits. For an extra energy boost, they may be mixed with *guaraná*, an energy-packed red berry.

Bahian Specialties

Bahian food from Brazil's Northeast revolves around seafood and is normally spicy and hot. Specialties include *moqueca*, a seafood stew cooked quickly in a clay pot over a high flame, and *acarajé*, a bean-meal patty deep-fried in *dendê* oil and filled with sun-dried shrimp and hot-pepper sauce. Brazilians from around the country lick their chops at the mention of *pirão de peixe*, a thick blended stew often made with fish heads and manioc flour.

BEACHGOING IN BRAZIL

Close your eyes, say the word "Brazil," and one of the first images to float up in your mind most likely will be of a tropical beach: white sands, azure water, and a fringe of palm trees. There's good reason for that. The country boasts 8,000 kilometers (5,000 miles) of coastline, and most of the population is concentrated along the coast, where the ocean's moderating influence tempers the tropical sun.

Beaches are often the center of social life, and there is one to suit every taste: kitsch paradises where you can sip juice cocktails under brightly colored umbrellas, chichi playgrounds for the rich, windswept gems, hard-to-reach fishing villages, and surfer havens with pounding waves.

In short, beaches are places to tan, strut, eat, drink, play sports, catch up with friends, and chat with strangers. Beaches are also worth a visit for people-watching and experiencing this quintessential aspect of Brazilian culture.

What to Expect

Brazilians are well known for being comfortable wearing very little. This goes for all ages and body types. Men often wear *sungas,* Speedo-style swimming trunks, though they avoid high-cut models that show too much leg. In recent years, the popular *sungao,* a wider model, has taken over as the outfit of choice. Surfers wear board shorts, and these are acceptable on and off the beach.

Women generally wear two-piece bathing suits, although stylish one-pieces have increasingly become a part of Brazilian beach fashion. Since details such as size, print, and design vary, fashionistas will buy several bikinis to alternate during the summer. Window-shop if you want to get a sense of this year's models. Although the infamous string bikini can still be found, it is no longer common.

Men and women will generally wear light, easy-to-remove clothes over their bathing suit so that they can undress easily at the beach and then compose themselves enough at the end of the day to make a stop at a beachside restaurant. *Havaianas,* rubber flip-flops that come in a rainbow of colors, are ubiquitous.

Finally, *kangas* (sarongs) are a must. The large rectangles of cloth come in a variety of prints and can be used to sit on the sand and to drape over your lounge chair or around your shoulders. Bringing a bulky towel to the beach is something a Brazilian generally wouldn't do.

Forget your kanga at the hotel? Never fear, Brazil's inventive beach vendors will happily sell you one, along with everything from sunblock, light summer dresses, bikinis, and even grilled shrimp. Usually, you can rent lounge chairs, sun umbrellas, and even children's paddling pools from them as well.

Food vendors offer cheese grilled over live coals, popsicles, savory pastries stuffed with spinach, meat, or cheese, frozen açaí slushies, and fresh fruit. Drinks range from the conventional—water, beer, sodas—to the uniquely Brazilian, such as green coconuts, sweet maté tea, and caipirinhas.

While beaches in Brazil are relatively free of hazards—no sharks or jellyfish—conditions vary. Always heed local warnings about riptides. When in Rio, check the newspaper section next to the weather to see if the beach you're planning to go to is clean. Heavy rain showers often wash sewage and trash into the ocean, rendering otherwise beautiful beaches unfit for bathing for at least 24 hours.

CARNIVAL IN BRAZIL

Brazilians can throw a party like no one else, and Carnival is the biggest party of the year. From dancing in the streets of the nation's smallest towns to the full-throttle revelry of Rio de Janeiro, this raucous bacchanal of music, drink, and flesh takes over the country. This is a time of transgression, when excesses are encouraged and lines are crossed: men dress as women, the poor dress as kings, strangers kiss in the streets, and rules are bent.

Like Mardi Gras, Carnival has its origins in pagan festivals of spring. These were co-opted by the advent of Christianity into a period of lenience, when one could rack up as many sins as possible before the 40 days of abstinence and withdrawal that comes with Lent.

Carnival is supposed to last five days, from the Friday until the Tuesday before Ash Wednesday. But the reality is that pre-Carnival parties begin a few weeks before the official opening ceremony. This is when the Mayor gives the keys of the city to the rotund King Momo, a jester-like figure who presides over the chaos and debauchery. The fun often continues for days after Ash Wednesday.

It can be an unforgettable experience if you're ready to plunge headlong into the joyful mayhem: Be prepared for days and nights fueled by light Brazilian beer and caipirinhas, and streets jammed with revelers following floats playing samba songs morning to night.

The crowds are surprisingly peaceful, but keep your wits about you. This is generally the hottest time of the year, so drink plenty of water and bring sunblock. The streets can get very crowded, making it easy to lose members of your party. Avoid traveling great distances through the city because traffic can turn nightmarish.

Since pickpockets work the masses, carry only cash you plan to spend that day and leave home any nice watches, jewelry, or sunglasses. Groping can be a real hassle for women, especially in Salvador. Travel in groups and avoid wearing a skirt—hands might get up there.

Plan your Carnival visit well in advance; be sure to make your hotel reservations early, and prepare to pay steeper prices. Lastly, do your research. The party takes on various regional flavors. Finding the best fit is important to enjoying the experience.

Rio de Janeiro

The best-known celebration is in Rio de Janeiro, which hosts the lavish culmination of the festival: the Carnival parades, in which *escolas de samba* (samba groups) compete for the top prize with elaborate, mechanized floats, sequin-and-spangled dancers, and huge percussion sections. In the weeks before the main event, you can catch the *ensaios*, or technical rehearsals, which are held on weekends at the Sambodromo. Free of charge, they are almost as dazzling as the real thing.

During the season, Rio's neighborhoods are also taken over by *blocos*—samba bands that parade through the streets, dragging behind them throngs of faithful revelers in a variety of costumes. There are nearly 500 of these spread around town. For many Rio residents, they are the heart of Carnival.

Most attract a mixed crowd, but some target a particular audience or have special characteristics: the traditional Banda de Ipanema draws a plethora of drag queens; among the Carmelitas, in the Santa Teresa neighborhood, you'll see many partygoers dressed as nuns. There are blocos for children, for journalists, for Michael

Jackson lovers—you name it. Street blocos are impossible to miss. In fact, if you are not interested in full-immersion Carnival, avoid Rio during this time period, because the party is unavoidable.

Carnival balls are a good option for those who prefer an enclosed, less chaotic setting. These are massive parties of mostly costumed revelers with live music, which can range from more staid, black-tie affairs like the famous Copacabana Palace ball to gay balls, balls for children, and smaller ones in samba joints.

Planning: To learn more about Carnival, from the schedules of the parading escolas de samba to where to find the street bloco of your dreams, visit the Riotur website (⊕ *www.rioguiaoficial.com.br*), or pick up their free Carnaval de Rua (street Carnival) guide. *Veja* magazine, sold at all newsstands, also has a Rio insert, *Veja Rio*, with a lot of good information about events during Carnival.

For tickets to see the Carnival parade, go to official league site: ⊕ *liesa.globo.com*. They go on sale as early as December. Alternately, you can check in with travel agencies. They snap up most of the tickets, and resell them at a higher cost in the months preceding Carnival.

Salvador

What makes Salvador's Carnival distinctive is the strong Afro-Brazilian presence in its music and traditions. While Rio's samba also derives from African rhythms, in Salvador this influence feels more immediate.

The centerpieces of Carnival in the Bahian capital are the *trios elétricos,*which are decorated sound trucks that parade through town at the head of a densely packed throng of dancers; and the *afoxes,* which are Afro-Brazilian groups that perform the rhythms and dances of *candomble,* the main Afro-Brazilian religion.

Getting close to the trio elétrico requires buying an *abada,* an outfit that allows the person wearing it to access a roped-off area. Those dancing around outside the cordoned area are called *pipoca,* or popcorn. It's cheaper and easier to "go popcorn," but the crowds can be suffocating. If you want to avoid the crush entirely, buy a ticket to the walled-off bleachers.

Planning: You can find more information at the official tourist office's website (⊕ *www.bahiatursa.ba.gov.br*). Tickets for camarotes and abadas are for sale year-round at ⊕ *home.centraldocarnaval.com.br*.

Elsewhere in Brazil

A multitude of smaller towns offer picturesque and lively Carnival bashes without the crowds. In Recife in Brazil's Northeast, people attend *baile* (dance) and *bloco* (percussion group) practice for months prior to the main Carnival festivities. The beat of choice is *frevo* (a fast-pace rhythm accompanied by a dance performed with umbrellas). Galo da Madrugada, the largest of Recife's 500 blocos, opens Carnival and has included up to 1,500,000 costumed revelers. The blocos are joined by *escolas de samba* (samba schools or groups), *caboclinhos* (wearing traditional Indian garb and bright feathers), and *maracatus* (African percussionists).

In addition, historic gold mining–era towns, like Paraty in Rio state and Ouro Preto in Minas Gerais, have plenty of dancing in their cobblestoned streets. Laid-back beach resorts like Arraial d'Ajuda in Bahia or Jericoacoara in Ceará offer a mellower atmosphere with more than enough fun to go around.

BRAZIL AND THE ENVIRONMENT

Since Brazil's colonization some five centuries ago, inhabitants have largely congregated along the country's coastline. The majority of Brazil's largest cities—Rio de Janeiro, São Paulo, Curitiba, Porto Alegre, Salvador, Recife—are along or very near the coast. Brazilian leaders grew so worried that its population did not "take advantage of its space" that former President Juscelino Kubitschek constructed and inaugurated in 1960 the planned capital city of Brasília in the country's center as a means to draw population inward.

Pushing Into the Interior

Take advantage of the interior they did, often to a fault. Brazilian agriculturalists, extraction industries, and infrastructure planners have long seemed to suffer from the mentality that land is extensive and cheap, and that pushing into new areas is easier than proper stewardship of the ones they already have. Deforestation has left the Atlantic Forest (*Mata Atlântica*) along Brazil's coast a tiny fraction of its original size, while the *cerrado* savanna in the country's center has lost an estimated half of its original territory. The Amazon rain forest loses thousands of square miles each year, in part because growing global demand for soy and cotton in Brazil's interior then pushes cattle farming into the Amazon. While deforestation had been on the wane since 2004, it sadly began to pick up pace again in 2013 and is once again a major cause of concern for environmentalists.

In addition to deforestation, bitter land disputes between commercial farmers and indigenous populations have a long and deadly history in Brazil. Killings of rural activists and indigenous leaders are common and justice can be scarce. In one of the most famous and chilling cases, the American nun and environmental activist Dorothy Stang was assassinated on her way to a meeting in the Amazon state of Pará. Another front for conflict has been the Brazilian government's push to build dozens of hydroelectric dams across the Amazon, which it says is necessary to satisfy urban Brazilians' growing demand for electricity.

Move Toward Sustainability

Concerns about the environment are beginning to be taken more seriously in Brazil. Major cities have imposed heavy fines for littering, and São Paulo banned stores from dispensing disposable plastic bags. Recycling is on the increase across the country, with São Paulo authorities introducing fines for those who don't appropriately separate their household waste.

A new seriousness about environmental causes was reflected by the political ascendency of Marina Silva. Born to an impoverished family in the Amazonian state of Acre, and illiterate until her teenage years, Silva later moved to the state's capital city and became an environmental activist alongside Chico Mendes, a famous rubber tapper and trade union leader who was assassinated in 1988. A former senator from the state of Acre and the environmental minister under former President Luiz Inácio Lula da Silva, she left his cabinet in protest over lack of commitment to environmental issues, and had a surprisingly strong performance as a third-party candidate in Brazil's 2010 elections.

In April 2014, Eduardo Campos, the Socialist Party presidential candidate, elected Silva as his vice candidate, and she was thrust into the role of presidential

contender months later when Campos was killed in a plane crash. Silva finished with 21 percent of the vote. She remains a political force, especially as a greater number of Brazilians begin to embrace what was once seen as a fringe cause.

Sustainability has become a mainstream value over the past two decades, especially since Brazil hosted the 1992 United Nations Earth Summit in Rio de Janeiro, then resurrected it 20 years later at the Rio+20 United Nations Conference on Sustainable Development. A more telling gauge of popular public opinion were the protests that erupted across Brazil in 2012 to fight against proposed changes in the national forestry code, which would have retroactively "amnestied" years of deforestation.

Such protests highlight how Brazil's civil society has learned to use the tools of accountability and manifestations. Social media has fueled the environmental movement by bringing urbanite organizers in Brazil's coastal cities in line with activists across Brazil's interior.

The Rise of Ecotourism

As a visitor, you will be able to appreciate the fruits of Brazil's sustainability efforts. Take note when you explore a park to see if it is a protected forest. Look at the map of Rio de Janeiro to understand just how large the Tijuca and Pedra Branca national parks are—all the more impressive in a city pressed for space, with real estate prices spiraling and green space coveted.

Many experts claim that Brazil still has few options for true ecotourism that involves education, study, and appreciation of local cultures and the environment. While ecotourism became a priority following the 1992 Earth Summit, the practice has taken some time to get off the ground in Brazil.

During the 1990s, economic turmoil and inconsistent government actions hampered the national industry. In addition, the high price of access to Brazil's Amazon region made it an expensive market in comparison with other destinations. A plane ticket from Rio or São Paulo to Manaus is often as expensive as one to Europe or Miami, and overland access to the Amazon is shaky, at best, with the Transamazônica highway, meant to cross the country's North and Northeast, still largely unpaved.

What Brazil has built up in the meantime is nature-based tourism, which includes responsible and respectful tourism that often lacks an educational component. The Instituto EcoBrasil is a superb resource for planning an eco-friendly trip to Brazil. On their informative, bilingual website (🌐 www.ecobrasil.org.br), you can browse a database of "Responsible Companies" and tour operators for the area that you hope to visit.

Overall, there are numerous options available for tourists who want to explore the country's vast natural wonders in an environmentally responsible manner. All visitors should simply keep in mind a phrase that rain forest activist Dorothy Stang often wore emblazoned on her shirt: "The death of the forest is the end of our lives." Brazil's forests are a verdant treasure to be enjoyed, open to those willing to tread lightly.

WILDLIFE IN BRAZIL

Brazil's biodiversity is a wonder to behold. The country itself occupies nearly half the South American continent, and Brazil's Amazon rain forest alone is larger than India. Its distinct ecosystems—the Pantanal wetlands in the Center-West, the Pampas temperate grasslands in the South, the Mata Atlântica tropical deciduous forest along the Atlantic coast, the *cerrado* savanna in the heart of the country, the *caatinga* tropical scrublands in the Northeast, and the Amazon rain forest in the North—contain more than 100,000 animal species and roughly 45,000 plant species.

According to the Brazilian government, some 700 new animals are discovered in the country each year. A new plant species is unearthed every two days.

Anaconda: The only contact that tourists most likely will have with this nocturnal snake is through the local's hyperbolic stories about its mammoth size. Tall tales of giant anacondas abound, and for good reason. The green anaconda is the world's heaviest snake, and also one of the longest, sometimes growing up to 16 feet. Anacondas lurk in the waters of the Amazon rain forest, although they rarely make their large presence known.

Capybara: The world's largest rodent, this scurrying beaver-like creature with a narrow head and rotund behind is prevalent in the Pantanal and Rio de Janeiro's parks.

Giant Anteater: This bushy-tailed creature with outsized claws and an undersized snout and head was once found in all Brazilian states; it has since become extinct in populous states like Rio de Janeiro and Espirito Santo, but is well represented in the Pantanal and Amazon area. The giant anteater digs up ants and termites with its claws and then laps them up with its long, sticky tongue.

Jaguar: This elegant big cat is one of the most alluring and elusive animals in

Brazil. The largest feline species in the Americas, the jaguar is recognizable by its golden fur and scattered black spots. Often solitary, they prowl about Brazil's Amazon region in search of prey, and are particularly adept at remaining in the jungle's shadows.

Pink dolphin: Tourists will likely spot these playful creatures during cruises along the Amazon River. The pink river dolphin, or boto, is an exclusively freshwater mammal with sharp rows of teeth on each side of its jaw. These animals catch fish by using echolocation, or sonar, and are particularly adept at prying fish out of the Amazon River's murky vegetation. In local lore, pink river dolphins can take human form as handsome men and seduce beautiful women.

Piranhas: These sharp-toothed freshwater fish are the stuff of legend. Visitors undoubtedly have heard unfounded tales of how piranhas can devour cows in seconds. Most jungle excursions include stops along the Amazon River to fish for piranhas, most likely to eat that night for dinner.

Tapir: This hefty mammal looks like a pig or a small rhino with a characteristically curved snout. Exceptional swimmers, tapirs in Brazil largely live close to the river in the Amazon rain forest.

Three-banded armadillo: The three-banded armadillo resides in the savanna and tropical scrublands. It's most renowned for its ability to roll up into a perfectly spherical, scaly ball.

Toco Toucan: Unmistakable for its large, orange beak, this black-and-white bird can be seen in Brazil's cerrado and Pantanal, and even in Brasília, an unexpected sight among its traffic jams and concrete. Perhaps the country's most emblematic animal, the toco toucan uses its distinctive bill to snatch fruit from trees.

IF YOU LIKE

Beaches

Along its coastline, Brazil has thousands of breathtaking beaches, so you're bound to find a slice of paradise wherever you are. In the Northeast you find sweeping expanses of dunes; warm aquamarine waters; and constant breezes. Rio's famous beaches are vibrant and beautiful. The South has glorious sands and cooler climes. A short list doesn't do them justice, but these are some of our favorite beach destinations:

Bahia. Praia do Forte has plenty of leisure activities, and is the number-one place to see sea turtles in Brazil.

Ceará. Canoa Quebrada, near Fortaleza, and Jericoacoara are our two favorite northeastern beaches for sheer beauty and relaxation.

Paraná. Ilha do Mel is known as the Paradise of the South Atlantic, and is one of the best ecotourism destinations in Brazil.

Rio de Janeiro. Barra da Tijuca, Prainha, and Grumari are the most naturally beautiful beaches in Rio. Copacabana and Ipanema are the best beach "scenes." Itacoatiara in Niterói is a hidden paradise locals sneak off to on the weekends to avoid crowds. Farther out, Búzios has some of the country's most gorgeous beaches, while Ilha Grande is home to unspoiled strands set amid rugged jungle.

Santa Catarina. It's difficult to choose one beach to recommend on Ilha de Santa Catarina and Florianópolis. Garopaba, Praia dos Ingleses, and Praia Mole are the most famous, and Jurerê Internacional is the favorite among the well-to-do.

São Paulo. Ilhabela is a paradise of more than 25 beaches, and a favorite destination for *paulistas* looking for a break from one of the world's most populous cities.

Nature

This is one of the best places on earth for nature lovers. There are so many places to see that you will need to carefully plan your itinerary. The Amazon and the Pantanal, Brazil's two ecological wonderlands, are givens, but some lesser-known gems are waiting to be discovered by tourists, like Curitiba, known as the "ecological city" because of its many parks and green areas. Our favorite nature destinations follow.

The Amazon Rain Forest. A visit to the world-famous Amazon is one of those "life-list" experiences. Its scope and natural wealth are truly awe-inspiring.

Pantanal Wetlands. This vast floodplain is the best place to see wildlife outside sub-Saharan Africa. Its savannas, forests, and swamps are home to more than 600 bird species as well as anacondas, jaguars, monkeys, and other creatures.

Parque Nacional da Chapada Diamantina, west of Salvador. One of Brazil's most spectacular parks, Chapada Diamantina was a former diamond mining center where intrepid tourists now camp amongst its plateaus and hidden pools.

Parque Nacional do Iguaçu. This preserve has one of the world's most fantastic waterfalls, in addition to winding hiking trails to take you to the fall's lookout points.

Projeto Tamar, Praia do Forte. Each year, September through March, more than 400,000 baby turtles are hatched along this beach northeast of Salvador.

Nightlife

Brazilians are famous for their Carnival, but any time of year is occasion for revelry here. Even small towns have multitudes of festivals that may start out with a Catholic mass and end with dancing in the streets. Nearly every town has live-music venues playing samba, axé, forró, and MPB (Brazilian pop music) year-round. Brazilians—men and women alike—seem to have been born shaking their hips. If you can't dance the wild-yet-elegant samba, don't worry, a lot of Brazilians can't either—they just know how to fake it.

Belo Horizonte. With more bars per capita than any other Brazilian city, it's obvious that BH knows how to party. Expect to find fine sipping cachaça. The music scene is quite lively here.

Rio de Janeiro. Music and dance clubs stay open all night long here, especially in Lapa. Brazilians arrive for their nights out late—expect the bars to fill around midnight and clubs and street parties around 1 am. This is one of the top places in Brazil to hear great samba and sultry bossa nova. Carnival is the biggest party of the year, but New Year's Eve in Rio is also a fabulous celebration on the Copacabana beach.

Salvador. The center of axé (Brazilian pop) music and Afro-Brazilian culture, Salvador has an easygoing party scene, but its Carnival is considered one of Brazil's best parties, where you can dance in the streets for eight days straight.

São Paulo. If you crave elite clubs and rubbing elbows with Brazilian cosmopolitan millionaires and sipping martinis at rooftop skyscraper bars, head to São Paulo. It's Brazil's poshest place to party.

Food and Drink

You will have your pick of diverse dishes to try in Brazil. Each region has its own specialties: exotic fish dishes and fruit juices in the Amazon; African spiced cassoroles in Bahia, and the seasoned bean paste tutu in Minas Gerais.

Açaí. This purple energy-packed berry from the Amazon makes a velvety, icy drink that wins addicts much as coffee does. Amazonians take it bitter, often accompanying savory dishes, whereas urbanite Brazilians in Rio and São Paulo sweeten it and drink it with granola or peanut dust, called *paçoca*.

Cafezinhos. These thimble-size cups of coffee with tons of sugar keep Brazilians going between meals. They are also offered after rodízios to sooth an achingly full stomach.

Caipirinha. The national drink is caipirinha—crushed lime, ice, sugar—and cachaça, a liquor distilled from sugarcane.

Churrasco. Served at churrascarias, churrasco is meat, poultry, or fish roasted on spits over an open fire. In a rodízio-style churrascaria, you get all the meat and side dishes you can eat at a fixed price.

Feijoada. The national dish is a thick stew with a base of black beans, combined with sausage, bacon, pork loin, and other meats. Traditional versions may include pig's feet, ears, and other "choice" meats. Feijoada is usually accompanied by *farofa* (toasted manioc flour), rice, and garlicky collard greens.

Guaraná. Be sure to try this carbonated soft drink made with the Amazonian fruit of the same name. It has a unique but subtle flavor.

GREAT ITINERARIES

ESSENTIAL BRAZIL: RIO, BRASÍLIA, SÃO PAULO, AND IGUAÇU

This itinerary is perfect for first-time visitors to Brazil who want to catch hidden highlights as well as world-famous attractions. The trip takes in Rio's golden sands, Brasília's modernist architecture, São Paulo's first class dining scene, and Iguaçu's mighty falls.

Day 1: Arrival

Land in **Rio de Janeiro** and take in the view on the way in from the airport to the Zona Sul, where you will pass several sprawling favelas (the slums that gave birth to samba, Carnival, and Brazilian funk) before reaching Guanabara Bay and Rio's packed commercial port. From here the cab will wind through the city's colonial-era downtown, and finally arrive at the beachside, where the open Atlantic greets you. Cool down with an icy açaí berry smoothie at sunset or enjoy the first caipirinha of your visit.

Logistics: Wear your breeziest clothes on the flight so that you can keep cool when you arrive in sunny Rio de Janeiro, where summer temperatures are the norm most of the year.

Day 2: Christ Statue, Sugarloaf, Ipanema Beach

Take the train up **Corcovado** to the **Christ the Redeemer statue**, where the 360-degree views of the city never fail to impress. Once you descend, a short trip through the charming neighborhood of Botafogo will take you to Urca. There, ride a cable car to the top of the iconic **Sugarloaf Mountain**, where you can enjoy a different perspective on the city. End your day at the **Praia do Arpoador**, right between Copacabana and Ipanema. Locals applaud there as the sun sets.

Logistics: Check the weather to make sure the Christ the Redeemer statue will not be above the clouds. Wear comfortable shoes for hiking, especially on rocky Arpoador. You can also hike the hill that leads up to **Morra da Urca**, the smaller hill next to Sugar Loaf that is the first port of call for the cable car.

Day 3: Rio's Hidden Corners

Since Rio bursts with beauty, travelers often overlook many of the city's indoor treasures. Try the **Roberto Burle Marx Farm**, a plantation-turned-museum dedicated to Brazil's most famous landscape designer. You should also make time for the **Museu de Arte Contemporânea**, designed by the one and only Oscar Niemeyer, in Rio's sister city, **Niterói**, across the Guanabara Bay. Top the night off with live music in Rio's famously hedonistic party district, **Lapa**.

Logistics: Enjoy the view as you cross the bay to Niterói, either by the Rio-Niterói bridge or the ferry from Praça 15.

Day 4: Beach bum

Rio's long coastline offers a beach for every taste. Want crowds and people-watching? Try **Copacabana**, with lunch in the Confeitaria Colombo along the Forte de Copacabana. A surfer's beach? The **Prainha** past Barra da Tijuca is for you. A beach for families? You can't go wrong at the low-key **Praia do Leblon**.

Logistics: Beyond Copacabana and Ipanema, you will need a car or long bus rides to get to the beaches farther southwest along the coast.

Days 5–6: Onward to Brasília

Make your way to the airport in Rio for a short flight to **Brasília**. Enjoy the view of Brasília at night—the **Esplanada dos Ministérios** is generally empty and feels elegant

and massive lit in the dark. Remember that Brasília was the city of the future—half a century ago. Enjoy Oscar Niemeyer's modernism and the clean lines of the government buildings of the Esplanada dos Ministérios. If you don't stay in Niemeyer's Brasília Palace, at least have dinner in the elegant Oscar restaurant to enjoy the grounds. Feel free to enter the boisterous Congress—just show an ID to get in.

Logistics: Take note of whether your flight leaves in Rio from Santos Dumont, the domestic airport, or Galeão, which is both international and domestic. The former is usually preferable and closer to Zona Sul hotels. Brasília has a speedy metro, but a taxi is a better option if you have difficulty orienting yourself on Brasília's highly organized map, which involves cardinal directions, "sectors," and numbered streets.

Day 7: Brasília to Foz do Iguaçu
Fly into **Foz do Iguaçu**, Brazil's side of the famous South American falls. Remember that the city is but a launching pad to the falls.

Logistics: Talk with local tour operators to decide whether to take a bus into the falls or a private taxi, which means you'll pay your own entrance fee separately. If you arrive early enough in the city, head straight to the falls—the Brazilian side has fewer trails and can be enjoyed in a few hours.

Day 8: The Falls from Argentina
The general wisdom is the following: Brazil's side of Iguaçu offers the best views, while Argentina's side offers the fun winding hikes that often directly overlook the falls. A boat trip into the falls is a thrilling way to enjoy its majesty.

Logistics: Crossing the border is a cinch, but make sure your Brazilian visa is in order so that you can return to Brazil afterward. Bring a towel if you plan on doing a boat ride.

Day 9: Into the Big City
Fly from Iguaçu to **São Paulo** to enjoy a day in the country's frenetic commercial capital. Wander anywhere in the city and you're likely to find a museum, top-notch restaurant, or a world-class boutique. Don't miss the outstanding collection at the **Museu de Arte de São Paulo**.

Day 10: Market Day

Stroll along **Avenida Paulista**, the packed heart of commercial São Paulo. The Jardins neighborhood will take you to more mouthwatering restaurants than you can handle. Check out the bustling **Mercado Municipal** for a light lunch and, if time permits, take a taxi to the massive CEAG-ESP wholesale market. The warehouses of fresh foods and endless stream of buyers will make you appreciate what a breadbasket Brazil has to offer.

Logistics: The metro in São Paulo is extensive, so make sure you grab a map before riding. Remember that distances in São Paulo can be quite far. Give yourself plenty of time between outings.

Day 11: Return to Rio

Try to fly in through the Santos Dumont airport so that you can hop out for an extra afternoon in Rio. Sunsets are glorious year-round.

Logistics: Give yourself cushion time, especially during holidays. Long lines for emigration can hold you back.

ADVENTURE BRAZIL: RIO, SALVADOR, AND THE AMAZON

Brazil is a dream destination for adventurous souls. This exciting itinerary takes in Rio's crashing waves and national park, the isolated beaches of Bahia, and the unrivalled nature-spotting opportunities of the Amazon.

Day 1: Arrive in Rio de Janeiro

Spend your first afternoon visiting either **Corcovado** and the **Christ the Redeemer statue** or **Sugarloaf**. Relax at night with caipirinhas from a beachside kiosk.

Logistics: To keep days in Rio stress-free, consult a map to see the distances between your outings. Remember that rush hour is not just in São Paulo—try to make sure you are set to wait out the worst afternoon traffic.

Day 2: Hiking

Explore Rio de Janeiro's Tijuca Forest, a sprawling national park in the middle of the municipality. Hike up the Pedra Bonita for great views. If you're feeling especially adventurous, you can then hang glide down to the São Conrado Beach.

Logistics: Start early to avoid the hottest part of the day. Wear sunscreen since the sun burns strong in Rio.

Day 3: Beach Day

Take a break after a strenuous day by lounging on either **Copacabana** or **Ipanema Beach**. Take several leisurely strolls to fully appreciate Rio's beach culture. The city's lagoon, called the Lagoa, offers a series of chic bars and restaurants behind Ipanema Beach.

Logistics: Be careful with Rio's strong undertow and waves. Bring only the bare minimum of belongings to the beach, and make sure someone from your group keeps an eye on them.

Day 4: Rio to Salvador

Say good-bye to Rio with breakfast at the Confeitaria Colombo, one of the city's oldest restaurants and known for its sweets, before flying to **Salvador,** the bayside capital of Bahia State. If you start in Pelourinho, you won't have to look hard to find live music in the evening.

Logistics: Keep in mind the difference it makes to fly from Rio de Janeiro's Santos Dumont, the centrally located domestic airport, or Galeão, the international airport about 45 minutes from it. Traffic leading toward Galeão during rush hour is often at a standstill.

Days 5–6: Historical Salvador

Stroll along **Pelourinho**, the center of historical Salvador, and the surrounding churches, art galleries, and museums. Start in the Largo do Pelourinho, where you can visit the impressive Museu da Cidade. Head up Rua Maciel de Baixo and stroll the cobblestone streets of the colonial district, flanked by houses in pastel shades. Continue through **Praça da Sé** to the **Municipal Square** towering above the Lower City, which offers spectacular views. Have a snack of acarajé, the traditional fried bean-meal patty stuffed with shrimp and spicy peppers.

Logistics: Wear comfortable shoes—you may need to hike up one of Salvador's steep streets.

Day 6: Afro-Brazilian Culture

Bahia is a seedbed of Brazilian culture. To learn more, visit the comprehensive **Museu Afro-Brasileiro (Afro-Brazilian Museum)** next to the Catedral Basilica. Many of the country's top musicians have come from here. Make a point to find live music and *capoeira*, a highly rhythmic form of martial arts. The Balé Folclórico de Bahia, stages exhilarating dance shows that showcase the region's Afro-Brazilian culture.

Logistics: Salvador's life often happens on the streets. Carry only what you need so that you can have your hands free.

Day 7: Salvador to Manaus

Manaus, the gateway to the Amazon region, is not just a hop from Brazil's coastal cities. You'll need to reserve at least half a day for this leg of the trip, since there are no direct flights from Salvador. When you arrive late in the day, check out a few Manaus sites, such as the iconic **Opera House** whose dome is tiled in the colors of Brazil's flag.

Logistics: Make an effort in advance to find a close connecting flight, often via Brasília, that will minimize your trip time. Flight service from Northeastern cities remains minimal to none.

Days 8–9: Cruise on the Amazon

Here, your options are limited only by your time. With five or more days, you can plan an excursion to a lonely river reserve, such as the breathtaking **Mamirauá**, with floating guest homes on the river and with pink dolphins jumping outside your window. A shorter trip could involve seeing the two-colored **"Meeting of the Waters,"** where the dark waters of the Rio Negro meets the sandy-colored Rio Solimões to form the mighty Rio Amazonas. If you don't have the time for a long trip on the river, try a short day trip, such as the Praia do Tupé, a half-hour riverboat ride along the Rio Negro from the center of Manaus. Gird yourself and hire a guide for a day of tree climbing up a 130-foot Amapazeiro.

Logistics: A normal "barco" (boat) will take you at the leisurely speed of a regular riverboat, often several days to get to popular Amazonian destinations, whereas the speedboat "lancha," sometimes called an "ajato," will fraction the time of your rides. Generously apply bug spray, as mosquitoes are a real threat. It is also highly recommended that you get a yellow fever vaccine before going to the Amazon.

Day 10: Shopping and Departure

Look for some of the only-in-the-Amazon products, such as the healing copaiba oil or the "milk" of the Amapazeiro tree, used for medicinal purposes. A bar of the energetic guaraná, which locals grind into a fine powder using the hard, dried tongue of the pirarucu fish, will keep you awake during your next adventure.

SOUNDS OF BRAZIL

Music is woven into the fabric of Brazilian life and is the art form that most completely translates this diverse nation's creativity and richness. Travelers will be exposed to it throughout their visit, whether it is an upbeat *forro* playing on the radio of your taxi or a traditional samba coming from a local bar where musicians have gathered for an afternoon jam session. You'll learn much about the country and the region you're in from music, since local rhythms usually say much about the place's unique ethnic makeup and history.

Samba

Samba, the music most associated with Brazil, was born in the mostly black neighborhoods near Rio de Janeiro's docks among stevedores and other laborers in the early 20th century. There are many varieties of it, generally all fast-paced and driven by percussion instruments including the deep bass *bumbo* and the smaller *atabaque*, tambourines, and complemented by stringed instruments like the *cavaquinho*, which looks like a tiny guitar.

There are great venues to see traditional samba in Rio's bohemian Lapa neighborhood, among them Semente and Carioca da Gema. Trapiche Gamboa, in the port-side neighborhood of Saude, has great bands in a beautifully restored old warehouse.

One of the real delights of Rio is to see samba played outdoors in samba circles much as it was over a century ago. These circles often spring up without notice, but there are parts of town where musicians traditionally gather. These include Ouvidor Street in downtown, which generally has music on Wednesdays and Saturdays, and Pedra do Sal, an outdoor space in Saude that hosts hugely popular samba circles on Monday and Friday evenings.

Bossa Nova

Bossa Nova, which means "new trend," is a fresh, jazzy take on percussion-heavy samba. Where samba is cathartic and communal and built on drums and powerful voices, bossa nova is intimate and contemplative, with the melody up front and percussion in the background, often played with brushes for a softer texture.

Bossa Nova was born in the bars of Rio's posh south side neighborhoods like Ipanema in the 1950s. It became famous worldwide with the song "The Girl from Ipanema." A good place to hear Bossa Nova is Rio's Vinicius Piano Bar, across the street from the Ipanema bar where the song's authors watched their muse saunter by.

Forro

Brazil's Northeast has the country's richest musical tradition. From these arid backlands sprung *coco, xaxado, baiao, xote, axe,* and *frevo,* among many others. The best known across Brazil is the *forro,* a fast, syncopated rhythm driven by the accordion and the *zabumba,* a rustic drum. It was brought to wealthier São Paulo and Rio de Janeiro by Northeastern migrants who left their impoverished hometowns in search of work.

Derided for years as the "music of maids and doormen," forro has gained a mainstream following. Good places to check it out are São Paulo's Canto da Ema or Feira Moderna, a charming little bar with Northeastern fare and music. In Rio de Janeiro, the Feira de Sao Cristovao—a huge indoor fair with about 700 stands selling Northeastern food, arts, and crafts—is the place to go.

RIO DE JANEIRO

Updated By
Lucy Bryson

Welcome to the Cidade Maravilhosa, or the Marvelous City, as Rio is known in Brazil. Synonymous with the girl from Ipanema, the dramatic views from Christ the Redeemer atop Corcovado mountain, and fabulously flamboyant Carnival celebrations, Rio is a city of stunning architecture, abundant museums, and marvelous food. Rio is also home to 23 beaches, an almost continuous 73-km (45-mile) ribbon of sand.

As you leave the airport and head to Rio's beautiful *Zona Sul* (the touristic South Zone), you'll drive for about 40 minutes on a highway from where you'll begin to get a sense of the dramatic contrast between beautiful landscape and devastating poverty. In this teeming metropolis of 12 million people (6.2 million of whom live in Rio proper), the very rich and the very poor live in uneasy proximity. You'll drive past seemingly endless cinder-block *favela*, but by the time you reach Copacabana's breezy, sunny Avenida Atlântica—flanked on one side by white beach and azure sea and on the other by condominiums and hotels—your heart will leap with expectation as you begin to recognize the postcard-famous sights. Now you're truly in Rio, where *cariocas* (Rio residents) and tourists live life to its fullest.

Enthusiasm is contagious in Rio. Prepare to have your senses engaged and your inhibitions untied. Rio seduces with a host of images: the joyous bustle of vendors at Sunday's Feira Hippie (Hippie Fair); the tipsy babble at sidewalk cafés as patrons sip their last glass of icy beer under the stars; the blanket of lights beneath the Pão de Açúcar (Sugarloaf Mountain); the bikers, joggers, strollers, and power walkers who parade along the beach each morning. Borrow the carioca spirit for your stay; you may find yourself reluctant to give it back.

ORIENTATION AND PLANNING

GETTING ORIENTED

Cariocas divide their city into four main sections: the suburban Zona Norte (North Zone), the chic Zona Sul (South Zone), the sprawling Zona Oeste (West Zone), and the urban Centro.

Most tourist activity takes place in the Zona Sul, with its mix of residential areas, office buildings, shops, restaurants, bars, hotels, and beaches. This is the city's most affluent section, with fancy condos housing Rio's middle and upper class, and dozens of theaters and music halls.

Centro and neighboring Lapa and Santa Teresa are filled with the remnants of the old Portuguese colony, including some impressive neoclassical structures housing churches, museums, and art galleries. The vast

TOP REASONS TO GO

Stunning Beaches: Unpack your Speedo or thong bikini and join the masses at Rio's miles of gorgeous beaches.

Carnival: Head to the streets or the Sambódromo, and revel in the celebration of Rio's biggest party.

Brazilian Beats: Tap your feet to the uniquely Brazilian styles of music [illegible] nova, funk,

and pagode that echo from the myriad clubs and live-music venues.

Scrumptious Meals: Tickle your taste buds with delicious dining experiences—there's a lot to like for meat lovers and vegetarians at Rio's diverse restaurants.

Breathtaking Landscapes: Bask in the beauty of the endlessly breathtaking landscapes that unfold between mountain and ocean.

Zona Norte is primarily residential and lower class, but the international airport and the legendary Maracanã soccer stadium are here. Zona Oeste is the "up and coming" part of Rio, occupied largely by the newly rich, and replete with malls, superstores, and untouched beaches. As the center of operations for the 2016 Rio Olympics, the West Zone is set to benefit from improved transport links to the rest of the city as well as a boost in hotel numbers.

Centro. Architectural gems left behind from the days of Portuguese colonialism share space with modern high-rises in Rio's financial district. Ornately decorated churches, museums, and palaces are just some of the highlights.

Catete and Glória. Historic Catete and Glória, two largely residential neighborhoods close to Centro, are well worth an afternoon's sightseeing. The national government formerly operated out of Catete, which still has its lovely palaces and old residences; the playground in Catete Palace grounds is one of the nicest spots in the city to bring young children. Glória is famous for its beautiful hilltop church.

Santa Teresa and Lapa. One of Rio's first residential neighborhoods, Santa Teresa is worth a visit to explore its narrow, cobblestone streets. Many of the beautiful colonial mansions lining them have been converted into stylish guesthouses and boutique hotels.

Adjacent to Centro, the Lapa neighborhood has some of the best music halls and dance clubs in the city. If you've come to Rio to explore its nightlife, you'll become intimately familiar with Lapa.

Flamengo and Botafogo. The middle-class neighborhoods of Flamengo and Botafogo, both good places to find value lodgings, are famed for their rival soccer teams, two of Brazil's biggest teams. Sports rivalry aside, the Parque de Flamengo, designed by the world-famous landscape architect Roberto Burle Marx, is an oasis of calm and a popular spot for walkers and joggers, while Botafogo is home to some of Rio's best independent bars and restaurants.

Urca. East of Botafogo is tiny, mainly residential Urca, where you can ascend the huge morro Sugarloaf by cable car. Praia Vermelha, a small, sheltered beach beneath Sugarloaf, is a wonderful spot for sunbathing, and on the easy walking trail nearby there's a good chance you'll see marmoset monkeys at play.

Copacabana and Leme. Copacabana Beach is the main attraction in the city's most tourist-packed neighborhood. It's the perfect place to sunbathe, stroll, people-watch, buy souvenirs at the open-air night market, sip a caipirinha at a beach kiosk, or gaze in awe at the giant apartment buildings and hotels (including the Copacabana Palace) that line the Avenida Atlântica. At its eastern end, Copacabana Beach becomes Leme, and this quieter spot is popular with families.

> **WHAT'S A CARIOCA?**
>
> The term *carioca* was an indigenous word meaning "white man's house" and was used in the city's early history to describe the Portuguese colonizers. Today the word is used more broadly, to identify residents of the city of Rio. But the word defines much more than birthplace, race, or residence: it represents an ethos of pride, a sensuality, and a passion for life. Poor or rich, cariocas share a common identity and a distinct local accent, considered by many foreigners and Brazilians alike to be the most beautiful within the Portuguese language.

Ipanema and Leblon. Famously the place where "The Girl from Ipanema" caught the eye of bossa nova songwriters Tom Jobim and Vinicius de Moraes in the 1960s, this affluent neighborhood is a collection of tree-lined streets harboring smart condos, fabulous restaurants, and trendy boutiques. The gorgeous beach, framed by the towering Dois Irmaos (Two Brothers) mountains, is the sunbathing spot of choice for Rio's young and beautiful. Extending west from Ipanema, affluent, intimate Leblon borrows some of its neighbor's trendy charms and is home to many of Rio's hippest restaurants.

São Conrado and Barra da Tijuca. West of Leblon, the well-heeled neighborhoods of São Conrado and Barra da Tijuca have long stretches of unspoiled beach. São Conrado contains some striking mansions, while towering condos and vast shopping malls have earned Barra da Tijuca the nickname Estados Unidos da Barra (United States of Barra). Rio's metro system is set to reach Barra da Tijuca in time for the Rio 2016 Olympics, which will be based here. Barra's beach is the longest in the city and tends to be much quieter than Copacabana and Ipanema.

Inland Zona Sul. The middle-class residential neighborhoods of Jardim Botânico, Gávea, Lagoa, Laranjeiras, and Cosme Velho are worth visiting for their stunning scenery and opportunities for peaceful strolls and nature-spotting rambles. The highlights here include the botanical garden in Jardim Botânico, the cable-car ride to the Christ the Redeemer statue in Cosme Velho, Gávea's planetarium, Laranjeiras's street fairs, and the massive city lake in Lagoa, which is good for a brisk stroll, run, or bike ride.

PLANNING

WHEN TO GO

Rio is a year-round destination, but Carnival, which usually takes place in February, is the best time to soak up the city's party spirit. Arrive a few days before the celebrations begin, or stay a few days after they end to enjoy the museums and other sights that close for the four days of revelry. Prices rise substantially during Carnival season, and accommodations need to be booked several months in advance.

Temperatures in Rio tend to be highest from January to March, when they often soar above 100 degrees. The city generally sees the most rain during December, when it might pour for days at a time. To tour the city at a quieter time, with smaller temperatures, and at lower prices, come in the off-season, from May to October (Brazil's winter). The temperature in the winter tends to be in the upper 70s during the day and rarely falls below 50 degrees at night.

PLANNING YOUR TIME

Rio has more than its fair share of stellar attractions—both natural and man-made—and good planning is key to fitting it all in. It is possible to visit the beaches of Copacabana, Ipanema, and Leblon in one day on foot. From Leblon it's just a short stroll down to Lagoa, home to the city's vast lake set against the mountains.

Set aside another full day to see the historic heart of the city in Lapa, Santa Teresa, Glória, and Catete. All are within close walking distance of each other, but the steep hills up to Santa Teresa can be a challenge in the heat, so grab a taxi or bus instead. Key attractions such as the Christ statue and Sugarloaf Mountain can be visited as part of a full-day or half-day city tour, which will make whistle-stop visits to other key locations in the city, too.

GETTING HERE AND AROUND

Rio's shuttle system currently extends from the Zona Norte to Ipanema, with shuttles to areas west of the final stop. By 2016 the metro should extend as far as Barra da Tijuca. Within Ipanema and Copacabana, it's easy to get around on foot, but some attractions are far apart, so a taxi might be in order. After dark you should always take a taxi if you're venturing into unexplored territory. Cabs are yellow and easy to hail on every main street. Public buses are cheap and cover every inch of the city, but can be difficult to figure out if you don't speak Portuguese.

AIR TRAVEL

Nearly three-dozen airlines regularly serve Rio, but most flights from North America stop first in São Paulo. Several international carriers offer Rio–São Paulo flights.

AIRPORTS All international flights and most domestic flights arrive and depart from the Aeroporto Internacional Antônio Carlos Jobim, also known as Galeão (GIG). The airport is about 40 minutes northwest of the beach area and most of Rio's hotels. Taxis are plentiful and operate on a fixed-fare basis (those outside the arrivals area are cheaper than those from kiosks inside), and comfortable, spacious air-conditioned buses leave the airport for Centro, the Zona Sul, and Barra da Tijuca.

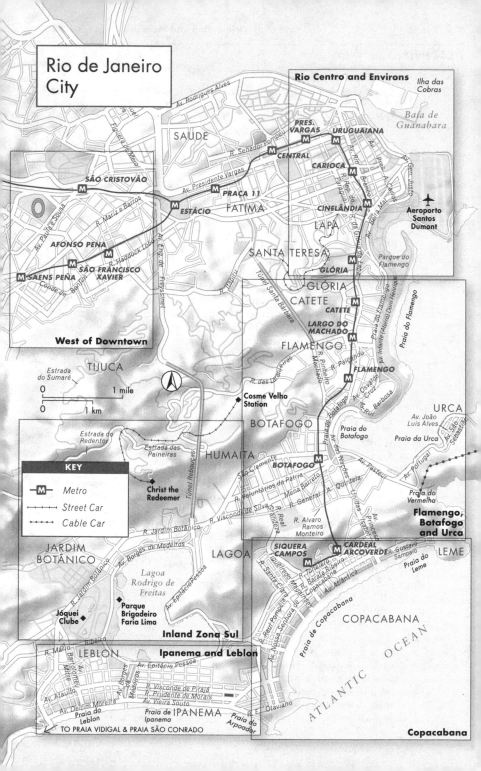

Aeroporto Santos Dumont (SDU), 20 minutes from the beaches and within walking distance of Centro, is served by the Rio–São Paulo air shuttle and other domestic flights.

Airport Information Aeroporto Internacional Antônio Carlos Jobim (*Galeão*, *GIG*). ✉ *Av. 20 de Janeiro s/n, Ilha do Governador* ☎ *021/3004-6050* ⊕ *www. riogaleao.com.* **Aeroporto Santos Dumont** (*SDU*). ✉ *Praça Senador Salgado Filho s/n, Centro* ☎ *021/3814-7070* ⊕ *www.aeroportosantosdumont.net.*

AIRPORT TRANSFERS: BUSES AND TAXIS

Most visitors arrive at Rio International Airport, about a 40-minute car ride from the tourist destinations. The speediest way to reach Centro and the Zona Sul is to take a taxi. Prices are steep, however. Expect to pay up to R$90 to reach Copacabana, and slightly more to Ipanema and Leblon. There are taxi booths in the arrival area, and passengers pay a set fare in advance, though drivers may charge extra if you have lots of luggage. Also trustworthy are the white radio taxis parked in front of arrivals; these metered vehicles cost an average of 20% less than the airport taxis.

Comfortable, air-conditioned buses run by Real (marked Real Premium) park curbside outside the arrivals lounge; there is plenty of luggage storage space, and staff will safely stow your luggage beneath the bus. The buses (R$14) make the hour-long trip from Galeão to the Zona Sul, following the beachfront drives and stopping at major hotels along the way. If your hotel is inland, the driver will let you off at the nearest corner. Buses operate from 5:30 am to 11:45 pm (*See Bus Travel, below, for contact information*).

BUS TRAVEL

ARRIVING AND DEPARTING

Long-distance and international buses leave from and arrive at the Rodoviária Novo Rio. Any local bus marked "rodoviária" will take you to the station. You can buy tickets at the depot or, for some destinations, from travel agents. To buy online you will need a CPF (Brazilian Social Security) number. A staff member at your hotel may be able to help you with online purchases.

Bus Stations Rodoviárla Novo Rio. ✉ *Av. Francisco Bicalho 1, Santo Cristo* ☎ *021/3213-1800, 021/3213-1800* ⊕ *www.novorio.com.br.*

TRAVEL WITHIN RIO DE JANEIRO

Rio's urban buses are cheap, frequent, and generally safe to use, but do not show cameras or wallets, and do not wear expensive-looking clothes or jewelry. Wear backpacks on your front, and avoid getting on or off the bus in deserted areas. Local buses have a fixed price (R$3), and can take you anywhere you want to go. Route maps aren't available, but local tourist offices (*See Visitor Information, below*) have route lists for the most popular sights. Enter buses at the front, pay the attendant, and pass through a turnstile. Have your fare in hand when you board to avoid flashing bills or your wallet. When you want to get off, pull the overhead cord and the driver will pause at the next designated stop. Exit from the rear of the bus.

The comfortable, privately run, and air-conditioned Real Premium buses serve the beaches, downtown, and Rio's two airports. These vehicles, which look like highway buses, stop at regular bus stops but also may be flagged down wherever you see them. Expect to pay around three times the price of the regular bus.

Bus Contacts Real Auto Onibus. ☎ *021/3035–6700, 021/3035–6700* ⊕ *www. realautoonibus.com.br.*

CAR TRAVEL

The carioca style of driving is passionate to the point of abandon: speeding is de rigueur, traffic jams are common, the streets aren't well marked, and red lights are often ignored by drivers. Although there are parking areas along the beachfront boulevards, finding a spot can be a real problem. If you do choose to drive, exercise extreme caution, wear seat belts at all times, and keep the doors locked.

Car rentals can be arranged through hotels or agencies and at this writing cost between R$1200 and R$200 a day for standard models. Major agencies include Avis, Hertz, and Unidas. Localiza is a local agency. Hertz and Unidas have desks at the international and domestic airports.

Turismo Clássico Travel can arrange for a driver to get you around the city, with or without an English-speaking guide (US$50 per hour). Clássico's owners, Liliana and Vera, speak English, and each has more than 20 years of experience in organizing transportation. They also lead sightseeing tours.

Car Rental Contacts Unidas. ☎ *021/4001–2222* ⊕ *www.unidas.com.br.*

SUBWAY TRAVEL

Metrô Rio, the subway system, is clean, relatively safe, and efficient, but it's not comprehensive. The system has two lines. Line 1 covers the Zona Sul, with 19 stops between Tijuca and Ipanema, along with integrated metro-bus services going to Barra da Tijuca, Gávea and Botafogo. Line 1 is being extended ahead of the 2016 Rio Olympics, with six more stations being added between Ipanema and Barra da Tijuca. Line 2 goes from the Zona Norte neighborhood of Pavuna to Cidade Nova in Rio's City Center (*Centro*). Reaching sights distant from metro stations can be a challenge, especially in summer, when beach traffic increases. Tourism offices and some metro stations have maps.

Trains operate daily between 5 am and midnight except on Sundays and holidays, when they run between 7 am and 11 pm. A single metro ticket costs R$3.50, but it is quicker and easier to use a pre-pay card. Machines at each metro station allow passengers to buy and load up cards from R$5 to the value of their choice, and although there are no financial savings, you'll avoid queues and hassle each time you take the subway.

Subway Information Metrô Rio. ✉ *Centro* ☎ *0800/595–1111 information line* ⊕ *www.metrorio.com.br.*

TAXI TRAVEL

Taxis are plentiful in Rio, and in most parts of the city you can easily flag one down on the street. Yellow taxis have meters that start at a set price and have two rates. The "1" rate applies to fares before 8 pm, and the "2" rate applies to fares after 8 pm, on Sunday, on holidays, throughout December, in the neighborhoods of São Conrado and

Barra da Tijuca, and when climbing steep hills, such as those in Santa Teresa. Drivers are required to post a chart noting the current fares on the inside of the left rear window. CentralTaxi has a fare calculator on its website that will give you a general idea of what the fare from one destination to another might be. ■ TIP➤ **Taxi drivers may be reluctant to make the steep climb to Santa Teresa, so if you are heading here wait until you are already inside the taxi before stating your destination, and stand your ground—by law drivers cannot refuse to take you here.**

Radio taxis and several companies that routinely serve hotels (and whose drivers often speak English) are also options. They charge 30% more than other taxis but are reliable and usually air-conditioned. Other cabs working with the hotels also charge more, normally a fixed fee that you should ~~agree on before you leave. Reliable radio-cab companies~~ include Coopacarioca and Coopatur.

Most carioca cabbies are pleasant, but there are exceptions. If flagging down a taxi on the street, check to see that an official phone number is displayed on the side and that the driver's official identity card is displayed. Remain alert and trust your instincts. Unless you've negotiated a flat fee with the driver, be sure the meter is turned on. ■ TIP➤ **Few cab drivers speak English, so it's a good idea to have your destination written down to show the driver, in case there's a communication gap.**

Taxi Companies CentralTaxi. ☎ *021/2195–1000* ⊕ *www.centraltaxi.com.br.* **Coopacarioca.** ☎ *021/2518–3857, 021/2158–1818* ⊕ *www.cooparioca.com.br.* **Coopatur.** ☎ *021/3885–1000.*

RESTAURANTS

With nearly a thousand restaurants, Rio's dining choices are broad, from low-key Middle Eastern cafés to elegant contemporary eateries with award-winning kitchens and first-class service. The succulent offerings in the *churrascarias* (restaurants specializing in grilled meats) can be mesmerizing for meat lovers—especially the places that serve *rodízio*-style (grilled meat on skewers is continually brought to your table—until you can eat no more). Hotel restaurants often serve the national dish, *feijoada* (a hearty stew of black beans and pork), on Saturday—sometimes on Friday, too. Wash it down with a *chopp* (the local draft beer; pronounced "shop") or a caipirinha (sugarcane rum, lime, and sugar).

HOTELS

Lodgings in Rio de Janeiro are among the most expensive in the world, though the price-to-quality ratio often disappoints. That said, there are some wonderful accommodation options in all price ranges if you know where to look. Copacabana and Ipanema are awash with lodgings and are the best bet for sun seekers, but expect to get more bang for your buck the farther you travel from the famous beaches. Leafy Santa Teresa contains many charming guesthouses and chic boutique hotels, while Centro, Flamengo, and Botafogo have solid options for business travelers. ■ TIP➤ **Note that "motels" are not aimed at tourists. They attract couples looking for privacy and usually rent by the hour.**

Expect to pay a premium for a room with a view. Most hotels include breakfast in the rate, and Brazilian breakfasts are usually a lavish affair involving everything from fresh fruit and juices to cakes, cold meats, and cheeses. If you're traveling during peak periods—from December to March—make reservations as far ahead of your visit as possible. *Hotel reviews have been shortened. For full information, visit Fodors.com.*

VISITOR INFORMATION

The Rio de Janeiro city tourism department, Riotur, operates a tourist information website in English and Portuguese ⊕ *www.rioguiaoficial. com.br* as well as a monthly free magazine with key tourist information and listings. The magazine, and city maps, can be picked up at Riotur booths at the bus station and airports, in Barra, Copacabana, Leblon, Gavea, at Sugarloaf, Lapa, and by Candelaria church in Centro. You can also try contacting Brazil's national tourism board, Embatur, via its Visit Brasil website.

Information Riotur information booth. ⊠ *Kiosk 15, Av. Atlantica, in front of Rua Hilário Gouveia, Copacabana* ☎ *021/2547-7522* ⊕ *www.rioguiaoficial.com. br* Ⓜ *Siqueira Campos.* **Turisrio.** ⊠ *Praça Pio X 119, Centro* ☎ *021/2271-7000* ⊕ *www.turisrio.rj.gov.br* Ⓜ *Cinelandia.* **Visit Brasil.** ⊕ *www.visitbrasil.com.*

TOURS

CITY TOURS

Fodor'sChoice
★
Be a Local. This well-established outfit conducts walking tours of Rocinha that make various stops inside the community, as well as trips to soccer matches, speedy city tours, and lively nocturnal visits to samba school rehearsals. On Sunday night, the fun favela funk-party tour (R$65) includes transport, entrance, and admission to a VIP area—be prepared to be the focus of locals' amorous attentions, and to head home just before daybreak. ⊠ *Rua Barata Ribeiro 111* ☎ *021/7816–9581* ⊕ *www. bealocal.com* ⊠ *From R$65.*

Brazil Expedition. This reliable tour company runs a hugely popular city tour–known as the Big Dude tour–which takes a scenic route through Tijuca National Park to the Christ statue before visiting other key Rio landmarks such as Santa Teresa and the Lapa Steps, with an optional visit to Sugarloaf Mountain. Other recommended excursions include trips to samba school rehearsals (August–February) and an interesting street-art tour. The English-speaking guides are knowledgeable and friendly. ☎ *021/9998–2907, 021/9376–2839* ⊕ *www.brazilexpedition. com* ⊠ *From R$200.*

Favela Tour. If you're interested in learning more about the favelas that cling to Rio's mountainsides, Favela Tour is the way to do it. Led by Marcelo Armstrong, this highly respected outfit conducts tours twice daily through Rocinha and Vila Canoas. Marcelo pioneered favela tourism in Rio and offers tours in English, Spanish, French, and Portuguese. Tours are informative but not voyeuristic, and there are opportunities to buy locally produced arts and crafts as you tour the communities. Hotel pickup and drop-off are included in the price. ☎ *021/3322–2727, 021/9989–0074* ⊕ *www.favelatour.com.br* ⊠ *From R$90.*

2

FAMILY

Fodor's Choice

★

Rio Cultural Secrets. This quality outfit has enthusiastic, knowledgeable English-speaking private guides who whisk visitors around the city in comfortable air-conditioned cars. Popular trips include visits to Tijuca National Park and Rio's Botanical Gardens, soccer games, and city tours that take in major attractions such as Sugar Loaf and the Christ statue. Rio Cultural Secrets can also take visitors up to the imperial city of Petrópolis, around an hour's drive from Rio. ☎ 21/98031–2692 ⊕ www.rioculturalsecrets.com ▥ From R$140.

Rio Free Walking Tour. Expert English-speaking guides lead free tours through Centro each weekday. Rain or shine, the guides will take you on a three-hour morning stroll, explaining the history of downtown Rio's major buildings, streets, statues, and monuments. The walk is followed by lunch at a pay-by-weight buffet restaurant. Tours leave from in front of the Theatro Municipal at 9:30 am Monday through Friday. There's no need to book in advance, just look out for the yellow-shirted guides. Although there's no charge, tips are welcomed. ☎ 021/97214–5095 ⊕ www.riofreewalkingtour.com ▥ Free.

Rio Hiking. This professional outfit leads hiking and climbing trips in Rio and the wider Rio de Janeiro state. All equipment is provided, guides are bilingual, and there are treks, tours, and adventure trips to suit all levels of experience. ✉ Laranjeiras ☎ 021/2552–9204 ⊕ www. riohiking.com.br ▥ From R$210.

HELICOPTER TOURS

Helisight. With landing pads at Morro da Urca (the smaller peak next to Sugarloaf), Lagoa, and Dona Marta view point in Tijuca National Park, Helisight conducts helicopter tours that pass over the Christ the Redeemer statue, the beaches of the Zona Sul, and other iconic sights. Prices start at R$260 for a seven-minute flight, while hour-long trips over this majestic city will set you back more than R$1,500. ✉ Conde de Bernadotte 26, Leblon ☎ 021/2259–6995 Lagoa, 021/2542–7935 Morro da Urca, 021/9602–1224 Dona Marta ⊕ www.helisight.com. br ▥ From R$260.

SAFETY AND PRECAUTIONS

IN THE CITY

As with any city its size, crime occurs in Rio, but taking a few basic precautions should keep you from becoming a victim of it. Crimes involving visitors generally occur in crowded public areas: beaches, busy

---

THE COPS

Once known as the murder capital of the world, Rio is now much less dangerous than it was a decade ago. Simple changes such as installing lights on the beaches have improved safety. An increased police presence has also helped. In Rio there are three types of police: the gray-uniformed Military Police, the beige-uniformed Municipal Guard, and the black-uniformed special forces called the BOPE (pronounced "boppy"). For a glimpse at Rio's SWAT team, the BOPE, check out the film *Tropa de Elite (Elite Squad)* (2007) and its Oscar-nominated sequel, *Tropa de Elite 2* (2010).

sidewalks, intersections, and city buses. Pickpockets, usually children, work in groups. One will distract you while another grabs a wallet, bag, or camera. Be particularly wary of children who thrust themselves in front of you and ask for money or offer to shine your shoes. Another member of the gang may strike from behind, grabbing your valuables and disappearing into the crowd. Another tactic is for criminals to approach your car at intersections. Always keep doors locked and windows partially closed. Leave valuables in your hotel safe, don't wear expensive jewelry or watches, and keep cameras hidden except when snapping shots. Avoid walking around after dark, and avoid deserted areas even in broad daylight. ■TIP→ **Keep large bills and cards in a hidden money belt, carry an inexpensive phone, and have a few notes ready to hand over just in case.**

ON THE BEACH

Don't shun the beaches because of reports of crime, but *do* take precautions. Leave jewelry, passports, and large sums of cash at your hotel; don't stroll the beaches at night; and be alert if groups of seemingly friendly youths attempt to engage you in conversation. They may be trying to distract you while one of their cohorts snatches your belongings. A big danger is actually the sun. From 10 am to 3 pm the rays are merciless, making heavy-duty sunscreen, hats, cover-ups, and plenty of liquids essential; you can also rent a beach umbrella from vendors on the beach or your hotel.

EXPLORING

When in Rio, don't be afraid to follow the tourist trail—the major attractions really are "must-sees." Contrary to tourist-board images, the sun doesn't always shine on the city, so when it does, make the most of it. If the skies are clear, waste no time in heading for Cosme Velho to visit the Christ the Redeemer statue atop Corcovado mountain, or to Urca to make the cable car ascent to the peak of Sugar Loaf. Time-pressed travelers will find that whistle-stop city tours are a good way to see many attractions in one day, while those lucky enough to spend a week or more here can afford to take a more leisurely approach. Cloudy days are a good time to visit the attractions of leafy Lagoa and Jardim Botânico and the breezily bohemian hilltop neighborhood of Santa Teresa. The historic buildings, museums, and cultural centers of Centro, Catete, Glória, and Lapa are ideal rainy-day options.

CENTRO

What locals generally refer to as Centro is actually several sprawling districts containing the city's oldest neighborhoods, churches, and most enchanting cafés. Rio's beaches, broad boulevards, and modern architecture may be impressive; but its colonial structures, old narrow streets, and alleyways in leafy inland neighborhoods are no less so. The metro stations that serve Centro are Cinelândia, Carioca, Uruguaiana, Presidente Vargas, Central, and Praça Onze.

Rio's settlement dates back to 1555. You can experience much of the city's rich history by visiting churches, government buildings, and villas in and around Centro. The metro is a good way to get downtown, but head here early, wear comfortable shoes, and be ready to walk multiple blocks as you explore this historic City Center. There are also daily free walking tours with English-speaking guides. If you're not up for a long walk, consider taking an organized bus tour.

TOP ATTRACTIONS

Biblioteca Nacional. Corinthian columns adorn the neoclassical National Library (built between 1905 and 1908), the first such establishment in Latin America. Its original archives were brought to Brazil by King João VI in 1808. The library contains roughly 13 million books, including two 15th-century printed Bibles, manuscript New Testaments from the 11th and 12th centuries, and volumes that belonged to Empress Teresa Christina. Also here are first-edition Mozart scores, as well as scores by Carlos Gomes, who adapted the José de Alencar novel about Brazil's Indians, *O Guarani*, into an opera of the same name. The library is accessible by guided tour only; tours are available in English. ⊠ *Av. Rio Branco 219, Centro* 🕾 *021/3095–3879* ⊕ *www.bn.br* 🎫 *Tours R\$4* 🕙 *Tours on the hr weekdays 10–5, weekends 12:30–4* Ⓜ *Cinelândia.*

Catedral de São Sebastião do Rio de Janeiro (*Catedral Metropolitana*). The exterior of this circa-1960 metropolitan cathedral, which looks like a concrete beehive, divides opinion. The daring modern design stands in sharp contrast to the baroque style of other churches in Rio, but don't judge until you've stepped inside. When light floods through the colorful stained-glass windows, it transforms the interior—which is 80 meters (263 feet) high and 96 meters (315 feet) in diameter—into a warm, serious place of worship that accommodates up to 20,000 people. An 8½-ton granite rock lends considerable weight to the concept of an altar. ⊠ *Av. República do Chile 245, Centro* 🕾 *021/2240–2669* ⊕ *www. catedral.com.br* 🎫 *Free* 🕙 *Daily 7–6* Ⓜ *Carioca or Cinelândia.*

Convento do Santo Antônio. The Convent of St. Anthony was completed in 1780, but some parts date from 1615, making it one of Rio's oldest structures. Its baroque interior contains priceless colonial art, including wood carvings and wall paintings. The sacristy is covered with traditional Portuguese *azulejos* (ceramic tiles). The church has no bell tower: its bells hang from a double arch on the monastery ceiling. An exterior mausoleum contains the tombs of the offspring of Dom Pedro I and Dom Pedro II. ⊠ *Largo da Carioca 5, Centro* 🕾 *021/2262–0129* ⊕ *www.conventosantoantonio.org.br* 🎫 *Free* 🕙 *By appointment only, call ahead or email conventorj@franciscanos.org.br to set up a visit* Ⓜ *Carioca.*

Igreja de São Francisco da Penitência. This baroque church was completed in 1737, nearly four decades after construction began. Today it's famed for its wooden sculptures and its rich gold-leaf interior. The nave contains a painting of St. Francis, the patron of the church—reportedly the first painting in Brazil done in perspective. ⊠ *Largo da Carioca 5, Centro* 🕾 *021/2262–0197* 🎫 *R\$2* 🕙 *Tues.–Fri. 9–noon and 1–4* Ⓜ *Carioca.*

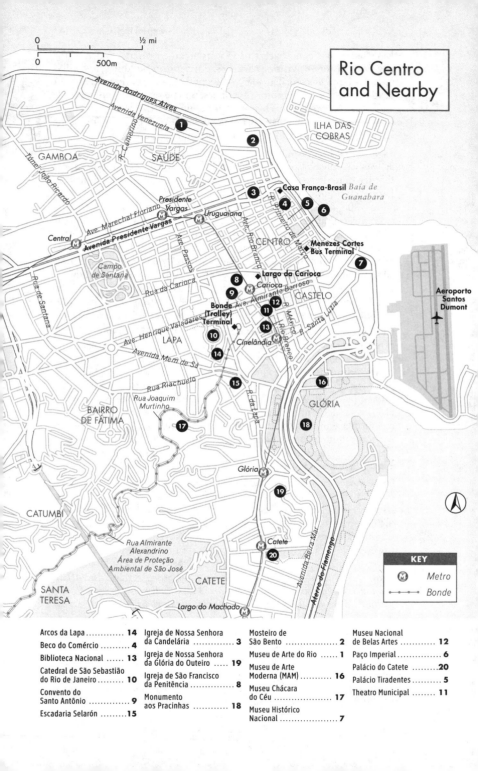

Rio Centro and Nearby

GAMBOA

SAÚDE

Avenida Rodrigues Alves

Avenida Venezuela

Túnel João Ricardo

R. Camerino

ILHA DAS
COBRAS

Casa França-Brasil

Baía de
Guanabara

Presidente
Vargas

Uruguaiana

Ave. Marechal Floriano

Avenida Presidente Vargas

Central

Campo
de Sántana

Rua da Carioca

Ave. Passos

Rua de Santana

Ave. Rio Branco

R. Primeiro de Março

CENTRO

Menezes Cortes
Bus Terminal

Largo da Carioca

Carioca

Ave. Almirante Barroso

CASTELO

Aeroporto
Santos
Dumont

Bonde
(Trolley)
Terminal

Ave. Henrique Valadares

LAPA

Cinelândia

R. México

R. Santa Luzia

R. Rio Branco

Avenida Mem de Sá

Rua Riachuelo

R. do Lavradio

R. do Riachuelo

GLÓRIA

BAIRRO
DE FÁTIMA

Rua Joaquim
Murtinho

Glória

CATUMBI

Ave. Beira Mar

Rua Almirante
Alexandrino
Área de Proteção
Ambiental de São José

Catete

Aterro do Flamengo

SANTA
TERESA

CATETE

Largo do Machado

KEY

- Ⓜ Metro
- •••• Bonde

0 ———— ½ mi
0 ———— 500m

Mosteiro de São Bento. Just a glimpse of the Monastery of St. Benedict's main altar can fill you with awe. Layer upon layer of curvaceous wood carvings coated in gold lend the space an opulent air, while spiral columns whirl upward to capitals topped by the chubbiest of cherubs and angels that appear lost in divine thought. Although the Benedictine monks arrived in 1586, work didn't begin on this church and monastery until 1617. It was completed in 1641, but artisans including Mestre Valentim (who designed the silver chandeliers) continued to add details almost to the 19th century. Sunday Mass at 10 am is accompanied by Gregorian chants. ⊠ *Rua Dom Gerardo 68, Centro* ☎ *021/2206–8100* ⊕ *www.osb.org.br* ✉ *Free* ⊙ *Daily 7–6.*

Museu de Arte do Rio. Rio's once run-down port zone is now the focus of a major investment and regeneration program, and the 2013 opening of the Museu de Arte do Rio (MAR) has provided a compelling reason for visitors to head to this part of town. The attention-grabbing museum structures—a colonial palace and a modernist former bus station, united visually by a wavelike postmodern form that floats on stilts above them—represent an impressive feat of architectural reimagination. The gallery celebrates depictions of Rio throughout the ages, and the eight gallery spaces inside the buildings contain permanent collections of surrealist, modernist, and *naif* artworks. Visiting exhibitions tend to be good, and the views from the top floor—looking out to sea and across Rio's port—are impressive. ⊠ *Praça Mauá 5, Centro* ☎ *021/2203–1235* ⊕ *www.museudeartedorio.org.br* ✉ *R$8, free on Tues.* ⊙ *Tues. 10–7, Wed.–Sun. 10–5* Ⓜ *Uruguiana.*

Museu de Arte Moderna (MAM). A great place to take the pulse of the vibrant Brazilian visual-arts scene, the Museum of Modern Art occupies a striking concrete-and-glass modernist building. Augmenting the permanent collection of about 6,400 works by Brazilian and international artists is the slightly larger Gilberto Chateaubriand Collection of modern and contemporary Brazilian art. MAM has earned respect over the years for its bold, often thought-provoking exhibitions, including a vibrant annual street-art festival. The venue also hosts events such as music performances and DJ sessions. Its theater screens Brazilian and international independent and art-house films. ⊠ *Av. Infante Dom Henrique 85, Centro* ☎ *021/2240–4944* ⊕ *www.mamrio.com.br* ✉ *R$8* ⊙ *Tues.–Fri. noon–6, weekends and holidays noon–7* Ⓜ *Cinelândia.*

Museu Histórico Nacional. The building that houses the National History Museum dates from 1762, though some sections—such as the battlements—were erected as early as 1603. It seems appropriate that this colonial structure should exhibit relics that document Brazil's history. Among its treasures are rare papers, Latin American coins, carriages, cannons, and religious art. ⊠ *Praça Marechal Ancora, Praça 15 de Novembro, Centro* ☎ *021/2550–9224, 021/2220–2328* ⊕ *www.museuhistoriconacional.com.br* ✉ *R$8, free Sun.* ⊙ *Tues.–Fri. 10–6, weekends noon–7* Ⓜ *Carioca or Cinelândia.*

Museu Nacional de Belas Artes. Works by Brazil's leading 19th- and 20th-century artists fill the space at the National Museum of Fine Arts. The most notable canvases are those by the country's best-known modernist,

Cândido Portinari, but be on the lookout for such gems as Leandro Joaquim's heartwarming 18th-century painting of Rio (a window to a time when fishermen still cast nets in the waters below the landmark Igreja de Nossa Senhora da Glória do Outeiro). After wandering the picture galleries, tour the extensive collections of folk and African art. ✉ *Av. Rio Branco 199, Centro* ☎ *021/2262–6067* ⊕ *www.mnba.gov.br/abertura/abertura.htm* ⊠ *R$8, free Sun.* ☉ *Tues.–Fri. 10–6, weekends noon–5* Ⓜ *Carioca or Cinelândia.*

Fodor's Choice **Theatro Municipal.** If you visit one place in Centro, make it the Munici-
★ pal Theater, modeled after the Paris Opera House and opened in 1909. Now restored to its sparkling best, the theater boasts Carrara marble, stunning mosaics, glittering chandeliers, bronze and onyx statues, gilded mirrors, German stained-glass windows, and brazilwood inlay floors. Murals by Brazilian artists Eliseu Visconti and Rodolfo Amoedo further enhance the opulent feel. The main entrance and first two galleries are particularly ornate. As you climb to the upper floors, the decor becomes simpler, a reflection of a time when different classes entered through different doors and sat in separate sections, but also due in part to the exhaustion of funds toward the end of the project. The theater seats 2,357—with outstanding sight lines—for its dance performances and classical music concerts. English-speaking guides are available. ✉ *Rua Marechal Floriano s/n, Centro* ☎ *021/2332-9195* ⊕ *www.theatromunicipal.rj.gov.br* ⊠ *Tours R$10* ☉ *Guided tours Tues.–Fri. on the hr noon–4, Sat. at 11, 1, and 9* Ⓜ *Cinelândia or Carioca.*

WORTH NOTING

Beco do Comércio. A network of narrow streets and alleys centers on this pedestrian thoroughfare, also called the Travessa do Comércio, whose name translates to Alley of Commerce. The area is flanked by restored 18th-century homes, now converted to offices, shops, and galleries. The best-known sight here is the Arco de Teles, a picturesque archway named in honor of the wealthy Teles de Menezes family, who built many of the street's most handsome buildings. Beco do Comércio is a good place to stop for lunch—the street is lined with everything from simple pay-by-weight buffet spots and casual bars to more upmarket restaurants and cafés. ✉ *Praça 15 de Novembro, Centro* Ⓜ *Uruguaiana/Carioca.*

Igreja de Nossa Senhora da Candelária. The classic symmetry of Candelária's white dome and bell towers casts an unexpected air of tranquillity over the chaos of downtown traffic. The church was built on the site of a chapel founded in 1610. Construction on the present church began in 1775, and although the emperor formally dedicated it in 1811, work on the dome wasn't completed until 1877. The sculpted bronze doors were exhibited at the 1889 World's Fair in Paris. ✉ *Praça Pio X, Centro* ☎ *021/2233–2324* ⊠ *Free* ☉ *Weekdays 7:30–4* Ⓜ *Uruguaiana.*

Paço Imperial. This two-story building with thick stone walls and an ornate entrance was built in 1743, and for the next 60 years was the headquarters for Brazil's captains (viceroys), appointed by the Portuguese court in Lisbon. When King João VI arrived, he made it his royal palace. After Brazil's declaration of independence, emperors Dom Pedro

I and II called the palace home, and when the monarchy was overthrown, the building became Rio's central post office. Restoration work in the 1980s transformed the palace into a cultural center and concert hall. The building houses a restaurant, a bistro, and a bit of shopping. The square on which the palace sits, Praça 15 de Novembro, known in colonial days as Largo do Paço, has witnessed some of Brazil's most significant historic moments: here two emperors were crowned, slavery was abolished, and Emperor Pedro II was deposed. The square's modern name is a reference to the date of the declaration of the Republic of Brazil: November 15, 1889. Praça 15, as it is widely known, sits in front of Rio's ferry terminal and is at the heart of a major regeneration project aiming to transform Rio's run-down docklands. ⊠ *Praça 15 de Novembro, 48, Centro* ⌖/₺₃₃₃-₄₃₃₇ ⊕ *www.pacoimperial.com.br* ⊠ *Free* ⊙ *Tues.–Sun. noon–6.*

Palácio Tiradentes. The Tiradentes Palace contains a permanent exhibit describing its history as the seat of the Brazilian parliament before Brasília was built in the late 1950s. Getúlio Vargas, Brazil's president for almost 20 years and by far the biggest force in 20th-century Brazilian politics, used the palace in the 1940s as a nucleus for disseminating propaganda. Free half-hour tours are given in Portuguese, English, and Spanish. ⊠ *Rua Primeiro de Março s/n, Centro* ☎ *021/2588-1000* ⊕ *www.alerj.rj.gov.br* ⊠ *Free* ⊙ *Mon.–Sat. 10–7, Sun. noon–5.*

CATETE AND GLÓRIA

Though a little run down, historic, residential Catete and Glória are well worth an afternoon's sightseeing. The Palácio do Catete, the presidential palace until the government moved to Brasília, itself warrants at least two hours. In addition to its hilltop church, Glória has a lovely marina that's perfect for a picnic or stroll, especially on a Sunday, when the main road is closed to traffic.

Handily located on the metro line between the Zona Sul and Centro, the two neighborhoods' subway stations are just a few minutes' walk from each other. From Ipanema or Copacabana take the 10-minute ride to Catete, and you'll emerge right in front of the Museum of the Republic. Set aside a couple of hours to see the exhibits and enjoy a coffee in the gardens before taking a stroll down to Glória's marina, taking in the monument to fallen soldiers. The surrounding area can be a little rough, so jump on a metro to Centro or the Zona Sul when you're done sightseeing.

TOP ATTRACTIONS

Igreja de Nossa Senhora da Glória do Outeiro. The aptly named Church of Our Lady of the Glory of the Knoll (Church of Glory for short) sits on top of a hill and is visible from many spots in the city, making it a landmark that's truly cherished by the cariocas. Its location was a strategic point in the city's early days, and the views from church grounds are impressive. Estácio da Sá took this hill from the French in the 1560s and then went on to expand the first settlement and to found a city for the Portuguese. The baroque church, which wasn't built until 1739, is notable for its octagonal floor plan, large dome, ornamental stonework, and vivid tile work. Tours are given by appointment only. As opening hours are sporadic, visitors might choose to arrive shortly before 9 am or 11 am on Sundays, when a Mass takes place and the church is open to the public. ⊠ *Praça Nossa Senhora da Glória 135, Glória* 🕾 *021/2225–2869* ⊕ *www.outeirodagloria.org.br* Ⓜ *Glória.*

FAMILY
Fodor'sChoice
★
Palácio do Catete. Once the villa of a German baron, this elegant, 19th-century granite-and-marble palace became the presidential residence after the 1889 coup overthrew the monarchy and established the Republic of Brazil. Eighteen presidents lived here. Gaze at the palace's gleaming parquet floors and intricate bas-relief ceilings as you wander through its **Museu da República** (Museum of the Republic). The permanent exhibits include a shroud-draped view of the bedroom where President Getúlio Vargas committed suicide in 1954 after the military threatened to overthrow his government. Presidential memorabilia, furniture, and paintings that date from the proclamation of the republic to the end of Brazil's military regime in 1985 are also displayed. The palace gardens are free, and worth a visit in themselves. With their imperial palm trees, water features, chattering monkeys, and strolling geese they are among the most pleasant—and safest, thanks to patrolling guards—parks in the city, and there's a well-equipped children's playground at the far end. A small contemporary art gallery, a movie theater, a café, and a bistro operate within the grounds, and there's free live music around 6 pm each weekday, courtesy of a group of senior local *sambistas.* ⊠ *Rua do Catete 153, Catete* 🕾 *021/3235–3693* ⊕ *www.museus. gov.br/os-museus* 🖾 *Tues. and Thurs.–Sat. R$6, Wed. and Sun. free* ☉ *Tues., Thurs., and Fri. noon–5, Wed. 2–5, weekends 2–6* Ⓜ *Catete.*

WORTH NOTING

Monumento aos Pracinhas. The Monument to the Brazilian Dead of World War II—the nation sided with the Allies during the conflict—is actually a combination museum and monument. The museum houses military uniforms, medals, stamps, and documents belonging to soldiers, and two soaring columns flank the tomb of an unknown soldier. The best time to visit is on a Sunday, when the road in front of the monument is closed to traffic, and joggers, dog-walkers, and strolling families fill the area. ⊠ *Parque Brigadeiro Eduardo Gomes, Glória* 🕾 *021/2240–1283* ⊕ *www.mnmsgm.ensino.eb.br* 🖾 *Free* ☉ *Tues.–Sun. 10–5* Ⓜ *Glória.*

SANTA TERESA AND LAPA

With its cobblestone streets and bohemian atmosphere, Santa Teresa is a delightfully eccentric neighborhood. Gabled Victorian mansions sit beside alpine-style chalets as well as more prosaic dwellings—many hanging at unbelievable angles from the flower-encrusted hills. Cafés, galleries, and antiques shops have nudged their way into nooks and crannies between the colorful homes, many of which house artists and their studios. Downhill from Santa Teresa, Lapa has some of the oldest buildings in the city and is home to the imposing Arcos da Lapa (Lapa Aqueduct) and the colorful Escadaria Selarón, also called the Lapa Steps, as well as the city's oldest street, the café-paved Rua do Lavradio.

By night, Lapa is transformed into the party heart of Rio, with countless bars and clubs and a notoriously wild weekend street party.

Santa Teresa and Lapa merit a full day's exploring, and Santa Teresa is at its bohemian best from Thursday through Saturday—many bars and restaurants don't open early in the week. Take the metro to Carioca metro station and stroll past the towering cubic Petrobras building to Rua do Lavradio to browse the antiques stores and sidewalk cafés. From here, the Lapa Steps and Lapa Aqueduct are a quick stroll, or take the bone-rattling cab ride up the cobbled steps. Jump off at Largo do Guimaraes and prepare to spend a few hours admiring the architecture, galleries, and museums and enjoying the café culture here; the area is best seen on foot but avoid deserted streets. If it's a weekend or holiday, make a night of it by starting with drinks in one of Santa Teresa's many lively bars before taking a cab or bus down to the Lapa street party around midnight.

TOP ATTRACTIONS

Arcos da Lapa. Formerly the Aqueduto da Carioca (Carioca Aqueduct), this structure with 42 massive stone arches was built between 1744 and 1750 to carry water from the Carioca River in the hillside neighborhood of Santa Teresa to Centro. In 1896 the city transportation company converted the aqueduct, by then abandoned, into a viaduct, laying trolley tracks along it. For decades, Santa Teresa's rattling yellow street cars (the "bonde" or "bondinho") passed over the aqueduct as they carried passengers from Centro up to the hillside neighborhood of Santa Teresa. After an accident in 2011, however, when the tram's brakes failed and six passengers were killed, the bonde was shut down pending major upgrades. Many of Santa Teresa's main roads are currently being ripped up as new tramlines are laid down, and as of this writing new trams were being tested on the first section of track. The trams are expected to be in service before the 2016 Rio Olympics, although the same was said of the 2014 FIFA World Cup, a target that proved wildly optimistic. ⊠ *Estação Carioca, Rua Professor Lélio Gama, Lapa* Ⓜ *Carioca or Cinelândia.*

Fodor's Choice ★ **Escadaria Selarón** (*Selarón's Staircase*). After traveling the world and living in more than 50 countries, Chilean painter Selarón began working in 1990 on the iconic tile staircase that is now one of the highlights of Lapa. With tiles from around the world, Selarón's staircase is the product of years of dedication, artistic vision, and donations of tiles from places far and near. Sadly, in 2013 Selarón was found murdered at his nearby home. The colorful stairs provide a great photo opportunity—Snoop Dogg and Pharell Williams shot the video for their song "Beautiful" here. ⊠ *Escadaria Selarón 24, Lapa.*

Museu Chácara do Céu (*Museum of the Small Farm of the Sky*). The collection of mostly modern works at this museum was left—along with the hilltop house that contains it—by one of Rio's greatest arts patrons, Raymundo de Castro Maya. Included are originals by 20th-century masters Picasso, Braque, Dalí, Degas, Matisse, Modigliani, and Monet. The Brazilian holdings include priceless 17th- and 18th-century maps and works by leading modernists. The views of the aqueduct, Centro, and the bay are splendid from the museum's grounds. The adjoining Parque das Ruinas (Ruins Park, free) is well worth a visit, too, and has some spectacular views from the top floor of a once-abandoned colonial mansion. ✉ *Rua Murtinho Nobre 93, Santa Teresa* ☎ *021/3970–1126* ⊕ *www.museuscastromaya.com.br/chacara.htm* ✉ *R$5, free Wed.* ⊙ *Wed.–Mon. 11–5.*

WORTH NOTING

Largo do Guimarães (*Guimarães Square*). Much of the activity in close-knit Santa Teresa takes place around its village-like squares, among them Largo do Guimarães, a social hub that frequently hosts street parties. The informal restaurant Bar do Arnaudo is a popular hangout for local artistic types; the neighborhood's main drinking and dining strip spans out from here. On weekends, live music spills out from bars opening onto the square, and street vendors sell beer and caipirinhas. If you follow the tram track 1.2 km (¾ mile) northwest from here you'll come to **Largo das Neves** (Neves Square), with its picturesque white-washed church. Families and other locals gather in this square until late at night. ✉ *Rua Paschoal Carlos Magno, Ladeira do Castro, and Rua Almirante Alexandrino, Santa Teresa.*

FLAMENGO AND BOTAFOGO

These largely residential neighborhoods connect the southern beach districts and Centro via a series of highways that intersect here. It's easy to reach these neighborhoods by metro. Apartment buildings dominate, but Rio Sul—one of the city's most popular shopping centers—is here, as are some of the city's best museums and public spaces.

The eponymous beach at Flamengo no longer draws swimmers (its gentle waters look appealing but are polluted; the people you see are sunning, not swimming). A marina sits on a bay at one end of the beach, which is connected via a busy boulevard to the smaller beach (also polluted), at Botafogo. The city's yacht club is here, and when Rio was Brazil's capital, it was also the site of the city's glittering embassy row. The embassies relocated to Brasília long ago, but the mansions that housed them remain. Among Botafogo's more interesting mansion- and tree-lined streets are Mariana, Sorocaba, Matriz, and Visconde e Silva.

TOP ATTRACTIONS

FAMILY
Fodor's Choice
★

Casa Daros. A grand 19th-century neoclassical building has been lovingly restored in conjunction with the acclaimed Swiss art institute Daros to create one of Rio's most impressive exhibition spaces. As well as housing the city's most comprehensive collections of South American art—including paintings, photos, videos, and installations—the center hosts interesting visiting exhibitions and film screenings. Even the restaurant—run by the team behind culinary hot spot Miam Miam—is a cut above your average gallery café, and the vast grounds are a great place for visiting children to burn off some energy. ✉ *Rua General Severiano 159, Botafogo* ☎ *21/2138–0850* ⊕ *www.casadaros.net* ✉ *R$14, free Wed.* Ⓜ *Botafogo.*

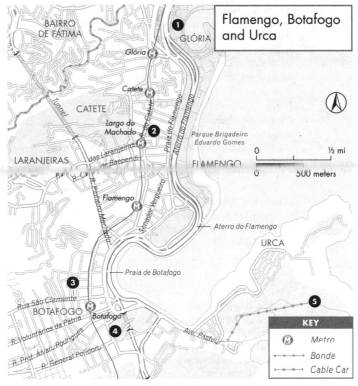

Flamengo, Botafogo and Urca

2

FAMILY **Oi Futuro Flamengo** (*Hi, Future*). This slick, ultramodern exhibition space also houses Rio's Telecommunications Museum. The museum itself delivers a unique multimedia adventure—lots of monitors, blinking lights, and media artifacts. After you've been oriented in the use of the MP3 headsets, a light- and mirror-filled airlock-like room awaits. The sights in this tiny exhibit space will likely mesmerize you, and if you don't speak Portuguese, the English guide will explain what you can't figure out from the visual cues. The other floors of the Oi Futuro building house cultural spaces devoted to theater performances, film screenings, and art exhibits. There's also a café whose rooftop terrace is a pleasant place to enjoy an iced cappuccino on a balmy day. ⊠ *Rua Dois de Dezembro 63, Flamengo* ☎ *021/3131–3060* ⊕ *www.oifuturo. org.br/en* ⊠ *Free* ☉ *Weekdays 11–5* Ⓜ *Largo do Machado or Catete.*

WORTH NOTING

FAMILY **Casa Rui Barbosa.** Steps away from Botafogo metro station is a museum in the former home of the 19th-century Brazilian statesman, writer, and scholar Rui Barbosa, a liberal from Bahia State who drafted one of Brazil's early constitutions. The pink mansion, which dates from 1849, is itself worth a visit. Stepping inside instantly transports you to the period when writers and other intellectuals inhabited this street's grand houses. Among the memorabilia and artifacts on display are Barbosa's 1913 car and legal, political, and journalistic works. The extensive libraries are testament to Rui Barbosa's love for literature. The well-tended gardens stretch for 9,000 meters and are filled with small pools and fountains, making them a pleasant place to take respite from the rush and crush of the city. There's a good children's library, regular kids' workshops and events, and free live music performances. ⊠ *Rua São Clemente 134, Botafogo* ☎ *021/3289–4600* ⊕ *www.casaruibarbosa.gov.br* ⊠ *R$2, free Sun.* ⊙ *Gardens daily 8–6, library Wed.–Fri. 10–5:30* Ⓜ *Botafogo.*

FAMILY **Parque do Flamengo.** The landscape architect Roberto Burle Marx designed this waterfront park that flanks the Baía de Guanabara from the Glória neighborhood to Flamengo. Frequently referred to as "Aterro do Flamengo," it gets its nickname from its location atop an *atêrro* (landfill). The park contains playgrounds and public tennis and basketball courts, and paths used for jogging, walking, and biking wind through it. On weekends the freeway beside the park is closed to traffic and the entire area becomes one enormous public space. For safety reasons, avoid wandering the park after dark. ⊠ *Inland of beach from Glória to Botafogo,* ⊠ *Free* Ⓜ *Glória or Flamengo.*

URCA

Tiny, sheltered Urca is home to one of Rio's most famous attractions, the Pão de Açúcar morro. As tranquil and bucolic as the rest of Rio is fast-paced and frenetic, Urca is a wonderful place for an afternoon's wandering. Fishing boats bob on a bay set against a spectacular view of Christ the Redeemer on his mountaintop perch, and the neighborhood contains some wonderful colonial architecture. The Pão de Açúcar separates Urca's tree-lined streets from Praia Vermelha, its small, coarse-sand beach. This beach is, in turn, blocked by the Urubu and Leme mountains from the 1-km (½-mile) Leme Beach at the start of the Zona Sul.

Urca is a little tricky to reach by public transport, so take a cab from Botafogo metro station. Come here in the morning and spend some time on the beaches. Take the pleasant 30-minute nature walk around the base of Sugar Loaf, and aim to be at the cable car station late afternoon to appreciate the stunning sunset views from the peak. Round off a perfect day by sipping a caipirinha by the harbor wall at Bar e Restaurante Urca.

TOP ATTRACTIONS

FAMILY
Fodor's Choice
★
Pão de Açúcar (*Sugarloaf Mountain*). The indigenous Tupi people originally called the soaring 396-meter (1,300-foot) granite block at the mouth of Baía de Guanabara *pau-nh-acugua* (high, pointed peak). To the Portuguese the phrase seemed similar to *pão de açúcar,* itself fitting because the rock's shape reminded them of the conical loaves in which refined sugar was sold. Italian-made bubble cars holding 75 passengers each move up the mountain in two stages. The first stop is at Morro da Urca, a smaller, 212-meter (705-foot) mountain; the second is at the summit of Pão de Açúcar itself. The trip to each level takes three minutes. In high season long lines form for the cable car; the rest of the year the wait is seldom more than 30 minutes. Consider visiting Pão

de Açúcar before climbing the considerably higher Corcovado, as the view here may seem anticlimactic if experienced second. ⊠ *Av. Pasteur 520, near Praia Vermelha, Urca* ☎ *021/2546–8400* ⊕ *www.bondinho. com.br* ⊠ *R$62* ⊙ *Daily 8–7:50.*

COPACABANA

2

Copacabana is Rio's most famous tourist neighborhood thanks to its fabulous beach and grande-dame hotels such as the Copacabana Palace. The main thoroughfare is Avenida Nossa Senhora de Copacabana, two blocks inland from the beach. The commercial street is filled with shops, restaurants, and sidewalks crowded with colorful characters. Despite having some of the best hotels in Rio, Copacabana's heyday is over, and the neighborhood is grittier than Ipanema or Leblon. It's no secret to thieves that tourists congregate here, so keep your eyes peeled for shady types when walking around after dark. *For a description of Copacabana Beach, see Beaches, below.*

Copacabana is Rio's most iconic neighborhood, and it's home to the city's largest concentration of hotels. The beach is the main attraction and is served by three metro stations. Cardeal Arcoverde is the closest to Leme, the quieter, family-oriented end of the beach, Siqueira Campos is right at the center, and Cantagalo is within walking distance of Ipanema. Plan to spend the best part of a day here, buying food and drink from beach vendors or the many kiosks that line the sidewalk.

TOP ATTRACTIONS

FAMILY **Forte de Copacabana and Museu Histórico do Exército.** Copacabana Fort was built in 1914 as part of Rio's first line of defense, and many original features, such as the thick brick fortification and old Krupp cannons, are still visible. In the '60s and '70s, during Brazil's military dictatorship, political prisoners were kept here. The fort is impressive in itself, and the entrance archway perfectly frames a postcard view of Sugar Loaf. The best views, however, follow the path to its end and climb the steep stairs to the cannon roof, which juts right out into the ocean and takes in sweeping vistas over the Zona Sul beaches. The on-site military-history museum is worth a stop, and there are two good cafés here as well as a gift shop. During the Brazilian summer, violin recitals, classical music performances, and outdoor cinema screenings are held here, many free of charge. ⊠ *Praça Coronel Eugênio Franco 1, Copacabana* ☎ *021/2287–3781* ⊕ *www.fortedecopacabana.com* ⊠ *R$6* ⊙ *Tues.–Sun. 10–6.*

IPANEMA AND LEBLON

Ipanema, Leblon, and the blocks surrounding Lagoa Rodrigo de Freitas are part of Rio's money belt. For an up-close look at the posh apartment buildings, stroll down beachfront Avenida Vieira Souto and its extension, Avenida Delfim Moreira, or drive around the lagoon on Avenida Epitácio Pessoa. The tree-lined streets between Ipanema Beach and the lagoon are as peaceful as they are attractive. The boutiques along Rua Garcia D'Ávila make window-shopping a sophisticated endeavor. Other

CLOSE UP

Gay Rio

Gay Rio rocks almost every night with a whole menu of entertainment options. During the day, dedicated areas of the beach in Copacabana (Posto 6) and Ipanema (in front of Rua Farme de Amoedo, near Posto 8) are gay and lesbian havens. After dark, the nightlife is welcoming and inclusive. Kick off the evening taking a walk along Farme do Amoeda in Ipanema, which is lined with GLS (Gay/Lesbian/Sympathiser) bars and restaurants. Close to the famous street, be sure to check out **Galeria Café,** also in Ipanema, or **Rainbow Kiosk,** right on the sands in front of the Copacabana Palace. As the night nudges 1 am, head toward **Le Boy** or the quieter **La Cueva,** one of Copacabana's longest-running

gay venues, which attracts a more mature male. Most of the livelier underground clubs, such as **Casa Rosa** and **Fosfobox,** run GLS nights during the week. The downtown party district of Lapa, previously lacking in appealing GLS options, was given a boost with the opening of **Sinônimo,** a three-story club incorporating live music, DJs, and a cocktail lounge. The sporadic circuit party B.I.T.C.H (Barbies in Total Control ⊕ *www.bitch.com.br*) has been one of the biggest events on the gay calendar since the 1980s. Many gay-focused parties and parades take place during carnival, while the annual Gay Pride parade along Copacabana Beach is one of the biggest and most colorful events on the international gay calendar.

chic areas near the beach include Praça Nossa Senhora da Paz, which is lined with wonderful restaurants and bars; Rua Vinicius de Moraes; and Rua Farme de Amoedo. Gourmands should make a beeline for Leblon's Rua Dias Ferreira, where top-notch restaurants thrill diners daily. The lively bar scene here encompasses everything from exclusive lounges and wine bars to relaxed post-beach watering holes. *For descriptions of Ipanema Beach and Leblon Beach, see Beaches, below.*

Ipanema is famous for its beach, beautiful people, and boutiques, so sun-seekers and shopaholics will want to spend at least a day here. There's a metro station a couple of blocks from the beach. Arrive at the beach early to bag a prime people-watching position and spend a few hours here—beach vendors will keep you refreshed with coconut water, soft drinks, beer, and snacks. In the afternoon head to Visconde de Piraja for shopping, before stopping at one of the many upscale restaurants for early evening food and drinks. Should you choose to make a night of it, there are plenty of lively bars here.

TOP ATTRACTIONS

Museu H.Stern. Hans Stern started his gem empire in 1945 with an initial investment of about $200. Today his company's interests include mining and production operations, as well as stores in Europe, the Americas, and the Middle East. The world headquarters of H.Stern contains a small museum that exhibits rare gems. On the self-guided workshop tour, you'll learn about the entire process of cutting, polishing, and setting stones. Afterward, you get a personal consultation with a salesperson, although you should not feel obliged to buy. The museum can arrange free transport to and from your hotel. ⊠ *Rua Garcia D'Avila 113, Ipanema* ☎ *021/2106–0000* ⊕ *www.hsterninrio. com* ✉ *Free* ☉ *Tours by appointment only; booking form on website* Ⓜ *Ipanema/General Osorio.*

SÃO CONRADO AND BARRA DA TIJUCA

West of the Zona Sul lie the largely residential (and considerably affluent) neighborhoods of São Conrado and Barra da Tijuca. If you're accustomed to the shop-lined and restaurant-filled streets of Copacabana and Ipanema, you're in for a shock if you head to these neighborhoods, dominated mainly by towering, modern apartment buildings. São Conrado's main attractions are the beach, which serves as a landing point for hang gliders and paragliders, and the chic Fashion Mall. Barra da Tijuca, often likened to Miami because of its wide avenues, towering condos, and sprawling malls, offers ample high-end dining opportunities as well as a white-sand beach that stretches for a staggering 15 km (9 miles).

Barra da Tijuca is not known as a cultural hot spot, but if you are looking for serious shopping it is the place to go. It's also home to Rio's largest beach, so set aside a day for both beachgoing and retail therapy. A metro station is set to open here ahead of the 2016 Olympics, but until that happens it is best reached by cab; ask the driver to stop at São Conrado so you can snap a few photos of the hang gliders, or alternatively visit this beach hangout as part of a group tour—until the metro arrives it is a little difficult to reach by public transport.

TOP ATTRACTIONS

FAMILY
Fodor'sChoice
★

Sitio Roberto Burle Marx (*Roberto Burle Marx Farm*). It's a cab ride out of town and visits need to be booked in advance, but nature lovers and architecture buffs will find it worth the effort to visit this plantation-turned-museum honoring Roberto Burle Marx, Brazil's legendary landscape architect. Marx, the mind behind Rio's swirling mosaic beachfront walkways and the Atêrro do Flamengo, was said to have "painted with plants," and he was the first designer to use Brazilian flora in his projects. More than 3,500 species—including some discovered by and named for Marx, as well as many on the endangered list—flourish at this 100-acre estate. Marx grouped his plants not only according to their soil and light needs but also according to their shape and texture. He also liked to mix the modern with the traditional—a recurring theme throughout the property. The results are both whimsical and elegant. In 1985 he bequeathed the farm to the Brazilian government, though he remained here until his death in 1994. His house is now a cultural center full of his belongings, including collections of folk art, and the beautiful gardens are a tribute to his talents. The grounds also contain his ultramodern studio (he was a painter, too) and a small, restored colonial chapel dedicated to St. Anthony. ⊠ *Estrada Roberto Burle Marx 2019, Pedra da Guaratiba* ✛ *At far end of Barra da Tijuca* ☎ *021/ 2410–1412* ⊕ *sitioburlemarx.blogspot.com.br* ✉ *R$10* ☉ *Tues.–Sun. by appointment only; tours at 9:30 am and 1:30 pm.*

FAMILY **Museu Casa do Pontal.** If you're heading toward the beaches of Prainha or Grumari, consider taking a detour to Brazil's largest folk-art museum. One room houses a wonderful mechanical sculpture that represents all of the *escolas de samba* (samba schools) that march in the Carnival parades. Another mechanical "scene" depicts a circus in action. This is the private collection of French expatriate Jacques Van de Beuque, who collected Brazilian treasures—including religious pieces—from his arrival in the country in 1946 until his death in 2000. ✉ *Estrada do Pontal 3295, Grumari* ☎ *021/2490–3278* ⊕ *www.museucasadopontal. com.br* 🖃 *R$10* ☉ *Tues.–Sun. 9:30–5.*

WORTH NOTING

São Conrado. The juxtaposition of the "haves" and "have nots" couldn't be more stark, or more startling, than it is in São Conrado, where mansions and expensive condos sit right next to sprawling favelas. As you approach the neighborhood heading west from Ipanema, Avenida Niemeyer, blocked by the imposing Dois Irmãos Mountain, snakes along rugged cliffs that offer spectacular sea views on the left. The road returns to sea level again in São Conrado, a natural amphitheater surrounded by forested mountains and the ocean. Development of this upper-class residential area began in the late 1960s with an eye on Rio's high society. A short stretch along the beach includes the condominiums of a former president, the ex-wife of another former president, an ex-governor of Rio de Janeiro State, and a onetime Central Bank president. The towering Pedra da Gávea, a huge flattop granite boulder, marks the western edge of São Conrado. North of the boulder lies Pedra Bonita, the mountain from which gliders depart. ✉ *Just west of Leblon, .*

INLAND ZONA SUL

In the western portion of the city north of Leblon, trees and hills dominate the landscape in the neighborhoods of Jardim Botânico, Lagoa, Cosme Velho, and Laranjeiras. In addition to their parks and gardens, these primarily residential neighborhoods have marvelous museums, seductive architecture, and tantalizing restaurants. The architecture is a blend of modern condominiums and colonial houses. These neighborhoods tend to be quieter during the day because they're not on the beachfront, but they do have some of the hippest nightclubs in Rio. You can't say you've seen Rio until you've taken in the view from Corcovado and then strolled through its forested areas or beside its inland Lagoa (Lagoon) Rodrigo de Freitas—hanging out just like a true carioca.

These picturesque inland neighborhoods lack metro stops, so the best way to visit them all in one day is as part of an organized tour or with a private guide. If you have time to spare, each neighborhood warrants at least half a day's exploring. Be sure to visit Lagoa, which can be reached on foot from Leblon, Ipanema, and Copacabana, and the nearby Botanical Gardens. Cosme Velho is home to impressive mansions as well as the station for trains up to the Christ statue, and it's a pleasant stroll along the main road from here to Laranjeiras, which has some good bars and restaurants as well as pleasant squares and street markets.

CLOSE UP

Favelas

A BIT OF HISTORY

Named after the flowers that grow on the hills of Rio, the first favela began as a squatter town for homeless soldiers at the end of the 19th century. Later, freed slaves illegally made their homes on these undeveloped government lands. The favelas flourished and expanded in the 1940s as the population in Brazil shifted from a rural-based to an urban-based one. In the 1970s, during the military dictatorship, the government moved favela dwellers into public housing projects.

RIO'S LARGEST FAVELA

Rocinha is Rio's largest and most developed favela. Between 150,000 and 300,000 people reside in this well-developed community (there are three banks, a nightclub, and many shops and small markets). Brace yourself for a variety of smells, both good and bad: you'll find savory-smelling, grilled *churrasquinho* (meat skewers) sold in the street, and any number of delicious aromas drifting out of nearby restaurants. On the flip side, residents dump their trash on the side

of the road (in designated areas) and in some places, raw sewage flows in open canals.

EXPLORING

The main thoroughfare, the Estrada da Gávea, begins in São Conrado and ends on the other side of Rocinha, in Gávea. Anyone can take a stroll up this steep, but urban, route and to hear English being spoken. If you're feeling intrepid and want to explore Rocinha on foot without a guide, be aware of the following: In 2012 police wrested control of Rocinha from the drug faction Amigos dos Amigos (ADA) as part of an ongoing citywide pacification project. Though UPPs (Police Pacification Units) have largely kept the peace since then, shoot-outs between police and faction members are not unheard of. Crime against tourists in the favela is rare, but unguided visitors stand a real chance of getting lost in the maze of streets. By far the safest way to visit Rocinha or other favelas is to take an organized tour. *For information about favela tours, see Tours, in Rio de Janeiro Planning, above.*

TOP ATTRACTIONS

FAMILY
Fodor's Choice
★

Corcovado and Christ the Redeemer. Rio's iconic *Cristo Redentor* (Christ the Redeemer) statue stands arms outstretched atop 690-meter-high (2,300-foot-high) Corcovado mountain. There's an eternal argument about which city view is better, the one from Pão de Açúcar (Sugarloaf) or the one from here. In our opinion, it's best to visit Sugarloaf *before* you visit Corcovado, or you may experience Sugarloaf only as an anticlimax. Corcovado has two advantages: it's nearly twice as high, and it offers an excellent view of Pão de Açúcar itself. The sheer 300-meter (1,000-foot) granite face of Corcovado (the name means "hunchback" and refers to the mountain's shape) has always been a difficult undertaking for climbers.

It wasn't until 1921, the centennial of Brazil's independence from Portugal, that someone had the idea of placing a statue atop Corcovado. A team of French artisans headed by sculptor Paul Landowski was assigned the task of erecting a statue of Christ with his arms apart as if embracing the city. (Nowadays, mischievous cariocas say Christ is getting ready to clap for his favorite escola de samba.) It took 10 years, but on October 12, 1931, Christ the Redeemer was inaugurated by then-president Getúlio Vargas, Brazil's FDR. The sleek, modern figure rises more than 30 meters (100 feet) from a 6-meter (20-foot) pedestal and weighs 700 tons. In the evening a powerful lighting system transforms it into an even more dramatic icon.

There are three ways to reach the top: by funicular railway, by official van, or on foot (not recommended without a guide for safety reasons). The train, built in 1885, provides delightful views of Ipanema and Leblon from an absurd angle of ascent, as well as a close look at thick vegetation and butterflies. (You may wonder what those oblong medicine balls hanging from the trees are, the ones that look like spiked watermelons tied to ropes—they're *jaca*, or jackfruit.) Trains leave the Cosme Velho station (*Rua Cosme Velho 513, Cosme Velho, 021/2558–1329, www.corcovado.com.br*) for the steep, 5-km (3-mile), 17-minute ascent. Late-afternoon trains are the most popular; on weekends be prepared for a long wait. Buy tickets online to avoid queueing twice: once to buy tickets and once to board the train. Official vans are slightly cheaper but not as much fun as the railway. There are boarding points for the vans in Copacabana and Largo do Machado, and at Paineiras inside the national park. Tickets can be bought online (*www.paineirascorcovado. com.br*). After disembarking you can climb up 220 steep, zigzagging steps to the summit, or take an escalator or a panoramic elevator. If you choose the stairs, you pass little cafés and shops selling souvenirs along the way. Save your money for Copacabana's night market; you'll pay at least double atop Corcovado. Once at the top, all of Rio stretches out before you. Visit Corcovado on a clear day; clouds often obscure the Christ statue and the view of the city. Go as early in the morning as possible, before people start pouring out of tour buses, and before the haze sets in. ⊠ *Estrada da Redentor, Cosme Velho* ⊕ *www.corcovado. com.br* ⊠ *R$62 by train, R$55 by minibus, R$30 on foot with guide* ⊙ *Daily 8–7; trains run every 30 minutes, vans 8–6 daily.*

FAMILY **Fundação Planetário.** Rio's planetarium is a great escape if your vacation gets rained on, or if you simply have a passion for astronomy. The adjoining interactive Museu do Universo (Museum of the Universe) illustrates the history of space exploration and travel in a futuristic exhibition area with lots of hands-on activities for kids. The planetarium frequently updates its programming, which consists of a mixture of fictitious adventures in space (recommended for kids) and nonfiction shows about the constellations and our solar system. If your aim is stargazing without the voice-over and music, the Praça dos Telescópios is open for sky observation from Tuesday to Friday, between 7:30 pm and 9:30 pm. ⊠ *Rua Vice-Governador Ruben Bernardo 100, Gávea* ☎ *021/2274–0046* ⊕ *www.planetariodorio.com.br* ⊠ *Museum R$4; museum and planetarium session R$16; weekends half price* ⊙ *Tues.– Fri. 9–5, weekends and holidays 2:30–5.*

FAMILY **Jardim Botânico.** The 340-acre Botanical Garden contains more than
Fodor's Choice 5,000 species of tropical and subtropical plants and trees, including 900
★ varieties of palms (some more than a century old) and more than 140

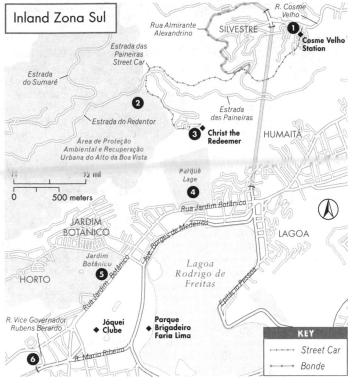

Inland Zona Sul

species of birds. The shady garden, created in 1808 by the Portuguese king João VI during his exile in Brazil, offers respite from Rio's sticky heat. In 1842 the garden gained its most impressive adornment, the Avenue of the Royal Palms, a 720-meter (800-yard) double row of 134 soaring royal palms. Elsewhere, the Casa dos Pilões, an old gunpowder factory, has been restored and displays objects pertaining to the nobility and their slaves. Also on the grounds are a museum dedicated to enviromental concerns, a library, two small cafés, and a gift shop. ⊠ *Rua Jardim Botânico 1008, Jardim Botânico* ☎ *021/3874–1808, 021/3874–1214* ⊕ *www.jbrj.gov.br* ⊠ *R$7* ⊙ *Mon. noon–7, Tues.–Sun. 8–5.*

FAMILY **Parque Lage.** This lush green space down the road from Jardim Botânico was acquired by Antônio Martins Lage Jr., whose grandson, Henrique Lage, fell head-over-heels in love with the Italian singer Gabriela Bezanzoni. The magnificent palace he had constructed for her was completed in 1922; the impressive mansion and grounds were turned into a public park in 1960. A visual-arts school and a café occupy the mansion. On the grounds are small aquariums and a few caves that have stalactites and stalagmites. If you want to tackle Corcovado on foot to make your pilgrimage to see Christ the Redeemer, start in Parque Lage; trails are clearly marked, though you shouldn't go alone. ⊠ *Rua Jardim Botânico*

414, Jardim Botânico ☎ *021/3257–1800* ⊕ *www.eavparquelage.rj.gov. br* ⬛ *Free* ⊙ *Daily 8–5.*

WORTH NOTING

FAMILY **Floresta da Tijuca** (*Tijuca Forest*). Surrounding Corcovado is the dense, tropical Tijuca Forest, also known as the Parque Nacional da Tijuca. Once part of a Brazilian nobleman's estate, it's studded with exotic trees and thick jungle vines and has several waterfalls, including the delightful Cascatinha de Taunay (Taunay Waterfall). About 180 meters (200 yards) beyond the waterfall is the small pink-and-purple Capela Mayrink (Mayrink Chapel), with painted panels by the 20th-century Brazilian artist Cândido Portinari.

The views are breathtaking from several points along this national park's 96 km (60 miles) of narrow winding roads. Some of the most spectacular are from Dona Marta, on the way up Corcovado; the Emperor's Table, supposedly where Brazil's last emperor, Pedro II, took his court for picnics; and, farther down the road, the Chinese View, the area where Portuguese king João VI allegedly settled the first Chinese immigrants to Brazil, who came in the early 19th century to develop tea plantations. A great way to see the forest is by Jeep or van; you can arrange tours through several agencies, among them Brazil Expedition (*www.brazilexpedition.com*) and Jeep Tour (*021/2108–5800, www.jeeptour.com.br*). ✉ *Estrada da Cascatinha 850, Alta da Boa Vista* ☎ *021/2492–2252* ⊕ *www.parquedatijuca.com.br* ⬛ *Free* ⊙ *Daily 8–5.*

FAMILY **Museu Internacional De Arte Naïf do Brasil** (*International Museum of Naïve Art from Brazil*). More than 6,000 works by Brazil's best self-taught painters, along with some by their counterparts from around the world, grace the walls of a colonial mansion that was once the studio of painter Eliseu Visconti. The museum is a few steps uphill from the station for the train to Corcovado, and entrance is half price for those with a train ticket for the same day. The works on display date from the 15th century to the present. Don't miss the colorful, colossal 7×4–meter (22×13–foot) canvas that depicts the city of Rio; it reportedly took five years to complete. There's a pleasant, kid-friendly organic café on the grounds. ✉ *Rua Cosme Velho 561, Cosme Velho* ☎ *021/2205–8612* ⊕ *www.museunaif.com/en* ⬛ *R$12* ⊙ *Tues.–Fri. 10–6, weekends and holidays noon–6.*

WEST OF DOWNTOWN

Neighborhoods west of downtown are mainly residential. Some are middle-class and some are poor. Unless you're a local, it's hard to know which areas are safe and which are not, so you should avoid wandering around. One exception is pleasant Quinta da Boa Vista, which is fine to wander. You can easily get here by metro, but avoid coming after dark.

Few visitors will make their base in the area west of downtown, but one compelling reason to visit is the mighty Maracana soccer stadium, which is open for tours on non–match days. If you want to catch a game it is easiest to go as part of a group trip. Nearby, the city zoo, national museum, and scenic gardens at Quinta da Boa Vista are worth a visit if you have the time.

TOP ATTRACTIONS

FAMILY

Fodor's Choice

★

Maracanã. Fans have witnessed many historic sports moments at this stadium that hosted the finals of the 1950 and 2014 FIFA World Cups and was the venue where the soccer star Pelé scored his 1,000th goal. Now seating 78,838 fans after a major makeover in anticipation of the 2014 World Cup, the stadium will host key matches during the 2016 Rio Olympics, and big local games are also held here during the seemingly never-ending Brazilian soccer season. The stadium is officially called Estádio Mário Filho, after a famous journalist, but it's best known as Maracanã, the name of the surrounding neighborhood and a nearby river. Guided and non-guided stadium tours can be booked on the official website. ✉ *Rua Professor Eurico Rabelo, Gate 16,* ☎ *0800/ 062-7222* ⊕ *www.maracana.com* ✉ *Match tickets R$30–R$100, non-guided tours from R$26, guided tours from R$40* Ⓜ *Maracanã.*

FAMILY

Museu Nacional. A little off Rio's main tourist track, the National Museum is well worth the metro ride to view its exhibits of botanical, anthropological, and animal specimens. With a permanent collection of 20 million objects (give or take a few), the supply is nearly endless. Temporary exhibitions focus on subjects such as meteorites, tribal art, and animal evolution. The opulent museum building—a former imperial palace—itself merits a visit, and the vast grounds are home to Rio's city zoo. ✉ *Quinta da Boa Vista, São Cristóvão* ☎ *021/2562–6900* ⊕ *www.museunacional.ufrj.br* ✉ *R$6* ☉ *Tues.–Fri. 10–5, Mon. noon–5* Ⓜ *Estação São Cristóvão.*

FAMILY

Quinta da Boa Vista. Complete with lakes and marble statuary, this vast public park on a former royal estate's landscaped grounds is a popular spot for family picnics. You can rent boats to pedal on the water, and bicycles to pedal on land. The former imperial palace now houses the Museu Nacional. The city zoo sits adjacent to the park, which often hosts live-music events. ✉ *Av. Paulo e Silva at Av. Bartolomeu de Gusmão, São Cristóvão* ✉ *Free* ☉ *Daily 10–6* Ⓜ *São Cristóvão.*

WORTH NOTING

FAMILY

Jardim Zoológico. For children and others with an interest in seeing birds and beasts up close, Rio's city zoo makes for a diverting day out. Colorful native birds and a variety of South American monkeys are among the attractions; the "nursery" for baby animals and the reptile house are always popular with younger visitors. The zoo has received criticism for the somewhat small enclosures the larger animals—including lions and bears—endure, but conditions overall have improved in recent years. ✉ *Quinta da Boa Vista, São Cristóvão* ☎ *021/3878–4200* ⊕ *www.rio. rj.gov.br/web/riozoo* ✉ *R$6* ☉ *Wed.–Sun. 9–4:30* Ⓜ *São Cristovão.*

BEACHES

Rio's circuit of *praias* (beaches) begins in the north with Flamengo, on Guanabara Bay, but the best strands are farther south. Beaches are the city's pulse points: exercise centers, gathering places, lovers' lanes.

Although cariocas wander into the water to cool off, most spend their time sunning and socializing, not swimming. Copacabana and Ipanema are the most active areas. As you head west from Barra da Tijuca the beaches become increasingly isolated and have little tourist infrastructure. Ruggedly beautiful, they are popular with surfers.

Zona Sul beaches can be easily reached by metro, but for the farther-flung strands, consider taking a taxi. City buses and chartered minivans drop you off along the shore, but they can be confusing if you don't speak Portuguese. Turismo Clássico can arrange for drivers and guides.

Beaches are listed geographically from north to south.

FLAMENGO AND BOTAFOGA

Praia do Flamengo. This small curved beach with a terrific view of Sugar Loaf is much busier from 5 to 7 in the morning than on a sunny afternoon. That's because Flamengo Beach is a great place to go for a walk, jog, run, or stroll, but not such a great place for a dip in the (usually brown) water. Vying with the beach for the attention of locals is Porcão Rio's, a not-to-be-missed churrascaria. **Amenities:** food and drink. **Best for:** walking. ⊠ *Rua Praia do Flamengo, Flamengo* Ⓜ *Flamengo.*

Praia do Botafogo. Though very much a strand, the Zona Sul's most polluted beach doesn't attract swimmers and sunbathers. Locals joke that the fish here come ready-coated in oil for frying, but don't let that stop you from jogging along the sidewalk if you're staying nearby. Early risers are often rewarded with a stunning sunrise from this shore. **Amenities:** none. **Best for:** sunrise. ⊠ *Between Praça Praia Nova and Praça Marinha do Brasil, Botafogo* Ⓜ *Botafogo.*

URCA

FAMILY   **Praia Vermelha.** Right at the foot of Sugar Loaf, this sheltered, rough-sand beach (the name means "red beach," a reference to the distinctive coarse sand here) is one of the safest places in the city for sunbathing thanks to its location next to a military base. Frequented more by local families than by tourists, and with only a few vendors, Vermelha is a tranquil spot to catch some rays. The water here is calm, but it's often too dirty for swimming. **Amenities:** food and drink. **Best for:** sunset. ⊠ *Praça General Tibúrcio, Urca.*

COPACABANA

FAMILY   **Praia do Leme.** Leme Beach is a natural extension of Copacabana Beach to the northeast, toward Pão de Açúcar. A rock formation juts into the water here, forming a quiet cove that's less crowded than the rest of the beach. This is a top spot for families, and small wading pools can be rented along with the usual beach chairs and sun umbrellas at the many *barracas* (beach tents selling food and drink). Along a sidewalk, at the side of the mountain overlooking Leme, anglers stand elbow to elbow with their lines dangling into the sea. Many locals swim here, but be wary of the strong undertow, and never head into the water when the

2

red flag is displayed on the beach. **Amenities:** food and drink; toilets; showers; lifeguards. **Best for:** walking; sunset. ☒ *From Av. Princesa Isabel to Morro do Leme, Leme* Ⓜ *Cardeal Arcoverde.*

Fodor's Choice ★ **Praia de Copacabana.** Maddening traffic, noise, packed apartment blocks, and a world-famous beach—this is Copacabana, or, Manhattan with bikinis. Walk along the neighborhood's classic ╌╌╌╌╌╌ to dive headfirst into Rio's beach culture, a cradle-to-grave lifestyle that begins with toddlers accompanying their parents to the water and ends with silver-haired seniors walking hand in hand along the sidewalk. Copacabana hums with activity: you're likely to see athletic men playing volleyball

NEW YEAR'S EVE IN RIO

Rio's New Year's celebration, or *Réveillon* as it's known in Brazil, is a whirling dervish of a party in which an estimated 3 million people truck over to Copacabana for drinks, dancing, and a spectacular fireworks show in Guanabara Bay. A word of warning: stay away from the stage. The area immediately surrounding the temporary stage on the beach becomes packed with people, and you run the risk of getting pickpocketed. Plan your hotel stay months in advance, and be prepared to pay more. Prices at least double, and rooms fill quickly.

using only their feet and heads, not their hands—a sport Brazilians have dubbed *futevôlei*. As you can tell by all the goal nets, soccer is also popular, and Copacabana has been a frequent host to the annual world beach soccer championships. You can swim here, although pollution levels and a strong undertow can sometimes be discouraging. Pollution levels change daily and are well publicized; someone at your hotel should be able to get you the information.

Copacabana's privileged live on beachfront Avenida Atlântica, famed for its wide mosaic sidewalks designed by Roberto Burle Marx, and for its grand hotels—including the Copacabana Palace Hotel—and cafés with sidewalk seating. On Sunday two of the avenue's lanes are closed to traffic and are taken over by joggers, rollerbladers, cyclists, and pedestrians. **Amenities:** food and drink; lifeguards; showers; toilets. **Best for:** sunset; walking. ☒ *Av. Princesa Isabel to Rua Francisco Otaviano, Copacabana* Ⓜ *Cardeal Arcoverde, Siqueira Campos, and Cantagalo.*

NEED A BREAK?

Manoel & Juaquim. For a cooling early evening drink after a walk along the beach, drop by this air-conditioned *boteco* (casual bar-restaurant) whose windows face the sand. Part of a chain whose branches you'll find elsewhere in Copacabana and in Ipanema, this is a fine place to settle in with a cold draft beer, order a few *empadas* (little pies filled with shrimp, chicken, or cheese), and watch carioca life unfold. ☒ *Av. Atlântica 1936, Copacabana* ☎ *021/2547–8192* ⊕ *manoelejuaquim.com.br/copacabanaposto3* ☉ *Closed Sun.* Ⓜ *Siqueira Campos.*

Praia do Diabo. A barely noticeable stretch of sand tucked away between Arpoador and a natural rock wall that extends to Copacabana's fort, Praia do Diabo is popular with local *surfistas* (surfers) but the dangerous waves, which can smash an unskilled surfer into the nearby rocks,

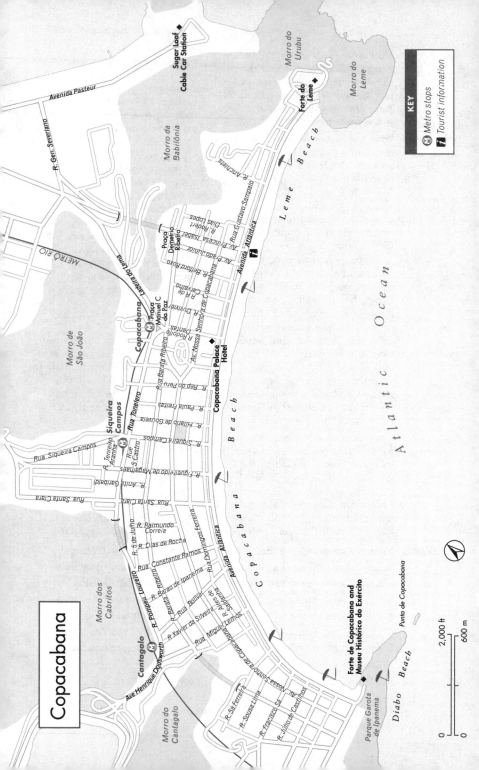

Copacabana

KEY

Ⓜ Metro stops
🛈 Tourist information

Sugar Loaf
Cable Car Station ◆

Avenida Pasteur

R. Gen. Severiano

Morro da
Babilônia

Morro do
Urubu

Morro do
Leme

**Forte do
Leme** ◆

Leme Beach

METRO RIO

Morro de
São João

Praça Demétrio Ribeiro

R. Rodolfo Dias Lopes
Av. P. Princesa Isabel

Avenida Atlântica

R. Anchieta

Ladeira do Leme

Praça
Manuel C
de Paz

Copacabana Ⓜ

Rua Barata Ribeiro

R. Duvivier
Ar. de
R. Belford Roxo
Av. Nossa Senhora de Copacabana

R. Rodolfo
Dantas

Av. Prado Júnior

Rua Gustavo Sampaio

**Copacabana
Palace Hotel**

R. Rep. do Peru

R. Paula Freitas

R. Hilário de Gouveia

Atlantic Ocean

Rua Tonelero

R. Siqueira Campos

**Siqueira
Campos** Ⓜ

Rua Siqueira Campos

R. Tenente Aranha

Rua
S. Castro

R. Figueiredo de Magalhães

Copacabana Beach

R. Anita Garibaldi

Rua Santa Clara

Rua Santa Clara

R. 5 de Julho

R. Raimundo
Correia

R. Dias de Rocha

Rua Constante Ramos

R. Pompeu Loureiro

Rua Barata Ribeiro

R. Barata Ribeiro

R. Barão de Ipanema

Rua Domingos Ferreira

Avenida Atlântica

Morro dos
Cabritos

Cantagalo Ⓜ

Ave Henrique Dodsworth

Rua Bolívar

R. Xavier da Silveira

R. Nossa Senhora de Copacabana

R. Miguel Lemos

Av. Rainha
Elisabeth

Morro de
Cantagalo

Parque Garota
de Ipanema

Punta de Copacabana

**Forte de Copacabana and
Museu Histórico do Exército** ◆

R. Sá Ferreira

R. Sousa Lima

R. Francisca Sá

R. Júlio de Castilhos

Av. Nossa Senhora de Copacabana

Parque Garota
de Ipanema

Diabo Beach

2,000 ft

600 m

0

0

leave no mystery as to why this beach is called the Devil's Beach in Portuguese. Take advantage of the exercise bars, but stay out of the water unless you are a very experienced surfer. Toilets and showers can be found at nearby Arpoador and Copacabana. **Amenities:** none. **Best for:** surfing. ⊠ *Between Arpoador rock and Copacabana Fort, Copacabana* Ⓜ *Ipanema/General Osório.*

IPANEMA AND LEBLON

Praia do Arpoador. At the point where Ipanema Beach meets Copacabana, Praia do Arpoador has great waves for surfing. They're so great that nonsurfers tend to avoid the water for fear of getting hit by boards. A giant rock jutting out into the waves provides panoramic views over the beaches and out to sea. Not surprisingly, the rock is a favorite haunt of romantic couples looking to catch the sunset. With more elbow room and fewer vendors than Ipanema, this beach is a prime spot for a relaxed sunbathing session. **Amenities:** food and drink; toilets; showers; lifeguards. **Best for:** sunset; surfing. ⊠ *Rua Francisco Otaviano, Arpoador* Ⓜ *Ipanema/General Osório or Cantagalo.*

FAMILY
Fodor'sChoice
★

Praia de Ipanema. As you stroll this world-famous beach you'll encounter a cross section of the city's residents, each favoring a particular stretch. Families predominate in the area near Posto (Post) 10, for instance, and the gay community clusters near Posto 8 by a giant rainbow flag. Throughout the day you'll see groups playing beach volleyball and soccer, and if you're lucky you might even come across the Brazilian Olympic volleyball team practicing here. At kiosks all along the boardwalk, you can sample all sorts of food and drink, from the typical coconut water to fried shrimp and turnovers. **Amenities:** food and drink; lifeguards; showers; toilets. **Best for:** walking; sunset. ⊠ *Avenida Viera Souto to Praça do Arpoador, Ipanema* Ⓜ *Ipanema/General Osório.*

FAMILY

Praia do Leblon. At the far end of Ipanema lies Praia do Leblon, a stretch of beach usually occupied by families and generally less lively as far as beach sports are concerned. The water tends to be rough and a strong undertow makes swimming unwise, but this a nice place for a paddle and a splash. Vendors pass by selling everything from ice-cold beer and coconut water to bikinis and sarongs, so come with a few reals to spend. As you stroll along the beautifully tiled sidewalk, take note of the sprawling Vidigal favela, which perches on the hillside overlooking the area. Continue up the road a bit to one of Leblon's *mirantes,* boardwalk-like areas that offer a great view of the entire beach from Leblon to Arpoador. **Amenities:** food and drink; lifeguards; toilets; showers. **Best for:** walking; sunset. ⊠ *Av. Epitácio Pessoa to Praça Escritor Antônio Callado, Leblon* Ⓜ *Ipanema/General Osorio.*

Praia do Vidigal. Quiet Vidigal Beach is next to the Sheraton hotel. The small stretch of sand was the playground of residents of the nearby Vidigal favela until the hotel was built in the 1970s. These days it's practically a private beach for hotel guests. The water is calm enough for swimming, but like others in Rio can be dirty after heavy rainfall. **Amenities:** food and drink. **Best for:** swimming. ⊠ *Av. Niemeyer at Sheraton, Vidigal.*

What's Your Beach Style?

To cariocas, where you hang out on the beach says a lot about you. Each of Rio's beaches has its own style, and the longer stretches of sand are themselves informally divided according to social groupings and lifestyles. There are sections of beach for singles, families, sporty types, and those looking for a quiet time. Cariocas who choose to bronze their bodies at Ipanema are generally considered to be more chic than those who catch their rays at Copacabana, with Ipanema's Posto Nove (lifeguard post 9) the hangout of choice for a young, fashionable crowd. Nearby, a vast rainbow flag in front of Rua Farme do Amoeda marks Ipanema Beach's gay and lesbian section. Families and beachgoers who prefer working on their tans to making new friends, on the other hand, largely populate Leblon Beach.

Wherever you choose to make your beach base, note that bringing along a beach towel constitutes a social faux pas. Women should equip themselves with a colorful sarong, and men are expected to remain either standing or engaged in sporting activity.

SÃO CONRADO AND BARRA DA TIJUCA

FAMILY **Praia da Barra.** Some cariocas consider the beach at Barra da Tijuca to be Rio's best, and the 18-km-long (11-mile-long) sweep of sand and jostling waves certainly is dramatic. Pollution isn't generally a problem, and in many spots neither are crowds. Barra's water is cooler and its breezes more refreshing than those at other beaches. The strong waves in some sections attract surfers, windsurfers, and jet-skiers, so you should swim with caution. The beach is set slightly below a sidewalk, where cafés and restaurants beckon. Condos have also sprung up here, and the city's largest shopping centers and supermarkets have made inland Barra their home. **Amenities:** food and drink; toilets; showers. **Best for:** walking; surfing. ⊠ *Av. Sernambetiba to Av. Lúcio Costa, Barra da Tijuca.*

FAMILY **Praia de Grumari.** A bit beyond Prainha, off Estrada de Guaratiba, is Grumari, a beach that seems a preview of paradise. What it lacks in amenities—it has only a couple of groupings of thatch-roof huts selling drinks and snacks—it makes up for in natural beauty: the glorious red sands of its quiet cove are backed by low, lush hills. Weekends are extremely crowded—arrive early. Take a lunch break at Restaurante Point de Grumari, which serves excellent fish dishes. If you've ventured this far, you might as well take a slight detour to the Museu Casa do Pontal, Brazil's largest folk-art museum, and, for an in-depth look at one of the world's greatest landscape artists, the Sítio Roberto Burle Marx. **Amenities:** food and drink. **Best for:** surfing; sunset. ⊠ *Av. Estado de Guanabara, Grumari.*

Praia de São Conrado. West of Leblon, Praia de São Conrado sits empty during the week but is often packed on weekends and holidays. The strand of soft sand attracts both wealthy locals and residents of the nearby Rocinha favela, and it provides a soft landing for hang gliders

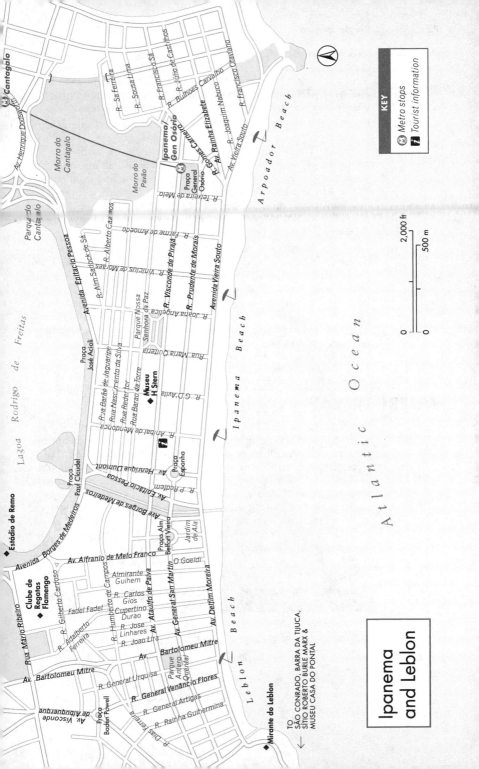

Ipanema
and Leblon

KEY

Ⓜ Metro stops
🛈 Tourist information

Atlantic Ocean

Ipanema Beach

Arpoador Beach

Leblon Beach

Lazoa Rodrigo de Freitas

Morro do Cantagalo

Morro do Pavão

Parque do Cantagalo

Ⓜ Cantagalo

Ipanema/Gen Osório
Ⓜ

Praça General Osório

Museu H Stern

Clube de Regatas Flamengo

Estádio de Remo

Mirante do Leblon

TO
SÃO CONRADO, BARRA DA TIJUCA,
SÍTIO ROBERTO BURLE MARX &
MUSEU CASA DO PONTAL

Av. Henrique Dodsworth
R. Sá Ferreira
R. Sousa Lima
R. Francisco Sá
R. Júlio de Castilhos
R. Bulhões Carvalho
R. Gomes Carneiro
Av. Rainha Elizabete
R. Joaquim Nabuco
Av. Vieira Souto
Av. Francisco Otaviano
R. Teixeira de Melo
Avenida Epitacio Pessoa
R. Alberto Campos
R. Prudente de Morais
R. Vinícius de Moraes
R. Visconde de Pirajá
R. Alm Sadock de Sá
R. Paul de Almeida
R. Joana Angélica
Avenida Vieira Souto
Parque Nossa Senhora da Paz
Praça José Acioli
Rua Maria Quitéria
Rua Barão de Jaguaripe
Rua Nasc. mento da Silva
Rua Redent tor
Rua Barão da Torre
R. G D'Avila
R. Aníbal de Mendonça
Av. Henrique Dumont
Praça Espanha
Praça Paul Claudel
R. P Redem
Av. Epitacio Pessoa
Ave Borges de Medeiros
Praça Alm Belfort Vieira
Jardim de Ala
Avenida Borges de Medeiros
Av. Alfranio de Melo Franco
O Goeldi
Atmirante Guihem
R. Carlos Gios
Cupertino Durao
R. Jose Linhares
R. Joao Lira
Humberto de Campos
Av. Ataulfo de Paiva
Av. General San Martin
Av. Delfim Moreira
Av. Bartolomeu Mitre
Fadel Fadel
R. Gilberto Cardoso
R. Adalberto Ferreira
Rua Mário Ribeiro
Av. Bartolomeu Mitre
R. General Urquisa
Parque Antero Quental
R. General Venâncio Flores
R. General Artigas
R. Rainha Guihermina
R. Dias Ferreira
Av. Visconde de Albuquerque
Praça Baden Powell

0   2,000 ft
0   500 m

swooping over the city. Surfers love the crashing waves, but swimmers should be cautious because of the undertow. It's worth remaining until sunset; the pumpkin sun often performs a dazzling show over Pedra da Gávea (Gávea Rock). **Amenities:** food and drink; water sports; lifeguards. **Best for:** sunset; surfing. ⊠ *Av. Niemeyer, São Conrado.*

Prainha. The length of two football fields, Prainha ("Little Beach") is a vest-pocket beach favored by surfers, who take charge of it on weekends. The swimming is good, but watch out for surfboards. On weekdays, especially in the off-season, the beach is almost empty; on weekends, particularly in peak season, the road to and from Prainha and nearby Grumari is so crowded it almost becomes a parking lot. **Amenities:** toilets; showers. **Best for:** swimming; surfing; sunset. ⊠ *35 km (22 miles) west of Ipanema on coast road; accessible only by car from Av. Lúcio Costa (Av. Sernambetiba), Grumari.*

FAMILY   **Recreio dos Bandeirantes.** At the far end of Barra's beachfront avenue—the name of the street was changed a few years back to Avenida Lúcio Costa, but locals still call it Sernambetiba—is this 1-km (½-mile) stretch of sand anchored by a huge rock that creates a small, protected cove. Recreio's quiet seclusion makes it popular with families. Although busy on weekends, the beach here is wonderfully quiet during the workweek. The calm, pollution-free water, with no waves or currents, is good for bathing, but don't try to swim around the rock—it's bigger than it looks. **Amenities:** food and drink. **Best for:** swimming; walking. ⊠ *Av. Lúcio Costa, Recreio dos Bandeirantes.*

WHERE TO EAT

Rio de Janeiro is world famous for its *churrascarias* (grilled-meat restaurants) but there's more to its dining scene than sizzling cuts of meat: the city embraces all types of cuisine, from traditional set meals of meat, rice, and black beans to upscale French cuisine. Unlike the states of Bahia and Minas Gerais, Rio doesn't have an identifiable cuisine, though its coastal location ensures that fish and seafood dishes are a staple of many menus here. Vegetarian cuisine has become more visible in recent years. Non-carnivores can feast on a vast range of vividly colored fruits and vegetables at a number of health-food spots. Don't leave Rio without enjoying a relaxed meal and drinks at a traditional *boteco* (casual bar-restaurant), or taking your pick from the heaping buffets at a *comida-a-kilo* (pay-by-weight) restaurant.

WHAT IT COSTS IN REALS			
$	**$$**	**$$$**	**$$$$**
AT DINNER under R$31	R$31–R$45	R$46–R$60	over R$60

Restaurant prices are the average cost of a main course at dinner or, if dinner is not served, at lunch.

CENTRO

$$$$ SEAFOOD

🍴 **Albamar Restaurante.** Open since 1933, the Albamar is not hard to spot: this outstanding seafood house is inside a distinctive green octagonal building with 360-degree views of Guanabara Bay. Chef Luiz Incao arrived here from Copacabana Palace in 2009 with a major reputation—he's cooked for Princess Diana, Bill Clinton, and Mick Jagger, among others—and he works wonders with dishes such as sautéed lobster with asparagus and saffron risotto. The attentive staff are happy to advise on wine pairings. Most main dishes are large enough for two people to share. If you're just looking to nibble, order a cocktail and some classic codfish balls, sit back, and take in the spectacular view across the bay. [$] *Average main: R$90* ✉ *Praça Marechal Âncora 186, Centro* ☎ *021/2240–8378* 🌐 *albamar.com.br* 🕒 *No dinner Sun.* [M] *Carioca* ✥ *1:F1.*

$$ BRAZILIAN

🍴 **Amarelinho.** The best spot for city-center people-watching, this vast pavement *boteco* (bar) sits directly in front of the Biblioteco Nacional, and to the side of the Theatro Nacional. An institution that's been around since 1921, the bar attracts hordes of lunchtime and afterwork diners, competing for the tables and chairs that sit directly on the flagstones of the busy Praça do Floriano. Waitstaffers in bright yellow waistcoats and bow ties flit among the tables delivering simple Brazilian dishes such as the mixed grill served with rice and fries. Pizzas are also popular here, as is the ice-cold draft beer, and the fresh fruit salad is a nice option on a hot day. Given the prime location, prices are surprisingly reasonable. Don't confuse Amerelinho with the adjoining bar, Vermelhino. Both have yellow roof canopies and yellow plastic chairs, but Amerelinho serves superior food. [$] *Average main: R$40* ✉ *Praça Floriano 55B, Cinelândia, Centro* ☎ *021/2240–8434* 🌐 *www.amarelinhodacinelandia.com.br* 🕒 *Closed Sun.* [M] *Cinelândia* ✥ *1:F2.*

$$ GERMAN

🍴 **Bar Luiz.** It's been well over a century since Bar Luiz first opened its doors—it's been at this location since 1927—and you could be excused for thinking that little has changed since, including the affable waiters. Claiming the best *chopp* (draft beer) in the city would arouse controversy from a lesser venue, but few in Rio would bother to argue. Tasty sausages and other German favorites are the culinary specialty; locals pop in for simple meals such as white bratwurst with potato salad dressed in a singular homemade mayonnaise. The chopp comes in light and dark varieties, both served *estupidamente gelado* (stupidly cold). The wooden tables, tiled floor, and wall-mounted photographs of old Rio combine to create a pleasingly nostalgic ambience. [$] *Average main: R$45* ✉ *Rua da Carioca 39, Centro* ☎ *021/2262–6900* 🌐 *www.barluiz.com.br* 🕒 *Closed Sun. No dinner* [M] *Carioca* ✥ *1:F1.*

$$ INTERNATIONAL

🍴 **Bistrô do Paço.** this is a good option for a light lunch and well placed for Centro sightseers. European influences abound, and the vegetarian-friendly menu includes salads, quiches, and grilled fish. Daily set plates include a soup or salad and a main. There are some tempting desserts, too, such as a popular apple strudel. [$] *Average main: R$38* ✉ *Praça Quinze de Novembro 48, Centro* ☎ *021/2262–3613* 🌐 *www.bistro.com.br* 🕒 *No dinner.* [M] *Uruguaiana* ✥ *1:F1.*

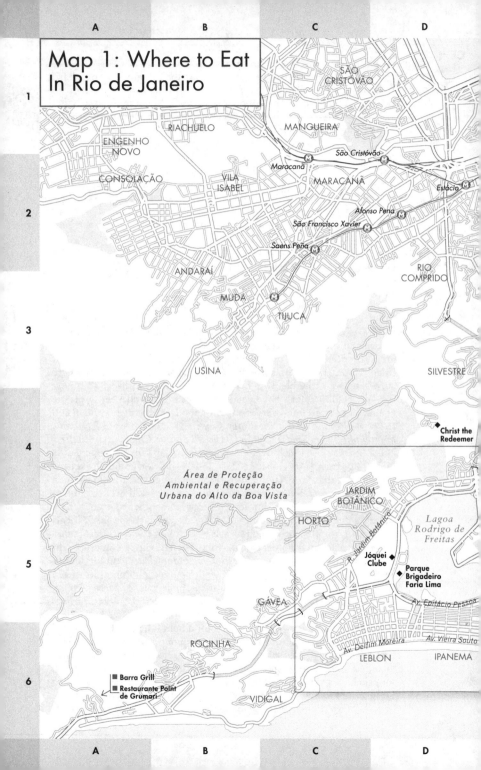

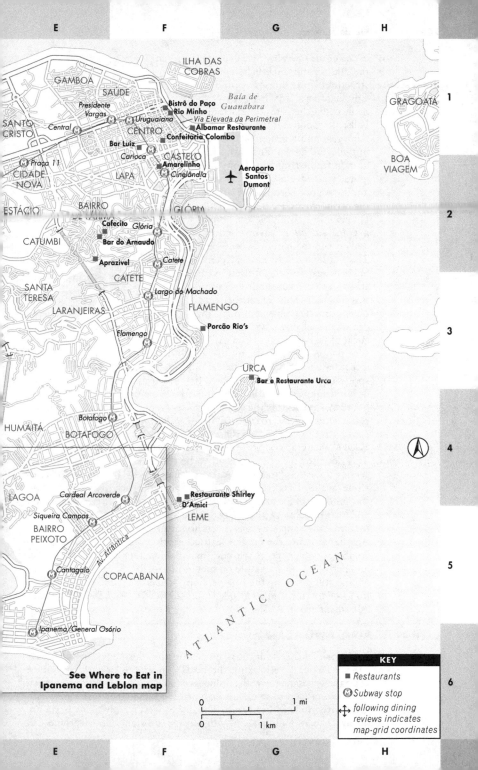

> **DINING TIPS**
>
> Some restaurants in Rio serve a *couvert* (a little something to nibble), usually bread, olives, or another type of munchie. The couvert is not free. If you don't want to pay for it, just hand it to your waiter. An "artistic" cover charge of around R$20 is usually applied when there's live music. Also, restaurants will include a 10% service charge, only half of which is distributed among the restaurant staff. Feel free to leave a little extra on the table for your server, but this is by no means obligatory.

$$$ CAFÉ Fodor's Choice ★ 🍴 **Confeitaria Colombo.** At the turn of the 20th century, the belle epoque structure that houses Colombo Confectionery was Rio's preeminent café, the site of elaborate balls, afternoon teas for upper-class *senhoras,* and a center of political intrigue and gossip. Enormous jacaranda-framed mirrors from Belgium, stained glass from France, and tiles from Portugal are among the art nouveau decor's highlights. Diners come to nibble on above-average *salgados* (savory snacks) and melt-in-the-mouth sweet treats. The waffles here are a local legend. Savory pastries are stuffed with shrimp and chicken, and vegetarian nosh includes spinach and ricotta quiche and heart-of-palm pie. You can wash it all down with a creamy coffee, a European lager, or a fruity cocktail (served virgin or laced with alcohol). If you want to experience the opulent side of city life, do so the way Rio's high society did a century ago: with *chá da tarde,* or afternoon tea. R$46 buys a lavish spread of cakes, sandwiches, breads, jams, fruit salad, and your choice of hot drink. Confeitaria Colombo now has a branch in Copacabana, but there's no beating the original. [$] *Average main: R$46* ✉ *Rua Gonçalves Dias 32, Centro* ☎ *021/2505–1500* 🌐 *www.confeitariacolombo.com.br* 🕒 *Closed Sun. No dinner* [M] *Carioca* ✣ *1:F1.*

$$$$ SEAFOOD 🍴 **Rio Minho.** Enjoy a slice of history along with your afternoon snack. This downtown restaurant said to be the oldest in the city has been serving up seafood to hungry cariocas since 1884. The simple blue-and-white facade of its pretty colonial building harks back to that time, as do the uniforms of the attentive waiters who show you to your seats. For a real taste of culinary history, order the Sopa Leáo Veloso—this fortifying Brazilian soup was created in honor of the Brazilian ambassador. An adaptation of the French seafood broth, *bouillabaisse marselhesa*- combines every type of seafood imaginable, along with onion, garlic, and herbs. It's now a staple on menus across Rio de Janeiro State, but Minho still serves up the best version. [$] *Average main: R$122* ✉ *Rua do Ouvidor 10, Centro* ☎ *021/2509–2338* 🕒 *Closed Sun. No dinner* [M] *Uruguaiana* ✣ *1:F1.*

COPACABANA AND LEME

$$$$ ITALIAN 🍴 **Cipriani.** This restaurant is housed in the plush environs of Copacabana Palace, overlooking the hotel's enormous pool. Start with a Cipriani—champagne with fresh peach juice (really a Bellini)—and then take your pick from an extensive Northern Italian menu prepared with great care by chef Luca Orini. The dishes with freshly made pasta are always a treat, and gnocchi with lobster is a standout. Meat and fish

entrées, such as wild boar, are appropriate to their lavish surroundings. Service, as one would expect, is excellent. The degustation menu costs R$228, or R$360 with wine. [$] *Average main: R$85* ✉ *Copacabana Palace Hotel, Av. Atlântica 1702, Copacabana* ☎ *021/2545–8747* 🌐 *www.copacabanapalace.com.br* ✍ *Reservations essential* [M] *Cardeal Arcoverde* ✥ *2:B6.*

2

$$$$ ITALIAN 🍴 **D'Amici.** A world away from the touristy restaurants that line Copacabana's beachfront, this refined Italian restaurant is easily overlooked but well worth seeking out. The menu celebrates Italy's diverse regional cuisines. The fish-stuffed ravioli with saffron and shrimp sauce stands out among many wonderful pastas, and the meat cuts are uniformly top-quality. Finish with that classic Italian dessert, tiramisu. The knowledgeable staff can advise you about appropriate wine pairings—helpful, as the list is extensive. [$] *Average main: R$76* ✉ *Rua Antônio Vieira 18, Leme* ☎ *021/2541–4477* 🌐 *www.damiciristorante.com.br* ✍ *Reservations essential* [M] *Cardeal Arcoverde* ✥ *1:F4.*

$$$$ FRENCH 🍴 **Le Pré-Catalan.** In an elegant space overlooking Copacabana Beach, this carioca version of the same-named Parisian restaurant serves some of Rio's best haute cuisine. Swarovski chandeliers illuminate the dining room, and chef Roland Villard, who's won numerous awards acknowledging his culinary skills, offers two prix-fixe menus. For the first he creates dazzling dishes using ingredients from the Amazon region; for the second he puts a chic French spin on traditional Brazilian cuisine. Each meal consists of a staggering 10 courses and costs R$290. You can also order à la carte and feast on sophisticated plates such as steak tartare with tomato and olive paste. Among some seriously tempting desserts, the dark chocolate mousse with raspberry sorbet and vanilla ice cream is a standout. [$] *Average main: R$90* ✉ *Sofitel Rio, Av. Atlântica 4240, Copacabana* ☎ *021/2525–1160* 🌐 *gastronomiasofitel.com.br* ⏲ *No lunch* ✍ *Reservations essential* [M] *Cantagalo* ✥ *2:D5.*

$$$$ SEAFOOD 🍴 **Nomangue.** Seafood fans will be in their element at this well-located restaurant specializing in Northeastern Brazilian fish dishes. The atmosphere is relaxed, the service attentive, and the food excellent. The *bolinjho de bobo de camarao* (fried balls of shrimp with potato) served with spicy tomato sauce are an excellent place to begin your culinary adventure. Don't miss the oysters au gratin or the *moqueca*—the classic Northeastern dish with seafood in a tomato, coconut, and palm oil sauce is made here with your choice of crab or octopus. [$] *Average main: R$90* ✉ *Rua Sa Ferreira 25, Copacabana* ☎ *021/2521–3237* 🌐 *www.nomangue.com.br* [M] *Cantagalo* ✥ *2:C5.*

$$$$ SPANISH 🍴 **Restaurante Shirley.** Traditional Spanish seafood casseroles are a strong suit at this small restaurant on a shady street, which has been attracting locals for more than 70 years. A line snakes around the block at peak hours, but it's worth the wait to find a table: the food is terrific. Seafood paella is among the most popular of the generously portioned traditional dishes. The waiters, clad in white suits, add to the old-time atmosphere. [$] *Average main: R$86* ✉ *Rua Gustavo Sampaio 610, Loja A, Leme* ☎ *021/2275–1398* ✍ *Reservations not accepted* [M] *Cardeal Arcoverde* ✥ *1:F4.*

$$$$ BRAZILIAN

🍴 **Siri Mole & Cia.** This restaurant takes its name from a soft-shell crab native to Brazil, and the signature dish here is *moqueca*—a Bahian stew that combines palm oil and coconut milk with seafood. For your stew, you can choose from squid, lobster, fish, or, of course, siri mole crab. Another delicious dish is *acaraje,* for which bean-flour patties are deep fried, split in two, and filled with shrimp, an okra paste, chili, and tomato. Vegetarians can opt for a shrimp-free version. This is one of Rio's best places for seafood served Bahia-style. [$] *Average main: R$120* ✉ *Rua Francisco Otaviano 50, Copacabana* ☎ *021/2267–0894* 🌐 *www.sirimole.com.br* 🕒 *No lunch Mon.* [M] *Ipanema/General Osório* ✣ *2:D5.*

FLAMENGO AND BOTAFOGO

$$$ ECLECTIC Fodor's Choice ★

🍴 **Miam Miam.** Blink and you could miss this hip Botafogo eatery housed in a tiny white colonial building and furnished entirely with pieces from the 1950s to the 1970s. The French–Brazilian owners have created a relaxed, casual dining space where they prepare hearty portions of tasty comfort food. The lentil ragu with sautéed mushrooooms, spiced okra, and roasted garlic is a treat for vegetarians, and the fish and meat dishes are unfailingly good. Leave room for dessert: the mini churros with *doce de leite*are an indulgent treat and a long-standing favorite on the menu. The relaxed vibe and kitsch decor ensures Miam Miam's popularity with Rio's bohemian crowd, and the award-winning cocktail list includes the *basel julep,* a vivacious concoction of rum, tangerine juice, and basil. [$] *Average main: R$55* ✉ *Rua General Góes Monteiro 34, Botafogo* ☎ *021/2244–0125* 🌐 *www.miammiam.com.br* 🕒 *Closed Sun. and Mon. No lunch* ✍ *Reservations essential* [M] *Botafogo* ✣ *2:A6.*

$$$$ BRAZILIAN FAMILY Fodor's Choice ★

🍴 **Porcão Rio's.** At lively Porcão, the ultimate in Brazilian churrascaria experiences, bow-tied waiters wielding giant skewers slip nimbly between linen-draped tables, slicing off portions of sizzling barbecued beef, pork, and chicken until you can eat no more. The buffet is huge, with salads, sushi, and pasta and rice dishes, and enough meat-free sides to keep the staunchest of vegetarians happy. Porcão is a chain, with three restaurants in Rio—including one in Ipanema—but the nearly floor-to-ceiling windows with a view over Guanabara Bay to the Sugar Loaf make the Flamengo branch, known as Porcão Rio's, the top choice. At all branches, children up to 6 eat free, while those aged 6–11 eat for half price. In the unlikely event you have room for dessert, these are charged separately. [$] *Average main: R$112* ✉ *Parque do Flamengo, Av. Infante Dom Henrique s/n, Flamengo* ☎ *021/3461–9020* 🌐 *www.porcao.com.br* [M] *Flamengo* ✣ *1:F3.*

IPANEMA AND LEBLON

$$$$ PORTUGUESE Fodor's Choice ★

🍴 **Antiquarius.** This pricey but much-loved establishment is famous for its flawless rendering of Portuguese classics, including many cod and lobster dishes. The couvert (R$29) includes tasty cod-and-potato balls, seafood rissoles, and imported cheeses. Seafood dishes are by far the best options. The chef prepares the shrimp cocktail simply but elegantly, and the vast seafood risotto is a knockout. The wine list is impressive, if predictably expensive, and the knowledgeable sommelier is always on hand to give tips on food and wine pairings; service is top-notch. [$] *Average main: R$145* ✉ *Rua Aristides Espínola 19, Leblon* ☎ *021/2294–1049* ✍ *Reservations essential* ⊕ *2:D1.*

$$$
SEAFOOD

🍴 **Azul Marinho.** You'll catch superb sunsets from the beachside tables at this spot in Arpoador that serves high-quality seafood and pasta dishes for lunch and dinner. Across from the beach on the Arpoador Inn's ground floor, the restaurant has a giant window with panoramic views. *Moqueca* is the house specialty, made with shrimp, cod, lobster, crab, or octopus—or a mix of them all. The service at Azul Marinho is excellent and the seafood is ultrafresh, but an even better reason to come here is to sit at one of the outdoor tables next to the sand and enjoy early-evening appetizers, drinks, and a marvelous sunset. [$] *Average main: R$60* ✉ *Arpoador Inn, Av. Francisco Bhering s/n, Arpoador* ☎ *021/2513–5014* [M] *Ipanema/General Osório* ⊕ *2:D5.*

$
VEGETARIAN

🍴 **Blyss Holy Foods.** Hidden away in a small arcade off Ipanema's main square, Blyss Holy Foods provides culinary delights for vegetarians, vegans, and anyone who fancies a break from the meat-centric Brazilian diet. The restaurant's organic lunch buffet is laden with fresh vegetable soups, colorful salads, fish-free sushi, savory pies and tarts, and a host of other dishes that are as tasty as they are nourishing. For a guilt-free feast after marveling at the parade of perfect beach bodies on Ipanema Beach, look no further. The friendly owners run yoga groups in the neighborhood and welcome out-of-towners to join the classes. [$] *Average main: R$23* ✉ *Rua Visconde de Pirajá 180, Loja H, Ipanema* ☎ *021/9218–5511* 🕓 *Closed weekends. No dinner* [M] *Ipanema/General Osório* ⊕ *2:D3.*

$$$$
ECLECTIC
Fodor's Choice ★

🍴 **Brigite's.** Leblon's Rua Dias Ferreira is a real go-to street for foodies, and the upmarket bar-restaurant Brigite's is a major reason why. As one might expect in body-conscious Leblon, there's an emphasis on fresh, organic ingredients, and vegetarians fare well here thanks to the emphasis on seasonal vegetables. The menu changes frequently, but seafood and pasta dishes are reliably good. The wine choices are extensive, and delicious, if pricey, cocktails can be enjoyed at the long balcony bar. Floor-to-ceiling plate-glass windows allow sunlight to flood Brigite's by day, and dim lighting creates a more atmospheric mood for after-dark drinking and dining. [$] *Average main: R$85* ✉ *Rua Dias Ferreira 247 A, Leblon* ☎ *021/2274–5590* 🌐 *www.brigites.com.br* 🕓 *No lunch Mon.* ⊕ *2:D1.*

$$
MEXICAN
Fodor's Choice ★

🍴 **La Calaca.** A labor of love from a Californian expat couple passionate about Mexican food, this casual-chic restaurant at the heart of Leblon sets culinary standards way above sour cream–heavy Tex Mex fare. Deliciously *picante*dishes are prepared according to traditional recipes and immaculately presented—the trio of tacos is a house specialty and looks (almost) too good to eat. The cocktails are a strong suit, with the frozen margaritas deliciously cooling on a balmy Rio evening, when the pavement tables are fiercely contested. The decor is modern and colorful with a nod toward kitsch, prices are more than reasonable, and the service is first-rate. Serious tequila fans will find plenty to keep them happy here, too—there's a wealth of imported varieties on offer. $ *Average main: R$40* ✉ *Av. Ataulfo de Paiva 1240, Leblon* 🕾 *021/3264–2217* ✛ *2:D2.*

$$$$
ITALIAN

✕ **Capricciosa.** Rio fairly bursts with pizza places, but this upmarket chain's Ipanema branch emerges at the top of the list. Wood-fired, thin-crust pizzas are made with imported Italian flour, and the toppings—from wild mushrooms and handmade buffalo mozzarella to wafer-thin Parma ham and fresh tuna—are of the highest quality. Capricciosa has branches in Jardim Botânico, Barra da Tijuca, Copacabana, and the beach resort of Búzios, but the Ipanema venue stands out for its location and tall glass windows that are perfect for people-watching. $ *Average main: R$65* ✉ *Rua Vinicius de Moraes 134, Ipanema* 🕾 *021/2523–3394* ⊕ *www.capricciosa.com.br* ☾ *No lunch* Ⓜ *Ipanema/General Osório* ✛ *2:D4.*

PIZZA RIO STYLE

Cariocas love pizza, and they've added some touches of their own to the established formula. As well as sharing the pan-Brazilian penchant for pizza bases covered in chocolate, Rio residents are also known to indulge in unusual topping combinations such as cheese with pepperoni, banana, and cinnamon. In one last break with tradition, many cariocas eschew the idea of tomato sauce *beneath* the cheese, in favor of squirting ketchup on the surface.

$$$$
BRAZILIAN
FAMILY

✕ **Casa da Feijoada.** Restaurants traditionally serve *feijoada*, Brazil's savory national dish, on Saturday, but here the huge pots of the stew simmer every day. You can choose which of the nine types of meat you want in your stew, but if it's your first time, waiters will bring you a "safe" version with sausage, beef, and pork—sans feet and ears. The feijoada comes with the traditional side dishes of rice, collard greens, *farofa* (toasted and seasoned manioc flour), *aipim* (cassava), *torresminho* (pork rinds), and orange slices. The set meal price includes an appetizer portion of black-bean soup and sausage, a choice of dessert, and a lime or passion-fruit *batida* (creamy cachaça cocktail). The menu also features options such as baked chicken, shrimp in coconut milk, grilled trout, and filet mignon. Desserts include *quindim* (a yolk-and-sugar pudding with coconut crust) and Romeo and Juliet (guava compote with fresh cheese). The caipirinhas are made not only with lime but also with tangerine, passion fruit, pineapple, strawberry, or kiwi. Be careful—they're strong. $ *Average main: R$78* ✉ *Rua Prudente de Morais 10, Ipanema* 🕾 *021/2247–2776* Ⓜ *Ipanema/General Osório* ✛ *2:D4.*

$$
VEGETARIAN

✕ **Celeiro.** One of an increasing number of organic eateries in Rio, Celeiro is a combination café and health-food store that's popular with models and other body-conscious locals. The restaurant operates on a pay-by-weight system, and the buffet features a staggering 50 types of salad, as well as oven-baked pies, wholemeal pastries, fish and chicken dishes, and low-calorie desserts. The homemade breads are delicious. $ *Average main: R$40* ✉ *Rua Dias Ferreira 199, Leblon* 🕾 *021/2274–7843* ⊕ *www.celeiroculinaria.com.br* ☾ *Closed Sun. No dinner* ✛ *2:D1.*

$
BRAZILIAN

✕ **Colher de Pau.** Sweet-toothed visitors should make a beeline for this little Leblon spot, which serves some of the most tempting cakes, pastries, and tarts in the city. If you try just one thing here, make it the *brigadeiro*, a much-loved traditional Brazilian treat made of condensed milk, butter, and chocolate. Colher de Pau's version is arguably the best in the city. [$] *Average main: R$8* ✉ *Rua Rita Ludolf 90, Loja A, Leblon* ☎ *021/2523–3018* 🌐 *www.colherdepaurio.com.br* 🕒 *No dinner* ✍ *Reservations not accepted* ✥ *2:D1.*

$$$$ FRENCH 🍴 **CT Boucherie.** The city's most celebrated chef—Claude Troisgros—has changed the face of the all-you-can-eat churrascaria with this chic bistro. Unlike at traditional rodizios, where waiters deliver cut after cut of meat, here they dash from table to table with steaming plates of roasted palm hearts, stuffed tomatoes, creamy mashed potatoes, and other meat-free sides to accompany meaty mains. Among the top picks are a substantial prime rib and the more accessibly priced house burger. As tempting as they are, consider skipping the entrées to save room for the never-ending flow of vegetable plates. [$] *Average main: R$90* ✉ *Rua Dias Ferreira 636, Leblon* ☎ *021/2529–2329* 🌐 *www.ctboucherie.com.br* 💳 *No credit cards* ✥ *2:D1.*

$$$$ BRAZILIAN 🍴 **Esplanada Grill.** This churrascaria is famed for the quality of its meats, among them T-bone steak and *picanha,* a tasty Brazilian cut of beef marbled with a little fat. All the grilled dishes come with fried palm hearts, seasoned rice, and a choice of fried, baked, or sautéed potatoes. [$] *Average main: R$86* ✉ *Rua Barão da Torre 600, Ipanema* ☎ *021/2512–2970* 🌐 *www.esplanadagrill.com.br* [M] *Ipanema/General Osório* ✥ *2:C3.*

$$$$ ITALIAN 🍴 **Gero.** This award-strewn and beautifully appointed restaurant is frequently cited as the best Italian in Rio. Choose from among wonderful pastas and risottos, as well as excellent fish and meat dishes. Vegetarian options are plentiful, and the tiramisu is a perfect blend of creamy, espresso-laced mascarpone. Owned by the Italian Fasano chain, the high-ceilinged, wooden-floor building exhibits the clean, contemporary design that is the Fasano hallmark. A second Rio branch operates in Barra da Tijuca, but the Ipanema location is a better option for Zona Sul–based visitors. [$] *Average main: R$90* ✉ *Rua Anibal de Mendonca 157, Ipanema* ☎ *021/2239–8158* 🌐 *www.fasano.com.br* ✍ *Reservations essential* ✥ *2:C3.*

$$ CAFÉ 🍴 **Gula Gula.** The salads at the upscale café chain Gula Gula are anything but boring. Beyond classics such as Caesar and chicken pesto, fresh local fruits and veggies are mixed into curried quinoa with tomatoes and marinated eggplant and bean sprouts, and the organic palm-heart salad comes with tomatoes, watercress, and raisins. Grilled fish or steak, baked potatoes, and soups are good nonsalad options, and there are some very fine desserts. A carioca favorite for over 30 years, Gula Gula operates a dozen restaurants in Rio, plus one in Niterói, but its location a few blocks from the beach makes the Ipanema branch an excellent choice. [$] *Average main: R$35* ✉ *Rua Henrique Dumont 57, Ipanema* ☎ *021/2259–3084* 🌐 *www.gulagula.com.br* [M] *Ipanema/General Osório* ✥ *2:D3.*

$$ BRAZILIAN Fodor's Choice ★ 🍴 **Jobi.** The post-beach hangout of choice for neighborhood locals since 1956, Jobi serves good coffee, super-chilled draft beer, and lip-smackingly delicious seafood. The bar's *bolinhos de bacalhau* (cod and potato balls) may well be the best in town. Because the restaurant is so small

and unassuming, it's only after you step inside and see the many awards hanging on the walls that you realize just how special Jobi is. This Leblon institution is open from 9 am to 4 am, so you should be able to squeeze it into your schedule. A cocktail favorite here is the *caipitequila*, a variation on the classic caipirinha that's made with tequila instead of sugarcane rum. [$] *Average main: R$35* ✉ *Rua Ataulfo de Paiva 1166, Leblon* ☎ *021/2274–0547* ✥ *2:D1.*

$$$$ ITALIAN 🍴 **Margutta.** A block from Ipanema Beach, Margutta has a reputation for outstanding Mediterranean-style seafood, such as shrimp panfried in olive oil, white wine, and garlic and lobster baked with butter and saffron rice. There's a handful of vegetarian options including mixed-vegetable risotto with truffle oil. [$] *Average main: R$62* ✉ *Av. Henrique Dumont 62, Ipanema* ☎ *021/2259–3887* 🌐 *www.margutta.com.br* ⏲ *No lunch weekdays* [M] *Ipanema/General Osório* ✥ *2:D3.*

$$ BRAZILIAN 🍴 **New Natural.** One of many buffet restaurants in Rio where you pay per 100 grams of food, this one stands out for its use of natural and organic products and its delicious fruit juices. The food is mainly vegetarian, with many soy-based dishes, but there are fish and chicken options. On hot days seek out the somewhat hidden upstairs dining room, which is air-conditioned. Attached to the restaurant is Emporia Natural—a health-food shop that sells oven-baked pastries to go. The palm heart with soft and creamy *catupiry* cheese is a winning combination. [$] *Average main: R$32* ✉ *Rua Barão da Torre 169, Ipanema* ☎ *021/2247–1335* [M] *Ipanema/General Osório* ✥ *2:D4.*

$$ BRAZILIAN 🍴 **Pipo.** The latest Rio venture from the high-profile Brazilian chef Felipe Bronze sees him apply his culinary wizardry to traditional boteco cuisine. The down-to-earth design features white walls and standard-issue boteco tables and chairs. But the food that emerges from the open kitchen is anything but standard. Neat tricks include a version of the traditional thick bean soup that here comes topped with a luminous green froth of *couve* (collard greens). Don't miss the chunky *aipim* (manioc) fries that come coated with coalho cheese foam for dipping. [$] *Average main: R$45* ✉ *Rua Dias Ferreira 64, Leblon* ☎ *021/ 2239–9322* 🌐 *www.piporestaurante.com* ⏲ *Closed Mon. No lunch Tues.–Sat.* ✥ *2:D1.*

$$$$ SEAFOOD Fodor's Choice ★ 🍴 **Satyricon.** Some of the best seafood in town is served at this smart restaurant that has impressed A-list visitors including Madonna and Jared Leto. A tank of snapping lobsters at the entrance gives diners an indication of the freshness of the fare served here, and the decor is low-key with plenty of exposed wood and sparkling white walls. The carpaccio entrée is a specialty—it and the daily specials, such as red snapper baked in red wine and herbs, are rendered beautifully, while sides such as rice with lemon are suitably simple companions to the main event. Grilled swordfish and sea bass are other popular orders, and the homemade Italian-style ice cream is a sweet way indeed to round off a meal. [$] *Average main: R$115* ✉ *Rua Barão da Torre 192, Ipanema* ☎ *021/2521–0627* 🌐 *www.satyricon.com.br* [M] *Ipanema/General Osório* ✥ *2:C4.*

$$$ ITALIAN 🍴 **Stuzzi.** Bringing the concept of Italian *stuzzichini* (tapas-style small plates of food for sharing), Stuzzi has evolved into a star of Leblon's

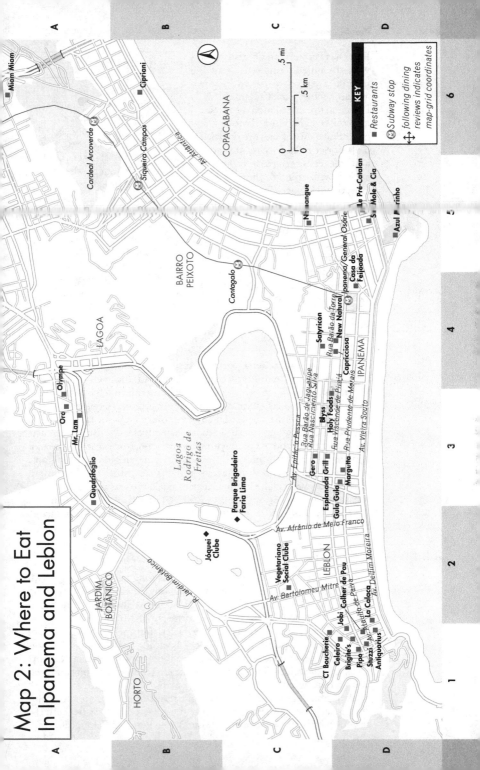

Map 2: Where to Eat
In Ipanema and Leblon

JARDIM BOTÂNICO

HORTO

LAGOA

Lagoa Rodrigo de Freitas

BAIRRO PEIXOTO

COPACABANA

LEBLON

IPANEMA

Miam Miam

Cipriani

Cardeal Arcoverde

Siqueira Campos

Olympe

Oro

Mr. Lam

Quadrifóglio

Cantagalo

Parque Brigadeiro Faria Lima

Jóquei Clube

Vegetariano Social Clube

CT Boucherie

Celeiro

Brigite's

Pipo

Jobi

Colher de Pau

La Calaça

Shuzzi

Antiquarius

Esplanada Grill

Gero

Gula Gula

Margutta

Myss

Holy Foods

Sahyricon

New Natural

Capricciosa

Casa da Feijoada

Nã-ãngue

Le Pré-Catalan

Sá Mole & Cia

Azul Marinho

Av. Bartolomeu Mitre

Av. Delfim Moreira

Av. Ataulfo de Paiva

Av. Afrânio de Melo Franco

Av. Epitácio Pessoa

Rua Barão de Jaguaripe

Rua Nascimento Silva

Rua Visconde de Piratá

Rua Prudente de Morais

Av. Vieira Souto

Rua Barão da Torre

Ipanema/General Osório

Av. Atlântica

R. Jardim Botânico

0   .5 mi

0   .5 km

KEY

■ Restaurants

Ⓜ Subway stop

✛ following dining reviews indicates map-grid coordinates

A   B   C   D

1   2   3   4   5   6

Rua Dias Ferreira foodie strip. Start with the mixed antipastos, which include a basket of baked breads and authentic Grana Padano cheese, Parma ham, marinated eggplant, and other light bites. Among the other don't-miss dishes are the fried balls of rice filled with meat ragout and the polenta *grissini* (breadsticks) with tomato chutney and Gorgonzola sauce. For something more substantial, head here on a Sunday for the Buffet da Mamma, a serve-yourself comfort-food feast. Arrive early to get a table on the leafy patio, and take your pick from the impressive cocktail menu; standouts include the *perfetto limone*—a sense-stimulating mix of bourbon, limoncello, lemon, passion fruit, and chili pepper. [$] *Average main: R$58* ✉ *Rua Dias Ferreira 48, Leblon* ☎ *021/2274–4017* 🌐 *www.stuzzibar.com.br* ⏲ *No lunch Mon.–Sat.* ✥ *2:D1.*

FOOD ON THE GO

There's a street snack for every taste in Rio—from low-cal treats such as corn on the cob and chilled pineapple slices to less virtuous, but absolutely delicious, barbecued sticks of grilled cheese served with or without herbs. Tasty bags of roasted and salted peanuts and cashews are found everywhere, as are giant hot dogs, served on a stick and covered in manioc flour. Barbecued chicken heart (*coraçao*) is not for the fainthearted, and the grilled shrimp at the beach is best avoided unless you want a side order of food poisoning.

$$ VEGETARIAN 🍴 **Vegetariano Social Clube.** Vegan restaurants are a growing trend in body-conscious Rio, but few are as established and well loved as the Vegetarian Social Club. The serve-yourself organic lunch buffet (R$28) includes tasty and wholesome soups, whole-grain rice, colorful salads, and many soy-based dishes. Dining in the evening is à la carte, with options such as quinoa with seasonal vegetables and tofu cream. The tempeh burgers with soya mayonnaise are a post-beach treat. Detoxifying juices and smoothies are on the drinks menu, along with organic wines and cachaças for those less in need of a cleansing. The Sunday feijoada, made with smoked tofu instead of pork, attracts vegetarians from across the city. [$] *Average main: R$32* ✉ *Rua Conde de Bernadotte 26, Loja L, Leblon* ☎ *021/2294–5200* 🌐 *www.vegetarianosocialclube.com.br* ✥ *2:C2.*

INLAND ZONA SUL

$$$$ CHINESE 🍴 **Mr. Lam.** In a city where Chinese food has long been associated with low-budget dining, this restaurant tossed out the rule book, attracting a discerning clientele with top-quality Peking-style cuisine. The menu is created by the famous Mr. Lam, formerly of Mr Chow, first at the London branch and then in New York City, and chef Chui Kwok Kam executes them to perfection. The decor is rather ostentatious—fixtures include a terra-cotta warrior, and a speedboat motor serves as support for one of the tables. The downstairs dining room is spacious and well illuminated by enormous windows, but for the ultimate experience book a table on the top floor. At night the roof retracts to allow dining beneath the stars, and you can request a spot directly beneath the gaze of Christ the Redeemer. The satay chicken and Peking duck are

two of the signature dishes. You can dine à la carte, but most patrons choose from one of the set menus (from R$139 to R$169 per person). [$] *Average main: R$98* ✉ *Av. Maria Angélica 21, Lagoa* ☎ *021/2286–6661* 🌐 *www.mrlam.com.br* 🕒 *No lunch Mon.–Sat.* ✍ *Reservations essential* ✥ *2:A3.*

$$$$ FRENCH Fodor's Choice ★ 🍴 **Olympe.** Claude Troisgros, of the celebrated Michelin-starred Troisgros family of France, today runs something of an empire of upscale restaurants in Rio, and this is his original and most celebrated venture. Troisgros creates the menu together with his equally talented son Thomas, applying nouvelle-cooking techniques to meals with all-Brazilian ingredients. Cases in point include quail stuffed with raisin and onion *farofa* (seasoned manioc flour) served with a kale confit, and duck with passion-fruit *jus*.At lunch on weekdays (1–4), there's a three-course set menu for R$115. [$] *Average main: R$130* ✉ *Rua Custódio Serrão 62, Jardim Botânico* ☎ *021/2539–4542* 🌐 *olympe.com.br* 🕒 *Closed Sun. No lunch Sat.* ✍ *Reservations essential* ✥ *2:A3.*

$$$$ CONTEMPORARY Fodor's Choice ★ 🍴 **Oro.** Food as theater is the theme of the acclaimed restaurant of celebrity chef Felipe Bronze, who has created an avant-garde dining experience like no other in the city. A pink-hued glass wall allows diners to watch his culinary team prepare ultracontemporary dishes, many using traditional Brazilian ingredients. There are à-la-carte dishes, but most diners here choose one of the tasting menus (from R$180 for four courses to R$295 for nine). The "mains" are really a series of small, elaborately prepared dishes, including a tiny burger made of duck confit and foie gras powder and served with guava "ketchup." Don't miss the *Brasilidades* dessert, which features no fewer than 10 tiny but perfectly rendered modern takes on classic Brazilian sweets. Clever tricks such as using liquid nitrogen to "freeze" chocolate mousse add to the stylish-yet-playful atmosphere, as do the waitstaff's uniforms, designed by Lenny Niemeyer, famous for her high fashion bikinis. [$] *Average main: R$160* ✉ *Rua Frei Leandro 20, Jardim Botânico* ☎ *021/2266–7591* 🌐 *www.ororestaurante.com* 🕒 *Closed Sun. No lunch* ✍ *Reservations essential* ✥ *2:A3.*

$$$$ ITALIAN Fodor's Choice ★ 🍴 **Quadrifoglio.** Many locals consider cozy Quadrifoglio to be Rio's best Italian restaurant. The restaurant has been around since 1991, and the service and the food are impeccable, the former perhaps because much of the original waitstaff still works here. Standout starters include a comforting white bean soup with shrimp, and a salad of arugula, goat cheese, walnuts, and pear in a balsamic reduction, while the potato gnocchi with steak and porcini mushrooms is one of many stellar mains. Ice cream with baked figs is among the justly famous desserts. [$] *Average main: R$78* ✉ *Rua J.J. Seabra 19, Jardim Botânico* ☎ *021/2294–1433* 🌐 *www.quadrifogliorestaurante.com.br* 🕒 *No dinner Sun* ✥ *2:A3.*

SANTA TERESA

$$$$ BRAZILIAN ECLECTIC FAMILY 🍴 **Aprazível.** A tropical garden filled with exotic plants, monkeys, and birds is the spectacular setting for this family restaurant serving pan-Brazilian dishes. The owner and chef, Ana Castilha, hails from Minas Gerais but received her formal training at New York City's French Culinary Institute. As a delightful consequence, there's a French twist

to dishes she has created with native ingredients, among them baked palm heart with pesto, basil, and cashews. The award-winning wine list includes many artisan Brazilian bottles, and their high quality may surprise those who have dismissed the country's wines. Dine in one of the straw-roofed gazebos to enjoy excellent views of downtown and Guanabara Bay, keeping an eye out for toucans overhead. By night hanging lanterns and twinkling fairy lights create a magical atmosphere in the garden. Call ahead to reserve, as opening hours can be erratic. $ *Average main: R$65* ⊠ *Rua Aprazível 62, Santa Teresa* ☎ *021/2508–9174* ⊕ *www.aprazivel.com.br* ⊗ *Closed Mon. No dinner Sun.* ⚞ *Reservations essential* ✚ *1:E2.*

$$$
BRAZILIAN
Fodor's Choice
★

✕ **Bar do Arnaudo.** A neighborhood favorite for more than three decades, this informal tavern in the heart of Santa Teresa serves excellent Northeastern cuisine in more than ample portions. Sun-dried beef is a popular choice among carnivores, and vegetarians will love the set meal of *queijo coalho* (grilled white cheese, similar to halloumi) with brown beans, rice, and seasoned farofa. Reservations aren't necessary, but the restaurant is always packed on weekend evenings. It's quieter at lunchtime, when you may be able to occupy one of the two tables that have views down to Guanabara Bay. Though the friendly staffers are speedy, the service never feels rushed. Wine isn't sold here, but your waiter will happily uncork any bottle you bring. $ *Average main: R$48* ⊠ *Rua Almirante Alexandrino 316B, Santa Teresa* ☎ *021/2252–7246* ⊗ *Closed Mon.* ✚ *1:E2.*

$
CAFÉ
Fodor's Choice
★

✕ **Cafecito.** Coffee culture is beginning to take off in Rio, and Argentine-owned Cafecito is one of just a few places so far to capture the essence of "café society." A leafy terrace overlooking Santa Teresa's main eating, drinking, and shopping strip provides a relaxed setting for brunches, lunches, and early-evening nibbles and cocktails. Chef Felipe Alves has previously worked at Copacabana Palace, and the dishes here are immaculately presented. The knickknack-strewn café serves what's arguably the city's best cappuccino—with a dusting of cinnamon and a morsel of gooey chocolate brownie—but the food menu also has plenty to recommend it. The standouts include the toasted ciabatta sandwiches (the Brie with artichoke hearts is delicious) and some pleasingly rustic baked mushrooms with melted Gorgonzola. $ *Average main: R$26* ⊠ *Rua Pashcoal Carlos Magno 121, Santa Teresa* ☎ *021/2221–9439* ⊟ *No credit cards* ⊗ *Closed Wed.* ✚ *1:E2.*

SÃO CONRADO AND BARRA DA TIJUCA

$$$$
BRAZILIAN

✕ **Barra Grill.** A nice place to stop after a long day at Barra Beach, this informal and popular steak house serves more than 30 cuts of top-quality meat. Choose from the menu or go the whole hog with the all-you-can-eat rodizio (R$109). The buffet is impressive in range and quality, with seafood and sushi as well as colorful, fresh salads. Prices for the rodízio-style feasts are slightly higher on weekends, when reservations are essential, but female diners eat for half price after 6 pm. $ *Average main: R$65* ⊠ *Av. Ministro Ivan Lins 314, Barra da Tijuca* ☎ *021/2493–6060* ⊕ *www.barragrill.com.br* ⊗ *No dinner Sun.* ✚ *1:A6.*

$$$$ ✗**Restaurante Point de Grumari.** From Grumari Beach, Estrada de Guara-
SEAFOOD tiba climbs up through dense forest, emerging atop a hill above the vast
Guaratiba flatlands. Here you'll come upon this restaurant famed for its
moqueca, the traditional seafood stew. Other standards on the seafood-
focused menu are lobster and grilled beefsteak, while the passion-fruit
caipirinha is nearly flawless. With its shady setting, colorful flora, and
glorious vistas, this is a fine spot for an early lunch after a morning
on the beach and before an afternoon visit to the Sítio Roberto Burle
Marx or the Museu Casa do Pontal. Or come here in the early evening
to catch the spectacular sunset. $ *Average main: R$62* ⊠ *Estrada do
Grumari 710, Grumari* ☎ *021/2410–1434* ⊕ *www.pointdegrumari.
com.br* ⊙ *No dinner* ⊹ *1:A6.*

URCA

$$ ✗**Bar e Restaurante Urca.** Dine indoors in this relaxed spot, or make like
BRAZILIAN the locals and enjoy a snack alfresco, propped against the harbor wall
across the street: the sea wall doubles as a makeshift table, and waiters
run to and fro delivering orders. You'll have a stunning backdrop to
your light meal—the panorama takes in bobbing boats, framed by a
clear view of Christ the Redeemer. Enjoy a cold beer and some finger
food while you contemplate the menu—the *salgadinhos* (little savory
snacks) are a strong suit, with the shrimp pastries a particular stand-
out. More substantial dishes can be enjoyed upstairs in the restaurant
and include some good Portuguese-influenced fare. Bar e Restaurante
Urca breaks with tradition and serves feijoada on Fridays instead of
Saturdays, and at a good price for what you get: R$68 for two. $ *Aver-
age main: R$38* ⊠ *Rua Cândido Gaffrée 205, Urca* ☎ *021/2295–8744*
⊕ *www.barurca.com.br* ⊟ *No credit cards* ⊙ *No dinner Sun.* ⊹ *1:G3.*

WHERE TO STAY

Rio's accommodations are among the most expensive in the world, with
beachfront lodgings in particular charging a premium for their envi-
able locations. Expect hotel rates to be the most expensive during high
season (from December through February), especially during Carnival
and New Year's, and for special events such as the 2016 Rio Olympics.
For stays during these times, it would be wise to book ahead as far as
possible. The low season (from March to November) sees prices fall
across the city.

As for the types of lodgings available, there are some excellent luxury
options on the beachfront—most notably the Belmond Copacabana
Palace and Ipanema's Fasano Rio—as well as standard chain hotels.
Ipanema and neighboring Leblon are more expensive than Copacabana,
but they are also safer and more pleasant to walk around at night. Rio's
expanding boutique-hotel scene centers largely around the Santa Teresa
and Gávea neighborhoods, while Botafogo and Flamengo offer some
decent midrange options. *Hotel reviews have been shortened. For full
information, visit Fodors.com.*

	WHAT IT COSTS IN REALS			
	$	$$	$$$	$$$$
FOR 2 PEOPLE	under R$251	R$251–R$375	R$376–R$500	over R$500

Hotel prices are the lowest cost of a standard double room in high season, excluding tax.

CENTRO

$$$ HOTEL **Windsor Guanabara.** One of the few solid hotel choices right in Centro, the Windsor Guanabara has reasonably sized and tastefully appointed rooms (although some are beginning to show signs of age), and the contemporary rooftop pool area—with white tiles, white trellises, and white patio furnishings—offers a welcome escape from the city swelter and stunning views of Guanabara Bay. The buffet breakfast is good, too, although the evening buffet served in the restaurant is a little steep. **Pros:** good transport links—close to metro and domestic airport; close to downtown attractions and nightlife; good pool with views. **Cons:** far from beaches; Centro is nearly deserted on Sunday. [$] *Rooms from: R$438* ✉ *Av. Presidente Vargas 392, Centro* ☎ *021/2195–5000* 🌐 *www.windsorhoteis.com.br* 🛏 *539 rooms, 3 suites* 🍴 *Breakfast* [M] *Uruguaiana* ✥ *B1.*

COPACABANA AND LEME

$$$$ HOTEL Fodor's Choice ★ **Belmond Copacabana Palace.** Built in 1923 for the visiting king of Belgium and inspired by Nice's Negresco and Cannes's Carlton, Copacabana Palace was the first luxury hotel in South America, and it's still one of the top hotels on the continent. **Pros:** historic landmark; front-facing rooms have spectacular ocean views; great on-site restaurants. **Cons:** area is a little seedy at night; need to take taxis to best bars and restaurants; "city view" rooms have poor views of backstreets. [$] *Rooms from: R$1,490* ✉ *Av. Atlântica 1702, Copacabana* ☎ *021/2548–7070* 🌐 *www.copacabanapalace.com.br* 🛏 *129 rooms, 116 suites* 🍴 *Breakfast* [M] *Cardeal Arcoverde* ✥ *G3.*

$$$$ B&B/INN **Casa Mosquito.** On a hillside between Ipanema and Copacabana, this stylish boutique guest house with just nine uniquely designed rooms has excellent service, a wonderful location, and a rooftop pool with lovely ocean views. **Pros:** boutique lodgings with character; personalized service; excellent in-house chef. **Cons:** it's a walk to beaches, nightlife, and metro. [$] *Rooms from: R$700* ✉ *Rua Saint-Roman 222, Copacabana* ☎ *21/3586–5042, 21/2523–1031* 🌐 *www.casamosquito.com* 🛏 *9 rooms* 🍴 *Breakfast* [M] *Cantagalo or Ipanema/General Osorio* ✥ *E5.*

$$$ HOTEL **Copacabana Rio Hotel.** The decor at this hotel may be a little dated, but rooms are spacious and the location—one block from Copacabana and a short walk from Ipanema—is spot on. **Pros:** comfortable rooms; handy to Copacabana and Ipanema beaches; fine breakfast. **Cons:** busy and noisy street; minimum seven-day stay in high season; decor looking dated. [$] *Rooms from: R$415* ✉ *Av. Nossa Senhora de Copacabana 1256, Posto 6, Copacabana* ☎ *021/3043–1111* 🌐 *www.*

copacabanariohotel.com.br 🛏 *90 rooms, 8 suites* 🍴 *Breakfast* [M] *Ipanema/General Osório* ✥ *E5.*

$$$ HOTEL 🏨 **Golden Tulip Regente Hotel.** The excellent location in front of Copacabana Beach is this hotel's main draw; the rooms are spic and span and reasonably tasteful, and some have been recently refurbished. **Pros:** good location; generous breakfast; small but well-equipped gym; pool. **Cons:** south-facing rooms have poor view; Copacabana isn't the safest area. [$] *Rooms from: R$486* ✉ *Av. Atlântica 3716, Copacabana* ☎ *021/3545–5400, 021/3545–5445 reservations* 🌐 *www.goldentulipregente.com* 🛏 *228 rooms, 2 suites* 🍴 *Breakfast* [M] *Cantagalo* ✥ *F5.*

$$$$ HOTEL 🏨 **JW Marriott Rio de Janeiro.** You could be walking into a Marriott anywhere in the world, which is a comfort for some and a curse for others: expect spotlessly clean rooms and public areas, an efficient English-speaking staff, and modern (and expensive) services and facilities. **Pros:** close to beach; efficient service; bountiful breakfasts; modern facilities. **Cons:** extra charge for Internet access; expensive; street noise heard in some rooms. [$] *Rooms from: R$1,100* ✉ *Av. Atlântica 2600, Copacabana* ☎ *021/2545–6500* 🌐 *www.marriott.com* 🛏 *229 rooms, 16 suites* 🍴 *Breakfast* [M] *Siqueira Campos* ✥ *F4.*

$$$ B&B/INN FAMILY Fodor's Choice ★ 🏨 **Marta's Rio Guesthouse.** Offering a personal touch that you won't find at Copacabana's larger hotels, this penthouse inn close to Ipanema enjoys sweeping views across Copacabana Beach and out to Sugarloaf Mountain. **Pros:** close to Copacabana Beach, restaurants, and nightlife; stunning views from the balcony; excellent value for the location; walking distance to Ipanema. **Cons:** rooms lack views. [$] *Rooms from: R$380* ✉ *Rua Francisco Sá 5, at the corner of Av. Atlântica, Copacabana* ☎ *021/2521–8568* 🌐 *www.martarioguesthouse.com* 🛏 *3 rooms, 3 suites* 🍴 *Breakfast* [M] *Cantagalo* ✥ *F5.*

$$$$ HOTEL 🏨 **Miramar Palace by Windsor.** With a prime beachfront location, this classic Copacabana hotel underwent a complete face-lift in 2013 and is now one of the neighborhood's best hotels. **Pros:** beachfront location; great service; modern decor. **Cons:** small pool. [$] *Rooms from:* ✉ *Av. Atlântica 3668, Copacabana* ☎ *021/956–200, 0800/23–2211* 🌐 *www.windsorhoteis.com* 🛏 *197 rooms, 3 suites* 🍴 *Breakfast* [M] *Cantagalo* ✥ *F5.*

$$$$ HOTEL 🏨 **Pestana Rio Atlântica.** This well-located hotel offers friendly service, a great breakfast, and a good location opposite Copacabana Beach, but the real stars of the show are the rooftop pool and bar—the sunset views are incredible. **Pros:** good value for the area; rooftop pool and bar; good beachfront location. **Cons:** some rooms need revamping; can feel a little crowded. [$] *Rooms from: R$760* ✉ *Av. Atlântica 2964, Copacabana* ☎ *021/2548–6332* 🌐 *www.pestana.com* 🛏 *109 rooms, 105 suites* 🍴 *No meals* [M] *Cantagalo* ✥ *F4.*

$$$$ HOTEL FAMILY 🏨 **Porto Bay Rio Internacional.** All rooms at this Copacabana landmark hotel have balconies with sea views, a rarity on Avenida Atlântica. **Pros:** excellent service; good views; beachfront location. **Cons:** some rooms quite small; Copacabana not as safe as Ipanema after dark; hotel beginning to look dated. [$] *Rooms from: R$755* ✉ *Av. Atlântica 1500, Copacabana* ☎ *021/2546–8000* 🌐 *www.portobay.com* 🛏 *117 rooms, 11 suites* 🍴 *Breakfast* [M] *Cardeal Arcoverde* ✥ *G3.*

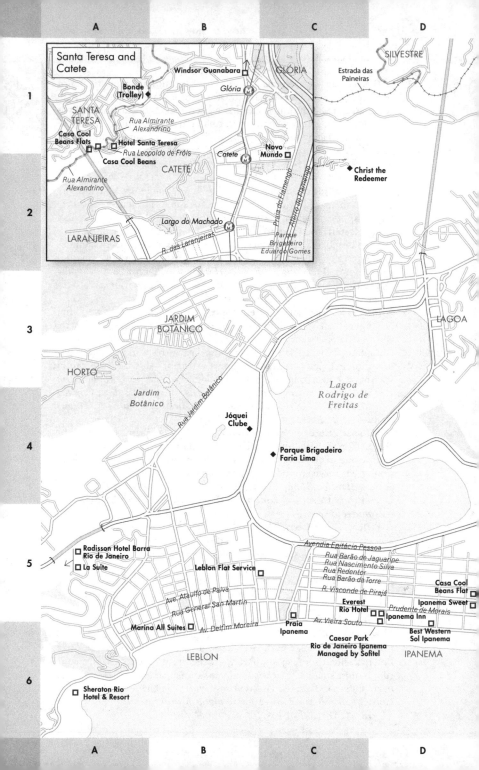

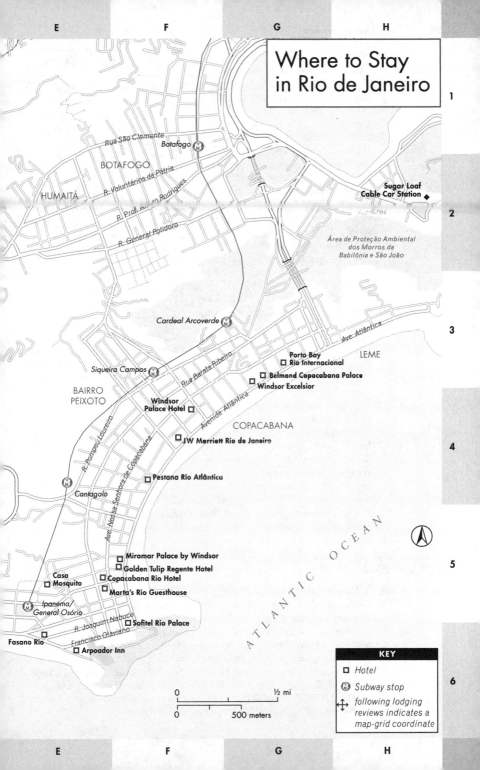

Where to Stay in Rio de Janeiro

E **F** **G** **H**

1

Rua São Clemente
Botafogo Ⓜ

BOTAFOGO

HUMAITÁ

R. Voluntários da Pátria

R. Prof. A...n Rodrigues

R. General Polidoro

Sugar Loaf
Cable Car Station ◆

2

Área de Proteção Ambiental
dos Morros da
Babilônia e São João

Cardeal Arcoverde Ⓜ

Ave. Atlântica

3

Porto Bay
□ Rio Internacional
LEME

Siqueira Campos Ⓜ

Rua Barata Ribeiro

□ Belmond Copacabana Palace
□ Windsor Excelsior

BAIRRO
PEIXOTO

Windsor
Palace Hotel □

Avenida Atlântica

COPACABANA

R. Pompeu Loureiro

□ JW Marriott Rio de Janeiro

4

Ⓜ

Cantagalo

Ave. Nossa Senhora de Copacabana

□ Pestana Rio Atlântica

ATLANTIC OCEAN

⊕ (compass)

5

□ Miramar Palace by Windsor
□ Golden Tulip Regente Hotel
Casa
□ Mosquito □ Copacabana Rio Hotel
□ Marta's Rio Guesthouse

Ⓜ
Ipanema/
General Osório

R. Joaquim Nabuco
□ Sofitel Rio Palace
Francisco Otaviano
□ Fasano Rio
□ Arpoador Inn

ATLANTIC

KEY	
□	Hotel
Ⓜ	Subway stop
⊕	following lodging reviews indicates a map-grid coordinate

0 _____ ½ mi
0 _____ 500 meters

6

E **F** **G** **H**

$$$$ HOTEL **Sofitel Rio Palace.** Anchoring one end of Copacabana Beach, and close to Ipanema, this huge hotel has an "H" shape that provides breathtaking views of the sea, the mountains, or both, from all the rooms' balconies. **Pros:** handy to Ipanema and Arpoador Beaches and nightlife; fantastic views. **Cons:** very large; somewhat impersonal; small bathrooms in some rooms. [$] *Rooms from: R$890* ✉ *Av. Atlântica 4240, Copacabana* ☎ *021/2525–1232* 🌐 *www.sofitel.com/gb/hotel-1988-sofitel-rio-de-janeiro-copacabana/index.shtml* 🛏 *388 rooms, 286 suites* 🍴 *No meals* [M] *Cantogalo* ✥ *F6.*

ALTERNATIVE HOUSING

Rio has accommodations to suit virtually every taste and wallet. There are plenty of self-catering options for those who value their own space over hotel luxury. Agencies specialize in everything from luxury Ipanema penthouses to pokey Copacabana digs. One good one, Alex Rio Flats (🌐 *www.alexrioflats.com*), has 10 air-conditioned studios and apartments, many with beachfront locations and full sea views, that cost R$220 and up per night. Alex, the English-speaking owner, provides friendly, personalized service and can help book trips and tours.

$$$$ HOTEL **Windsor Excelsior.** This beachfront hotel, part of the Windsor chain, may have been built in the 1950s, but its look is sleek and contemporary—from the sparkling marble lobby to the guest-room closets paneled in gleaming Brazilian redwood. **Pros:** top-notch service; rooftop pool; good breakfast. **Cons:** slightly impersonal chain feel; busy street can be dangerous at night. [$] *Rooms from: R$603* ✉ *Av. Atlântica 1800, Copacabana* ☎ *021/2195–5800* 🌐 *www.windsorhoteis.com.br* 🛏 *230 rooms, 3 suites* 🍴 *Breakfast* [M] *Cardeal Arcoverde* ✥ *G3.*

$$$ HOTEL **Windsor Palace Hotel.** Close to Copacabana's main shopping area, handy for the metro and just a couple of blocks from the beach, the Windsor Palace is a solid midrange option with decent services and standard, cookie-cutter hotel rooms, many of which have recently been refurbished. **Pros:** rooftop views; good amenities; two blocks from metro. **Cons:** bland rooms; so-so location. [$] *Rooms from: R$480* ✉ *Rua Domingos Ferreira 6, Copacabana* ☎ *021/2195–6600* 🌐 *www.windsorhoteis.com* 🛏 *73 rooms, 1 suite* 🍴 *Breakfast* [M] *Siqueira Campos* ✥ *F4.*

FLAMENGO

$$$ HOTEL **Novo Mundo.** A short walk from the Catete metro station, next door to Palacio de Catete, and five minutes by car from Santos Dumont Airport, this traditional hotel occupies an attractive art deco building overlooking Guanabara Bay. Convention rooms are popular with the business crowd. **Pros:** close to metro; some rooms have great views; good playground at palace gardens next door; children under 12 free. **Cons:** metro ride away from the best beaches; some rooms past their prime. [$] *Rooms from: R$390* ✉ *Praia do Flamengo 20, Flamengo* ☎ *021/2105–7000, 0800/25–3355* 🌐 *www.hotelnovomundo.com.br* 🛏 *209 rooms, 22 suites* 🍴 *Breakfast* [M] *Catete* ✥ *C2.*

IPANEMA AND LEBLON

$$$
HOTEL
⬚ **Arpoador Inn.** This pocket-size hotel is functional rather than luxurious, but it benefits from one of the best beachfront locations in the city at Arpoador, the point at which Ipanema meets Copacabana. **Pros:** great sunsets; right-on-the-beach location; good restaurant; reasonable prices. **Cons:** front rooms can be noisy; hotel often busy with groups of surfers. $ *Rooms from: R$475* ✉ *Rua Francisco Otaviano 177, Ipanema* ☎ *021/2523–0060* ⊕ *www.arpoadorinn.com.br* ↝ *50 rooms, 1 suite* ⊚ *Breakfast* Ⓜ *Ipanema/General Osório or Cantagalo* ✣ *E6.*

$$$$
HOTEL
FAMILY
⬚ **Best Western Sol Ipanema.** Another of Rio's tall, slender hotels, this one has a great location at the eastern end of Ipanema Beach between Rua Vinicius de Moraes and Farme de Amoedo, and though it isn't luxurious, the hotel has comfortable accommodations with crisp, clean, and modern interiors. **Pros:** great beach location; near lively Ipanema nightlife; friendly staff; decent value for Ipanema. **Cons:** standard facilities; tiny pool. $ *Rooms from: R$780* ✉ *Av. Vieira Souto 320, Ipanema* ☎ *021/2525–2020* ⊕ *www.solipanema.com.br* ↝ *90 rooms* ⊚ *Breakfast* Ⓜ *Ipanema/General Osório* ✣ *D6.*

$$$$
HOTEL
⬚ **Caesar Park Rio de Janeiro Ipanema Managed by Sofitel.** In the heart of Ipanema, close to high-class shops and gourmet restaurants, this beachfront hotel has established itself among business travelers, celebrities, and heads of state, who appreciate its impeccable service; and while the suites are impressive, other rooms feel more functional than luxurious. **Pros:** great location; good business facilities; good views. **Cons:** no balconies; small pool; uninspired decor. $ *Rooms from: R$780* ✉ *Av. Vieira Souto 460, Ipanema* ☎ *021/2525–2525* ⊕ *www.sofitel.com* ↝ *221 rooms, 28 suites* ⊚ *No meals* Ⓜ *Ipanema/General Osório* ✣ *D6.*

$$$
RENTAL
Fodor's Choice
★
⬚ **Casa Cool Beans Flats.** A block from the beach in Ipanema, this lodging in a converted 1940s building has eight flats that have stylish, contemporary furnishings and artworks by popular Rio artist Paulo Freire. **Pros:** excellent value for Ipanema; close to beach, bars, restaurants, shopping, and the metro; gay-friendly. **Cons:** two-night minimum (three for major holidays and events); no guests under age 18; no elevator. $ *Rooms from: R$460* ✉ *Rua Vinicius de Moraes 72, Ipanema* ☎ *021/2262–0552, 202/470–3548 in the U.S.* ⊕ *flats.casacoolbeans.com* ↝ *5 suites, 3 studios* ⊚ *No meals* Ⓜ *Ipanema/General Osório* ✣ *D5.*

$$$$
HOTEL
⬚ **Everest Rio Hotel.** In the heart of Ipanema's shopping and dining district, a block from the beach, this hotel has standard accommodations and in-room amenities but a great rooftop view—a postcard shot of Corcovado and the lagoon. **Pros:** rooftop views and pool; good business amenities; fine location close to beach, restaurants, and nightlife. **Cons:** noisy air-conditioning; other buildings hamper some views. $ *Rooms from: R$530* ✉ *Rua Prudente de Morais 1117, Ipanema* ☎ *021/2525–2200, 0800/709–2220* ⊕ *www.everest.com.br* ↝ *148 rooms, 8 suites* ⊚ *Breakfast* Ⓜ *Ipanema/General Osório* ✣ *D5.*

$$$$
HOTEL
⬚ **Fasano Rio.** The Italian-owned Fasano Group is renowned for its stylish, elegant hotels and restaurants, and Fasano Rio has the added glamour of having been crafted by the French designer Philippe Starck. **Pros:** chic decor; wonderful views from pool; glamorous clientele. **Cons:**

standard rooms lack views; expensive; street noise. $ Rooms from: R$1,600 ⊠ Av. Viera Souto 80, Ipanema ☏ 021/3202–4000 ⊕ www. fasano.com.br ⮌ 82 rooms, 10 suites ⦿ Breakfast Ⓜ Ipanema/General Osório ✛ E6.

$$$ ⛩ **Ipanema Inn.** If you want to stay in Ipanema and avoid the ultrahigh
HOTEL   prices of beachfront accommodations, this no-frills hotel with great service is a wise choice. **Pros:** great location; good value. **Cons:** basic rooms; no views. $ Rooms from: R$460 ⊠ Rua Maria Quitéria 27, Ipanema ☏ 021/2523–6092, 021/2529–1000 ⊕ www.ipanemainn.com. br ⮌ 56 rooms ⦿ Breakfast Ⓜ Ipanema/General Osório ✛ D5.

$$$ ⛩ **Ipanema Sweet.** In this smart residential building in the heart of
RENTAL   Ipanema—two blocks from the beach and steps away from the neigh-
FAMILY   borhood's best bars, restaurants, and shops—one- and two-bedroom apartments are rented out by the night, week, or month. **Pros:** great location; stylish public areas; more space than standard hotel rooms. **Cons:** not all apartments have safe boxes; small pool; maid service costs extra. $ Rooms from: R$420 ⊠ Rua Visconde de Pirajá 161, Ipanema ☏ 021/8201–1458, 021/98137–2774 Raissa Cordeiro ⮌ 10 apartments ⦿ No meals Ⓜ Ipanema/General Osório ✛ D5.

$$$ ⛩ **Leblon Flat Service.** A good option for those who want to save money
RENTAL   by cooking some meals, this hotel-like complex with an excellent loca-
FAMILY   tion three blocks from Leblon Beach rents simply decorated, small fur- nished apartments with one or two bedrooms and balconies and has a small pool. **Pros:** good rate for Leblon area; kitchens; near shopping, restaurants, and nightlife. **Cons:** unattractive building; basic lodgings. $ Rooms from: R$500 ⊠ Rua Professor Antônio Maria Teixeira 33, Leblon ☏ 021/ 2127–7700 for information, 021/3722–5053 for reser- vations, 021/3722–5054 ⮌ 120 apartments ⦿ Breakfast ✛ C5.

$$$$ ⛩ **Marina All Suites.** In front of Leblon Beach and surrounded by designer
HOTEL   stores and upmarket restaurants, this hotel is a favorite with chic vaca- tioners (Gisele Bundchen and Calvin Klein are regulars). **Pros:** good location; spacious, well-equipped suites; excellent service; pool with sea views. **Cons:** expensive; Leblon Beach is not quite as pretty as Ipanema; small pool. $ Rooms from: R$1,100 ⊠ Av. Delfim Moreira 696, Leblon ☏ 021/2172–1001 ⊕ www.marinaallsuites.com.br ⮌ 37 suites ⦿ Breakfast ✛ B6.

$$$$ ⛩ **Praia Ipanema.** This hotel between Ipanema and Leblon may not be
HOTEL   deluxe, but it's across from the beach, and each room has a sea view and a private balcony. **Pros:** great views; beachfront location; close to Ipanema and Leblon shopping and nightlife. **Cons:** some furnishings a little shabby. $ Rooms from: R$740 ⊠ Av. Vieira Souto 706, Ipanema ☏ 021/2141–4949 ⊕ www.praiaipanema.com ⮌ 103 rooms ⦿ Break- fast Ⓜ Ipanema/General Osorio ✛ C5.

$$$$ ⛩ **Sheraton Rio Hotel & Resort.** Between the upmarket neighborhoods
RESORT   of São Conrado and Leblon, this hotel has the most spacious leisure
FAMILY   area in the city, with three pools, two tennis courts, and a children's playground; however, the leisure area is less than pristine, and the hotel's location directly in front of the sprawling favela of Vidigal may make some guests uncomfortable. **Pros:** great for families; wonder- ful beach; good amenities. **Cons:** isolated location means taxi rides;

some furnishings past their prime; pool area is not clean. [$] *Rooms from: R$690* ✉ *Av. Niemeyer 121, Leblon* ☎ *021/2529 1122* 🌐 *www.sheraton-rio.com* 🛏 *500 rooms, 59 suites* 🍴 *Breakfast* ⊕ *A6.*

SANTA TERESA

$$
B&B/INN
Fodor's Choice ★

🏨 **Casa Cool Beans.** American expats Lance and David opened Casa Cool Beans in 2010, determined to raise the bar for accommodations in Rio, and their guests' raves about the attentive service, chill atmosphere, and gorgeous decor testify to their success. **Pros:** excellent service; characterful building; peaceful neighborhood; breakfast alfresco. **Cons:** difficult for taxis to find; far from the beach; two-night minimum stay. [$] *Rooms from: R$290* ✉ *Rua Laurinda Santos Lobo 136, Santa Teresa* ☎ *021/2262–0552, 202/470–3548 in U.S.* 🌐 *www.casacoolbeans.com* 🛏 *10 rooms* 🍴 *Breakfast* ⊕ *A1.*

$$$$
HOTEL
Fodor's Choice ★

🏨 **Hotel Santa Teresa.** This five-star hotel, located in the historic hilltop neighborhood of Santa Teresa, is housed in a regenerated coffee plantation mansion that pays homage to Brazil's cultures and traditions with folk art and handicrafts from across the nation. **Pros:** sense of place; highlights Brazilian artists; stylish setting; excellent restaurant; close to Santa Teresa's drinking and dining scene. **Cons:** it's a cab ride to the beach; hotel bar sometimes closed for private events. [$] *Rooms from: R$1,100* ✉ *Rua Almirante Alexandrino 660, Santa Teresa* ☎ *021/3380–0204* 🌐 *www.santa-teresa-hotel.com* 🛏 *44 rooms* 🍴 *Breakfast* ⊕ *A1.*

SÃO CONRADO, BARRA DA TIJUCA, AND BEYOND

$$$$
HOTEL
Fodor's Choice ★

🏨 **La Suite.** If you're looking for an extra-special place to spend a romantic night in Rio, this luxurious cliffside hideaway is the one to book: La Suite's off-the-beaten-track location amid the secluded mansions of Joatinga—often referred to as "the Beverly Hills of Rio"—gives it an ultra-exclusive feel, and the French owners have imbued their boutique hotel with real Parisian chic. **Pros:** impossibly scenic location; exclusive feel; romantic ambience. **Cons:** it's a cab ride to bars and restaurants. [$] *Rooms from: R$1,300* ✉ *Rua Jackson de Figueiredo 501, Joatinga* ☎ *021/2484–1962* 🛏 *7 rooms* 🍴 *Breakfast* ⊕ *A5.*

$$$$
HOTEL
FAMILY

🏨 **Radisson Hotel Barra Rio de Janeiro.** Each of the spacious and comfortable rooms in this mammoth hotel has a balcony overlooking Barra Beach, and while the hotel is in need of modernization, it has a large heated pool as well as tennis courts and a fitness center. **Pros:** good facilities; Barra Beach is quieter than Zona Sul. **Cons:** traffic is bad; neighborhood is more like Miami than Rio. [$] *Rooms from: R$720* ✉ *Av. Lúcio Costa 3150, Barra da Tijuca* ☎ *021/3139–8000* 🌐 *atlanticahotels.com.br* 🛏 *264 rooms, 28 suites* 🍴 *Breakfast* ⊕ *A5.*

NIGHTLIFE AND PERFORMING ARTS

Rio supports a rich variety of cultural activity and cutting-edge nightlife. The classic rhythms of samba can be heard in many clubs and bars, and on street corners, but it's possible to find something to suit every kind of musical taste almost every night of the week. Major theater, opera, ballet, and classical-music performances are plentiful, and smaller, more intimate events happen in most neighborhoods. Arts enthusiasts should pick up the bilingual *Guia do Rio* published by Riotur, the city's tourist board, which is available free at tourist information kiosks and hotel reception. The Portuguese-language newspapers *Jornal do Brasil* and *O Globo* publish schedules of events in the entertainment supplements of their Friday editions, which can be found online at ⊕ *www.jb.com.br* and ⊕ *www.oglobo.com.br*. Finally, *Veja Rio* is the city's most comprehensive entertainment guide, published every Saturday and available at all newsstands.

> ### PLAYING IT SAFE
>
> Safety after dark is a paramount concern in Rio. Be aware of your surroundings at all times. Always take a taxi after dark, and be sure it has the company name and phone number painted on the outside before you get in. Pickpockets love Copacabana and Lapa, so keep valuables either at the hotel or well hidden. If you're heading to Lapa, arrange a meeting point in case you get separated from your group, as it's easy to get lost in the crush of people.

NIGHTLIFE

It's sometimes said that cariocas would rather expend their energy on the beach and that nighttime is strictly for recharging their batteries and de-sanding their swimsuits, but witnessing the masses swarming into Lapa at 10 pm on a Friday night make this a tricky argument to endorse. New nightclubs and bars continue to sprout up with remarkable regularity, and there are cutting-edge underground rhythms and musical styles competing with samba, chorro, and Brazilian pop (MPB) for the locals' hearts.

Live music is nighttime Rio's raison d'être, with street corners regularly playing host to impromptu renditions. During Carnival the entire city can feel like one giant playground. The electronic-music scene is also very much alive, and the underground popularity of funk (the city's own X-rated genre, not to be confused with the James Brown version) is slowly seeping into the mainstream, down from the huge *bailes* or open-air parties held weekly in the city's favelas. In addition to samba and MPB, hip-hop, electronica, and rock can be heard in clubs around the city.

COPACABANA

BARS

Bip Bip. Here the *roda de samba*—where musicians sit and play instruments around a central table (in fact the *only* table in this tiny bar)—is legendary, as is the help-yourself beer policy. The gnarled old owner makes drink notations and keeps the crowd in check. The standards of the music here are as high as the bar is simple: big-name Brazilian musicians have been known to drop in for a jam session, and on weekend evenings the revelry often spills out onto the street. ⊠ *Rua Almirante Gonçalves 50, Copacabana* ☎ *021/2267–9696.*

Cervantes. This no-frills Copacabana institution marries great beer with great sandwiches made with fresh beef, pork, and cheese crammed into French bread (with the obligatory pineapple slice). It's closed on Monday, but merely to give the staff a chance to recover: the rest of the week everyone's up until all hours catering to the lively late night–early morning crowd. ✉ *Rua Barata Ribeiro 7, Loja B, Copacabana* ☎ *021/2275–6147* ⊕ *www. restaurantecervantes.com.br.*

NIGHTCLUBS AND LIVE MUSIC

Fosfobox. For the more serious dance-music enthusiast, Fosfobox, in the heart of Copacabana, plays the best underground tunes, as well as rock and pop. Dancers cram onto the floor in the industrial-feeling basement, while an upstairs bar offers opportunity for conversation. It's closed on Monday and Tuesday. ✉ *Rua Siqueira Campos 143, Loja 22A, Copacabana* ☎ *021/2548–7498* ⊕ *www.fosfobox.com.br* 🎟 *R$50.*

Le Boy. The focal point of Rio's gay scene, this classic club has expansive dance floors and lively DJ sets as well as outrageous stage shows. The liveliest action takes place after 1 am, and one dance floor only opens at 6 am. ✉ *Rua Paul Pompéia 102, Posto 6, Copacabana* ☎ *021/2513–4993* ⊕ *www.leboy.com.br* 🎟 *R$15, men free before midnight.*

FLAMENGO AND BOTAFOGO

BARS

Belmonte. If you find yourself in need of refreshment after a stroll through the beautiful Parque do Flamengo, then your best stop is Belmonte. The original outlet of a now successful chain, it keeps the carioca spirit alive and well with its carefree air, great tapas and Brazilian snacks, and icy chopp. ✉ *Praia do Flamengo 300, Flamengo* ☎ *021/2552–3349.*

Cobal do Humaitá. Occupying a vast outdoor space under the gaze of Christ the Redeemer, this collection of bars, restaurant, and shops throngs with people after dark, when the air is filled with the tipsy chatter of locals relaxing over dinner and drinks. ✉ *Cobal do Humaitá, Rua Voluntarios Da Patria 446, Loja 3/4 A, Humaitá.*

NIGHTCLUBS AND LIVE MUSIC

Casa da Matriz. With its multiroom layout, old-school arcade games, and small junk shop, this shabby-chic venue has the look and feel of a house party. The club's youngish crowd appreciates the adventurous musical policy: don't be surprised if the DJ follows a 1960s Beatles track with down-and-dirty favela funk. It's closed Sunday to Tuesday. ✉ *Rua Henrique de Novaes 107, Botafogo* ☎ *021/2226–9691* ⊕ *casadamatriz. com.br* 🎟 *R$15–R$20.*

BAR TALK

A few useful Portuguese words under your belt will make the bar experience even more enjoyable and help you feel like a local. *Chopp* is the ubiquitous draft beer served in small glasses, while *cerveja* is the universal word for bottled beer. A simple *mais uma* will get you "one more," and a *saideira* will get you "one for the road." Finally, ask for *a conta* or "the bill" when you want to settle your tab.

2

IPANEMA AND LEBLON

BARS

Fodor's Choice ★ **Academia da Cachaça.** Not merely *the* place in Rio to try caipirinhas (made here with a variety of tropical fruits), Academia da Cachaça is a veritable temple to cachaça. The small bar sells close to 100 brands of cachaça by the glass or bottle, as well as mixing the famous sugarcane rum into dangerously drinkable concoctions such as the *cocada geladinha*—frozen coconut, coconut water, brown sugar, and cachaça. The Northeastern bar snacks here include sun-dried beef, baked palm hearts, and delicious black-bean soup. ✉ *Rua Conde de Bernadotte 26, Leblon* ☎ *021/2239–1542* ⊕ *www.academiadacachaca.com.br.*

Bar Garota de Ipanema. This is the original Garota (there are branches all over the city), where Tom Jobim and Vinicius de Moraes penned the timeless song "The Girl from Ipanema." The place serves well-priced food and drink that no doubt originally appealed to the two songsmiths. Occasional live-music events take place in the upstairs lounge. ✉ *Rua Vinicius de Moraes 39, Ipanema* ☎ *021/2523–3787* ⊕ *www.bargarotadeipanema.com* Ⓜ *Ipanema/General Osório.*

Bracarense. A trip to Bracarense after a hard day on the beach is what Rio is all about. Crowds spill onto the streets while parked cars double as chairs and the sandy masses gather at sunset for ice-cold chopp and some of Leblon's best pork sandwiches, fish balls, and empadas. ✉ *Rua José Linhares 85, Leblon* ☎ *021/2294–3549* ⊕ *www.bracarense.com.br.*

Devassa. Another cross-city bar chain, Devassa is notable for its house-brand beers, including delicious pale ales and *chopp escuro* (dark beer). The bar also has a great menu of meat-related staples and lighter bites as well as a lunch buffet. This branch has a plum location a couple of blocks from Ipanema Beach and is a popular post-beach hangout for sociable locals. ✉ *Rua Visconde de Pirajá 539, Ipanema* ☎ *021/2540–8380* ⊕ *www.devassa.com.br* Ⓜ *Ipanema/General Osório.*

Jobi Bar. Authentically carioca and a fine place to experience Rio spirit, the bar at down-to-earth Jobi stays open on weekends until the last customer leaves. Don't be fooled by the unassuming exterior—Jobi serves some of Rio's most delicious bar snacks and is one of the best-loved bars in the Zona Sul. ✉ *Av. Ataulfo de Paiva 1166, Loja B, Leblon* ☎ *021/2274–0547* ⊕ *jobibar.com.br/wp.*

THE REAL GIRL FROM IPANEMA

Have you ever wondered if there really *was* a girl from Ipanema? The song was inspired by schoolgirl Heloisa Pinheiro, who caught the fancy of songwriter Antônio Carlos (aka Tom) Jobim and his pal, lyricist Vinicius de Moraes, as she walked past the two bohemians sitting in their favorite bar. They then penned one of last century's classics. That was in 1962, and today the bar has been renamed **Bar Garota de Ipanema.** Its owners have further capitalized on their venue's renown, with "Garota de..." bars across the city, with the appropriate neighborhood names appended.

NIGHTCLUBS AND LIVE MUSIC

House of Music. The fashionable nightclub and live-music venue attracts a young, photogenic crowd. There's an interesting and varied program of live music and DJs, taking in everything from *sertanejo* (Brazilian country music) and samba to hip-hop. ✉ *Rua Rita Ludolf 47, Leblon* ☎ *021/2249–9309* ✆ *From R$25.*

Plataforma. Although Plataforma is very tourist-oriented, if you're in Rio outside of Carnival season, then seeing the shows here will give you a taste of the festival's costumes, music, and energy. Capoeira martial-arts displays complete an enjoyable if expensive look at some great Brazilian traditions. Reservations can be made on the venue's website (also for the restaurant). ✉ *Rua Adalberto Ferreira 32, Leblon* ☎ *021/2274 4022* ⊕ *www.plataformashow.com* ✆ *R$60–R$100.*

INLAND ZONA SUL

BARS

FAMILY **Assis Garrafeira.** Just a few minutes' stroll from the station for the funicular railway that whisks tourists up to the Christ statue, this welcoming bar prides itself on its enormous selection of quality beers. In a building once occupied by the late fiction writer Machado do Assis—a giant of Brazilian literature—the walls of the lounge are occupied by well-stocked bookshelves. Staff are hugely knowledgeable about drink pairings and beer, and can help you choose from the list of almost 200 bottles, which includes many imported Belgian beers. ✉ *Rua Cosme Velho 174* ☎ *021/2205–3598.*

Boteco D.O.C. A pleasant 10-minute walk from the Corcovado railway station, this gastrobar is run by talented young chef Gabriel Carvalho, who has worked at some of the best restuarants in the city. Food is a main focus—try the *bolinha da bacalhau 90%*, a version of the classic cod-and-potato ball that comes with more fish and less filler than standard. There are good cocktails, including one made with cashew, gin, and tonic. It's a small space, so things get full quickly—come early if you want a seat. ✉ *Rua das Laranjeiras 486, Laranjeiras* ☎ *021/3486–2550* ⊕ *www.botecodoc.com.*

Lagoa. Rio's beautiful city lake is flanked with bars and informal kiosks. Along with the usual beers and cocktails, the food—Italian, Arabian, burgers, and other nontraditional Brazilian—may not be spectacular, but the view of surrounding water and mountains, with Christ the Redeemer lighted up in the distance, most certainly is. In November and December a giant floating Christmas tree lit by millions of twinkling lights adds to the spectacle.The kiosks close down around 1 am. ✉ *Parque Brigadeiro Faria Lima, turnoff near BR gas station, Av. Epitácio Pessoa 1674, Lagoa* ☎ .

NIGHTCLUBS AND LIVE MUSIC

Fodor's Choice ★ **00 (Zero Zero).** Alongside the Gávea Planetarium, 00 is at once a buzzing nightclub, chic sushi restaurant, and open-air bar. Music at this enduringly popular carioca hangout ranges from modern Brazilian samba and house to drum and bass. ✉ *Av. Padre Leonel Franca 240, Gávea* ☎ *021/2540–8041* ⊕ *www.00site.com.br* ✆ *From R$30.*

Casa Rosa. A former brothel in a bright-pink mansion on the Laranjeiras hillside is now a hot spot for live music and dancing. The Sunday-afternoon *feijoada* and samba on the terrace is a must for anyone seeking out a true carioca experience. ⊠ *Rua Alice 550, Laranjeiras* ☎ *021/2557–2562* ⊕ *www.casarosa.com.br* ⊠ *From R$20.*

SANTA TERESA AND LAPA

BARS

FodorśChoice
★

Bar do Gomez. Officially Armazem São Thiago, this neighborhood institution is universally referred to by its nickname, Bar do Gomez, in honor of the owner, whose family has run the business for close to 100 years. Pictures documenting the bar's history adorn the high wooden walls, and surveying the scene in the present, you get the pleasant impression that little has changed over the years. The draft beer flows like water, locals swap stories at the long wooden bar, and new friendships are forged at the outdoor drinking posts. Favorites among the bar snacks include the giant olives, a pastrami sandwich, and the shrimp plate. Early on a Friday night, this is a good place to strike up a conversation with locals before heading down the hill to Lapa. ⊠ *Rua Aurea 26, Santa Teresa* ☎ *021/2232–0822* ⊕ *www.armazemsaothiago.com.br.*

Bar do Mineiro. The liveliest of Santa Teresa's many drinking dens and the hub of much social activity, this enduringly popular *boteco* anchors one end of the neighborhood's main drinking and dining strip. Some excellent snacks are served here—the *pasteis de feijao* (fried pastries filled with black beans) being a firm favorite with locals—as well as hearty plates of meat-based *comida mineira* (cuisine from Minas Gerais State). A street-party atmosphere prevails on Sunday afternoon, when the bar is standing room only and revelers spill out onto the road outside. ⊠ *Rua Paschoal Carlos Magno 99, Santa Teresa* ☎ *021/2221–9227.*

Mangue Seco Cachaçaria. Specializing in some of Brazil's finest institutions—strong and fine-tasting cachaças (Brazilian rum), mouthwatering *moquecas* (stews), and, of course, live samba—Mangue Seco's location on the popular Rua do Lavradio makes it a perfect place to start a night out. Arrive at sundown, grab one of the sidewalk tables, and watch Lapa life unfold as you sip a caipirinha and browse the menu. ⊠ *Rua do Lavradio 23, Lapa* ☎ *021/3852–1947* ⊕ *www.manguesecocachacaria. com.br.*

NIGHTCLUBS AND LIVE MUSIC

Carioca da Gema. A favorite among local *sambistas*, Carioca da Gema is one of Lapa's liveliest spots, with talented musicians performing seven nights a week. By 11 pm, finding a place to stand can be difficult, but regulars still find a way to samba. Call ahead and book a table if you are more keen to be a spectator. There's a good pizzeria downstairs. ⊠ *Rua Mem de Sá 79, Lapa* ☎ *021/2221–0043* ⊕ *www.barcariocadagema. com.br* ⊠ *From R$23.*

FodorśChoice
★

Circo Voador. A great venue in an excellent location right by the Lapa arches, Circo Voador hosts club nights during the week, but it's the varied live shows that really stand out, with a big stage set under a huge open-sided circular tent and room for up to 1,500 people to dance the night away. ⊠ *Rua dos Arcos s/n, Lapa* ☎ *021/2533-0354* ⊕ *www. circovoador.com.br* 🖳 *From R$25.*

Lapa Street Party. Lapa's transformation from no-go area to must-go party district has been dramatic, and the ongoing gentrification of this formerly neglected part of downtown has extended to the weekend street parties held in the area surrounding the Arcos da Lapa (Lapa Aqueduct). On Fridays and Saturdays, smart-looking canvas kiosks sprout up, offering everything from super-strong fruit cocktails to alcohol-absorbing pizzas and burgers, and thousands of revelers come to rub shoulders. The lively scene often involves impromptu music performances, and the party doesn't wind down until the sun rises. Both men and women should be prepared for an onslaught of attention from locals. If this attention is unwanted, be polite but clear and walk away—small talk may be perceived as flirting. An increased police presence has made Lapa safer than it was, but pickpocketing remains a problem, so don't bring valuables here. ⊠ *Rua dos Arcos, Lapa* Ⓜ *Carioca.*

Leviano. Among the best of the slick modern bars to crop up as part of the ongoing gentrification of Lapa, Leviano is situated at the heart of the action. A glass frontage allows patrons to look out onto the hedonistic hordes from the comfort of an air-conditioned lounge, and the second floor features live bands—jazz nights here have been a particular success—while downstairs circus acrobats whirl and twirl from the ceiling. Should you be loathe to tear your eyes away, there's an extensive menu of light meals to accompany those ice-cold beers and caipirinhas. ⊠ *Av. Mem de Sá 49, Lapa* ☎ *021/2507-5779* ⊕ *www.levianobar.com. br* Ⓜ *Carioca or Cinelandia.*

Fodor's Choice **Rio Scenarium.** Despite the hordes of samba-seeking tourists, Rio Sce-
★   narium somehow manages to retain its authenticity and magic. This is partly due to the incredible setting—a former movie-props warehouse still crammed to the rafters with old instruments, bikes, furniture, and puppets—but also to the great bands and persevering locals who love to show off their moves and entice novices onto the dance floor. On weekends arrive before 9 pm to avoid the lines, or call ahead and book a table. It's closed on Sunday and Monday. ⊠ *Rua do Lavrádio 20, Lapa* ☎ *021/3147-9005* ⊕ *www.rioscenarium.com.br* 🖳 *From R$30* Ⓜ *Carioca or Cinelandia.*

PERFORMING ARTS

Theater, classical music (*música erudita*), and opera may be largely the preserve of the affluent upper classes in Rio, but tickets remain reasonably priced by international standards and can be purchased easily from box offices. Although understanding Portuguese may prove difficult for some visitors, musicals provide a good opportunity to catch the glitzier side of Rio, and the international language of song and dance is considerably more comprehensible. Since many of the venues are in downtown or more out-of-the-way areas, use taxis to get to and from them, as the surrounding streets can feel dangerously deserted by night.

Visual-art venues and museums are also very well endowed, with privately funded cultural centers hosting a rich variety of exhibitions,

CLOSE UP

Carnival in Rio

The four-day Carnival weekend, marked on every Brazilian's calendar, is by far the biggest event of the year, with planning and preparation starting months ahead. What began as a pre-Lent celebration has morphed into a massive affair of street parties, masquerades, and samba parades. Elaborate costumes, enormous floats, and intensive planning all unfurl magically behind the scenes as Brazilians from all walks of life save their money for the all-important *desfile* (parade) down the Sambódromo. Even though Carnival has set dates based on the lunar calendar that determine when Lent occurs, the *folia* (Carnival festivities) start at least a week before and end at least a week after the samba schools parade. Five-star hotels such as the Sheraton and Copacabana Palace have balls that are open to the public, as long as you can afford tickets (which run upward of R$3,000). A cheaper option is partying at the Carnival *blocos* (street parties), along the streets of Centro and Santa Teresa and the beaches of the Zona Sul. If you really want to get close to the action, then you'll need to buy tickets (well in advance) for a seat at the Sambódromo. Most samba schools begin their rehearsals around October; if you're in Rio from October to January, visit one of the samba schools *(see Performing Arts)* on a rehearsal day. Whether your scene is hanging out at the bars, partying in the street, parading along the beach, masked balls for the elite, or fun in a stadium, Rio's Carnival is an experience of a lifetime.

specific details of which are again best sought out in the Friday editions of the Rio press.

CLASSICAL MUSIC

FAMILY **Centro Cultural Municipal Parque das Ruinas.** With a glorious view of Guanabara Bay and downtown, the Parque das Ruinas houses the remains of a mansion building that was Rio's bohemian epicenter in the first half of the 20th century. Today live music and theater performances are held here, and the panoramic views from the top of the building are stunning. Occasional music and art events take place during the summer. ⊠ *Rua Murtinho Nobre 169, Santa Teresa* ☎ *021/2252–1039.*

Escola de Música da UFRJ. The music school auditorium, inspired by the Salle Gaveau in Paris, has 1,100 seats, and you can listen to chamber music, symphony orchestras, and opera, all free of charge. ⊠ *Rua do Passeio 98, Lapa* ☎ *021/2222–1029* Ⓜ *Cinelândia.*

Instituto Moreira Salles. Surrounded by beautiful gardens, the institute creates the perfect atmosphere for classical music. Listen to musicians performing pieces from Bach, Chopin, Debussy, and other classical composers. Outdoor cinema screenings are held here, too. ⊠ *Rua Marquês de São Vicente 476, Gávea* ☎ *021/3284–7400* ⊕ *www.ims.com.br.*

Sala Cecília Meireles. A popular concert venue for classical music in the city, the Sala hosts regular performances in a midsize hall. ⊠ *Largo da Lapa 47, Lapa* ☎ *021/2332–9223* ⊕ *www.salaceciliameireles.com.br* ⌦ *From R$25* Ⓜ *Cinelândia.*

CONCERT HALLS

Cidade das Artes. This enormous cultural complex and live-music venue opened in 2013 and is now the largest concert hall in South America, seating 1,780. Designed by French architect Christian de Portzamparc, the Cidade das Artes (City of Arts) complex covers around 90,000 square meters and houses theaters and cinemas, and is home to the Brazilian Symphony Orchestra, and hosts major rock and pop shows. ⊠ *Av. das Americas 5300, Barra da Tijuca* ☎ *021/3325–0102* ⊕ *www. cidadedasartes.org.*

Citibank Hall. This huge venue hosts some of the biggest Brazilian and international names playing in Rio, such as Caetano Veloso, Adele, Smashing Pumpkins, and Lady Gaga. ⊡ *Via Parque Shopping, Av. Ayrton Senna 3000, Barra da Tijuca* ☎ *0300/789–6846* ⊕ *www. citibankhall.com.br* ⊠ *From R$90.*

HSBC Arena. HSBC Arena hosts big-name rock and pop stars. ⊠ *Av. Embaixador Abelardo Bueno 3401, Barra da Tijuca* ☎ *021/3035–5200.*

FILM

Estação Net Ipanema. The charming two-screen Estação Net Ipanema cinema is part of a lively area of small restaurants and bookstores, perfect for hanging out before or after the films (the theater itself has a coffee shop). Other locations of the Estação chain of small art-house cinemas can be found on the Ipanema beachfront (Estação Net Laura Alvim), in Flamengo (Estação Paissandu), Barra da Tijuca (Estação Barra Point), and two in Botafogo (Estação Net Rio and Estação Botafogo). ⊠ *Av. Visconde de Pirajá 605, Ipanema* ☎ *021/2279–4603* ⊕ *www. grupoestacao.com.br* ⊠ *From R$15.*

FAMILY **UCI New York City Center.** This 18-screen, American-style multiplex is located in a large mall that comes complete with a model of the Statue of Liberty outside. Fittingly, it shows many Hollywood blockbusters. ⊠ *Av. das Américas 5000, Loja 301, Barra da Tijuca* ☎ *021/2461–1818* ⊕ *www.ucicinemas.com.br* ⊠ *From R$20.*

OPERA

Fodor'sChoice **Theatro Municipal.** Built in 1909, the stunning Municipal Theater at
★ Cinelândia is the city's main performing-arts venue, hosting dance, opera, symphony concerts, and theater events for most of the year. The season officially runs from March to December, so don't be surprised to find the theater closed in January and February. The theater also has its own ballet company. ⊠ *Praça Floriano, Rua Manuel Carvalho s/n, Centro* ☎ *021/2332–9134, 021/2332–9191, 021/2262–3501, 021/2299–1717* ⊕ *www.theatromunicipal.rj.gov.br* Ⓜ *Cinelândia.*

SAMBA-SCHOOL SHOWS

Weekly public rehearsals (*ensaio*) attract crowds of samba enthusiasts and visitors alike to the *escolas de samba* (samba schools) from August through to Carnival (February or March). As the schools frantically ready themselves for the high point of the year, the atmosphere in these packed warehouses is often electric, and with Mangueira and Beija Flor, always sweaty. This may prove one of your liveliest and most chaotic nights on the town. Ticket prices range from R$15 to R$35. The tour company Brazil Expedition *(See Tours, in the Rio de Janeiro*

Planner) offers trips to samba school rehearsals, including transport and entrance, for R$75. On weekends during the run up to Carnival, technical rehearsals are held at the Sambodromo. Entrance is free, crowds are relatively small, and the spectacle is almost as exciting as the real thing. Check local listings for details.

Acadêmicos do Salgueiro. The samba school Salguiero holds its pre-Carnival rehearsals only on Saturdays, from 10 pm. The school also runs Samba Experience events from 9:30 pm, which include a limb-loosening caipirinha, samba classes, and entry to the rehearsals. ⊠ *Rua Silva Teles 104, Andaraí* ☎ *021/2238-0389* ⊕ *www.salgueiro.com.br* 🎫 *From R$30.*

Beija-Flor. The several-times winner of Rio's annual Samba School competition, Beija-Flor holds public rehearsals on Thursdays at 9 pm in the months leading up to Carnival. ⊠ *Pracinha Wallace Paes Leme 1025, Nilópolis* ☎ *021/2247–4800* ⊕ *www.beija-flor.com.br* 🎫 *From R$30.*

Estação Primeira de Mangueira. One of the most popular schools and always a challenger for the Carnival title, Estação Primeira holds its rehearsals on Saturdays at 10 pm. ⊠ *Rua Visconde de Niterói 1072, Mangueira* ☎ *021/2567–4637* ⊕ *www.mangueira.com.br* 🎫 *From R$30.*

THEATER

Fodor'sChoice
★ **Centro Cultural Banco do Brasil.** Formerly the headquarters of the Banco do Brasil, in the late 1980s this opulent six-story domed building with marble floors was transformed into a space for plays, art exhibitions, and music recitals. Today the CCBB is one of the city's most important cultural centers, with a bookstore, three theaters, a video hall, four individual video booths, a movie theater, two auditoriums, a restaurant, a coffee shop, a children's library, and a tearoom. It's open Wednesday through Sunday between 10 am and 9 pm, and there are regular children's shows on weekends. ⊠ *Rua 1° de Março 66, Centro* ☎ *021/3808–2020* ⊕ *www.bb.com.br/cultura* ☉ *Tues.–Sun 10 am–9 pm* Ⓜ *Uruguaiana.*

FAMILY **Teatro das Artes.** Located in a shopping mall in well-heeled Gavea, this theater hosts popular productions. Two smaller theaters are reserved for less commercial productions. ⊠ *Shopping Center da Gávea, Rua Marques de São Vicente 52, Loja 264, Gávea* ☎ *021/2540–6004, 021/2294–1096* ⊕ *www.teatrodasartes.com.br* 🎫 *From R$40.*

Teatro João Caetano. The city's oldest theater dates to 1813, and while the building itself is less than spectacular, the 1,200-seat venue hosts some interesting productions. These tend to be accessibly priced so it's worth a look, especially since the once-seedy area around the theater has been smartened up. ⊠ *Praça Tiradentes, Centro* ☎ *021/2332–9166* ⊕ *www.cultura.rj.gov.br/espaco/teatro-joao-caetano* 🎫 *From R$20* Ⓜ *Presidente Vargas.*

SPORTS AND THE OUTDOORS

Simply put, Rio de Janeiro is sports mad. Though much of the frenzy centers on soccer, other sports—among them volleyball, basketball, beach soccer, beach volleyball, and *futevolei* (a soccer-volleyball hybrid)—are taken extremely seriously. Invigorated by the success of the 2014 FIFA World Cup, it is with a sense of fevered anticipation that Rio awaits the 2016 Olympics, whose impact on the city cannot be understated. In addition to the vast sums spent to renovate existing and create new sports facilities and an Olympic village in the city's West Zone, significant investments are being made to upgrade the public-transportation system.

> ### CYCLE RIO
>
> With its many bike paths, Rio is a great place to explore by bicycle, and Bike Rio, a citywide bicycle-sharing system, has made it easier than ever to do so. Locals and visitors can pick up one of hundreds of bicycles at many stations along the beach front and at other bike-friendly locations, returning the bikes to similar stations at journey's end. Daily passes cost R$5 and can be purchased online at ⊕ *www.mobilicidade.com.br*.

BOATING AND SAILING

Dive Point. Schooner tours around the main beaches of Rio and as far afield as Búzios and Arraial do Cabo are offered here, as well as deep-sea and wreck diving. Be sure to ask if prices include all the necessary equipment and training (if required). ✉ *Av. Ataulfo da Paiva 1174, SS 04, Leblon* ☎ *021/2239–5105, 021/2239–5105* ⊕ *www.divepoint.com.br*.

FAMILY **Saveiro's Tour.** Take a trip down the coast to Angra or catch one of the two-hour daily cruises around Guanabara Bay—views of Sugar Loaf, Botafogo Bay, and the Rio-Niterói Bridge are among the highlights. Saveiro's also hires out speedboats and sailboats by the day. ✉ *Marina da Glória, Av. Infante Dom Henrique s/n, Lojas 13 e 14, Glória* ☎ *021/2225–6064* ⊕ *www.saveiros.com.br* 🕙 *From R$55* Ⓜ *Gloria*.

GOLF

Gávea Golf and Country Club. With a stunning setting overlooking the ocean and framed by the towering Pedra da Gávea mountain, Gávea Golf and Country Club has an impeccably groomed course. It's members-only on weekends, but nonmembers can play during the week. ✉ *Estrada da Gávea 800, São Conrado* ☎ *021/3322–4141* ⊕ *www.gaveagolfclub.com.br* 🕙 *R$350 weekdays* 🏌 *18 holes, 5986 yards, par 18* Ⓜ *No metro*.

FAMILY **Golden Green Golf Club.** This small but well-maintained golf course may only have six holes, but given the exclusivity and prices of the alternatives, this could be your best option for getting in a little play in Rio. Nonmembers are welcome every day, but it's a little out of town. ✉ *Av.*

Prefeito Dulcídio Cardoso 2901, Barra da Tijuca ☎ *021/2434–0696*
✉ *R$80 weekdays, R$100 weekends* ⛳ *6 holes, 2637 yards, par 54.*

HANG GLIDING

Just Fly. This highly reputable and experienced outfit will collect you from your hotel, take you through the basics, and then run you off Pedra Bonita mountain into the sky high above Tijuca Forest. The excellent instructors can also film or photograph the experience for an extra charge. ✉ *Ipanema* ☎ *021/2268–0565, 021/9985–7540* ⊕ *justflyinrio. blogspot.co.uk* ✉ *From R$240.*

São Conrado Eco-Aventura. This reliable and experienced team can provide you with a bird's-eye view of Rio either by hang glider or paraglider as well as leading jungle treks and Jeep tours. It is possible to book adventure packages combining several activities for a discounted price. ✉ *São Conrado* ☎ *021/2522–5586* ⊕ *www.saoconradoecoaventuras. com.br* ✉ *From R$250.*

HIKING AND CLIMBING

Given the changeable weather and the harsh terrain, guides are recommended for all major walks and climbs in Rio. Of particular note within the city itself are the hikes up Corcovado from Parque Lage and the trip through Tijuca Forest to Pico da Tijuca.

Centro Excursionista Brasileiro. The largest and oldest mountaineering organization in Brazil, Centro Excursionista Brasileiro runs climbing courses and leads treks throughout Rio State and as far away as Minas Gerais, providing guides, maps, and all the gear you'll need. ✉ *Av. Almirante Barroso 2, 8th fl., Centro* ☎ *021/2252–9844* ⊕ *www.ceb.org.br.*

Rio Adventures. This professional outfit with English-speaking guides runs a range of adventure sports activities and tours, including stand-up paddleboarding, white-water rafting, jungle treks, and climbing trips. ✉ *Praça Radial Sul 25, Botafogo* ☎ *021/2705–5747, 021/9768–5221* ⊕ *rioadventures.com* Ⓜ *Botafogo.*

Rio Ecoesporte. This ecotourism outfit specializes in exploring Rio's West Zone on foot and horseback, as well as running rappel and surf excursions. The excursions set off from Vargem Grande, a rural neighborhood west of Rio, and the tour company also has its own hostel, Rio Ecoesporte Hostel. ✉ *Estrada dos Bandeirantes 24081, Vargem Grande* ☎ *021/ 96416–4930 Activities, 021/3734–0744 Hostel* ⊕ *www. rioecoesporte.com.br* Ⓜ *No metro.*

HORSE RACING

Jóquei Clube. This beautiful old racetrack conjures up a bygone era of grandeur with its impeccably preserved betting hall, 1920s grandstand, and distant beach views framed by Cristo Redentor and the Dois Irmaos mountain. When the big event of the year, the Grande Premio, comes around in August, expect the crowds to swell and everyone to be dressed to the nines. Entry is free year-round, but you need to dress smart–casual, with no shorts or flip-flops allowed in the main stand. ✉ *Praça Santos Dumont 31, Gávea* ☎ *021/2512–9988* ⊕ *www.jcb.com. br* Ⓜ *No metro.*

SOCCER

FAMILY
Fodor'sChoice
★

Estádio Maracanã. The vast stadium is nothing short of legendary, and watching a soccer game here is a must if the season (from mid-January to November) is in swing. As entertaining as some of the games are the obsessive supporters, devoted to their team colors but not afraid to trash their own players, the opposition, other fans, and of course the referee. The huge flags and fireworks are always spectacular. Tickets are available in advance and often on game day from the stadium ticket office. The *branco* or white section of the *archibancado*, or upper tier, is the safest option for the neutral fan. Expect to pay around R$35 for a ticket there, and arrive in good time to grab the best seats and soak up the atmosphere. Major refurbishments were made to prepare the 78,838-seat stadium for the FIFA 2014 World Cup, and the stadium will also host decisive soccer matches—including the final—of the 2016 Rio Olympics. On non–match days visitors can take tours of the stadium. ✉ *Rua Prof. Eurico Rabelo s/n, Maracanã* ☎ *0800/062–7222 Freephone info number* ⊕ *www.maracana.com/site* 💳 *From R$35* Ⓜ *Maracana.*

> **RIO SURF BUS**
>
> The Surf Bus travels seven days a week from Botafogo to Prainha, which is considered to be the best surfing beach close to the city. The two-hour trip takes in the best surf breaks west of Rio, including all 12 km (7½ miles) of Barra, Recreio, and Macumba. There's no snobbery if you don't have a board and are just going along for the ride. Catch the bus from anywhere along the Copacabana, Ipanema, or Leblon beachfront for an easy route to some stunning out-of-town beaches. Check outward and return times at ⊕ *www.surfbus com.br*, because you do not want to be left stranded.

SURFING

Surfing remains hugely popular in Rio, and stand-up paddleboarding is a current trend—kiosks offer stand-up paddleboards and classes all along the Zona Sul beaches. Kite surfing is growing rapidly, too, with several schools opening on Barra beachfront and out of town toward Cabo Frio.

Escola de Surf do Arpoador. The most consistent break in the city has its own surf school based on the beach; call up or stop by to book an early-morning appointment. ✉ *Av. Francisco Bhering s/n, in front of Posto 7, Arpoador* ☎ *021/99438–2980 surf and stand-up paddle, 021/9180–2287 stand-up paddle* ⊕ *www.surfrio.com.br* 💳 *From R$120* Ⓜ *Cantagalo or Ipanema/General Osorio.*

Kitepoint Rio. One of several companies based in beach kiosks along Avenida do Pepê near Posto 7, Kitepoint provides all the equipment and training you'll need to master the sport of kite surfing. Wind conditions have to be just right, though, so patience is a virtue when seeking lessons. ⊠ *Av. do Pepê, Kiosk 7, next to Bombeiro, Barra da Tijuca* ☎ *021/8859–2112, 021/9200–0418* ⊕ *www.kitepointrio.com. br* 🖃 *From R\$110* Ⓜ *No metro.*

SHOPPING

Rio shopping is most famous for its incomparable beachwear and gemstone jewelry, both of which are exported globally. Brazil is one of the world's largest suppliers of colored gemstones, with deposits of aquamarines, amethysts, diamonds, emeralds, rubellites, topazes, and tourmalines. If you're planning to go to Minas Gerais, do your jewelry shopping there; otherwise stick with shops that have certificates of authenticity and quality. Other good local buys include shoes, Havaianas flip-flops, arts and crafts, coffee, local music, and summer clothing in natural fibers. With lots of low-quality merchandise around, the trick to successful shopping in Rio is knowing where to find high-quality items at reasonable prices.

Ipanema is Rio's most fashionable shopping district. Its many exclusive boutiques are in arcades, with the majority along Rua Visconde de Pirajá. Leblon's shops, scattered among cafés, restaurants, and newspaper kiosks, are found mainly along Rua Ataulfo da Paiva. Copacabana has souvenir shops, bookstores, and branches of some of Rio's better shops along Avenida Nossa Senhora de Copacabana and connecting streets. For cheap fashion finds and Carnival costumes, head to the maze of shopping streets behind the Uruguaiana metro station.

CENTRO

BOOKS

Livraria Leonardo da Vinci. One of Rio's best sources for foreign-language titles, this bookstore has a wide selection of titles in English, Spanish, and French. ⊠ *Av. Rio Branco 185, Subsolo, Centro* ☎ *021/2533–2237* ⊕ *www.leonardodavinci.com.br* Ⓜ *Carioca.*

CAHAÇA

Lidador. Deli goods and more than 30 types of cachaça are sold at Lidador. ⊠ *Rua da Assembléia 65, Centro* ☎ *021/2533–4988* Ⓜ *Carioca.*

DEPARTMENT STORES

Lojas Americanas. Rio's largest chain department store sells casual clothing, toys, records, candy, cosmetics, and sporting goods. There are branches in virtually every neighborhood of the city, some of which are smaller "Express" stores. ⊠ *Rua do Passeio 42–56, Centro* ☎ *021/2524–0284* ⊕ *www.americanas.com.br* Ⓜ *Cinelândia.*

MARKETS

Feira de Antiquários da Praça 15 de Novembro. This open-air antiques fair held on Saturdays attracts more locals than tourists—it's a good place to pick up vintage clothing, sunglasses, rare vinyl, and antique furniture and jewelry. Arrive early to get the best buys, and be prepared to haggle.

Serious collectors arrive as early as 6 am, often with an eye to grabbing a bargain and reselling it a few hours later at a higher price. Sellers begin to close up shop by early afternoon. ⊠ *Praça 15 de Novembro, Centro* ⊘ *Sat. 7 am–2 pm.*

FAMILY

Fodor's Choice

★

Feira do Rio Antigo (*Rio Antiques Fair*). Vendors at this outdoor fair sell antiques, rare books, records, and all types of objets d'art on the first Saturday afternoon of the month. New and vintage fashion is also a strong suit. Live samba music and capoeira performances create a festival-like atmosphere, and the pavement bars and restaurants buzz with locals and visitors. ⊠ *Rua do Lavradio, Centro* ☎ *021/2224–6693* ⊕ *www.polonovorioantigo.com.br* Ⓜ *Carioca or Cinelandia.*

Cristóvão, better known as the Feira Nordestina, is a social hub for Brazilians from the country's Northeast who live in Rio. They gather to hear their own distinctive music, eat regional foods, and buy arts, crafts, home furnishings, and clothing. With two stages for live music, the fair takes on a nightclub vibe after dark, and there are some seriously impressive displays of *forro* dancing. This fair is at its busiest and most exciting on the weekends. It's best to take a taxi here. ⊠ *Campo de São Cristóvão, Pavilhão de São Cristóvão, 7 km (4½ miles) northwest of Centro, São Cristóvão* ☎ *021/2580–0501, 021/2580–5335* ⊕ *www. feiradesaocristovao.org.br* ⊘ *Tues.–Thurs. 10–6, Fri. 10 am–Sun. 8 pm (continuously)* Ⓜ *São Cristóvão.*

MUSIC

Musical Carioca. A paradise for musicians and music lovers, Musical Carioca shares a street with many other music stores. Brazilian percussion instruments are also sold here. ⊠ *Rua da Carioca 89, Centro* ☎ *021/2524–6029, 021/3814–3400* ⊕ *www.musicalcarioca.com.br.*

COPACABANA AND LEME

BEAUTY

Spa do Pé. If touring and shopping have left you in need of revival, stop by Spa do Pé for a massage, manicure, or a foot treatment. The Copacabana branch is one of several across the city. ⊠ *Av. Nossa Senhora de Copacabana 680, Loja L, Copacabana* ☎ *021/2547–0459, 021/2523–8430* ⊕ *www.spadope.com.br* Ⓜ *Siqueira Campos.*

CENTERS AND MALLS

Shopping Center Cassino Atlântico. Antiques shops, jewelry stores, art galleries, and souvenir outlets predominate at this mall adjoining the Royal Rio Palace hotel. ⊠ *Av. Nossa Senhora de Copacabana 1417, Copacabana* ☎ *021/2523–8709* Ⓜ *Ipanema/General Osorio.*

COFFEE

Pão de Açúcar. The upscale supermarket Pão de Açúcar is a good bet for coffee that's cheaper than you'd pay at a coffee shop. ⊠ *Av. Nossa Senhora Copacabana 749, Copacabana* ☎ *021/2547–0372* ⊕ *www. paodeacucar.com.br* Ⓜ *Siqueira Campos.*

MARKETS

Avenida Atlântica. In the evening and on weekends along the median of Avenida Atlântica, artisans spread out their wares. You can find paintings, carvings, handicrafts, handmade clothing, and hammocks. ⊠ *Av. Atlântica, Copacabana* Ⓜ *Siqueira Campos.*

Feirarte. This street fair similar to the Sunday Feira Hippie in Ipanema takes place on weekends from 8 to 6. Handmade clothes, jewelry, and artsy knickknacks can be found here. ⊠ *Praça do Lido, Copacabana* Ⓜ *Cardeal Arcoverde.*

> ### BARGAINING IN RIO
>
> Bargaining in shops is unusual, but you can try your luck and ask if there's a discount for paying in cash, especially if it's a high-priced item. When granted, you can expect a 5% to 10% discount. Market or street-vendor shopping is a different story—bargain to your wallet's content.

SURF AND EXTREME SPORTS GEAR

Centauro. The massive Centauro store caters to the needs of all sorts of sporting enthusiasts. ⊠ *Shopping Leblon, Av. Afrânio de Melo Franco 290, Loja 106 and 107 A, Leblon* ☎ *021/2512–1246, 021/2512–1246* ⊕ *www.centauro.com.br.*

Galeria River. Stores at this youth-focused arcade sell all the clothing and equipment you'll need for a surfing or sporting vacation, as well as gear for climbing, rapelling, and other extreme sports. ⊠ *Rua Francisco Otaviano 67, Copacabana* ☎ *021/2267–1709* ⊕ *www.galeriariver.com. br* Ⓜ *Ipanema/General Osório.*

FLAMENGO AND BOTAFOGO

CENTERS AND MALLS

FAMILY **Rio Sul.** The popular Rio Sul retail complex has more than 400 stores, plus a cineplex, bars, and a giant food court where you can chow down on anything from sushi to coffee and cakes. ⊠ *Av. Lauro Müller 116, Botafogo* ☎ *021/2122–8070* ⊕ *www.riosul.com.br.*

SHOES, BAGS, AND ACCESSORIES

Mr. Cat. The stylish Mr. Cat carries handbags and leather shoes for men and women and has stores all over the city. ⊠ *Botafogo Praia Shopping, Praia de Botafogo 400, Lojas 124 and 125, Botafogo* ☎ *021/2552–5333* ⊕ *www.mrcat.com.br* Ⓜ *Botafogo.*

Victor Hugo. A Uruguayan who began making handbags when he came to Brazil in the 1970s, Victor Hugo has become famous nationally for chic leather handbags that are similar in quality to those of more expensive brands such as Louis Vuitton, Gucci, and Prada. ⊠ *Shopping Rio Sul, Av. Lauro Müller 116, Loja B19, Botafogo* ☎ *021/2542–2999* ⊕ *www.victorhugo.com.br.*

IPANEMA AND LEBLON

ART

Gam Arte e Molduras. A good place to find high-quality modern and contemporary paintings and sculptures, this gallery, which ships items abroad for customers, also sells photographs that can be made to size. ⊠ *Rua Garcia D'Ávila 145, Loja C, Ipanema* ☎ *021/2247–8060* ⊕ *www.gamarteemolduras.com.br* Ⓜ *Ipanema/General Osório.*

BEACHWEAR

Bumbum Ipanema. Alcindo Silva Filho, better known as Cidinho, opened Bumbum in 1979 after deciding to create the smallest (and by some accounts, the sexiest) bikinis in town. Bumbum remains a solid beach wear brand, and today sells slightly more modest styles as well as the trademark teeny bikinis. ⊠ *Forum Ipanema, Rua Visconde de Pirajá 351, Loja B, Ipanema* ☎ *021/2227-4080* ⊕ *www.bumbum.com.br* Ⓜ *Ipanema/General Osório.*

Espaço Brazilian Soul. For funky T-shirts and high-quality swimsuits, go to Brazilian Soul. The two-floor department store sells pricey but hip clothes and accessories from Brazilian designers and carries international brands such as Osklen. ⊠ *Rua Prudente de Moraes 1102, Ipanema* ☎ *021/2522–3641* Ⓜ *Ipanema/General Osório.*

Garota de Ipanema Shop. Come here for killer bikinis as well as T-shirts, tanks, colorful beach bags, and everything else you'll need to look fabulous at the beach. ⊠ *Rua Vinicius de Moraes 53, Loja A, Ipanema* ☎ *021/2521–3168* ⊕ *www.garotadeipanemabrasil.com.br* Ⓜ *Ipanema/ General Osório.*

Fodor's Choice ★ **Lenny.** Upmarket swimwear store Lenny sells sophisticated, exquisitely cut pieces in a range of sizes, and lots of fashionable beach accessories. Prices are high, but the bikinis are particularly creative. ⊠ *Forum Ipanema, Rua Visconde de Pirajá 351, Loja 114/115, Ipanema* ☎ *021/ 2523–3796* ⊕ *www.lenny.com.br* Ⓜ *Ipanema/General Osório.*

Lenny Off. If you are looking for an affordably priced designer bikini and don't mind last season's models, check out Lenny Off, selling slashed-rate pieces from the celebrated bikini designer Lenny Niemeyer. ⊠ *Rua Carlos Góis 234, Loja H, Leblon* ☎ *021/2511–2739* ⊕ *www.lenny. com.br.*

BEAUTY

Farma Life. The drugstore Farma Life has a wide selection of beauty products. ⊠ *Av. Ataulfo de Paiva 285, Loja B/C, Leblon* ☎ *021/2239– 1178* ⊕ *www.farmalife.com.br.*

O Boticario. This shop carries soaps, lotions, perfumes, shampoos, and cosmetics made from native Brazilian plants and seeds. There are branches across the city, but the Ipanema branch is handy for post-beach shopping. ⊠ *Rua Visconde de Pirajá 371, Ipanema* ☎ *021/2287– 2944* ⊕ *www.oboticario.com.br* Ⓜ *Ipanema/General Osório.*

Shampoo Cosmeticos. This shop sells local and imported beauty products. ⊠ *Rua Visconde de Pirajá 581, Loja A, Ipanema* ☎ *021/2529–2518* ⊕ *www.shampoocosmeticos.com.br.*

BOOKS

Argumento. Its large selection of books in English has made this bookstore popular with expats and vacationers. There's also a CD section. The very fine Café Severino, in the back, has coffee, pastries, salads, crepes, and sandwiches. ⊠ *Rua Dias Ferreira 417, Leblon* ☎ *021/2239-5294.*

CACHAÇA

Academia da Cachaça. You can buy close to 100 brands of cachaça here. The bar serves amazing caipirinhas and other cachaça-based drinks. ⊠ *Rua Conde Bernadote 26, Loja G, Leblon* ☎ *021/2239-1542* ⊕ *www.academiadacachaca. com.br.*

Garapa Doida. At Garapa Doida you can learn how to prepare a good caipirinha and purchase everything you need to make it, including glasses, straws, barrels to conserve the alcohol, and cachaça from all over the country. ⊠ *Rua Carlos Góis 234, Loja F, Leblon* ☎ *021/2274-8186.*

A Garrafeira. The charming liquor store Garrafeira sells a wide range of cachaça, including excellent versions from Minas Gerais State. ⊠ *Rua Dias Ferreira 259, Loja A, Leblon* ☎ *021/2512-3336* ⊕ *www. agarrafeira.com.br.*

CENTERS AND MALLS

Shopping Leblon. International designers and chic local boutiques can be found at this upmarket fashion mall in Leblon. There is some seriously good food to be found in the food court—think fine dining rather than fast food—and the mall has free Wi-Fi and a modern four-screen cineplex. ⊠ *Av. Afrânio de Melo Franco 290, Leblon* ☎ *021/2430-5122* ⊕ *www.shoppingleblon.com.br* Ⓜ *No metro.*

CLOTHING

Alessa. For fashion-forward designs, visit Alessa. Pay special attention to Alessa's fabulously fun underwear, which makes for great presents. ⊠ *Rua Nascimento Silva 399, Ipanema* ☎ *021/2287-9939* ⊕ *www. alessa.com.br* Ⓜ *Ipanema/General Osorio.*

Animale. A favorite among local fashionistas, Animale carries casual wear and formal wear that's both sophisticated and sexy. If you want to make an impression in Rio's social scene, head here for slinky dresses, chic cover-ups, and showstopping shoes and accessories. ⊠ *Rua Joana Angelica 116, Ipanema* ☎ *021/2227-3336* ⊕ *www.animale.com.br* Ⓜ *Ipanema/General Osório.*

THE BRAZILIAN BIKINI

Urban myth has it that Brazilian model Rose de Primo fashioned the Brazilian string bikini when she hurriedly sewed a bikini for a photo shoot with too little material. Whatever its history, the Tanga (string bikini) provides less than half the coverage of conventional bikinis, and makes the itsy bitsy teeny-weeny yellow polka-dot bikini look rather conservative. If you're looking to buy a Brazilian bikini but want a little more coverage, ask for a "sunkini." Happily for those reluctant to bare almost all, recent years have seen chic cariocas increasingly embrace one-piece swimwear.

Farm. Fun colors and bold patterns make Farm popular with cariocas. It's a great place to find feminine dresses and cute tops. ⊠ *Rua Visconde de Pirajá 365, Loja C–D, 202–204, Ipanema* ☎ *021/3813–3817* ⊕ *www.farmrio.com.br* Ⓜ *Ipanema/General Osório.*

Osklen. The Osklen brand is synonymous with fashionable sportswear, and all the clothes and accessories are designed to help you look good in the great outdoors. The brand is popular with sports-loving locals, and there are several stores in Rio. ⊠ *Rua Maria Quitéria 85, Ipanema* ☎ *021/2227–2911* ⊕ *www.osklen.com.br* Ⓜ *Ipanema/General Osório.*

Richards. A classic Brazilian clothing store selling tasteful, well-made pieces, Richards was originally just for men but now also carries women's clothing and children's wear. It's the place to go to for good-quality linen clothing. ⊠ *Rua Maria Quiteria 95, Ipanema* ☎ *021/2522–1245* ⊕ *www.richards.com.br* Ⓜ *Ipanema/General Osório.*

COFFEE

Armazém do Café. The "Coffee Store" chain has several branches in Rio, including ones in Ipanema and Leblon where you can enjoy a cappuccino or espresso and a pastry at the café before browsing the coffees and coffee-making devices for sale. ⊠ *Rua Visconde de Pirajá 595, Loja 101/102, Ipanema* ☎ *021/3874–2920* ⊕ *www.armazemdocafe.com.br* Ⓜ *Ipanema/General Osório.*

Zona Sul. Branches of this upscale supermarket can be found throughout Rio's South Zone, and they're good places to pick up deli goods, coffee, chocolate, and fresh fruit and vegetables. The promotional prices displayed usually apply only to those holding Zona Sul loyalty cards. ⊠ *Prudente de Morais 49, Ipanema* ☎ *021/2267–0361* Ⓜ *Ipanema/General Osório.*

JEWELRY

Amsterdam Sauer. One of Rio's top names in jewelry, this is the perfect place to pick up an elegant gift. The on-site gemstone museum is open weekdays between 10 and 6 and Saturday between 9 and 2 for free guided tours that can be booked online. ⊠ *Rua Visconde de Pirajá 484, Ipanema* ☎ *021/3539–0165, 021/2512–9878 for the museum* ⊕ *www. amsterdamsauer.com* ☸ *Closed Sun.* Ⓜ *Ipanema/General Osório.*

Francesca Romana Diana. The store's namesake designer, who has five shops in Rio, creates great gold and silver jewelry and works with semiprecious stones. Check out the wonderful bangles featuring the famous Copacabana or Ipanema sidewalk pattern. ⊠ *Rua Visconde de Pirajá 547, Ipanema* ☎ *021/2274–8511* ⊕ *www.francescaromanadiana.com.*

H.Stern. The award-winning designers at H.Stern create distinctive contemporary pieces—the inventory runs to about 300,000 items. The shops downstairs sell more affordable pieces and folkloric items. Around the corner at the company's world headquarters, you can see exhibits of rare stones and watch craftspeople transform rough stones into sparkling jewels. ⊠ *Rua Visconde de Pirajá 490, Ipanema* ☎ *0800/227–442* ⊕ *www.hstern.com.br* Ⓜ *Ipanema/General Osorio.*

Sobral. Visit Sobral for chunky, colorful resin jewelry, accessories, and decorative items, including its signature multicolored replicas of the

2

THE 7 WONDERS OF RIO SHOPPING

Arts and crafts. The hills of Santa Teresa brim with arts and crafts stores selling paintings, colorful wooden animals, and other works by local artists. (R$10 and up)

Brazilian soccer shirt. You just can't leave Brazil without one of the country's most emblematic gifts. (R$35 and up)

Cachaça. While showing your friends your vacation pictures, you can impress them with a caipirinha made with genuine cachaça. (R$10 and up)

Chic swimwear. You can show off your Rio tan back home in a daringly revealing bikini—Lenny and Bumbum have some of the best designs—or a more modest, but still sexy, one-piece suit. (R$90 and up)

Gilson Martins bag. Whatever style or size you buy from the hip designer's stores will make a cool souvenir or gift. (R$30 and up)

Havaianas. The brand's stores in Ipanema and Centro sell its flip-flops at such low prices, how can you not take home a bagful? (R$17 and up)

Mini-Cristo. Sobral makes a colorful miniversion of one of the seven wonders of the modern world. (R$50)

Christ statue. Reclaimed materials are used to make the store's funky goods, and its owners invest in social projects such as jewelry-making classes for young people in disadvantaged communities. ⊠ *Forum Ipanema, Rua Visconde de Pirajá 351, Loja 105, Ipanema* ☎ *021/2267–0009* ⊕ *www.rsobral.com.br* Ⓜ *Ipanema/General Osório.*

MARKETS
FAMILY **Feira Hippie** (*Hippie Fair*). The colorful handicrafts street fair takes place on Sundays between 9 am and 7 pm. Shop for high-quality jewelry, hand-painted dresses, paintings, wood carvings, leather bags and sandals, rag dolls, knickknacks, furniture, and samba percussion instruments, among many other items. It's fun to browse here even if you're not looking to buy anything. ⊠ *Praça General Osório, Ipanema* ⊕ *www.feirahippieipanema.net* Ⓜ *Ipanema/General Osório.*

MUSIC
Fodor'sChoice **Toca do Vinicius.** Tiny Toca do Vinicius bills itself as a "cultural space
★ and bossa nova salon," and indeed the shop feels like more than just a place of business. Bossa nova aficionados from around the world gather here, and if you're one of them, there's a good chance you'll leave with the email address of at least one new pal. You'll also find sheet music, T-shirts, CDs, and books on music, including a few in English. One Sunday a month the shop hosts an intimate bossa nova concert. ⊠ *Rua Vinicius de Moraes 129, Loja C, Ipanema* ☎ *021/2247–5227* ⊕ *www. tocadovinicius.com.br* Ⓜ *Ipanema/General Osório.*

SHOES, BAGS, AND ACCESSORIES
Constança Basto. Costly women's shoes made of crocodile and snake leather in original styles are the specialty of Constança Basto. ⊠ *Shopping Leblon, Av. Ataulfo de Paiva 290, Loja 311j, Leblon* ☎ *021/2511–8801.*

Fodor'sChoice **Gilson Martins.** The shops of one of Brazil's most gifted and acclaimed
★ designers sell his colorful Rio-inspired bags and accessories at affordable prices. ⊠ *Rua Visconde de Pirajá 462, Ipanema* ☎ *021/2227–6178*
⊕ *www.gilsonmartins.com.br* Ⓜ *Ipanema/General Osorio.*

Havaianas Store. The Ipanema Havaianas store carries the fun and funky
flip-flops in all colors, styles, and sizes, for men, women, and kids. The
range is staggering, from classic Brazil-flag designs to limited-edition
gem-encrusted versions. The prices start at R$15 and creep over R$100.
Alongside the legendary flops, the store also sells canvas deck shoes and
sturdier sandals, as well as opinion-dividing "flip flop socks." Other
locations around town include one in Centro. ⊠ *Rua Farme de Amoedo
76A, Ipanema* ☎ *021/2247–7321* Ⓜ *Ipanema, ... General*
eral Osório.

Via Mia. You'll find a large selection of reasonably priced shoes, bags,
and accessories at Via Mia. ⊠ *Rua Anibal de Mendonça 55, Loja F,
Ipanema* ☎ *021/2274–9996* ⊕ *www.viamia.com.br* Ⓜ *Ipanema/Gen-
eral Osório.*

INLAND ZONA SUL

ART
Contorno. The gallery Contorno exhibits and sells an eclectic selection of
Brazilian art. ⊠ *Gávea Trade Center, Rua Marquês de São Vicente 124,
Loja 102, Gávea* ☎ *021/2274–3832* ⊕ *www.contornoartes.com.br.*

CENTERS AND MALLS
Shopping da Gávea. The brand-name stores and smaller boutiques at
the fashionable Shopping da Gávea mall sell designer fashions, accessories, and swimwear, and there are several good cafés and coffee shops.
⊠ *Rua Marquês de São Vicente 52, Gávea* ☎ *021/2294–1096* ⊕ *www.
shoppingdagavea.com.br.*

HANDICRAFTS
Fodor'sChoice **O Sol Artesanato.** Exhibiting Brazilian craftsmanship at its finest, O
★ Sol is a nonprofit, nongovernmental shop promoting and selling the
handiwork of artisans from all regions of Brazil. It's one of Rio's best
handicraft stores, and well worth a visit. ⊠ *Rua Corcovado 213, Jardim
Botânico* ☎ *021/2294–6198.*

Pé de Boi. A popular arts and crafts store that carries woodwork pieces,
ceramics, weaving, and sculptures created by artists from around Brazil, Pé de Boi specializes in objects from the states of Pernambuco and
Minas Gerais. ⊠ *Rua Ipiranga 55, Laranjeiras* ☎ *021/2285–4395*
⊕ *www.pedeboi.com.br.*

MARKETS
Babilônia Feira Hype (*Babylon Hype Fair*). This fair that takes place
roughly every couple of months combines fashion, design, art, and
gastronomy. It's good not only for shopping, but also for watching the
parade of beautiful people. ⊠ *Clube Monte Líbano, Avenida Borges de
Medeiros s/n, Leblon* ☎ *021/2267–0066* ⊕ *www.babiloniafeirahype.
com.br* 🎫 *R$10.*

FAMILY **Feira de General Glicério.** Browse for local crafts, enjoy delicious snacks,
Fodor's Choice sip a caipirinha, and listen to the delicate sounds of live *choro* at this
★ laid-back Saturday street market in the leafy residential neighborhood
of Laranjeiras. Vendors selling fruit and veggies set up stalls on the
streets surrounding a small neighborhood square, but the main focus of
attention are the clothing and crafts stalls on the square itself, as well as
food and drink sellers and the famous Barraca do Luiz—a tent selling
caipirinhas and rare music CDs as choro bands perform nearby. Come
early: the market opens at 10 am and the fun is over by midafternoon.
⌂ *Rua General Glicério, Laranjeiras* Ⓜ *No metro.*

SANTA TERESA

CLOTHING

Eu Amo Vintage. Bohemian Santa Teresa is a hotbed of vintage fashions,
and the style-savvy team behind I Love Vintage has put together the biggest and best collection of all. If you find yourself envying the effortless,
thrift store–chic of the neighborhood's gals and guys about town, the
staff here can help you join their ranks. The store sits right behind the
lively Bar do Gomez, so you can slip into your new threads and instantly
fit in with the bar's hipster throngs. ⌂ *Rua Monte Alegre 374, Loja R,
Santa Teresa* ☎ *021/2221–2855* ⊕ *blogeuamovintage.blogspot.co.uk.*

HANDICRAFTS

La Vereda. Head to this Santa Teresa arts and crafts store for colorful
ceramics, ornate mirrors, and original works by local artists. For the
quality and inventiveness of the objects it sells, La Vereda warrants a
lengthy browsing session. ⌂ *Rua Almirante Alexandrino 428, Santa
Teresa* ☎ *021/2507–0317* ⊕ *www.lavereda.com.br.*

SÃO CONRADO AND BARRA DA TIJUCA

CENTERS AND MALLS

Barra Shopping. By far Rio's largest mall, this is the place to come for a
serious shopping spree. There are some 600 stores here, ranging from
high-street names such as C&A to small and seriously chic boutique
fashion, jewelry, and lingerie stores. A branch of the legendary bikini
store Bumbum Ipanema is here, and there's a wealth of good dining
options. ⌂ *Av. das Américas 4666, Barra da Tijuca* ☎ *021/4003–4131*
⊕ *www.barrashopping.com.br.*

São Conrado Fashion Mall. The shops at Rio's least crowded and most
sophisticated mall sell domestic and international fashions to a clientele
that knows how to splurge. High-end Brazilian and international labels
can be found here, and there are some very decent restaurants as well
as a four-screen movie theater. ⌂ *Estrada da Gávea 899, São Conrado*
☎ *021/2111–4444* ⊕ *www.fashionmall.com.br/contato.asp.*

SIDE TRIPS
FROM RIO

Updated By
Lucy Bryson

Rio's frenetic pace can be as exhausting as it is exhilarating, so it's handy that the city is surrounded by idyllic beaches and peaceful historic towns that are perfect for recharging the batteries. Just a couple of hours' drive east is the chic beach resort of Búzios, with its 23 beaches, boutiques and lively nightlife, while to the west is the unspoiled, untamed beauty of Ilha Grande. Nearby lies Paraty, Brazil's best preserved colonial town.

The Costa do Sol (Sun Coast), famed for its beautiful beaches, enjoys more sunny days than anywhere else in Rio de Janeiro State. Here, the hip resort town of Búzios is a playground for Rio de Janeiro's *gente bonita* (beautiful people), who come to relax on the beaches by day and socialize in the stylish bars and clubs by night. En route to Búzios is the quieter beach resort of Arraial do Cabo, an unpretentious fishing town known as the "Caribbean of Brazil" because of its crystal clear waters and white-sand beaches.

Sitting west of the city on the verdant Costa Verde (Green Coast), pretty Paraty's pedestrianized historical center has changed little since the 18th century. The vast nature-reserve island of Ilha Grande, just off the Green Coast, provides virtually unlimited opportunities for beach hopping, hiking on nature trails, and just relaxing.

Heading inland from Rio, the stifling temperatures drop a little as steep mountain roads deliver you to the imperial city of Petrópolis, summer residence of Emperor Pedro II.

ORIENTATION AND PLANNING

GETTING ORIENTED

The Sun Coast. En-route to the gorgeous beaches and scorched mountains of the Costa do Sol is the small city of Niterói, whose ancient forts stand in stark contrast to its contemporary Museu de Arte Contemporânea. Farther east is the coastal town of Cabo Frio, one of the country's oldest settlements, and the small village of Arraial do Cabo, whose clear turquoise waters make it one of Brazil's top spots for diving. Nearby Búzios, with its many beaches, year-round sunshine and vibrant nightlife, is a popular weekend holiday destination for wealthy *cariocas* as well as foreign visitors to Rio.

North of Rio de Janeiro. Northeast of Rio de Janeiro lies Petrópolis, whose opulent imperial palace was once the emperor's summer home. A twisting road through the mountains takes you to Teresópolis, named for Empress Teresa Christina. Nestled between these two towns is Parque Nacional da Serra dos Órgãos, famous for its curious rock formations.

TOP REASONS TO GO

Glamorous Búzios: Hang out with the young and beautiful on the beach at Búzios in the morning, then enjoy the sunset on Orla Bardot.

Water Sports: Sail a schooner to a deserted island for some scuba diving, then watch the dolphins play in your wake on the way home.

Mountain Excursions: Got lost in time at the Imperial Museum in mountainous Petrópolis.

Glorious Ilha Grande: Take an early-morning hike through the Atlantic rain forests of Ilha Grande.

Historic Paraty: Stroll the cobbled streets of this colonial town, before boarding a sailboat for an island-hopping afternoon.

Fresh Beach Food: Tuck into freshly caught sardines at beach kiosks in Búzios and Arraial do Cabo, washing them down with coconut water sipped straight from the shell.

The Green Coast. West of Rio de Janeiro, the Costa Verde sees wild jungle tumbling down rocky mountains to a seemingly endless string of beaches. Angra dos Reis is the jumping-off point for 365 islands that pepper a picturesque bay. The largest, Ilha Grande, is a short boat ride from Angra dos Reis or nearby Conceição de Jacareí. Paraty, a UNESCO World Heritage Site, is a perfectly preserved colonial town farther down the coast whose proximity to secluded beaches makes it one of the region's highlights.

PLANNING

WHEN TO GO

The towns along the Costa do Sol and Costa Verde are packed solid between Christmas and Carnival, so reservations should be made well in advance. The populations of Paraty and Búzios can more than double as young people arrive from nearby Rio de Janeiro and São Paulo on the weekend. Paraty books up well ahead of its annual literary festival (July) and cachaça festival (August).

The weather along the coast is fairly predictable: summers are hot. During low season, from March to June and September to November, the weather is milder and there is plenty of elbow room on the beach. To top it off, prices can be half of what they are in high season. In the interior, Petrópolis and Teresópolis provide a refreshing change from the oppressive heat of the coast.

PLANNING YOUR TIME

The many attractions of Rio de Janeiro fan out in all directions from the city itself, so it makes sense to focus your time on one region, whether it be the mountainous inland, the Sun Coast, or the Green Coast. Whichever direction you head, trips along the coast invariably merit a few days. Anyone heading down the Costa Verde should allow for at least a couple of nights' stay on lovely Ilha Grande, and once back on the mainland, it's a couple of hours' scenic drive to Paraty. While the

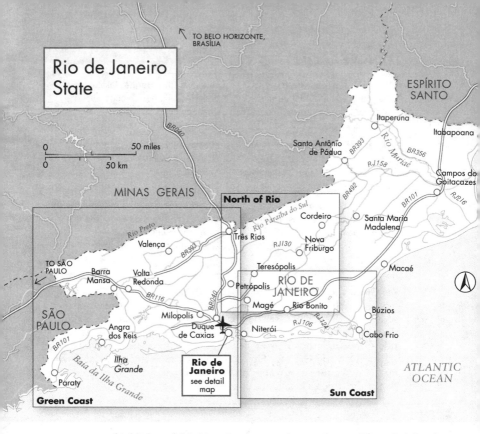

highlights of this historic town can be seen in one day and night, those who can spare the time may well want to head to the tranquil beach village of Trindade nearby.

The highlights of Rio's sister city, Niterói, can be seen in a morning or afternoon, and sun lovers will want to set aside at least a couple of nights to visit the beach resorts that lie farther up the coast. The aptly named Costa do Sol is home to some of the best beaches in the state. Make your base in Búzios, where chic accommodation options abound, and take a day trip to the beaches of Cabo Frio and Arraial do Cabo as well as setting aside at least one full day to take a boat trip to some of Búzios's best beaches. Partiers should allow time in their schedules for late nights and lazy mornings.

The mountainous north is often visited as a day trip from Rio, taking in the imperial town of Petrópolis, but hikers and climbers may want to spend a couple of days scaling the peaks that surround nearby Teresópolis.

GETTING HERE AND AROUND
While most resort towns boast an airport of some kind, the area is small enough that few people fly to destinations within the state. The roads along the coasts and to the towns in the mountains tend to be well maintained, so most Brazilians travel by car or bus. Check weather

conditions before heading to the mountains, however, as heavy rains can cause serious landslips.

Along the Green Coast, collective transfer services such as Easy Transfer provide door-to-door services, complete with boat connections that are a convenient and cost-effective way to travel in the region. At the beach resorts of Búzios, driving from beach to beach in a buggy is great fun, and the cost of renting works out to be a reasonable value.

Driving within the city of Rio can be a daunting experience, but outside the city it's fairly easy to get around. The roads, especially to the major tourist destinations, are well signposted. Buses are cheap, comfortable, and efficient, but the vast terminal in Rio can be uncomfortably hot and the surrounding area is a little edgy. It's best to leave plenty of time to buy tickets and locate your boarding point. Don't rely on using the ATMs here as they are frequently out of service. Note that non-Brazilians may have problems buying advance tickets online, as a CPF (Brazilian social security number) is usually required. At popular times, it may be preferable to arrange a group or private transfer, or to book through a travel agent.

■ TIP→ Avoid leaving the city on Friday afternoons when residents flee the city en masse and the traffic is horrific. For the same reason, try to avoid returning on a Monday.

BUS TRAVEL

As a rule, private buses in Rio such as Autoviacao 1001 and Costa Verde tend to be clean, punctual, air-conditioned, and comfortable. Buses leave from the Rodoviária Novo Rio, and most destinations are within three hours of the city. Expect to catch a taxi from the bus station to your hotel.

Outside the city, local bus service within towns, or districts, tends to be regular and cheap, but buses rarely have air-conditioning and are not well maintained. There are few routes, and the bus driver will either nod or shake his head if you tell him where you want to go. You can buy your ticket on the bus, but don't use large notes. Bus terminals and stands are easy to spot. Beware of pickpockets if the stand or bus is particularly crowded.

Bus Contacts Autoviacao 1001. ⊠ *Estrada Velha Da Usina 444, Centro, Búzios* ☎ *022/2623-2050* ⊕ *www.autoviacao1001.com.br.* **Costa Verde.** ⊠ *Rio de Janeiro* ☎ *021/3622-3123* ⊕ *www.costaverdetransportes.com.br.* **Easy Transfer.** ⊠ *Rio de Janeiro* ☎ *21/ 99386-3919* ⊕ *www.easytransferbrazil.com.* **Rodoviária Novo Rio.** ⊠ *Av. Francisco Bicalho 1, Santo Cristo, Rio de Janeiro* ☎ *021/3213-1800* ⊕ *www.novorio.com.br* Ⓜ *No metro.*

CAR TRAVEL

The roads in Rio de Janeiro State are generally in good condition and well marked, especially in the areas frequented by holidaymakers. If you plan to travel around and spend a few nights in different towns, it makes sense to rent a car in Rio, although it can be a bit tricky finding your way out of the city. Remember that if you travel to Ilha Grande, you will have to leave your car on the mainland, so be sure to remove all valuables.

■TIP➜ Car-rental prices in resort towns can be exorbitant, so if you plan to rent a car, do it in Rio. In Cabo Frio and Búzios, it is a better value and more fun to rent a beach buggy—numerous agencies offer this service.

RESTAURANTS

The food here is nothing if not eclectic. Expect to find sushi bars, Italian restaurants, and German *biergartens* sitting alongside restaurants selling typical Brazilian cuisine. Coastal towns serve a large selection of fresh seafood, and most have a local specialty that's worth trying. Beachfront restaurants, especially the ubiquitous *baracas* (kiosks), can be a pleasant surprise and most will bring food and drink right up to your chosen spot on the sands.

Paraty and Búzios have excellent restaurants serving international cuisine. During high season they fill up beginning at 10 pm and may not close until after sunrise. Restaurants in Petrópolis and Teresópolis serve European cuisine and *comida mineira*, the hearty, meaty fare from Minas Gerais. Generally, dinner starts at seven and restaurants close around midnight.

■TIP➜ To be on the safe side, don't buy seafood from venders strolling along the beach. Be especially careful about the oysters in Búzios and Cabo Frio, which may not be as fresh as the vendor claims.

HOTELS

There are hotels for all budgets and all tastes, from beachfront *pousadas* offering simple rooms with barely more than a bed and a ceiling fan to boutique hotels with luxurious amenities and on-site spas. Paraty and Petrópolis have gorgeous 18th-century inns, some of which can be a bit drafty in winter. *Hotel reviews have been shortened. For full information, visit Fodors.com.*

WHAT IT COSTS IN REALS			
$	**$$**	**$$$**	**$$$$**
Restaurants	under R$31	R$31–R$45	R$46–R$60	over R$60
Hotels	under R$251	R$251–R$375	R$376–R$500	over R$500

Restaurant prices are the average cost of a main course at dinner or, if dinner is not served, at lunch. Hotel prices are the lowest cost of a standard double room in high season, excluding tax.

TOURS

Fodor's Choice ★ **Cruz the Coast Brazil.** A fun way for time-pressed travelers to see as much of Rio's coastline as possible is to take a bus tour with Cruz the Coast Brazil. This hassle-free hop-on, hop-off service makes a four-day loop from Rio to Paraty and Ilha Grande, or from Rio to Cabo Frio and Búzios, with all travel and accommodations prearranged and excursions such as boating trips, surfing lessons and even Portuguese classes included. ⊠ *Rio de Janeiro* ☎ *021/97827-3256* ⊕ *www. cruzthecoastbrazil.com* 🖃 *From R$400 for Rio State Loops.*

Rio Xtreme. Rio Xtreme offers group and private adventure tours and activities in Rio de Janeiro State. The friendly, English-speaking guides and instructors can take you scuba diving in Cabo Frio, zip-lining in

CLOSE UP

A Bit of History

The history of Rio de Janeiro State is as colorful as it is bloody. The first Portuguese trading post was established in 1502 in Cabo Frio to facilitate the export of *Pau-Brasil* (brazilwood). This led to confrontations with Tamoios Indians and their French allies.

The discovery of gold in the state of Minas Gerais in 1696 and the construction of the "Caminho de Ouro" (Path of Gold) from the mines to Paraty brought prosperity. In its wake came pirates and corsairs who used the islands and bays of Angra dos Reis as cover while they plundered the ships bound for Rio de Janeiro.

The mines gave out in the late 1700s, but the relatively new crop called coffee, introduced to the state around 1770, brought another boom. In the mid-19th century the state produced more than 70% of Brazil's coffee. Sadly, vast tracts of Atlantic rain forest were destroyed to make room for the crop across the interior of the state.

In 1808, threatened by Napoléon, King Dom João VI of Portugal moved his court to Rio. He returned to Portugal in 1821 and left his son, Dom Pedro I, behind as prince regent. The following year Dom Pedro I was called back to Portugal, but he refused to leave. Instead, he declared Brazil an independent state and himself its emperor. In 1847, his son, Dom Pedro II, inaugurated Petrópolis as the summer capital of Brazil.

Rio, or hiking through thick jungle on Ilha Grande. Climbing tours in and around Teresópolis and Petrópolis can be arranged on demand. ☎ *021/98516–1146* ⊕ *www.rioxtreme.com* ✉ *From R$200.*

THE SUN COAST

This stretch of coastline is where you'll find the resort towns of Cabo Frio, Arraial do Cabo, and Búzios. The most popular of the three is Búzios, reminiscent of the French Riviera gone tropical. On its 8-km (5-mile) peninsula are 23 beaches. Cabo Frio is a family town famous for its bikini shops and blue water. Arraial do Cabo, jutting into the Atlantic Ocean, still retains the rustic charms of a fishing village. The wind blows year-round, and sports such as windsurfing, kitesurfing, and sailing are popular.

NITERÓI

14 km (9 miles) east of Rio.

Cariocas joke that the best thing about Niterói is the view—on a clear day you can see Rio de Janeiro with the Corcovado and Sugarloaf across the bay. But Niterói has the last laugh, as the city is ranked as having the highest quality of life in the state.

Catch a ferry from Rio's Praça 15 de Novembro and cross the bay in 20 minutes. From the Praça Araribóia or at the Terminal Hidroviário de

Charitas, walk along the esplanade to the Forte de Gragoatá and then walk to Museu de Arte Contemporânea, whose Oscar Niemeyer–designed building and views of Rio are more impressive than the art exhibitions, which rarely thrill. Icaraí beach attracts local beach lovers, and offers spectacular panoramic views of Rio. If you have time, enjoy a beer on the beach and watch the sunset over Sugarloaf and the Corcovado. Don't plan to spend more than one afternoon in Niterói. Instead head up the Costa do Sol to Búzios or Cabo Frio. The tourist office is located next to the ferry terminal.

POUSADA DEFINED

Wherever you travel in Rio de Janeiro State, you're likely to stay in a *pousada*. The name translates as "rest stop," and a pousada may be anything from a simple guesthouse to a luxury boutique lodging with pool and spa. The one thing all pousadas have in common is that they are independently run and managed. Generally smaller than hotels, they tend to offer more personalized service. For detailed listings of quality pousadas throughout Brazil, visit the website of Hidden Pousadas Brazil ⊕ *www.hiddenpousadasbrazil.com.*

GETTING HERE AND AROUND
The best way to get to Niterói is by passenger ferry from the Praça 15 de Novembro in Rio de Janeiro. The trip takes about 20 minutes with CCR Barcas boats (R$4.80). Don't travel here by car unless you have somebody driving for you. The roads in Niterói are even more confusing than in Rio. Viação Mauá's Bus 100 (R$4.35) departs for Niterói from Praça 15 de Novembro (in front of the ferry terminal). The trip takes 15 minutes, not counting traffic delays, which can be severe during rush hour.

ESSENTIALS
Boat Contact CCR Barcas. ⊠ *Praça Araribóia 6–8, Niterói* ☎ *0800/721-1012 toll-free information line* ⊕ *www.grupoccr.com.br/barcas.*

Bus Contact Viação Mauá. ☎ *021/2607-0485* ⊕ *www.vmaua.com.br.*

Taxi Contact Rádio Táxi Niterói. ⊠ *Niterói* ☎ *021/2610-0609.*

Visitor Information Niterói Tourism Office. ⊠ *Estrada Leopoldo Fróes 773, Niterói* ☎ *021/2710-2727* ⊕ *www.neltur.com.br.*

EXPLORING
Fortaleza de Santa Cruz. Built in 1555, the impressive Fortaleza de Santa Cruz was the first fort on Guanabara Bay. The cannons are distributed over two levels, but more impressive are the 17th-century sun clock and Santa Barbara Chapel. The views over Rio de Janeiro span out in all directions, so keep your camera on hand. It takes 15 minutes by taxi to reach the fort from downtown Niterói, and costs about R$35. The on-site restaurant serves good coffee and light meals. ⊠ *Estrada General Eurico Gaspar Dutra, Jurujuba, Niterói* ☎ *021/2710-2354* ⊠ *R$6* ⊗ *Tues.–Sun. 9–4.*

Fodor's Choice ★ Museu de Arte Contemporânea. Designed by the late, great modernist architect Oscar Niemeyer, the cliff-top Museum of Contemporary Art looks like a spaceship that has touched down to admire the views. The

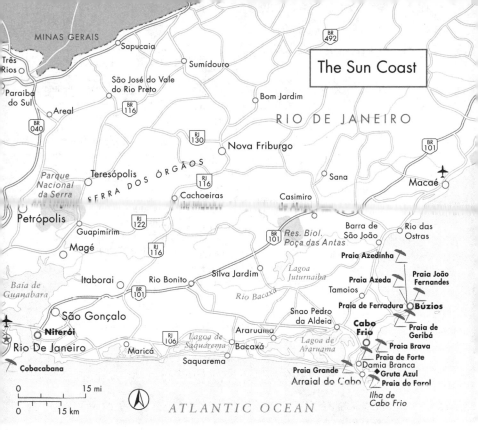

museum's visiting art exhibits tend to be underwhelming, but it's worth
a trip here just to see the building. The museum is a five-minute cab ride
from Praça Araribóia, by the ferry terminal in downtown Niterói, or
take the 47B bus. The on-site bistro is a good spot for lunch. ⊠ *Mirante
de Boa Viagem s/n, Niterói* ☎ *021/2620–2400* ⊕ *www.macniteroi.com.
br* ⊠ *R$10, free Wed.* ☉ *Tues.–Sun. 10–6.*

CABO FRIO

155 km (101 miles) east of Rio.

One of the oldest settlements in Brazil, Cabo Frio was established in
the early 1500s as a port from which wood was shipped to Portugal.
Today it's best known for its beaches with clear blue waters, its party
scene, and its water sports. However, it has recently been dogged by
crime problems, and the town itself is less than beautiful. Of far greater
appeal is the smaller and more tranquil Arraial do Cabo, with its crystal
clear waters—making it a top spot for diving—and icing-sugar beaches.

Hotels in Cabo Frio are both less appealing and more expensive than
those in nearby Búzios. If you are looking for chic lodgings, you're better off staying in Búzios and taking a day trip to Cabo Frio.

GETTING HERE AND AROUND

From Rio de Janeiro, drive across the Rio–Niterói Bridge (officially the President Costa e Silva Bridge) and bear left, following the BR 101. At Rio Bonito take the exit to the Region dos Lagos and follow the signs to Cabo Frio. The trip takes approximately two-and-a-half hours—expect to be held up in traffic outside Niterói for some time. Cabo Frio–bound 1001 buses leave the Rodoviária every half hour. The trip takes around three hours and costs R$57. Tourist information desks at Cabo Frio's bus station can provide maps. Shuttle transfers from Rio hotels and airports can be arranged for around R$100—speak to hotel staff.

> ### BATHING BEAUTIES
>
> No visit to Cabo Frio is complete without a walk past the bikini shops along Rua das Biquínis. Local lore has it that everything began with a woman selling her homemade bathing suits on the street here. Today more than 70 stores—the largest collection of bikini stores in Latin America, according to the Guinness World Records—sell all manner of beach fashions. In summer, many shops stay open past midnight.

ESSENTIALS

Bus Contact Terminal Rodoviário Cabo Frio. ⊠ *Av. Julia Kubitschek s/n, Parque Riviera, Cabo Frio.*

Taxi Contact Associação dos Taxistas de Cabo Frio. ⊠ *Cabo Frio* ☎ *022/2645–5463* ⊕ *www.cabofriotaxi.com.br.*

EXPLORING

FAMILY
Fodor'sChoice
★

Arraial do Cabo. Nicknamed the "Caribbean of Brazil" in honor of its translucent white sands and crystal clear warm waters, Arraial do Cabo is a favorite destination for divers and sunseekers alike and lies just 10 km (6 miles) south of Cabo Frio. The village is surrounded by gorgeous beaches and craggy rock formations—don't miss the Gruta Azul—a 15-meter-tall cave over the blue sea. PADI-accredited dive schools can be found in abundance here, and skippers wait at the harbor to whisk visitors to the best beaches and vantage points, often stopping for lunch at a floating restaurant. The sunsets over the small beach Prainha Pontal do Atalaia are often quite stunning. There's a handful of pousadas here, but there are cheaper and better options in nearby Búzios, which is a quick bus or cab ride away. ⊠ *Arraial do Cabo, Cabo Frio.*

BEACHES

FAMILY
Praia do Forte. The longest and most famous of Cabo Frio's beaches, Praia do Forte is very popular with families for its soft sands and gentle waves. On summer weekends it's jammed with colorful beach umbrellas, swimmers, sun lovers, and food kiosks that extend their services to tables on the sand. Praia do Forte is also very popular with partiers and after dark, during the summer, live music (and dancing) take over the beach. **Amenities:** food and drink. **Best for:** swimming; partiers. ⊠ *Avenida do Contôrno, Cabo Frio.*

Praia do Foguete. This beach is famous for its almost transparent soft white sand and the equally clear waters that shelter sea creatures such as turtles, dolphins, and even penguins. The 6-km (4-mile) strand is almost deserted in low season, and while even in summer the water is chilly, the constant strong breeze here creates waves that are perfect for surfing and bodyboarding. During summer, a few vendors operate kiosks with food and drink, but if you visit between March and November you should bring your own refreshments. **Amenities:** food and drink (in summer). **Best for:** solitude; surfing. ✉ *Foguete, Cabo Frio.*

WHERE TO STAY

$$ HOTEL FAMILY 🏨 **Malibu Palace Hotel.** Cabo Frio's most convenient option for partiers and beachgoers sits across the avenue from Praia do Forte and mere blocks from the shops and restaurants of the town center. **Pros:** rooms have great views; hotel provides umbrellas on the beach; delicious breakfast. **Cons:** can be noisy at night; somewhat rowdy area; property showing signs of wear and tear. [$] *Rooms from: R$300* ✉ *Av. do Contorno 900, Praia do Forte, Cabo Frio* ☎ *022/2647–8000* 🌐 *www.malibupalace.com.br* 🛏 *102 rooms, 6 suites* 🍴 *Breakfast.*

SPORTS AND THE OUTDOORS

TOUR OPERATORS

Over Sea Dive Center. This PADI-accredited diving school and trip operator offers highly professional service, with modern boats, well-maintained equipment, and enthusiastic English-speaking staff. Over Sea Dive Center runs dive trips to the best spots around Cabo Frio and farther afield. ✉ *Rua Jose Augusto Saraiva 2, Ilha da Draga, Cabo Frio* ☎ *22/2647–5375* 🌐 *www.overseadivecenter.com.br* 🎫 *Dives from R$200.*

BÚZIOS

24 km (15 miles) northeast of Cabo Frio; 176 km (126 miles) northeast of Rio.

Fodor's Choice ★ Around two hours from Rio de Janeiro, Búzios is a string of beautiful beaches on an 8-km-long (5-mile-long) peninsula. It was the quintessential sleepy fishing village until the 1960s, when the French actress Brigitte Bardot holidayed here to escape the paparazzi and the place almost instantly transformed into a vacation sensation. Búzios has something for everyone. Some hotels cater specifically to families and provide plenty of activities and around-the-clock child care. Many have spa facilities, and some specialize in weeklong retreats. For outdoor enthusiasts, Búzios offers surfing, windsurfing, kitesurfing, diving, hiking, and mountain biking, as well as leisurely rounds of golf.

GETTING HERE AND AROUND

From Rio de Janeiro, drive across the Rio–Niterói Bridge and bear left, following the BR 101. At Rio Bonito take the exit to the Region dos Lagos. At São Pedro de Aldeia, turn left at the sign for Búzios. The trip takes about three hours, of which at least an hour may be spent caught in traffic around Niterói.

Búzios-bound 1001 buses leave from Rio's Novo Rio bus station every half hour. The trip takes around 3½ hours and costs R$48. Transfers from Rio hotels can be arranged for around R$150. Speak to hotel staff who should be happy to set this service up for you. Shuttle transfers from Rio's airports are also available for about the same price. Malizia Tour is a reliable shuttle operator and provides currency exchange services as well.

ESSENTIALS

Taxi Information Búzios Radio Taxi. ☎ *22/2623–2509.*

Visitor and Tour Information
Búzios Tourism Office. ✉ *Praça Santos Dumont s/n, Centro, Búzios* ☎ *022/2623–2099* ⊕ *www.buziosonline.com.br.*

TOURS
Malizia Tour. This prominent tourist agency provides collective and private shuttle transfers to Rio de Janeiro, stopping at airports and Zona Sul hotels, as well as sightseeing trips in and around Búzios. ✉ *Shopping Praia do Canto, Estrada José Bento Ribeiro Dantas, Loja 16, Centro, Búzios* ☎ *22/2623–1226* ⊕ *www.maliziatour.com.br.*

BRIGITTE & BÚZIOS

A walk along the Orla Bardot will bring you to the bronze statue of a seated woman looking out over the cobalt-blue waters. This is the statue of the actress Brigitte Bardot, who put Búzios on the map when she came here on holiday. Bardot, world-famous at the time for her role in director Roger Vadim's provocative *And God Created Woman* and other films, declared the city the one place where she was able to relax. She stayed in Búzios until photographer Denis Albanèse's candid shots allowed the international press to discover her and, in turn, Búzios.

SAFETY AND PRECAUTIONS
A few simple rules: don't eat fresh oysters sold anywhere but in a restaurant, and make sure you only take boat trips with accredited groups or individuals. Crime here is rare, but don't walk along dark and deserted streets after dark, and don't leave your belongings unattended on the beach.

BEACHES
Búzios boasts 23 beautiful beaches, which can be reached by schooner boat trips or speedier taxi boats. There is a taxi boat "terminal" on Orla Bardot, with skippers ready to whisk passengers off to any of the beaches on the island. Prices are per person and start at R$7 to get to the closest beaches, rising to around R$30 for farther-flung sands. There's a minimum two-person fare but solo travelers can wait for others to come along and bump up the numbers. Schooners depart from the end of a small pier nearby and take groups on beach-hopping trips that might last from a couple of hours to a full day. Prices start at around R$40 per person for a two-hour trip, rising to around R$150 for a full-day trip with stops for swimming and snorkeling.

Praia Azeda. Two beaches, Praia Azeda and its smaller neighbor, Praia Azedinha, have clear, calm waters and are accessible via a trail from Praia dos Ossos, or by taxi boat (R$10). The view as you descend to the beach on foot is breathtaking. Vendors at kiosks on the beach sell coconut water and frozen caipirinhas, and you can rent beach chairs and umbrellas. Azedinha is one of the few beaches here where women can sunbathe topless. During summer, arrive early to secure a good spot—the beaches start to get crowded by 11 am. **Amenities:** food and drink; toilets. **Best for:** swimming. ✉ *João Fernandes, Búzios.*

FAMILY **Praia da Ferradura.** On a cove that protects it from the winds that often blow elsewhere on the peninsula, Praia da Ferradura has calm waters that make it a perfect choice for families with children. The beach adjoins one of Búzios' most exclusive areas—some mansions back right onto it—but maintains a relaxed ambience. Sun loungers and umbrellas are provided as a courtesy for clients of the many beach *barracas* (simple makeshift kiosks selling food and drink). Arrive early for a good spot on summer weekends. **Amenities:** food and drink; toilets; water sports. **Best for:** swimming. ✉ *Ferradura, Búzios.*

Fodor's Choice ★ **Praia de Geribá.** This long half-moon of white sand is fashionable with a young crowd, and its breaks and swells make it popular with surfers and windsurfers. The walk from one end to the other takes 30 minutes, so there's plenty of elbow room here even in high season. The relaxed bars and beach kiosks make it easy to while away whole days here. The surrounding Geribá neighborhood makes a great base for beach lovers, with plenty of good pousadas near the sands. **Amenities:** food and drink; water sports. **Best for:** walking; surfing. ✉ *Geribá, Búzios.*

FAMILY **Praia João Fernandes.** Praia João Fernandes and the smaller adjoining beach, Praia João Fernandinho, are a short taxi-boat ride (R$10) from the center of town; both are beloved for their crystal waters and soft sands. The sounds of live samba music at nearby restaurants and bars can be heard on the beach, and you can bring cocktails out to your chosen spot on the sand if you're not ready to abandon your sun lounger. This beach can get a little busy, but the sunset here is spectacular. **Amenities:** food and drink; toilets; water sports. **Best for:** sunset; swimming. ✉ *João Fernandes, Búzios.*

WHERE TO EAT

$$ BRAZILIAN FAMILY 🍴 **Buzin.** Behind fashionable Rua das Pedras is a buffet restaurant featuring many varieties of seafood, steaks, salads, and pizzas. The reasonable prices, ample choices, and casual atmosphere make it a great post-beach stop. Try the shrimp fried in oil and garlic or the *picanha* beef, a very tender cut found in every churrascaria. The house opens at noon and closes when the last person leaves in the evening. [$] *Average main: R$45* ✉ *Rua Manoel Turíbio de Farias 273, Centro, Búzios* ☎ *022/2633–7051* 🌐 *www.buzinbuzios.com.*

$$$ PIZZA 🍴 **Capricciosa.** The Búzios branch of this pizzeria serves the same high-quality pies as the main location in Rio. The Margarita Gourmet is a classic, with a thin crust topped with tomatoes and buffalo mozzarella. Imported Italian cheeses and pizza flour make Capricciosa a hit with foodies in Búzios. [$] *Average main: R$50* ✉ *Orla Brigitte Bardot 500, Centro, Búzios* ☎ *022/2623–2691* 🌐 *www.capricciosa.com.br* 🕒 *No lunch.*

$ BELGIAN FAMILY 🍴 **Chez Michou.** A pancake house might seem an unlikely meeting point for partiers, but this Belgian-owned *crêperie* is indeed the hangout of choice for many hip young things in Búzios. Locals and tourists alike flock to the street-side tables after dark to soak up the scene and listen to live DJ sets while tucking into their choice of over 50 savory and sweet fillings. By day it's a quieter affair and popular with families. [$] *Average main: R$25* ✉ *Av. José Bento Ribeiro Dantas 90, Centro, Búzios* ☎ *022/2623–2169* 🌐 *www.chezmichou.com.br.*

$$$ FRENCH Fodor's Choice ★ 🍴 **Cigalon.** Often cited as the best restaurant in Búzios, Cigalon is an elegant establishment with a veranda overlooking the beach. Though the waiters are bow-tied and the tables covered with crisp linens and lighted by flickering candles, the place still has an unpretentious feel. The food is French-inspired and includes thyme-infused lamb steak, braised duck breast, and prawns in a lemongrass sauce with almonds. Set menus start at R$60 including a starter, a main, and a dessert, and are a terrific value. [$] *Average main: R$55* ✉ *Rua das Pedras 199, Centro, Búzios* ☎ *022/2623–6284* 🌐 *www.cigalon.com.br.*

$$ ARGENTINE FAMILY 🍴 **Estancia Don Juan.** Take a walk through the center of Búzios and you could be forgiven for thinking you've suddenly landed in Argentina. The country's cuisine has arrived in the city in a big way, and you'll hear restaurant staff speaking Spanish almost as much as Portuguese. Argentina's beef is legendary and is traditionally served grilled at a *parrilla*. Of the several parrillas in town, Estancia Don Juan is the most established. Its perfectly grilled cuts of prime beef can be washed down with a glass of Malbec from the well-stocked cellar as you take in a live tango show. [$] *Average main: R$45* ✉ *Rua das Pedras 178, Centro, Búzios* ☎ *22/2623–2169* ⏲ *No lunch* 💳 *No credit cards.*

$$$$ MEDITERRANEAN Fodor's Choice ★ 🍴 **Mistico.** With dazzling views over the bay and out across the mountains, the intimate restaurant at boutique hotel Abracadabara offers impeccable service and exquisitely presented dishes. Enjoy the sunset while sipping a signature cocktail of sugarcane rum with ginger, mango, and orange, and choose from light, fresh dishes such as quinoa salad with avocado, cherry tomato, and basil, or potato croquettes with cod and salmon. The seafood taster plate of tuna ceviche, octopus carpaccio with citrus sauce, and grilled calamari is a wonderful dish for two to share. The creative amuse-bouches surprise the palate with offerings such as tiny cups of tangy chilled kiwi soup. [$] *Average main: R$80* ✉ *Pousada Abracadabara, Alto do Humaitá 13, Centro, Búzios* ☎ *22/2623–1217* 🌐 *www.abracadabrapousada.com.br* ✍ *Reservations essential.*

$$$$ SEAFOOD 🍴 **Rocka Beach Lounge & Restaurant.** Overlooking beautiful Praia Brava, relaxed but sophisticated Rocka is one of Búzios's gastronomic highlights. Superbly fresh locally sourced seafood is combined with seasonal fruit, vegetables, and herbs to wonderful effect. Order a frozen cocktail, or splurge on a bottle of Veuve Clicquot, and soak up the ambience as you wait for your food. The fish and shrimp ceviche is terrific, while the chocolate fondant with hazelnut makes for an appropriately decadent closer. If you're here for lunch (all that's served during low season), you can enjoy your meal from the comfort of a sun bed—literally, a bed, not a plastic lounger—on a grassy slope with perfect beach views. Aim to be here at sunset for a romantic end to the day. [$] *Average main: R$85* ✉ *Praia Brava 13, Brava, Búzios* ☎ *022/2623–6159* ⏲ *No dinner Mar.–Nov.* ✍ *Reservations essential.*

$$$$ SEAFOOD 🍴 **Satyricon.** The Italian fish restaurant famous in Rio has a branch here as well, and the beachfront location adds an extra dash of romance to

the proceedings. The dishes are expensive, but seafood lovers will find them worth the splurge. Go all out and try the grilled mixed-seafood plate with cream-of-lemon risotto. On weekends, reservations are normally required for parties of four or more. [$] *Average main: R$110* ✉ *Av. José Bento Ribeiro Dantas (Orla Bardot) 500, Centro, Búzios* ☎ *022/2623–2691* 🌐 *www.satyricon.com.br* ⏲ *No lunch* ✍ *Reservations essential.*

3

WHERE TO STAY

Be sure to book well in advance if you plan to visit Búzios on a weekend between Christmas and Carnival. You'll find good accommodation options in the center of town—handy for nightlife, shopping, and organized tours—but there's no real beach there. For beachfront lodgings, you'll have to head a little out of town.

$$$$ HOTEL Fodor's Choice ★

🏨 **Abracadabra.** Rooms at this gorgeous, centrally located boutique hotel are simply but stylishly appointed and have soft white linens and fresh flowers, but the crowning glory is an infinity pool that has stunning views over the bay and out to sea. **Pros:** stunning views; wonderful breakfasts; excellent service. **Cons:** the best beaches are a taxi boat ride away. [$] *Rooms from: R$550* ✉ *Alto do Humaitá 13, Centro, Búzios* ☎ *022/2623–1217* 🌐 *www.abracadabrapousada.com.br* 🛏 *16 rooms* 🍴 *Breakfast.*

$$$ B&B/INN

🏨 **Aquabarra Boutique Hotel and Spa.** A Zen-like calm pervades the rooms and living spaces at this casual-chic spot just a few-minutes' walk from Geribá Beach. **Pros:** gorgeous space; excellent spas; most rooms have lovely views; close to beach. **Cons:** need to cab or bus to get to Centro. [$] *Rooms from: R$456* ✉ *Rua de Corina 16, Centro, Búzios* ☎ *022/2623–6186* 🌐 *www.aquabarra.com* 🛏 *15 rooms* 🍴 *Breakfast.*

$$$$ HOTEL Fodor's Choice ★

🏨 **Casas Brancas.** Each of the 32 rooms at this timelessly chic hotel is unique, and many have deep baths, beach views, and private balconies. **Pros:** unique accommodations; friendly service; multilingual staff; pool with stunning views; beautiful setting; excellent spa and restaurants; relaxed ambience. **Cons:** a taxi ride to the best beaches. [$] *Rooms from: R$900* ✉ *Alto do Humaitá 10, Centro, Búzios* ☎ *022/2623–1458* 🌐 *www.casasbrancas.com.br* 🛏 *32 rooms, 3 suites* 🍴 *Breakfast.*

$$$$ HOTEL

🏨 **Hotel le Relais de la Borie.** This historic villa sits right on the edge of Gériba Beach and has a pool area with sweeping views out to sea. **Pros:** on the beach; great restaurant; friendly staff. **Cons:** it's a bus or cab ride from the center. [$] *Rooms from: R$900* ✉ *Rua dos Gravatás 1374, Geribá, Búzios* ☎ *022/2620–8504* 🌐 *www.laborie.com.br* 🛏 *38 rooms, 1 suite* 🍴 *Breakfast.*

$ B&B/INN FAMILY

🏨 **Maresia de Búzios.** Small but stylish, this guesthouse close to Geribá Beach provides clean, budget-friendly accommodations. **Pros:** friendly staff; contemporary decor; fine buffet breakfast; pleasant communal spaces; children welcome. **Cons:** small rooms; no TVs in rooms; need to take a taxi to get to town. [$] *Rooms from: R$160* ✉ *Rua das Pitangueiras 12, Bosque de Geribá, Geribá, Búzios* ☎ *022/8822–2384* 📧 *contato@maresiadebuzios.com* 💳 *No credit cards* 🛏 *5 rooms, 1 dorm* 🍴 *Breakfast.*

$ B&B/INN FAMILY

🏨 **Pousada Barcarola.** With a large pool and sun terrace, bright and spacious rooms, generous breakfasts, and free parking and Wi-Fi, this family-friendly guesthouse offers excellent value for its price range. **Pros:** spacious rooms; helpful staff; lovely pool and gardens. **Cons:** 10 minutes' walk to the beach or town center. [$] *Rooms from: R$150* ✉ *Rua G-5 Lote 14, Ferradura, Búzios* ☎ *22/ 2623–7254* 🌐 *www.pousadabarcarola.com* 🛏 *16 rooms* 🍴 *Breakfast.*

$$$ HOTEL FAMILY 🏨 **Rio Búzios Beach Hotel.** This hotel has a great location a few steps from João Fernandes Beach, and a glass-walled elevator provides sweeping views over the sands. **Pros:** good games room; fantastic breakfast; helpful, friendly staff. **Cons:** 20-minute walk to the center. [$] *Rooms from: R$420* ✉ *Praia de João Fernandes s/n, João Fernandes, Búzios* ☎ *022/2633–6400* 🌐 *www.riobuzios.com.br* 🛏 *63 rooms* 🍴 *Breakfast.*

NIGHTLIFE

BARS

Anexo. A slightly lower-key alternative to the city's more frenetic clubs, Anexo plays ambient house and has a veranda where you can kick back and enjoy one of the many specialty cocktails alongside the *gente bonita* of Búzios. ✉ *Av. José Bento Ribeiro Dantas 392, Centro, Búzios* ☎ *022/2623–6837* 🌐 *www.anexobarbuzios.com.br.*

Terraço no Morro. Head here in the early evening for relaxed drinks and *petiscos* (light snacks) on the wooden patio and enjoy a perfect view as the pumpkin sun dips over the harbour. A place where you won't feel out of place in beachwear and Havaianas, this casual bar holds regular Sunday afternoon *feijoadas*, a hit with locals and visitors looking to soothe their hangovers with Brazil's hearty national dish and a caipirinha. ✉ *Av. José Bento Ribeiro Dantas 575, Centro, Búzios* ☎ *022/2623–0859.*

DANCE CLUBS

Pacha. If you want to sip potent cocktails with beautiful people in scanty clothing, this slick beachfront nightclub is the place to do it. The party set dances here until dawn to contemporary tunes spun by visiting DJs from Europe and the United States, as well as some of the biggest names on the Brazilian dance-music circuit. With room for 1,000 party people, the vast, colorfully lit space can feel a little empty in the low season, but it's packed to the rafters during the summer high season. Tickets for New Year's celebrations sell out well in advance. ✉ *Rua das Pedras 151, Centro, Búzios* ☎ *022/2633–0592* 🌐 *www.pachabuzios.com* 🎟 *From R$50* ⏲ *Closed Sun.–Wed.*

Privilège. A vast space with room for more than 1,000 people, Privilège is one of the top places to party in Búzios. There are six separate areas, including a lounge, two dance floors, four bars, a sushi restaurant, and a pizzeria. Resident DJs play techno on Thursdays and Sundays, while top DJs from around the world fly in to spin tunes on Fridays and Saturdays. This is also a late-night hangout for the rich and famous, who head to the two exclusive VIP areas. ✉ *Av. José Bento Ribeiro Dantas 550, Orla Bardot, Manguinhos, Búzios* ☎ *022/2620–8585* 🌐 *www.privilegebrasil.com/casa/buzios* 🎟 *From R$70* ⏲ *Closed Mon.–Wed. except for Carnival and other major holidays.*

SPORTS AND THE OUTDOORS

BOATING

FAMILY **Babylon Búzios.** Babylon Búzios runs a number of water-based trips and activities, the most popular of which whisks passengers to the peninsula's best beaches during a 2½-hour excursion, with stops for swimming and snorkeling (masks provided). A great option for families, the schooner *Babylon Búzios* is equipped with a splash pool and a waterslide that flows right into the ocean. It departs three times a day from the main pier in Búzios. ⊠ *Rua das Pedras 232, Centro, Búzios* ☎ *022/2623–2350* ⊕ *www.babylonbuzios.com.br* ⊠ *R$50 per person* ☉ *Daily departures 11:45, 2:45, 5:45.*

DIVING

The clear waters of Búzios teem with colorful marine life, making the peninsula a thrilling place to dive.

Mares del Sur Brasil. This professional dive outfit has 5-Star PADI accreditation and operates daily dive trips in Búzios as well as nearby Arraial do Cabo, and offers a full range of instruction from diving "baptisms" to advanced courses. Instructors speak English as well as Spanish and Portuguese. Look out for special promotions such as two diving for the price of one. ⊠ *Rua Lagosta 114, Ferradurinha, Ferradura, Búzios* ☎ *22/99233–7035* ✍ *buceomares@gmail.com.*

GOLF

Búzios Golf Club and Resort. Designed by the acclaimed American golf-course architects Pete and Perry Dye, this well-maintained 18-hole course is challenging thanks to the winds that blow here, but the scenic backdrop of hills, natural pools, and tropical vegetation makes a round here worth the effort. The course is about 10 km (6 miles) from the town center, but it's easily accessed by car or taxi. ⊠ *Av. José Bento Ribeiro Dantas 9, Búzios* ☎ *022/2629–1240* ⊕ *www.buziosgolf.com.br* ⊠ *R$190* ⅄ *18 holes, 6652 yards, par 72.*

KITE SURFING

Búzios Kitesurf School. The certified instructors here are an upbeat team dedicated to helping you get the most out of your lessons. ⊠ *José Bento Ribeiro Dantas 9, Praia Raza, Búzios* ☎ *022/9956–0668* ⊕ *www.kitenews.com.br* ⊠ *R$500.*

SURFING

Surf schools set up tents along Geribá Beach, and also rent out boards. Expect to pay around R$70 an hour for a private lesson, including board rental, and R$300 to rent a board for an hour.

Shark's Surf School. With a kiosk at the western end of Geribá Beach, this outfit rents equipment and offers personalized classes for children and adults of all experience levels. The energetic, enthusiastic instructor, Marcio, has years of experience, and the school has International Surfing Association accreditation. ⊠ *Praia de Geribá, Geribá, Búzios* ⚓ *At the right hand corner of the beach as you face the sea* ☎ *022/2623–1134.*

TOUR OPERATORS

FAMILY **Tour Shop Búzios.** The largest tour operator in Búzios conducts whitewater rafting and boat trips, 4x4 adventures in the dunes, and a popular trolley tour that takes in 12 of the peninsula's best beaches and some spectacular view points. Alongside a wealth of adventure activities, there are family-friendly pursuits such as horseback riding. ⊠ *Orla Bardot 550, Centro, Búzios* ☎ *022/2623–4733, 022/2623–0292* ⊕ *www. tourshop.com.br* ✉ *From R$50.*

SHOPPING

Adriana Fernandez Bikinis. There are branches of chic bikini stores Bum-Bum Ipanema and Lenny on Rua das Pedras, but for something with a little more local flavor check out the sexy-but-stylish swimwear at Adriana Fernandez Bikinis, where curve-enhancing bikinis are sold alongside one-pieces whose striking prints, deep-scooped backs, and cut-out side panels keep frumpiness firmly at bay. ⊠ *Rua das Pedras 199, Centro, Búzios* ☎ *22/2623–6121* ⊕ *www.adrianafernandezbikinis.com.*

Gatos de Rua. This store sells gorgeous beaded bags, artsy home furnishings, and even bikinis, all made using recycled materials by young people working as part of a community arts project aimed at helping adolescents at risk. The project is admirable, but the pieces stand out as works of art in their own right. The cute beaded cats make great souvenirs or gifts for folks back home. ⊠ *Travessa dos Pescadores 306, Passeio das Palmeiras, Loja 3, Búzios* ⚓ *Next to the pier* ☎ *22/2623–4602* ⊕ *www.gatosderua.com.br.*

NORTH OF RIO

Petrópolis is a charming historical village that was once the summer home of the imperial family. If you enjoy hiking, visit the Parque National da Serra dos Órgãos between Teresópolis and Petrópolis. Temperatures in the mountains are low by Brazilian standards—an average of 55°F (13°C) in winter—providing a welcome change from the stifling heat of the city.

PETRÓPOLIS

68 km (42 miles) northeast of Rio.

The highway northeast of Rio de Janeiro rumbles past forests and waterfalls en route to a mountain town so refreshing and picturesque that Dom Pedro II, Brazil's second emperor, moved there with his summer court. From 1889 to 1899 it was the country's year-round seat of government. Horse-drawn carriages clip-clop between the sights, passing flowering gardens, shady parks, and imposing pink mansions. Be sure to visit the Crystal Palace and the Gothic cathedral, São Pedro de Alcântara. The city is also home to the Encantada—literally "Enchanted"—the peculiar house created by Santos Dumont, an inventor and early aviator. Fashion-conscious bargain hunters from across Rio de Janeiro State generally make a beeline for Rua Teresa, a hilly street just outside the historic center that's lined with discount clothing stores.

GETTING HERE AND AROUND

From Rio by car head north along BR 040 to Petrópolis. The picturesque drive (once you leave the city) takes about an hour if traffic isn't heavy. Única buses leave every 40 minutes—less often on weekends—from

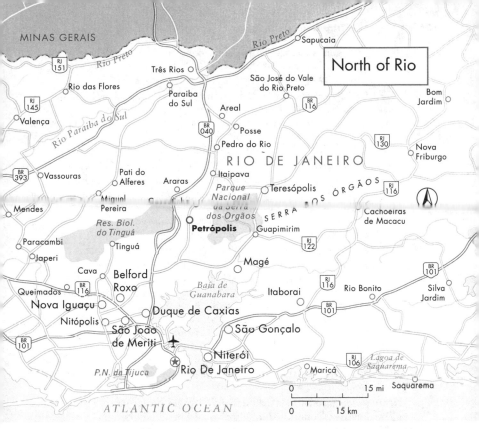

Rio's Rodoviária Novo Rio. The 90-minute journey costs R$22. Upon arrival at Rodoviária Petrópolis, the bus station, you'll be several miles from downtown, so you'll need to take a taxi (R$15–30, depending on traffic), especially if you're laden with luggage.

The easiest and safest way to get to Petrópolis from Rio, though, is to arrange a shuttle at your hotel or to take a tour either privately or as part of a group.

ESSENTIALS

Bus Contacts Rodoviária Petrópolis. ⊠ *BR 40–Rodovia Washington Luiz, Km 82.9–Fazenda Inglesa, Petrópolis* ☎ *024/2249–9858.* **Única.** ☎ *024/2244–1600* ⊕ *www.unica-facil.com.br.*

Taxi Contact Ponto de Taxi Elite. ⊠ *Petrópolis* ☎ *024/2242–4090.*

Visitor Information Petrópolis Tourism Office. ⊠ *Centro de Cultura Raul de Leoni, Praça Visconde de Mauá 305, Petrópolis* ☎ *024/2233–1200* ⊕ *www.petropolis.rj.gov.br.*

TOURS

FAMILY

Fodor'sChoice

★

Rio Cultural Secrets. The private tours to Petrópolis run by Rio Cultural Secrets are led by knowledgeable English-speaking guides and include door-to-door transport in comfortable air-conditioned cars. Ask for Fabio, who runs the tours with great enthusiasm and knowledge of

Petrópolis's history. Trips take around six hours, including a stop for lunch. ⊠ *Rio de Janeiro* 🕾 *021/ 98031–2692* ⊕ *www.rioculturalsecrets. com.br* 🖃 *From R$220, excluding entrance fees.*

Rio Turismo Radical. This well-established Rio company leads hiking trips up to Teresópolis, Petrópolis, and the surrounding mountains. Treks last from a few hours up to two days, and hikers can expect cascading waterfalls, mammoth granite walls, and astonishing views over dense jungle. 🕾 *021/9224–6963* ⊕ *www.rioturismoradical.com.br/petropolis.htm.*

Terra Vertical. Adventurous types can enjoy white-knuckle activities including rappelling, cascading, and hiking in the mountains with this experienced and professional group. There's a strong emphasis on safety, and the team, led by the highly experienced Anderson, has enormous enthusiasm for their high-altitude adventures. ⊕ *www. terravertical.com.br* 🖃 *From R$100.*

EXPLORING
TOP ATTRACTIONS

Fodor'sChoice
★

Catedral São Pedro de Alcântara. The imposing Cathedral of Saint Peter of Alcantara, a fine example of Gothic architecture and the city's most recognizable landmark, sits at the base of a jungle-clad hill. Inside the building, whose construction began in 1884, lie the tombs of Dom Pedro II, his wife, Dona Teresa Cristina, and their daughter, Princesa Isabel. Elegant sculptures and ornate stained-glass windows add to the interior's visual appeal. Drift further back in time by arriving via a horse-drawn carriage, easily hailed in the historic center of town. ⊠ *Rua São Pedro de Alcântara 60, Petrópolis* 🕾 *024/2242–4300* ☉ *Daily 8–6.*

FAMILY

Museu Imperial. The magnificent 44-room palace that was the summer home of Dom Pedro II, emperor of Brazil, and his family in the 19th century is now the Imperial Museum. The colossal structure is filled with polished wooden floors, artworks, and grand chandeliers. You can also see the diamond-encrusted gold crown and scepter of Brazil's last emperor, as well as other royal jewels. Visitors are handed soft slippers on arrival and asked to slip them over their own shoes to avoid damaging the antique floors. (Children will love sliding around on the polished floors in their slippered feet.) ⊠ *Rua da Imperatriz 220, Petrópolis* 🕾 *024/2245–5550* ⊕ *www.museuimperial.gov.br* 🖃 *R$8* ☉ *Tues.–Sun. 11–6.*

Palácio de Cristal. The Crystal Palace, a stained-glass and iron building made in France and assembled in Brazil, is rather less grand than its name suggests, resembling a large and very ornate greenhouse, but is worth a visit nonetheless. The palace was a wedding present to Princesa Isabel from her consort, the French Count d'Eu. Their marriage was arranged by their parents—Isabel, then 18, learned of Dom Pedro II's choice only a few weeks before her wedding. The count wrote to his sister that his bride to be was "ugly," but after a few weeks of marriage decided he rather liked her. During the imperial years the palace was used as a ballroom: the princess held a celebration dance here after she abolished slavery in Brazil in 1888. Surrounded by pleasant gardens, the Crystal Palace is now open to the public and often hosts live classical music performances. ⊠ *Praça da Confluência, Rua Alfredo Pachá*

s/n, Petrópolis ☎ *024/2247–3721*
🕓 *Tues.–Sun. 9–6.*

WORTH NOTING

FAMILY **Casa de Santos Dumont.** Known as "Encantado" or "enchanted," this diminutive cottage wouldn't look out of place in a fairy-tale wood. Santos Dumont, one of the world's first aviators, built the house in 1918 to a scale in keeping with his own tiny size. The eccentric genius's ⟨⟨⟨⟨⟨⟨⟨⟨, ⟨⟨⟨ ⟨⟨⟨ ⟨⟨⟨⟨⟨, ⟨⟨⟨⟨⟨⟨ ing a heated shower he developed before most homes even had running water. The home doesn't have a kitchen because Dumont ordered his food from a nearby hotel—the first documented restaurant delivery service in Brazil. ✉ *Rua do Encantado 22, Petrópolis* ☎ *024/2247–3158* 💲 *R$5* 🕓 *Tues.–Sun. 9:30–5.*

WALKING IN THE CLOUDS

The Parque Nacional da Serra dos Órgãos, created in 1939 to protect the region's natural wonders, covers more than 101 square km (39 square miles) of mountainous terrain between Petrópolis and Teresópolis. The Petrópolis to Teresópolis trail—a tough three-day hike with spectacular views— is a must for hard-core hikers. Inexperienced hikers should go with a guide, but everyone should check weather forecasts in advance as heavy rainfall in the region has caused mudslides in recent years.

WHERE TO EAT

$$$ ✕ **Churrascaria Majórica.** A classic steak house in the heart of Petrópolis's
BRAZILIAN historic center, Majórica has been a huge hit with meat lovers since
FAMILY it opened in 1962. Every cut is cooked to perfection and served with flair by attentive waitstaff, and there are excellent fish dishes and sides, too. There's a decent wine list, although it may be even more tempting to opt for one of the very well-made caipirinhas. 💲 *Average main: R$50* ✉ *Rua de Emperador 754, Petrópolis* ☎ *024/2242–2498* ⊕ *www. majorica.com.br.*

$$ ✕ **Trutas do Rocio.** It's off the beaten track—ask a local for directions—
SEAFOOD and only open on weekends, but this rustic, riverside restaurant is really something special. "Trutas" means trout and that's what you'll find on the menu—trout, trout, and more trout served fresh from the river in many imaginative ways: as appetizers mashed into a pâté or baked in cassava-dough pastry, and as entrées grilled or cooked with a choice of almond, mustard, or orange sauce. The restaurant seats only 22, so reservations are a must. On sunny afternoons, the food is served alfresco. 💲 *Average main: R$40* ✉ *Estrada da Vargem Grande 6333, Rocio, Petrópolis* ☎ *024/2291–5623* ⊕ *www.trutas.com.br* 💳 *No credit cards* 🕓 *No dinner. Closed Mon.–Thurs.* ✍ *Reservations essential.*

WHERE TO STAY

$$$$ 🏨 **Locanda della Mimosa.** Sitting in a valley with walking trails winding
B&B/INN through colorful bougainvillea trees, this cozy pousada has six well-appointed suites decorated in a classical style with imperial influences. **Pros:** spacious rooms; great restaurant; massages and afternoon tea service are included in the rates. **Cons:** need to book well in advance; some suites have traffic noise; minimum two-night stay. 💲 *Rooms from: R$700* ✉ *BR 040, Km 71.5, Alameda das Mimosas 30, Vale*

Florido, Petrópolis ☎ *024/2233–5405* 🌐 *www.locanda.com.br* 🛏 *6 suites* 🍴 *Breakfast.*

$$$ B&B/INN FAMILY 🏨 **Pousada de Alcobaça.** Just north of Petrópolis, this 1914 mansion is owned by descendents of the family that built it, and great pride is taken in managing the building and its beautiful flower-filled gardens. **Pros:** tasty food; great views; breakfast can be taken at any hour. **Cons:** need to book far in advance; 15-minute drive from the city. [$] *Rooms from: R$385* ✉ *Agostinho Goulão 298, Correias, Petrópolis* ☎ *024/2221–1240* 🌐 *www.pousadadaalcobaca.com.br* 🛏 *11 rooms* 🍴 *Breakfast.*

$ B&B/INN 🏨 **Pousada Monte Imperial.** A 10-minute walk from downtown, this Bavarian-style inn has a lobby with a fireplace, a comfortable restaurant and bar area, and rustic rooms that are cozy, if a bit spartan. **Pros:** close to downtown; friendly, attentive staff; great sunset views. **Cons:** spartan rooms; chilly in winter; uphill walk from the city. [$] *Rooms from: R$245* ✉ *Rua José de Alencar 27, Centro, Petrópolis* ☎ *024/2237–1664* 🌐 *www.pousadamonteimperial.com.br* 🛏 *15 rooms* 🍴 *Breakfast.*

$$$ HOTEL FAMILY Fodor's Choice ★ 🏨 **Solar do Imperio.** Occupying a tastefully restored 1875 neoclassical building and smaller outlying houses amid Petrópolis's historic center, this elegant hotel provides stylish, comfortable accommodations. **Pros:** excellent location; good in-house restaurant; great service; modern spa facilities. **Cons:** insects from the gardens occasionally find their way into the rooms. [$] *Rooms from: R$500* ✉ *Av. Koeler 376, Petrópolis* ☎ *024/2242–0034* 🌐 *www.solardoimperio.com.br* 🛏 *24 rooms* 🍴 *Breakfast.*

THE GREEN COAST

Italy has the charming Costa Azurra, but Brazil has the Costa Verde. The emerald waters in the bay at Angra dos Reis have fabulous diving spots, with abundant marine life and near year-round visibility. If you're not a diver, though, don't fret. There are plenty of boat tours to places like Ilha Grande. With its unspoiled beaches and rough-hewn nature trails, the bay's biggest island attracts sunseekers and adventure tourists alike.

During Carnival, pristine nature takes a backseat when the normally quiet Paraty celebrates its roots with Bloco da Lama, a parade for which participants get down and dirty—literally—and smear mud from local Praia do Jabaquara on one another. The ritual reenacts one the region's prehistoric tribes practiced to drive away evil spirits.

ANGRA DOS REIS

168 km (91 miles) west of Rio.

Angra dos Reis (Bay of Kings) has it all: colonial architecture, beautiful beaches, and clear green waters. Schooners, yachts, and fishing skiffs drift among the bay's 365 islands, one for each day of the year. Indeed, Angra dos Reis's popularity lies in its strategic location near the islands. Some are deserted stretches of sand, others patches of Atlantic rain forest surrounded by emerald waters perfect for swimming or snorkeling.

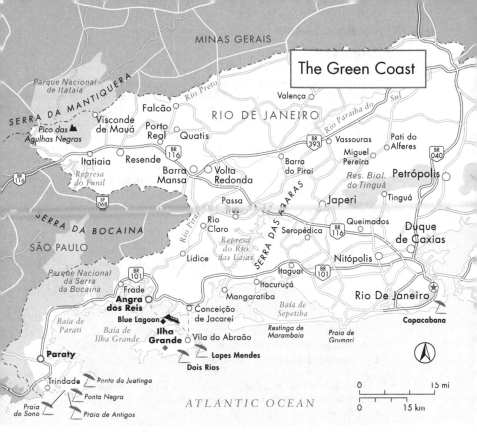

GETTING HERE AND AROUND

Angra dos Reis-bound Costa Verde buses leave Rio every hour. The 2½-hour trip costs R$48. Ferries leave the terminal at Angra dos Reis for Ilha Grande every day at 3:30 pm. The 90-minute trip costs R$14.

From Rio by car, get onto the Rio-Santos highway (BR 101) and follow it south for 190 km (118 miles) until you get to Angra dos Reis. Expect the trip to take between two and three hours, depending on traffic.

ESSENTIALS

Bus Contact Rodoviária Angra dos Reis. ⊠ *Av. Almirante Jair Toscano de Brito 110, Balneário, Angra dos Reis* ☎ *024/3365–2041* ⊕ *www.socicam.com.br/ terminais/terminais_rodoviarios.php?ID=15.*

Ferry Contact CCR Barcas. ⊠ *Cais da Lapa, 15-113 Avenida Júlio Maria, Angra dos Reis* ☎ *0800/ 721–1012 toll free* ⊕ *www.grupoccr.com.br.*

Taxi Contact Ponto de Táxi. ⊠ *Rua do Comércio 201, Centro, Angra dos Reis* ☎ *024/3365–2792.*

Visitor Information Angra dos Reis Tourism Office. ⊠ *Av. Ayrton Senna da Silva 580, Praia do Anil, Angra dos Reis* ☎ *024/3367–7826, 024/3367–7789* ⊕ *www.turisangra.com.br.*

TOURS

Associação dos Barqueiros. This group runs boat tours to the islands around Angra dos Reis, and rents out boats, plus skipper, for up to 10 people. One great tour is to Ilha da Gipóia and its beautiful beaches, such as the famous Jurubaíba, which is perfect for snorkeling or diving. Some boats have a reputation for playing loud music. Check before you book if you prefer a tranquil environment. ⊠ *Rua Júlio Maria 92, Centro, Angra dos Reis* ☎ *024/3365–3165* 💲 *From R$50.*

FAMILY **Mar de Angra.** This reliable outfit sails its schooners, catamarans, and other boats on day trips to the islands around Angra dos Reis with stops for swimming, snorkeling, and sunbathing. Fresh fruit and soft drinks are provided on board. The boats are also available for private group hire, with skipper. ⊠ *Av. Júlio Maria 16, Angra dos Reis* ☎ *024/3365–1097* ⊕ *www.mardeangra.com.br* 💲 *From R$50.*

WHERE TO STAY

$$$$ 🏨 **Hotel do Bosque.** Inside Parque Perequê, this resort hotel has boat
HOTEL service to its private beach across the river and lays on breakfast, dinner, and activities such as boat trips, kayaking, water skiing, fishing, and rafting. **Pros:** plenty of activities; private beach; spacious rooms. **Cons:** out-of-the-way location. 💲 *Rooms from: R$2,150* ⊠ *BR 101, Km 533, Mambucaba, Angra dos Reis* ☎ *024/3362–3130* ⊕ *www. hoteldobosque.com.br* 🛏 *98 rooms, 4 suites* 🍽 *Some meals.*

$ 🏨 **Pousada dos Corsarios.** Its location right on the beach at scenic Praia
HOTEL do Bonfim makes this simple hotel a great option for its price range.
FAMILY **Pros:** beachfront location; abundant breakfast; friendly service. **Cons:** few frills; a half-hour walk or 10-minute taxi ride to town center. 💲 *Rooms from: R$216* ⊠ *Praia do Bonfim 5, Bonfim, Angra dos Reis* ☎ *024/3365–4445* ⊕ *www.corsarios.com.br* 🛏 *10 rooms* 🍽 *Breakfast.*

ILHA GRANDE

21 km (13 miles) south of Angra dos Reis or Mangaratiba via 90-minute ferry ride.

Ilha Grande, 90 minutes via ferry from Angra dos Reis, is one of the most popular island destinations in Brazil. It boasts 86 idyllic beaches, some of which are sandy ribbons with backdrops of tropical foliage, while others are densely wooded coves with waterfalls tumbling down from the forest.

Ferries, catamarans, and schooners arrive at Vila do Abraão. As there are no cars, it's wise to take only what you can carry. Men waiting at the pier make a living helping tourists carry luggage for about R$10 per bag. Take cash out in Angra. There aren't any ATMs on the island, and credit cards aren't always accepted.

GETTING HERE AND AROUND

By far the simplest and most cost-effective way to get to the island is by a bus and boat transfer service. Easy Transfer's comfortable, air-conditioned vans pick travelers up from their lodgings in Rio (the service covers the South Zone, Centro, and Santa Teresa) and make the two-hour journey to Conceição de Jacareí, where the company's own double-decker schooner boat waits to ship passengers over to Abraão, Ilha Grande's only real town. Traveling with a transfer service works out cheaper (R$85 with Easy Transfer) and is far easier than arranging taxis to the bus station, buses down the coast, and then a boat trip out to the island. Easy Transfer and its competitors offer the same service back to Rio, as well as transfers between Ilha Grande and Paraty.

For those that choose to make the trip independently, the quickest route is to go via Conceição de Jacareí. Comfortable coaches leave from Rio's Novo Rio bus station approximately once an hour, a journey of around one-and-a-half hours. Several operators run schooners (40 minutes) and speedier flexboats (15 minutes) to Ilha Grande roughly every hour, with the first crossing at 7:30 am and the last at 9 pm. The fare starts at R$20 per person.

Most boats used to sail to Ilha Grande from Angra dos Reis, and it's still possible to take this route, although most travelers coming from Rio make the quicker trip via Conceição de Jacareí. Buses from Rio's Novo Rio bus station take 2 hours and 15 minutes to reach Angra dos Reis's bus station, from where it's a 10-minute cab ride or hot 20-minute walk to the town center and the boat terminal. Catamarans (R$25) leave at 10:30 am and take 40 to 50 minutes, while the ferry (R$14) takes about 1 hour 40 minutes, leaving at 3:30 pm on weekdays, 1:30 pm on weekends and holidays. A daily ferry also sails from Mangaratiba, but it's slow and inconveniently scheduled at 8 am daily, except on Fridays when it leaves at 10 pm.

SAFETY AND PRECAUTIONS

Avoid taking unlicensed boats. Verify the condition of any boat you plan to board, and check that it has a life preserver for every person aboard.

ESSENTIALS

Boat Contacts Saveiro Andréa. ⊠ *Cais de Conceição de Jacareí ✛ A couple of minutes' downhill walk from the bus stop* ☎ *024/9744–0732.*

Visitor Information Tourist Information Center. ⊠ *Estacao Abraao, Abraão, Ilha Grande ✛ At the entrance to the pier* ☎ *024/3365–5186* ⊕ *www.angra. rj.gov.br/turisangra/atendimento.asp.*

TOURS

FAMILY
Fodor'sChoice
★

Pinguim Tours. Book a full-day or half-day boat trip around Ilha Grande taking in highlights such as the Blue Lagoon and Lopes Mendes. The excursions are family-friendly with a strong emphasis on water safety. There are stops for swimming and lunch, but it's a good idea to bring along a cool box with fruit, drinks and sandwiches as food at the beach restaurants tends to be heavy on both stomach and wallet. ⊠ *Rua da Praia s/n, Abraão, Ilha Grande ✛ Facing the pier* ☎ *024/9814–4307* ⊠ *From R$40.*

EXPLORING

Visitors to Ilha Grande can follow well-marked nature trails that lead to isolated beaches and waterfalls and past the ruins of the former prison. Walks may last from 20 minutes to six hours, and there are maps at strategic points. Bring along water and insect repellent, and wear lightweight walking shoes. For a less taxing experience, take a schooner or taxi boat out to the unspoiled beaches. Schooners make regular trips out to the most popular beaches and lagoons, with stops for swimming and snorkeling, while the taxi boats whisk passengers to any point on the island.

FAMILY **Blue Lagoon.** This natural pool forms at low tide and is home to thousands of brightly colored fish that will literally eat out of your hands. Many tour operators include a stop here as part of their boat trips around the island, and most provide floats for children. Be sure to bring a mask and snorkel. ✉ *Lagoa Azul, Ilha Grande.*

BEACHES

Dois Rios. With its pristine white sands and turquoise waters, this beautiful, unspoiled beach sits in stark contrast to the dark prison ruins that sit behind it. Visitors have the place practically to themselves, as few people make the arduous 5-km (3-mile) trek through hot jungle to get here. Those who do are rewarded with one of the island's most gorgeous beaches, and the sense of achievement that comes with really getting off the beaten track. The prison ruins are worth exploring, but be sure to head back several hours before sundown. **Amenities:** none. **Best for:** solitude. ✉ *Dois Rios, Ilha Grande.*

Fodor's Choice ★ **Lopes Mendes.** Locals and visitors alike regard Lopes Mendes, a 3-km (2-mile) stretch of dazzling-white sand lapped by emerald waters, as the most beautiful beach on Ilha Grande. It's often cited as one of the most beautiful in all Brazil. Strict environmental protection orders have kept the jungle-fringed beach from being spoiled by development: expect makeshift beach kiosks, not upscale bars. Take a taxi boat from Vila do Abraão (R$15), if you don't feel up to the two-hour hike through the forest, or hike here and take the boat back—the rough jungle trail and sticky heat can tax even the most hearty of ramblers. While here, use plenty of sunblock, as the rays rebounding off the white sand are particularly strong. **Amenities:** food and drink. **Best for:** swimming; walking. ✉ *Lopez Mendes, Ilha Grande.*

WHERE TO EAT

$$ SEAFOOD 🍴 **Lua e Mar.** Expect fresh, well-prepared seafood at this longtime favorite. It's a casual establishment, so you can stroll in from the beach still wearing your Havaianas. Try Dona Cidinha's specialty, fish with half-ripe bananas, or the famous *moqueca* (seafood stew), which many islanders claim is the best in Rio de Janeiro State. [$] *Average main: R$45* ✉ *Praia do Canto, Abraão, Ilha Grande* ☎ *024/3361–5113* 🌐 *www.ilhagrande.org/luaemar* 🕒 *Closed Wed.*

$$ SEAFOOD 🍴 **O Pescador.** Inside the pousada of the same name, this restaurant serves local seafood prepared using Italian cooking techniques. The specialty is grilled fish (the types vary according to the season) bought from local fishermen. After dark, you can dine alfresco on the beach by candlelight, or just pop in for a cocktail and nibbles from the bar. [$] *Average main: R$45* ✉ *Rua da Praia 647, Abraão, Ilha Grande* ☎ *024/3361–5114* 🌐 *www.opescador.org.*

$$$ BRAZILIAN 🍴 **Pé Na Areia.** For the ultimate I'm-on-vacation feeling, take a seat at a straw-roofed table right on the sands at this relaxed beachfront

restaurant. Quirky illuminated parasols hang from the trees overhead, musicians strum acoustic guitars, and waiters bring delicious *moquecas* (seafood stew with palm oil and coconut milk) to diners as they sit sipping caipirinha cocktails. The candlelit tables and gentle music—a change from the reggae that's played everywhere else on the island—make Pé Na Areia an ideal option for a romantic dinner. $ *Average main: R$55* ✉ *Rua da Praia s/n, Abraão, Ilha Grande* ✛ *About five minutes' walk along the beach from the pier* ☎ *024/ 3361-9572* ☽ *No lunch. Closed Mon.* ▭ *No credit cards.*

> ## ILHA GRANDE'S SWEET SPOT
>
> They appear late in the afternoon to tempt you with their sweet aromas and delicate flavors. We're talking about Vila do Abraão's sweet carts, of course. They first appeared in 1998, when a resident of the island started producing baked goods at his home. His success inspired other dessert makers to sell their sweets on the streets of Abraão. The carts stay out late at night, tempting even the most resolute of travelers.

3

$$
$$ PIZZA FAMILY ✗**Pizza na Praça.** On the flagstones of Ilha Grande's main square, this simple restaurant serves up more than four-dozen types of pies, from simple margheritas to exotic seafood combinations. There are low-cal versions made with fresh vegetables and soft ricotta cheese on a wholegrain base, but also indulgent options such as the sweet pizzas with chocolate, or *doce de leite* (thick sweet milk), or both. The pizza menu is available from 6 pm until the early hours, while at lunchtime the restaurant serves vast, tasty salads and good-value set meals. This is a great spot for evening meals on Friday and Saturday nights, when live bands play in the square. $ *Average main: R$40* ✉ *Praça São Sebastião, Abraão, Ilha Grande* ☎ *024/3361-9566* ▭ *No credit cards.*

WHERE TO STAY

$$ B&B/INN **Fodor's**Choice ★ ⌨**Aratinga Inn.** Cooled by gentle hill breezes and shaded by trees and coconut palms, Aratinga Inn is rated by Hidden Pousadas Brazil—experts in chic lodgings across the country—as one of the best in the region. **Pros:** lovely gardens; complimentary afternoon teas; knowledgeable and helpful owner. **Cons:** an uphill walk from the pier. $ *Rooms from: R$330* ✉ *Rua das Flores 232, Abraão, Ilha Grande* ☎ *024/3361-9559* ⊕ *aratingailhagrande.com.br* ↩ *7 chalets* ⍭ *Breakfast.*

$ HOTEL FAMILY ⌨**Farol dos Borbas.** Practical rather than luxurious, Farol do Borbas has simple but comfortable and well-equipped rooms, a vast buffet breakfast, and attentive staff who are happy to arrange trips around the island on guests' behalf. **Pros:** walking distance from the pier; close to everything; attentive staff; private schooner. **Cons:** can be noisy at night. $ *Rooms from: R$250* ✉ *Rua da Praia 881, Abraão, Ilha Grande* ☎ *024/3361-5832* ⊕ *www.ilhagrandetour.com.br* ↩ *14 rooms* ⍭ *Breakfast.*

$$ B&B/INN FAMILY ⌨**Pousada do Canto.** In a colonial-style house, this family-friendly pousada with a tropical atmosphere faces lovely Praia do Canto. **Pros:** on the beach; pretty pool. **Cons:** rooms can get chilly in winter; small bathrooms; a bit of a walk to the boat pier, shops, and restaurants. $ *Rooms from: R$265* ✉ *Rua da Praia 121, Vila do Abraão, Ilha*

Grande ☎ *021/3717–3262* 🌐 *www.canto-ilhagrande.com* 🛏 *11 rooms* 🍴 *Breakfast.*

$ B&B/INN 🏨 **Pousada Naturalia.** A beachfront location, excellent service, and sumptuous breakfasts all contribute to the appeal of Pousada Naturalia. **Pros:** excellent service; sumptuous breakfasts; sea views; lush tropical gardens. **Cons:** 10-minute walk to the ferry terminal means that you may need to pay a carrier at the harbor around R$20 to transport your luggage. [$] *Rooms from: R$230* ✉ *Rua da Praia 149, Abraão, Ilha Grande* ☎ *024/3361–9583* 🌐 *www.pousadanaturalia.net* 🛏 *14 rooms* 🍴 *Breakfast.*

A POTENT BREW

One telling has it that cachaça was invented around 1540 by slaves working on the sugarcane plantations. A liquid called *cagaço* was removed from the sugarcane to make it easier to transport. The slaves noticed that after a few days this liquid would ferment into a potent brew.

SPORTS AND THE OUTDOORS

Elite Dive Center. This PADI-accredited dive school offers diving classes from beginner to Dive Master level, rents out equipment, and runs daytime and nocturnal diving excursions to numerous places around the island. ✉ *Travessa Bouganville, Loja 1, Vila do Abraão, Ilha Grande* ☎ *024/99936–4181* 🌐 *www.elitedivecenter.com.br.*

PARATY

99 km (60 miles) southwest of Angra dos Reis; 261 km (140 miles) southwest of Rio.

Fodor's Choice ★ This stunning colonial city—also spelled Parati—is one of South America's gems. Giant iron chains hang from posts at the beginning of the mazelike grid of cobblestone streets that make up the historic center, closing them to all but pedestrians, horses, and bicycles. Until the 18th century this was an important transit point for gold plucked from the Minas Gerais—a safe harbor protected by a fort. (The cobblestones are the rock ballast brought from Lisbon, then unloaded to make room in the ships for their gold cargoes.) In 1720, however, the colonial powers cut a new trail from the gold mines straight to Rio de Janeiro, bypassing the town and leaving it isolated. It remained that way until contemporary times, when artists, writers, and others "discovered" the community and UNESCO placed it on its list of World Heritage Sites.

Paraty isn't a city peppered with lavish mansions and opulent palaces; rather, it has a simple beauty. By the time the sun breaks over glorious Paraty Bay each morning—illuminating the whitewashed, colorfully trimmed buildings—the fishermen have begun spreading out their catch at the outdoor market. The best way to explore is simply to begin walking winding streets banked with centuries-old buildings that hide quaint inns, tiny restaurants, shops, and art galleries.

Paraty holds Brazil's largest literary festival, FLIP (Festival Literaria de Paraty) each July, followed in quick succession by the more raucous Festival da Pinga (Cachaça Festival), at which cachaça producers from around the country unveil their latest brews. The Carnival celebrations here are also a spectacle to behold, with costumed revelers covering themselves in mud to parade through the streets at the Bloco da Lama. Book well in advance if you plan to visit during the festivals.

GETTING HERE AND AROUND

From Rio de Janeiro, it's a four-hour drive along the BR 101 to Paraty. Costa Verde buses leave Rio daily every two hours, more frequently before noon. The journey costs R$63, and buses arrive at the *rodoviária* in the new town, about 20 minutes' walk from the pedestrianized historic center. It pays to travel light as taxis may not be able to take you to your hotel door.

ESSENTIALS

Bus Contact Rodoviária Paraty. ⊠ *Rua Jango Pádua, Centro, Paraty* ☎ *024/3371–1238.*

Taxi Contact Tuim Taxi Service. ⊠ *Centro, Paraty* ☎ *024/9918–7834* ⊕ *www. eco-paraty.com/taxi.*

Visitor Information Paraty Tourism Office. ⊠ *Rua Dr. Samuel Costa 29, Centro Histórico, Paraty* ☎ *024/3371–1897* ⊕ *www.paraty.com.br.*

TOURS

Paraty Tours. This outfit conducts six-hour Jeep tours that head into Serra da Bocaina National Park, crossing rivers and visiting fantastic waterfalls, with stops for swimming in natural pools, hiking through rain forest, and even visiting sugarcane-rum distilleries (complete with tastings). Paraty Tours also runs boat trips, adventure sports excursions, and transfers to Rio and São Paulo. ⊠ *Av. Roberto Silveira 11, Centro, Paraty* ☎ *024/3371–2651* ⊕ *www.paratytours.com.br* 🎫 *From R$100.*

EXPLORING

TOP ATTRACTIONS

Forte Defensor Perpétuo. Paraty's only fort was built in the early 1700s, and rebuilt in 1822, as a defense against pirates. It's a pleasant short climb through jungle to get here and the views from the fort itself are terrific. Visitors can also see heavy British-made cannons, still in their original positions. ⊠ *Morro da Vila Velha, Paraty* ☎ *024/3371–2289* 🎫 *R$4* ⊗ *Wed.–Sun. 9–12 and 1–5.*

Igreja de Nossa Senhora dos Remédios. Also known as Igreja Matriz, the neoclassical Church of Our Lady of Remedies was built in 1787 and is one of Paraty's most iconic buildings, with its gray-and-white facade shaded by a towering imperial palm tree. The small art gallery within, Pinacoteca Antônio Marino Gouveia, has paintings by modern artists such as Djanira, Di Cavalcanti, and Anita Malfatti. ⊠ *Rua da Matriz, Centro Histórico, Paraty* ☎ *024/ 3371–1467* ⊕ *www.igrejaparati.com. br* 🎫 *R$4* ⊗ *Tues.–Sun. 8–noon and 1–4.*

Igreja de Santa Rita. The oldest church in Paraty, the simple whitewashed Church of Saint Rita sits on a grassy square with a mountain backdrop and makes for a terrific photo opportunity. The church was built in 1722 by and for freed slaves and has a typical Jesuit layout with a bell tower and domed front. Inside, the carved angels and ornate wood and iron work catch the eye, and there are many valuable religious artifacts on display in the church's small religious art museum. ✉ *Largo de Santa Rita, Rua Santa Rita s/n, Centro Histórico, Paraty* ☎ *024/3371–1206* 🌐 *www.igrejaparati.com.br* 🎟 *R$4* 🕒 *Wed.–Sun. 9–noon and 2–5.*

FAMILY **Trindade.** About 30 km (20 miles) from Paraty, Trindade was once a hippie hangout. Today Trindade's several gorgeous beaches attract everybody from backpackers to Cariocas on vacation, and the natural pools are perfect for children. Regular buses run from the bus station in Paraty. If you're looking to stay overnight, you'll find simple lodgings and campsites near the beaches. ✉ *Trindade, Paraty.*

WORTH NOTING

Casa da Cultura. The largest cultural center in Paraty, Casa da Cultura is dedicated to telling the story of the city and its people. Permanent and visiting exhibitions illustrate the area's rich history and its abundant native flora and fauna. There's a pleasant coffee shop and patio, and the gift shop downstairs, one of the best in town, sells crafts made by local artisans. ✉ *Rua Dona Geralda 177, at Rua Dr. Samuel Costa, Centro Histórico, Paraty* ☎ *024/3371–2325* 🌐 *www.cultura.rj.gov.br/espaco/casa-da-cultura-de-paraty* 🎟 *R$8* 🕒 *Wed.–Mon. 10–6:30.*

BEACHES

Praia de Antigos. An environmental protection order keeps beautiful Antigos Beach wonderfully unspoiled—you can swim amid rugged nature here. The thick jungle reaches right down to the sands, and the beach is famous for the large rocks that jut into the transparent water, separating Antigos from the adjoining smaller beach, Antiginhos, whose calmer waters are better for swimming. The beach can be reached via a 20-minute walking trail from equally scenic Sono Beach, which in turn can be reached by boat from Paraty. **Amenities:** none. **Best for:** solitude; snorkeling; sunbathing. ✉ *Take trail from Sono Beach, Trindade, Paraty.*

Praia do Sono. Secluded Sono Beach is one of the Paraty area's most beautiful strands, with thick jungle framing the crescent of light, soft sand bordering crystal clear waters teeming with colorful fish. Campers base themselves here during the summer, when there's a relaxed, bohemian air. In the off-season, the beach is virtually deserted—sunbathers bask in what feels like a private tropical paradise. Although Sono is a bit off the beaten track, the gorgeous setting makes it worth the effort to reach it. The best way to access the beach is by boat from Paraty (about R$35); otherwise you must take a one-hour bus ride and then hike for about 40 minutes. **Amenities:** food and drink (in high season). **Best for:** solitude; swimming; walking. ✉ *Trindade, Paraty.*

WHERE TO EAT

$$$ BRAZILIAN 🍴 **Banana da Terra.** Seafood is always excellent at this long-standing favorite on Paraty's dining scene, and it's a great place to try giant shrimp when they are in season. The restaurant is in a colonial house decorated with cachaça labels (the caipirinhas here are another strong suit) and 19th-century pictures of the city. The name of the place comes from another of its specialties: *banana da terra* (plantain), which is incorporated into many dishes, among them grilled fish with garlic butter, herbs, plantains, and rice. [$] *Average main: R$55* ✉ *Rua Doutor*

Samuel Costa 198, Centro Histórico, Paraty ☎ *024/3371–1725* 🕐 *No lunch Wed. and Thurs. Closed Tues.*

$$$ ITALIAN Fodor'sChoice ★ 🍴 **Punto Divino.** A covered outdoor space means that diners at Punto Divino can enjoy meals alfresco even when the famously torrential Paraty rains start to pour. Tuscan and Sicilian dishes are at the fore, and are prepared with care. Evening live-music performances lend a touch of festivity to the proceedings, and the crisp, generously topped pizzas here are the best in town. The salads are fresh and tasty, and dishes such as the risotto with squid, squid ink, and chili peppers will tempt adventurous eaters. The restaurant's convenient location, at the heart of the historic center opposite the main square, only adds to its popularity. [$] *Average main: R$55* ✉ *Rua Marechal Deodoro 130, Centro Histórico, Paraty* 🕐 *No lunch.*

$$$ SEAFOOD 🍴 **Refúgio.** Near the water in a quiet part of town, this seafood restaurant is a great place for a romantic dinner, with candle-lit tables and a good wine list. It serves excellent cod, sea bass, and shellfish dishes as well as colorful, fresh salads. On chilly days, heat lamps warm the café tables out front. Note that there is an extra "artistic cover" charged when live music is performed. [$] *Average main: R$60* ✉ *Praça do Porto 1, Centro, Paraty* ☎ *024/3371–2447* 🌐 *www.restauranterefugio.com.*

$$$ BRAZILIAN 🍴 **Restaurante do Hiltinho.** The specialty at this elegant restaurants is *camarão casadinho*, fried colossal shrimp stuffed with hot *farofa* (cassava flour). Even if you're familiar with jumbo shrimp, you might be astonished at the size of these beauties. Seafood outnumbers other dishes two to one, but the filet mignon is very good. Glass doors that open onto the street are both welcoming and lend a meal here a touch of grandeur, as does the gracious, professional service. [$] *Average main: R$60* ✉ *Praça da Matriz, Rua Marechal Deodoro 233, Centro, Paraty* ☎ *024/3371–1432* 🌐 *www.hiltinho.com.br.*

WHERE TO STAY

$$ B&B/INN Fodor'sChoice ★ 🏨 **Pousada do Príncipe.** Owned by the great-grandson of Emperor Pedro II, this inn at the edge of the Centro Histórico has rooms decorated in colonial style that face either the interior garden or the swimming pool, which is set in a pleasant courtyard. **Pros:** historic building; good location a short walk from the bus station; nice pool and courtyard; welcoming, attentive staff. **Cons:** small rooms; some rooms need repainting. [$] *Rooms from: R$268* ✉ *Av. Roberto Silveira 289, Centro, Paraty* ☎ *024/3371–2266* 🌐 *www.pousadadoprincipe.com.br* 🛏 *34 rooms, 3 suites* 🍽 *Breakfast.*

$$$ B&B/INN 🏨 **Pousada do Sandi.** This welcoming, centrally located pousada offers terrific service and a great location close to the main square in Paraty's historic center. **Pros:** close to all the main sights; large rooms; welcoming lobby and pool area; noteworthy restaurant; great breakfasts. **Cons:** street noise and creaky building; hard to maneuver for people with some disabilities; two-night minimum stay. [$] *Rooms from: R$490* ✉ *Largo do Rosário 1, Centro, Paraty* ☎ *024/3371–2100* 🌐 *www.pousadadosandi.com.br* 🛏 *25 rooms, 1 suite* 🍽 *Breakfast.*

$$$$ HOTEL Fodor'sChoice ★ 🏨 **Pousada Literária de Paraty.** A totally renovated colonial mansion is the setting for this timelessly chic luxury guesthouse that celebrates the literary spirit of Paraty. **Pros:** elegant decor; great heated pool; superb Old Town location. **Cons:** books up well ahead of July literary

festival; streets nearby can flood during rainy season. [$] *Rooms from: R$860* ✉ *Rua Ten Francisco Antônio 36, Centro Histórico, Paraty* ☎ *024/3371–1568* 🌐 *www.pousadaliteraria.com.br/pousada-literaria* 🛏 *20 rooms, 3 suites* 🍴 *Breakfast.*

$$$ B&B/INN 🏨 **Pousada Pardieiro.** This is one of the oldest guesthouses in Paraty, and the residences that make up this property are decorated in 19th-century colonial style. **Pros:** close to the historic center; great pool and garden. **Cons:** no TVs in rooms; cold floors in winter. [$] *Rooms from: R$440* ✉ *Rua Tenente Francisco Antônio 74, Centro Histórico, Paraty* ☎ *024/3371–1370* 🌐 *www.pousadapardieiro.com.br* 🛏 *27 rooms, 2 suites* 🍴 *Breakfast.*

SHOPPING

Paraty is known countrywide for its fine cachaça, including brands like Coqueiro, Corisco, Vamos Nessa, Itatinga, Murycana, Paratiana, and Maré Alta.

Empório da Cachaça. This shop stocks more than 300 brands—both local and national—of sugarcane liquor as well as bottled chili peppers and locally produced preserves. It stays open well into the evening. ✉ *Rua Doutor Samuel Costa 22, Centro Histórico, Paraty* ☎ *024/3371–6329.*

Porto da Pinga. If you're looking for cachaça, Porto da Pinga is a worthy stop. It stocks many brands of the liquor, along with fiery bottled chilis, *doce de leite* (thick, sweet milk), and other local specialties. ✉ *Rua da Matriz 12, Centro Histórico, Paraty* ☎ *024/3371–1563.*

SÃO PAULO

Updated By
Claire Rigby

A sprawling, high-rise megacity, São Paulo might not have Rio's beaches and sultry good looks, but for urban explorers, it's a thoroughly rewarding destination. Blessed with its own unique charisma and a kind, courteous population, charmingly unused to tourists, it's brimming with culture and boasts some of the most varied options for eating out on the continent. The incessant urban landscape in this 20-million-strong metropolis won't be to everyone's taste, but for most visitors, one taste of São Paulo will leave them wanting more.

São Paulo is Brazil's main financial hub and its most cosmopolitan city, with top-rate nightlife and restaurants and impressive cultural and arts scenes. Most of the wealthiest people in Brazil live here—and the rest of them drop by at least once a year to shop for clothes, shoes, accessories, luxury items, and anything else money can buy. *Paulistanos* (São Paulo inhabitants) work hard and spend a lot, and there's no escaping the many shopping and eating temptations.

Despite—or because of—these qualities, many tourists, Brazilian and foreigners alike, avoid visiting the city. Too noisy, too polluted, too crowded, they say, and they have a point. São Paulo is hardly a beautiful city with nothing as scenic as Rio's hills and beaches. But for travelers who love big cities and prefer nights on the town to days on the sand, São Paulo is the right place to go. It's fast-paced and there's a lot to do. So even as the sea of high-rise buildings obstructs your view of the horizon, you'll see there's much to explore here.

ORIENTATION AND PLANNING

GETTING ORIENTED

Situated 70 km (43 miles) inland from the Atlantic Ocean with an average elevation of around 800 meters (2,625 feet), São Paulo has a flat and featureless metropolitan area, apart from a few elevated areas, including those around Avenida Paulista and Centro. A major expressway called the "Marginal" runs along the city's northern edge, accompanying the polluted River Tietê, and down the western side along the equally fetid River Pinheiros, with most business and tourist activity occurring in the southeastern, western, and central neighborhoods. No matter where you are, though, it's difficult to gain a visual perspective of your relative location, thanks to the legions of buildings in every direction. A good map or app is a necessity.

TOP REASONS TO GO

Shop Till You Drop: Shop along with Brazil's rich and famous in the Jardins or Itaim areas, or at one of the city's many fashion malls.

Food, Glorious Food: Adventurous eating is a sport in São Paulo. The 12,500 restaurants here serve dozens of different cuisines, from across Brazil and beyond.

Art Attack: Some of the finest galleries on the continent make up São Paulo's buzzing art scene.

Hopping Nightlife: Bars of all shapes, styles, and sizes beckon the thirsty traveler—quench your thirst with a cold beer or strong caipirinha.

The Beautiful Game: *Futebol,* or soccer, is truly "the beautiful game" in Brazil. São Paulo, with no fewer than three major teams, is a great place to feel the passion.

4

Centro. This downtown area has the city's most interesting historic architecture and some of its most famous sights; however, many parts are also quite daunting and dirty, so be prepared. Area highlights include Praça da Sé, geographical center of the São Paulo municipal district, and attractions around the revitalized Vale do Anhangabaú. Some of São Paulo's prime guilty pleasures can be snacked on at Mercado Municipal. Parque da Luz is just to the north and next to a number of important buildings, including the Estação da Luz railway station, part of which now houses the Museum of the Portuguese Language.

Liberdade. Southeast of Centro, Liberdade (meaning "freedom" or "liberty" in Portuguese) is the center of São Paulo's Japanese, Korean, and Chinese communities, and features a range of Asian-style streetscapes and shopfronts. It's a popular area with travelers, thanks to the many culturally motivated markets and restaurants.

Barra Funda. Once a desert of abandoned warehouses, this region has experienced a renaissance in recent years. The construction of various high-rise apartment buildings and trendy nightlife venues has returned life to a neighborhood boasting many of São Paulo's samba schools, architecture by Oscar Niemeyer, and the Allianz Parque stadium, home to Palmeiras soccer club.

Avenida Paulista. The imposing Avenida Paulista is home to some of the city's best-located hotels, biggest financial companies, and most important businesses. Many of São Paulo's cultural institutions center around this impressive, eight-lane-wide thoroughfare. Just 2.8 km (1.7 miles) long, the avenue begins west of Centro and spans several of the city's chicest neighborhoods as it shoots southeast toward the Atlantic.

Bixiga. Officially called Bela Vista, this is São Paulo's Little Italy. Here are plenty of restaurants, theaters, and nightlife hot spots. Southwest of Centro and right next to Avenida Paulista, Bixiga is an old, working-class neighborhood—the kind of place where everybody knows everybody else's business.

Jardins. On the southern side of Avenida Paulista sits Jardins, an upscale neighborhood that's ideal for shopping and eating out. The gently sloping, tree-filled area is one of the nicer parts of São Paulo for walking around; it's also one of the city's safest neighborhoods.

Itaim Bibi. Moving farther south, Itaim (locals always drop the Bibi part) is similar to Jardins because it's also filled with fashionable bars, restaurants, and shops. Another of the city's most impressive roads transects the suburb, Avenida Brigadeiro Faria Lima, which, along with its many cross-streets, has a ton of expensive and exclusive nightlife options. At its western border, Itaim stretches down to the Marginal.

Pinheiros. Just north of Itaim and west of Jardins sits Pinheiros (pine trees), another nightlife hot spot chock-full of bars, clubs, and late-night restaurants. The area, with some of the city's most expensive low-rise housing, is also traversed by the popular Avenida Brigadeiro Faria Lima and has the Marginal as its western boundary.

Vila Madalena. One of the hillier parts of São Paulo with impressive views across the city from the uppermost buildings, Vila Madalena is a relatively small enclave just to the north of Pinheiros. It's yet another nightlife mecca with bohemian-style haunts that stay open until dawn. Bars are stacked one on top of the other, making it a great place for a pub crawl, particularly because it's also one of the city's safest after-dark spots. Scores of boutiques, bookstores, cafés, galleries, and street-art displays also contribute to the neighborhood's pull on the free-spirited.

PLANNING

WHEN TO GO

Cultural events—film and music festivals, and fashion and art exhibits—usually take place between April and December. In South American summer (from January through March) the weather is rainy, and floods can disrupt traffic. Be sure to make reservations for beach resorts as far in advance as possible, particularly for weekend stays. In winter (June and July), follow the same rule for visits to Campos do Jordão. Summers are hot—35°C (95°F). In winter temperatures rarely dip below 10°C (50°F). ■TIP➜ **The air pollution might irritate your eyes, especially in July and August (dirty air is held in the city by thermal inversions), so pack eye drops.**

PLANNING YOUR TIME

A walk along Avenida Paulista is a good way to ease gently in to São Paulo while still soaking up the big-city atmosphere. A long, prominent ridge topped with huge TV and radio antennae, Paulista is a handy geographical reference: you can stroll down into chic, leafy Jardins from here, or grab a cab and head the other way into revitalizing Centro. On Paulista itself, the boxlike MASP art museum has to be seen to be believed, while the little park just opposite, Trianon, is a beautiful scrap of native forest. Centro is where much of the city's remaining historic architecture can be found—don't miss a trip to the foodie-heaven market, the Mercado Municipal, and close to Praça da República, the view from the top of towering Edifício Itália is truly spectacular.

Parque do Ibirapuera is a great favorite with paulistanos, especially on weekends, when a stroll in the park is a chance to see locals of all stripes taking their leisure; while a day spent sauntering around Vila Madalena is a pleasant, undemanding way to see another side to the city. The neighborhood is packed with boutiques, cafés, restaurants and bars—but beware the steep hills. Don't miss Beco do Batman, a copiously graffitied pair of alleyways. Finish up at one of the many lovely restaurants here, or in neighboring Pinheiros.

GETTING HERE AND AROUND
Navigating São Paulo is not easy, and staying either in the central areas or at least near an inner-city subway station is advisable, especially if you don't plan on renting a car or taking cabs. The subway is quick, easy, inexpensive, and covers much of the city, with stops near the most interesting sites for travelers. Buses can be hard to navigate if you don't speak Portuguese. Driving in São Paulo, particularly in peak hours, can be slow and difficult. For longer stays, obtain a provisional driver's license and a good map or GPS—with a little care and a lot of confidence, you can get by. Parking can be perplexing, so it's probably best to use a parking lot (*estacionamento*), which are numerous and relatively cheap, depending on the neighborhood. Cabs are reasonably priced, safe, and abundant in the popular neighborhoods.

AIR TRAVEL
Nearly all international flights stop in São Paulo, so it's easy to get from São Paulo to everywhere else in Brazil. There are flights every half hour covering the short (around one hour) trip between São Paulo and Rio (starting from around R$100 one-way). There are also multiple departures per day to other major cities such as Brasília and Belo Horizonte.

AIRPORTS São Paulo's international airport, Aeroporto Internacional de São Paulo/Guarulhos (GRU) or "Cumbica," is in the suburb of Guarulhos, 30 km (19 miles) and a 45-minute drive (longer during rush hour or on rainy days) northeast of Centro. Much closer to the Zona Sul region is Aeroporto de Congonhas (CGH), 14 km (9 miles) south of Centro (a 15- to 45-minute drive, depending on traffic), which serves regional airlines, including the Rio–São Paulo shuttle.

Airports Aeroporto Internacional de Congonhas (*CGH*). ✉ *Avenida Washington Luís s/n, Campo Belo* ☎ *011/5090–9000* ⊕ *www.infraero.gov.br.* **Aeroporto Internacional de São Paulo/Guarulhos** (*GRU*). ✉ *Rod. Hélio Smidt s/n, Guarulhos* ☎ *011/2445–2945* ⊕ *www.infraero.gov.br.*

AIRPORT TRANSFERS: BUSES AND TAXIS State government–operated EMTU's Airport Bus Service buses (air-conditioned blue-and-white vehicles) shuttle between Guarulhos and Congonhas airports every 30 to 40 minutes from 5:30 am to midnight and every 60 to 90 minutes from midnight to 5:30 am (R$36.50). Look for the EMTU stand near the private bus and cab stalls outside the arrivals terminal. You may also be able to arrange a free transfer with your airline as part of your ticket.

The EMTU buses travel between Guarulhos and the Tietê bus terminal (which is also on the main subway line) from 5 am to midnight, every 30 to 60 minutes; the downtown Praça da República (5:40 am to midnight, every 60 to 90 minutes); and Avenida Paulista (5:50 am to 11:10 pm,

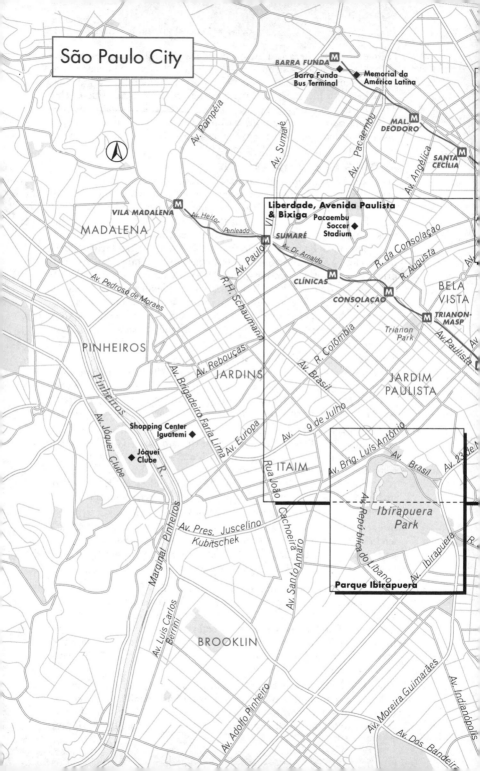

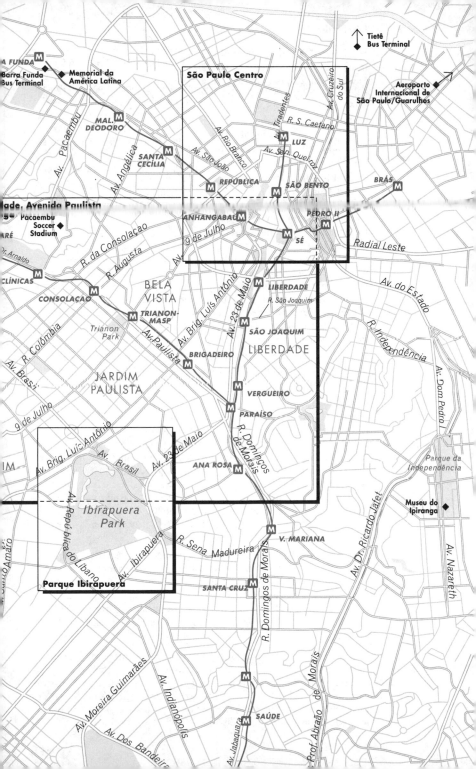

every 60 to 70 minutes), stopping at most major hotels around Avenida Paulista. Lines also connect Guarulhos to the Barra Funda bus terminal, Brooklin, and Itaquera. The cost is R$36.50. Alternatively, there is also a local, non-air-conditioned line that connects to metro Tatuapé for R$4.45.

The blue-and-white, air-conditioned Guarucoop radio taxis are the official taxis at Guarulhos Airport and can take you to Centro for around R$105 and Paulista for around R$125. It can cost up to R$170 to more distant destinations such as Morumbi. The price is set before the trip based on your drop-off address or suburb and can take from 45 minutes to two hours in peak traffic. The line for the cabs forms just outside the arrivals terminal and moves quickly. Congonhas is much closer to downtown and the Zona Sul, so it usually costs no more than R$50 with the airport's offical radio taxi company, Vermelho e Branco. Prices are not set before the trip, so fares can vary.

Transfer Contacts EMTU. ☎ 0800/770–2287 ⊕ www.airportbusservice.com.br. **Guarucoop.** ☎ 011/2440–7070 ⊕ www.guarucoop.com.br. **Rádio Taxi Vermelho e Branco.** ☎ 011/3146-4000 ⊕ www.radiotaxivermelhoebranco.com.br.

BUS TRAVEL

The three key bus terminals in the city of São Paulo are connected to metro (subway) stations and serve more than 1,100 destinations combined. The huge main station—serving all major Brazilian cities (with trips to Rio every 10 minutes during the day and every half hour at night, until 2 am) as well as Argentina, Uruguay, Chile, and Paraguay—is the Terminal Tietê in the north, on the Marginal Tietê Beltway. Terminal Jabaquara, near Congonhas Airport, serves coastal towns. Terminal Barra Funda, in the west, near the Memorial da América Latina, has buses to and from western Brazil. Socicam, a private company, runs all the bus terminals in the city of São Paulo.

Bus Contacts EMTU. ☎ 0800/7702287 ⊕ www.airportbusservice.com.br. **Socicam.** ☎ 011/3866–1100 ⊕ www.socicam.com.br. **Terminal Barra Funda.** ✉ Rua Auro Soares de Moura Andrade, 664, Barra Funda ☎ 011/3866–1100 ⊕ www.socicam.com.br Ⓜ Barra Funda. **Terminal Jabaquara.** ✉ Rua dos Jequitibás, s/n, Jabaquara ☎ 011/3866–1100 ⊕ www.socicam.com.br Ⓜ Jabaquara. **Terminal Tietê.** ✉ Av. Cruzeiro do Sul, 1800, Santana ☎ 011/3866–1100 ⊕ www.socicam.com.br Ⓜ Tietê.

TRAVEL WITHIN SÃO PAULO Municipal bus service is frequent and covers the entire city, but regular buses are overcrowded at rush hour and when it rains. If you don't speak Portuguese, it can be hard to figure out the system and the stops. The stops are clearly marked, but routes are spelled out only on the buses themselves. Buses don't stop at every bus stop, so if you're waiting, you'll have to flag one down.

> ### A VIEW OF THE PAST
>
> Although modern-day São Paulo is a tough place to navigate thanks to the jungle of tall buildings, this wasn't always the case. During the city's first few hundred years, before skyscrapers appeared, there were impressive views from Avenida Paulista, which runs along a natural ridgeline extending all the way to Vila Madelena and beyond.

Bus fare is R$3.50. You enter at the front of the bus, pay the *cobrador* (fare collector) in the middle, and exit from the rear of the bus. To pay, you can use either money or a rechargeable electronic card *bilhete único*. The card allows you to take four buses in three hours for the price of one fare. Cards can be bought and reloaded at special booths at major bus terminals or at lottery shops.

For bus numbers and names, routes, and schedules, go to the (Portuguese-language) website of Transporte Público de São Paulo (SPTrans), the city's public transport agency, or use Google Maps, which is linked to the SPTrans system and shows all bus routes. The *Guia São Paulo Ruas,* published by Quatro Rodas and sold at newsstands and bookstores for about R$15, is another option.

4

Contact **Transporte Público de São Paulo.** ☎ *156* ⊕ *www.sptrans.com.br.*

CAR TRAVEL
The principal highways leading into São Paulo are: the Dutra, from the northeast (and Rio); Anhangüera and Bandeirantes, from the north; Washington Luis, from the northwest; Raposo Tavares, from the west; Régis Bittencourt, from the south; and Anchieta-Imigrantes, from Santos in the southeast. Driving in the city isn't recommended, however, because of the heavy traffic (nothing moves at rush hour, especially when it rains), daredevil drivers, and inadequate parking. You'll also need to obtain a temporary driver's license from *Detran,* the State Transit Department, which can be a time-consuming endeavor.

MAJOR HIGHWAYS AND ROADS The high-speed beltways along the Rio Pinheiros and Rio Tietê rivers—called Marginal Tietê and Marginal Pinheiros—sandwich the main part of São Paulo. Avenida 23 de Maio runs south from Centro and beneath the Parque do Ibirapuera via the Ayrton Senna Tunnel. Avenida Paulista splits Bela Vista and Jardins with Higienópolis and Vila Mariana as bookends.

You can cut through Itaim en route to Brooklin and Santo Amaro by taking avenidas Brasil and Faria Lima southwest to Avenida Santo Amaro. Avenida João Dias and Viaduto José Bonifácio C. Nogueira cut across the Pinheiros River to Morumbi. The Elevado Costa e Silva, also called Minhocão, is an elevated road that connects Centro with Avenida Francisco Matarazzo in the west.

PARKING In most commercial neighborhoods you must buy hourly tickets (called Cartão Zona Azul) to park on the street during business hours. Buy them at newsstands, not from people on the street, who may overcharge or sell counterfeited copies. Booklets of 10 one-hour tickets cost R$45. Fill out each ticket, one for every hour you plan to park, with the car's license plate and the time you initially parked. Leave the tickets in the car's window so they're visible to officials from outside. After business hours or at any time near major sights, people may offer to watch your car. If you don't pay these "caretakers," there's a chance they'll damage your car (R$2 is enough to keep your car's paint job intact). But to truly ensure your car's safety, park in a guarded lot, where rates are R$5–R$7 for the first hour and R$1–R$2 each hour thereafter.

Invest in the *Guia São Paulo Ruas,* published by Quatro Rodas, which shows every street in the city. It's sold at newsstands and bookstores for about R$30.

SUBWAY TRAVEL

Five color-coded lines compose the São Paulo Metrô, known simply as the metro by locals, which interconnects with six train lines administered by the Companhia Paulista de Trens Metropolitanos (CPTM) to blanket most of São Paulo in rail. The most glaring gaps exist around the Ibirapuera, Moema, and Morumbi neighborhoods, as well as near the airports. You can print maps of the entire network from the metro's English-language website, where you'll also find ticket prices and schedules. The first four lines are the most useful to tourists. Most notably they cover the center, Avenida Paulista, and Vila Madalena.

Kiosks at all metro and train stations sell tickets; vendors prefer small bills for payment. You insert the ticket into the turnstile at the platform entrance, and it's returned to you only if there's unused fare on it. Seniors (65 or older) ride without charge by showing photo IDs at the turnstiles. Transfers within the metro system are free. A single ticket costs R$3.50. You can also buy a rechargeable *bilhete único* (good for combination tickets for the bus and the metro, R$5.45) at metro stations.

Subway Information Metrô. ☎ *0800/770–7722* ⊕ *www.metro.sp.gov.br.*

TAXI TRAVEL

Taxis in São Paulo are white. Owner-driven taxis are generally well maintained and reliable, as are radio taxis. Fares start at R$4.10 and run from R$2.70 for each kilometer (½ mile) or R$0.55 for every minute sitting in traffic. After 8 pm and on weekends, fares rise up to 50%. You'll pay a tax if the cab leaves the city, as is the case with trips to Cumbica Airport. Good radio-taxi companies, among them Coopertax, Ligue-Taxi, and Radio Taxi Vermelho e Branco, usually accept credit cards, but you must call ahead and request the service. Smartphone apps like Easy Taxi and 99Taxis are popular, reliable, and highly recommended.

Taxi Contacts Coopertaxi. ☎ *011/2095–6000, 011/3511–1919* ⊕ *www. coopertax.com.br.* **Ligue-Taxi.** ☎ *011/2101–3030, 011/3873–3030* ⊕ *www. ligue-taxi.com.br.* **Radio Taxi Vermelho e Branco.** ☎ *011/3146–4000* ⊕ *www. radiotaxivermelhoebranco.com.br.*

SAFETY

Stay alert and guard your belongings at all times. Avoid wearing expensive sneakers or watches and flashy jewelry, and be careful with cameras, smartphones, and tablets—all of which attract attention. Muggers love to target the airports, tourist-frequented neighborhoods, and ATMs, so be vigilant while in these spaces.

If driving, stay alert during traffic jams and at stop signs, especially at night, and don't deviate from the main streets and beltways. Watch out for motorcycles with pillion passengers, as this is a popular mode of transport for thieves. It's best to keep your windows up and doors locked.

VISITOR INFORMATION

The most helpful contact is the São Paulo Convention and Visitors Bureau, open weekdays from 9 to 6. Branches of the city-operated São Paulo Turismo are open daily from 9 to 6. The Secretaria de Turismo do Estado de São Paulo, open weekdays from 9 to 6, is less helpful, but has maps and information about the city and state of São Paulo. The Secretaria also has a booth at the arrivals terminal in Guarulhos airport; it's open daily from 9 am to 10 pm.

Visitor Information São Paulo Convention and Visitors Bureau. ☒ *Alameda Ribeirão Preto 130, conjuntos 121, Jardins* ☏ *011/3736–0600, 011/3289–7588* ⊕ *www.spcvb.com.br.* São Paulo Turismo S/A. ☒ *Anhembi Convention Center, Av. Olavo Fontoura 1209, Santana* ☏ *011/2226–0400* ⊕ *www.spturis.com.* São Paulo Turismo S/A. ☒ *Praça da República, Rua 7 de Abril, Centro* ⊕ *www.spturis. com* Ⓜ *República.* São Paulo Turismo S/A. ☒ *Av. Paulista 1853, Cerqueira César* ⊕ *www.spturis.com* Ⓜ *Trianon-Masp.* São Paulo Turismo S/A. ☒ *Bus station, Av. Cruzeiro do Sul 1800, Tietê* ⊕ *www.spturis.com* Ⓜ *Tietê.* São Paulo Turismo S/A. ☒ *Guarulhos Airport Terminals 1 and 2, Aeroporto de Guarulhos* ⊕ *www.spturis. com.* Secretaria de Turismo do Estado de São Paulo. ☒ *Praça Antônio Prado 9, Centro* ☏ *011/3241–5822* ⊕ *www.turismo.sp.gov.br.*

TOURS

You can hire a bilingual guide through a travel agency or a hotel concierge (about R$15 an hour with a four-hour minimum), or you can design your own itineraries. The São Paulo tourist board's Cidade São Paulo website offers various themed walking itineraries and English language audio guides, and it outlines tours facilitated by subway through the TurisMetrô program. SPTuris conducts three half-day bus tours on Sunday, one covering the parks, one centered on the museums, and one focused on the historical downtown area. Officially, the board's guides don't speak English, but it's sometimes possible to arrange for an English speaker.

Check Point. Check Point's daily tours specialize in general sightseeing. They don't have a physical location, so reservations are online-only. ☏ *011/2791–1316 business hours, 011/99187–1393 after-hours* ⊕ *www.checkpointtours.com.br* ☒ *From R$450 for three people.*

Easygoing Brazil. Brazilian cooking lessons, kart rides at the Interlagos Formula One racetrack, and fly-and-dine tours that include a helicopter trip are part of Easygoing's personalized services. You can book tours in English if you reserve by phone. ☒ *Perdizes* ☏ *011/3801–9540* ⊕ *www. easygoing.com.br* ☒ *From R$373.*

Gol Tour Viagens e Turismo. This company offers half-day city tours, and they also do custom and out-of-town tours for small groups to cities such as Campos do Jordão. ☒ *Centro* ☏ *011/3256–2388* ⊕ *www. goltour.com.br* ☒ *From R$155.*

Sampa Bikers. Specializing in city bicycle tours and excursions outside town, Sampa Bikers has a two-hour tour every Wednesday. ☒ ☏ *011/5517–7733* ⊕ *www.sampabikers.com.br* ☒ *From R$50.*

SP Free Walking Tours. To explore the city's historic center or the gleaming towers and old mansions around Avenida Paulista, join one of the free, English-language group tours run by this outfitter. Tours are around three hours long and leave from Praça República and Avenida Paulista. ⊕ *www.saopaulofreewalkingtour.com.*

Terra Nobre. This company's four-hour car tours include a driver and an English-speaking guide, for one or two people. ⊠ *Rua Tagipuru 235, Conjuntos 44, Perdizes* ☎ *011/3662–1505* ⊕ *www.terranobre.com.br* ▧ *From US$310.*

EXPLORING SÃO PAULO

CENTRO

The downtown district is one of the few places in São Paulo where a significant amount of pre-20th-century history remains visible. You can explore the areas where the city began and view examples of architecture, some of it beautifully restored, from the 19th century. Petty criminals operate in this area, so keep your wits about you while you tour. The best way to get here is by metro.

> ### STAY ALERT
>
> Pickpocketing can be a problem in Centro, so keep a low profile, don't wear expensive jewelry or watches, and bring only what money you absolutely need. Touring with a guide usually provides some extra security.

For an easy glimpse of Centro, start at the Anhangabaú metro station and head northwest along the valley (Vale do Anhangabaú). Pass under the historic Viaduto do Chá viaduct and take in the sight of the magnificent, baroque Theatro Municipal to your left. A bit farther along near the São Bento metro station, find your way to the monastery of the same name, uphill to the right. Then continue on over the hill, and make your way downhill, zigzagging through the crowded shopping streets towards Mercado Municipal.

TOP ATTRACTIONS

Catedral da Sé. The imposing, 14-tower neo-Gothic Catedral da Sé occupies the official center of São Paulo—the 0 Km point, as it's called here. Tours of the church wind through the crypt, which contains the remains of Tibiriçá, a native Brazilian who helped the Portuguese back in 1554. ⊠ *Praça da Sé s/n, Centro* ☎ *011/3106–2709, 011/3107–6832 for tour information* ⊕ *www.catedraldase.org.br/site* ▧ *Tour R$5* ⊙ *Church weekdays 8–7, Sat. 8–5, Sun. 8–1 and 2–6; tours weekdays 1–4:30, weekends 9–3* Ⓜ *Sé.*

Edifício Itália. One way to catch the astounding view from atop the Itália Building is to drop in for lunch or dinner at the Terraço Itália restaurant, starting on the 41st floor. The main dining room features central columns, candlelit tables, and a terrace. A live band and dance floor jazz up the panoramic parlor upstairs Monday to Saturday. The restaurant is expensive, making a drink at the piano bar, with its upholstered seating and wood lining, a more affordable strategy. Thriftier still is a visit to the outside terrace, which is free weekdays 3–4 pm. ⊠ *Av. Ipiranga 344, Centro* ☎ *011/2189–2929 restaurant* ⊕ *www.*

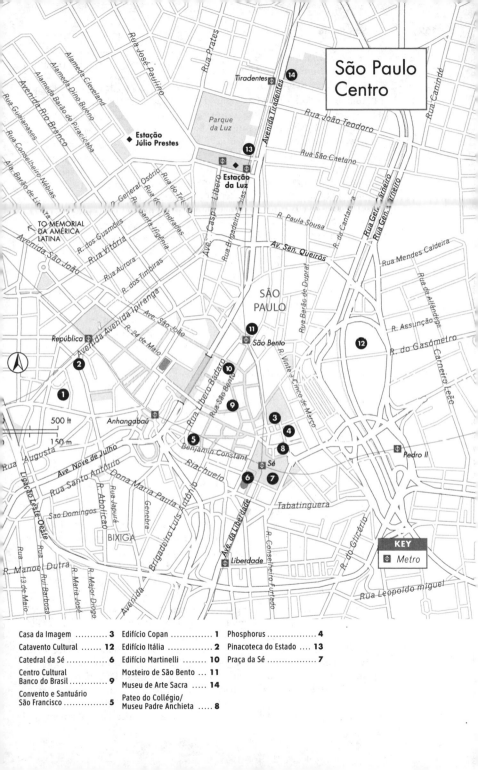

São Paulo
Centro

Tiradentes **14**

*Parque
da Luz*

◆ Estação
Júlio Prestes

13

Estação
da Luz

TO MEMORIAL
DA AMÉRICA
LATINA

SÃO
PAULO

11

República
São Bento

12

2

10

1

9

500 ft
Anhangabaú
3

150 m
4

5

Benjamin Constant
8

Sé
6 **7**

BIXIGA
Tabatinguera

Liberdade

Pedro II

KEY

⊞ *Metro*

terracoitalia.com.br 🖵 *Piano bar R$30 entrance fee* ⊙ *Daily noon–midnight* Ⓜ *República.*

Fodor's Choice
★ **Edifício Martinelli.** Amid São Paulo's modern 1950s-era skyscrapers, the Gothic Martinelli Building is a welcome anomaly. Built in 1929 by Italian immigrant–turned-count Giuseppe Martinelli, it was the city's first skyscraper. The whimsical penthouse is worth checking out, and the rooftop has a great view. ✉ *Av. São João 35, Centro* ☎ *011/3104–2477* ⊕ *www.prediomartinelli.com.br/visitas.php* 🖵 *Free* ⊙ *Weekdays 9:30–11:20 and 2–4, weekends 9–1* Ⓜ *São Bento.*

Mosteiro de São Bento. The German architect Richard Berndl designed this Norman–Byzantine church that was completed in 1922. Ecclesiastical imagery abounds, and soaring archways extend skyward. The church's enormous organ has some 6,000 pipes, and its Russian image of the Kasperovo Virgin is covered with 6,000 pearls from the Black Sea. On the last Sunday of each month, paulistanos compete for space at the church's popular brunch (noon–3:30, R$178 per person), which also includes a tour and varying performances, from dance to choir. To join the party, call *011/2440–7837* early to reserve your seat. The don't-miss religious event at Mosterio de São Bento is Sunday Mass at 10 am, when the sound of monks' Gregorian chants echoes through the chamber. ✉ *Largo de São Bento, Centro* ☎ *011/3328–8799* ⊕ *www.mosteiro.org.br* 🖵 *Free* ⊙ *Weekdays 6–6, weekends 6–noon and 4–6* Ⓜ *São Bento.*

Museu de Arte Sacra (*Museum of Sacred Art*). If you can't get to Bahia or Minas Gerais during your stay in Brazil, you can get a taste of the fabulous baroque and rococo art found there at the Museum of Sacred Art. On display are 4,000 wooden and terra-cotta masks, jewelry, and liturgical objects from all over the country (but primarily Minas Gerais and Bahia), dating from the 17th century to the present. The on-site convent was founded in 1774. ✉ *Av. Tiradentes 676, Centro* ☎ *011/5627–5393* ⊕ *www.museuartesacra.org.br* 🖵 *R$6, free Sat.* ⊙ *Tues.–Fri. 9–5, weekends 10–6* Ⓜ *Tiradentes or Luz.*

Pinacoteca do Estado. The highlights of the State Art Gallery's permanent collection include paintings by the renowned Brazilian artists Tarsila do Amaral and Cândido Portinari. Amaral, who died in São Paulo in 1973, applied avant-garde techniques, some of which she acquired while hanging out with the cubists in 1920s Paris, with Brazilian themes and content. Portinari, born in São Paulo State and known for his neo-realistic style, also dealt with social and historical themes. The museum occupies a 1905 structure that was renovated in the late 1990s. The exterior recalls a 1950s brick firehouse, while the view through the

A Bit of History

São Paulo wasn't big and important right from the start. Jesuit priests founded it in 1554 and began converting native Indians to Catholicism. The town was built strategically on a plateau, protected from attack and served by many rivers. It remained unimportant to the Portuguese crown until the 1600s, when it became the departure point for the *bandeira* (literally, "flag") expeditions, whose members set out to look for gemstones and gold, to enslave Indians, and, later, to capture escaped African slaves. In the process, these adventurers established roads into vast portions of previously unexplored territory. São Paulo also saw Emperor Dom Pedro I declare independence from Portugal in 1822, by the Rio Ipiranga (Ipiranga River), near the city.

It was only In the late 19th century that São Paulo became a driving force in the country. As the state established itself as one of Brazil's main coffee producers, the city attracted laborers and investors from many countries. Italians, Portuguese, Spanish, Germans, and Japanese put their talents and energies to work. By 1895, 70,000 of the 130,000 residents were immigrants. Their efforts transformed the place from a sleepy mission post into a dynamic financial

and cultural hub, with people of all colors and religions living and working together peacefully.

Avenida Paulista was once the site of many a coffee baron's mansion. Money flowed from these private domains into civic and cultural institutions. The arts began to flourish, and by the 1920s São Paulo was promoting such great artists as Mário and Oswald de Andrade, who introduced modern elements into Brazilian art.

In the 1950s the auto industry began to develop and contributed greatly to São Paulo's contemporary wealth—and problems. Over the next 30 years, people from throughout Brazil, especially the Northeast, came seeking jobs, which transformed the city's landscape by increasing slums and poverty. Between the 1950s and today, the city's main revenue has moved from industry to banking and commerce.

Today, like many major European or American hubs, São Paulo struggles to meet Its citizens' transportation and housing needs, and goods and services are expensive. Like most of its counterparts elsewhere in the world, it hasn't yet found an answer to these problems.

4

central courtyard's interior windows evokes the cliffs of Cuenca, Spain. Admission is valid for same-day admission to the Estação Pinacoteca, the Pinacoteca's second branch, which is a short walk away at Largo General Osório 66. The area is sketchy so stay alert as you go, especially at night. ⊠ *Praça da Luz 2, Centro* ☎ *011/3324–1000* ⊕ *www. pinacoteca.org.br* ⊠ *R$6, free Thurs. 5–10 and Sat.* ☉ *Mon.–Wed. and weekends 10–8, Thurs. 10–10* Ⓜ *Luz.*

Praça da Sé. Two major metro lines cross under the busy Praça da Sé, the large plaza that marks the city's geographical center and holds its main cathedral. Migrants from Brazil's poor Northeast often gather here to enjoy their music and to purchase and sell regional items such as medicinal herbs, while street children hang out and try to avoid the periodic police sweeps to remove them. ⊠ *Praça da Sé s/n, Centro* Ⓜ *Sé.*

WORTH NOTING

Casa da Imagem. This museum dedicated to São Paulo–themed photography opened in 2012 on the site of Casa No. 1, named for its original address in 1689. The 84,000-image collection, which traces the city's expansion and increasing complexity, includes flashbacks to the days when nearby park Vale do Anhangabaú hosted ceremonies for the rich and regal. Casa da Imagem speaks to São Paulo's earliest foundations, but also captures its contemporary composition. ⊠ *Rua Roberto Simonsen 136-B, Centro* ☎ *011/3106–5122* ⊕ *www.museudacidade.sp.gov. br/casadaimagem.php* 🎫 *Free* ⏰ *Tues.–Sun. 9–5* Ⓜ *Sé.*

> ### GAROA
>
> One of São Paulo's most famous nicknames is *terra da garoa*, which basically means land of drizzling rain. A dearth of sufficient rain in recent years has put an end to that nickname, but especially in the summertime, when afternoon rains wash over the city most days, a lightweight umbrella is a sensible item to carry.

FAMILY **Catavento Cultural.** Traveling families will find education and entertainment for their children at this interactive science museum in the former city hall building. For architecture fans, the early-20th-century structure, with its interior courtyard, alone justifies a visit. Stepping into human-size soap bubbles or touching actual meteorites, meanwhile, are the big attractions for kids. The museum's exhibits are organized along four thematic lines: the universe, life, ingenuity, and society. ⊠ *Parque Dom Pedro II, Palácio das Indústrias s/n, Brás* ☎ *011/3315–0051* ⊕ *www.cataventocultural.org.br* 🎫 *R$6* ⏰ *Tues.–Sun. 9–5, last admission 4* Ⓜ *Pedro II.*

Centro Cultural Banco do Brasil. The greenhouse-size skylight of this cultural center's 1901 neoclassical home makes the modern and contemporary art exhibits here seem almost to sprout organically. Past ones include "The Magic World of Escher." Plays and small film festivals, the latter celebrating filmmakers from Quentin Tarantino to Louis Malle, further broaden the venue's appeal. The center's facilities include a theater, an auditorium, a movie theater, a video room, and three floors of exhibition rooms. ⊠ *Rua Álvares Penteado 112, Centro* ☎ *011/3113–3651, 011/3113–3652* 🎫 *Free; performances R$10; movies R$4* ⏰ *Wed.–Mon. 9–9* Ⓜ *Sé.*

Convento e Santuário São Francisco. One of the city's best-preserved Portuguese colonial buildings, this baroque structure—two churches, one run by Catholic clergy and the other by lay brothers—was built between 1647 and 1790. The image inside of Saint Francis was rescued from a fire in 1870. ⊠ *Largo São Francisco 133, Centro* ☎ *011/3291–2400* ⊕ *www.franciscanos.org.br* 🎫 *Free* ⏰ *Mon.–Sat. 7:30–5:50* Ⓜ *Sé or Anhangabaú.*

Edifício Copan. The architect of this serpentine apartment and office block, Oscar Niemeyer, went on to design much of Brasília, the nation's capital. The building has the clean, white, undulating curves characteristic of Niemeyer's work. The Copan was constructed in 1950, and its 1,160 apartments house about 5,000 people. Pivô (*www.pivo. org.br*), a stunning new art gallery inside the Copan, has exhibitions, workshops, residencies, and educational activities; admission is free. ⊠ *Av. Ipiranga 200, Centro* ☎ *011/3257–6169* ⊕ *www.copansp.com. br* Ⓜ *República.*

NEED A BREAK? **Café Floresta.** Drop in at this standing-room-only coffee bar for a cup of java and to soak up the atmosphere inside the Copan building, which includes shops, restaurants, and cafés on the ground floor. ⊠ *Av. Ipiranga 200, Loja 21, Centro* ☎ *011/3259-8416* ⊕ *www.cafefloresta.com.br* Ⓜ *República.*

4

Pateo do Collegio / Museu Padre Anchieta. São Paulo was founded by the Jesuits José de Anchieta and Manoel da Nóbrega in the College Courtyard in 1554. The church was constructed in 1896 in the same style as the chapel built by the Jesuits. In the small museum you can see a fascinating relief map of Centro in colonial times and an exhibition of early sacred art and relics. ⊠ *Praça Pateo do Collegio 2, Centro* ☎ *011/3105–6899* ⊕ *www.pateocollegio.com.br* 🎫 *Museum R$6* ☉ *Museum Tues.–Sun. 9–4:30; church Mon.–Sat. 8:15–7, Sun. Mass at 10* Ⓜ *Sé.*

Phosphorus. This wonderful contemporary art gallery, which also encompasses a second gallery, Sé, on the top floor, occupies one of the oldest buildings in the area, which it shares with a vintage clothing company, Casa Juisi. ⊠ *Rua Roberto Simonsen 108, Centro* ☎ *011/3107–7074* ⊕ *www.phosphorus.art.br/about* 🎫 *Free* ☉ *Thurs.–Fri. noon–7, Sat. noon–5* Ⓜ *Sé.*

NEED A BREAK? **Café do Páteo.** A great place to rest your feet while touring Centro, this café on a large balcony overlooking the east side of town serves cold and hot drinks along with typical snacks, such as *pão de queijo* (cheese bread). ⊠ *Praça Pateo do Collegio 2, Centro* ☎ *011/3105–6899* ⊕ *www. pateodocollegio.com.br* ☉ *Tue.–Sun. 9–4:30* Ⓜ *São Bento.*

LIBERDADE

The red-porticoed entryway to Liberdade (which means "Freedom") is south of Praça da Sé, behind the cathedral. The neighborhood is home to many first-, second-, and third-generation Nippo-Brazilians, as well as to more recent Chinese and Korean immigrants. Clustered around Avenida Liberdade are shops with everything from imported bubble gum to miniature robots and Kabuki face paint.

The best time to visit Liberdade is on Sunday during the street fair at Praça Liberdade, where Asian food, crafts, and souvenirs are sold. The fair will very likely be crowded, so keep your wits about you and do not wander around at night.

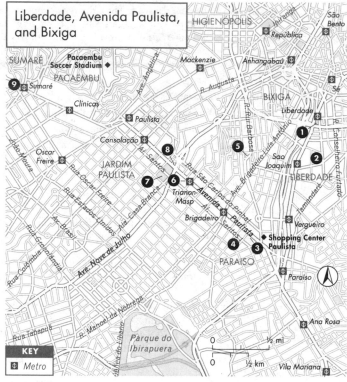

Liberdade, Avenida Paulista, and Bixiga

TOP ATTRACTIONS

Museu Histórico da Imigração Japonesa no Brasil. The three-floor Museum of Japanese Immigration has exhibits about Nippo-Brazilian culture and farm life, and about Japanese contributions to Brazilian horticulture. There are also World War II memorials. Relics and life-size re-creations of scenes from the Japanese diaspora line the walls, and paintings hang from the ceiling like wind chimes. Most of the museum's labels are in Portuguese. ⊠ *Rua São Joaquim 381, Liberdade* ☎ *011/3209–5465* ⊕ *www.museubunkyo.org.br* ⊠ *R$7* ☉ *Tues.–Sun. 1:30–5:30* Ⓜ *São Joaquim.*

WORTH NOTING

Praça Liberdade. To experience the eclectic cultural mix that keeps São Paulo pulsing, visit Praça Liberdade on a weekend, when the square hosts a sprawling Asian food and crafts fair. You might see Afro-Brazilians dressed in colorful kimonos hawking grilled shrimp on a stick, or perhaps a religious celebration such as April's Hanamatsuri, commemorating the birth of the Buddha. Many Japanese shops and restaurants worth a stop can be found near the square. ⊠ *Av. da Liberdade and Rua dos Estudantes, Liberdade* ☉ *Fair weekends 10–7* Ⓜ *Liberdade.*

AVENIDA PAULISTA AND BIXIGA

Money once poured into and out of the coffee barons' mansions that lined Avenida Paulista, making it, in a sense, the financial hub. And so it is today, though the money is now centered in the major banks. Like the barons before them, many of these financial institutions generously support the arts. Numerous places have changing exhibitions—often free—in the Paulista neighborhood. Nearby Bixiga, São Paulo's Little Italy, is full of restaurants—Italian, of course.

TOP ATTRACTIONS

Casa das Rosas. Peek into the Paulista's past at one of the avenue's few remaining early-20th-century buildings, the House of the Roses. A 1935 French-style mansion with gardens inspired by those at Versailles, it seems out of place next to the surrounding skyscrapers. The famous paulistano architect Ramos de Azevedo designed the home for one of his daughters, and the same family occupied it until 1986, when it was made an official municipal landmark. The site, now a cultural center, hosts classes and literary events. Coffee drinks and pastries are served at the café on the terrace. ⊠ *Av. Paulista 37, Paraíso* ☎ *011/3285–6986, 011/3288–9447* ⊕ *www.casadasrosas.org.br* ⬚ *Free* ☉ *Tues.–Sat. 10–10, Sun. 10–6; café noon–5* Ⓜ *Brigadeiro.*

NEED A BREAK?

Ponto Chic. Stop here for a delicious *bauru*—a sandwich with roast beef, tomato, cucumber, and a mix of melted cheeses. This branch of the Paissandu restaurant that invented the bauru is a block east of the Instituto Itaú Cultural, across Avenida Paulista. ⊠ *Praça Osvaldo Cruz 26, Paraíso* ☎ *011/3289-1480* ⊕ *www.pontochic.com.br* ☉ *Daily 11 am–2 am.*

Fodor'sChoice **Museu de Arte de São Paulo (MASP).** A striking low-rise building elevated ★ on two massive concrete pillars holds one of the city's premier fine-arts collections. The highlights include works by Van Gogh, Renoir, Delacroix, Cézanne, Monet, Rembrandt, Picasso, and Degas. The baroque sculptor Aleijadinho, the expressionist painter Lasar Segall, and the expressionist/surrealist painter Cândido Portinari are three of the many Brazilian artists represented. The huge open area beneath the museum is often used for cultural events and protests, and is the site of a charming Sunday antiques fair. ⊠ *Av. Paulista 1578, Bela Vista* ☎ *011/3251–5644* ⊕ *www.masp.art.br* ⬚ *R$15; free Tues.* ☉ *Tues.–Wed. and Fri.–Sun. 10–6, Thurs. 10–8* Ⓜ *Trianon-MASP.*

Parque Trianon. Created in 1892 as a showcase for local vegetation, the park was renovated in 1968 by Roberto Burle Marx, the Brazilian landscaper famed for Rio's mosaic-tile beachfront sidewalks. You can escape the noise of the street and admire the flora and the 300-year-old trees while seated on one of the benches sculpted to look like chairs. ⊠ *Rua Peixoto Gomide 949, Jardim Paulista* ☎ *011/3289–2160, 011/3253–4973* ⬚ *Free* ☉ *Daily 6–6* Ⓜ *Trianon-MASP.*

WORTH NOTING

Centro Cultural FIESP–Ruth Cardoso. Adorned with LED lights, the cultural center's pyramid-shaped facade serves as an open-air digital-art gallery. Past exhibits at this facility of São Paulo State's Federation of

TAKE A WALK

The imposing and almost dead-straight Avenida Paulista is a great place to explore on foot. Running from Paraíso (paradise) to Consolação (consolation), two bookending metro stations, the avenue also serves as paulistanos' tongue-in-cheek comparison to marriage, but many couples of all ages will be found strolling here hand-in-hand. The Museu de Arte de São Paulo (MASP) has one of Brazil's best collections of fine art. Right across the street is shady Parque Trianon, where locals hang out and eat lunch. Leaving the park, veer right and head for the Centro Cultural FIESP. Here you may be able to catch one of its art shows or performances. A few blocks away is the Instituto Itaú Cultural, a great place to see contemporary Brazilian art. Finally, rest your weary feet in Casa das Rosas, a cultural center and café, with a pretty rose garden attached.

Industry have broadcast towering games of Pac-Man and Space Invaders to pedestrians and nearby residents. The center has a theater, a library of art and photography, galleries that host temporary exhibitions, and areas for lectures, films, and other events. ⊠ *Av. Paulista 1313, Jardim Paulista* ☎ *011/3146–7405* ⊕ *www.fiesp.com.br/centro-cultural-fiesp-ruth-cardoso* ⊠ *Free* ☉ *Mon. 11–8, Tues.–Sat. 10–8, Sun. 10–7* Ⓜ *Trianon-MASP.*

Centro da Cultura Judaica. A short cab or metro trip northwest of Avenida Paulista, this Torah-shape concrete building is one of the newest architectural hot spots in town. Inaugurated in 2003 to display Jewish history and culture in Brazil, it houses a theater and an art gallery and promotes exhibits, lectures, and book fairs. The center's café was inspired by New York delis and serves local Jewish cuisine. ⊠ *Rua Oscar Freire 2500, Pinheiros* ☎ *011/3065–4333* ⊕ *www.culturajudaica. org.br* ⊠ *Free* ☉ *Tues.–Sun. noon–7* Ⓜ *Sumaré.*

Feira do Bixiga. Strolling through this flea market is a favorite Sunday activity for paulistanos. Crafts, antiques, and furniture are among the wares. Walk up the São José staircase to see **Rua dos Ingleses,** a typical and well-preserved fin-de-siècle Bixiga street. ⊠ *Praça Dom Orione s/n, Bixiga* ⊠ *Free* ☉ *Sun. 8–5.*

Itaú Cultural. Maintained by Itaú, one of Brazil's largest private banks, this cultural institute has art shows as well as lectures, workshops, and films. It also maintains an archive with a photographic history of São Paulo, a library that specializes in works on Brazilian art and culture, and a new permanent exhibition tracing the formation of Brazil. ⊠ *Av. Paulista 149, Paraíso* ☎ *011/2168–1777* ⊕ *www.itaucultural.org.br* ⊠ *Free* ☉ *Tues.–Fri. 9–8, weekends 11–8* Ⓜ *Brigadeiro.*

PARQUE IBIRAPUERA

Ibirapuera is São Paulo's Central Park, though it's slightly less than half the size and is often more crowded on sunny weekends than its New York City counterpart. In the 1950s the land, which originally contained the municipal nurseries, was chosen as the site of a public park to commemorate the city's 400th anniversary. Architect Oscar Niemeyer and landscape architect Roberto Burle Marx joined the team of professionals assigned to the project. The park was inaugurated in 1954, and some pavilions used for the opening festivities still sit amid its 160 hectares (395 acres). It has jogging and biking paths, a lake, and rolling lawns. You can rent bicycles near some of the park entrances for about R$5 an hour.

TOP ATTRACTIONS

Museu Afro Brasil. Among Parque Ibirapuera's various attractions, natural and architectural, this museum might easily pass unnoticed. But in terms of its content—a thorough if sometimes patchily organized survey of Brazil's profoundly important but underreported black history—it's highly recommended. English available only to download as audio, so bring your headphones. ⊠ *Av. Pedro Álvares Cabral, Gate 10, Parque Ibirapuera* ☎ *011/3320–8900* ⊕ *www.museuafrobrasil.org.br* ⊠ *R$6, free Thurs. and Sat.* ☺ *Tues.–Sun. 10–5* Ⓜ *Brigadeiro.*

Museu de Arte Contemporânea (MAC). The Museum of Contemporary Art expanded its Ibirapuera presence in 2012 by renovating and moving into the eight-floor former Department of Transportation building. Now shorn of its bureaucratic coldness, the space ranks among Parque Ibirapuera's architectural highlights (even though it is just over the road, rather than inside the park). The museum houses the MAC's entire 10,000-piece collection, including works by Picasso, Modigliani, and Chagall. ⊠ *Av. Pedro Álvares Cabral 1301, Parque Ibirapuera* ☎ *011/5573–9932 direct line, 011/3091–3039* ⊕ *www.macvirtual.usp. br* ⊠ *Free* ☺ *Tues. 10–9, Wed–Sun. 10–6.*

Museu de Arte Moderna (MAM). More than 4,500 paintings, installations, sculptures, and other works from modern and contemporary artists such as Alfredo Volpi and Ligia Clark are part of the Museum of Modern Art's permanent collection. Temporary exhibits often feature works by new local artists. The giant wall of glass, designed by Brazilian architect Lina Bo Bardi, serves as a window beckoning you to glimpse inside; an exterior mural painted in 2010 by Os Gêmeos, São Paulo twin brothers famous for their graffiti art, shows a little of MAM's inner appeal to the outside world. ⊠ *Av. Pedro Álvares Cabral, Gate 3, Parque Ibirapuera* ☎ *011/5085–1300* ⊕ *www.mam.org.br* ⊠ *R$6, free Sun.* ☺ *Tues.–Sun. 10–6.*

NEED A BREAK? **Prêt no MAM.** The café inside the Museum of Modern Art serves dishes from many lands, Brazil, France, and Italy among them. Except for hot-dog stands, this is one of the few places in Parque Ibirapuera to buy food. It's open for lunch only (buffet R$49.90). ⊠ *Av. Pedro Álvares Cabral, Gate 3, Parque Ibirapuera* ☎ *011/5085–1306* ⊕ *www.mam.org.br* ☺ *Tues.-Sun. noon–4.*

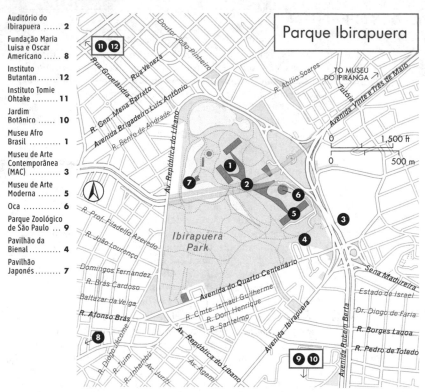

Pavilhão da Bienal. In even-numbered years this pavilion hosts the *Bienal* (Biennial), an exhibition that presents the works of artists from more than 60 countries. The first such event was held in 1951 in Parque Trianon and drew artists from 21 countries. After Ibirapuera Park's inauguration in 1954, the Bienal was moved to this Oscar Niemeyer– designed building that's noteworthy for its large open spaces and floors connected by circular slopes. ⊠ *Av. Pedro Álvares Cabral, Gate 3, Pavilhão Ciccillo Matarazzo, Parque Ibirapuera* ☎ *011/5576–7600, 011/5576–7641* ⊕ *www.bienal.org.br.*

WORTH NOTING

Auditório do Ibirapuera. The final building in Oscar Niemeyer's design for the park, the Auditório opened in 2005. It has since become one of São Paulo's trademark sights, with what looks like a giant red lightning bolt striking a massive white daredevil ramp. Seating up to 800, the concert hall regularly welcomes leading Brazilian and international musical acts. Its back wall can be retracted to reveal the stage to thousands more on the lawn outside. ⊠ *Gate 3, Av. Pedro Álvares Cabral, Parque Ibirapuera* ☎ *011/3629–1075* ⊕ *www.auditorioibirapuera.com.br.*

Oca. A spacecraft-like building that's pure Oscar Niemeyer, the Oca often hosts popular temporary art exhibitions. The building isn't usually open to the public when there is no show on. ⊠ *Av. Pedro Álvares*

Cabral, Gate 3, Parque Ibirapuera ☎ *011/3105–6118, 011/5082–1777* ⊕ *www.parqueibirapuera.org* 🎫 *Price varies depending on show.*

Pavilhão Japonês. An exact replica of the Katsura Imperial Palace in Kyoto, Japan, the Japanese Pavilion is one of the structures built for the Parque Ibirapuera's inauguration. Designed by professor Sutemi Horiguti of the University of Tokyo, it was built in Japan and reassembled here beside the man-made lake in the Japanese-style garden. The main building displays samurai clothing, pottery, and sculpture from several dynasties; rooms upstairs are used for traditional tea ceremonies. ⊠ *Av. Pedro Álvares Cabral, Gate 10, Parque Ibirapuera* ☎ *011/5081–7296* ⊕ *www.bunkyo. org.br* 🎫 *R$6* ☯ *Wed. and weekends 10–noon and 1–5.*

GREATER SÃO PAULO

Several far-flung sights are worth a taxi ride to see. West of Centro is the Universidade de São Paulo (USP), which has two interesting museums: a branch of the Museu de Arte Contemporânea and the Instituto Butantã, with its collection of creatures that slither and crawl. Close by, Parque Villa-Lobos is a smaller but still significant alternative to Ibirapuera for sporty locals. Head southwest of Centro to the Fundação Maria Luisa e Oscar Americano, a museum with a forest and garden in the residential neighborhood of Morumbi. In the Parque do Estado, southeast of Centro, are the Jardim Botânico and the Parque Zoológico de São Paulo.

TOP ATTRACTIONS

Fundação Maria Luisa e Oscar Americano. A beautiful, quiet private wooded estate is the setting for the Maria Luisa and Oscar Americano Foundation. Paintings, furniture, sacred art, silver, porcelain, engravings, tapestries, sculptures, and personal possessions of the Brazilian royal family are among the 1,500 objects from the Portuguese colonial and imperial periods on display here, and there are some modern pieces as well. Having afternoon high tea here is an event, albeit an expensive one, and Sunday concerts take place in the auditorium. ⊠ *Av. Morumbi 4077, Morumbi* ☎ *011/3742–0077* ⊕ *www.fundacaooscaramericano. org.br* 🎫 *R$10* ☯ *Tues.–Sun. 10–5:30.*

Memorial da América Latina. The memorial's massive concrete hand sculpture, its fingers reaching toward the São Paulo sky, is one of the city's signature images. Part of a 20-acre park filled with Oscar Niemeyer–designed structures, the Memorial da América Latina was inaugurated in 1989 in homage to regional unity and its greatest champions, among them Simón Bolívar and José Martí. Aside from the monument, the grounds' highlights include works by Cândido Portinari and an auditorium dedicated to musical and theatrical performances.

Free two-hour guided visits for individuals or groups of up to 40 people can be scheduled in advance for Tuesday and Sunday at 10 am or 3 pm. ✉ *Av. Auro Soares de Moura Andrade 664, Barra Funda* ☎ *011/3823-4600, 011/3823-4655 For guided visit reservations only, Tues.–Fri. 2–6* ⊕ *www.memorial. org.br* ✉ *Free* ⊗ *Tues.–Sun. 9–6* Ⓜ *Barra Funda.*

FAMILY **Parque Zoológico de São Paulo.** The 200-acre São Paulo Zoo has more than 3,200 animals, and many of its 410 species—such as the *micoleão-dourado* (golden lion tamarin monkey)—are endangered. If you visit the zoo, don't miss the monkey houses, built on small islands in the park's lake, and the Casa do Sangue Frio (Cold-Blooded House), with reptilian and amphibious creatures. ✉ *Av. Miguel Stéfano 4241, Água Funda, Parque do Estado* ☎ *011/5073-0811* ⊕ *www.zoologico.com.br* ✉ *R$18* ⊗ *Tues.–Sun. 9–5* Ⓜ *Jabaquara.*

WORTH NOTING

FAMILY **Instituto Butantan.** In 1888 a Brazilian scientist, with the aid of the state government, turned a farmhouse into a center for the production of snake serum. Today the Instituto Butantan has more than 70,000 snakes, spiders, scorpions, and lizards in its five museums. It still extracts venom and processes it into serum that's made available to victims of poisonous bites throughout Latin America. ✉ *Av. Vital Brasil 1500, Butantã* ☎ *011/3726-7222* ⊕ *www.butantan.gov.br* ✉ *R$6* ⊗ *Tues.–Sun. 9–4:30* Ⓜ *Butantã.*

Instituto Tomie Ohtake. The futuristic green, pink, and purple exterior of this contemporary art museum designed by Ruy Ohtake makes it one of the city's most recognizable buildings. The institute, named for Ohtake's mother, a renowned painter who emigrated from Japan to Brazil, mounts interesting photography and design-related exhibitions. It also houses the independently operated Brazilian restaurant Santinho, which has a popular Sunday brunch. ✉ *Av. Brigadeiro Faria Lima 201, Pinheiros* ☎ *011/2245-1900* ⊕ *www.institutotomieohtake. org.br* ✉ *Free* ⊗ *Tues.–Sun. 11–8* Ⓜ *Faria Lima.*

FAMILY **Jardim Botânico.** A great spot for a midday picnic, the Botanical Gardens contain about 3,000 plants belonging to more than 340 native species. Orchids, aquatic plants, and Atlantic rain-forest species thrive in the gardens' greenhouses. The hundred-plus bird species that have been observed at Jardim Botânico make it a favorite stopover for São Paulo birders. ✉ *Av. Miguel Stéfano 3031, Água Funda, Parque do Estado* ☎ *011/5073-6300* ⊕ *www.ibot.sp.gov.br* ✉ *R$5* ⊗ *Tues.–Sun. 9–5.*

WHERE TO EAT

São Paulo's dynamic social scene centers on dining out, and among the 12,500-plus restaurants, most of the world's cuisines are covered. The most popular options include Portuguese, Japanese, Italian, French, and Lebanese; contemporary fusions are popular and plentiful. The city also offers a massive selection of pizza and hamburger joints with some world-class offerings. Most places don't require jacket and tie, but paulistanos tend to dress to European standards, so if you're going to pricey establishments, looking elegant is key.

On the domestic front the Brazilian *churrascarias* are a carnivore's dream, with their all-you-can-eat skewers of barbecued meats and impressive salad buffets. For in-between times, just about every bar will offer a selection of grilled meats, sandwiches, and deep-fried favorites for casual grazing. On Wednesday and Saturday, head to a Brazilian restaurant for *feijoada*—the national dish of black beans and pork. Ask about the other traditional and regional Brazilian dishes as well.

WHAT IT COSTS IN REAIS

	$	$$	$$$	$$$$
AT DINNER	under R$31	R$31–R$45	R$46–R$60	over R$60

Restaurant prices are the average cost of a main course at dinner or, if dinner is not served, at lunch.

BIXIGA

$$$ ITALIAN 🍴 **Cantina Roperto.** Wine casks and bottles adorn the walls at this typical Bixiga cantina, located on a street so charmingly human-scaled you'll hardly believe you're still in São Paulo. You won't be alone if you order the ever-popular fusilli—either *ao sugo* (with tomato sauce) or *ao frutos do mar* (with seafood)—or the traditional baby goat's leg with potatoes and tomatoes. [$] *Average main: R$60* ✉ *Rua 13 de Maio 634, Bixiga* ☎ *011/3288–2573* 🌐 *www.cantinaroperto.com.br* 🕒 *Closed Sun.* [M] *Brigadeiro* ✛ *2:C5.*

$$ ITALIAN 🍴 **Lazzarella.** Generous portions at reasonable prices and live music—that's the Lazzerella way. The cantina, a classic Italian joint founded in 1970, is hardly extravagant, but the rich flavors of a meal here and the Neapolitan stylings of the crooners circling among the red-and-white checkered tabletops linger in memory. The signature house lasagna dish, made old-style with ground beef and mozzarella in a Bolognese sauce, is meal enough for two. All the pastas here are worth a try. [$] *Average main: R$40* ✉ *Rua Treze de Maio 589, Bixiga* ☎ *011/3289–3000* 🌐 *www.lazzarella.com.br* ✛ *2:C5.*

$$$$ ITALIAN PIZZA 🍴 **Speranza.** One of the most traditional pizzerias in São Paulo, this restaurant is famous for its margherita pie. In 2010, Speranza became the first pizzeria in Latin America to win recognition from the Italian pizza quality-control board Associazione Verace Pizza Napoletana. The crunchy *pão de linguiça* (sausage bread) appetizers have a fine reputation as well. Pastas and chicken and beef dishes are also

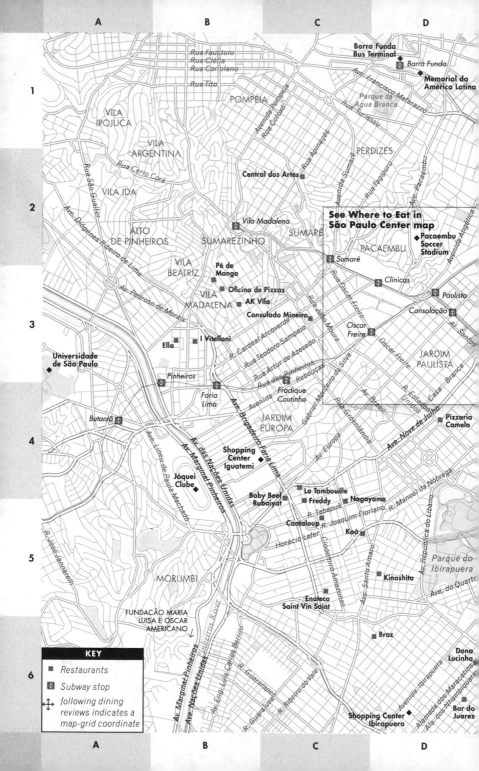

KEY

■ Restaurants
Ⓢ Subway stop
↕ following dining reviews indicates a map-grid coordinate

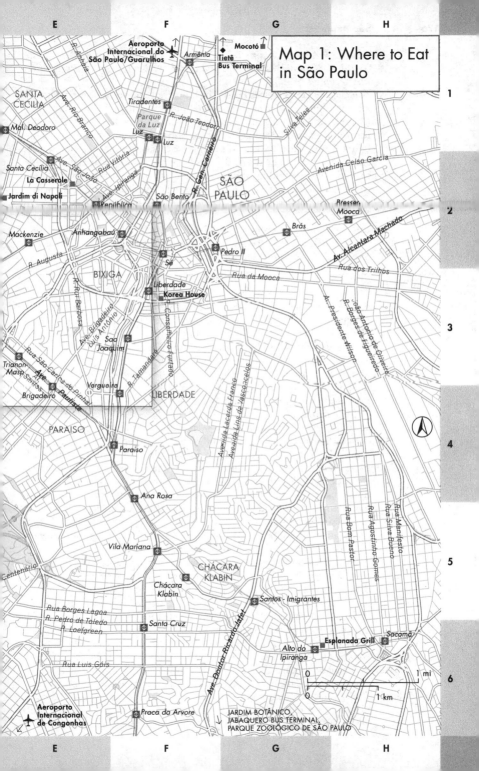

served. $ *Average main: R$80* ⊠ *Rua 13 de Maio 1004, Bela Vista* ☎ *011/3288–8502* ⊕ *www.pizzaria.com.br* ⊙ *No lunch* ♨ *Reservations not accepted* ✛ *2:C5.*

$$$$
BRAZILIAN

✕ **Templo da Carne Marcos Bassi.** The brainchild of the late Marcos Bassi, a former butcher turned restaurateur and radio host, Templo da Carne (Temple of Meat) makes no bones about its specialty. *Contrafilé* (sirloin) and famed Brazilian *picanha* (rump cap) are among the highlights. Unlike at all-you-can-eat churrascarias, dining here is an à la carte experience. The decor departs from the nostalgic interiors found in Bixiga's surrounding Italian cantinas without entirely abandoning the neighborhood's traditional coziness. The wait for a table regularly exceeds an hour, so try to arrive before your hunger peaks. You can fill the time perusing the emporium for wines and other items used in the restaurant. $ *Average main: R$150* ⊠ *Rua Treze de Maio 668, Bixiga* ☎ *011/3288–7045* ⊕ *www.marcosbassi.com.br* ⊙ *No dinner Sun.* ♨ *Reservations essential* ✛ *2:C5.*

CENTRO

$
CAFÉ

✕ **Café Girondino.** Photos of old São Paulo, a winding wooden bannister, and antique light fixtures transport Café Girondino's patrons back to the trolley-car era. On the ground floor is a coffee shop known for its espresso drinks and the wildly flavorful Miguel Couto (ice cream, espresso, bourbon, whipped cream, and cinnamon). Typical café fare and mouthwatering desserts are also served—the *arroz doce* (rice pudding) is among the city's best. (A saloon occupies the second floor, and a full restaurant is on the third.) $ *Average main: R$30* ⊠ *Rua Boa Vista 365, Centro* ☎ *011/3229–1287, 011/3229–4574* ⊕ *www.cafegirondino. com.br* ⊙ *No dinner weekends* Ⓜ *São Bento* ✛ *2:A6.*

$$$
FRENCH

✕ **La Casserole.** Facing a little Centro flower market, this romantic Parisian-style bistro has been around for five decades and has witnessed more than its share of wedding proposals. Surrounded by wood-paneled walls decorated with art that nods at famous French artists, you can dine on such delights as *gigot d'agneau aux soissons* (roast leg of lamb in its own juices, served with white beans), *canard à l'orange* (roast duck in an orange sauce), and cherry strudel. $ *Average main: R$50* ⊠ *Largo do Arouche 346, Centro* ☎ *011/3331–6283* ⊕ *www.lacasserole.com.br* ⊙ *Closed Mon. No dinner Sun.* Ⓜ *República* ✛ *1:E2.*

$
DELI

✕ **Estadão Bar & Lanches.** Quests for quick, cheap, and good food should start near São Paulo's origins at this greasy spoon that's open 24 hours a day. Estadão's recipe for staying in business for more than four decades is its succulent *pernil* (roast pork) sandwich, a staple of the local street-food scene. Depending on the hour, the clientele ranges from partygoers and bohemians to politicians and bus drivers. $ *Average main: R$25* ⊠ *Av. Nove de Julho 193, Centro* ☎ *011/3257–7121* ⊕ *www.estadaolanches. com.br* ♨ *Reservations not accepted* Ⓜ *Anhangabaú* ✛ *2:A6.*

$$$$
ITALIAN
Fodor's Choice
★

✕ **Famiglia Mancini.** This busy little cantina is well loved for both its cuisine and location. It's on an unforgettable restaurant-lined strip of Rua Avandhandava, where you may find yourself admiring the cobblestones on the street as you wait for a table. An incredible buffet with cheeses, olives, sausages, and much more makes finding a tasty appetizer a cinch. The menu has many terrific pasta options, such as the cannelloni with palm hearts and a four-cheese sauce. All dishes serve two people. [$] *Average main: R$120* ✉ *Rua Avanhandava 81, Centro* ☎ *011/3256–4320* 🌐 *www.famigliamancini.com.br* ✍ *Reservations not accepted* [M] *Anhangabaú* ✥ *2:A5.*

$$$$ ITALIAN 🍴 **Gigetto.** When the menu of this São Paulo classic was slimmed down a few years back, dedicated locals successfully lobbied to have its more than 150 delicious options restored. Try the cappelletti *à romanesca* (pasta with chopped ham, peas, mushrooms, and white cream sauce), osso buco with polenta, or the popular *cabrito com batata e brócolis* (baby goat with potatoes and broccoli). Main courses serve two people. [$] *Average main: R$90* ✉ *Rua Avanhandava 63, Centro* ☎ *011/3256–9804* 🌐 *www.gigetto.com.br* [M] *Anhangabaú* ✥ *2:A5.*

4

CERQUEIRA CÉSAR

$ PIZZA 🍴 **Pedaço da Pizza.** At one of São Paulo's few pizzerias where you can order by the slice (R$6), the options for toppings range from pepperoni and other traditional favorites to shimeji mushrooms, kale, and other innovative ingredients. Open until 4 am on Friday and Saturday night, this is a good place to stop after clubbing. [$] *Average main: R$30* ✉ *Rua Augusta 1463, Cerqueira César* ☎ *011/3061–0004* 🌐 *www.opedacodapizza.com.br* 🕒 *No lunch Sun.* [M] *Consolação* ✥ *2:D2.*

$$$$ ECLECTIC 🍴 **Spot.** A few blocks west of MASP, this quaint yet futuristic glass-encased diner occupies a lonely single-story building tucked between government skyscrapers. Entrées—Argentine beef is a favorite—don't come with sides, so you'll have to order a dish such as rice with broccoli to fill the plate. Come early if you want to eat—as the night wears on, the extensive drink menu becomes the focus of partying patrons. [$] *Average main: R$70* ✉ *Alameda Rocha Azevedo 72, Cerqueira César* ☎ *011/3284–6131* 🌐 *www.restaurantespot.com.br* [M] *Consolação or Trianon-Masp* ✥ *2:C4.*

$$$$ BRAZILIAN 🍴 **Tordesilhas.** Typically Brazilian from its decor to its daily specials, rustic-elegant Tordesilhas prides itself on spotlighting recipes from across the republic. Feijoada takes center stage on Wednesdays and Saturdays, while a Brazilian tasting menu is served from Tuesday through Saturday. Among the daily staples you'll find *tacacá* (shrimp soup), from Brazil's northern region, and *moqueca* (fish and shrimp stew), from Espírito Santo State. [$] *Average main: R$80* ✉ *Alameda Tietê 489, Cerqueira César* ☎ *011/3107–7444* 🌐 *www.tordesilhas.com* 🕒 *Closed Mon. No lunch weekdays. No dinner Sun.* [M] *Paulista* ✥ *2:C3.*

CONSOLAÇÃO

$$$$ ECLECTIC 🍴 **Mestiço.** Even the fabulous people have to hang at the bar before being shown to a table in this large, sleek dining room; but especially for vegetarians, dishes such as the tofu and vegetable curry make the wait worthwhile. The restaurant makes a point of using free-range chicken and other ecologically responsible ingredients. The decidedly eclectic menu includes Italian, Brazilian, Bahian, and even Thai cuisine. [$] *Average main: R$80* ✉ *Rua Fernando de Albuquerque 277, Consolação*

☎ 011/3256–3165 🌐 *www.mestico.com.br* ✍ *Reservations essential* [M] *Consolação* ✥ *2:B3.*

$$$ BRAZILIAN 🍴 **Sujinho–Bisteca d'Ouro.** Occupying corners on both sides of the street, the modest Sujinho honors its roots as an informal bar by serving churrasco without any frills: this is the perfect place for diners craving a gorgeous piece of meat to down with a cold bottle of beer. The portions are so Jurassic in size that one dish can usually feed two. Sujinho stays open until 5 am, making it a leading stop on the post-bar circuit. [$] *Average main: R$50* ✉ *Rua da Consolação 2078, Cerqueira César* ☎ *011/3231–1299* 🌐 *www.sujinho.com.br* 💳 *No credit cards* [M] *Consolação or Paulista* ✥ *2:B3.*

MEAL TIME

Eating out in São Paulo can be an all-night affair, so most restaurants open late and close even later. The majority will officially throw their doors open around 8 pm but will only get busy after 9 pm, regardless of what day it is. Try a bar that has a good happy hour if you want to eat earlier.

$$$$ FRENCH 🍴 **La Tartine.** An ideal place for an intimate dinner, this small bistro has a good wine selection and an upstairs bar furnished with mismatched sofas and armchairs. The menu changes daily; a favorite is the classic coq au vin, but you can also fill up on entrées such as beef tenderloin, pasta, soups, and quiches. The frogs' legs come off like a Tangier-style chicken wing. If Moroccan couscous is being served, don't pass it up. The trendy set loves La Tartine; on weekends you might have to wait a bit to get a table. [$] *Average main: R$65* ✉ *Rua Fernando de Albuquerque 267, Consolação* ☎ *011/3259–2090* ⏲ *Closed Sun. No lunch* [M] *Consolação* ✥ *2:B3.*

HIGIENÓPOLIS

$$$$ CONTEMPORARY 🍴 **Carlota.** TV host, author, and chef Carla Pernambuco introduces Brazilian elements to a multicultural array of recipes at her popular restaurant. The four-cheese polenta and the red-rice risotto with lobster are among the many well-calibrated dishes served here. All-white brick walls outside and inside lend Carlota a soothing, stylish feel. The clientele, befitting the neighborhood's demographics, tends to be older than elsewhere in town. Save room for the signature dessert, a guava jam soufflé with melted-cheese sauce. [$] *Average main: R$95* ✉ *Rua Sergipe 753, Higienópolis* ☎ *011/3661–8670* 🌐 *carlota.com.br* ⏲ *No dinner weekends. Closed Mon.* ✥ *2:A3.*

$$$$ ITALIAN 🍴 **Jardim di Napoli.** The classic neon sign that adorns this restaurant's exterior cues diners about what to expect inside: traditional Italian cuisine. No surprises here, but dishes such as the unchanging and unmatchable *polpettone alla parmigiana,* a huge meatball with mozzarella and tomato sauce, inspire devotion among the local clientele. Many other meat dishes can be found on the menu, along with pastas and pizzas. [$] *Average main: R$70* ✉ *Rua Doutor Martinico Prado 463, Higienópolis* ☎ *011/3666–3022* 🌐 *www.jardimdenapoli.com.br* ✥ *1:E2.*

$$$$ PIZZA Fodor's Choice ★ 🍴 **Veridiana.** Owner Roberto Loscalzo transformed a 1903 mansion into a remarkable dining space; expansive yet intimate, grandiose yet welcoming. At one end of the room chefs pull Napoli-style pizzas from the three mouths of a two-story brick oven that looms over diners like a

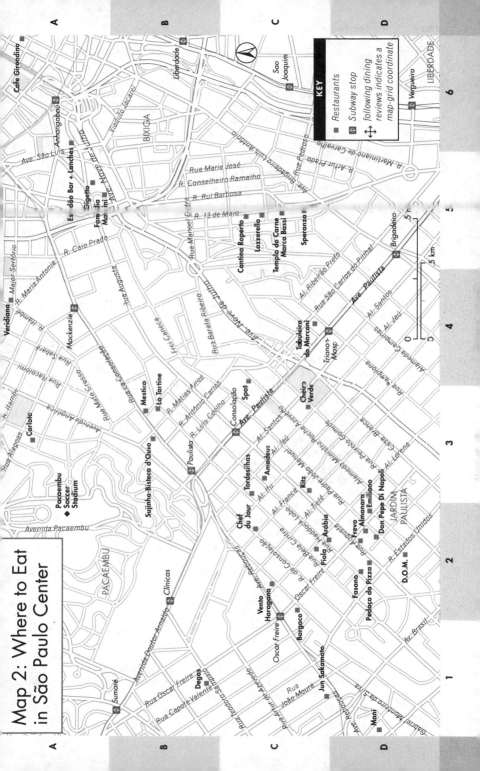

Map 2: Where to Eat in São Paulo Center

KEY

■ Restaurants

■ Subway stop

↔ following dining reviews indicates a map-grid coordinate

Café Girondino

Liberdade

São Joaquim

BIXIGA

LIBERDADE

Vergueiro

Estádão Bar + Lanches
Gigetto
Família Mancini
Anhangabaú
Ave. São Luís

Rua Maria José
R. Conselheiro Ramalho
R. Rui Barbosa
R. 13 de Maio

Cantina Roperto
Lazzerella
Templo da Carne
Marco Bassi
Speranza

Veridiana
R. Maria Antonia
Mackenzie
R. Caio Prado

R. Martiniano de Carvalho
Ave. Brigadeiro Luís Antônio
Ave. Arthur Prado
Rua Pedroso

Carlota
R. Itambé
Rua Sabará
Rua Maceió

Mestico
La Tartine
R. Matias Aires
R. Antônio Carlos
R. Luís Coelho
Consolação

Tabuleiro
do Marconi

Brigadeiro

Sujinho-Bisteca d'Ouro
Paulista
Ave. Paulista
Spot
Ave. Paulista

Al. Ribeirão Preto
Rua São Carlos do Pinhal
Ave. Paulista

Al. Santos
Al. Jaú

Cheiro
Verde

Trianon-Masp

Alameda Campinas

PACAEMBU

Pacaembu Soccer Stadium
◆

Avenida Pacaembu

Clínicas

Tordesilhas
Amadeus
Al. Itu

Ritz
Al. Tietê

Al. Santos
Al. Jaú
Al. Lorena

Alameda Ministro Rocha Azevedo
Rua Peixoto Gomide
Casa Branca

Rua Pádre João Manuel

Chef
du Jour

Al. França

Rua Haddock Lobo
Al. Itu
Piola
Arábia

Frevo
Almanara
Emiliano
Don Pepe Di Napoli

JARDIM PAULISTA

R. Estados Unidos

D.O.M.

Avenida Doutor Arnaldo

Sumaré

Rua Oscar Freire
Degas
Rua Capote Valente

Vento
Haragano

Bargaço
Oscar Freire

Fasano
Pedaço da Pizza

Av. Brasil

Jun Sakamoto

Mani

Rua João Moura

Rua Artur de Azevedo
Rua Henrique Schaumann
Rua Gabriel Monteiro da Silva

0   5 km
0   5 mi

cathedral organ. Different place-names lead to different taste combinations: Napoli in Beruit blends goat cheese and za'atar, a spice mixture that includes herbs and sesame seeds, while Napoli in Brasili contains sun-dried meat and Catupiry, the creamy Brazilian cheese invented in Minas Gerais a century ago. If you don't feel like globe-trotting, go for the Do Nonno, topped with juicy grilled tomatoes. A sister branch of Veridiana operates in the Jardins neighborhood. The Higienópolis location is not well marked. The restaurant is directly across from the Iate Clube (Yacht Club) de Santos. $ *Average main: R$70* ⊠ *Rua Dona Veridiana 661, Higienópolis* ☎ *011/3120–5050* ⊕ *www.veridiana.com. br* ☉ *Closed Sun. No lunch* Ⓜ *Santa Cecilia* ✛ *2:A4.*

ITAIM BIBI

$$$$
BRAZILIAN
✕ **Baby Beef Rubaiyat.** The family that owns and runs this restaurant serves meat from its ranch in Mato Grosso do Sul State. Charcoal-grilled fare—baby boar (request at least two hours in advance of your visit), steak, chicken, salmon, and more—is served at the buffet, and options abound at the salad bar. Wednesday and Saturday are feijoada nights, and on Friday the emphasis is on seafood. $ *Average main: R$150* ⊠ *Av. Brigadeiro Faria Lima 2954, Itaim Bibi* ☎ *011/3165– 8888* ⊕ *www.rubaiyat.com.br* ☉ *No dinner Sun.* Ⓜ *Faria Lima* ✛ *1:C5.*

$$
BRAZILIAN
✕ **Bar do Juarez.** With the look of an old-style saloon, Bar do Juarez has won awards for its draft beers and buffet of *petiscos* (small tapas-like dishes), but *picanha* (rump cap of beef) is this gastropub's calling card. Served raw on a mini-grill, the platter is perfect for small groups and gives individuals direct control over how their meat is done. Bow-tied waiters with A-plus attentiveness add to Juarez's appeal. The Itaim location is the best of four in the city, with the Moema, Pinheiros, and Brooklin houses coming close. $ *Average main: R$40* ⊠ *Av. Pres. Juscelino Kubitschek 1164, Itaim Bibi* ☎ *011/3078–3458* ⊕ *www. bardojuarez.com.br* ☉ *No lunch weekdays* ✛ *1:D6.*

$$$$
EUROPEAN
✕ **Cantaloup.** That paulistanos take food seriously has not been lost on the folks at Cantaloup. The converted warehouse has two dining areas: oversize photos decorate the walls of the slightly formal room, while a fountain and plants make the second area feel more casual. Try the veal cutlet with blinis of yucca or the stuffed shrimp with clams. Save room for macerated strawberries in port wine sauce or a particularly velvety crème brûlée with ice cream. $ *Average main: R$130* ⊠ *Rua Manoel Guedes 474, Itaim Bibi* ☎ *011/3078–9884, 011/3078–3445* ⊕ *www. cantaloup.com.br* ☉ *No dinner Sun.* ✛ *1:C5.*

$$$$
FRENCH
✕ **Freddy.** A pioneer in bringing French cuisine to São Paulo, Freddy opened originally in 1935. Despite moving from its original location, Freddy has managed to retain the feel of an upscale Parisian bistro, thanks to a number of small touches as well as some larger ones, like the grand chandeliers hanging from its ceiling. Try the duck with Madeira sauce and apple purée, coq au vin, or the hearty cassoulet with white beans, lamb, duck, and garlic sausage. $ *Average main: R$100* ⊠ *Rua Pedroso Alvarenga 1170, Itaim Bibi* ☎ *011/3167–0977* ⊕ *www. restaurantefreddy.com.br* ☉ *No dinner Sun. No lunch Sat.* ✛ *1:C5.*

$$$$ JAPANESE 🍴**Nagayama.** Low-key, dependable, and well loved, Nagayama consistently serves excellent sushi and sashimi. The chefs like to experiment: the California *uramaki* Philadelphia has rice, cream cheese, grilled salmon, roe, cucumber, and spring onions rolled together. [$] *Average main: R$110* ✉ *Rua Bandeira Paulista 369, Itaim Bibi* ☎ *011/3079–7553* 🌐 *www.nagayama.com.br* ⏰ *Closed Sun.* ✣ *1:C5.*

$$$$ ECLECTIC 🍴**La Tambouille.** This Italo-French restaurant with a partially enclosed garden isn't just a place for businesspeople and impresarios to see and be seen; it also has some of the best food in town. Among chef Giancarlo Bolla's recommended dishes are the linguine with fresh mussels and prawn sauce, the eggplant Parmesan, and the filet mignon *rosini* (served with foie gras and saffron risotto). [$] *Average main: R$100* ✉ *Av. Nove de Julho 5925, Itaim Bibi* ☎ *011/3079–6277, 011/3079–6276* 🌐 *www.tambouille.com.br* ✣ *1:C4.*

A TASTE OF LEBANON

While in São Paulo, be sure to try a *beirute*, a Lebanese sandwich served hot on toasted Syrian bread and filled with roast beef, cheese, lettuce, and tomato. Another quick bite from Lebanon that has established itself in the city is *esfiha*, an open-faced pastry topped with cheese or spiced meat. Fast-food restaurants serving these snacks are scattered around the city.

JARDINS

$$$ LEBANESE 🍴**Almanara.** Part of a chain of Lebanese semifast-food outlets, Almanara is perfect for a quick lunch of hummus, tabbouleh, grilled chicken, and rice. A full-blown restaurant also on the premises offers up Lebanese specialties *rodízio* style, meaning you're served continuously until you can ingest no more. [$] *Average main: R$60* ✉ *Rua Oscar Freire 523, Jardins* ☎ *011/3085–6916* 🌐 *www.almanara.com.br* ✣ *2:D2.*

$$$$ SEAFOOD 🍴**Amadeus.** Because São Paulo isn't on the ocean, most restaurants here don't base their reputations on seafood, but Amadeus is an exception. Appetizers such as fresh oysters and salmon and endive with mustard, and entrées like shrimp in cognac sauce make it a challenge to find better fruits of the sea elsewhere in town. The restaurant is popular with the business-lunch crowd. [$] *Average main: R$100* ✉ *Rua Haddock Lobo 807, Jardins* ☎ *011/3061–2859* 🌐 *restauranteamadeus.com.br* ⏰ *No dinner Sun.* [M] *Consolação* ✣ *2:C3.*

$$$$ LEBANESE 🍴**Arábia.** For almost 20 years Arábia has served traditional Lebanese cuisine at this beautiful high-ceilinged restaurant. Simple dishes such as hummus and stuffed grape leaves are executed with aplomb, and the lamb melts in your mouth. Meat-stuffed artichokes are great for sharing, and the reasonably priced "executive" lunch menu includes one appetizer, one cold dish, one meat dish, a drink, dessert, and coffee. Don't miss the crepe-like *ataife*, filled with pistachio nuts or cream, for dessert. [$] *Average main: R$70* ✉ *Rua Haddock Lobo 1397, Jardins* ☎ *011/3061–2203* 🌐 *www.arabia.com.br* ✣ *2:D2.*

$$$ ECLECTIC 🍴**Chef du Jour.** Despite the name, there's indeed a permanent chef installed here: Renato Frias, who hails from the state of Pernambuco, though his cuisine straddles France and Italy. Take your pick from a vast buffet with more than 30 different salads, along with sushi, risottos and pastas, and fish and meat dishes. Colorful tiles decorate the spacious dining room. [$] *Average main: R$60* ✉ *Rua da Consolação 3101, Jardins* ☎ *011/3845–6843* 🕒 *No dinner. Closed Sun.* ✥ *2:C2.*

$ VEGETARIAN 🍴 **Cheiro Verde.** A São Paulo pioneer in meat-free dining, Cheiro Verde has attracted a devoted following over the past three decades for its simple but tasty vegetarian fare. (One couple fancied the restaurant so much they ended up buying it.) Whole-wheat mushroom pasta and delicious empanadas are among the many good bets here. [$] *Average main: R$30* ✉ *Rua Peixoto Gomide 1078, Jardim Paulista* ☎ *011/3289–6853* 🌐 *www.cheiroverderestaurante.com.br* 🕒 *No dinner. Closed Sun.* [M] *Trianon-MASP* ✥ *2:C3.*

$$$$ CONTEMPORARY 🍴 **D.O.M.** Regularly named among the best restaurants in South America and the world, D.O.M. is synonymous with exclusivity in São Paulo's gastronomic circles—its popularity is limited only by a self-imposed cap on the number of customers served. This is some of the finest food to be had on the continent, with prices as dizzying as celebrity chef Alex Atala's inspired cooking. The focus is on Brazilian fare with added flair, such as *filhote* (Amazonian catfish) with tapioca in *tucupi* (manioc root) sauce and sweet potato in a Béarnaise made from maté, a South American tea. Try the tapas-esque tasting menu for the full, unforgettable experience, at R$380 for four courses, or R$527 for eight. Make your reservations at least a week in advance. [$] *Average main: R$250* ✉ *Rua Barão de Capanema 549, Jardins* ☎ *011/3088–0761* 🌐 *www.domrestaurante.com.br* 🕒 *Closed Sun. No lunch Sat.* ✍ *Reservations essential* ✥ *2:D2.*

$$$$ ITALIAN 🍴 **Don Pepe Di Napoli.** Good and simple Italian food is what you'll find at this traditional spot. Choose from a great variety of pastas, salads, and meat dishes. A good option is *talharina a Don Pepe,* pasta with meat, broccoli, and garlic. [$] *Average main: R$70* ✉ *Rua Padre Joao Manoel 1104, Jardins* ☎ *011/3081–4080* 🌐 *www.donpepedinapoli.com.br* ✥ *2:D2.*

$$$$ ITALIAN 🍴 **Fasano.** A family-owned Northern Italian classic tucked away behind the elegantly modern lobby of the hotel of the same name, this restaurant is as famous for its superior cuisine as for its exorbitant prices. The luxe decor oozes class—marble, mahogany, and mirrors, all crowned by a breathtaking skylight—and suggests that proof of one's captainship of industry or other such mastery of the universe must be shown at the door for entrance. In the kitchen, a 20-strong brigade of chefs, butchers, and bakers commanded by Luca Gozzani sends out exquisite, sinfully rich dishes like agnollottis of Angola chicken on heart-of-mozzarella cream. [$] *Average main: R$120* ✉ *Rua Vittorio Fasano 88, Jardins* ☎ *011/3062–4000* 🌐 *www.fasano.com.br* 🕒 *Closed Sun. No lunch* ✍ *Reservations essential* ✥ *2:D2.*

$ BRAZILIAN 🍴 **Frevo.** Paulistanos of all types and ages flock to this luncheonette on the stylish Rua Oscar Freire for its *beirute* sandwiches, filled with ham and cheese, tuna, or chicken, and for its draft beer and fruit juices in flavors such as *acerola* (Antilles cherry), passion fruit, and papaya. [$] *Average main: R$30* ✉ *Rua Oscar Freire 603, Jardins* ☎ *011/3082–3434, 011/4003–2665 delivery* 🌐 *www.frevinho.com.br* ✥ *2:D2.*

> **PURPLE POWER**
>
> Açai, an antioxidant-rich super fruit, has recently made its way to juice bars around the world. Don't miss your chance to get it close to the source, where it's cheaper and purer than the versions you'll find back home. Always frozen, scoops of it are blended together with syrup of the energy-filled guaraná berry. The most popular way to get it is *na tigela*, in a glass bowl with bananas and granola, though juice stands dedicated to the fruit should serve up a pure milk-shake-thick *suco* (juice) as well.

$$$ CONTEMPORARY Fodor's Choice ★ 🍴**Maní.** With world-class chef-proprietor Helena Rizzo at the helm, Maní has made its way to the top of the restaurant charts in São Paulo. A sophisticated take on Brazilian country cuisine meshed with modern cooking techniques, dishes like chicken and rice with okra might not sound like much, but one bite will be enough to explain why local and visiting foodies beat a path to Maní's door. Go for the tasting menu (R$195) or for the great-value lunch platters (around R$40). [$] *Average main: R$50* ✉ *Rua Joaquim Antunes 210, Jardins* ☎ *011/3085-4148* 🌐 *www.manimanioca.com.br* ⏲ *Closed Mon. No dinner Sun.* [M] *Faria Lima* ✣ *2:D1.*

$$$ PIZZA FAMILY 🍴**Piola.** Part of a chain started in Italy, this restaurant serves pizzas loaded with toppings like Gorgonzola, Brie, ham, salami, mushrooms, and anchovies. It also has good pasta dishes, like the penne with smoked salmon in a creamy tomato sauce. The young, hip crowd matches the trendy contemporary decor, and there's also a recreational area for kids to play while the grown ups finish their meals. [$] *Average main: R$55* ✉ *Alameda Lorena 1765, Jardins* ☎ *011/3064–6570, 011/3061–2221 delivery* 🌐 *www.piola.com.br* ⏲ *No lunch* ✣ *2:C2.*

$$ PIZZA 🍴**Pizzaria Camelo.** Though it's neither fancy nor beautiful, Pizzaria Camelo has kept paulistanos enthralled for ages with its many thin-crust pies. The *chopp* (draft beer) is great, too. Avoid Sunday night unless you're willing to wait an hour for a table. [$] *Average main: R$45* ✉ *Rua Pamplona 1873, Jardins* ☎ *011/3887–8764* 🌐 *www.pizzariacamelo.com.br* ⏲ *No lunch* ✣ *1:D4.*

$$ ECLECTIC 🍴**Ritz.** An animated, gay-friendly crowd chatters at this restaurant with Italian, Brazilian, French, and mixed cuisine, as contemporary pop music plays in the background. Although Ritz serves some of the best hamburgers in the city, another popular dish is *bife à milanesa* (breaded beef cutlet) with creamed spinach and french fries. [$] *Average main: R$40* ✉ *Alameda Franca 1088, Jardins* ☎ *011/3088–6808 delivery, 011/3062–5830* 🌐 *www.restauranteritz.com.br* ⏲ *No dinner Mon.–Wed.* [M] *Consolação* ✣ *2:C3.*

LIBERDADE

$$$ KOREAN 🍴**Korea House.** Camper cooking meets Korean at this Liberdade mainstay. For the *bul go gui* (Korean barbecue), diners blend raw meat, spices, sauces, and veggies and cook them over small, do-it-yourself gas stoves. One order feeds two. You can prepare other Korean dishes, and there are Chinese options, including several involving tofu. Everything is reasonably priced. The design is unimpressive but the atmosphere is lively, with hipsters and gringos sprinkled among neighborhood

residents. $ *Average main: R$60* ✉ *Rua Galvão Bueno 43, 1° andar, Liberdade* ☎ *011/3208–3052* ◷ *Closed Wed.* Ⓜ *Liberdade* ✛ *1:F3.*

MOEMA

$$$
PIZZA
Fodor's Choice
★
✕ **Bráz.** This restaurant's name comes from one of the most traditional Italian neighborhoods in São Paulo, and no one argues that Bráz doesn't have the right. The pies are of a medium thickness with high, bubbly crusts. And each of the nearly 20 varieties is delicious, from the traditional margherita to the house specialty, pizza *Bráz,* with tomato sauce, zucchini, and mozzarella and Parmesan cheeses. The *chopp* (draft beer) is also very good. Reservations aren't accepted on weekends. $ *Average main: R$60* ✉ *Rua Graúna 125, Moema* ☎ *011/5561–1736* ⊕ *www. brazpizzaria.com.br* ◷ *No lunch* ✛ *1:D6.*

$$$
BRAZILIAN
✕ **Dona Lucinha.** Mineiro dishes are the specialties at this modest eatery with plain wooden tables. The classic cuisine is served as a buffet only: more than 50 stone pots hold dishes like *feijão tropeiro* (beans with manioc flour) and *frango com quiabo* (chicken with okra). Save room for a dessert of ambrosia. The menu is in English, French, and Spanish. $ *Average main: R$60* ✉ *Av. Chibarás 399, Moema* ☎ *011/5051–2050* ⊕ *www.donalucinha.com.br* ◷ *Closed Mon. No dinner Sun.* ✛ *1:D6.*

$$$
JAPANESE
Fodor's Choice
★
✕ **Kinoshita.** Contemporary Japanese plates with international influences are the draw at Kinoshita, where foie gras might accompany a Kobe beef hamburger or truffles might enliven salmon roe and shellfish. The freshness of the ingredients available on any given day determines the fare of chef Tsuyoshi Murakami, one of São Paulo's culinary superstars. Geishas serve guests in the Krug Room (available only for groups of 6 to 12), where slippers replace shoes and diners sit on floor mats. For a real, if pricey, treat opt for one of the *omakase* (tasting) menus—seven or nine courses, plus dessert—and let chef Murakami decide what you eat. $ *Average main: R$50* ✉ *Rua Jacques Félix 405, Moema* ☎ *011/3849– 6940, 011/5318–9014* ⊕ *restaurantekinoshita.com.br* ◷ *Closed Sun.* ⌘ *Reservations essential* ✛ *1:D5.*

MORUMBI

$$$
BRAZILIAN
✕ **Esplanada Grill.** The beautiful people hang out in the bar of this highly regarded churrascaria. The thinly sliced *picanha* (similar to rump steak) is excellent; it goes well with a house salad (hearts of palm and shredded, fried potatoes), onion rings, and creamed spinach. The version of the traditional *pão de queijo* (cheese bread) served here is widely viewed as among the city's best. $ *Average main: R$50* ✉ *Morumbi Shopping Center, Av. Roque Petroni Jr. 1089, Morumbi* ☎ *011/5181–8156* ✛ *1:G6.*

PINHEIROS

$$$$
BRAZILIAN
Fodor's Choice
★
✕ **Consulado Mineiro.** During and after the Saturday crafts and antiques fair in Praça Benedito Calixto, it may take an hour to get a table at this homey restaurant. Among the shareable, traditional *mineiro* (from Minas Gerais State) dishes are the *mandioca com carne de sol* (cassava

with salted meat) appetizer and the *tutu* (pork loin with beans, pasta, cabbage, and rice) entrée. The cachaça menu is extensive, with rare, premium, and homemade brands of the sugarcane-based spirits, and several types of *batidas* (fruit-and-alcohol mixtures) and caipirinhas are served. [$] *Average main: R$70* ✉ *Rua Praça Benedito Calixto 74, Pinheiros* ☎ *011/3064–3882* 🌐 *www.consuladomineiro.com.br* ⏲ *Closed Mon.* ✥ *1:C3.*

WOK THIS WAY

In a street-food scene dominated by hamburgers and hot dogs, Yakisoba stands out—keep an eye peeled for the spectacle of stir-fried noodles tossed over an open flame in the middle of the crowded sidewalk. Another delicious option is homemade *espetinhos* or *churrascos*, wooden kebabs of beef, chicken, or pork whose juices send towers of fragrant smoke into the air. A calmer alternative is the corn cart. Rather than on the cob, try *pamonha*, steam-cooked sweetened cornmeal wrapped in a husk, or *curau*, sweet creamed corn.

$$ ITALIAN FAMILY
🍴 **Degas.** Humble-looking Degas owes its more than 50 years in existence to word-of-mouth among the residents of São Paulo's western neighborhoods. Its famed filet mignon Parmigiana has gained near-legendary status, attracting foodies from across the city. The dish, along with almost anything else on the menu, easily feeds two, if not a family of four. Even the salads seem to be small vegetable gardens on a platter. Lunchtime usually brings a business crowd. Dinner, when the restaurant fires up its pizza ovens, is more of a family affair. [$] *Average main: R$35* ✉ *Rua Teodoro Sampaio 568, Pinheiros* ☎ *011/3062–1276, 011/3085–3545* 🌐 *www.degasrestaurante.com.br* [M] *Clinicas* ✥ *2:B1.*

$$ ITALIAN **Fodor's Choice** ★
🍴 **Ella.** A diminutive restaurant tucked away on a nondescript Pinheiros street, Ella is all about the simple pleasure of fresh homemade pasta, risotto, and the like, with a fantastic-value executive lunch menu, at R$37 for three courses. Try the ruby-red beetroot tortelloni with sage and ricotta. [$] *Average main: R$45* ✉ *Rua Costa Carvalho 138, Pinheiros* ☎ *011/3034–1267* ⏲ *Closed Mon. No dinner Sun.* [M] *Pinheiros* ✥ *1:B3.*

$$$ PIZZA
🍴 **I Vitelloni.** At perhaps the most creative pizza restaurant in town, owner Hamilton Mello Júnior combines disparate ingredients for his specialty pies, while serving up tasty classics as well. In the Pinheiros neighborhood, lively at night, the restaurant sits on a quiet residential street, away from the sidewalk bars an avenue away, so it's prized by locals and well worth searching out. We recommend the authentic arugula pie. There's a stand-up bar outside that's a nice place to finish your drinks before you head off. [$] *Average main: R$50* ✉ *Rua Conde Sílvio Álvares Penteado 31, Pinheiros* ☎ *011/3819–0735* 🌐 *www.ivitelloni.com.br* ⏲ *No lunch. Closed Mon.* ✥ *1:B3.*

$$$ JAPANESE **Fodor's Choice** ★
🍴 **Jun Sakamoto.** Arguably the best Japanese restaurant in a town famous for them, Jun Sakamoto stands out for serving fish of the highest quality and for employing the most skillful of sushi chefs to slice them. This is haute gastronomy at its haughtiest. You're best served if you let the waiters wearing futuristic earpieces guide you through the menu based

on what's freshest the day you visit. 🟨 *Average main: R$60* ⊠ *Rua Lisboa 55, Pinheiros* ☎ *011/3088–6019* ⊗ *No lunch. Closed Sun.* ✛ *2:C1.*

$$$$ ✗**Vento Haragano.** São Paulo has a certain fame for its all-you-can-eat
BARBECUE steak houses. Vento Haragano, just a few blocks from Avenida Paulista,
Fodors Choice has the best location in town, attentive staff in slightly kitsch historic-
★ reenactment-style garb, and a truly magnificent salad bar. And, naturally, a never-ending parade of succulent meat, served table-side until you cry uncle. 🟨 *Average main: R$116* ⊠ *Av. Rebouças 1001, Pinheiros* ☎ *011/3083-4265* ⊕ *www.ventoharagano.com.br* Ⓜ *Consolação* ✛ *2:C2.*

POMPÉIA

$ ✗**Central das Artes.** Come for the view, stay for the crepes. Or vice
ECLECTIC versa. A back wall made of windows faces out to a verdant valley and,
beyond that, Avenida Paulista. The panorama makes Central das Artes
a popular place to grab drinks as well. Crepes are named for famous
artists. The Cocteau, with salmon, shiitake, and cream, is as smooth on
the taste buds as its namesake was with the written word. 🟨 *Average
main: R$25* ⊠ *Rua Apinajés 1081, Pompéia* ☎ *011/3865–0116* ⊕ *www.
centraldasartes.com.br* ✛ *1:C2.*

VILA MADALENA

$$$ ✗**AK Vila.** Putting a premium on freshness, chef Andrea Kaufmann
CONTEMPORARY shifts her menu weekly to keep pace with seasonal ingredients. Her
restaurant's multicultural, contemporary cuisine ranges from salads and
sandwiches to ceviche and octopus couscous. The chef made her name
cooking Jewish favorites, and she often makes room on her menu for
bagels or salads with smoked salmon. A touch of the burlesque softens
AK Vila's industrial-sleek design. On nice nights, sit outside and soak
in the Vila Madalena scene. 🟨 *Average main: R$50* ⊠ *Rua Fradique
Coutinho 1240, Vila Madalena* ☎ *011/3231–4496, 011/3231–4497*
⊕ *www.akvila.com.br* ⊗ *No dinner Sun.–Mon.* ✛ *1:B3.*

$$$ ✗**Oficina de Pizzas.** This restaurant looks like something designed by the
PIZZA Spanish architect Gaudí had he spent his later years in the tropics, but
the pizzas couldn't be more Italian and straightforward. Try a pie with
mozzarella and toasted garlic. 🟨 *Average main: R$50* ⊠ *Rua Purpurina
517, Vila Madalena* ☎ *011/3816–3749* ⊕ *www.oficinadepizzas.com.br*
⊗ *No lunch* ✛ *1:B3.*

$$ ✗**Pé de Manga.** The restaurant's name and charm come from a mas-
BRAZILIAN sive mango tree. Tables surrounding the trunk spread across a shaded
patio, which is usually packed with professionals in their 30s and 40s.
A two-story covered seating area lends the whole affair a Robinson
Crusoe touch. High-end, Brazilian-style pub grub pads stomachs for Pé
de Manga's beers and caipirinhas. The feijoada buffet is a top option on
Saturdays. 🟨 *Average main: R$35* ⊠ *Rua Arapiraca 152, Vila Madalena*
☎ *011/3032–6068* ⊕ *www.pedemanga.com.br* ✛ *1:B3.*

VILA OLÍMPIA

$$$$ WINE BAR

🍴 **Enoteca Saint Vin Saint.** A snug bistro on as secluded a street as you're apt to find in São Paulo's hip southern neighborhoods, Enoteca triples as a wineshop, restaurant, and live-music venue. Marble-top tables fill two rooms brimming with bottle racks, bookshelves, and bullfighting posters. Friends and thirtysomething couples toast each other with an international array of wines, many from France, Spain, Italy, and Chile. The kitchen's specialty is a risotto with wine-braised beef whose taste more than compensates for its plain appearance. There's a $R15 cover for live tango, jazz, and flamenco music from Wednesday through Saturday night, but it's well worth it. [$] *Average main: R$100* ✉ *Rua Professor Atílio Innocenti 811, Vila Olímpia* ☎ *011/3846–0384* 🌐 *www.saintvinsaint.com.br* ⏲ *Closed Sun. No lunch Sat.* ✥ *1:C5.*

JAPANESE FRUIT

Along with the famous Japanese cuisine, which can be found just about everywhere in São Paulo, Brazil's Japanese immigrants are credited with introducing persimmons, azaleas, tangerines, and kiwis to Brazil.

$$$ CONTEMPORARY Fodor's Choice ★

🍴 **Kaá.** Contemporary cuisine, attentive service, and a luxurious, secret-garden charm help Kaá maintain its status as one of São Paulo's leading fine-dining establishments. The gorgeously designed restaurant, complete with fountains, a sunken bar, and a rain forest–like wall, attracts a mostly mature and well-to-do clientele. The crayfish au gratin in endive cream is a top choice among the appetizers; appealing entrées include rack of lamb ribs and beer-cooked duck. Though the wine list is extensive, many diners opt for the signature orchid martini. [$] *Average main: R$60* ✉ *Av. Presidente Juscelino Kubitschek 279, Vila Olímpia* ☎ *011/3045–0043* 🌐 *kaarestaurante.com.br* ⏲ *No dinner Sun.* ✥ *1:C5.*

$$ BRAZILIAN Fodor's Choice ★

🍴 **Mocotó.** This far-flung restaurant is an exceptional take on the classic boteco, run by the young, charismatic chef Rodrigo Olveira. Try his Northeastern Brazilian classics like *escondidinho*, a rich little meat-and-manioc pie, and don't miss the homemade *torresmo*, crunchy morsels of pork rind. [$] *Average main: R$40* ✉ *Av. Nossa Senhora do Loreto 1100* ☎ *011/2951-3056* 🌐 *www.mocoto.com.br* ⏲ *No dinner Sun.* ✥ *1:G1.*

$$ BRAZILIAN

🍴 **Tabuleiro do Marconi.** Owner Marconi Silva started his little slice of Bahia by selling *acarajé* (deep-fried bean balls usually stuffed with paste made from shrimp and other ingredients) on the sidewalk in front of where his restaurant now stands. Since moving indoors, he's expanded his menu to include favorites such as *escondidinho* (a lasagna-like dish with cheese, meat, and manioc) and shrimp risotto in a coconut shell. Kitsch is this tiny eatery's other calling card: keepsakes and curios line the walls. [$] *Average main: R$45* ✉ *Rua Ribeirão Claro 319, Vila Olímpia* ☎ *011/3846–9593* 🌐 *www.tabuleirodomarconi.com.br* ⏲ *Closed Mon.* ✥ *2:C4.*

WHERE TO STAY

São Paulo puts an emphasis on business, and for the most part so do its hotels. Most of them are near Avenida Paulista, along Marginal Pinheiros, or in the charming Jardins neighborhood, where international businesses are located. But catering to business doesn't mean they've forgotten about pleasure. On the contrary, if you're willing to pay for it, the city can match London or New York for unfettered elegance.

Because of the business influence, rates often drop on weekends. Breakfast is a sumptuous affair and is oftentimes included in the room rate. International conventions and the annual Brazilian Grand Prix in November can book hotels completely, so it's wise to make reservations in advance. *Hotel reviews have been shortened. For full information, visit Fodors.com.*

WHAT IT COSTS IN REAIS				
	$	$$	$$$	$$$$
FOR 2 PEOPLE	under R$251	R$251–R$375	R$376–R$500	over R$500

Hotel prices are the lowest cost of a standard double room in high season, excluding tax.

BELA VISTA

$ HOTEL **Ibis São Paulo Paulista.** One of the best bargains on Avenida Paulista, all rooms at this large hotel feature queen-size beds and contemporary decor, with the focus on function, not beauty. **Pros:** a nonaffiliated airport shuttle bus has a stop next door; close to major thoroughfares. **Cons:** heavy traffic all day long. [$] *Rooms from: R$229* ✉ *Av. Paulista 2355, Bela Vista* ☎ *011/3523–3000* 🌐 *www.ibishotel.com* 🛏 *236 rooms* 🍴 *No meals* [M] *Consolação or Paulista* ✥ *D3.*

$ HOTEL **San Gabriel.** Expect no frills at this budget hotel in a lively neighborhood close to Avenida Paulista—rooms are small (though there are some larger suites), but have all the basics and are clean, and the rates are unbeatable for this part of town. **Pros:** close to malls, bars, and restaurants; in-house convenience store. **Cons:** surrounding area isn't well lighted; room rate doesn't include breakfast; no Internet. [$] *Rooms from: R$172* ✉ *Rua Frei Caneca 1006, Bela Vista* ☎ *011/3253–2279* 🌐 *www.sangabriel.com.br* 🛏 *134 rooms* 🍴 *No meals* [M] *Consolação* ✥ *E3.*

BROOKLIN

$$ HOTEL **Hilton São Paulo Morumbi.** The brightest star in Brooklin and the hot spot of the São Paulo business world, this venue is one of three skyscrapers that form an office park loaded with Fortune 500 companies. **Pros:** attached by tunnel to D&D Shopping mall; art exhibits at Canvas Bar; spa uses treatments from the Amazon. **Cons:** far from anything cultural or historical; charge for Internet access. [$] *Rooms from: R$320* ✉ *Av. das Nações Unidas 12901, Torre Leste, Brooklin* ☎ *011/2845–0000* 🌐 *www.hiltonmorumbi.com.br* 🛏 *503 rooms, 13 suites* 🍴 *Breakfast* ✥ *B6.*

CENTRO

$$ HOTEL **Bourbon.** Rich woodwork runs at waist level throughout the halls of this small, classy hotel near Praça da República, just one block away from Largo do Arouche, a bar-lined square that sees a largely gay

crowd at night. **Pros:** great location for exploring Centro; next door to metro. **Cons:** small workstations; Praça da República can be dodgy at night. $ *Rooms from: R$290* ⊠ *Av. Vieira de Carvalho 99, Centro* 🏨 *011/3337-2000, 011/3331-8187, 011/3337-1414* ⊕ *www.bourbon. com.br* ⇨ *127 rooms* ⦿ *Breakfast* Ⓜ *República* ✛ *E2.*

$ 🖭 **Novotel São Paulo Jaraguá Conventions.** Built in 1951 to be the head-
HOTEL quarters of one of the main newspapers in the city, the building that now houses this hotel is a landmark in downtown São Paulo and has hosted Queen Elizabeth II, Fidel Castro, and Errol Flynn. **Pros:** pleasant rooms at good prices; close to many restaurants and sights; 10-minute taxi ride to Paulista. **Cons:** no pool; weak water pressure; area can be spooky at night. $ *Rooms from: R$250* ⊠ *Rua Martins Fontes 71, Centro* 🏨 *011/2802-7000* ⊕ *www.novotel.com.br* ⇨ *415 rooms, 99 suites* ⦿ *No meals* Ⓜ *Anhangabaú* ✛ *E2.*

CERQUEIRA CÉSAR

$$$$ 🖭 **Tivoli São Paulo–Mofarrej.** The five-star Tivoli Mofarrej reopened a
HOTEL few years ago after renovations that raised the standard of lavishness
Fodor'sChoice for São Paulo hotels. **Pros:** chance of meeting a prince or princess (lit-
★ erally); Thai spa's Rainmist Steam Bath; steps from Avenida Paulista. **Cons:** Wi-Fi access not included in price; extremely expensive. $ *Rooms from: R$720* ⊠ *Alameda Santos 1437, Cerqueira César* 🏨 *011/3146-5900* ⊕ *www.tivolihotels.com* ⇨ *220 rooms, 35 suites* ⦿ *No meals* Ⓜ *Tirianon-MASP* ✛ *D3.*

CONSOLAÇÃO

$ 🖭 **Ibis Budget.** With hotels at both ends of Paulista and other properties
HOTEL in Jardins, Morumbi, and the city center, the Ibis Budget (formerly the Formule 1) is a great choice if you value location and price over luxury. **Pros:** close to metro and convenience stores; perfect for travelers who plan to be out and about. **Cons:** unspectacular breakfast; often fully booked; no pool. $ *Rooms from: R$175* ⊠ *Rua da Consolação 2303, Consolação* 🏨 *011/3123-7755* ⊕ *www.ibisbudget.com* ⇨ *399 rooms* ⦿ *No meals* Ⓜ *Paulista* ✛ *D3.*

HIGIENÓPOLIS

$$ 🖭 **Hotel Ville.** In the lively Higienópolis neighborhood of apartment
HOTEL buildings, bars, and bookstores abutting Mackenzie University, this hotel has plain, clean rooms with little decoration. **Pros:** walking distance to shopping mall; supermarket next door is open until midnight; university campus is pretty. **Cons:** only one person at desk on weekends; heavy evening-rush-hour traffic. $ *Rooms from: R$290* ⊠ *Rua Dona Veridiana 643, Higienópolis* 🏨 *011/3257-5288* ⊕ *www.hotelville.com. br* ⇨ *56 rooms* ⦿ *Breakfast* Ⓜ *Santa Cecilia* ✛ *E2.*

$$$ 🖭 **Tryp Higienópolis.** Tucked imperceptibly among stately apartment
HOTEL buildings in one of the city's oldest and most attractive residential neighborhoods, this hotel built in 2000 has bright and spacious rooms with contemporary light-wood furnishings. **Pros:** cool half-indoor,

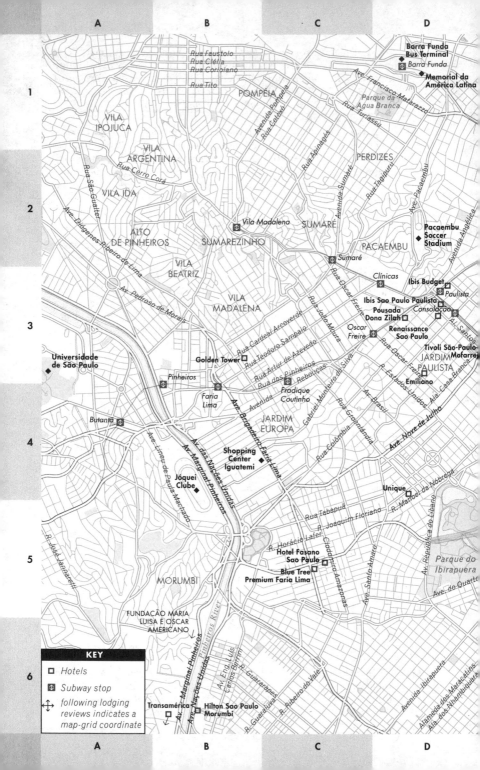

Where to Stay in São Paulo

half-outdoor pool; breakfast menu in Braille; 10-minute taxi ride from Centro. Cons: small bathrooms; boring furniture. $ *Rooms from: R$500* ✉ *Rua Maranhão 371, Higienópolis* ☎ *011/3665–8200, 0800/892–1356* ⊕ *www.melia.com* ➫ *207 rooms* ⎮○⎮ *No meals* Ⓜ *Paulista* ✢ *E2.*

ITAIM BIBI

$$ ⌗ **Blue Tree Premium Faria Lima.** Techno beats enliven the lobby of this
HOTEL chic business hotel halfway between Paulista and Brooklin whose rooms have clean lines and dark-wood furnishings that contrast with the bright-white walls and fabrics. Pros: courteous staff; on major thoroughfare close to many multinationals; close to restaurants. Cons: taxi needed to visit sights; heavy rush hour. $ *Rooms from: R$310* ✉ *Av. Brigadeiro Faria Lima 3989, Itaim Bibi* ☎ *011/3896–7544, 011/3896–7545* ⊕ *www. bluetree.com.br* ➫ *338 rooms* ⎮○⎮ *Breakfast* Ⓜ *Faria Lima* ✢ *C5.*

JARDINS

$$$$ ⌗ **Emiliano.** For pure luxury, the Emiliano would match any modern
HOTEL hotel in Europe's best cities: rooms are large, with blonde-wood floors and furnishings—including Eames lounge chairs—and creamy leather sofas and banquettes. Pros: on São Paulo's chicest avenue; pillow menus; complimentary wine bottles. Cons: stratospheric prices. $ *Rooms from: R$1,780* ✉ *Rua Oscar Freire 384, Jardins* ☎ *011/3069–4369* ⊕ *www.emiliano.com.br* ➫ *56 rooms, 19 suites* ⎮○⎮ *No meals* Ⓜ *Trianon-Masp* ✢ *D3.*

$$$$ ⌗ **Hotel Fasano São Paulo.** With a decor that hints at 1940s modern but
HOTEL is undeniably 21st-century chic, the Hotel Fasano caters to those for
Fodor'sChoice whom money is a mere detail. Pros: attentive, knowledgeable staff; top-
★ floor pool with stunning view. Cons: paying for it all. $ *Rooms from: R$1,240* ✉ *Rua Vittorio Fasano 88, Jardins* ☎ *011/3896–4000* ⊕ *www. fasano.com.br* ➫ *60 rooms, 10 suites* ⎮○⎮ *No meals* Ⓜ *Consolação* ✢ *C5.*

$$$$ ⌗ **L'Hotel Porto Bay São Paulo.** Compared to the top-of-the line chain
HOTEL hotels on Paulista, L'Hotel stands out as a truly special experience. Pros: small number of rooms makes for personalized service; L'Occitane bath products. Cons: expensive. $ *Rooms from: R$700* ✉ *Alameda Campinas 266, Jardins* ☎ *011/2183–0500, 011/2183–0505* ⊕ *www.lhotel. com.br* ➫ *83 rooms, 8 suites* ⎮○⎮ *Breakfast* Ⓜ *Trianon-MASP* ✢ *E3.*

$$$$ ⌗ **InterContinental São Paulo.** One of the city's most attractive top-tier
HOTEL establishments, the InterContinental consistently receives rave reviews because of the attention paid to every detail, including the pillows (guests choose among six different types). Pros: Japanese breakfast; PlayStation in rooms; gym with personal trainers. Cons: suites aren't much bigger than regular rooms. $ *Rooms from: R$941* ✉ *Alameda Santos 1123, Jardins* ☎ *011/3179–2600, 0800/770–0858, 011/3179–2666* ⊕ *www.intercontinental.com* ➫ *195 rooms, 38 suites* ⎮○⎮ *No meals* Ⓜ *Trianon-MASP* ✢ *E3.*

$$$ ⌗ **Maksoud Plaza.** Once the top choice for luxury accommodations in
HOTEL São Paulo, Maksoud must now share the bill with a bevy of high-end hotels; still, its facilities, comfort, and good location make it one of the best choices in the city. Pros: four full-service restaurants and five bars;

huge atrium. **Cons:** dingy exterior; rush-hour traffic. $ *Rooms from: R$400* ✉ *Alameda Campinas 1250, Jardins* ☎ *011/3145–8000, 888/551–1333 toll-free in U.S.* ⊕ *www.maksoud.com.br* ⟷ *416 rooms* ⟨○⟩ *Breakfast* Ⓜ *Trianon-MASP* ✛ *E3.*

$$ ⊡ **Pousada Dona Zilah.** Marvelously
B&B/INN located in the retail-heavy part of the Jardins district and easily navigable both to and from, this homey pousada, while not exactly cheap, might be a more affordable alternative if you're seeking to momentarily escape the skyscraper experience. **Pros:** close to Oscar Freire shopping; excellent breakfast. **Cons:** can be noisy. $ *Rooms from: R$275* ✉ *Alameda Franca 1621, Jardins* ☎ *011/3062–1444* ⊕ *www.zilah.com* ⟷ *14 rooms* ⟨○⟩ *Breakfast* Ⓜ *Paulista* ✛ *D3.*

MOTELS AND POUSADAS

If you check into a reasonably priced motel with the hope of humble-but-cheap lodging alternative, you may be surprised to find a heart-shape bed and strategically placed mirrors. Yes, motels in Brazil are specifically set aside for romantic rendezvous. The market is large because most unmarried people live with their parents until well into their 20s or 30s, not to mention the soap-opera lives that many Brazilians lead. If you're looking for a bed that doesn't vibrate, the name of what you seek is *pousada*.

$$$ ⊡ **Renaissance São Paulo.** In case the rooftop helipad doesn't say it all,
HOTEL the striking lines of the red-and-black granite lobby announce one serious business hotel. **Pros:** you never have to leave hotel; professional staff. **Cons:** Internet and breakfast aren't included; uninspired decor. $ *Rooms from: R$400* ✉ *Alameda Santos 2233, Jardins* ☎ *011/3069–2233, 888/236–2427 in U.S.* ⊕ *www.renaissancehotels.com* ⟷ *444 rooms, 56 suites, 45 club rooms* ⟨○⟩ *No meals* Ⓜ *Consolação* ✛ *D3.*

$$$$ ⊡ **Unique.** It's hard not see a familiar shape (some say watermelon, some
HOTEL say boat, but neither hits the mark) in the wild but harmonious design of
Fodor'sChoice this boutique hotel. **Pros:** steps from Ibirapuera Park and a taxi ride to
★ many top restaurants; attractive, modern design. **Cons:** nonstop techno music in public spaces; very expensive. $ *Rooms from: R$1,000* ✉ *Av. Brigadeiro Luís Antônio 4700, Jardins* ☎ *011/3055–4700, 011/3889–8100* ⊕ *www.unique.com.br* ⟷ *95 rooms* ⟨○⟩ *No meals* ✛ *D4.*

PINHEIROS

$$$ ⊡ **Golden Tower.** Its ideal location close to important hubs and to Vila
HOTEL Madalena and spacious rooms make this a good choice. **Pros:** close to Marginal Pinheiros; quiet neighborhood. **Cons:** far from Centro. $ *Rooms from: R$400* ✉ *Rua Deputado Lacerda Franco 148, Pinheiros* ☎ *011/3094–2200* ⊕ *www.goldentowerhotel.com.br* ⟷ *96 rooms, 8 suites* ⟨○⟩ *Breakfast* Ⓜ *Faria Lima* ✛ *B3.*

SANTO AMARO

$$$$ ⊡ **Transamérica.** Directly across the Pinheiros River from the Centro
HOTEL Empresarial office complex, the home of many U.S. companies, this hotel is a convenient choice for those working in the area. **Pros:** great

location for business travelers; free Wi-Fi; tennis courts; 3-hole chip-and-putt golf course. **Cons:** Pinheiros River smells terrible; traffic paralyzes the area at rush hour. [$] *Rooms from: R$835* ✉ *Av. das Nações Unidas 18591, Santo Amaro* ☎ *011/5693–4050, 0800/012–6060* 🌐 *www.transamerica.com.br* 🛏 *400 rooms, 11 suites* 🍴 *Breakfast* [M] *Santo Amaro* ✣ *B6.*

VILA MARIANA

$$$$ HOTEL 🏨 **Hotel Pullman São Paulo Ibirapuera.** Renovated in 2013 and looking fresh, the Pullman brings contemporary design and reasonable prices to the Ibirapuera area. **Pros:** near Ibirapuera Park, Avenida Paulista, and museums; affordable. **Cons:** considerable ride from main business and nightlife districts; small pool. [$] *Rooms from: R$900* ✉ *Rua Joinville 515, Vila Mariana* ☎ *011/5088–4000* 🌐 *www.pullmanhotels.com* 🛏 *350 rooms* 🍴 *No meals* [M] *Paraíso* ✣ *E4.*

$$$$ HOTEL 🏨 **Grand Mercure São Paulo Ibirapuera.** Near the Congonhas Airport and Ibirapuera Park, this modern, luxury hotel is noted for its French style, and its restaurant serves French cuisine. **Pros:** many amenities; convenient helipad for millionaires; park views. **Cons:** afternoon traffic; far from business centers. [$] *Rooms from: R$505* ✉ *Rua Sena Madureira 1355, Bloco 1, Vila Mariana* ☎ *011/3201–0800, 011/5575–4544* 🌐 *www.accorhotels.com.br* 🛏 *215 rooms* 🍴 *No meals* ✣ *E5.*

NIGHTLIFE AND PERFORMING ARTS

NIGHTLIFE

São Paulo's nightlife options are seemingly endless, so knowing where to go is key. The chic and wealthy head for establishments, most of which serve food, in the Vila Olímpia, Jardins, and Itaim neighborhoods. The Pinheiros and Vila Madalena neighborhoods have a large concentration of youthful clubs and bars, and many trendy clubs have opened in Barra Funda. Jardins and Centro have many gay and lesbian spots, with the area around Rua Augusta catering to hipsters.

Most clubs open at 9 pm, but people tend to arrive late (around midnight) and dance until 5 or 6 am. Still, you should arrive early to be at the front of the lines. Don't worry if the dance floor appears empty at 11 pm; things will start to sizzle an hour or so later.

Clubbing can get expensive. Most clubs charge at least R$20 at the door (sometimes women are allowed in for free), and the most popular and upscale places as much as R$300 just for entry. At the hottest clubs, expect to wait in line for a bit, especially if you head out late. Expect to wait in line on the way out again, too—the system is usually that you charge your drinks on an electronic tab, presenting the card and paying upon leaving. It can mean long queues: smart clubbers think ahead and pay up in good time.

A word about happy hour: Unlike in some countries, where the term refers to those few early-evening hours when drinks are cheaper, happy hour (pronounced and written in English) in Brazil simply means the time just after the work day ends, around 6 pm, when you might head to a bar for a drink with friends or colleagues. Despite the lack of discounted cocktails, paulistanos love to use the term, and many bars are judged purely on their suitability as a happy hour venue.

> ### GETTING AROUND AFTER DARK
>
> For safety reasons, we strongly suggest taking cabs at night—it's convenient and relatively cheap. Ask your concierge about transportation if finding a cab proves difficult.

BARRA FUNDA, ÁGUA BRANCA, AND LAPA

DANCE CLUBS

D.Edge. Electronic music is the main attraction at this popular club with a Death Star–meets–Studio 54 appeal. As many as nine DJs, often including internationally renowned turntablists, spin music on Thursday, Friday, and Saturday nights; on Sunday the party starts at 6 am and runs into the afternoon, and Monday is rock night. The terrace here has views of a park of Oscar Niemeyer design. Cover charges dip as low as R$20 but sometimes exceed R$100. ⌂ *Av. Auro Soares de Moura Andrade 141, Barra Funda* ☎ *011/3665–9500, 011/3667–8799* ⊕ *www.d-edge.com.br* ⛁ *Average entry R$20* Ⓜ *Barra Funda.*

Villa Country. This is *the* place to dance to American country music and *sertanejo,* Brazilian country music. The huge club has a restaurant, bars, shops, game rooms, and a big dance floor. The decor is strictly Old West. ⌂ *Av. Francisco Matarazzo 774, Água Branca* ☎ *011/3868–5858* ⊕ *www.villacountry.com.br* ⛁ *Average entry R$40 women, R$60 men* Ⓜ *Barra Funda.*

GAY AND LESBIAN BARS AND CLUBS

Blue Space. In a huge colonial blue house in an old industrial neighborhood, Blue Space is one of the largest gay nightclubs in São Paulo. Every Saturday and Sunday, two dance floors and four bars, along with lounge and private rooms, fill with a large crowd, mostly 40 and over, interested in the house DJs and go-go-boy and drag shows. ⌂ *Rua Brigadeiro Galvão 723, Barra Funda* ☎ *011/3666–1616, 011/3665–7157* ⊕ *www.bluespace.com.br* ⛁ *Average entry R$30* Ⓜ *Marechal Deodoro.*

The Week. Occupying a nearly 6,000-square-meter (64,500-square-foot) space, this club popular with gay men has two dance floors, three lounge rooms, a deck with a swimming pool, six bars, and a massage bed. Several DJs playing house, electro, and techno animate an often shirtless crowd on Friday and Saturday night. ⌂ *Rua Guaicurus 324, Lapa* ☎ *011/3868–9944* ⛁ *Average entry R$100.*

BELA VISTA

MUSIC CLUBS

Café Piu Piu. The café is best-known for its live-rock nights—Thursday, Friday, and Saturday. On other nights, it hosts groups that play rock jazz, blues, bossa nova, and sometimes tango. Potato latkes are among the menu highlights. ⌂ *Rua 13 de Maio 134, Bela Vista* ☎ *011/3258–8066* ⊕ *www.cafepiupiu.com.br* ⛁ *Average entry R$20.*

CENTRO
BARS

Bar Brahma. First opened in 1948, Bar Brahma used to be the meeting place of artists, intellectuals, and politicians. The decor is a time warp to the mid-20th century, with furniture, lamps, and a piano true to the period. This is one of the best places in São Paulo for live music, with traditional samba and Brazilian pop groups scheduled every week. Caetano Veloso immortalized the intersection of Ipiranga and São João Avenues, where the bar is located, in his 1978 song "Sampa." ⊠ *Av. São João 677, Centro* ☎ *011/3224–1250 reservations, 011/3367–3601* ⊕ *www.barbrahmacentro.com* ▣ *Average entry R$35* Ⓜ *República.*

DANCE CLUBS

Alberta #3. A linchpin of the nightlife revival pulling hipsters back to Centro, this club across from the Novotel Jaraguá caters to crowds from happy hour to the bewitching hours. Head upstairs to the lounge for cocktails and imported beers or downstairs to shake it out on the dance floor to indie and classic rock. ⊠ *Av. São Luís 272, Centro* ☎ *011/3151–5299* ⊕ *www.alberta3.com.br* ▣ *Average entry R$30* Ⓜ *República.*

Cine Joia. One of the city's newer live-music venues, Cine Joia may also be its loveliest. It takes the form of a resurrected vintage cinema, minus the seating but with the added attraction of a top-notch video-mapping system. See the site for live dates, or check out regular club nights like Talco Bells, spinning soul classics for a faithful party crowd. ⊠ *Praça Carlos Gomes 82, Centro* ☎ *011/3101–1385* ⊕ *www.cinejoia.tv* ▣ *Average entry R$40* Ⓜ *Liberdade.*

CONSOLAÇÃO
BARS

Drosophyla. Your creepy aunt's house filled with bizarre keepsakes meets quaint garden bar at Drosophyla. Young professionals and midlife free spirits assemble here for exotic caipirinhas, shots of vodka with cranberry syrup, and other zesty cocktails. If here for a meal, try the *huahine*, a French-Polynesian dish with marinated raw tuna, carrot, peppers, cherry tomatoes, and coconut milk. ⊠ *Rua Pedro Taques 80, Consolação* ☎ *011/3120–5535* ⊕ *www.drosophyla.com.br* Ⓜ *Consolação or Paulista.*

Riviera Bar. A firm nighttime favorite, Riviera reinvented a much-loved corner bar dating from 1949 as a chic, modern nightspot owned by star chef Alex Atala and nightclub entrepreneur Facundo Guerra. Drop in for a drink at the curvaceous bar, head upstairs and find a table for an evening of dinner and jazz, or stop by for the good buffet lunch. ⊠ *Av. Paulista 2584, Consolação* ☎ *011/3258–1268* ⊕ *www.rivierabar. br* ▣ *Average entry R$30* Ⓜ *Paulista.*

GAY AND LESBIAN BARS AND CLUBS

A Lôca. A mixed gay, lesbian, and straight crowd often dances until dawn at A Lôca to everything from pop and rock to disco and techno. ⊠ *Rua Frei Caneca 916, Consolação* ☎ *011/3159–8889* ⊕ *www.aloca. com.br* ▣ *Average entry R$40* Ⓜ *Consolação.*

FREGUESIA DO Ó

BARS

Frangó. A stop at off-the-beaten-path Frangó, northwest of Centro, makes you feel as if you've been transported to a small town. The bar has more than 300 varieties of beer, including the Brazilian craft beer Colorado. The Indica brew, an IPA made with sugarcane, nicely complements the bar's unforgettable *coxinhas de frango com queijo* (fried balls of chicken with cheese). ✉ *Largo da Matriz de Nossa Senhora do Ó 168, Freguesia do Ó* ☎ *011/3932–4818* ⊕ *www.frangobar.com.br.*

> ### GAY PRIDE PARADE
>
> São Paulo hosts one of the world's biggest and most famous gay parades each year on the Sunday of the Corpus Christi holiday, which generally falls at the end of May or in early June. The Gay Pride Parade, which was first held in 1997, runs along Avenida Paulista and attracts more than 1 million people.

ITAIM BIBI

BARS

Na Mata Café. Close to the northern border of Itaim, Na Mata ranks among the city's best live-music venues. It's a great place to catch some upmarket Brazilian entertainment. ✉ *Rua da Mata 70, Itaim* ☎ *011/3079–0300* ⊕ *www.namata.com.br* ▥ *Average entry R$45 women, R$55 men.*

GAY AND LESBIAN BARS AND CLUBS

Vermont Itaim. A major lesbian hangout in Itaim, this venue offers dining, live music, and dancing. Ten acts divvy up the showtimes from Wednesday to Saturday; on Sunday a nine-piece all-girl samba band takes the stage. When the bands stop playing, DJs spin music late into the night. ✉ *Rua Pedroso Alvarenga 1192, Itaim Bibi* ☎ *011/3071–1320, 011/3707–7721* ⊕ *www.vermontitaim.com.br* ▥ *Average entry R$20.*

MUSIC CLUBS

Kia Ora Pub. Rock and pop cover bands perform at this Down Under–themed pub. Seven international draft beers and happy hour specials make Kia Ora popular after businesses close. ✉ *Rua Dr. Eduardo de Souza Aranha 377, Itaim* ☎ *011/3846–8300* ⊕ *www.kiaora.com.br* ▥ *Average entry R$30 women, R$70 men.*

JARDIM PAULISTA

BARS

Balcão. Balcão means "bar" in Portuguese, and this artsy place has a long, curving one. If you'd like a little food to accompany your drinks and conversation, try one of the famous sandwiches on ciabatta bread. ✉ *Rua Doutor Melo Alves 150, Jardim Paulista* ☎ *011/3063–6091* Ⓜ *Consolação.*

DANCE CLUBS

8 Bar. The DJs at this intimate space play electronic, disco, and hip-hop, often interacting with the crowd on the dance floor and accepting requests. The bar closes occasionally for private events, so call ahead to be sure it's open. ✉ *Rua José Maria Lisboa 82, Jardim Paulista*

☎ *011/3889–9927, 011/97085–5718* ⊕ *www.8bar.com.br* 📧 *Average entry R$10.*

JARDINS

BARS

O'Malley's. A self-proclaimed "gringo" hangout, this is a good place to catch international sporting events, perhaps that major one back home it's killing you to miss. O'Malley's has three bars, a game room, and more than a dozen TVs spread across two floors. Seven beers are on tap, along with more than four dozen by the bottle. Bands play nightly, so there's always a cover after happy hour ends. ✉ *Alameda Itú 1529, Jardins* ☎ *011/3086–0780* ⊕ *www.omalleysbar.net* 📧 *Average entry R$10* Ⓜ *Consolação.*

MOEMA

MUSIC CLUBS

Bourbon Street. With a name right out of New Orleans, it's no wonder that Bourbon Street is where the best jazz and blues bands, Brazilian and international, play. Performances start at 9:30 pm. On Sunday, you can merengue and mambo at the Caribbean dance party. ✉ *Rua dos Chanés 127, Moema* ☎ *011/5095–6100* ⊕ *www.bourbonstreet.com.br* 📧 *Average entry R$30.*

PARAÍSO

BARS

Barnaldo Lucrécia. Live MPB and pub fare such as the *carne seca com mandioca frita* (sun-dried beef with fried manioc) draws an intense but jovial crowd to this bohemian spot. ✉ *Rua Abílio Soares 207, Paraíso* ☎ *011/3885–3425* ⊕ *www.barnaldolucrecia.com.br* 📧 *Average entry R$35* Ⓜ *Paraíso.*

Fodor's Choice ★ **Veloso.** Tables here are as disputed as a parking spot in front of a downtown apartment. An intimate corner bar on a quiet cobblestone plaza, Veloso dispenses some of São Paulo's best caipirinhas, including exotic versions such as tangerine with red pepper, and *coxinhas* (fried balls of chicken with cheese). ✉ *Rua Conceição Veloso 56, Paraíso* ☎ *011/5572–0254* ⊕ *www.velosobar.com.br* Ⓜ *Ana Rosa.*

PINHEIROS

DANCE CLUBS

Bar Secreto. Madonna and band members from U2 are former patrons of this once esoteric and invitation-only dance club. Though entrance is no longer just for Bruce Wayne, to make sure you can mingle with the moneyed partygoers, you should still try to put your name on the list—through the website or by email invitation. List or not, you'll still have to pay a cover charge that might wade into the triple digits. Bar Secreto opens at 11 pm from Wednesday to Saturday, and at 7 on Sunday. Or does it? ✉ *Rua Álvaro Anes 97, Pinheiros* ⊕ *barsecreto.com.br* 📧 *Average entry R$40* Ⓜ *Faria Lima.*

Casa 92. Giving new meaning to the concept house party, Casa 92 was fashioned out of a converted domicile. The living room has been fitted with disco lighting; the patio and terrace each have bars. An upstairs dance floor resides where a bedroom otherwise would. The music is eclectic with an emphasis on (what else?) house. ✉ *Rua Cristovão Gonçalves 92, Pinheiros* ☎ *011/3032–0371* ⊕ *www.casa92.com.br* 🍽 *Average entry R$50* Ⓜ *Faria Lima.*

GAY AND LESBIAN BARS AND CLUBS

Bubu Lounge Disco. Disco balls dangle over the dance floor at gay Bubu, where shirtless is the new fully clothed. Drag performers strut their stuff at Sunday matinees, and the last Thursday of the month is girls-only night. ✉ *Rua Dos Pinheiros 791, Pinheiros* ☎ *011/3081–9546, 011/3081–9659* ⊕ *www.bubulounge.com.br* 🍽 *Average entry R$30* Ⓜ *Faria Lima.*

MUSIC CLUBS

Canto da Ema. At what's widely considered the best place in town to dance *forró* (music/dance from Brazil's Northeast), you'll find people of different ages and styles coming together on the dance floor. *Xiboquinha* is the official forró drink, made with *cachaça* (a Brazilian sugarcane-based alcohol), lemon, honey, cinnamon, and ginger. The doors open at 10:30 pm from Wednesday through Saturday; the hours on Sunday are from 7 pm to midnight. ✉ *Av. Brigadeiro Faria Lima 364, Pinheiros* ☎ *011/3813–4708* ⊕ *www.cantodaema.com.br* 🍽 *Average entry R$25.*

Carioca Club. A *carioca* is a person from Rio de Janeiro, and Carioca Club has the decor of old-style Rio clubs. Its large dance floor attracts an eclectic mix of up to 1,200 college students, couples, and professional dancers who move to samba, *gafieira*, and *pagode* from Thursday through Saturday starting at varying times. ✉ *Rua Cardeal Arcoverde 2899, Pinheiros* ☎ *011/3813–8598, 011/3813–4524* ⊕ *www. cariocaclub.com.br* 🍽 *Average entry R$25* Ⓜ *Faria Lima.*

VILA MADALENA

BARS

Astor. The 1960s and 1970s bohemian-chic decor here sends you back in time. The quality draft beer and tasty snacks and meals mean that Astor is always hopping—the menu is full of specialties from classic bars in Brazil. Don't miss the *picadinho:* beef stew with rice and black beans, poached eggs, banana, farofa, and beef *pastel* (a type of dumpling). To finish up, head downstairs, where SubAstor, a speakeasy-style sister bar, serves the kind of cocktails that inspire you to attempt knockoffs at your next house party. ✉ *Rua Delfina 163, Vila Madalena* ☎ *011/3815–1364* ⊕ *www.barastor.com.br.*

Filial. When it comes to ending the night, Filial is considered by many to be the best bar in town. Many musicians stop by for an after-hours taste of its draft beer, along with the flavorful snacks (such as *bolinho de arroz,* or rice fritters) and meals (try *galinha afogada,* a stew with incredibly moist chicken and rice). ✉ *Rua Fidalga 254, Vila Madalena* ☎ *011/3813–9226* ⊕ *www.barfilial.com.br.*

Gràcia. A flirtatious clientele frequents this hot spot. Named for a Barcelona neighborhood, Gràcia is clothed in Catalan imagery and serves tapas and Sangria from the region. Sidewalk seating is available when the weather cooperates. ✉ *Rua Coropes 87, Vila Madalena* ☎ *011/3034–1481* ⊕ *graciabar.com.br* Ⓜ *Faria Lima.*

Posto 6. One of four comparable and fashionable bars at the corner of Mourato Coelho and Aspicuelta streets, Posto 6 pays homage to Rio de Janeiro and its Botafogo soccer club. The bar gets gold stars for its chopp and *escondidinho de camarão* (a lasagna-type dish with shrimp). ⊠ *Rua Aspicuelta 646, Vila Madalena* ☏ *011/3812–4342.*

DANCE CLUBS

Fodor's Choice
★
Ó do Borogodó. With live samba and MPB music every night of the week, this packed little club is a firm local favorite and provides a reliably good time, every time. ⊠ *Rua Horácio Lane 21, Vila Madalena* ☏ *011/3814–4087* ◻ *Average entry R$20.*

UP Club. DJs spin hip-hop and rap, and dancers pack the floor on Friday night at the UP Club. If things get too steamy, you can take a breather in the backyard garden. ⊠ *Rua Harmonia 21, Vila Madalena* ☏ *011/2309–7159* ⊕ *www.upclubsp.com.br* ◻ *Average entry R$20.*

MUSIC CLUBS

Grazie a Dio. The fashionable patrons at this club may vary in age, but they all appreciate good music. The best time to go is at happy hour for daily live performances. Samba, soul, and jazz figure prominently, with Brazilian pop represented as well. The natural decorations, including trees and constellations, complement the Mediterranean food served in the back. ⊠ *Rua Girassol 67, Vila Madalena* ☏ *011/3031–6568* ⊕ *www. grazieadio.com.br* ◻ *Average entry R$10.*

Fodor's Choice
★
Madeleine. The riffs heard at Madeleine place it in an exclusive stratum of São Paulo music clubs, but it's the mix of music, food, drinks, and atmosphere that lends the bar its comprehensive appeal. Jazz ensembles play in the exposed-brick lounge, which has clear sightlines from the mezzanine. Better for chatting are the candlelit tables in the well-stocked wine cellar, and the seats on the veranda, with its panoramic views of Vila Madalena. Wherever you sit, the gourmet pizzas go great with the craft beers poured here. ⊠ *Rua Aspicuelta 201, Vila Madalena* ☏ *011/2936–0616* ⊕ *www.madeleine.com.br.*

VILA OLÍMPIA

BARS

Bar Do Arnesto. More than 500 types of the rumlike liquor cachaça—the main ingredient in caipirinhas, Brazil's national cocktail—line a huge wall at this traditional Brazilian *botequim.* These casual bars generally specialize in cold bottled beer, snack foods, and caipirinhas. ⊠ *Rua Ministro Jesuíno Cardoso 207, Vila Olímpia* ☏ *011/3848–9432, 011/3848-6041 after 6 pm* ⊕ *www.bardoarnesto.com.br* ◻ *Average entry R$20.*

DANCE CLUBS

Disco. Big names in electronic music command the turntables at Disco, where you might end up sharing the dance floor with members of the national glitterati—or just some very–São Paulo playboys. ⊠ *Rua Professor Atílio Innocenti 160, Brooklin* ☏ *011/3078–0404* ⊕ *www. clubdisco.com.br* ◻ *Average entry men R$150, women free.*

Rey Castro. Salsa, merengue, zouk, and Latin pop predominate at Rey Castro; and during the breaks between live performances, you can take dance classes. The Caribbean-influenced drinks and snacks include mojitos and ham croquettes. ⊠ *Rua Ministro Jesuíno Cardoso 181, Vila Olímpia* ☏ *011/3842–5279* ⊕ *www.reycastro.com.br* ◻ *Average entry R$40.*

MUSIC CLUBS

All of Jazz. People come here to listen quietly to good jazz and bossa nova in an intimate environment—there's even a CD store upstairs with more than 3,000 discs. Local musicians jam from 10 pm on except on Sunday. The club gets crowded on weekends, when it's best to reserve a table. ⊠ *Rua João Cachoeira 1366, Vila Olímpia* ☎ *011/3849–1345* ⊕ *www.allofjazz.com.br* 💲 *Average entry R$30.*

PERFORMING ARTS

The world's top orchestras, opera and dance companies, and other troupes always include São Paulo in their South American tours. Many free concerts—with performances by either Brazilian or international artists—are presented on Sunday in Parque Ibirapuera. City-sponsored events are frequently held in Centro's Vale do Anhangabaú area or in Avenida Paulista.

The Centro Cultural São Paulo near Paraíso metro and an ample network of Serviço Social do Comércio (SESC) cultural centers feature inexpensive dance, theater, and musical performances daily. Listings of events appear in the "Veja São Paulo" insert of the newsweekly *Veja.* The arts sections of the dailies *Folha de São Paulo* and *O Estado de São Paulo* also have listings and reviews. Both papers publish a weekly guide on Friday. The Portuguese-language website Catraca Livre (⊕ *catracalivre.com.br/brasil*)is the authority on free entertainment options.

Tickets for many events are available through the Ingresso Rápido, Ingresso, and Tickets for Fun websites. Many of these venues and sites offer ticket delivery to your hotel for a surcharge.

Ticket Information Ingresso Rápido. ☎ *011/4003–1212* ⊕ *www. ingressorapido.com.br.* **Ingresso.com.** ☎ *011/4003–2330* ⊕ *www.ingresso.com. br.* **Show Tickets.** ⊠ *Iguatemi São Paulo, Av. Brigadeiro Faria Lima 1191, 3rd fl., Jardim Paulistano* ☎ *011/3031–2098* ⊕ *www.showtickets.com.br.* **Tickets for Fun.** ☎ *011/4003–5588* ⊕ *premier.ticketsforfun.com.br.*

CLASSICAL MUSIC AND OPERA

Fodor'sChoice **Sala São Paulo.** Despite being housed in a magnificent old train station, Sala São Paulo is one of the most modern concert halls for classical music in Latin America. It's home to the **São Paulo Symphony** (OSESP). ⊠ *Praça Júlio Prestes 16, Centro* ☎ *011/3367–9500* ⊕ *www. salasaopaulo.art.br* Ⓜ *Luz.*

★

Theatro São Pedro. Built in the neoclassical style in 1917, São Paulo's second-oldest theater is one of its best venues for chamber concerts and operas. Free morning events take place on Sunday and Wednesday. ⊠ *Rua Albuquerque Lins 207, Barra Funda* ☎ *011/3667–0499 ticket booth* ⊕ *www.theatrosaopedro.org.br* Ⓜ *Marechal Deodoro.*

CONCERT HALLS

Credicard Hall. One of the biggest theaters in São Paulo, Credicard Hall can accommodate up to 7,000 people. The venue frequently hosts concerts by famous Brazilian and international artists. Tickets can be bought by phone or online through Tickets for Fun. ⊠ *Av. das Nações Unidas 17995, Santo Amaro* ☎ *011/4003–5588* ⊕ *www.credicardhall.com.br.*

SESC Pompéia. Part of a chain of cultural centers throughout the city, SESC Pompéia incorporates a former factory into its design. There are multiple performance spaces, but the *choperia* (beer hall) and theater host the most prominent Brazilian and international musical acts—from jazz and soul to rock and hip-hop. ⊠ *Rua Clélia 93, Vila Olímpia* ☎ *011/3871–7700* ⊕ *www.sescsp.org.br.*

Teatro Alfa. International musicals and ballet, as well as occasional musical performances, are held at Teatro Alfa, which seats more than a thousand people. The sound and lighting technology are top of the line. Tickets can be bought by phone and through Ingresso Rápido, then picked up a half hour before the performance. ⊠ *Rua Bento Branco de Andrade Filho 722, Santo Amaro* ☎ *011/5693–4000, 0300/789–3377* ⊕ *www.teatroalfa.com.br.*

Theatro Municipal. Inspired by the Paris Opéra, the Municipal Theater was built between 1903 and 1911 with art nouveau elements. *Hamlet* was the first play presented, and the house went on to host such luminaries as Isadora Duncan in 1916 and Anna Pavlova in 1919. Plays and operas are still staged here; local newspapers, as well as the theater's website, have schedules and information on how to get tickets. The auditorium, resplendent with gold leaf, moss-green velvet, marble, and mirrors, has 1,500 seats and is usually open only to those attending cultural events, although prearranged visits are also available. A museum dedicated to the theater's history is located close by at Praça das Artes. Call the theater to arrange a free guided tour in English. ⊠ *Praça Ramos de Azevedo, Centro* ☎ *011/3397–0300, 011/3397–0327* ⊕ *www.prefeitura.sp.gov.br/cidade/secretarias/cultura/ theatromunicipal* Ⓜ *Anhangabaú.*

DANCE

Balé da Cidade. The City Ballet, São Paulo's official dance company, has performed for many years at the magnificent Theatro Municipal. ⊠ *Rua João Passaláqua 66, Bela Vista* ☎ *011/3241–3883, 011/3241–1740* Ⓜ *Anhangabaú.*

Ballet Stagium. The ballet performs contemporary works incorporating Brazilian pop and bossa nova music. Founded in 1971 during Brazil's period of dictatorship, the company made its name performing dances with political and social-justice themes. ⊠ *Rua Augusta 2985, 2nd fl., Cerqueira César* ☎ *011/3085–0151.*

FILM

Centro Cultural São Paulo. The cultural center has temporary alternative film screenings, particularly of Brazilian titles, but also presents plays, concerts, and art exhibits. Major renovations finished in 2013 added new projection and sound equipment and saw improvements in the lighting and acoustics. Admission is free or low-price for some events. ⊠ *Rua Vergueiro 1000, Paraíso* ☎ *011/3397–4002* ⊕ *www. centrocultural.sp.gov.br* Ⓜ *Vergueiro.*

Cidade Jardim Cinemark. The prices are elite but so are the amenities, such as gourmet food service. Cidade Jardim Cinemark set the bar much higher for blockbuster-screening, luxury theaters in São Paulo. ⊠ *Av.*

Magalhães de Castro 12000, Morumbi ☎*011/3552–1800* ⊕*www. shoppingcidadejardim.com/cinema.*

CineSESC. Titles already out of other theaters and independent openings show for discounted prices at CineSESC. The screen is visible from the snack bar. ✉ *Rua Augusta 2075, Cerqueira César* ☎ *011/3087–0500* ⊕ *www.sescsp.org.br* Ⓜ *Consolação.*

Espaço Itaú de Cinema, Augusta. Brazilian, European, and other non-block-buster films are shown at the Espaço Itaú. ✉ *Rua Augusta 1475, Consolação* ☎ *011/3288–6780* ⊕ *www.itaucinemas.com.br* Ⓜ *Consolação.*

Reserva Cultural. The complex contains four movie theaters, a small library, and a deck-style restaurant from which you can see—and be seen by—pedestrians on Paulista Avenue. ✉ *Av. Paulista 900, Jardim Paulista* ☎ *011/3287–3529* ⊕ *www.reservacultural.com.br* Ⓜ *Trianon-MASP or Brigadeiro.*

SAMBA SHOWS

Escolas de samba or samba schools are the heart and soul of many communities. Most people only associate them with the dancing groups that perform during Carnival, but they keep busy all year round. In addition to samba lessons, they organize a range of community services, especially education and health outreach programs. Check them out anytime, but from November to February they're gearing up for Carnival, and often open their rehearsals to the public.

Mocidade Alegre. Up to 3,000 people at a time attend rehearsals at Mocidade Alegre just before Carnival. ✉ *Av. Casa Verde 3498, Limão* ☎ *011/3857–7525* ⊕ *www.mocidadealegre.com.br.*

Rosas de Ouro. One of the most popular rehearsals takes place at Rosas de Ouro. ✉ *Rua Coronel Euclides Machado 1066, Freguesia do Ó* ☎ *011/3931–4555* ⊕ *www.sociedaderosasdeouro.com.br.*

SPORTS AND THE OUTDOORS

Maybe it's the environment or maybe the culture, but participating in organized sports isn't usually a huge part of a paulistano's regime. An exception is soccer, or *futebol*, which you will see being played in most parks, either on full fields, half-size arenas, or even sandy courts, every weekend and on weeknights. Basketball and volleyball also have loyal, if smaller, followings at parks and SESC centers around the city.

AUTO RACING

Brazilian Grand Prix. Racing fans from all over the world come to São Paulo in November for the Brazilian Grand Prix, a Formula 1 race that attracts massive national attention, especially when a Brazilian driver is in the mix. The race is held at Autódromo da Interlagos, which at other times hosts auto races on weekends. ✉ *Autódromo da Interlagos, Av. Senador Teotônio Vilela 261* ☎ *021/2221–4895 tickets* ⊕ *www. gpbrasil.com.*

CYCLING AND JOGGING

Parque Ibirapuera. Going for a ride or a run in one of São Paulo's parks is a good choice if you want a little exercise. For cyclists there are usually plenty of rental options (from R$5 per hour) available and special lanes just for riders. Parque Ibirapuera gets busy on the weekends, but it's still worth coming here. ✉ *Av. Pedro Álvares Cabral, Parque Ibirapuera* ☎ *011/5574–5045* ⊕ *www.parqueibirapuera.org.*

Parque Villa-Lobos. It may have fewer trees and less of a history than Parque Ibirapuera, but Parque Villa-Lobos is big and has plenty of winding pathways wide enough to accommodate cyclists and runners. There are bike-rental stands inside the park (from R$7 per hour), as well as a few soccer pitches and a big, concrete square with basketball half-courts. There are some food-and-drink options, too. ✉ *Av. Professor Fonseca Rodrigues 2001, Alto de Pinheiros* ☎ *011/3021–6285* ⊕ *www.ambiente.sp.gov.br/parquevillalobos* ☉ *Daily 6–6.*

SOCCER

São Paulo State has several well-funded teams with some of the country's best players. The four main teams—Corinthians, São Paulo, Palmeiras, and Santos—attract fans from other states. Corinthians and Palmeiras opened new stadiums in 2014. São Paulo's Morumbi and the municipally run Pacaembu, meanwhile, continue to host matchups featuring Brazilian clubs. Covered seats offer the best protection, not only from the elements but also from rowdy spectators.

Buy tickets at the stadiums or online at ⊕ *www.ingressofacil.com.br.* Futebol Tour (⊕ *www.futeboltour.com.br*) also sells packages starting at R$60 for select games that include transportation to and from the stadiums, admission, and information folders. Regular games usually don't sell out, but finals and classicos between the big four—for which you can buy tickets up to five days in advance—generally do. For a history lesson on the "beautiful game," check out the interactive Soccer Museum at the Pacaembu stadium.

Allianz Parque (*Nova Arena*). This new arena opened in 2014 and is configured to seat about 46,000 people for soccer and other events. The home team, Palmeiras, plays here. ✉ *Rua Turiassu 1840, Barra Funda* ☎ *011/3874–6500* ⊕ *www.allianzparque.com.br* Ⓜ *Barra Funda.*

Arena Corinthians. The home of Corinthians soccer club hosted the opening of the 2014 World Cup. It holds 48,000 spectators. ✉ *Av. Miguel Inácio Curi 111, Vila Carmosina* ☎ *011/2095–3000, 011/2095–3175* ⊕ *www.corinthians.com.br/arena* Ⓜ *Corinthians-Itaquera.*

Canindé. The home team, Portuguesa, is the main attraction here, though the *bolinhos de bacalhau* (salt-cod fritters), popular among the Portuguese immigrants filling the stadium's 21,000 seats, run a close second. ✉ *Rua Comendador Nestor Pereira 33, Canindé* ☎ *011/2125–9400* ⊕ *www.portuguesa.com.br.*

Estádio da Javari (*Estádio Conde Rodolfo Crespi*). The 4,000-seat Estádio da Javari, also known as Estádio Conde Rodolfo Crespi, is where third-division Juventus plays. It's an ideal place to soak up some

Italian atmosphere—Moóca is an Italian neighborhood—and eat a cannoli while cheering for the home team. ✉ *Rua Javari 117, Moóca* ☎ *011/2693–4688, 011/2292–4833* ⊕ *www.juventus.com.br* Ⓜ *Moóca.*

Morumbi. The home stadium of São Paulo Futebol Clube seats 67,000 people. When soccer isn't being played here, other events take place, including concerts by stars such as Lady Gaga. ✉ *Praça Roberto Gomes Pedroza 1, Morumbi* ☎ *011/3742–3377, 011/3749–8000* ⊕ *www.saopaulofc.net.*

Pacaembu (*Estádio Municipal Paulo Machado de Carvalho*). The first games of the 1950 World Cup were played at this stadium. The plaza it inhabits is named for the Englishman who introduced Brazil to soccer. While it isn't used by any team in particular, it does host games occasionally and still houses the Museu de Futebol (soccer museum). ✉ *Praça Charles Miller s/n, Pacaembú* ☎ *011/3664–4650, 011/3663–6888* Ⓜ *Clínicas.*

SHOPPING

Fashionistas from all over the continent flock to São Paulo for the clothes, shoes, and accessories. In fact, shopping is a tourist attraction in its own right. You can get a sampling of what's on offer six days a week: stores are usually open on weekdays from 9 to 6:30 and Saturdays from 9 to 1; many are closed on Sunday. Mall hours are generally weekdays and Saturday from 10 am to 10 pm; some malls only open on Sunday around 2 pm.

Well-heeled paulistanos famously love shopping malls, and there are plenty of those in the city. Perhaps of more interest for visitors, almost every neighborhood has a weekly outdoor food market, complete with loudmouthed hawkers, exotic scents, and mountains of colorful produce. Nine hundred of them happen every week in São Paulo, so you'll be able to hit at least one; ask around to find out when and where the closest one happens.

Antiques and secondhand furniture are the big draws at the Sunday flea market at the Praça Dom Orione in **Bela Vista**. You'll also find clothing, CDs, and other (mostly) reasonably priced items here. In **Centro**, Rua do Arouche is noted for leather goods. Rua Barão de Paranapiacaba is lined with jewelry shops and is nicknamed the "street of gold." The area around Rua João Cachoeira in **Itaim** has evolved from a neighborhood of small clothing factories into a wholesale- and retail-clothing sales district. Several shops on Rua Tabapuã sell small antiques. Also, Rua Dr. Mário Ferraz is stuffed with elegant clothing, gift, and home-decoration stores.

In **Jardins,** centering on Rua Oscar Freire, double-parked Mercedes-Benzes and BMWs point the way to the city's fanciest stores, which sell leather items, jewelry, gifts, antiques, and art. Shops that specialize in high-price European antiques are on or around Rua da Consolação. Lower-price antiques stores and thrift shops line Rua Cardeal Arcoverde in **Pinheiros**. Flea markets with secondhand furniture, clothes, and CDs take place on Saturday at the popular Praça Benedito Calixto in Pinheiros, where you can also eat at food stands and listen to music all day long. Arcades along Praça Benedito Calixto and many streets in neighboring **Vila Madalena**, like Ruas Aspicuelta and Harmonia, house boutique clothing stores.

BOM RETIRO

BEACHWEAR

Beira Mar Beachwear. This Brazilian brand, founded in 1948, is known for innovative and high-quality products. Beira Mar has its own factory and produces many types of bikinis and swimming suits. ⊠ *Rua Silva Pinto 254, 3rd fl.*, *Bom Retiro* ☎ *011/3222–7999* ⊕ *www. maiosbeiramar.com.br* Ⓜ *Tiradentes.*

CENTRO

BEAUTY

O Boticário. The Brazilian brand O Boticário was founded by dermatologists and pharmacists from Curitiba in the 1970s. The company creates products for men, women, and children, and through its foundation funds ecological projects throughout Brazil. The shops can be found in most neighborhoods and malls in the city. ⊠ *Av. Brig. Luis Antonio 282, Centro* ☎ *011/3115–0712* ⊕ *www.oboticario.com.br.*

LEATHER GOODS AND LUGGAGE

Inovathi. A shop you'll find in many malls all over town, Inovathi has leather accessories at good prices. ⊠ *Av. Ipiranga 336, Centro* ☎ *011/2179–2050* ⊕ *www.inovathi.com.br* Ⓜ *República.*

MARKETS

Fodor'sChoice
★

Mercado Municipal. The city's first grocery market, this huge 1928 neo-baroque-style building is the quintessential hot spot for gourmets and food lovers. The building, nicknamed Mercadão (Big Market) by locals, houses about 300 stands that sell just about everything edible, including meat, vegetables, cheese, spices, and fish from all over Brazil. It also has restaurants and traditional snack places. The Hocca Bar is justly famous for its *pastel de bacalhau* (salt-cod pastry) and heaping mortadella sandwich. ⊠ *Rua da Cantareira 306, Sé, Centro* ☎ *011/3313–3365, 011/3313–7456* ⊕ *www.oportaldomercadao.com.br* ☞ *Free* ☾ *Mon.–Sat. 6–6, Sun. 6–4* Ⓜ *São Bento.*

Praça da República arts and crafts fair. Vendors sell jewelry, embroidery, leather goods, toys, clothing, paintings, and musical instruments at the Sunday-morning arts-and-crafts fair in Praça da República. If you look carefully, you can find reasonably priced, out-of-the-ordinary souvenirs. ⊠ *Praça da República, Centro* Ⓜ *República.*

MUSIC

Baratos Afins. Heaven for music collectors, Baratos Afins opened inside the popular Galeria do Rock in 1978 and is also a record label. The company was the brainchild of Arnaldo Baptista, guitar player in the influential 1960s Brazilian rock band Os Mutantes. The store sells all kinds of music, but it specializes in Brazilian popular music. If you're looking for rare records, ask for the owner, Luiz Calanca. ✉ *Galeria do Rock, Av. São João 439, 2nd fl.*, *Centro* ☎ *011/3223-3629* ⊕ *www. baratosafins.com.br* Ⓜ *República.*

Ventania. Browse through more than 100,000 records at this huge store that specializes in Brazilian popular music. You can find old 78s, contemporary CDs, and everything in between. ✉ *Rua 24 de Maio 188, 1st fl.*, *Centro* ☎ *011/3331-0332* ⊕ *www.ventania.com.br* Ⓜ *República.*

CERQUEIRA CÉSAR

ANTIQUES
Patrimônio. Head to Patrimônio for Brazilian antiques at reasonable prices. The shop also sells Indian artifacts, as well as modern furnishings crafted from iron. ✉ *Alameda Ministro Rocha Azevedo 1077, 1st fl.*, *Cerqueira César* ☎ *011/99225-7570* ⊕ *www.patrimonioantiguidades. com* ⊙ *Fri. and by appointment other days.*

CONSOLAÇÃO

JEWELRY
Antonio Bernardo. Carioca Antonio Bernardo is one of the most famous jewelry designers in Brazil. He creates custom pieces with gold, silver, and other precious metals and stones. ✉ *Rua Bela Cintra 2063, Consolação* ☎ *011/3083-5622* ⊕ *www.antoniobernardo.com.br* ⊙ *Closed Sun.*

HIGIENÓPOLIS

BEACHWEAR
Cia. Marítima. The Brazilian beachwear brand known for its bikinis and swimsuits has a presence in this and many other high-class malls. ✉ *Shopping Pátio Higienópolis, Av. Higienópolis, Higienópolis* ☎ *011/3661-7602* ⊕ *www.ciamaritima.com.br.*

CENTERS AND MALLS
Shopping Pátio Higienópolis. One of the most upscale shopping malls in São Paulo, Shopping Pátio Higienópolis is a mixture of old and new architecture styles. It has plenty of shops and restaurants, as well as six screens in the Cinemark movie theater. ✉ *Av. Higienópolis 618, Higienópolis* ☎ *011/3823-2300* ⊕ *www.patiohigienopolis.com.br.*

ITAIM BIBI

ANTIQUES
Pedro Corrêa do Lago. The shop's namesake owner, a consultant for Sotheby's auction house, sells and auctions rare and used books, as well as antique maps, prints, and drawings of Brazil. ✉ *Rua Afonso Braz 473, Conjuntos 31 and 32, Itaim* ☎ *011/3063-5455.*

CENTERS AND MALLS
JK Iguatemi. Natural light illuminates the atrium and walkways of this luxury mall for the elite, where international brands from AW Store to Zara mix it up with national brands like Animale and Carlos Miele.

There are plenty of fancy dining spots. If scheduled beforehand, the mall will supply you with a personal shopper. ⊠ *Av. Presidente Juscelino Kubitschek 2041, Itaim Bibi* ☎ *011/3152–6800, 011/3152–6809 Schedule personal shopper* ⊕ *www.jkiguatemi.com.br.*

JARDIM PAULISTA

HANDICRAFTS

Amoa Konoya Arte Indigena. Inspired by contact with indigenous peoples, Walter Gomes opened this store to promote awareness about and economic opportunities for Brazil's native communities. Artisans of 230 indigenous tribes create the crafts and artworks, from musical instruments to earthenware, sold here. ⊠ *Rua João Moura 1002, Jardim Paulista* ☎ *011/3061–0639* ⊕ *www.amoakonoya.com.br.*

JARDIM PAULISTANO

ANTIQUES

Juliana Benfatti. The antiques shop run by Juliana Benfatti and her two sons has inventory that dates back to the 18th century. The buyers have a discerning eye for what was unique and special in many lands over many generations. ⊠ *Rua Sampaio Vidal 786, Jardim Paulistano* ☎ *011/3083–7858* ⊕ *www.julianabenfatti.com.br* Ⓜ *Faria Lima.*

CENTERS AND MALLS

Iguatemi São Paulo. This may be the city's oldest mall, but it has the latest in fashion and fast food. The Cinemark movie theaters often show films in English with Portuguese subtitles. The Gero Caffé, built in the middle of the main hall, has a fine menu. If you're in São Paulo at Christmastime, the North Pole–theme displays here are well worth a detour. ⊠ *Av. Brigadeiro Faria Lima 2232, Jardim Paulistano* ☎ *011/3816–6116* ⊕ *www.iguatemisaopaulo.com.br.*

JEWELRY

Tiffany & Co. The world-famous store sells exclusive pieces for the very wealthy. Go for the diamonds—you know you want to. ⊠ *Iguatemi São Paulo, Av. Brigadeiro Faria Lima 2232, Jardim Paulista* ☎ *011/3815–7000* ⊕ *www.tiffany.com.*

JARDINS

On Sunday there are antiques fairs near the Museu de Arte de São Paulo (MASP).

ANTIQUES

Legado. At this antiques showroom that holds monthly auctions you'll find plenty of heirlooms looking for new homes—Baccarat bowls and vases, art nouveau and art deco sideboards, and a slew of silver trays and tea sets among them. Past oddities include the helmet of the late race-car legend Ayrton Senna. ⊠ *Alameda Lorena 882, Jardins* ☎ *011/3063–3400* ⊕ *www.legadoantiguidades.com.br.*

Renée Behar Antiques. This shop has that prim and proper look one expects from a reputable, longtime dealer known for classic 18th- and

19th-century silver, ceramics, and other antiques. The craftsmanship in the items for sale here is consistently top-drawer. ✉ *Rua Peixoto Gomide 2088, Jardins* ☎ *011/3085–3622* ⊕ *www.reneebehar.com.br.*

ART GALLERIES

Arte Aplicada. A respected Jardins gallery, Arte Aplicada is known for its high-quality Brazilian paintings, sculptures, and prints. ✉ *Rua Haddock Lobo 1406, Jardins* ☎ *011/3062–5128, 011/3064–4725* ⊕ *www.arteaplicada.com.br.*

Bel Galeria. Paintings and sculptures from Brazilian and international artists go up for auction at Bel Galeria. ✉ *Rua Paraguaçú 334, Perdizes* ☎ *011/3663–3100* ⊕ *www.belgaleriadearte.com.br.*

Dan Galeria. Specializing in 20th-century Brazilian art, this gallery is a must for serious art lovers and monied collectors, and educational for interested amateurs. Look out for works by modernist stars such as Tarsila do Amaral and di Cavalcanti. ✉ *Rua Estados Unidos 1638, Jardins* ☎ *011/3083–4600* ⊕ *www.dangaleria.com.br* ⊙ *Closed Sun.*

Galeria Luisa Strina. One of the city's oldest and best established galleries, Luisa Strina is a serious player in the international art world, representing artists of the stature of Cildo Meireles and Anna Maria Maiolino, as well as a stable of young stars such as Renata Lucas, Clarissa Tossin, and Fernanda Gomes. ✉ *Rua Padre João Manuel 755, Jardins* ☎ *011/3088–2471* ⊕ *www.galerialuisastrina.com.br.*

Galeria Renot. At this gallery you'll find oil paintings by such Brazilian artists as Vicente Rego Monteiro, Di Cavalcanti, Cícero Dias, and Anita Malfatti. ✉ *Alameda Ministro Rocha Azevedo 1327, Jardins* ☎ *011/3083–5933.*

Mônica Filgueiras Galeria. Many a trend has been set at this gallery, which sells all types of art but mostly paintings and sculpture. ✉ *Rua Bela Cintra 1533, Jardins* ☎ *011/3082–5292* ⊕ *www.monicafilgueiras.com.br.*

BEAUTY

Granado. As with the other locations of this Brazilian beauty-supplies chain that dates back to 1870, the Jardins shop maintains the old-time appearance of an apothecary. ✉ *Rua Haddock Lobo 1353, Jardins* ☎ *011/3061–0891* ⊕ *www.granado.com.br.*

BEACHWEAR

Track & Field. This brand's shops, which you'll find in nearly every mall in São Paulo, are good places to buy beachwear and sports clothing. The store sells bikinis and swimsuits from Cia. Marítima, a famous Brazilian beachwear brand. ✉ *Rua Oscar Freire 959, Jardins* ☎ *011/3062–4457* ⊕ *www.tf.com.br.*

BOOKS

Livraria Cultura. São Paulo's best selection of travel literature can be found here, along with many maps. ✉ *Av. Paulista 2073, Jardins* ☎ *011/3170–4033* ⊕ *www.livrariacultura.com.br* Ⓜ *Consolação.*

CLOTHING

Alexandre Herchcovitch. The Brazilian designer Alexandre Herchcovitch sells prêt-à-porter and tailor-made clothes at his store. ⊠ *Rua Melo Alves 561, Jardins* ☎ *011/3063-2888* ⊕ *www.herchcovitch.com.br.*

Animale. With a deft line in cool, sophisticated fashion, Animale has long been a go-to brand for hip young Brazilian women. Known for its striking prints and sultry yet wearable garments, Animale isn't cheap—but these are clothes you'll be slipping into for years. ⊠ *Rua Bela Cintra 2164, Jardins* ☎ *011/3063-2038* ⊕ *www.animale.com.br* Ⓜ *Consolação.*

BO.BÔ. Brazilian models and soap-opera stars wear this brand, which blends bohemian and bourgeois (coincidentally, the type of bank account needed to shop here). ⊠ *Rua Oscar Freire 1039, Jardins* ☎ *011/3062-8145* ⊕ *www.bobo.com.br.*

Fórum. High-class evening attire for young men and women is the specialty of Fórum, which also sells sportswear and shoes. ⊠ *Rua Oscar Freire 916, Jardins* ☎ *011/3085-6269* ⊕ *www.forum.com.br.*

Le Lis Blanc. This chain is Brazil's exclusive purveyor of the French brand Vertigo. Look for party dresses in velvet and sheer fabrics. ⊠ *Rua Oscar Freire 1119, Jardins* ☎ *011/3809-8950* ⊕ *www.lelis.com.br.*

Lita Mortari. The designer Lita Mortari sells her feminine festive wear in four stores in São Paulo, including two in Jardins. ⊠ *Rua Bela Cintra 2195, Jardins* ☎ *011/3064-3021* ⊕ *litamortari.com.br.*

Mulher Elástica. Outfits built around leggings are no stretch for Mulher Elástica. Looks range from sporty to business casual. ⊠ *Rua Dr. Melo Alves 381, Jardins* ☎ *011/3060-8263* ⊕ *mulherelastica.com.br.*

Reinaldo Lourenço. Sophisticated, high-quality women's clothing is Reinaldo Lourenço's calling card. ⊠ *Rua Bela Cintra 2167, Jardins* ☎ *011/3085-8150* ⊕ *www.reinaldolourenco.com.br.*

Richards. The collections at Richards include casualwear for men, women, and kids. ⊠ *JK Iguatemi, Av. Presidente Juscelino Kubitschek 2041, Vila Olímpia* ☎ *011/3073-1332* ⊕ *www.richards.com.br.*

HANDICRAFTS

Galeria de Arte Brasileira. Since 1920 Galeria de Arte Brasileira has specialized in art and handicrafts from all over Brazil. Look for objects made of *pau-brasil* (brazilwood), hammocks, jewelry, T-shirts, *marajoara* pottery (from the Amazon), and lace. ⊠ *Alameda Lorena 2163, Jardins* ☎ *011/3062-9452* ⊕ *www.galeriaartebrasileira.com.br.*

JEWELRY

H.Stern. An internationally known Brazilian brand for jewelry, especially featuring precious Brazilian gems, H.Stern has shops in more than 30 countries. This one has designs made especially for the Brazilian stores. ⊠ *Rua Oscar Freire 652, Jardins* ☎ *011/3068-8082* ⊕ *www. hstern.com.br.*

LEATHER GOODS AND LUGGAGE

Le Postiche. One of the biggest brands for luggage and leather goods in Brazil, Le Postiche has 96 shops around the country. You can find one in almost any mall in São Paulo. ⊠ *Rua Haddock Lobo 1307, Jardins* ☏ *011/3081–9702* ⊕ *www.lepostiche.com.br.*

Schutz. Boots, sandals, wedges, stilettos—if you can't find a pair of shoes you like at Schutz, you're probably not looking properly. This flagship store carries a huge variety of fashion footwear, from statement heels to fun prints on sneakers. ⊠ *Rua Oscar Freire 944, Jardins* ☏ *011/4508–1499* ⊕ *www.schutz.com.br* Ⓜ *Consolacão.*

MOEMA

4

CLOTHING

Fil du Fil. The women's clothing brand Fil du Fil maintains three locations across Moema and Vila Olímpia. This address is dedicated to plus-size attire. Looks are casual with colorful blouses and dresses featuring prominently. ⊠ *Rua Canário 1253, Moema* ☏ *011/5561–2645* ⊕ *www.fildufil.com.br.*

Vila Romana Factory Store. The prices for suits, jackets, jeans, and some women's clothing (silk blouses, for example) at Vila Romana Factory Store are unbeatable. The store is a 40-minute drive from Centro. In-town mall branches are more convenient, but prices are higher. ⊠ *Via Anhanguera, Km 17.5, Rua Robert Bosch 1765, Osasco* ☏ *011/3604–5293* ⊕ *www.vilaromana.com.br.*

HANDICRAFTS

Casa do Amazonas. As its name suggests, Casa do Amazonas has a wide selection of products from the Amazon. ⊠ *Alameda dos Jurupis 460, Moema* ☏ *011/5051–3098* ⊕ *www.arteindigena.com.br.*

MUSIC

Painel Musical. In shopping malls, look out for Painel Musical, a small record shop that carries CDs and DVDs. It usually has a good selection of instrumental Brazilian music and local rock. ⊠ *Shopping Ibirapuera, Av. Ibirapuera 3103, Moema* ☏ *011/5561–9981.*

MORUMBI

CENTERS AND MALLS

MorumbiShopping. Though it's taken a backseat to newer malls Cidade Jardim and JK Iguatemi, MorumbiShopping is still a slice of São Paulo's upper crust, seasoned with swank boutiques, record stores, bookstores, and restaurants. The atrium hosts art exhibits. ⊠ *Av. Roque Petroni Jr. 1089, Morumbi* ☏ *011/4003–4132* ⊕ *www.morumbishopping.com.br.*

Shopping Cidade Jardim. The feeling here is almost as though archaeologists have uncovered a lost jungle city's ancient temples—only they're to upscale shopping and gourmet dining, not deities and potentates. Trees outside sprout three stories high, and a bevy of plants inside shrouds boutiques with names like Valentino, Omega, and Louis Vuitton. For resting, there's a huge open garden with splendid city views. If you get hungry, head to the Argentine steak house Pobre Juan for a hearty meal or, for lighter fare, drop in at bright and breezy The Gourmet Tea. ⊠ *Av. Magalhães de Castro 12000, Morumbi* ☎ *011/3552–1000* ⊕ *www.shoppingcidadejardim.com.*

CLOTHING

FAMILY **Camu Camu.** Founded in 1974, Camu Camu sells stylish clothing for young girls and boys. ⊠ *Shopping Marketing Place, Av. Dr. Chucri Zaidan 902, Morumbi* ☎ *011/5181–1567* ⊕ *www.camucamu.com.br.*

PARAÍSO

HANDICRAFTS

Marcenaria Trancoso. The wooden products this shop sells are an elegant mixture of interior design and handicraft. ⊠ *Rua Mateus Grou 282, Pinheiros* ☎ *011/3816–1298* ⊕ *www.marcenariatrancoso.com.br.*

LEATHER GOODS AND LUGGAGE

Arezzo. A leader in the leather game, with stores in most São Paulo shopping malls, Arezzo is best known for its footwear. The brand also has an extensive line of bags, wallets, and accessories. ⊠ *Shopping Paulista, Rua Treze de Maio 1947, Paraíso* ☎ *011/3171–1183* ⊕ *www.arezzo. com.br* Ⓜ *Brigadeiro.*

VILA MADALENA

ART

Galeria Fortes Vilaça. This fine gallery is one of the city's big hitters and always worth a look. ⊠ *Rua Fradique Coutinho 1500, Vila Madalena* ☎ *011/3032–7066* ⊕ *www.fortesvilaca.com.br.*

CLOTHING

Uma. Women of all ages lust after the simple elegance of Uma's swimsuits, dresses, shorts, shirts, and pants—they're not cheap, but they're good. ⊠ *Rua Girassol 273, Vila Madalena* ☎ *011/3813–5559* ⊕ *www. uma.com.br.*

HANDICRAFTS

Ôoh de Casa. Souvenirs and presents, from vividly colored hammocks to papier-mâché piggy banks (cows, actually), are for sale here. ⊠ *Rua Fradique Coutinho 899, Vila Madalena* ☎ *011/3812–4934, 011/3815–9577* ⊕ *www.oohdecasa.com.br.*

VILA MARIANA

ART

Galeria Jacques Ardies. If you like *art naif*—as the name suggests, the art is simple, with a primitive and handcrafted look—Galeria Jacques Ardies is a must. ⊠ *Rua Morgado de Mateus 579, Vila Mariana* ☎ *011/5539–7500* ⊕ *www.ardies.com* Ⓜ *Paraíso.*

SIDE TRIPS FROM SÃO PAULO

Updated By
Angelica Mari

São Paulo's surroundings are perfect for all types of getaways with the peaks of the Serra da Mantiqueira inland and the area's finest beaches up the North Coast. The state has the best highways in the country, making it easy to travel by car or bus to its many small, beautiful beaches, and beyond to neighboring states (Paraná, Rio de Janeiro, and Minas Gerais). Although the North Coast's sandy stretches require two-hour drives, good side trips from the city can be as close as the 30-minute trip to Santos's long strip of sand, Embu's weekend craft market, or Santana de Parnaíba's historical streets.

For a weekend of relaxation, soak up the healing properties of Águas de São Pedro's spas and springs. If you like mountains, head to Campos do Jordão, where cafés and clothing stores are often crowded with ohso-chic *paulistanos* (natives of São Paulo city; inhabitants of São Paulo State are called *paulistas*). Serra Negra and its surrounding region offer mineral waters and an immersion in the coffee production history of Brazil, as well as several activities for families and couples looking for a romantic getaway. Favor the coast's North Shore beaches and Ilhabela (the name means "beautiful island") if you prefer sun and sand. The island is part of the Mata Atlântica (Atlantic Forest) and has many waterfalls, trails, and diving spots.

ORIENTATION AND PLANNING

GETTING ORIENTED

Along the Coast. On weekends, paulistanos flock to the easily accessible beaches of Santos just south of São Paulo. Farther up the coast, the North Shore has beautiful stretches of sand for every kind of sun or sports enthusiast. In the 1990s the area experienced a building boom, with condos popping up seemingly overnight. Luckily, the North Shore still managed to maintain its pristine environment.

Inland. Just a stone's throw from São Paulo, Embu das Artes is famous for its big handicraft fair with paintings, toys, and candles, as well as scrumptious pastries and breads. Campos do Jordão, known as the Switzerland of Brazil, attracts hordes of chill-seekers in winter, when temperatures drop below tepid. Serra Negra is the main city of São Paulo's Circuito das Águas (Water Circuit) and offers plenty of events and activities for families as well as a refuge for couples seeking romance.

TOP REASONS TO GO

Beach Paradises: Bask on a range of beautiful beaches, from surfer paradises in Ubatuba to coastal islands and sandy rain-forest coves on Ilhabela.

Rich History: Witness Brazil's colonial and rural history in Embu and Santana de Parnaíba.

Great Nightlife: Dance until dawn with a seaside view at Maresias, São Sebastião.

Gorgeous Landscapes: Luxurious forests in Campos do Jordão combine with impressive wildlife and bodies of water in Águas de São Pedro and Serra Negra.

Scrumptious Food: Sample a variety of local dishes made with the freshest ingredients, including artisanal sausages and locally brewed beer.

5

PLANNING

WHEN TO GO

The area around São Paulo is lovely year-round. Most places have a steady stream of visitors, so it's always wise to book hotels well in advance. Summers are hot and humid, and it's the rainy season, so it's good to have some indoor plans in the back of your mind. In winter, temperatures drop into the 40s°F (5°C–10°C), so be sure to bring some warm clothing.

PLANNING YOUR TIME

Those who crave a couple of days of sunning themselves on a beach should head up to the resort towns and rain-forest fringed sands of the North Shore about 210 km (130 miles) from São Paulo (two to three hours by car; longer by bus). Alternatively squeeze in an afternoon on the sands by joining the paulistanos heading to the port city of Santos less than an hour away. If you prefer spending time in the mountains and have two or three days to spare, aim for Campos do Jordão, Águas de São Pedro, or Serra Negra. For a quicker day-trip, Embu das Artes or Santana de Parnaíba make great choices, especially for those interested in arts, crafts, and architecture, and they can even be reached by taxi.

GETTING HERE AND AROUND

Bus travel to and from the towns around São Paulo can be a time-consuming affair because of heavy traffic to and from the big city to commuter towns along the coast and inland, particularly on weekends. It is also possible to rent a car or take a taxi, particularly as roads are good and traffic isn't too chaotic once you're out of the city. Reaching many of the destinations around São Paulo is feasible by taxi, but expect to pay upwards of R$200 for one-way trips, even for relatively nearby destinations such as Embu das Artes and Santana de Parnaíba. Your taxi driver might agree to a flat fee over turning on the meter.

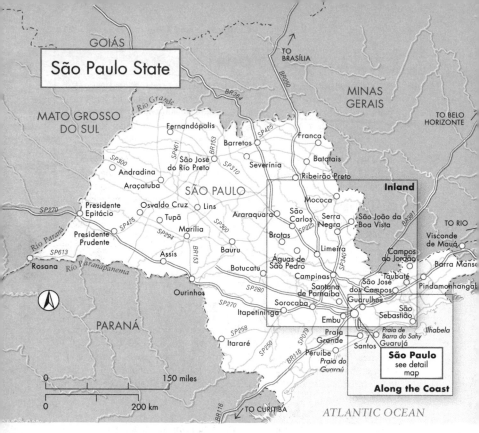

São Paulo State

GOIÁS

TO BRASÍLIA

MINAS GERAIS

MATO GROSSO DO SUL

Rio Grande

Fernandópolis

Barretos

Franca

TO BELO HORIZONTE

SP300

Andradina

São José do Rio Preto

SP310

Severínia

Batatais

Araçatuba

SÃO PAULO

Ribeirão Preto

Inland

SP270

Presidente Epitácio

Osvaldo Cruz

Lins

Mococa

TO RIO

Tupã

Araraquara

São Carlos

Serra Negra

São João da Boa Vista

Visconde de Mauá

Presidente Prudente

Marília

SP294

SP300

Brotas

Limeira

Campos do Jordão

Barra Mansa

SP613

Rosana

Rio Paranapanema

Assis

BR153

Bauru

Águas de São Pedro

São José dos Campos

Taubaté

Pindamonhangaba

PARANÁ

Botucatu

Campinas

Santana de Parnaíba

Guarulhos

São Sebastião

Ourinhos

SP280

Sorocaba

Embu

Praia de Barra do Sahy

Ilhabela

SP270

Itapetininga

Praia Grande

Santos

Guarujá

São Paulo
see detail map

0   150 miles

Itararé

SP250

Peruíbe

Praia do Guaraú

Along the Coast

0   200 km

BR116

TO CURITIBA

ATLANTIC OCEAN

RESTAURANTS

Restaurants in coastal towns tend to be of the rustic beach-café sort, and predictably serve lots of seafood. For a change of taste, visit Ubatuba and these three neighborhoods in or near São Sebastião—Maresias, Boiçucanga, and Camburi—where you can find good pizzerias and Japanese restaurants. In Campos do Jordão, a popular paulistano mountain retreat, you can find a Brazilian version of Swiss fondue (both the chocolate and the cheese varieties are delicious). In Serra Negra, you'll find typical countryside food, including lots of fresh meat and farm produce, as well as a vast range of local sweets, artisanal beers, and wine.

HOTELS

São Paulo has by far the best lodgings in the state. Elsewhere you can generally find basic *pousadas* (sort of like bed-and-breakfasts), with the occasional gems like Porto Pacuíba on Ilhabela and Shangri-Lá in Serra Negra. Coastal towns are packed in summer (from December to March) and it's almost impossible to get anything without advance reservations. The same holds true for Campos do Jordão and Serra Negra in winter (June and September). *Hotel reviews have been shortened. For full information, visit Fodors.com.*

WHAT IT COSTS IN REAIS			
$	**$$**	**$$$**	**$$$$**
Restaurants	under R$31	R$31–R$45	R$46–R$60	over R$60
Hotels	under R$251	R$251–R$375	R$376–R$500	over R$500

Restaurant prices are the average cost of a main course at dinner or, if dinner is not served, at lunch. Hotel prices are the lowest cost of a standard double room in high season, excluding tax.

ALONG THE COAST

After visiting the concrete jungle of São Paulo, you'll be pleased to find that there are some lovely beaches in São Paulo State that are within easy reach. The beaches of the South Shore in and around Santos are more urban than those farther up the coast, but pleasant enough for a quick escapade from the big city. The cleanest and best *praias* (beaches) in the region are along what is known as the Litoral Norte (North Shore), where mountains and bits of Atlantic Forest hug numerous small, sandy coves.

Beaches generally have restaurants nearby, or at least vendors in tents selling soft drinks, beer, and *porções* (platters of savory snacks such as shrimp and french fries, perfect for sharing). They often don't have bathrooms or phones right on the sands. Vendors rent beach umbrellas or chairs, especially in summer and on holidays and weekends. It is standard practice on Brazilian beaches to set up a *conta* (tab) with vendors, so you can order food and drinks during your stay and pay it all when you leave. On weekdays when school is in session, the beaches are gloriously deserted.

SANTOS

70 km (43 miles) south of São Paulo.

The biggest city on the São Paulo coast, Santos is the home of the largest container port in South America. At the turn of the 20th century, the local economy was focused on coffee exports, which contributed to the city's wealth and development. Lined with neoclassical buildings, the cobblestone streets of the historic center are compact enough to explore on foot. The main attraction here, though, is the coastline, a full 7 km (4½ miles) long, and adorned with a large beachfront garden. Try visiting on weekdays or Saturday.

GETTING HERE AND AROUND

Buses to Santos leave every 10–15 minutes from São Paulo's Jabaquara terminal, at the south end of the Linha 1 (Blue) of the underground. The journey takes just over an hour and offers views of the spectacular mountain range Serra do Mar. Santos's bus station is located right in the center and is a 10-minute walk to the Museu do Café in the historic center and the Museu Pelé in Valongo. A five-minute cab ride will drop

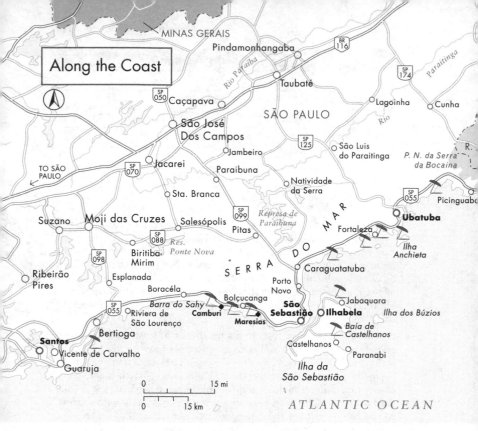

you off at the Gonzaga and José Menino Beaches, where most of the hotels, bars, and restaurants are located.

ESSENTIALS

Bus Contacts Terminal Rodoviário de Santos. ⊠ *Praça dos Andradas 45, Centro* ☎ *013/3213-2290.*

Visitor Information Tourist Information. ⊠ *Terminal Rodoviário de Santos, Praça dos Andradas 45, Centro* ☎ *0800 /173-887.*

TOURS

FAMILY **Bonde Turístico de Santos.** This delightful tour is on board a restored 1920s tram, which stops at all the main points of interest in the historic center. It's a hop-on, hop-off service, which allows you to jump off, have a look around, and get on the next tram when you're ready to move on. ⊠ *Praça Mauá, Centro* ☎ *013/3201-8000* 🎫 *R$6* ☺ *Tues.–Sun. 11–5.*

SAFETY AND PRECAUTIONS

When walking around at night, prefer the beaches of José Menino and Gonzaga; at these times, avoid walking around the area near the port and the bus station. If you need to get on a bus back to São Paulo at night, get a taxi straight to the station.

A BIT OF HISTORY

In the 19th century, farming, first of sugarcane, and then of coffee, was São Paulo's major industry and brought prosperity to the region. At the beginning of the 20th century, São Paulo became the center for industry in Brazil, as factories were built at a rapid pace, mostly by an immigrant workforce. By mid-century, São Paulo was one of the largest industrialized centers in Latin America and the state with the highest population in Brazil, thanks in part to mass migration from within Brazil.

Today São Paulo is the richest and most multicultural state in the country. It has about 1 million people of Middle Eastern descent, approximately 6 million people of Italian descent and the largest Japanese community outside of Japan (an estimated 1 million people).

EXPLORING

Museu do Café (*Coffee Museum*). The grand neoclassical Palácio da Bolsa de Café, where the Coffee Museum is located, was home to the coffee exchange up to 1957. Rosewood chairs are set out for traders in the trading hall, whose walls are hung with panels painted by Brazilian Benedicto Calixto. Upstairs are exhibits related to the world of coffee. Visitors can also sample the drink at the museum's cafeteria. ✉ *Rua 15 de Novembro 95* ☎ *013/3213–1750* ⊕ *www.museudocafe.com.br* ⛁ *R$6* ⊘ *Tues.–Sat. 9–5, Sun. 10–5.*

Fodor's Choice
★ **Museu Pelé.** Edson Arantes do Nascimento's, or simply Pelé's, self assessment—"I was born for soccer, just as Beethoven was born for music."—may seem a tad self-important, but to many soccer fans, who regard him as one of the world's greatest footballers, it is not far from the truth. Housed in a 19th-century mansion and opened during the 2014 World Cup, Museu Pelé honors Santos's most famous son through displays of his personal items and trophies, plus photos, videos, and documents concerning the footballer. The area surrounding the museum, the Valongo district, is currently being revitalized with restaurants, bars, and cultural centers. ✉ *Largo Marquês de Monte Alegre s/n, Valongo* ☎ *013/3704–6260* ⊕ *museupele.org.br* ⛁ *R$18* ⊘ *Tues.–Sun. 10–6.*

BEACHES

Praia do Santos. The massive, 7-km (4½-mile) strip of sand along Santos's shoreline is made up of a series of lively beaches. The city is crossed by seven channels, which act as borders between districts, and separate each of the beaches from one another. The busiest beaches—José Menino, Gonzaga, and Boqueirão—are between channels 1 and 4, and this is where you'll find the greatest concentration of hotels and restaurants. The sea conditions do not differ greatly from one beach to another, but at José Menino (channels 1 to 2) the waves are a bit stronger and better for surfing. Partiers gather at Gonzaga Beach (channels 2 to 3), where open air concerts often take place. Boqueirão (channels 3 to 4) has Santos's best infrastructure with ATMs, toilets, and showers, as well as a crafts fair on the weekend. Embaré Beach (channels 4 to 5) has many kiosks and bars and is a magnet for the younger set. Aparecida Beach (channels 5 to 6) is the meeting point for families with children, as well as seniors, and the location of the biggest beachfront garden in the world. The calm, almost flat sea at Ponta da Praia (channels 6 to 7) is suitable for water sports such as sailing, windsurfing, and jet skiing. **Amenities:** food and drink; lifeguards; showers; toilets. **Best for:** partiers; walking. ✉ *From Av. Presidente Wilsom 1900 (José Menino beach) to Av. Saldanha da Gama (Ponta da Praia).*

WHERE TO EAT AND STAY

$$$ CONTEMPORARY Fodor's Choice ★ 🍴 **Guaiaó.** A hidden gem and a favorite among well-informed locals, Guaiaó serves up a (successfully) adventurous menu of world dishes with a Brazilian twist created by chef André Ahn, including watermelon carpaccio and smoked *vieira*, a local fish specialty. The coffee pudding is highly recommended, as is the fresh seasonal fruit salad with lemon mousse. [$] *Average main: R$60* ✉ *Rua Dom Lara 65, Boqueirão* ☎ *013/3877–5379* 🕒 *No lunch. Closed Sun.* ✍ *Reservations essential* 💳 *No credit cards.*

$$ HOTEL 🏨 **Mercure Santos Hotel.** Hotel chain Mercure offers a practical base for a short visit to Santos, located near the beach and the historical center, as well as the main bars and restaurants. **Pros:** beach location; rooftop terrace. **Cons:** room service is rather slow. [$] *Rooms from: R$300* ✉ *Av. Washington Luiz 565, Boqueirão, Santos* ☎ *013/3036–1013* 🌐 *mercure.com* 🛏 *107 rooms* 🍽 *Breakfast.*

SÃO SEBASTIÃO

204 km (127 miles) southeast of São Paulo.

São Sebastião stretches along 100 km (62 miles) of the North Shore. Its bays, islands, and beaches attract everyone from the youngsters who flock to Maresias and Camburi to the families who favor Barra do Sahy and Camburizinho. Boating enthusiasts, hikers, and wildlife-seekers also come here, especially on weekends, when hotels are often crowded. Nightlife is good here—the main spots are in Maresias and Boiçucanga. The "beautiful island" of Ilhabela *(below)* is a 15-minute ferry ride away from downtown São Sebastião.

GETTING HERE AND AROUND

Litorânea buses travel four times daily to São Sebastião (to the ferry dock) from São Paulo's Tietê terminal, close to the international airport of Guarulhos, and take about four hours.

The drive from São Paulo to São Sebastião is about three hours if it is not raining. Some of the North Shore's most beautiful houses line the Rio-Santos Highway (SP 055) on the approach to Maresias. However, extra care is required when driving along the 055, as the road conditions and lighting are precarious, particularly past Maresias. To reach the 055, take the Ayrton Senna (SP 070) highway, followed by Mogi-Bertioga (SP 098). Alternatively if you want to get straight to the center of São Sebastião where the Ilhabela ferry docks, take Rodovia Ayrton Senna–Carvalho Pinto (SP 070), followed by Rodovia Tamoios (SP 099) to Caraguatatuba, and then follow the signs.

ESSENTIALS

Bus Contacts **Litorânea.** ☎ *011/3775–3850, 0800/285–3047* 🌐 *www.litoranea.com.br.* **Terminal Rodoviário.** ✉ *Praça Vereador Venino Fernandes Moreira 10, São Sebastião.*

Visitor Information **Sectur.** ✉ *Avenida Altino Arantes 174, São Sebastião* ☎ *012/3892–2620.*

BEACHES

FAMILY **Barra do Sahy.** Families with young children favor small, quiet Barra do Sahy. Its narrow strip of sand (with a bay and a river on one side and rocks on the other) is steep but smooth, and the water is clean and calm. Kayakers paddle about, and divers are drawn to the nearby Ilha das Couves. Area restaurants serve mostly basic fish dishes with rice and salad, as well as sharing platters of snacks, seafood, and fries. Note that Barra do Sahy's entrance is atop a slope and appears suddenly—be on the lookout around marker Km 174. **Amenities:** food and drink; lifeguards; parking (no fee). **Best for:** snorkeling; sunrise. ✉ *Rio-Santos Hwy., SP 055, São Sebastião* ✣ *157 km (97 miles) southeast of São Paulo.*

Camburizinho and Camburi. Wealthy paulistanos flock to Camburizinho and Camburi, to sunbathe, surf, and party. While the first beach is more secluded and also where the families head to, the latter, on the other side of the river Camburi, is where the action is, with night owls heading here to play guitar by the moonlight. At the center of the beaches is a cluster of cafés, ice-cream shops, bars, and restaurants. The two beaches are located just north of Barra do Sahy. If you're coming from the south, take the second entrance, which is usually in better shape than the first entrance, at Km 166. **Amenities:** food and drink; lifeguards; parking (fee). **Best for:** partiers; sunset; surfing. ✉ *Rio-Santos Hwy., SP 055, São Sebastião* ✣ *162 km (100 miles) southeast of São Paulo.*

Maresias. Maresias is a 4-km (2-mile) stretch of white sand with clean, green waters that are good for swimming and surfing. Maresias is popular with a young crowd and compared with the others along the North Coast, its beach village is large and has a good infrastructure, with banks, supermarkets, and a wide choice of nightlife entertainment. **Amenities:** food and drink; lifeguards; parking (fee); toilets. **Best for:** partiers; surfing; windsurfing. ✉ *Rio-Santos Hwy, Km 151, SP 055, São Sebastião* ✣ *177 km (109 miles) southeast of São Paulo.*

WHERE TO EAT

$ PIZZA 🍴 **Candeeiro.** On the main street of Camburi, Candeeiro serves delicious Neapolitan-style pizza, as well as crepes. The little gallery where it is located has a very good ice-cream shop, Gelateria Parmalat, tucked at the back, so save room for dessert. [$] *Average main: R$30* ✉ *Estrada do Camburi 87, Camburi, São Sebastião* ☎ *012/3865–3626* 🕒 *No lunch* 💳 *No credit cards.*

$$$$ ITALIAN FAMILY 🍴 **Ristorante Mergellina Maresias.** A traditional restaurant run by a Neopolitan chef, Mergellina serves good, fuss-free Italian fare with generous portions and great desserts. The prices are a little higher than the local average, but this place is absolutely worthwhile. Try the Gorgonzola paste with freshly baked Italian bread to start, followed by risotto Brasil, with heart of palm, zucchini, and mushrooms, and the chocolate

and nut tart to finish. The well-rounded wine list has about 40 local and international varieties. Ask to sit outside, under a giant parasol. [$] *Average main: R$100* ✉ *Rua Dos Navegantes 139, Maresias, São Sebastião* ☎ *012/3865–7272* ⏲ *No lunch Mon. and Tues. Closed Wed.*

WHERE TO STAY

$$$$ HOTEL 🏨 **Amora Boutique Hotel.** Right on São Sebastião's beachfront, with easy access to the town center, this hotel has cozy rooms and a heated outdoor pool, hot tub, and sauna, perfect for days when agitated seas make the beach less appealing. **Pros:** beach service; comfortable rooms. **Cons:** limited and expensive food options. [$] *Rooms from: R$600* ✉ *Av. Dr. Francisco Loup 1285, São Sebastião* ☎ *012/3865–7377* 🌐 *www.amorahotel.com.br* 🌐 🛏 *23 suites* 🍴 *Breakfast.*

$$$$ HOTEL Fodor's Choice ★ 🏨 **Nau Royal.** Tucked away from the main cluster of Camburi's bars and all the noise of weekend partiers, this very special boutique hotel is the perfect choice for couples looking for peace and quiet. **Pros:** unparalled service; good restaurant; beach service. **Cons:** suites near reception area can be noisy. [$] *Rooms from: R$1,000* ✉ *Alameda Patriarca Antônio José Marques 1533, Camburi, São Sebastião* ☎ *012/3865–4486* 🌐 *www.nauroyal.com.br* 🛏 *15 suites* 🍴 *Breakfast.*

$$$ B&B/INN FAMILY 🏨 **Pousada Porto Mare.** On the main street just a stone's throw from the town's clubs and bars, Pousada Port Mare is a great choice for those who like to be close to the action, with plenty of amenities thrown in—a nice pool and sauna facilities, and beach service, too. **Pros:** excellent breakfast; good outdoor facilities. **Cons:** rooms near the breakfast area can be noisy; poor Wi-Fi. [$] *Rooms from: R$400* ✉ *Rua Sebastião Romão César 400, Maresias, São Sebastião* ☎ *012/3865–5272* 🌐 *www.pousadaportomare.com.br* 🛏 *28 rooms* 🍴 *Some meals.*

$$ B&B/INN 🏨 **Villa Bebek.** The owners of this chic hotel sought inspiration from Bali to create the beautiful gardens inlaid with pebbles, sculptures, and tropical plants surrounding the pool and sauna areas. **Pros:** beautiful decor; good service; perfect for relaxing poolside. **Cons:** fewer options at breakfast during low season. [$] *Rooms from: R$300* ✉ *Rua Zezito 251, Camburi, São Sebastião* ☎ *012/3865–3320* 🌐 *www.villabebek.com.br* 🛏 *15 rooms* 🍴 *Breakfast.*

NIGHTLIFE

Morocco. Combining dining with a club environment, Morocco hosts a wide range of live bands. When Sirena (*below*) doesn't appeal, partiers head here to dance. ✉ *Rua Silvina Auta Salles 375, São Sebastião* ☎ *012/3077–0020.*

Santo Gole. Santo Gole is an informal beach-style bar run by three friends that attracts a younger crowd and stays open until dawn. Come here for live rock music, draft beer, and light snacks. ✉ *Av. Rua Sebastião Romão César 477, São Sebastião* ☎ *012/3865–5044.*

Sirena. Wealthy, sun-kissed paulistanos head to Sirena to see and be seen, sip cocktails, and dance the night away, watching the sun rise from the external dance floor. ✉ *Rua Sebastião Romão César 418, Maresias, São Paulo* ☎ *011/3865–6681* 🌐 *www.sirena.com.br.*

ILHABELA

7 km (5 miles)/15-minute boat ride from São Sebastião.

Fodor's Choice Ilhabela is favored by those who like the beach and water sports; indeed,
★ many sailing competitions are held here as well as scuba diving. This is the biggest sea island in the country, with 22 calm beaches along its western shore, which faces the mainland. The hotels are mostly at the north end, though the best sandy stretches are the 13 to the south, which face the open sea. Eighty percent of the island is in a state park area, with some parts accessible by car and others by boat only.

There are two small towns on the island: one is where the locals live; the other is where most visitors stay because of its hotels, restaurants, and stores. During the winter months most businesses that cater to tourists, including restaurants, are open only on weekends.

Scuba divers have several 19th- and early-20th-century wrecks to explore—this region has the most wrecks of any area off Brazil's coast—and hikers can set off on the numerous inland trails, many of which lead to a waterfall (the island has more than 300). ■TIP➔ **Mosquitoes are a problem; bring plenty of insect repellent.**

5

GETTING HERE AND AROUND
Balsas (ferries) from São Sebastião to Ilhabela run every 30 minutes from 6 am to midnight and hourly during the night. The São Sebastião Balsa transports vehicles as well as passengers. Fares range from R$15 (weekdays) to R$22.50 (weekends), including a car. To get to the ferry dock in São Sebastião, take Avenida São Sebastião from town to the coast. Make advance ferry reservations, particularly December through February. On rainy days, it is worth checking whether ferries are operating at all.

The best way to get around Ilhabela is by car. There are no rental agencies on the island (or connecting bridges) so be sure to make arrangements beforehand. Public buses also cross the island from north to south daily.

ESSENTIALS
Ferry Information São Sebastião Balsa (Ferry). ⊠ *São Sebastião* ☎ *012/3892–1576.*

Visitor and Tour Information Ilhabela Secretaria do Turismo. ⊠ *Praça Vereador José Leite dos Passos 14, Ilhabela* ☎ *012/3895–7492* ⊕ *www.ilhabela. sp.gov.br.*

TOURS
Maremar Turismo. Maremar Turismo offers a range of scuba diving, Jeep, horseback riding, and hiking tours around Ilhabela's most popular areas, as well as some off-the-beaten track tours. ⊠ *Av. Princesa Isabel 90, Ilhabela* ☎ *012/3896–1418* ⊕ *www.maremar.tur.br* 🖼 *From R$50.*

BEACHES
Praia da Armação. The long strip of white sand and calm sea attract sailing, windsurfing, and kitesurfing aficionados. Busy during most of the year, Praia da Armação has an excellent infrastructure, with bars, restaurants, and kiosks serving food and drinks and renting parasols and beach chairs. Bathrooms, baby changing facilities, and parking

bays are available. There is a church on-site, which is said to be one of the oldest buildings on the island. The beach was also once the site of a factory for processing blubber and other resources from whales caught in the waters around Ilhabela. **Amenities:** food and drink; lifeguards; parking (fee); toilets; water sports. **Best for:** snorkeling; sunset; walking; windsurfing. ✉ *14 km (9 miles) north of ferry dock, Ilhabela.*

Praia do Curral. Curral is one of the most famous beaches on Ilhabela, and is popular with tourists as well as young people. It has clear and slightly rough waters and also a large green area, which serves as a refuge for those needing a break from sunbathing. The local vendors provide tables and chairs, fresh showers with clean water, bathrooms, and parking. At night people gather at the many restaurants and bars—some with live music—and there are places to camp. The wreck of the ship *Aymoré* (1921) can be found off the coast of this beach, near Ponta do Ribeirão, where you can also look for a waterfall trail. **Amenities:** food and drink; lifeguards; showers; toilets. **Best for:** partiers; sunset. ✉ *6 km (4 miles) south of Praia Grande, Ilhabela.*

Praia Grande. It's busy, but some of the best infrastructure in Ilhabela can be found here: the kiosks have tables in the shade; you can rent a chair from most vendors along the long sandy strip; showers are available free of charge; and there's even a chapel. The beach is popular for windsurfing, diving, and surfing. The sandy strip is rather inclined, with a tumble in the central part. The sands are thick and yellowish. On the far left there is a small river that ends in the sea. **Amenities:** food and drink; lifeguards; showers; toilets. **Best for:** partiers; surfing; walking; windsurfing. ✉ *13 km (8 miles) south of ferry dock, Ilhabela.*

WHERE TO EAT

$$$$ SEAFOOD 🍴 **Ilha Sul.** The best option on the menu at Ilha Sul is the grilled shrimp with vegetables. Fish and other seafood are also available. [$] *Average main: R$90* ✉ *Av. Riachuelo 287, Ilhabela* ☎ *012/3894–9426* 🕒 *Closed Mon.–Thurs. in the months of Apr.–June and Aug.–Nov.*

$$$$ SEAFOOD FAMILY 🍴 **Viana.** *Camarão* (shrimp) is prepared in various ways at this traditional, petite restaurant with just a few tables. It's popular among locals, who come here to eat and enjoy the gorgeous view and sunsets. Grilled fish is also on the menu. It's open for breakfast Tuesday and on weekends. [$] *Average main: R$65* ✉ *Av. Leonardo Reale 2301, Ilhabela* ☎ *012/3896–1089* 💳 *No credit cards* 🕒 *No lunch Mon. and Thurs. Closed Wed.* ✍ *Reservations essential.*

WHERE TO STAY

$$$$ HOTEL Fodor's Choice ★ 🏨 **DPNY Beach Hotel & Spa.** This luxury hotel is geared up for couples looking for romance and relaxation, with modern, comfortable rooms and direct access to Praia do Curral, one of Ilhabela's most famous beaches. **Pros:** luxuriously comfortable rooms; excellent food; perfect for poolside relaxation. **Cons:** service can be slow at busy times. [$] *Rooms from: R$738* ✉ *Praia do Curral, Av. Jose Pacheco do Nascimento 7668, Ilhabela* ☎ *012/3894–3000* 🛏 *79 suites* 🍽 *Breakfast* 💳 *No credit cards.*

$$$$ HOTEL 🏨 **Maison Joly.** Past guests of this exclusive hotel at the top of the Cantagalo Hill range from kings of Sweden to the Rolling Stones. **Pros:** beautiful surroundings; excellent restaurant. **Cons:** service a little erratic

in busy seasons. [$] *Rooms from: R$575* ✉ *Rua Antônio Lisboa Alves 278, Ilhabela* ☎ *012/3896–1201, 012/3896–2364* 🌐 *www.maisonjoly.com.br* 🛏 *9 rooms* 🍴 *Breakfast.*

$$$ HOTEL FAMILY 🏨 **Porto Pacuíba.** Peaceful and family-friendly, Porto Pacuíba is close to a beach and has easy access to good hikes nearby. **Pros:** excellent service; good restaurant; well-decorated rooms. **Cons:** far from the town center and ferry dock. [$] *Rooms from: R$400* ✉ *Av. Leonardo Reale 2392, Viana, Ilhabela* ☎ *012/3896–2466* 🛏 *29 suites* 🍴 *Breakfast.*

$ B&B/INN 🏨 **Pousada dos Hibiscos.** North of the ferry dock, this red house has midsize rooms, all at ground level. **Pros:** great service; hearty breakfast. **Cons:** couples looking for poolside relaxation may be disturbed by large groups; rooms may feel a little small. [$] *Rooms from: R$220* ✉ *Av. Pedro de Paula Moraes 720, Ilhabela* ☎ *012/3896–1375* 🌐 *www.pousadadoshibiscos.com.br* 🛏 *13 suites* 🍴 *Breakfast.*

SPORTS AND THE OUTDOORS

BOATING AND SAILING

Ilha Sailing Ocean School. Sailing courses here run 12 hours and cost about R$500. ✉ *Av. Pedro de Paula Moraes 578, Ilhabela* ☎ *012/9766–6619* 🌐 *www.ilhasailing.com.br.*

KITE- AND WINDSURFING

BL3. You can take kitesurfing, windsurfing, and sailing lessons at BL3, the biggest school in Ilhabela. Individual lessons are priced from R$200. ✉ *Av. Perimetral Norte 4260, Ilhabela* ☎ *012/3286–5885* 🌐 *www.bl3.com.br.*

SCUBA DIVING

Diving is a popular activity for those visiting Ilhabela. In the calm, transparent waters, you can explore the marine wildlife as well as discover the mysteries surrounding the island's various shipwrecks. It is said that Ilhabela has more than 100 close to its shore. These vessels have formed huge submerged artificial reefs, and are now home to a wide variety of aquatic species such as turtles, octopuses, and the like. It is still possible to actually see the ships. Beginning divers should aim for the most popular wrecks, such as the *Aymoré* (1914; Curral Beach; 3–7 meters) and the *Darth* (1894; Itaboca Beach; 5–15 meters). There are numerous diving schools along nearly every beach, which also rent equipment if you are happy to go solo.

Colonial Diver. You can rent equipment, take diving classes, and arrange for a dive-boat trip through Colonial Diver. The basic course takes up to three days and costs around R$1,190, which includes equipment for the classes, course material, and an international certificate. ✉ *Av. Brasil 1751, Ilhabela* ☎ *012/3894–9459* 🌐 *www.colonialdiver.com.br.*

Fodor's Choice ★ **Ilha das Cabras.** The main attractions of this little piece of paradise—besides the white sand and clear water—are the tiny bars that serve delicious, fresh seafood and the Ecological Sanctuary of Ilha das Cabras. The park, created in 1992, is a secluded reserve around the island and is also a great diving and fish-watching site. While most "baptisms" of diving beginners take place here, seasoned divers head off to their underwater adventures at the diving/snorkeling sanctuary off the shore of the isle, where a statue of Neptune can be found at the 22-foot depth. ⊠ *2 km (1 mile) south of ferry, Ilhabela.*

Fodor's Choice **Ilha de Búzios.** A nearly two-hour boat trip separates Ilhabela from Ilha
★ de Búzios, but the effort is totally worthwhile. Because it is located far
from the coast, the water is very transparent, meaning divers will be able
to see plenty of colorful fish and other underwater fauna such as rays
and sea turtles. The main stars, however, are the dolphins, which fear-
lessly approach boats. ⊠ *25 km (15 miles) offshore; take boat from São
Sebastião, Ilhabela.*

Itaboca. One of best places for diving is Itaboca, where British ship
Darth sank in 1884, leaving bottles of wine and porcelain dishes that
can still be found. ⊠ *17 km (11 miles) south of ferry dock, Ilhabela.*

UBATUBA

234 km (145 miles) southeast of São Paulo.

Many of the more than 70 beaches around Ubatuba are more than
beautiful enough to merit the long drive from São Paulo. Young people,
surfers, and couples with and without children hang out in the 90-km
(56-mile) area, where waterfalls, boat rides, aquariums, diving, and
trekking in the wild are major attractions. Downtown Ubatuba also
has an active nightlife, especially in summer.

GETTING HERE AND AROUND
Litorânea buses travel eight times a day to Ubatuba from São Paulo. The
journey takes about four hours. By car from São Paulo, take Rodovia
Ayrton Senna–Carvalho Pinto (SP 070), followed by Rodovia Tamoios
(SP 099) to Caraguatatuba. Turn right and head north on SP 055.

ESSENTIALS
Bus Contacts Litorânea. ☎ *011/3775–3850* ⊕ *www.litoranea.com.br.*
Rodoviária. ⊠ *Av. Thomas Galhardo 513, Ubatuba* ⊕ *www.rodoviariaubatuba.
com.*

BEACHES
Praia Grande. For those seeking a party atmosphere, Praia Grande is a
great option. It has bars and restaurants by the sea, with local samba
and country music playing all day. Chairs and parasols can be hired
from beach vendors. The waters here are clean and green, and the hard
sands are ideal for football, volleyball, and racquetball; it's also a great
place for hiking. Praia Grande is a major surf spot in Ubatuba, with
consistent, perfect waves. **Amenities:** food and drink; lifeguards; parking
(fee). **Best for:** partiers; surfing; walking. ⊠ *Off Tamoios (SP 099) and
Rio-Santos intersection, Ubatuba.*

Praia do Prumirim. Surrounded by rain forest and lined with summer
holiday mansions, Prumirim is a small beach of coarse sands and tur-
quoise calm waters. Despite its exuberant natural beauty, Prumirim is
not very busy. There's good surfing, but the waves are generally smaller
than those at Praia Grande. About a kilometer out to sea, Prumirim
Island also has magnificent scenery and is a great place for diving. To
reach the island you can pay one of the local fishermen to ferry you
out there or, if you're particularly fit, you could even swim. The access

to Praia do Prumirim is near Km 29 of SP 055, past the entrance to a private condominium. A beautiful waterfall with a natural pool can also be accessed nearby off the highway. **Amenities:** food and drink. **Best for:** snorkeling; solitude; sunrise; walking. ✉ *Near Km 29 of BR 101 (Rio-Santos), Ubatuba.*

WHERE TO EAT AND STAY

$ BRAZILIAN FAMILY 🍴 **Padaria Integrale.** This popular, centrally located *padaria* (bakery) offers a range of healthy sandwiches and drinks, as well as an excellent deli selection. Even if the place is packed, service is still agile and friendly. You can either have your breakfast or light meal here, or take it away like many locals do. [$] *Average main: R$25* ✉ *Rua Dr. Esteves da Silva 360, Ubatuba* ☎ *012/3836–1036.*

$$$$ HOTEL Fodor's Choice ★ 🏨 **Pousada Picinguaba.** A luxury pousada in the beautiful, unspoiled fishing village of Picinguaba, this place is ideal for couples looking for peace and quiet. **Pros:** beautiful surroundings; excellent food; unparalleled service. **Cons:** the pousada is up a steep hill. [$] *Rooms from: R$1,120* ✉ *Rua G 130 , Picinguaba, Ubatuba* ☎ *012/3836–9105* 🌐 *www.picinguaba.com* 🛏 *10 suites* 🍽 *Some meals.*

$ B&B/INN FAMILY 🏨 **Pousada Torre del Mar.** A simple but comfortable and very clean pousada, Torre del Mar is just a stone's throw from the town's main attractions, beaches, and restaurants. **Pros:** comfortable beds; excellent homemade breakfast; central location. **Cons:** rooms facing the street can be noisy; rooms can be quite small. [$] *Rooms from: R$200* ✉ *Av. Milton de Holanda Maia 210, Itaguá, Ubatuba* ☎ *012/3832–2751* 🛏 *18 suites* 🍽 *Breakfast* 💳 *No credit cards.*

INLAND

São Paulo's inland region has beautiful mountains, springs, rivers, and waterfalls perfect for outdoor activities like hiking and rafting. Historic attractions are generally fewer than in other states. Save some time for clothing and crafts shopping, and for the lavish regional cuisine.

Highways that lead to inland towns are some of the best in the state. To get to Águas de São Pedro, take Anhangüera–Bandeirantes (SP 330/SP 348); to Santana de Parnaíba, take Castelo Branco (SP 280); and to Campos de Jordão, take Ayrton Senna–Carvalho Pinto (SP 70). Embu is the exception—it's a 30-minute drive from the capital on the not-so-well-maintained Régis Bittencourt (BR 116). To go by bus, choose between the daily departures from the Tietê and Barra Funda terminals in São Paulo. Both are next to subway stations, making access fairly easy.

ÁGUAS DE SÃO PEDRO

180 km (112 miles) northwest of São Paulo.

Although Águas de São Pedro is one of the smallest cities in Brazil, at a mere 3.9 square km (1.5 square miles), its sulfurous waters made it famous countrywide in the 1940s and '50s. The healing hot springs were discovered by chance in the 1920s when technicians were drilling for oil.

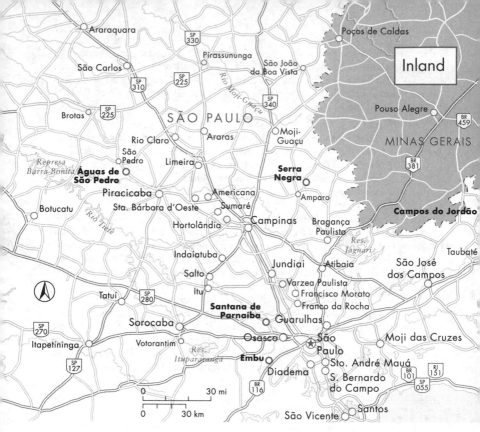

You can access the springs at the Balneário Publico (public bathhouse) or through some hotels. Though a number of illnesses respond to the water, most visitors are just healthy tourists soaking in relaxation. Águas de São Pedro is compact, so it's easy to get around on foot.

GETTING HERE AND AROUND

Águas de São Pedro is about a 2½-hour drive north of São Paulo on Anhangüera-Bandeirantes (SP 330/SP 348) and then SP 304.

ESSENTIALS

Visitor Information **Tourist Information.** ⊠ *Praça Pref Geraldo Azevedo 153, Águas de São Pedro* ☎ *019/3482–1652* ⊕ *www.aguasdesaopedro.sp.gov.br.*

EXPLORING

Balneário Municipal Dr. Octávio Moura Andrade. Want immersion baths in sulfurous springwater? You can swim in the pool or sweat in the sauna while you wait for your private soak, massage, or beauty treatment. A snack bar and a gift shop round out the spa services. The surrounding forested grounds are perfect for a leisurely stroll or a ride on horseback (R$10 for half an hour). The park is free and open to the public in the morning on weekdays and all day on weekends. ⊠ *Av. Carlos Mauro, Águas de São Pedro* ☎ *019/3482–1333* 🎟 *R$8–R$50* ⊙ *Mon.–Thurs. 7:30 am–12:30 pm, Fri. and Sat. 7 am–noon and 3–6 pm, Sun. 7 am–12:30 pm.*

WHERE TO STAY

$$ HOTEL

🏨 **Avenida Charme Hotel.** This hotel, resembling a large ranch house, has an arcaded veranda and well-maintained, but rather dated, rooms. **Pros:** excellent breakfast; friendly service; good pool area. **Cons:** rooms are spacious but plain and sparsely decorated. [$] *Rooms from: R$300* ✉ *Av. Carlos Mauro 246, Águas de São Pedro* ☎ *019/3482–7900,* 🌐 *www.hotelavenida.com.br* 🛏 *53 rooms* 🍴 *All-inclusive.*

$$$$ HOTEL Fodor'sChoice ★

🏨 **Grande Hotel São Pedro.** In the middle of a 300,000-square-meter (3.2 million-square-foot) park with more than 1 million trees and local wildlife, this hotel is in a beautiful art deco building that was a casino during the 1940s. **Pros:** beautiful location; excellent service. **Cons:** requires booking months in advance, especially during the winter season. [$] *Rooms from: R$800* ✉ *Parque Dr. Octávio de Moura Andrade, Águas de São Pedro* ☎ *019/3482–7600* 🌐 *www.grandehotelsenac.com.br* 🛏 *96 rooms, 16 suites* 🍴 *No meals.*

$ HOTEL

🏨 **Hotel Jerubiaçaba.** In a 17,000-square-meter (183,000-square-foot) green area with springs and a bathhouse, this hotel features rooms bathed in light colors. **Pros:** excellent location. **Cons:** rather simple furnishings; not very comfortable mattresses. [$] *Rooms from: R$200* ✉ *Av. Carlos Mauro 168, Águas de São Pedro* ☎ *0800/13–1411* 🌐 *www.hoteljerubiacaba.com.br* 🛏 *120 rooms, 8 suites* 🍴 *No meals.*

5

CAMPOS DO JORDÃO

184 km (114 miles) northeast of São Paulo.

In the Serra da Mantiqueira at an altitude of 5,525 feet, Campos do Jordão and its fresh mountain air are paulistanos' favorite winter attractions. In July temperatures drop as low as 32°F (0°C), though it never snows; in warmer months temperatures linger in the 13°C–16°C (55°F–60°F) range.

In the past some people came for their health (the town was once a tuberculosis treatment area), others for inspiration—including such Brazilian artists as writer Monteiro Lobato, dramatist Nelson Rodrigues, and painter Lasar Segall. Nowadays the arts continue to thrive, especially during July's Festival de Inverno (Winter Festival), which draws classical musicians from around the world.

Exploring Campos do Jordão without a car is difficult, as attractions are far-flung. The neighborhood of Vila Capivary is where most restaurants and cafés are located.

GETTING HERE AND AROUND

Six Passaro Marron buses leave São Paulo for Campos do Jordão daily. The journey takes three hours and costs R$43. To reach Campos do Jordão from São Paulo (a 2½-hour drive), take Rodovia Carvalho Pinto (SP 070) and SP 123.

ESSENTIALS

Bus Contacts Passaro Marron. ☎ *0800/2853–047, 011/3775–3890* 🌐 *www.passaromarron.com.br.* **Terminal Rodoviário.** ✉ *Rua Benedito Lourenço 285, Campos do Jordão.*

Visitor Information **Campos do Jordão Tourist Office.** ✉ *At entrance to town, Campos do Jordão* ☎ *012/3664–3525* 🌐 *www.camposdojordao.com.br.*

EXPLORING

TOP ATTRACTIONS

FAMILY **Amantikir Garden.** The Amantikir Garden consists of 17 areas inspired by various ecosystems and famous gardens around the world. On the grounds you can find a cafeteria and a learning center, where there are courses on gardening. Plans arc in the works for expanding the area and building a bird-watching center. Reservations are mandatory, as the place receives a limited number of guests per day. An English-speaking guide is available if booked in advance. ✉ *Rodovia Campos do Jordão Eugênio Lefreve 215, Estrada Gavião Gonzaga, Campos do Jordão* ☎ *012/3662–5044* 🌐 *www.parqueamantikir.com.br* 🎟 *R$25* 🕒 *Daily 8–5.*

FAMILY **Estação Ferroviária Emílio Ribas.** A wonderful little train departs from Estação Ferroviária Emílio Ribas for tours of the city and its environs, including the 47-km (29-mile) trip to Reino das Águas Claras, where there's a park with waterfalls and models of Monteiro Lobato's characters (Lobato is a well-loved children's-book author). Be sure to book in advance. ✉ *Av. Dr. Emílio Ribas s/n, Vila Capivari, Campos do Jordão* 🎟 *R$11* 🕒 *Daily departures every hr apart from noon.*

Horto Florestal. Horto Florestal is a natural playground for *macacos-prego* (nail monkeys), squirrels, and parrots, as well as people. The park has a trout-filled river, waterfalls, and trails—all set among trees from around the world and one of the last *araucária* (Brazilian pine) forests in the state. ✉ *Av. Pedro Paulo, Km 13, Campos do Jordão* ☎ *012/3663–3762* 🎟 *R$13* 🕒 *Daily 9–6.*

Morro do Elefante (*Elephant Hill*). Outside town a chairlift ride to the top of Morro do Elefante is a good way to enjoy the view from a 5,850-foot height. ✉ *Av. José Oliveira Damas s/n, Campos do Jordão* ☎ *012/3663–1530* 🎟 *R$7* 🕒 *Tues.–Fri. 1–5, weekends 9–5:30.*

Palácio Boa Vista. Palácio Boa Vista, the official winter residence of the state's governor, has paintings by such famous Brazilian modernists as Di Cavalcanti, Portinari, Volpi, Tarsila do Amaral, and Anita Malfatti. On the same property, the Capela de São Pedro (São Pedro Chapel) has sacred art from the 17th and 18th centuries. ✉ *Av. Dr. Adhemar de Barros 3001, Campos do Jordão* ☎ *012/3662–1122* 🎟 *Free* 🕒 *Wed., Thurs., Sat., and Sun. 10–noon and 2–5.*

WHERE TO EAT AND STAY

$$$ GERMAN Fodor's Choice ★ 🍴 **Baden-Baden.** One of the specialties at this charming German restaurant and *chopperia* in the heart of town is sauerkraut *garni* (sour cabbage with German sausages). The typical dish serves two and is almost as popular as Baden-Baden's cold draft beer from the attached brewery, open 10–5 on weekdays. [$] *Average main: R$60* ✉ *Rua Djalma Forjaz 93, Loja 10, Campos do Jordão* ☎ *012/3663–3610.*

$$$ SWISS 🍴 **Baronesa Von Leithner.** This Switzerland-inspired restaurant on a working berry farm is surrounded by beautiful Brazilian pine trees. Typical fare such as fondue is served and you can buy homemade jellies, fudges, and jams made on-site. [$] *Average main: R$60* ✉ *Av. Fausto Arruda Camargo*

CLOSE UP

Os Bandeirantes

In the 16th and 17th centuries, groups called *bandeiras* (literally meaning "flags" but also an archaic term for an assault force) set out on expeditions from São Paulo. Their objectives were far from noble. Their initial goal was to enslave Native Americans. Later, they were hired to capture escaped African slaves and destroy *quilombos* (communities the slaves created deep in the interior). Still, by heading inland at a time when most colonies were close to the shore, the *bandeirantes* (bandeira members) inadvertently did Brazil a great service.

A fierce breed, bandeirantes often adopted indigenous customs and voyaged for years at a time. Some went as far as the Amazon River; others only to what is today Minas Gerais, where gold and precious gems were found. In their travels they ignored the 1494 Treaty of Tordesilhas, which established a boundary between Spanish and Portuguese lands. (The boundary was a vague north–south line roughly 1,600 km (1,000 miles) west of the Cape Verde islands.) Other Brazilians followed the bandeirantes, and towns were founded, often in what was technically Spanish territory. These colonists eventually claimed full possession of the lands they settled, and thus Brazil's borders were greatly expanded.

Near Parque Ibirapuera in the city of São Paulo, there's a monument, inaugurated in 1953, to honor the bandeirantes. It's a huge granite sculpture created by Victor Brecheret, a famous Brazilian artist. A major São Paulo highway is named Bandeirantes and several roads across the state are named after these supposedly brave, honorable men. Protests are occasionally staged at the Ibirapuera statue by those who don't believe the bandeirantes deserve any kind of monument whatsoever.

5

2815, Alto da Boa Vista, Campos do Jordão ☎ *012/3662–1121* 🌐 *www.baronesavonleithner.com.br* 🕑 *Closed Mon.* 💳 *No credit cards.*

$ CAFÉ 🍴 **Chocolates Montanhês.** A well-known chocolate shop and café, and a perfect stop after a meal, where you can stock up on chocolate lollipops and slabs. Don't forget to try the extra-creamy hot chocolate. [$] *Average main: R$20* ✉ *Praça São Benedito 45, Loja 6, Campos do Jordão* ☎ *012/3663–1979* 🌐 *www.chocolatemontanhes.com.br* 💳 *No credit cards.*

$$$$ RESORT FAMILY Fodor's Choice ★ 🏨 **Grande Hotel Campos do Jordão.** A former 1940s casino—just like its sister hotel in Águas de São Pedro—the Grande Hotel is a teaching hotel that boasts extensive grounds with beautiful gardens and plenty of outdoor activities. **Pros:** excellent food; unparalled service; plenty of activities for adults and children. **Cons:** few dining options for vegetarians and others with dietary restrictions. [$] *Rooms from: R$800* ✉ *Av. Frei Orestes Girardi 3549, Vila Capivary, Campos do Jordão* ☎ *012/3668–6000, 0800/770–0790 for reservations* 🛏 *95 suites* 🍽 *All meals* 💳 *No credit cards.*

$$ HOTEL 🏨 **Pousada Villa Capivary.** A stay at this cozy guesthouse puts you in the gastronomic and commercial center of Campos. **Pros:** friendly, helpful, and efficient staff; central location. **Cons:** booking well in advance

required, particularly in the winter months. $ *Rooms from: R$350* ✉ *Av. Victor Godinho 131, Campos do Jordão* ☎ *012/3663–1746* ⊕ *www.capivari.com.br* ⤴ *15 rooms* ⦿ *Breakfast.*

SHOPPING

Boulevard Genéve. This mall in the busy Vila Capivari district is lined with cafés, bars, and restaurants, making it a nightlife hub. You can also find plenty of clothing stores, and candy shops selling chocolate, the town's specialty. ✉ *Rua Doutor Djalma Forjas 93, Vila Capivari, Campos do Jordão* ☎ *012/3663–5060* ⊕ *www.boulevardgeneve.com.br.*

Maison Genéve. The best handmade embroidered clothing in town is at Maison Genéve, open weekdays 10–7 and weekends 10–10. It also has a café offering a range of cakes, pastries, and drinks. ✉ *Av. Dr. Januário Miráglia 3224, Vila Jaguaribe, Campos do Jordão* ☎ *012/3663–3922* ⊕ *www.lojageneve.com.br.*

SERRA NEGRA

142 km (88.2 miles) northeast of São Paulo.

At 4,265 feet above sea level in the Serra da Mantiqueira, Serra Negra attracts hordes of paulistanos and cruising motorbike fans looking for a bucolic weekend break in the mountains. In addition to various mineral water fountains, there is the Coffee Route, where you can drive through thousands of acres of coffee fields until you reach Cachoeira dos Sonhos (Dreams Waterfall), where it's possible to swim and have a snack. You can also head over to Alto da Serra, the town's highest point, where paragliding aficionados gather on the weekends. To get there, follow the signs from Avenida João Gerosa and drive up Rua 14 de Julho all the way past Hotel São Mateus, until you reach an unpaved road on the left that will lead to the top. The main shopping street in Serra Negra is Rua Coronel Pedro Penteado, where you can find plenty of knitwear, leather bags and clothing, as well as sweets and cheeses of all kinds. The town center is small enough to be explored by foot.

GETTING HERE AND AROUND

Nine Fênix buses leave São Paulo's Tietê bus terminal for Serra Negra daily. The journey takes 3½ hours and costs R$37. To reach Serra Negra from São Paulo (a 2½-hour drive), take Rodovia Fernão Dias (SP 381) to Atibaia, Rodovia Dom Pedro I (SP 065) toward Itatiba, then the SP 360.

ESSENTIALS

Bus Contacts Rápido Fênix. ✉ *Praça Sesquicentenário s/n, Serra Negra* ☎ *019/3892–2098* ⊕ *www.rapidofenix.com.br.*

Visitor Information Serra Negra Tourist Office. ✉ *Praça Sesquicentenário, Serra Negra* ✛ *Behind the bus station and next to chairlift* ☎ *019/3842–2109.*

EXPLORING

Monte Alegre do Sul. If you have more than a day to spare and are driving, pay a quick visit to the delightful little town of Monte Alegre do Sul, just 6 km (4 miles) from Serra Negra and known for its September strawberry festival. The buildings of the historic center, including the town's church, Santuario Bom Jesus, date from the 19th century. Check out the shop of local artisan group Associarte, as well as the traditional sweet shop Peschiera nearby. At the old train station, a steam engine used for transporting coffee waits at a decommissioned platform. ✉ *Monte Alegre do Sul, Serra Negra.*

WHERE TO EAT

$$$ FUSION

🍴 **Bar da Fonte.** A delightful restaurant oozing charm, Bar da Fonte serves excellent dishes based on a mix of cuisines. Choices range from risottos to Indian-inspired stews and steaks, as well as feijoada served on Saturdays. A small cachaça distillery is based on-site, and the owner Marcos Kaloy offers tours that include a tasting. Local beers are also available. There's often live music in the evening on weekends. [$] *Average main: R$60* ✉ *Rua Joaquim de Oliveira 116, Monte Alegre do Sul* ☎ *019/3899–1239* 🕒 *Closed Mon.–Wed.* 💳 *No credit cards.*

$$$ BRAZILIAN FAMILY Fodor's Choice ★

🍴 **Café Boteco.** Located by João Zelante Square in what was once a department store, Café Boteco incorporates elements of the traditional Brazilian *boteco* (dive bar) in some of its recipes and decor, but the comparisons end there: smartly dressed, friendly waiters serve excellent *picanha* (rump steak) and *costelinha com polenta* (pork ribs with polenta chips), as well as salad and pasta dishes with a local twist. Draft lager and a range of local beers are available. On weekends, sit outside to hear bands playing in the square. The owners also run a small shop next door selling souvenirs, fine wines, and cold cuts. [$] *Average main: R$60* ✉ *Travessa Tenente Mário Dallari 20 (Praça João Zelante), Serra Negra* ☎ *019/3892–3481* 🌐 *www.cafeboteco.com.br* 🕒 *Closed Mon. and Tues.*

$ CAFÉ FAMILY

🍴 **Gelato Donato.** A small ice-cream parlor at Praça João Zelante, Gelato Donato is a good destination for dessert and a coffee after a meal. The ice cream is made in Serra Negra using locally sourced ingredients, and the typically Brazilian flavors, such as the strange sounding but delicious guava and cheese, change often. [$] *Average main: R$10* ✉ *Travessa Sargento Agostinho de Oliveira 47 (Praça João Zelante), Serra Negra* ☎ *019/3892–7794* 🕒 *Closed Mon.* 💳 *No credit cards.*

$ BRAZILIAN FAMILY

🍴 **Padaria Serrana.** Located at the heart of Serra Negra, Serrana is a bakery that serves breakfast, light snacks, and also meals, as well as sharing platters. The *bolinhos de bacalhau* (cod fritters) are a popular choice, as is Ecobier, the local draft beer. Grab a *pao na chapa* (grilled bread) and coffee for breakfast here on a Sunday morning and sit at one of the tables outside to watch the hordes of motorcycling aficionados—they flock to Serra Negra on weekends from other cities on their amazing touring bikes. [$] *Average main: R$20* ✉ *Rua Padre Joao Batista Lavello 21, Serra Negra* ☎ *019/3892–2289* 💳 *No credit cards.*

WHERE TO STAY

$$ HOTEL FAMILY Fodor's Choice ★

🏨 **Hotel Firenze.** The choice of wealthy paulistanos, the Firenze is the smartest hotel in Serra Negra; its location, a stone's throw from the shopping area and the town's main square, is the primary draw. **Pros:** excellent breakfast; comfortable rooms; unparalled service. **Cons:** the bar and games room close early. [$] *Rooms from: R$350* ✉ *Rua Sete de Setembro 118, Serra Negra* ☎ *019/3942–9999* 🌐 *www.hotelfirenzeserranegra.com.br* 🛏 *76 suites* 🍽 *All-inclusive.*

$$ B&B/INN 🏨 **Shangri-Lá.** At the edge of town, 3,600 feet above sea level, this little gem offers a wonderful pool area open 24 hours and gazebos with breathtaking views of the mountains. **Pros:** amazing views; good restaurant; comfortable beds. **Cons:** need to drive to reach the town center. [$] *Rooms from: R$270* ✉ *Estrada das Tabaranas, Km 4 at the end of Av. Juca Preto, Serra Negra* ☎ *019/3892–3765* 🛏 *17 suites* 🍴 *Breakfast* 💳 *No credit cards.*

EMBU

27 km (17 miles) west of São Paulo.

Founded in 1554, Embu, or Embu das Artes, is a tiny Portuguese colonial town of whitewashed houses, old churches, wood-carvers' studios, and antiques shops. It has a downtown handicrafts fair every weekend. On Sunday the streets sometimes get so crowded you can barely walk, so it's worth arriving early. Embu also has many stores that sell handicrafts and wooden furniture; most of these are close to where the street fair takes place.

GETTING HERE AND AROUND

EMTU runs an *executivo* (executive or first-class) bus from São Paulo to Embu–Engenho Velho on Line 179, which departs hourly from Anhangabaú. Regular (intermunicipal) buses travel more often: every 20 minutes, Line 033 leaves from Clínicas to Embu. The ride is less comfortable, though: you might have to stand up.

To make the 30-minute drive from São Paulo to Embu, drive from Avenida Professor Francisco Morato to Rodovia Régis Bittencourt (BR 116) and then follow the signs.

ESSENTIALS

Bus Contacts EMTU. ✉ *Embu* ☎ *0800/724–0555* 🌐 *www.emtu.sp.gov.br.*

Visitor Information Tourist Information. ✉ *Largo 21 de Abril 139, Embu* ☎ *011/4704-6565* 🌐 *www.embu.sp.gov.br.* **Gol Tour Viagens e Turismo.** ✉ *São Paulo* ☎ *011/3256-2388* 🌐 *www.goltour.com.br.*

EXPLORING

FAMILY **Cidade das Abelhas** (*City of the Bees*). In the Atlantic Rain Forest you can visit the Cidade das Abelhas, a farm with a small museum where you can watch bees at work. You can buy honey and other bee-related natural products while your kids climb the gigantic model of a bee. It's about 10 minutes from downtown; just follow the signs. ✉ *Km 7, Estrada da Ressaca, Embu* ☎ *011/4703-6460* 🎟 *R$20* 🕑 *Tues.–Sun. 8:30–5.*

Igreja Nossa Senhora do Rosário. Igreja Nossa Senhora do Rosário was built in 1690 and it's worth seeking out if you won't have a chance to visit the historic cities of Minas Gerais. The church contains baroque images of saints and is next to a 1730 monastery now turned into a museum of sacred art. ✉ *Largo dos Jesuítas 67, Embu* ☎ *011/4704-2654* 🎟 *R$2* 🕑 *Tues.–Sun. 9–5.*

WHERE TO EAT

$$ BRAZILIAN **🍴 Casa do Barão.** In this colonial-style spot you find contemporary versions of country plates. Go for the exotic *picadinho jesuítico* (round-steak stew), served with corn, fried bananas, and *farofa* (cassava flour sautéed in butter). Unlike most restaurants in the city, Casa do Barão serves single-person portions. Note that there are no salads or juices on the menu. [$] *Average main: R$40* ✉ *Rua Joaquim Santana 12, Embu* ☎ *011/4704–2053* 🕒 *No lunch Thurs. and Fri. Closed Mon.–Wed.*

$$$ ECLECTIC **🍴 O Garimpo.** Sit in either the beautiul garden or the dining room with fireplace of Embu's most famous restaurant, and then choose between Brazilian regional dishes such as the house specialty, *moqueca de badejo* (spicy fish-and-coconut-milk stew), and German classics such as *eisbein* (pickled and roasted pork shank). There is live music on weekends, but note that it stops at 10:30 on the dot, regardless of how much patrons might be enjoying themselves. Service is patchy on weekends, when the place is busy. [$] *Average main: R$60* ✉ *Rua da Matriz 136, Embu* ☎ *011/4704–6344* 🕒 *No lunch Mon.–Fri.*

$ ECLECTIC **🍴 Os Girassóis Restaurante e Choperia.** A great variety of dishes is served at this downtown restaurant next to an art gallery and at the center of the weekend hustle and bustle of the artisan fair. The *picanha brasileira* (barbecued steak) with fries and farofa is recommended. [$] *Average main: R$30* ✉ *Rua Nossa Senhora do Rosário 3, Embu* ☎ *011/4781–6671* 🕒 *Closed Mon.*

SHOPPING

Associação dos Artesãos de Embu das Artes. Maintained by the artisan association of Embu das Artes, this shop has a mix of locally produced craft, with some occasional gems. Many of the artisans help run the shop and so are on hand to answer questions about the work. ✉ *Rua Siqueira Campos 100, Embu* ☎ *011/4781–9387* 🕒 *Wed.–Fri. 9–5, weekends 10–6.*

Cantão Móveis e Galeria. Cantão Móveis e Galeria is a good place to buy ceramics, paintings, sculptures, and antique decorations. ✉ *Largo dos Jesuítas 169, Embu* ☎ *011/4781–6671* 🕒 *Weekends 9–5.*

Fodor's Choice ★ **Oficina da Cor.** Clovis Fau-Nasser runs a collective featuring plenty of interesting paintings and sculptures including some of his own works. Many of the pieces are small enough to easily pack away while traveling. ✉ *Rua Nossa Senhora do Rosário 45, Embu* ☎ *011/3433–1290* 🕒 *Fri.–Sun. 10–5.*

SANTANA DE PARNAÍBA

42 km (26 miles) northwest of São Paulo.

With more than 200 preserved houses from the 18th and 19th centuries, Santana de Parnaíba is considered the "Ouro Preto from São Paulo"—a town rich with history and colonial architecture. Santana was founded in 1580; by 1625 it was the most important point of departure for the bandeirantes.

In 1901 the first hydroelectric power station in South America was built here. Throughout the 20th century, Santana managed to retain its houses and charm while preserving a local tradition: a rural type of samba called "de bumbo," in which the pacing is marked by the *zabumba* (an instrument usually associated with rhythms from the northeastern states of Brazil). The proximity to a couple of São Paulo's finest suburbs explains the region's fine dining. Outdoors lovers feel at home with the canopy-walking and trekking options.

GETTING HERE AND AROUND

EMTU's *executivo* (executive or first-class) bus from Barra Funda in São Paulo to Pirapora do Bom Jesus (Line 385) stops in Santana de Parnaíba daily and takes one hour.

To reach Santana de Parnaíba from São Paulo—a 40-minute drive—take the express lane of Rodovia Castelo Branco (SP 280) and pay attention to the road signs. On weekends parking is scarce in Santana de Parnaíba, and parking lots can be expensive.

ESSENTIALS

Bus Contacts EMTU. ✉ *Santana de Parnaíba* ☎ *0800/724–0555.*

Visitor Information Santana de Parnaíba Secretaria de Cultura e Turismo. ✉ *Largo da Matriz 19, Santana de Parnaíba* ☎ *011/4154–1874, 011/4154–2377* 🌐 *www.santanadeparnaiba.sp.gov.br.*

EXPLORING

Centro Histórico. The best place to begin your trip to Santana de Parnaíba is in the Centro Histórico, where you'll be able to appreciate numerous examples of 17th- and 18th-century colonial architecture. The more than 200 well-preserved houses are concentrated around three streets: Suzana Dias, André Fernandes, and Bartolomeu Bueno—two of which are named after famous bandeirantes. ✉ *Santana de Parnaíba.*

Igreja Matriz de Sant'Anna. Baroque Igreja Matriz de Sant'Anna was built in 1610 and restored in 1892. It has terra-cotta sculptures and an altar with gold-plated details. ✉ *Largo da Matriz, Santana de Parnaíba* ☎ *011/4154–2401* 🎫 *Free* 🕒 *Daily 8–5.*

Museu Casa do Anhanguera. Museu Casa do Anhanguera provides a sharp picture of the bandeirantes era. In a 1600 house (the second-oldest in the state) where Bartolomeu Bueno—nicknamed Anhanguera, or "old devil," by the Indians—was born, the museum displays objects and furniture from the past four centuries. ✉ *Largo da Matriz 9, Santana de Parnaíba* ☎ *011/4154–5042* 🎫 *R$2* 🕒 *Weekdays 8–4:30, weekends 11–5.*

WHERE TO EAT

$$$ BRAZILIAN FAMILY 🍴 **Bartolomeu.** In a 1905 house, this restaurant serves regional specialties like feijoada and *picadinho* (steak stew served with rice and beans, farofa, fried banana, and fried egg). Salmon and boar ribs are some additional choices. [$] *Average main: R$60* ✉ *Praça 14 de Novembro 101, Santana de Parnaíba* ☎ *011/4154–6566* 🕒 *Closed Mon.*

$$ BRAZILIAN 🍴 **São Paulo Antigo.** In a century-old ranch-style house, a hearty buffet lunch is served with dishes such as *feijão tropeiro* (beans with bacon), *dobradinha com feijão branco* (intestines and white-bean stew), or *galinha atolada* (rural-style hen stew). [$] *Average main: R$40* ✉ *Rua Álvaro Luiz do Valle 66, Santana de Parnaíba* ☎ *011/4154–2726* 🕒 *No dinner.*

THE SOUTH

6

Updated By
Catherine
Balston

Too often overlooked by visitors to Brazil, the southern states of Paraná, Santa Catarina, and Rio Grande do Sul are a delightful surprise. From pristine beaches rising up into fertile highlands to the spectacular Iguaçu Falls, on the border with Argentina and Paraguay, the Região Sul (South Region) has a more varied topography and cooler climate than the rest of Brazil. As the country's wealthy, industrial heart, the standard of living down South also sets it apart. Here, you'll find the legacy of its German, Italian, and Portuguese immigrants alive and well, in the food, the viniculture, the architecture, and the cultural celebrations, which include the largest Oktoberfest outside of Germany.

The southern section of the Serra do Mar, a mountain range flanking the coast, stretches well into Rio Grande do Sul, and separates the interior from the shore. Much of it is still covered with the luxuriant Mata Atlântica (Atlantic Forest), which is as diverse and impressive as the Amazon rain forest. The Serra do Mar gives way to hills that roll gently westward to the valleys of the *rios* (rivers) Paraná and Uruguay. Most of these lands were originally covered with dense subtropical forests interspersed with natural rangelands such as the Campos Gerais, in the north, and the Brazilian Pampas, in the south.

ORIENTATION AND PLANNING

GETTING ORIENTED

Touring the three states of the region—roughly the size of France—in a short time is a challenge, despite a relatively efficient transportation network. The South can be divided into two major areas: the coast and the interior. Coastal attractions, along a 700-km (450-mile) line from Curitiba south to Porto Alegre, include fantastic beaches, forested slopes, canyons, and the Serra do Mar mountains. In the interior, Foz do Iguaçu, far to the west, should not be missed.

Paraná. The state of Paraná has a very short coastline of about 100 km (62 miles), with islands and historical cities. Curitiba, the capital, known internationally as a green city for its innovative urban planning and many parks, is about 90 km (56 miles) from the coast, on a plateau. West of Curitiba lies the vast interior, which incorporates Vila Velha State Park, with its ancient sandstone formations, and stretches all the way to the Paraguayan border and Foz do Iguaçu.

TOP REASONS TO GO

■ **Waterfalls and More Waterfalls:** Get up close and personal to the mighty Iguaçu Falls, either on foot or on a spray-soaked boat ride into the waterfalls.

■ **Atlantic Forest:** Take a train or a breathtaking hike through Paraná coast's stunning virgin rain forest.

■ **Lovely Beaches:** Soak up the sun on the glamorous beaches of Florianópolis.

■ **Brazilian Vineyards:** Sip wine on the slopes of the Vale dos Vinhedo and explore the country's burgeoning wineries.

■ **Outdoor Adventures:** Hike through the impressive green-clad canyons in northeastern Rio Grande do Sul.

Iguaçu Falls. The grandeur of this vast sheet of white water cascading in constant cymbal-banging cacophony makes Niagra Falls and Victoria Falls seem sedate. Allow at least two full days to take in this magnificent sight, and be sure to see it from both the Argentine and Brazilian sides.

Santa Catarina. Geographically, Santa Catarina is the opposite of Paraná: a long coastline of about 500 km (310 miles) and narrow interior. Most of the attractions are on or near the coast. Santa Catarina has some of the best beaches in the South Atlantic. The capital, Florianópolis, an ideal hub for exploring the state's attractions, is on the Ilha de Santa Catarina (Santa Catarina Island).

Rio Grande do Sul. Most tourist attractions in this state, with equal parts coast and interior, are in the heavily populated northeastern corner, including the capital, Porto Alegre, about 100 km (62 miles) from the coast. One highlight in the west is the Jesuit mission ruins in São Miguel.

PLANNING

WHEN TO GO

November through March is normally hot and humid. Rainfall is quite frequent, but less intense than in northern Brazil. Some years might have extremely rainy El Niño-related summers or, conversely, quite dry La Niña-affected years. January and February are top vacation months, so expect crowded beaches, busy highways, and higher prices. Winter (April–November) brings much cooler temperatures, sometimes as low as the upper 20s in the higher elevations at night. Major cold fronts blowing in from Patagonia can bring some gray, blustery days, usually followed by chilly days with deep blue skies.

GETTING HERE AND AROUND

You'd need at least 20 days to visit all of the South's main attractions, but if you have only about a week, fly to Florianópolis and make it your hub to the South. From there visit the attractions in Ilha de Santa Catarina and choose one of the beaches up or down the coast. You can get a rental car or take regular bus lines. One side trip you shouldn't miss is to Foz do Iguaçu, on the Argentina border. Either join an organized (three-day) bus tour or fly on your own to the falls.

BORDER CROSSINGS AT FOZ DO IGUAÇU

U.S., Canadian, and British citizens need only a valid passport for stays of up to 90 days in Argentina, so crossing the border at Iguaçu isn't a problem. Crossing back into Brazil from Argentina, however, is a thorny issue. In theory, *all* U.S. citizens need a visa to enter Brazil, so make sure your paperwork is in order before you depart.

Many local taxis (both Argentine and Brazilian) have "arrangements" with border control and can also get you across with no visa. Most charge 150–200 pesos for the return trip. Though the practice is well-established (most hotels and travel agents in Puerto Iguazú have deals with Brazilian companies and can arrange a visa-less visit), it *is* illegal. Enforcement of the law is generally lax, but sudden crackdowns and on-the-spot fines of hundreds of dollars have been reported.

RESTAURANTS

Churrasco (slow-grilled and -roasted meat), one of the most famous foods of Brazil, originated in Rio Grande do Sul. But the cuisine is eclectic here in cowboy country, and rice and beans sit on southern tables beside Italian and German dishes, thanks to the South's many European immigrants. Look for *barreado*, a dish from coastal Paraná made by stewing beef, bacon, potatoes, and spices for hours in a clay pot made airtight with moistened manioc flour. *Café colonial* is the elaborate 5 pm tea—with breads, pies, and German kuchen—popular among the Germans in the South.

HOTELS

The South has a great variety of hotels and inns. Except for in the smallest towns and most remote areas, however, you shouldn't have a problem finding comfortable accommodations. Pousadas in historic buildings are common, particularly in beach towns. Hotel-*fazendas* (farmhouse hotels) are popular in rural areas. Southern beaches attract many South American tourists, and seaside cities might become crowded and highway traffic nightmarish from December through March. Make advance reservations. *Hotel reviews have been shortened. For full information, visit Fodors.com.*

WHAT IT COSTS IN REAIS				
	$	**$$**	**$$$**	**$$$$**
Restaurants	under R$31	R$30–R$45	R$46–R$60	over R$60
Hotels	under R$251	R$251–R$375	R$376–R$500	over R$500

Restaurant prices are the average cost of a main course at dinner or, if dinner is not served, at lunch. Hotel prices are the lowest cost of a standard double room in high season, excluding tax.

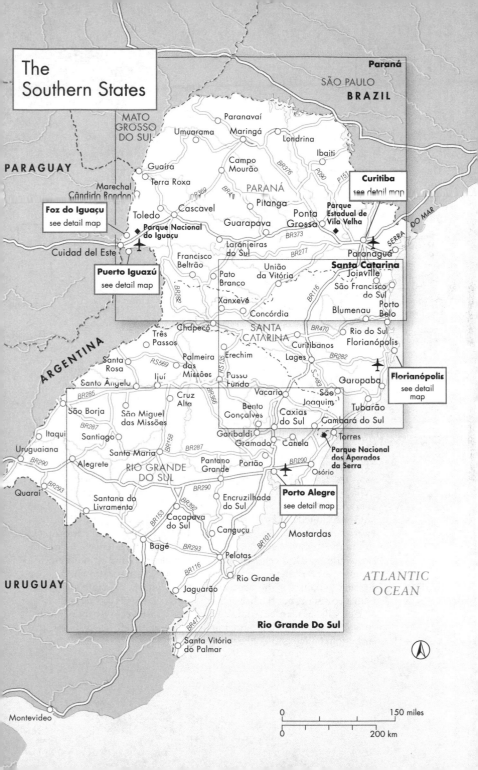

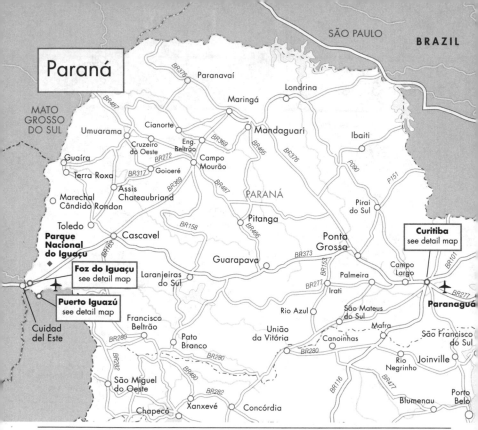

PARANÁ

The state of Paraná is best known for Iguaçu Falls, a natural wonder, and the Itaipú Dam, an engineering marvel. But also worth a visit is Vila Velha, a series of strange sandstone formations in the center of Paraná that might remind you of the eerily moving landscapes of the western United States. At one time the rolling hills of the state's plateau were covered with forests dominated by the highly prized Paraná pine, an umbrella-shape conifer. Most of these pine forests were logged by immigrants half a century ago, and the cleared land of the immense interior is now where soybeans, wheat, and coffee are grown. (Still, be on the lookout for the occasional Paraná pine.) The state has a very short coastline, but the beaches are spectacular, as is the Serra do Mar, which still has pristine Atlantic Forest and coastal ecosystems. Curitiba, the upbeat capital, ranks as a top Brazilian city in efficiency, innovative urban planning, and quality of life.

CURITIBA

408 km (254 miles) south of São Paulo, 710 km (441 miles) north of Porto Alegre.

Curitiba is on the Paraná Plateau, at an elevation of 2,800 feet. It owes its name to the Paraná pinecones, which were called *kur-ity-ba* by the native Guaranis. In a region that already differs considerably from the rest of the country, this city of 1.8 million is unique for its temperate climate (with a mean temperature of 16°C/61°F) and the 50% of its population that is of non-Iberian European ancestry.

With one of the highest densities of urban green space in the world, Curitiba is known as the environmental capital of Brazil. This is not only because of its array of parks but also because since the 1980s it has had progressive city governments that have been innovative in their urban planning. The emphasis on protecting the environment has produced an efficient public transportation system and a comprehensive recycling program that are being used as models for cities around the globe.

GETTING HERE AND AROUND

The flight from São Paulo to Curitiba is about an hour. A bus takes six hours. Curitiba's Aeroporto Internacional Afonso Pena is 21 km (13 miles) east of downtown. A cab ride to downtown is around R$70. A minibus service (R$12) provides transportation between Rua 24 Horas and Estação Rodoferroviária, passing by several downtown hotels on its way to the airport.

You can drive from Curitiba to Foz do Iguaçu on BR 277, which traverses Paraná State. It's a long drive, but this toll highway is kept in good shape. To visit the picturesque seaside around historic Paranaguá, it's best to join a tour, especially one that includes a train ride on the Serra Verde Express.

The coastal, single-lane BR 101 is the most direct route from Curitiba to other southern communities, but it's one of the country's busiest roads, with heavy truck traffic night and day. The stretch south of Florianópolis to Porto Alegre is dangerous during the January and February vacation months.

BR 116, the Mountain Route, runs from Curitiba to Porto Alegre. Although it's scenic for much of the way—and a little shorter than other routes—it's also narrow, with many curves and trucks.

Curitiba is renowned for its modern and efficient public transportation system. Buses take you quickly to any place in the city. There are regular lines (R$2.85) and *ligeirinho* express lines (R$2.85). Moreover, tourists can make the most of the hop-on, hop-off bus service connecting the city's principal attractions, the 2½-hour Linha Turismo tour (R$30). Taxis are easy to find in Curitiba. A ride from downtown to the Jardim Botânico costs about R$30.

ESSENTIALS

Airport Aeroporto Internacional Afonso Pena (*CWB*). ✉ *Av. Rocha Pombo s/n, Águas Belas, São José dos Pinhais* ☎ *041/3381–1515* ⊕ *www.infraero.gov. br/index.php/aeroportos/parana/aeroporto-afonso-pena.*

Bus Contacts **Estação Rodoferroviária** (*Bus Station*). ⊠ *Av. Pres. Affonso Camargo 330, Jardim Botânico, Curitiba* ☎ *041/3320–3000* ⊕ *www.urbs.curitiba. pr.gov.br/comunidade/rodoferroviaria.* **Linha Turismo.** ⊠ *Praça Tiradentes, Centro, Curitiba* ☎ *041/3320–3232.*

Taxi Contacts **Rádio Táxi.** ☎ *0800/600–6666, 041/3264-6464* ⊕ *www. radiotaxicapital.com.br.*

Train Contacts **Serra Verde Express.** ⊠ *Estação Rodoferroviária, Av. Pres. Affonso Camargo 330, Centro, Curitiba* ☎ *041/3888-3488* ⊕ *serraverdeexpress. com.br.*

Visitor and Tour Information **Paraná Turismo** (*State Tourism Board*). ⊠ *Alameda Dr. Muricy 950, Centro, Curitiba* ☎ *041/3313–3500, 041/3352–6443* ⊕ *www. turismo.pr.gov.br/modules/turista-en.*

TOURS

BWT. A local operator, BWT packages include a half-day Curitiba city tour as well as trips to Ilha do Mel, Parque Nacional Superaguí, and Parque Estadual Vila Velha, as well as the Serra Verde Express train to Morretes. ⊠ *Estação Rodoferroviária, Av. Pres. Affonso Camargo 330, Centro, Curitiba* ☎ *041/3888–3499, 041/3323–4007* ⊕ *www. bwtoperadora.com.br* ✆ *From R$130.*

Gondwana Brasil Ecoturismo. Specializing in nature tourism and ecotourism, Gondwana organizes trips and trekking in national parks, the Pantanal, the Amazon, Iguaçu Falls and the Atlantic Forest. Special-interest excursions include bird-watching and nature photography. ⊠ *Av. República Argentina 369, Room 804, Água Verde, Curitiba* ☎ *041/3566-6339* ⊕ *gondwanabrasil.com.br* ✆ *From R$977.*

EXPLORING

Much as in other Brazilian cities, the history of the downtown district of Curitiba revolves around the first church built in the city, Igreja de São Francisco. In the early days it was the focal point where roads and streets converged, businesses set up shop, the government established its representation, and urban sprawl unfolded. Development in the last 50 years moved the administrative and commercial district away from the original center, where symbols of early days are preserved.

It would be a shame to visit Brazil's environmental capital without seeing one of its many parks, especially the Jardim Botânico, east of downtown.

TOP ATTRACTIONS

Fodor'sChoice **Jardim Botânico.** Although not as old and renowned as its counterpart in
★ Rio, the Botanical Garden has become a Curitiba showplace. Its most outstanding feature is the tropical flora in the two-story steel-and-glass greenhouse that was inspired by London's Crystal Palace. The Municipal Botanical Museum, with its library and remarkable collection of rare Brazilian plants, is also worth visiting. There are several paths for jogging or just wandering. ⊠ *Rua Eng. Ostoja Roguski s/n, Jardim Botânico, Curitiba* ☎ *041/3264–6994* ✆ *Free* ☉ *Daily 6 am–7:30 pm in winter, 6 am–8 pm in summer.*

Museu Oscar Niemeyer. Pictures of Oscar Niemeyer's projects throughout the world are on display at this museum designed by the late architect himself. Museu Oscar Niemeyer also incorporates a collection of the works of Paraná's artists from the former Museu de Arte do Paraná. The main building, a suspended eye-shape structure overlooking the adjacent John Paul II Wood, hosts temporary modern art exhibitions. ⊠ *Rua Marechal Hermes 999, Centro Cívico, Curitiba* ☏ *041/3350–4400* ⊕ *www.museuoscarniemeyer.org.br* ⊡ *R$6* ⊗ *Tue.–Sun. 10–6.*

Museu Paranaense. Founded in 1876, the State Museum of Paraná moved several times before installing its collections in this imposing art nouveau building, which served as city hall from 1916 to 1969. The permanent displays contain official documents, ethnographic materials of the native Guaraní and Kaigang peoples, coins and photographs, and archaeological pieces related to the state's history. ⊠ *Rua Kellers 289, Centro Histórico, Curitiba* ☏ *041/3304–3300* ⊕ *www. museuparanaense.pr.gov.br* ⊡ *Free* ⊗ *Weekdays 9–6, weekends 10–4.*

Parque das Pedreiras. This cultural complex was built in the abandoned João Gava quarry and adjacent wooded lot. The quarry itself was converted into an amphitheater that can accommodate 60,000 people. The 2,400-seat **Ópera de Arame** (Wire Opera House), also on the grounds here, was constructed from tubular steel and wire mesh above a water–field quarry pit. National and international musical events have given this facility world renown. ⊠ *Rua João Gava s/n, Pilarzinho, Curitiba* ☏ *041/3355–6071* ⊡ *Free* ⊗ *Daily 8–6.*

OFF THE BEATEN PATH
Santa Felicidade. What was once an Italian settlement, dating from 1878, is now one of the city's most popular neighborhoods, drawing hungry crowds especially on Sunday. It has been officially designated as Curitiba's "gastronomic district," and, indeed, you'll find some fantastic restaurants—as well as wine, antiques, and handicrafts shops—along Via Veneto and Avenida Manuel Elias. The area also has some colonial buildings, such as the Igreja Matriz de São José (St. Joseph's Church). ⊠ *Santa Felicidade, Curitiba.*

WORTH NOTING

Igreja de São Francisco. Curitiba's oldest church, St. Francis was built in 1737 and fully restored in 1981. Check out its gold-plated altar before ducking into the attached **Museu de Arte Sacra** (Sacred Art Museum), with its baroque religious sculptures made of wood and terra-cotta. ⊠ *Largo da Ordem s/n, Curitiba* ☏ *041/3223–7545 church*, *041/3321–3265 museum* ⊡ *Free* ⊗ *Weekdays 9–6, weekends 9–2.*

Parque Tangüá. The most-visited park in the city, Tangüá shows creative landscaping in an abandoned quarry with its pond, tunnel (dug 160 feet into the rock wall), artificial waterfall, and walkway over the water, all surrounded by woods, with many imposing Brazilian pines. ⊠ *Rua Dr. Bemben s/n, Pilarzinho, Curitiba* ☏ *041/3352–7607* ⊡ *Free* ⊗ *Daily dawn–dusk.*

Passeio Público. Opened in 1886, the Public Thoroughfare was designed as a botanical and zoological garden and soon became a favorite place for the affluent to spend their weekend afternoons. The main gate is a replica of that at the Cimetière des Chiens in Paris. Although it's no

Igreja de São Francisco ... 2
Museu Oscar Niemeyer 4
Museu Paranaense 1
Passeio Público 3

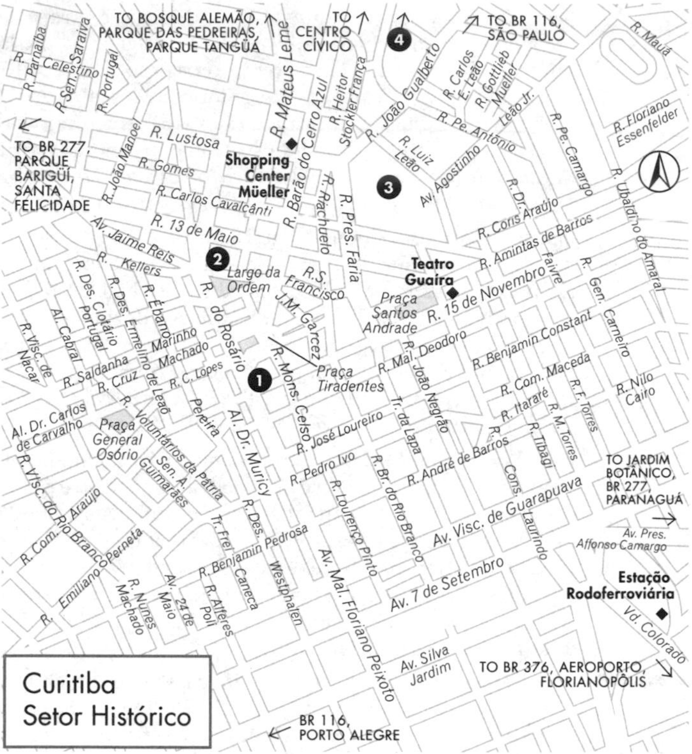

Curitiba Setor Histórico

longer the official city zoo, you can observe several Brazilian primates and birds still kept in the park, as well as majestic sycamores, oaks, and the *ipê amarelo,* a striking Brazilian tree with vibrant yellow flowers. ✉ *Main Gate, Rua Pres. Faria at Pres. Carlos Cavalcanti, Setor Histórico, Curitiba* ☎ *041/3350–9920* 🎟 *Free* ⏲ *Tues.–Sun. 6 am–8 pm.*

WHERE TO EAT

$$$ PIZZA

🍴 **Baviera.** Recommended for those on a budget, Baviera is essentially a pizzeria, but the menu also includes Brazilian-style steak (thin-cut fillet, usually rare), grilled chicken, and hamburgers, with most dishes serving two. The restaurant, in the basement of an imposing house on a hillside, has an Italian cantina look, with wine barrels at the entrance, rustic wood furniture, and candlelighted tables. [$] *Average main: R$50* ✉ *Rua Augusto Stellfeld 18, Centro, Curitiba* ☎ *041/3232–1995* ⏲ *No lunch.*

$$ ITALIAN

🍴 **Madalosso.** One of the best-known establishments for Italian cuisine in Curitiba, Madalosso is also possibly the largest restaurant in Brazil: the hangarlike building seats 4,600 diners. The prix-fixe menu includes a huge selection of pastas and sauces, chicken dishes, and salads. The gnocchi and lasagna are particularly noteworthy. The restaurant keeps a large wine cellar, with many renowned Brazilian and international wines, as well as a house wine, made for the restaurant in the vineyards

CLOSE UP

The Mata Atlântica

Such is the renown of the Amazonian rain forest that most tourists are amazed to learn that Brazil's eastern seaboard was once covered by an equally lush humid forest, teeming with animal and plant biodiversity. The Mata Atlântica (Atlantic Forest), essentially a series of adjoining forests, originally covered about a fourth of Brazil. One of the most complex ecosystems on Earth, these evergreen forests contained about 7% of all known vertebrates and more than 20,000 plant species.

The major difference between the Amazon and the Mata Atlântica is the flora. In the Amazon, plants are essentially lowland types adapted to the humid climate; those in the Atlantic forests have adapted to mountainous terrain, less rainfall, and lower mean annual temperatures. Unique Mata Atlântica fauna includes primates like the *mico-leão dourado* (goldenlion tamarin) and the *muriqui* (spider monkey), parrots, toucans, *arapongas* (bell birds), and the *anta* (tapir).

The flora includes rich *pau-brasil* (brazilwood) and, at higher elevations, *araucária* (Brazilian pine). The hundreds of orchid species, the yellow flowers of the *ipê* (Brazil's national flower), and the flowers of the *manacá* (princess flower tree) that turn from white to purple to violet within days, compose a colorful spectacle.

The Mata Atlântica has suffered intense deforestation as a result of coastal development and agricultural land conversion, with recent estimates indicating that only 8.5% of the original forest remains. Preservation, conservation, and recovery efforts by the national government and private organizations are ongoing. "Bright spots" include Foz do Iguaçu, Superagüí National Park (near Paranaguá), a golden tamarin reserve in southern Bahia State, and organizations that train farmers in sustainable agriculture practices.

6

---

of Rio Grande do Sul. $ *Average main: R$39* ⊠ *Av. Manoel Ribas 5875, Santa Felicidade, Curitiba* ☎ *041/3372–2121* ⊕ *www.madalosso. com.br* ☾ *No dinner Sun.*

$$$$
CONTEMPORARY

✕ **Restaurante Manu.** A top-end option in Curitiba, Restaurant Manu is an intimate spot with a dozen tables, and a constantly evolving menu that emphasizes local ingredients with creative flair. Submit to one of chef Manu's tasting menus—3 courses (R$118), 7 courses (R$158), or 11 courses (R$190)—for a show-and-tell of bite-sized dishes and surprising combinations: think seared fish with bacon, caramel, and sour melon. For a behind-the-scenes view, book the table by the kitchen window, just inches away from where the dishes are plated up. Expect to pay top dollar for wine. $ *Average main: R$158* ⊠ *Alameda Dom Pedro II 317, Batel, Curitiba* ☎ *041/3044-4395* ⊕ *restaurantemanu. com.br* ☾ *No lunch. Closed Sun. and Mon.*

$$
GERMAN

✕ **Schwarzwald (Bar do Alemão).** The city's most popular German bar–restaurant, Schwarzwald has carved a name for itself with great draft beer, including some imported brands and local bocks (German-style dark beers). Highly recommended entrées are the house version of *eisbein* (pig's leg served with mashed potatoes), *kassler* (beef fillet with a cream sauce), and duck with red cabbage. The restaurant is somewhat small and packed with tables, but there's plenty of space on the sidewalk in front. $ *Average main: R$40* ⊠ *Rua Claudino dos Santos 63, Setor Histórico, Curitiba* ☎ *041/3223–2585* ⊕ *www.bardoalemaocuritiba. com.br.*

WHERE TO STAY

$ ⊞ **Duomo Park Hotel.** At this small, comfortable hotel, the rooms and
HOTEL suites are unusually spacious and come with large beds, blond-wood furniture, and carpeting. **Pros:** great service and location. **Cons:** furniture needs updating; small commons area. $ *Rooms from: R$156* ⊠ *Rua Visconde de Rio Branco 1710, Centro, Curitiba* ☎ *041/3321–1900* ⊕ *www.hotelduomo.com.br* ⇗ *48 rooms* ⫯⊙⫯ *Breakfast.*

$$$$ ⊞ **Four Points by Sheraton.** Widely regarded as Curitiba's finest hotel, the
HOTEL Four Points is geared toward the discriminating business traveler. **Pros:** great business facilities; central location. **Cons:** expensive; few amenities for leisure travelers. $ *Rooms from: R$515* ⊠ *Av. Sete de Setembro 4211, Água Verde, Curitiba* ☎ *041/3340–4000, 0800/368–7764 toll-free* ⊕ *www.fourpoints.com/curitiba* ⇗ *165 rooms* ⫯⊙⫯ *Breakfast.*

$$ ⊞ **Johnscher.** This small, hip hotel in Curitiba's historic center dates
HOTEL back to 1917 and features a curious mix of original features and bold design. **Pros:** interesting, historic building; large rooms; city center location. **Cons:** not safe to walk around the area at night; some rooms are noisy. $ *Rooms from: R$305* ⊠ *Rua Barão do Rio Branco 354, Centro, Curitiba* ☎ *041/3302–9600* ⊕ *johnscher.com.br* ⇗ *22 rooms, 2 suites* ⫯⊙⫯ *Breakfast* ⊟ *No credit cards.*

$$$$ ⊞ **Radisson Hotel Curitiba.** The imposing 17-story façade of the Radis-
HOTEL son may seem incongruous with its setting, but the bright, spacious rooms and location in upmarket Batel make this a good choice for business travelers and tourists alike. **Pros:** close to bars, restaurants, and shopping malls; excellent breakfast spread; spacious, light rooms. **Cons:** lack of towel-hanging space; small pool for a hotel of this size. $ *Rooms from: R$539* ⊠ *Praça do Japão, Av. Sete de Setembro 5190, Batel, Curitiba* ☎ *041/3351–2222* ⊕ *www.radisson.com/curitiba-hotel-br-80240-000/bracurt* ⇗ *191 rooms, 3 suites* ⫯⊙⫯ *Breakfast.*

$ ⊞ **Slaviero Slim Centro Hotel.** In a landmark building overlooking the
HOTEL Rua das Flores walkway, Slaviero Slim in downtown Curitiba has large rooms with wood paneling and matching furniture. **Pros:** central location; good value for the better rooms. **Cons:** some rooms are small; few amenities. $ *Rooms from: R$195* ⊠ *Av. Luiz Xavier 67, Centro, Curitiba* ☎ *041/3322–2829, 0800/704–3311* ⊕ *slavierohoteis.com.br* ⇗ *89 rooms, 3 suites* ⫯⊙⫯ *Breakfast.*

NIGHTLIFE AND PERFORMING ARTS

Curitiba has a bustling cultural scene, a reflection of the European background of many of its citizens. Complete listings of events are published in the *Gazeta do Povo*, the major daily newspaper.

NIGHTLIFE

Fodor's Choice **Rua São Francisco.** Buzzing with life, the once down-at-heel stretch of
★ Rua São Francisco between Rua Pres. Faria and Rua Barão do Cerro
Azul has been given a face-lift by city hall, restoring its cobbled stones,
installing new street lights, and giving the colonial era houses a lick of
paint. The result is a hotbed of hipsters and new creative spaces, from
boutiques to cafés and bars. ⊠ *Rua São Francisco, Centro Histórico,
Curitiba.*

PERFORMING ARTS

Teatro Guaíra. Formerly the Teatro São Teodoro (circa 1884), the Teatro
Guaíra was rebuilt in its present location and reopened in 1974. It
has a modern, well-equipped 2,000-seat auditorium, as well as two
smaller rooms. Shows include plays, popular music concerts, and the
occasional full-fledged opera. ⊠ *Rua 15 de Novembro 971, Centro,
Curitiba* ☎ *041/3304–7900* ⊕ *www.tguaira.pr.gov.br.*

SHOPPING

Feira do Largo. Buy directly from the artisans every Sunday from 9 to
3 at the Feira de Artesanato do Largo da Ordem, a popular fair with
paintings from local artists, pottery, tapestry, handicrafts, and antiques.
⊠ *Largo da Ordem and Praça Garibaldi, Setor Histórico, Curitiba*
⊕ *www.feiradolargo.com.br.*

Shopping Center Müller. One of the city's prime shopping destinations,
Shopping Center Müeller includes branches of national chains, upscale
fashion and jewelry stores, as well as some small handicraft shops,
restaurants and cafés, bookstores, and movie theaters. ⊠ *Rua Candido de Abreu 127, São Francisco, Curitiba* ☎ *041/3074–1000* ⊕ *www.
shoppingmueller.com.br.*

FAMILY **Shopping Estação.** In what was once a railway terminal, the Shopping
Estação is a 700,000-square-foot covered area with a colorful and noisy
collection of bars and restaurants, amusement arcades, exhibits, a railway museum, a cineplex, daily live music shows, and more than 100
shops. ⊠ *Av. 7 de Setembro 2775, Centro, Curitiba* ☎ *041/3094–5300*
⊕ *www.shoppingestacao.com.br* ☾ *Mon.–Sat. 10–10, Sun. 2–8.*

PARANAGUÁ

90 km (56 miles) east of Curitiba.

Most of Brazil's coffee and soybeans are shipped out of Paranaguá, the
nation's second-largest port, which also serves as chief port for landlocked Paraguay. Downtown holds many examples of colonial architecture and has been designated an official historic area. The city, founded
in 1565 by Portuguese explorers, is 30 km (18 miles) from the Atlantic
on the Baía de Paranaguá. The bay area is surrounded by the Mata
Atlântica, of which a great swathe on the northern side is protected;
several islands in the bay also have rain forests as well as great beaches.
You'll find other less scenic but popular sandy stretches farther south,
toward the Santa Catarina border.

GETTING HERE AND AROUND

Although you can reach Paranaguá from Curitiba on BR 277, consider taking the more scenic Estrada da Graciosa, which follows the route taken by 17th-century traders up the Serra do Mar. This narrow, winding route—paved with rock slabs in parts—is some 30 km (18 miles) longer than BR 277, but the breathtaking peaks and slopes covered with rain forest make the extra travel time worthwhile. You can drive or take a Viação Graciosa bus (75 minutes; R$26), but most tourists take the Serra Verde Express scenic train to Morretes, and then a minibus on down to Paranaguá, as part of an organized tour.

ESSENTIALS

Currency exchange is difficult in the Paranaguá area. Exchange reais in Curitiba.

Bus Contacts Terminal Municipal Rodoviário *(Municipal Bus Station).* ✉ *Rua João Estevam at Rua João Regis, Centro, Paranaguá* ☎ *041/3423–1215.*

Taxi Contacts Ponto de Taxi. ☎ *041/3423–4548.*

Visitor Information Informações Turísticas. ✉ *Praça dos Povos Árabes, Rua João Regis s/n, Setor Histórico, Paranaguá* ✛ *In the square opposite the Municipal Bus Station* ☎ *041/3422–6290.*

SAFETY AND PRECAUTIONS

Paranaguá has some difficult neighborhoods, but the historic district downtown, where most attractions are, is fairly safe. All the same, be extra careful with valuables.

EXPLORING

TOP ATTRACTIONS

Fodor's Choice ★ **Ilha do Mel** *(Honey Island).* The 10-km-long (6-mile-long) Ilha do Mel, a state park in the Baía de Paranaguá, is the most popular destination on Paraná's coast. The island is crisscrossed by hiking trails—cars aren't allowed, and the number of visitors is limited to 5,000 at any one time—and has two villages, Encantadas and Nova Brasília, and several pristine beaches. Local lore has it that the east shore's Gruta das Encantadas (Enchanted Grotto) is frequented by mermaids. On the south shore check out the sights around Farol das Conchas (Lighthouse of the Shells) and its beach. From Forte de Nossa Senhora dos Prazeres (Our Lady of Pleasures Fort), built in 1767 on the east shore, take advantage of the great views of the forest-clad northern bay islands. The most scenic ferry rides leave from Paranaguá between 8 am and 1 pm (2 hours; R$39). More convenient are the ferries that depart from Pontal do Sul, 30 miles east of Paranaguá, every 30 minutes. Prices start at R$29. Both ferry routes are operated by Abaline. To ensure admission in the high season (December–March), book an island tour before you leave Curitiba. ✉ *Abaline in Paranaguá, Rua General Carneiro 366, Centro, Paranaguá* ☎ *041/3455–2616 Abaline, Pontal do Sul, 041/3925–6325 Abaline, Paranaguá* ⊕ *abaline.com.br.*

Fodor's Choice ★ **Reserva Ecológica do Sebuí.** A private, protected nature reserve near Pinheiros Bay, the Reserva Ecológica do Sebuí is an immersive way to experience the Atlantic Forest, in one of the best preserved stretches of forest that remains on Brazil's coast. Owned and run by the eccentric Italian

Enzo Sebastiani, the reserve contains 1,000 acres of primary rain forest, as well as saltwater mangroves, rivers, waterfalls, and forested islands, all of which can be explored on foot and by boat, with Enzo—or an English-speaking biologist—as your guide. Built in a former banana plantation, the lodging consists of wooden huts and a house built on stilts, all powered by solar energy, and is only accessible via boat. A minimum of two nights and four people is required. Per person, for two nights, all-inclusive prices are R$750 from Guaraqueçaba (160-km/100-mile drive from Curitiba), R$950 from the port of Paranaguá, and R$1,250 from Cananéia, on the São Paulo border. ☎ *041/8403–8056 operator Vivo, 041/9803–4342 operator Tim* 🌐 *cormorano.com.br* 🎫 *2 nights from R$750.*

WORTH NOTING

Museu de Arqueologia e Etnologia (*Archaeology and Ethnology Museum*). Built in 1755, the Museu de Arqueologia e Etnologia (MAE) occupies a building that was once part of a Jesuit school. The collection here includes pieces found in excavations in the area, mostly in *sambaquis*—burial sites in shell-mounds built by native coastal-dwelling people. The museum also hosts temporary art exhibits. ✉ *Rua XV de Novembro 575, Setor Histórico, Paranaguá* ☎ *041/3721–1200* 🎫 *Free* 🕓 *Tues.–Sun. 8–8.*

6

WHERE TO EAT AND STAY

$$$ BRAZILIAN

🍴 **Casa do Barreado.** This small, family-run, buffet-style restaurant specializes in the traditional dish most associated with Paraná State: the *barreado* (meat stew simmered in a sealed clay pot). Because *barreado* takes 24 hours to cook, you must order it a day in advance. The prix-fixe menu includes *galinha na púcara* (chicken cooked in wine, tomato, and bacon sauce), several salads, and *cachaças* (Brazilian liquor distilled from sugarcane). Although the restaurant is officially open only on weekends, you can call ahead to arrange a dinner during the week. [$] *Average main: R$60* ✉ *Rua José Antônio Cruz 78, Ponta do Cajú, Paranaguá* ☎ *041/3423–1830* 🌐 *casadobarreado.com.br* 🕓 *No dinner. Closed weekdays* ✍ *Reservations essential.*

$$ RESORT

🏨 **Camboa Resort.** Right in the historic district, Camboa Resort has comfortable facilities, a long roster of activities, and a dedicated staff that can arrange tours in the region. **Pros:** close to historic district; many amenities. **Cons:** busy in summer months; poor Internet connection. [$] *Rooms from: R$289* ✉ *Rua João Estevão s/n, Ponta do Cajú, Paranaguá* ☎ *041/3420–5200 lobby, 041/3323–5546 reservations* 🌐 *www.hotelcamboa.com.br* 🛏 *134 rooms* 🍽 *Breakfast.*

IGUAÇU FALLS

1,358 km (843 miles) north of Buenos Aires; 637 km (396 miles) west of Curitiba; 544 (338 miles) west of Vila Velha.

Iguaçu consists of some 275 separate waterfalls—in the rainy season there are as many as 350—that plunge more than 200 feet onto the rocks below. They cascade in a deafening roar at a bend in the Iguazú River (Río Iguazú in Spanish, Rio Iguaçu in Portuguese) where the borders of Argentina, Brazil, and Paraguay meet. Dense, lush jungle surrounds the falls: here the tropical sun and the omnipresent moisture produce a towering pine tree in two decades instead of the seven it takes in, say, Scandinavia. By the falls and along the roadside, rainbows and butterflies are set off against vast walls of red earth, which is so ubiquitous that eventually even paper currency in the area turns red from exposure to the stuff.

The falls and the lands around them are protected by Argentina's Parque Nacional Iguazú (where the falls are referred to by their Spanish name, the Cataratas de Iguazú) and by Brazil's Parque Nacional do Iguaçu (where the falls go by the Portuguese name of Cataratas do Iguaçu).

To visit the falls, you can base yourself in the Argentine town of Puerto Iguazú, or its sprawling Brazilian counterpart, the city of Foz do Iguaçu. The two cities are 18 km (11 miles) and 25 km (15 miles) northwest of the falls, respectively, and are connected by an international bridge, the Puente Presidente Tancredo Neves.

PUERTO IGUAZÚ, ARGENTINA

Fodor's Choice
★
Originally a port for shipping wood from the region, Puerto Iguazú now revolves around tourism. This was made possible in the early 20th century when Victoria Aguirre, a wealthy visitor from Buenos Aires, funded the building of a road to the falls. Despite the constant stream of visitors from Argentina and abroad, Puerto Iguazú remains small and sleepy. Many of its secondary roads still aren't paved.

Many travelers to the falls—including those from Brazil—opt to stay on the Argentine side of the border because it's less expensive than the Brazilian side. The town is also a good place to wind down after a day or two of high-energy adventure before heading back to Buenos Aires. So spare some time to experience being surrounded by hummingbirds in a garden, or just grab some *helado* (ice cream) and meander to el Hito Tres Fronteras.

Prices for restaurants and hotels in the Argentina sections are given in Argentine pesos. As of this writing, the exchange rate was 1 Brazilian real to 2.81 Argentine pesos.

GETTING HERE AND AROUND
Aerolíneas Argentinas flies four to five times daily between Aeroparque Jorge Newbery in Buenos Aires and the Aeropuerto Internacional de Puerto Iguazú, which is about 20 km (12 miles) southeast of Puerto Iguazú; the trip takes 1¾ hours. LAN does the same trip two or three times daily. Normal rates start at about 800 pesos each way. Four Tourist Travel runs shuttle buses from the airport to hotels in Puerto Iguazú. They leave after every flight lands and cost 60 pesos. Taxis to Puerto Iguazú cost 100 pesos.

Vía Bariloche operates several daily buses between the Retiro bus station in Buenos Aires and the Puerto Iguazú Terminal de Omnibus in the center of town. The trip takes 16–18 hours, so it's worth paying the little extra for *coche cama* (sleeper) or *cama ejecutivo* (deluxe sleeper) services, which cost about 1,144 pesos one-way (regular semi-cama

Puerto Iguazú

BRAZIL

services cost around 1,005 pesos). You can travel direct to Rio de Janeiro (22 hours) and São Paulo (15 hours) with Crucero del Norte; the trips cost 1,035 and 904 pesos, respectively.

From Puerto Iguazú to the falls or the hotels along RN12, take El Práctico from the terminal or along Avenida Victoria Aguirre. Buses leave every 15 minutes from 7 to 7 and cost 20 pesos round-trip.

There's little point in renting a car around Puerto Iguazú: daily rentals start at 260 to 300 pesos, more than twice what you pay for a taxi between the town and the falls.

Crucero del Norte runs an hourly cross-border public bus service (60 pesos) between the bus stations of Puerto Iguazú and Foz do Iguaçu. Locals don't have to get on and off for immigration, but be sure you do so. To reach the Argentine falls, change to local minibus service El Práctico at the intersection with RN12 on the Argentine side. For the Brazilian park, change to a local bus at the Avenida Cataratas roundabout.

Argentinean travel agency Sol Iguazú Turismo organizes door-to-door transport to both sides of the falls, and can reserve places on the Iguazú Jungle Explorer trips.

Bus Contacts Crucero del Norte. ☎ 11/4315–1652 in Buenos Aires, 3757/421–916 in Puerto Iguazú ⊕ www.crucerodelnorte.com.ar. **Four Tourist**

CLOSE UP

Iguaçu Falls Itineraries

One Day: If you have only one day, limit your visit to the Argentine park. Arrive when it opens, and get your first look at the falls aboard one of Iguazú Jungle Explorer's Zodiacs. The rides finish at the Circuito Inferior: take a couple of hours to explore this. Grab a quick lunch at the snack bar, then blitz the shorter Circuito Superior. Finally, catch the train from Estación Cataratas to Estación Garganta del Diablo, where the trail to the viewing platform starts (allow two hours for this).

Two Days: Two days gives you enough time to see both sides of the falls. Visit the Brazilian park on your second day to get the panoramic take on what you've experienced up close in Argentina. If you arrive at 9 am, you've got time to walk the entire trail, take photos, have lunch, and be back at the park entrance at 1 pm.

Three Days: With three days, you can explore both parks at a leisurely pace. Follow the one-day itinerary, then return to the Argentine park on your second day. Make a beeline for the Garganta del Diablo, which looks different in the morning, then spend the afternoon exploring the Sendero Macuco and Isla San Martín. You could spend all of your third day in the Brazilian park.

Travel. ☎ *3757/420–681.* **Vía Bariloche.** ☎ *0810/333-7575 in Buenos Aires, 3757/420-854 in Puerto Iguazú* ⊕ *www.viabariloche.com.ar.*

Visitor Information **Cataratas del Iguazú Visitors Center.** ⊠ *Off Ruta Nacional 101, Puerto Iguazú* ☎ *3757/491–469* ⊕ *www.iguazuargentina.com.* **Iguazú Tourist Information.** ⊠ *Puerto Iguazú* ☎ *3757/491–469* ⊕ *www. iguazuargentina.com.* **Puerto Iguazú Tourist Office.** ⊠ *Av. Victoria Aguirre 311, Puerto Iguazú* ☎ *3757/420-800* ⊕ *www.iguazuturismo.gov.ar.* **Sol Iguazú Turismo.** ⊠ *Puerto Iguazú* ☎ *3757/421-008* ⊕ *www.soliguazu.com.ar.*

TOURS

Iguazú Forest. It's all about adrenaline with Iguazú Forest. The full-day expedition involves kayaking, rappelling, waterfall climbing, mountain biking, and canopying all within the Argentine side of the park. ⊠ *Puerto Iguazú* ☎ *3757/42–1140* ⊕ *www.iguazuforest.com.*

Iguazú Jungle Explorer. Iguazú Jungle Explorer runs trips within the Argentine park. The standard trip, the Gran Aventura, includes a truck ride through the forest and a Zodiac ride to Isla San Martín, Bossetti, and the Salto Tres Mosqueteros (be ready to get soaked). ⊠ *Puerto Iguazú* ☎ *3757/42–1696* ⊕ *www.iguazujungle.com* 🚌 *From 450 Argentine pesos.*

EXPLORING

The falls are not the only sites to see in these parts, though few people actually have time (or make time) to go see others.

TOP ATTRACTIONS

Argentina's side of the falls is in the **Parque Nacional Iguazú,** which was founded in 1934 and declared a World Heritage Site in 1984. The park is divided into two areas, each of which is organized around a train station: Estación Cataratas or the Estación Garganta del Diablo. (A third, Estación Central, is near the park entrance.) Paved walkways lead from the main entrance past the visitor center. Colorful visual displays provide a good explanation of the region's ecology and human history. To reach the park proper, you cross through a small plaza containing a food court, gift shops, and ATM. From the nearby Estación Central, the gas-propelled Tren de la Selva (Jungle Train) departs every 20 minutes.

Expect to get up close and personal with the waterfalls on the Argentine side (in other words, you're going to get wet). Two-thirds of the falls are in the Parque Nacional Iguazú, including the Garganta del Diablo, a massive, raging waterfall that is the area's star attraction. The catwalks and trails of the Circuito Superior and Circuito Inferior have numerous scenic overlooks where you can snap photos of the raging waterfalls. From the Circuito Inferior, you can catch a ferry to Isla San Martín, which has walking trails that lead to scenic viewing points of the falls. For a truly soaking experience, you can take Zodiac boat rides that steer you directly into the gushing falls.

WORTH NOTING

La Aripuca. It looks like a cross between a log cabin and the Pentagon, but this massive wooden structure—which weighs 551 tons—is a large-scale replica of a Guaraní bird trap. La Aripuca officially showcases different local woods, supposedly for conservation purposes—ironic, given the huge trunks used to build it and the overpriced wooden furniture that fills the gift shop. ⊠ *RN 12, Km 5, Puerto Iguazú* ☎ *3757/425–857* ⊕ *www.aripuca.com.ar* ⌦ *40 pesos* ⊙ *Daily 9–6.*

Güira Oga. Although Iguazú Falls is home to around 450 bird species, the parks are so busy these days that you'd be lucky to see so much as a feather. It's another story at Güira Oga, which means "House of the Birds" in Guaraní. Birds that were injured, displaced by deforestation, or confiscated from traffickers are brought here for treatment. The large cages also contain many species you rarely see in the area, including the fearsome harpy eagle and the gorgeous red macaw. The sanctuary is in a forested plot just off RN 12, halfway between Puerto Iguazú and the falls. The entrance price includes a 90-minute guided visit (in English and Spanish). ⊠ *RN 12, Km 5, Puerto Iguazú* ☎ *3757/423–980* ⊕ *www.guiraoga.com.ar* ⌦ *85 pesos* ⊙ *Daily 9–5.*

Jardín de los Picaflores. With more than 400 species of birds in the national parks surrounding Iguazú Falls, bird-watchers will be kept happily busy. After trekking in the forest for a day or two, the sight of scores of hummingbirds in a more intimate setting might be a birder's dream. This tiny garden north of Puerto Iguazú serves as more of a feeding station than a refuge, but it's busy with the little powerhouses zipping about. ⊠ *Fray Luis Beltran 150, Puerto Iguazú* ☎ *3757/424–081* ⌦ *30 pesos* ⊙ *Daily 8–noon and 3:30–7.*

Hito Tres Fronteras. This viewing point west of the town center stands high above the turbulent reddish-brown confluence of the Iguazú and Paraná Rivers, which also form the Triple Frontera, or Triple Border. A mini pale-blue-and-white obelisk reminds you you're in Argentina;

Iguazu Falls

KEY

♿	Wheelchair-accessible
🍴	Restaurant
🌲	Scenic Viewpoint
– – –	Walking/Hiking Trails
🚢	Ferry Lines
+––+	Rail Lines

Estación Central

Estación Cataratas

Estación Garganta del Diablo

Garganta del Diablo

ARGENTINA

Parque Nacional Iguazú

Circuito Superior

Circuito Inferior

Dos Hermanas

Isla San Martin

Río Iguazú

Parque Nacional do Iguaçu

BRAZIL

across the Iguazú River is Brazil's green-and-yellow equivalent; farther away, across the Paraná, is Paraguay's, painted red, white, and blue. A row of overpriced souvenir stalls stands alongside it. ✉ *Av. Tres Fronteras, Puerto Iguazú.*

WHERE TO EAT

$$$$ MODERN ARGENTINE 🍴 **Aqva.** Locals are thrilled: finally, a date-night restaurant in Puerto Iguazú. Although the high-ceilinged split-level cabin seats too many to be truly intimate, the owners make up for it with well-spaced tables, discreet service, and low lighting. Softly gleaming timber from different local trees lines the walls, roof, and floor. Local river fish like *surubí* and *dorado* are the specialty: have them panfried, or, more unusually, as pasta fillings. Forget being romantic at dessert time: the chef's signature dessert, fresh mango and pineapple with a Torrontés sabayon, is definitely worth keeping to yourself. Reservations are essential on weekends. [$] *Average main: 150 pesos* ✉ *Av. Córdoba at Carlos Thays, Puerto Iguazú* ☎ *3757/422–064* 🌐 *www.aqvarestaurant.com.*

$$$$ ARGENTINE 🍴 **La Rueda.** This parrilla is so popular that it starts serving dinner as early as 7:30 pm—teatime by Argentine custom. The local beef isn't quite up to Buenos Aires standards, but La Rueda's perfectly cooked *bife de chorizo* is one of the best in town. Locally caught surubí is another house specialty, but skip the traditional Roquefort sauce, which overwhelms the fish's flavor. The surroundings stay true to the restaurant's rustic roots: hefty tree trunks hold up the bamboo-lined roof, and the walls are adorned by a curious wooden frieze carved by a local artist. [$] *Average main: 200 pesos* ✉ *Av. Córdoba 28, Puerto Iguazú* ☎ *3757/422–531* 🌐 *www.larueda1975.com.ar* ⏲ *No lunch Mon. and Tues.* ✍ *Reservations essential.*

WHERE TO STAY

$$$$ HOTEL 🏨 **Panoramic Hotel Iguazú.** The falls aren't the only good views in Iguazú: half the rooms of this chic hotel look onto the churning, jungle-framed waters of the Iguazú and Paraná Rivers. **Pros:** river views; great attention to detail; the gorgeous pool. **Cons:** the in-house casino makes the lobby noisy; staff can seem indifferent; in-house transportation is overpriced. [$] *Rooms from: 2,650 pesos* ✉ *Calle Paraguay 372, Puerto Iguazú* ☎ *3757/498–100, 3757/498–050* 🌐 *www.panoramichoteliguazu.com* 🛏 *91 rooms* 🍽 *Breakfast.*

$$$ B&B/INN 🏨 **Posada 21 Oranges.** Friendly owners Rémy and Romina give you a warm welcome at this rootsy B&B, which is surrounded by a lush garden. **Pros:** wonderfully helpful and attentive owners; peaceful surroundings; abundant homemade breakfasts served on a terrace in the garden. **Cons:** too far from the town center to walk to; low on luxury. [$] *Rooms from: 800 pesos* ✉ *Montecarlo s/n, near RN 12, Km 5, Puerto Iguazú* ☎ *3757/494–014* 🌐 *www.21oranges.com* 💳 *No credit cards* 🛏 *10 rooms* 🍽 *Breakfast.*

$$$$ B&B/INN 🏨 **Secret Garden Iguazú.** Dense tropical vegetation overhangs the wooden walkway that leads to this tiny guesthouse's three rooms, tucked away in a pale-blue clapboard house. **Pros:** wood deck overlooking the back-to-nature garden; owner's charm and expert mixology; home-away-from-home vibe. **Cons:** the three rooms book up fast; no pool; comfortable but not luxurious. [$] *Rooms from: 994 pesos* ✉ *Los Lapachos 623,*

Puerto Iguazú ☎ *3757/423–099* 🌐 *www.secretgardeniguazu.com* 💳 *No credit cards* 🛏 *3 rooms* 🍴 *Breakfast.*

$$$$ HOTEL 🏨 **Sheraton International Iguazú.** That thundering you hear in the distance lets you know how close this hotel is to the falls—the lobby opens right onto the park trails, and half the rooms have big balconies with fabulous falls views. **Pros:** the falls are on your doorstep; great buffet breakfasts; well-designed spa. **Cons:** rooms are in need of a complete makeover; mediocre food and service at dinner; other restaurants are an expensive taxi ride away. [$] *Rooms from: 3,132 pesos* ✉ *Within Parque Nacional Iguazú, off Ruta Nacional 101, Puerto Iguazú* ☎ *3757/49–1800, 3757/491–800* 🌐 *www.sheraton.com* 🛏 *176 rooms, 8 suites* 🍴 *Breakfast.*

FOZ DO IGUAÇU, BRAZIL

The construction of the Itaipú Dam (now the world's second largest) in 1975 transformed Foz do Iguaçu into a bustling city with seven times more people than nearby Puerto Iguazú. It's precisely because of the city's size that many visitors to the falls arrange accommodations in or near Foz do Iguaçu. After daytime adventures in the national park, the city's nightlife extends the fun. Aside from pubs, clubs, and all kinds of live music, there's even a samba show.

GETTING HERE AND AROUND

There are direct flights between Foz do Iguaçu and São Paulo (1½ hours; $230), Rio de Janeiro (2 hours; $260), and Curitiba (1 hour; $280) on TAM, which also has connecting flights to Salvador, Recife, Brasilia, other Brazilian cities, and Buenos Aires. Low-cost airline GOL operates slightly cheaper direct flights on the same three routes.

The Aeroporto Internacional Foz do Iguaçu is 13 km (8 miles) southeast of downtown Foz. The 20-minute taxi ride should cost R$40 to R$50; the 45-minute regular bus ride about R$2.60. Note that several major hotels are on the highway to downtown, so a cab ride from the airport to these may be less than R$30. A cab ride from downtown hotels directly to the Parque Nacional in Brazil costs about R$70.

Via bus, the trip between São Paulo and Foz do Iguaçu takes 15 hours (R$184). The Terminal Rodoviário in Foz do Iguaçu is 5 km (3 miles) northeast of downtown. There are regular buses into town; they stop at the Terminal de Transportes Urbano (local bus station, often shortened to TTU) at Avenida Juscelino Kubitschek and Rua Mem de Sá. From platform 2, Bus No. 120 (labeled "Parque Nacional") also departs every 20 minutes (from 7 to 7) to the visitor center at the park entrance; the fare is R$2.60. The buses run along Avenida Juscelino Kubitschek and Avenida Jorge Schimmelpfeng, where you can also flag them down.

There's no real reason to rent a car in Foz do Iguaçu, as you can't cross the border in a rental car. There are *pontos de taxi* (taxi stands) at intersections all over town. Hotels and restaurants can call you a cab, but you can also hail them on the street.

Bus Contacts Pluma. ☎ *045/3522–2988 in Foz do Iguaçu* 🌐 *www.pluma.com.br.*

Visitor Information **Foz do Iguaçu Tourist Office.** ✉ *Praça Getúlio Vargas 69, Foz do Iguaçu* ☎ *045/3521–1455* ⊕ *www.iguassu.tur.br.*

TOURS

Cânion Iguaçu. In Brazil, Cânion Iguaçu offers rafting and canopying, as well as abseiling over the river from the Salto San Martín. It also offers wheelchair-compatible equipment. ✉ *Foz do Iguaçu* ☎ *045/3529–6040* ⊕ *www.macucosafari.com.br.*

Macuco Ecoaventura. Macuco Ecoaventura is one of the official tour operators within the Brazilian side of the park. Its Trilha do Pozo Negro trip combines a 9-km (5½-mile) guided hike or bike ride with a thrilling boat trip along the upper river (the bit before the falls). The aptly named Floating trip is more leisurely; shorter jungle hikes are also offered. ✉ *Foz do Iguaçu* ☎ *045/3529–9665* ⊕ *www. macucoecoaventura.com.br.*

Macuco Safari. You can take to the water on the Brazilian side with Macuco Safari. The signature trip is a Zodiac ride around (and under) the Salto Tres Mosqueteros. You get a more sedate ride on the *Iguaçu Explorer*, a 3½-hour trip up the river. ✉ *Foz do Iguaçu* ☎ *045/3574– 4244, 045/3529–6262* ⊕ *www.macucosafari.com.br.*

EXPLORING

TOP ATTRACTIONS

In Brazil, the falls can be seen from the **Parque Nacional Foz do Iguaçu.** Much of the park is protected rain forest, off-limits to visitors and home to the last viable populations of panthers as well as rare flora.

Buses and taxis drop you off at a vast plaza alongside the park entrance building. As well as ticket booths, there's an ATM, a snack bar, gift shop, and information and currency exchange. Next to the entrance turnstiles is the small visitor center, where helpful geological models explain how the falls were formed. Double-decker buses run every 15 minutes between the entrance and the trailhead to the falls, 11 km (7 miles) away; the buses stop at the entrances to excursions run by private operators Macuco Safari and Macuco Ecoaventura.

The top reason to go to the Brazil side of the falls is to revel in the panoramic perspective of the Garganta do Diablo, the raging waterfall on the Argentine side. There are also scenic viewing points along the trails in the park that give visitors full views of the falls. For truly fabulous views, consider taking a helicopter ride over the park.

Itaipú Dam and Hydroelectric Power Plant. It took more than 30,000 workers eight years to build this 8-km (5-mile) dam, voted one of the Seven Wonders of the Modern World by the American Society of Civil Engineers. The monumental structure, which produces roughly 17% of Brazil's electricity and 75% of Paraguay's, was the largest hydroelectric power plant in the world until China's Three Gorges Dam was completed.

You get plenty of insight into how proud this makes the Brazilian government—and some idea of how the dam was built—during the 30-minute video that precedes the hour-long guided panoramic bus tours of the complex. Although commentaries are humdrum, the sheer size of

KEY

❶ Exploring sights

① Hotels & Restaurants

Foz do Iguaçu

the dam is an impressive sight. To see more than a view over the spill-ways, consider the special tours, which take you inside the cavernous structure and into the control room. Night tours—which include a light-and-sound show—begin at 8 on Friday and Saturday, 9 during the summer months (reserve ahead). ⊠ *Av. Tancredo Neves 6702, Foz do Iguaçu* ☎ *800/645–4645, 0800/645–4645* ✉ *reservas@turismoitaipu. com.br* ⊕ *www.turismoitaipu.com.br* ✇ *Panoramic tour R$26, special tour R$64* ☉ *Regular tours daily 8–4 (on the hour). Special tours daily 8, 8:30, 10, 10:30, 1:30, 2, 3:30, and 4.*

Parque das Aves (*Bird Park*). Flamingos, parrots, and macaws are some of the more colorful inhabitants of this privately run park. Right outside the Parque Nacional Foz do Iguaçu, it's an interesting complement to a visit to the falls. A winding path leads you through untouched tropi-cal forest and walk-through aviaries containing hundreds of species of birds. One of the amazing experiences is the toucan enclosure, where they are so close you could touch them. Iguanas, alligators, and other nonfeathered friends have their own pens. ⊠ *Rodovia das Cataratas, Km 17.1, Foz do Iguaçu* ☎ *045/3529–8282, 045/3529–8282* ⊕ *www. parquedasaves.com.br* ✇ *R$24 for Brazilians, R$34 for international visitors* ☉ *Daily 8:30–5.*

WORTH NOTING

Ecomuseu de Itaipú (*Itaipú Eco-Museum*). At the Ecomuseu de Itaipú you can learn about the geology, archaeology, and efforts to preserve the flora and fauna of the area since the Itaipú Dam was built. This museum is funded by the dam's operator, Itaipú Binacional, so the information isn't necessarily objective. ✉ *Av. Presidente Tancredo Neves 6731, Foz do Iguaçu* ☎ *045/3529–2892* ⊕ *www.turismoitaipu.com.br* 💳 *R$10* ☉ *Tues.–Sun 8–4:30.*

WHERE TO EAT

$$$$ ✕**Búfalo Branco.** The city's finest and largest churrascaria does a killer
BRAZILIAN rodízio (all you can eat meat buffet). The *picanha* (beef rump cap) stands out among the dozens of meat choices, but pork, lamb, and chicken find their way onto the metal skewers they use to grill the meat. Never fear, vegetarians—the salad bar is also well stocked. The dining room is bright and cheerful, and bow-tied waiters serve your food. 💲 *Average main: R$75* ✉ *Av. Rebouças 530, Foz do Iguaçu* ☎ *045/3523–9744* ⊕ *www.bufalobranco.com.br.*

$$$$ ✕**Tempero da Bahia.** If you're not traveling as far as Salvador and the state
BRAZILIAN of Bahia, you can at least check out its flavors at this busy restaurant. It specializes in northeastern fare like *moquecas* (a rich seafood stew made with coconut milk and palm oil). The version here is unusual for mixing prawns with local river fish. Spicy panfried sole and salmon are lighter options. The flavors aren't quite so subtle at the all-you-can-eat seafood buffets served several times a week. At R$60, it certainly pulls in crowds. 💲 *Average main: R$80* ✉ *Rua Marechal Deodoro 1228, Foz do Iguaçu* ☎ *045/3025–1144* ⊕ *www.restaurantetemperodabahia.com* ☉ *No lunch Mon.–Sat. No dinner Sun.*

$$$ ✕**Zaragoza.** On a tree-lined street in a quiet neighborhood, this tra-
SPANISH ditional restaurant's Spanish owner is an expert at matching Iguaçu's fresh river fish to authentic Spanish seafood recipes. Brazilian ingredients sneak into some dishes—the *surubi à Goya* (catfish in a tomato and coconut-milk sauce) definitely merits a try. 💲 *Average main: R$50* ✉ *Rua Quintino Bocaiúva 882, Foz do Iguaçu* ☎ *045/3028–8084* ⊕ *www.restaurantezaragoza.com.br.*

WHERE TO STAY

$$$$ 🏨 **Hotel das Cataratas.** Not only is this stately hotel *in* the national park,
RESORT with views of the smaller falls from the front-side suites, but it also pro-
Fodor's Choice vides the traditional comforts of a colonial-style establishment: large
★ rooms, terraces, vintage furniture, and hammocks. **Pros:** right inside the park, a short walk from the falls; serious colonial-style charm; friendly, helpful staff. **Cons:** rooms aren't as luxurious as the price promises; far from Foz do Iguaçu so you're limited to the on-site restaurants; only the most expensive suites have views of the falls. 💲 *Rooms from: R$960* ✉ *Rodovia das Cataratas, Km 32, Foz do Iguaçu* ☎ *045/2102–7000,* *0800/726–4545* ⊕ *www.hoteldascataratas.com.br* ⬆ *197 rooms, 5 suites* ⭐ *Breakfast.*

6

SANTA CATARINA

The 560 km (350 miles) of coastline, with beautiful beaches galore, are the calling card of Santa Catarina, the smallest state in the South. The most popular beaches are on Ilha de Santa Catarina, an island best known as Florianópolis, home to the state capital of the same name. Visitors can explore the island's 42 beaches, from the upmarket, high-rise hotels and resorts on the northern shores, where thousands of Brazilian and foreign tourists flock every summer, to the wilder, quieter beaches down south. For surf, head to the stunning beaches around Praia do Rosa, where southern right whales go to breed in the winter months.

BALNEÁRIO CAMBORIÚ

81 km (50 miles) north of Florianópolis, 616 km (382 miles) south of São Paulo.

At a glance, the beachside city of Balneário Camboriú could be straight out of the Jetsons, with its futuristic skyline of tall, thin buildings (one of which is the tallest in Brazil). On the ground, it bears a passing resemblance to Rio's Copacabana, from the long, sweeping beach and black-and-white tiled boardwalk to the statue of Christ up on a hill. In the summer, the population increases almost tenfold, and the traffic grinds to a halt, with tourists flocking to the beaches, restaurants, and bars. For quieter beaches, head just south to Praia do Estaleiro and beyond.

GETTING HERE AND AROUND

If arriving by car, Balneário Camboriú can be easily accessed from both the north and south via a number of exits off the BR101. The nearest airport is Navegantes, 33 km (20 miles) to the north. To get from Navegantes airport to Balneário Camboriú, you can either hire a car at the airport, take a taxi (around R\$86), or travel by bus with Lufer (R\$28.50). Both Catarinense and Pluma run regular bus services from Florianópolis (80 km/50 miles, around R\$23), and from Curitiba (220 km/137 miles, around R\$43). To get around the city and neighboring beaches, Expressul has a number of routes (R\$3.15), and a tourist bus, the Bondindinho (R\$4.25), does a circular route up the main avenues, Avenida Brasil and Avenida Atlántica.

ESSENTIALS

Bus contacts Catarinense. ☎ *048/4002–4700* ⊕ *www.catarinense.net.* **Pluma.** ☎ *0800/646–0300* ⊕ *pluma.com.br.* **Viação Lufer.** ☎ *047/3342–8141* ⊕ *luferviagem.com.br.* **Terminal Rodoviário de Balneário Camboriú** (*Bus Station*). ✉ *Av. Santa Catarina 347, Balneário Camboriú* ☎ *047/3367–2901.*

Taxi contacts Rádio Táxi. ☎ *047/3367–0066.*

Tourist information Posto de Informação Turística (*Tourist Information Point*) ✉ *Av. do Estado 5041* ☎ *047/3367–8005* ⊕ *secturbc.com.br.*

BEACHES

Praia Balneário Camboriú. Crowded in the summer months, Balneário Camboriú's main beach stretches for 6 km (3.7 miles), with the sweeping boardwalk a favorite for joggers, cyclists, and casual strollers. The quality of the water, however, is tested regularly by the state's environment agency, and regularly deemed unsuitable for swimming. **Amenities:** food and drink. **Best for:** partiers; walking. ✉ *Balneário Camboriú.*

Praia Brava. Just a couple of miles around the headland from busy Balneário Camboriú, Praia Brava and connecting Praia dos Amores are where the party animals go in the summer. The seafront restaurants and bars stake their claim on the soft sand with a warren of chairs, parasols, and waiter service. A handful of beach clubs raise the volume with guest DJs and drinks promos during weekends. **Amenities:** food and drink. **Best for:** partiers; walking. ✉ *Av. José Medeiros Viêira, Balneário Camboriú.*

Praia do Estaleiro. Clean and tranquil, with soft, yellow sand, Praia do Estaleiro is an attractive beach that has escaped the clutches of the property developers thanks to its environmental protection status. The beach never gets too crowded and the water stays clean. **Amenities:** food and drink. **Best for:** solitude; swimming. ✉ *Balneário Camboriú.*

WHERE TO EAT AND STAY

\$\$\$\$
CONTEMPORARY ✕ **L'Assiette Cozinha de Autor.** Decked out in purple leathers and black laminate, L'Assiette Cozinha de Autor has an enviable location looking out over the sweeping bay in Balneário Camboriú. Unlike the decor,

there's nothing of dubious taste on the menu here, with imaginative dishes emerging from a small kitchen. For maximum Franco-Brazilian flair, adventurous diners should book ahead to try the chef's excellent tasting menu (six courses R$128, nine courses R$178), packed with surprises like a trio of tomatoes (powder, jelly, and chutney) and funghi ice cream with white chocolate foam. [$] *Average main: R$70* ✉ *Rua 4100, 21, Centro, Balneário Camboriú* ☎ *047/3363–9818* ⏲ *No lunch.*

$$$$ B&B/INN 🏨 **Estaleiro Guest House.** A well-manicured hotel with direct access to a clean, quiet beach, Estaleiro Guest House has 21 rooms, split across a trio of colorful, three-story buildings. **Pros:** on-site bistro; direct beach access. **Cons:** regularly booked out for events. [$] *Rooms from: R$690* ✉ *Avenida Interpraias 3987, Balneário Camboriú* ☎ *047/3264–5717, 047/3363–5071* 🌐 *praiadoestaleiro.com.br* 🛏 *19 rooms, 2 suites* 🍴 *Breakfast.*

$$$$ B&B/INN 🏨 **Felissimo Exclusive Hotel.** What started as an upmarket guesthouse in a quiet, residential suburb is now a self-styled "exclusive hotel," with a vibe that's design-conscious and hip. **Pros:** good food; gated parking lot. **Cons:** new construction spoils the sea view; busy with outside guests at weekends. [$] *Rooms from: R$690* ✉ *Rua Ales Blaun 201, Balneário Camboriú* ☎ *047/3360–6291* 🌐 *felissimoexclusivehotel.com.br* 🛏 *10 rooms* 🍴 *Breakfast.*

$$ B&B/INN 🏨 **Pousada Estaleiro Village.** Simple and rustic, this pousada is one of the few on this stretch of coastline to have direct access to the beach. **Pros:** the garden will delight nature lovers; direct access to the beach; friendly service. **Cons:** basic furnishings; swimming pool showing its age. [$] *Rooms from: R$340* ✉ *Av. Interpraias 3996, Balneário Camboriú* ☎ *047/9112–5200* 🌐 *estaleirovillage.com* 🛏 *17 rooms, 7 suites* 🍴 *Breakfast.*

GOVERNADOR CELSO RAMOS

62 km (38 miles) south of Balneário Camboriú, 49 km (30 miles) north of Florianópolis.

Just across the water from Florianópolis, this charming stretch of coastline is dotted with fishing villages still stuck in the past and quaint beaches, largely unspoiled by tourism.

GETTING HERE AND AROUND

Hiring a car in Florianópolis is the easiest way to access the peninsula. Take route BR 101 and exit on the SC410, either at Km 183 for the more circuitous road counterclockwise round the coast, or at Km 180 for a more direct route to the towns on the peninsula's north coast. A regular Biguaçú bus service runs every 40 minutes from the central Florianópolis bus station to the town of Governador Celso Ramos, stopping in a few towns on route. This service takes 80 minutes and costs R$6.20.

BEACHES

Praia da Armação da Piedade. At the tip of the peninsula, a couple of miles down a dead-end dirt road, you'll find one of the most tranquil and best-preserved of the fishing villages on this stretch of coast. The

WELCOME TO THE RIO OLYMPICS

In August 2016 athletes from more than 200 nations will head to Rio de Janeiro, one of the world's most stunning cities, to compete in South America's first Olympic Games. Hosting the games is a major coup for Brazil, allowing the nation to bask in the world's attention as it flaunts its spectacular natural beauty and vibrant cultures.

Brazil has a strong performance history at the Olympics: since the 1920s, Brazilian athletes have brought home 108 medals. Surprisingly, Brazil has never won a gold medal in soccer; and the national team will be keen to correct that on its hallowed home turf.

No matter the number of medals earned by the hosts in 2016, visitors can expect to find Rio in full party mode during the 17-day festivities.

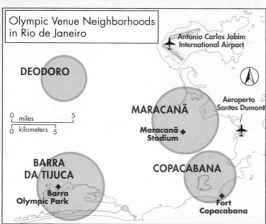

Olympic Venue Neighborhoods in Rio de Janeiro

Antonio Carlos Jobim International Airport

DEODORO

0 miles 5
0 kilometers 5

MARACANÃ

Aeroperto Santos Dumont

Maracanã Stadium

BARRA DA TIJUCA

Barra Olympic Park

COPACABANA

Fort Copacabana

BARRA DA TIJUCA

With vastly more available land than Rio's built-up urban heart, Barra da Tijuca was an obvious choice as the hub of the 2016 Olympics. Known locally as Barra (pronounced "Baha"), this affluent beach suburb feels like a city apart from the rest of Rio, even though it's only 25 miles west of the city center.

Although Barra has towering condos, wide avenues, and large shopping malls that make the area feel less "Brazilian" than most of Rio (indeed, it is often referred to by locals as "the United States of Barra"), its soft sand beach is the biggest in the city, stretching for more than 13 km (8 miles). The bars, restaurants, and nightclubs attract a hip crowd.

The **Olympic Village** and press camp will be located in Barra, and the largest concentration of games, including many of the big-ticket events such as diving, swimming, and gymnastics, will be held at a total of 14 competition venues making up the **Olympic Park**. Golf will also return to

the Summer Olympics after an absence of more than a century; the new **Olympic Golf Course** will be in Barra da Tijuca.

Occupying a peninsula jutting out into the ocean, the Olympic Park will have venues connected by curved pathways that are designed to resemble Brazil's twisty Amazon River. Those without tickets can watch the games live on giant screens at a green waterfront space within the park.

Barra has traditionally suffered from poor transpor-

(top left) The sprawling beach in Barra da Tijuca. (top right) Gabby Douglas of the U.S. national team.

tation links to Rio's South Zone and downtown, but it is fast becoming better connected. The first of several rapid bus corridors is already in place, and the metro is scheduled to reach Barra by late 2015.

DEODORO

This nondescript area of Rio holds little tourist appeal outside of its Olympic events, but it will be the setting for the second-largest concentration of venues during the Games. Nine venues will be located here. The zone is best accessed by rail, with trains leaving for Deodoro rail station from Central do Brasil in downtown Rio.

FAST FACTS

Dates: August 5–21, 2016

Total Sports: 42

Total Medal Events: 306

Total Venues: 33

Opening and Closing Ceremonies: Maracanã Stadium

Ticket Prices: $25–$350

Where to Purchase Tickets: www.rio2016.org/tickets

The official Rio 2016 website: www.rio2016.org/en

The official Olympics website: www.olympic.org/rio-2016-summer-olympics

Brazil Tourism Board website: www.visitbrasil.com

Deodoro will host a mix of traditional and more modern events at venues such as the Olympic Shooting Stadium and Equestrian Arena. The modern X-Park includes an Olympic BMX Centre and will leave a legacy for future extreme sporting events. In addition, Deodoro will host rugby, which returns to the Olympics after a 92-year absence.

With little visual appeal and limited tourist infrastructure in the immediate vicinity of the venues, the area is not a good base for visitors.

(top left) The Maracanã Stadium. (top right) Rio's famed Copacabana beach.

MARACANÃ

This area north of the city center will host events in three locations: the iconic **Maracanã Stadium**; the nearby **Sambódromo,** where Rio's famous Carnival parades take place; and the **Engenhão Stadium** in the residential neighborhood of Engenho de Dentro.

The Maracanã Stadium was given a multimillion-dollar overhaul ahead of the 2014 FIFA World Cup. It is here that Rio's spectacular opening and closing ceremonies will be held. Appropriately, the men's and women's soccer finals will take place in the Maracanã Stadium as well.

One of the Olympics' most popular sports, volleyball, will take place in the **Maracanãzinho Gymnasium,** next to the Maracanã Stadium.

The marathon will begin and end in Rio's Sambódromo, which was recently renovated and can now hold up to 72,000 spectators.

The J. Havelange Olympic Stadium, or "Engenhão," was built for the 2007 Pan-American Games and will host high-profile track-and-field events during the Olympics.

The area is not Rio's most beautiful, but good metro links mean that visitors making their base in Centro or the South Zone will be able to reach the stadiums without much trouble.

COPACABANA

For many people, Copacabana *is* Rio. The long, curved ribbon of sand here is one of the world's most famous beaches, anchored by a perfect view of Sugar Loaf and frequented by bronzed beauties in skimpy swimsuits. It's fitting that Copacabana is the location for the Olympic beach volleyball events in **Copacabana Stadium**, which was purpose-built for the games.

Marathon swimming will take place at the western end of Copacabana beach, and the scenic surrounding area will host some of the Olympics' most exciting events, including cycling at **Flamengo Park** and the triathlon at **Fort Copacabana.**

Copacabana is one of Rio's liveliest neighborhoods, and the beach here is sure to teem with sports fans eager to touch up their tans in between games. Free-flowing caipirinhas, impromptu music performances, and cooling breezes will create a party atmosphere on the beach throughout the games.

Even though hotels are plentiful here, visitors should expect to pay a premium for beachfront lodgings, and loud parties are likely to continue late into the night. Those looking for quieter accommodations will find good options in nearby Ipanema, while budget visitors will find a lively scene in nearby Botafogo.

WHERE TO SEE SELECT EVENTS

Basketball: Barra da Tijuca and Deodoro

Beach Volleyball: Copacabana

Boxing: Barra da Tijuca

Diving: Barra da Tijuca

Equestrian Events: Deodoro

Fencing: Barra da Tijuca

Field Hockey: Deodoro

Golf: Barra da Tijuca

Gymnastics: Barra da Tijuca

Road Cycling: Barra da Tijuca and Copacabana

Rowing: Copacabana

Rugby: Deodoro

Sailing: Copacabana

Soccer: Maracanã

Swimming: Barra da Tijuca

Tennis: Barra da Tijuca

Track and Field: Maracanã

Triathlon: Copacabana

Volleyball: Maracanã

Water Polo: Barra da Tijuca and Maracanã

Weight Lifting: Barra da Tijuca

Wrestling: Barra da Tijuca

Four additional cities will host soccer games during the Olympics: São Paulo, Belo Horizonte, Brasília, and Salvador.

Hurdlers compete for the gold.

For sports fans visiting Rio during the 2016 Olympics, finding lodging and getting around will be the most pressing issues. The games will take place in four neighborhoods spread across this sprawling city.

LODGING

Most sporting events, along with the newly constructed Olympic Village, will be in Barra da Tijuca, an upscale beach community 25 miles west of the city center. Many new hotels are being built here ahead of the games to accommodate the throngs of visitors seeking a convenient base near the main venues.

Those looking for more independence or affordable lodgings will have plenty of options. As happened during the 2014 FIFA World Cup in Brazil, numerous locals will rent out apartments or spare rooms, while residents in some of Rio's favelas have proven themselves excellent hosts for those priced out of lodgings in the city's touristic heartland.

Visitors can use online agencies such as *Booking.com* to get the best prices for Olympic stays. *Airbnb.com* is widely used by Rio locals renting everything from spare sofa beds to penthouse apartments. The go-to source for chic guesthouse accommodation across Brazil is Hidden Pousadas Brazil *(www.hiddenpousadasbrazil.com)*. Those curious to try a favela stay should look to agencies such as Favela Experience *(www.favelaexperience.com)*, which was a reliable and socially responsible operator during the 2014 FIFA World Cup.

TRAVEL

Flights to Rio de Janeiro are available via major carriers from most global destinations, and the city's international airport is getting much-needed renovations as it prepares to receive a mass influx of international visitors. It is wise to book airline tickets as far in advance as possible to avoid ramped-up last-minute prices.

A major overhaul of Rio de Janeiro's public transportation system has been initiated ahead of the games, with plans to extend the metro system to the Olympic Village in Barra da Tijuca. A new light railway system and fast bus corridors will improve transportation connections between the city's airports, inter-city bus terminal, tourist hot spots, and the Olympic Village.

There will be four Bus Rapid Transit (BRT) fast bus corridors. The first connects the international airport with Barra da Tijuca, the main competition zone for the games. The other three will be completed by the time the games begin, and will transport athletes and spectators between the city and the Olympic pavilions. The bus lanes will be open to the general public, with tickets bought on board at the time of travel.

However you get around the city, leave plenty of travel time in your schedule and don't try to cram too many events in multiple venues into one day. Attempts to fit in games in different neighborhoods on the same day may not be realistic unless the schedule allows for several hours of travel. While taxis are widely available and affordable, the metro and fast bus corridors will provide speedier links between venues.

TICKETS TO THE EVENTS
Tickets will be available on the official site: *www.rio2016.org*. Of the 7.5 million tickets available, roughly half will cost US$30 or less. The Olympics Organizing Committee has announced that it will use multiple official vendors and round-the-clock sales in order to ensure that venues are filled to capacity.

Carnival parades at Rio's Sambódromo.

TIPS FOR ATTENDING AN EVENT

- Arrive an hour or so early to soak up the atmosphere and sample traditional snacks from the street sellers. Be on the lookout for white-clad Bahian women selling Northeastern specialties such as tapioca pancakes and spicy acaraje bean meal patties.

- Save queuing time with a pre-pay metro card. With machines (cash only) available at all metro stations, these cards can be preloaded with amounts from R$5–R$50.

- Allow plenty of extra time when heading to a game for any transportation disruptions.

- Don't plan on walking around the areas surrounding stadiums in Deodoro or Maracanã, especially after dark.

- Bring a lightweight jacket and an umbrella; it can be chilly after dark in Rio.

- If you plan to take a taxi and don't speak Portuguese, write down the name of the destination to show the driver.

- Don't bring outside food or drinks into the stadium.

Visitors marvel at the Escadaria Selarón in Lapa, one of the best neighborhoods for nightlife in Rio.

TEAM SPIRIT

If you don't have tickets to the events, you can still find ways to root for your country. Most bars and restaurants will have their televisions permanently tuned to the sports channels. It is also common during sporting events to see someone's living room television hooked up on the street—a scene that is often accompanied by locals selling cold beers and soft drinks from a cooler.

There will be three live sites scattered through Rio where crowds will be able to follow Olympic events on massive screens. For a peek at the local sporting scene, simply stroll along Rio's many beachfronts to watch cariocas engage in beach volleyball, water sports, and, in particular, soccer, the national sport.

To show your team spirit, paint your country's colors on your nails. At Rio's legendary beauty salons, skilled technicians are renowned for their devotion to perfectly painted nails. Nearly every street in the city has a salon where you can receive an affordable mani-pedi that would cost a fortune elsewhere.

HIT THE TOWN

Rio's downtown Port Zone is currently being transformed into a cultural hot spot through the **Porto Maravilha** project. The **Museum of Tomorrow**, a modern science museum designed by renowned architect Santiago Calatrava, is scheduled to open here before the Games, along with a wealth of upscale restaurants and shops. As of this writing, work is under way to construct a new 28-km (17-mile) light-rail network that will connect the port with Rio's metro system and domestic airport.

For nightlife, Barra da Tijuca draws a sophisticated crowd at its chic wine bars and nightclubs, while Copacabana has a livelier, more casual vibe with beachfront kiosks enticing tourists with bargain caipirinhas. But if you really want to party with the locals, head to the downtown district of **Lapa**. This formerly rundown neighborhood is now Rio's party hub, filled with live music venues where you can dance samba or just watch while fleet-footed locals show how it's done. It's the perfect place to barhop or just wander through street stalls selling potent cocktails.

sand is more suited to walking than sunbathing, so park up by the 18th-century colonial chapel at one end of the beach and stroll down to the handful of beach bars at the other. **Amenities:** food and drink. **Best for:** walking. ✉ *Governador Celso Ramos.*

WHERE TO STAY

$$$$ RESORT Fodor's Choice ★ 🏨 **Ponta dos Ganchos.** Taking luxury to new levels, this little patch of paradise has its own small beach, helipad, a private island for candlelit dinners, and an infinity pool and/or hot tub in each of the 25 Balinese-style villas. **Pros:** multilingual staff; great views; spacious, well-appointed rooms. **Cons:** no outdoor swimming pool; food not always worth the price tag. [$] *Rooms from: R$1,950* ✉ *Rua Eupídeo Alves do Nascimento 104, Governador Celso Ramos* ☎ *048/3262–5000* 🌐 *pontadosganchos.com.br* 🛏 *25 villas* 🍴 *Breakfast.*

FLORIANÓPOLIS

300 km (187 miles) southeast of Curitiba, 476 km (296 miles) northeast of Porto Alegre.

Fodor's Choice ★ The nickname "Magic Island" is an appropriate moniker for Florianópolis (officially called Ilha de Santa Catarina, but known to most as Florianópolis, or simply "Floripa") with a breathtaking shoreline, easy-to-reach beaches, and seemingly endless vacation activities. The northern *praias* (beaches) are considered the best—because of their warm waters—and are therefore the busiest. Impressive seascapes dominate the Atlantic beaches, and southern beaches have fewer sun worshippers and a more laid-back atmosphere. Scuba diving, surfing, kitesurfing, sailing, and parasailing are among the many water sports. You can also go for nature walks along trails with the ocean as backdrop.

GETTING HERE AND AROUND

Flights from São Paulo to Florianópolis take just over an hour. The Aeroporto Internacional Hercílio Luz is 12 km (8 miles) south of downtown Florianópolis. Taking a cab into town costs about R$45. In addition, there's the *amarelinho* (minibus) service from the airport for R$7.

Several bus companies have regular services to and from Florianópolis's Terminal Rodoviário Rita Maria. For the 12-hour journey to São Paulo, the 2-hour trip to Blumenau, or the 14-hour trip to Foz do Iguaçu, use Catarinense. Pluma buses travel to Curitiba (5 hours). União Cascavel/Eucatur and Catarinense travel to Porto Alegre (6 hours).

To drive to Ilha de Santa Catarina from the mainland, take the BR 262 exit off BR 101. Downtown Florianópolis is 7 km (4½ miles) from the exit. The island is joined to the mainland by two bridges: the modern, multilane Ponte Colombo Sales and the 89-year-old Ponte Hercílio Luz, which is being restored (albeit slowly) after being closed off to cars for safety reasons for more than 30 years.

Attractions are spread about the island, so a rental car is recommended. A quick, convenient way to visit the beaches is by *amarelinho* (also called *executivo*), express minibuses that cost R$5.50. They leave regularly from designated places around Praça XV and are convenient if you plan to spend the day on one beach. If you want to move about and see different beaches and attractions in one day, a car is your only viable option.

ESSENTIALS

Airport Information Aeroporto Internacional Hercílio Luz *(FLN)*. ⊠ *Km 12, Av. Deomício Freitas 3393, Carianos, Florianópolis* ☎ *048/3331–4000.*

Bus Contacts Catarinense. ☎ *048/4002–4700* ⊕ *www.catarinense.net.* **Pluma.** ☎ *0800/646–0300* ⊕ *pluma.com.br.* **Terminal Rodoviário Rita Maria** *(Bus Terminal).* ⊠ *Av. Paulo Fontes 1101, Centro, Florianópolis* ☎ *048/3212– 3100.* **Eucatur.** ☎ *0800/45–5050* ⊕ *www.eucatur.com.br.*

Taxi Contact Rádio Táxi. ☎ *048/3240–6009.*

Visitor Information SanTur *(State Tourist Board).* ⊠ *Rua Felipe Schmidt 249, 9th fl., Centro, Florianópolis* ☎ *048/3212–6300, 0800/644-6300* ⊕ *turismo. sc.gov.br.*

TOURS

Scuna Sul. This company operates several schooner tours that visit some of the historic forts and various islands. They also traverse the Baía dos Golfinhos (Dolphin Bay), home to dozens of gray dolphins. Tours depart from the downtown harbor (near Hercílio Luz Bridge) or Canasvieiras Pier and last about five hours. English-speaking staff is sometimes on hand to take reservations; otherwise, make arrangements through your hotel. ⊠ *Albatross Bldg., Rua Antonio Heil 605, Suite 01, Canasvieiras, Florianópolis* ☎ *048/3266–1810* ⊕ *www.scunasul.com.br* 🎟 *From R$70 (cash only).*

EXPLORING

TOP ATTRACTIONS

Fodor's Choice **Mercado Público** *(Public Market).* The picturesque Mercado Público is in
★ a Portuguese colonial structure with a large central patio. Even though the interior of the market was destroyed in a fire in 2005, the renovated space—filled with stalls selling fish, fruit, and vegetables—preserves its lively bazaar atmosphere. ⊠ *Rua Conselheiro Mafra 255, Centro, Florianópolis* ☎ *048/3225–8464* 🎟 *Free* ☉ *Weekdays 7 am–9 pm, Sat. 8–4.*

Museu Histórico de Santa Catarina. This museum is in the 18th-century baroque-and-neoclassical Palácio Cruz e Souza; its stairways are lined with Carrara marble. The sidewalks around the building are still paved with the original stones brought from Portugal. Exhibits revolve around state history: documents, personal items, and artwork that belonged to former governors (this used to be the governor's home). ⊠ *Praça 15 de Novembro 227, Centro, Florianópolis* ☎ *048/3665–6367* ⊕ *fcc.sc.gov. br/mhsc* 🎟 *R$5* ☉ *Tues.–Fri. 10–6, weekends 10–4.*

BEACHES

Praia da Joaquina. Surfers have staked claims to this beach, the site of several surfing events, including one round of the world professional circuit. **Amenities:** food and drink; lifeguards; parking; water sports. **Best for:** surfing. ⊠ *15 km (9 miles) east of Florianópolis, SC-406, Lagoa da Conceição, Florianópolis.*

Praia da Lagoinha do Leste. This secluded mile-long beach is surrounded by hills covered with lush tropical vegetation (now mostly protected by a municipal park) and offers breathtaking views of the Atlantic. It can only be reached by boat or by a steep, 5-km (3-mile) path that starts at the entrance of the Pântano do Sul village. **Amenities:** none. **Best for:** solitude. ✉ *18 km (11 miles) south of Florianópolis, SC-406, Pantano do Sul, Florianópolis.*

Praia do Canasvieiras. This sophisticated beach has calm, warm waters, and great services and facilities. **Amenities:** food and drink; parking; water sports. **Best for:** swimming. ✉ *27 km (17 miles) north of Florianópolis, SC 401, Canasvieiras, Florianópolis.*

Praia do Campeche. This long stretch of beach, backed by dunes, is as yet largely undeveloped, and is popular with a local crowd of walkers and joggers. From here, you can also join a boat tour over to Campeche Island. **Amenities:** food and drink. **Best for:** walking. ✉ *SC 405, Florianópolis* ✣ *15 km (9 miles) east of Florianópolis.*

Praia do Pântano do Sul. This small beach community is surrounded by hills and has good restaurants and fishing-boat rides to other beaches and smaller islands nearby. **Amenities:** food and drink; water sports. **Best for:** walking. ✉ *24 km (15 miles) south of Florianópolis, SC 406, Pantano do Sul, Florianópolis.*

6

Fodor's Choice ★ **Praia dos Ingleses.** Named for a British sailboat that sank here in 1700, this narrow beach has an unparalleled lineup of hotels and restaurants for all budgets, making it one of the most popular beaches on the island. In summer Spanish with an Argentine accent is the local language. **Amenities:** food and drink; lifeguards; parking; showers; toilets; water sports. **Best for :** swimming. ✉ *34 km (21 miles) northeast of Florianópolis, SC-403, Ingleses, Florianópolis.*

Praia Jurerê. Located about 24 km (15 miles) north of Florianópolis city center and home to an upscale resort and condominiums, Jurerê normally has bigger waves than its neighbors. The increased development of beachfront hotels, restaurants, and shops has attracted many out-of-state visitors. **Amenities:** food and drink; parking; toilets. **Best for:** walking. ✉ *Km 24, SC 402, Jurerê, Florianópolis.*

Praia Mole. This white-sand beach mostly attracts surfers and foreign tourists. You can paraglide here, and there are a number of beachfront bars. Walk left along the beach and over the point to reach the smaller Praia da Galheta, where nudism is tolerated. **Amenities:** food and drink; water sports. **Best for:** nudists; surfing. ✉ *14 km (8½ miles) east of Florianópolis, SC 406, Lagoa da Conceição, Florianópolis.*

WHERE TO EAT

$$$$ BRAZILIAN 🍴 **Bistrô Isadora Duncan.** An eccentric little gem, Bistrô Isadora Duncan is best known for its romantic vibe and views over Lagoa da Conceição. The dark, wood-paneled interior is softly lighted by lamps and chandeliers at night. The food includes mystically named dishes such as enchanted shrimp (flambéed with orange and green pepper) and blessed shrimp (with a Gorgonzola sauce). Book a table on the veranda and marvel at the moon and the crab-catchers below, who wade out with nets and flashlights in the shallows of the lake. [$] *Average main: R$85* ✉ *Rodovia Jornalista Manuel de Menezes 2658, Florianópolis*

☎ *048/3232–7210* 🌐 *www.bistroisadoraduncan.com.br* ⏲ *Closed Sun.–Tues. and Aug. No lunch.*

$$$$ SEAFOOD Fodor's Choice ★ 🍴 **Chef Fedoca.** On the second floor of the Marina Ponta da Areia complex, this restaurant has a grand view of the Lagoa da Conceição, with surrounding green hills as the backdrop. The fare, carefully created by chef Fedoca, a diver himself, includes a wide variety of seafood and pasta options. Fedoca's *moqueca* (a fish, shrimp, octopus, and mussel stew), inspired by the famed Bahian dish, is the house specialty, as are the lobster dishes. [$] *Average main: R$77* ✉ *Rua Sen. Ivo D'Aquino Neto 133, Marina Ponta da Areia, Lagoa da Conceição, Florianópolis* ☎ *048/3232–0759.*

$$$ SEAFOOD 🍴 **Gugu.** This off-the-beaten-path restaurant combines no-frills service and undistinguished decor with an outstanding seafood menu. Start with the steamed oysters and then move on to the seafood stew or fish fillet with shrimp sauce. [$] *Average main: R$60* ✉ *Rua Fernando José de Andrade 147, Sambaqui, Florianópolis* ☎ *048/3335–0288* ⏲ *Closed Mon.*

$$$$ SEAFOOD Fodor's Choice ★ 🍴 **Ostradamus.** The village of Riberão da Ilha, a mere 21 km (13 miles) away from Florianópolis, is worth an afternoon jaunt to try the local specialty: oysters. There's no better place for oysters than Ostradamus, right on the beach overlooking the oyster beds. Seafood doesn't get more local and fresh than this. Ask for a table out on the pier, or opt for air-conditioning inside, where the decor and staff are decked out in a nautical theme. Oysters are served numerous ways, from raw to au gratin. In winter, when the bivalves are plumper, you can opt for the *degustação* (tasting)—a sequence of oysters prepared 16 different ways. [$] *Average main: R$70* ✉ *Rodovia Baldicero Filomeno 7640, Florianópolis* ☎ *48/3337–5711* 🌐 *ostradamus.com.br* ⏲ *Closed Mon. No dinner Sun.* 💳 *No credit cards.*

WHERE TO STAY

$$$$ RESORT Fodor's Choice ★ 🏨 **Costão do Santinho Resort.** The ocean view from the north-facing rooms is one reason to stay at the island's most sophisticated resort; the surrounding 100-acre Atlantic Forest is another. **Pros:** many amenities; large and comfortable rooms. **Cons:** hectic when hosting conventions; service not as attentive in high season; 3-day minimum stay. [$] *Rooms from: R$1,520* ✉ *Rua Ver. Onildo Lemos 2505, Praia do Santinho, Florianópolis* ☎ *048/3261–1000, 0800/48–1000* 🌐 *www.costao.com.br* 🛏 *696 rooms* 🍽 *All-inclusive.*

$$ HOTEL 🏨 **Hotel Plaza Baía Norte.** Lush, meticulously furnished suites with hot tubs await discerning guests at this popular hotel. **Pros:** great service; spectacular views. **Cons:** cramped rooms; small bathrooms. [$] *Rooms from: R$360* ✉ *Av. Beira-Mar Norte 220, Centro, Florianópolis* ☎ *048/3229–3144, 0800/702–2021* 🌐 *www.baianorte.com.br* 🛏 *105 rooms, 9 suites* 🍽 *Breakfast.*

$$$$ HOTEL FAMILY 🏨 **Hotel Ponta das Canas.** Cozy up in the poolside Jacuzzi to watch an epic sunset over the mainland at this hotel on the northern tip of Florianópolis. **Pros:** the best sunset view on the island; excellent service. **Cons:** nearby beaches crowded in high season. [$] *Rooms from: R$600* ✉ *Rua Dep. Fernando Viegas 560, Florianópolis* ☎ *048/3261–0800* 🌐 *hoteiscostanorte.com.br* 🛏 *55 rooms* 🍽 *Some meals.*

$ **Íbis Florianópolis.** If you're looking for service and basic facilities like
HOTEL those you can find back home, Íbis is a reliable choice. **Pros:** convenient
location for business travelers; bargain price. **Cons:** far from beaches;
small common area. $ *Rooms from: R$159* ✉ *Av. Rio Branco 37, Centro, Florianópolis* ☎ *048/3216–0000, 0800/703–7000* ⊕ *www.ibis.com.
br* ⇌ *198 rooms* �� *No meals.*

$$$$ **Jurerê Beach Village.** This renowned hotel has lush rooms with verandas, most of which give ample views of the beach; some are apartments
HOTEL
Fodor'sChoice with a small kitchen, perfect for longer stays. **Pros:** many amenities
★ and sports; friendly staff. **Cons:** expensive; some rooms are small and
cramped. $ *Rooms from: R$1,000* ✉ *Alameda César Nascimento 646,
Praia de Jurerê, Florianópolis* ☎ *048/3261–5100, 048/3231–9128*
⊕ *www.jurerebeachvillage.com.br* ⇌ *222 apartments* ⓘ *Some meals.*

$$$$ **Quinta das Videiras.** The only boutique hotel on the island, Quinta das
HOTEL Videiras has tastefully adorned rooms with antique-style furnishings,
from stained-glass windows to porcelain doorknobs and an abundance
of Portuguese tiles. **Pros:** packed with characterful details; solar-heated
tiled swimming pool; close to shops and restaurants. **Cons:** some rooms
have poor views; nearest beach 3 km (2 miles) away. $ *Rooms from:
R$660* ✉ *Rua Afonso Luiz Borba 113, Lagoa da Conceição, Florianópolis* ☎ *048/3232–3005* ⊕ *quintadasvideiras.com.br* ⇌ *10 rooms,
1 suite* ⓘ *Breakfast.*

$$$ **Vila Tamarindo Eco Lodge.** A 10-minute stroll from Praia Campeche,
B&B/INN Vila Tamarindo is a clean and tidy pousada with a manicured garden where kids can splash about in a fenced off swimming pool. **Pros:**
FAMILY
friendly staff; pleasant garden; free yoga and tai chi lessons. **Cons:**
no sea view; no on-site dining options. $ *Rooms from: R$460* ✉ *Av.
Campeche 1836, Florianópolis* ☎ *048/3237–3464* ⊕ *tamarindo.com.
br* ⇌ *14 rooms, 1 suite* ⓘ *Breakfast.*

NIGHTLIFE
BARS
Fodor'sChoice **Bar DeRaiz.** This breezy, out-of-the-way live-music bar has a final frontier
★ feel—a glorified wooden shack perched on the edge of the sand dunes
that roll down to nearby Praia da Joaquina. The bar mostly opens on
nights when other bars are shut, with different local musical styles for
different nights. It's worth checking the bar is indeed open before turning up. ✉ *Av. Prefeito Acácio Garibaldi São Tiago 1777, Florianópolis*
☎ *048/9609–4734, 048/3232–5479* ⊕ *barderaiz.com* ⓘ *R$15–R$25.*

John Bull Pub. This popular pub is *the* place for live music on the island.
A roster of local and nationally known bands performs everything from
blues, rock and roll, and reggae to Brazilian popular music. It's also a
great place for drinks and snacks. ✉ *Av. das Rendeiras 1046, Lagoa da
Conceição, Florianópolis* ☎ *048/3232–8535* ⊕ *www.johnbullfloripa.
com.br.*

SPORTS AND THE OUTDOORS
BOATING
Marina Ponta da Areia. This is the place to go for boat rentals on Florianópolis. ✉ *Rua Sen. Ivo D'Aquino Neto 133, Lagoa da Conceição,
Florianópolis* ☎ *048/3232–0759.*

6

KITESURFING
OpenWinds. This company gives kitesurfing lessons. A 90-minute lesson costs R$220. Surfing and windsurfing lessons can be arranged here and they also sell and rent gear. ⊠ *Servidão dos Coroas 41, Lagoa da Conceição, Florianópolis* ☎ *048/9962–3778* ⊕ *www.openwinds.com.br.*

PARASAILING
Parapente Sul. A center for parasailing—a popular sport on this mountainous, windy coast of Santa Catarina—Parapente Sul leads tandem flights with an instructor for R$170. For enthusiasts, a full course is available as well as equipment rental. ⊠ *Rua João Antônio da Silveira 201, Lagoa da Conceição, Florianópolis* ☎ *048/3232–0791* ⊕ *www.parapentesul.com.br.*

SNORKELING AND SCUBA DIVING
Parcel Dive Center. Snorkeling and scuba diving are popular on the northern beaches; check out Parcel Dive Center for internationally accredited diving lessons, diver's certification, and for equipment sale and rentals. The cost to rent basic gear is about R$260 a day. ⊠ *Av. Luiz B. Piazza 3257, Cachoeira do Bom Jesus, Florianópolis* ☎ *048/3284–5564* ⊕ *www.parcel.com.br.*

PRAIA DO ROSA

86 km (53 miles) south of Florianópolis, 390 km (242 miles) northwest of Porto Alegre.

Once a simple fishing hamlet, Praia do Rosa is one of the most beautiful beaches in the South, with a winning combination of good surf, stunning topography, and an eco-conscious tourist setup that strikes a nice balance beween hippy and chic. Choose from dozens of guesthouses to suit all budgets, as well as restaurants and a laid-back nightlife in the summer months. One of the few beaches that attracts tourists year-round, Praia do Rosa has grown popular in the winter months (July through November), too, when the warm waters attract the *baleia-franca* (southern right whales) from Patagonia to breeding grounds off the coast. The nearby town of Garopaba (17 km/10½ miles north) also has great beaches, as well as the conveniences of a larger town, including an ATM and a bus station.

GETTING HERE AND AROUND
The easiest way to reach Praia do Rosa is to fly to Florianópolis. Paulo-Tur bus lines offers hourly services between Florianópolis and Garopaba, between 6 am and 8 pm, from where you can take a taxi to Praia do Rosa.

ESSENTIALS
Bus Contacts Estação Rodoviária (Bus Station). ⊠ *Rua Teonaz Israel 111, Centro, Garopaba* ☎ *048/3254-4188.* **PauloTur.** ☎ *048/3244-2777, 048/3223-7424* ⊕ *www.paulotur.com.br.*

Taxi Contacts Ponto de Taxi. ⊠ *Praça Governador Ivo Silveira s/n, Centro, Garopaba* ☎ *048/3223-1198.*

EXPLORING

OFF THE BEATEN PATH

Laguna. The city of Laguna is the second-oldest Portuguese settlement in the state of Santa Catarina. Most downtown buildings reflect the early colonial days. Known for its many beaches, Laguna has one of the liveliest Carnival festivities of southern Brazil. Part of the city faces Laguna Imaruí (Imaruí Lagoon), which connects to the Atlantic 5 km (3 miles) farther east. You can drive or hire a boat on the beaches to get to the Imaruí Lake delta, where exploring the imposing Santa Marta Lighthouse and nearby beaches is well worth a day's outing. ⊠ *62 km (38 miles) south of Garopaba on BR 101, Laguna.*

BEACHES

Praia da Ferrugem. Busy in summer months thanks to its abundance of guesthouses and proximity to Garopaba, Praia da Ferrugem is a popular choice with surfers. A small rocky outcrop marks the division with neighboring Praia da Barra, and it's an easy amble from one to the other across a channel where, depending on the tide, the ocean connects with the Lagoa da Encantada lake. **Amenities:** food and drink. **Best for:** surfing. ⊠ *8 km (5 miles) south of Garopaba on SC 434 and Estrada Velha, Praia do Rosa.*

Fodor's Choice ★

Praia do Rosa. Known nationally for its awesome beauty and laid-back atmosphere, Praia do Rosa boasts sand dunes, lagoons, and green, forest-covered hills that end right in the ocean. The 3-km (2-mile) beach is popular with surfers, while its sheltered lagoons are excellent swimming spots for children. **Amenities:** food and drink. **Best for:** surfing; swimming; walking. ⊠ *15 km (9 miles) south of Garopaba, Praia do Rosa.*

WHERE TO EAT

$$
FRENCH FUSION

✕ **Bistrô Pedra da Vigia.** A cozy little restaurant in a converted flour mill, Bistrô Pedra da Vigia is an enduring Praia do Rosa favorite, both for its candlelit ambience and its crowd-pleasing cuisine that covers steak, seafood, and homemade pastas. Some original features remain, including the exposed tiled roof, while a liberal approach with a paintbrush has the woodwork coated in bright shades of yellows, blues, and pinks. $ *Average main: R$40* ⊠ *Caminho do Alto do Morro s/n, Praia do Rosa* ☎ *048/3355–6066* ⊕ *reginagh.com.br.*

$$$$
BRAZILIAN

✕ **Urucum.** The soft orange glow of lanterns sets a sultry tone by night at this top-end dining option in Praia do Rosa. Named after a bright red seed that's used as a natural colorant, the restaurant's focus is Brazilian cuisine, and in particular the hearty seafood stew, *moqueca.* . Whether you order yours with fish, shellfish, or extra spice, the *moquecas* more than feed two, and are served bubbling in clay pots, along with rice, *farofa* (toasted manioc flour), and *pirão* (a spicy seafood stock thickened with manioc flour). For dessert, don't miss the creamy tapioca with frozen açaí. $ *Average main: R$65* ⊠ *Estrada Geral do Rosa s/n, Praia do Rosa* ☎ *048/3355–7330* ⊕ *restauranteurucum.com.br* ⊟ *No credit cards.*

WHERE TO STAY

$$$$
B&B/INN

⚟ **Pousada Solar Mirador.** Indulge in the extraordinary views of Rosa Beach while sitting, drink in hand, by the pool at this luxurious pousada. **Pros:** heated indoor swimming pool; majestic sea views. **Cons:**

6

patchy Wi-Fi in the rooms; multiple steps to get about the property; beach access is via a boat ride across a small lake. $ *Rooms from: R$730 ⊠ Estrada Geral do Rosa s/n, Praia do Rosa ☎ 048/3355–6144, 048/3355–6697 ⊕ solarmirador.com.br ⤳ 12 rooms ❍❘ Breakfast.*

$$$$

B&B/INN

Fodor's Choice

★

⛭ **Quinta do Bucanero.** The ultimate in barefoot luxury, this stunning hotel in Praia do Rosa is carved in and around the hillside some 100 feet above the beach, with rooms perched on wooden supports and vast slabs of rocks in the sitting area. **Pros:** swimming pool with sea view; walking distance to shops and restaurants; gym, sauna, and hot tub. **Cons:** no under-14s allowed; beach access is via boat. $ *Rooms from: R$780 ⊠ Estrada Geral Praia do Rosa s/n, Praia do Rosa ☎ 048/3355–6056 ⊕ bucanero.com.br ⤳ 10 rooms, 2 suites ❍❘ Breakfast.*

SPORTS AND THE OUTDOORS
WHALE-WATCHING
Instituto Baleia Franca (*Right Whale Institute*). This not-for-profit organization provides whale-watching tours on foot, guided by biologists, from July to November, when the southern right whales from Antarctica come to the warmer waters near Garopaba to breed. As of this writing, boat tours have been suspended. ⊠ *Vida, Sol e Mar Beach Village, Km 6, Estrada Geral do Rosa, Imbituba* ☎ 048/3355–6111 ⊕ www. baleiafranca.org.br.

RIO GRANDE DO SUL

The state of Rio Grande do Sul is almost synonymous with the *gaúcho,* the South American cowboy who is glamorized as much as his North American counterpart. There's more to this state, however, than the idyllic cattle-country lifestyle of the early days. As it's one of Brazil's leading industrial areas, its infrastructure rivals that of any country in the Northern Hemisphere. Its mix of Portuguese, German, and Italian cultures is evident in the food and architecture. Indeed, to be *gaúcho* (which is a term for all people and things from this state) may mean to be a vintner of Italian heritage from Caxias do Sul or an entrepreneur of German descent from Gramado as much as a cattle rancher with Portuguese lineage out on the plains.

The state capital, Porto Alegre, is a sophisticated metropolis of 1.5 million that rivals Curitiba in quality of life. This important industrial and business center has universities, museums, and convention centers. It's also one of the greenest cities in Brazil, with many parks and nature preserves. The slopes of the Serra Gaúcha were settled by Italian immigrants; thanks to their wine-making skills, the state now produces quality wines, particularly in the Caxias do Sul and Bento Gonçalves areas. Along the coast, basaltic cliffs drop into a raging Atlantic and provide an impressive backdrop for the seaside resort towns. Farther inland, straddling the state's highest elevations, is the Aparados da Serra National Park, whose gargantuan canyons are the result of millions of years of erosion.

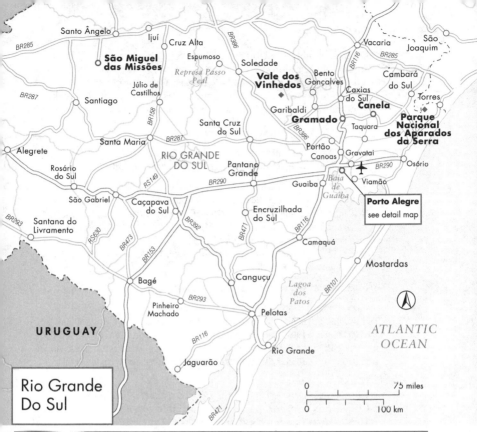

Rio Grande
Do Sul

PORTO ALEGRE

476 km (296 miles) southwest of Florianópolis, 760 km (472 miles) southwest of Curitiba, 1,109 km (690 miles) southwest of São Paulo.

Porto Alegre's hallmark is the hospitality of its people, a trait that has been acknowledged over and over by visitors, earning it the nickname "Smile City." The capital of one of Brazil's wealthiest states, it has many streets lined with jacaranda trees that create violet tunnels when in full spring bloom.

GETTING HERE AND AROUND

It takes about 90 minutes to fly from São Paulo to Porto Alegre. The Aeroporto Internacional Salgado Filho is one of Brazil's most modern air terminals. It's only 8 km (5 miles) northeast of downtown. The cost of a cab ride is around R$30. At a booth near the arrivals gate you can prepay your cab ride. There's also a minibus shuttle into town for about R$5.

Penha bus has service to São Paulo (19 hours); Pluma buses travel to Curitiba (12 hours); Florianópolis (6 hours) is served by Eucatur or Catarinense. To reach Foz do Iguaçu (14 hours), Unesul is the only option. Public bus service to São Miguel das Missões is painfully slow; instead, book a tour from Porto Alegre via a flight or charter bus.

Ask your hotel reception which lines to take. Alternatively, the Linha Turismo bus, a double-decker tour bus, stops at most tourist attractions. It departs from the Cidade Baixa SAT location; one ticket for the 80-minute ride costs R$25 during the week and R$30 on the weekends. Another option is to take a cab downtown, where most sights are within walking distance of each other.

ESSENTIALS
Airport Aeroporto Internacional Salgado Filho (*POA*). ✉ *Av. Severo Dulius 90010, São João, Porto Alegre* ☎ *051/3358-2000, 051/3358-2000.*

Bus Contacts Catarinense. ☎ *051/3228-8900, 0800/470-470* ⊕ *www. catarinense.net.* **Estação Rodoviária** (*Bus Station*). ✉ *Largo Vespasiano Veppo 70, Centro, Porto Alegre* ☎ *051/3228-0699, 051/3210-0101 timetables* ⊕ *www. rodoviaria-poa.com.br.* **Eucatur.** ☎ *051/3901-5920, 0800/455-050* ⊕ *www. eucatur.com.br.* **Penha.** ☎ *0800/646-2121* ⊕ *vendas.nspenha.com.br.* **Pluma.** ☎ *051/3228-5112* ⊕ *pluma.com.br.* **Unesul.** ☎ *051/3375-9000, 0800/888-0809* ⊕ *www.unesul.com.br.*

Taxi Contacts Rádio Táxi. ☎ *051/3472-3448.*

Visitor Information Secretaria de Turismo (*State Tourism Authority*). ✉ *Avenida Borges de Medeiros 1501, 10th fl., Praia de Belas, Porto Alegre* ☎ *051/3288-5400* ⊕ *www.turismo.rs.gov.br.* **Serviço de Atenção ao Turista** (*Municipal Tourist Board*). ✉ *Travessa do Carmo, 84, Cidade Baixa, Porto Alegre* ☎ *0800/51-7686, 051/3289-6700* ⊕ *www.portoalegre.rs.gov.br/turismo.*

TOURS
Cisne Branco. Cruise around the Guaíba estuary aboard the 200-seater Cisne Branco motorboat, which has tables up on the roof deck. At 10:30 am, a one-hour excursion takes in the estuary's main islands while the happy hour trip at 6 pm heads along the shoreline as the sun sets. Drinks and snacks are available on board. More expensive lunch and dinner cruises can also be arranged. ✉ *Port of Porto Alegre, Main Gate, Av. Mauá 1050, Centro, Porto Alegre* ☎ *051/3224–5222* ⊕ *www. barcocisnebranco.com.br* ⊴ *From R$28.*

Noiva do Caí. Leaving from the Usina do Gasômetro, Noiva do Caí runs three boat tours per day, taking in the city shoreline and some of the islands in the Guaíba estuary. On Sunday, an extended 2½-hour boat ride includes a stop-off for lunch in a fishing village. ✉ *Usina do Gasômetro, Av. João Goulart 551, Centro, Porto Alegre* ☎ *051/3211–7662* ⊴ *From R$25.*

SAFETY AND PRECAUTIONS
Some neighborhoods of Porto Alegre, such as the central district, are sketchy at night. Ask your hotel reception about the safety of your destination. During the day, pickpockets are generally the only concern.

EXPLORING
The heart of Porto Alegre lies within a triangle formed by Praça da Alfândega, the Mercado Público, and the Praça da Matriz. Not only is this the main business district, it's also the site of many cultural and historical attractions. Outside this area, Casa de Cultura Mário Quintana and Usina do Gasômetro are active cultural centers, with

movies, live performances, art exhibits, and cafés.

TOP ATTRACTIONS

Fundação Iberê Camargo. Set up in 1995 to promote the work of the 20th-century *gaúcho*painter Iberê Camargo, this foundation is the jewel in the city's cultural crown. The award-winning building was designed by Portuguese architect Álvaro Siza Vieira, and is in itself worth the schlep downriver just to wander through the striking, four-story white atrium, and round the curving walkways that snake inside and out of the curvaceous building. Known for his poetic expressionism, Iberê Camargo's paintings arc on display, alongside a changing roster of modern artists. ⊠ *Av. Padre Cacique 2000, Praia de Belas, Porto Alegre* ☎ *051/3247–8000* ⊕ *iberecamargo.org.br* ⊡ *Free* ◔ *Tues.–Wed. and Fri.–Sun. noon–7, Thurs. noon 9.*

BEAUTIFUL VIEWS

From Morro de Santa Teresa (Santa Teresa Hill), you get a grand view of the skyline as it meets the expanse of the Rio Guaíba. From here, or in the numerous waterfront parks, the great spectacle of Porto Alegre's sunset draws out the locals to sit, watch, and sip *chimarrão* (maté tea). As local poet Mário Quintana put it: "Skies of Porto Alegre, how could I ever take you to heaven?" For a different view of the city, consider taking a riverboat tour of the Rio Guaíba and its islands, or hire a bike at one of the orange BikePOA bicycle-sharing points and roll along the waterfront beyond the Usina do Gasômetro.

6

Memorial do Rio Grande do Sul. Built to house the post-office headquarters at the turn of the 20th century, this building was declared a national architectural landmark in 1981. It now houses a state museum. Although the overall style is neoclassical, German baroque influences are strong; the asymmetrical corner towers with their bronze rotundas are said to resemble Prussian army helmets. A permanent exhibit focuses on the state's history and the lives of important gaúchos, and the second floor houses one of the country's largest collections of documents and manuscripts about Brazilian society. ⊠ *Praça da Alfândega, Rua Sete de Setembro 1020, Centro, Porto Alegre* ☎ *051/3224–7159* ⊡ *Free* ◔ *Tues.–Sun. 10–6.*

Museu de Arte do Rio Grande do Sul. At this art museum housed in the old, neoclassical customs building you can also see paintings, sculptures, and drawings by gaúcho and other Brazilian artists. Stop for a coffee or a bite to eat in the museum's bistro. ⊠ *Praça da Alfândega s/n, Centro, Porto Alegre* ☎ *051/3227–2311* ⊕ *www.margs.rs.gov.br* ⊡ *Free* ◔ *Tues.–Sun. 10–7.*

Museu Júlio de Castilhos. The small Júlio de Castilhos Museum is the oldest in the state. On display is an impressive collection of gaúcho documents, firearms, clothing, and household utensils. The home belonged to Governor Julio de Castilhos, who lived here at the turn of the 20th century, before the Palácio Piratini was built. ⊠ *Rua Duque de Caxias 1231, Centro, Porto Alegre* ☎ *051/3221–3959* ⊕ *www. museujuliodecastilhos.rs.gov.br* ⊡ *Free* ◔ *Tues.–Sat. 10–5.*

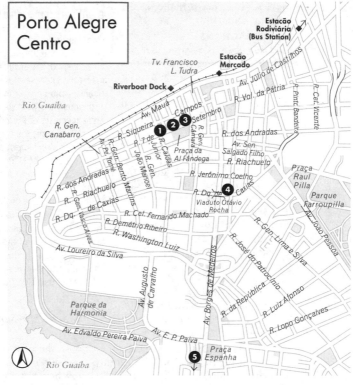

Porto Alegre
Centro

WORTH NOTING

Centro Cultural Santander. This stately building, constructed in 1927–32 and the former headquarters of various banks, is now owned by Banco Santander, which has transformed it into a cultural center and gallery. Guided tours (Portuguese only) show the intricate ironwork of the entrance door and second-floor balcony as well as the ceiling's neoclassical paintings. The massive bank vault now houses a café. ⊠ *Rua Sete de Setembro 1028, Centro, Porto Alegre* ☎ *051/3287–5940* ⊕ *www. santandercultural.com.br* ⊠ *Free* ⊙ *Tues.–Sat. 10–7, Sun. 1–7.*

Parque Estadual de Itapuã. Where the Rio Guaíba flows into Lagoa dos Patos, 57 km (35 miles) south of Porto Alegre, Itapoã State Park protects 12,000 acres of granitic hills and sandy beaches. Although the infrastructure is minimal, visitors can bathe in the river, walk along marked trails, and watch magnificent sunsets. Rare cacti, bands of *bugios* (howler monkeys), and a century-old lighthouse round out the list of park highlights. ⊠ *Park entrance, Estrada Dona Maria Leopoldina s/n, Itapoã, Viamão* ☎ *051/3494–8083* ⊠ *R$5.75* ⊙ *Wed.–Sun. 9–6.*

WHERE TO EAT

$$$ NORTHERN ITALIAN Fodor's Choice ★

🍴 **Al Dente Ristorante.** You may be surprised at the quality and authenticity of the Northern Italian cuisine at this small restaurant in Porto Alegre. Among many excellent choices are *garganelli* (a variety of pasta from Emilia-Romagna) with salmon in wine sauce and fettuccine *nere* (fettuccine with a black tinge of squid ink) with caviar sauce. A house novelty is the Italian-gaúcho risotto, made with sun-dried meat, tomatoes, and squash. The decor is sober, with candlelit tables and cream drapes covering most of the walls. [$] *Average main: R$55* ✉ *Rua Mata Bacelar 210, Auxiliadora, Porto Alegre* ☎ *051/3343–1841* 🌐 *www.aldenteristorante.com.br* 🕒 *Closed Sun. No lunch weekends.*

$$ CAFÉ

🍴 **Café do Porto.** One of the trendiest cafés in town, Porto serves several types of coffee, plus drinks, sandwiches, pies, and pastries. Try the *espetinho* (little skewer of meats and vegetables) combined with a glass of Chardonnay or the house cappuccino. All coffee is Brazil's finest, from the Mogiana region in São Paulo. [$] *Average main: R$33* ✉ *Rua Padre Chagas 293, Moinhos de Vento, Porto Alegre* ☎ *051/3346–8385* 🌐 *www.cafedoporto.com.br.*

$$$ MEDITERRANEAN

🍴 **Constantino Café.** The real draw at this informal eatery is the setting, in a converted colonial house on one of the city's liveliest streets. Wind your way through a warren of cozy rooms, or just head straight to the lush, green garden out back, where candles add a romantic glow at night. The menu—Mediterranean with an Asian touch—won't win awards for imagination, but dishes are well presented and tasty nonetheless. [$] *Average main: R$50* ✉ *Rua Fernando Gomes 44, Moinhos de Vento, Porto Alegre* ☎ *051/3346–8589* 🌐 *constantinocafe.com.br* 🕒 *Closed Sun.*

$$$$ CONTEMPORARY

🍴 **Floriano Spiess Cozinha de Autor.** On a leafy square in an upscale suburb, this place serves contemporary cuisine at its most creative. The eponymous chef offers a tasting menu (which must be booked the day before) of small, stunning dishes that are loaded with flavor. The dazzle and glitz extends to the space—all grays and blacks with mirrors and LED tube lights, with a well-dressed clientele. À la carte options are also available, and the wine list is extensive, albeit with few Brazilian options. [$] *Average main: R$80* ✉ *Praça Japão 155, Boa Vista, Porto Alegre* ☎ *051/3237–7601* 🌐 *florianospiess.blogspot.com.br* 🕒 *Closed Sun. and Mon. No lunch Tues.–Fri.* ✍ *Reservations essential.*

$$$$ BRAZILIAN

🍴 **Galpão Crioulo.** One of Porto Alegre's largest churrascarias, Galpão Crioulo serves traditional *espeto-corrido*—a prix-fixe, never-ending rotation of tender roasted and grilled meats brought to the table, accompanied by a salad buffet. If a full *espeto-corrido* sounds too much, ask for the *miniespeto* (a small sampler skewer of all meats). Another option is the *comidas campeiras* (countryside food) buffet, with plenty of dishes featuring rice, beans, and squash. You can also try *chimarrão* (a maté tea) at a tasting booth where the staff demonstrates the traditional way to drink it. Gaúcho musical performances take place in the evening. [$] *Average main: R$74* ✉ *Parque Maurício Sirotsky Sobrinho, Rua Otávio Francisco Caruso da Rocha, Centro,*

Porto Alegre ☎ *051/3226–8194* 🌐 *www.churrascariagalpaocrioulo.com.br.*

$$$ BRAZILIAN Fodor's Choice ★ 🍴 **Gambrinus.** Porto Alegre's best-known restaurant has been in business at the same spot, steps from city hall at the Mercado Público, since 1889. The walls are covered with Portuguese tiles, antiques, and period photographs exalting those early days. The restaurant is a popular happy-hour spot for politicians and businesspeople. The menu varies daily from beef to fish dishes. One of the highlights is the large Brazilian grey mullet stuffed with shrimp (served Friday and Saturday). [$] *Average main: R$50* ✉ *Rua Borges de Medeiros 85, Centro, Porto Alegre* ☎ *051/3226–6914* 🌐 *www.gambrinus.com.br* ⏲ *No dinner Sat. Closed Sun.*

WHERE TO STAY

$$ HOTEL 🏨 **Laghetto Viverone Moinhos.** Part of a local hotel chain, Laghetto Viverone Moinhos is a reasonably priced option for the upmarket Moinhos de Vento neighborhood, with small but functional rooms. **Pros:** easy walk to bars and restaurants; rooftop pool; charming period features. **Cons:** service is minimal; small bathrooms. [$] *Rooms from: R$359* ✉ *Rua Dr. Vale 579, Porto Alegre* ☎ *051/2102–7272* 🌐 *hotellaghettomoinhos.com.br* 🛏 *132 rooms* 🍽 *Breakfast.*

$$$$ HOTEL Fodor's Choice ★ 🏨 **Sheraton Porto Alegre.** In the fashionable neighborhood of Moinhos de Vento, the Sheraton sets the city's standard of luxury; the level of comfort is outstanding, from the lobby to the top-floor rooms. **Pros:** top-notch service; prime location; many amenities. **Cons:** can be hectic during conferences; high charges for Internet. [$] *Rooms from: R$580* ✉ *Rua Olavo Barreto Viana 18, Moinhos de Vento, Porto Alegre* ☎ *051/2121–6000* 🌐 *www.sheraton-poa.com.br* 🛏 *170 rooms, 22 suites* 🍽 *Breakfast.*

NIGHTLIFE AND PERFORMING ARTS

NIGHTLIFE

Dado Bier Bourbon Country. The city's first microbrewery, Dado Bier has expanded into a full-fledged restaurant, an ample space decked out in expanses of dark wood. Dado biers include a *weiss bier*, a red ale, and a chocolate stout. ✉ *Bourbon Country Center, Av. Túlio de Rose 80, Três Figueiras, Porto Alegre* ☎ *051/3378–3000* 🌐 *www.dadobier.com.br* ⏲ *No dinner Sun.*

PERFORMING ARTS

Casa de Cultura Mário Quintana. Occupying what was Porto Alegre's finest hotel at the turn of the 20th century, the salmon-pink Casa de Cultura Mário Quintana has two art-house cinemas, one theater, and several exhibit rooms. The popular Café Santo da Casa, on the seventh floor, has regular jazz and classical music performances and gets busy with an after-work crowd. ✉ *Rua dos Andradas 736, Centro, Porto Alegre* ☎ *051/3221–7147* 🌐 *ccmq.com.br.*

Centro Cultural Usina do Gasômetro. With its conspicuous 350-foot brick smokestack, the Centro Cultural Usina do Gasômetro was the city's first coal-fired power plant—built in the late 1920s, when the city experienced rapid growth. Today it holds theaters, meeting rooms, and exhibit spaces on the banks of the Rio Guaíba. A terrace café overlooking the river is the perfect place to take in a sunset. The center is open Tuesday–Sunday 9–9. To find out what's on, it's best to call ahead, as there is little up-to-date information published online. ⊠ *Av. João Goulart 551, Centro, Porto Alegre* ☎ *051/3289–8100, 051/3289–8111.*

SHOPPING

Fodor's Choice
★

Brique da Redenção. Originally a flea market that took place on the sidewalks of Parque Farroupilha, Brique da Redenção has expanded into a full-blown Sunday antiques, crafts, and arts fair that spills over the full length of Avenida José Bonifácio on the southeast side. ⊠ *Av. José Bonifácio, Bom Fim, Porto Alegre* ⊕ *briquedaredencao.com.br/ brique* ⊙ *Sun. 9–6.*

Mercado Público. Constructed in 1869, the neoclassical Public Market has undergone repeated renovations, the last of which added the glass roof that now covers the central inner plaza. With these changes, some of the produce stalls have been replaced by souvenir shops, cafés, and restaurants, taking away a bit of the boisterous bazaar ambience but increasing the options for visitors. One of the best restaurants in the city, Gambrinus, is here. ⊠ *Largo Glenio Peres s/n, Centro, Porto Alegre* ⊕ *www.portoalegre.rs.gov.br/mercadopublico* ⊙ *Weekdays 7 am–7:30 pm, Sat. 7:30–6:30.*

Shopping Iguatemi. The city's largest mall, Shopping Iguatemi includes branches of large chain stores as well as high-end specialty shops. ⊠ *Rua João Wallig 1800, Três Figueiras, Porto Alegre* ☎ *051/3131–2000* ⊕ *iguatemiportoalegre.com.br.*

Vinhos do Mundo. If you don't have the time to venture into Brazilian wine country, look for a sample to buy at Vinhos do Mundo. ⊠ *Rua Cristóvão Colombo 1493, Floresta, Porto Alegre* ☎ *051/3028–1998* ⊕ *www.vinhosdomundo.com.br.*

VALE DOS VINHEDOS

124 km (77 miles) north of Porto Alegre.

The Serra Gaúcha—the mountainous region of Rio Grande do Sul—produces 90% of Brazilian wine. Grapevines grow throughout the hilly terrain, but the heart of the wine-making country is within the municipality of Bento Gonçalves, settled by Italian immigrants in the late 19th century. Because the best-known Brazilian wineries are within a few miles in this region, the name Vale dos Vinhedos (Vineyard Valley) has become synonymous with quality wines.

GETTING HERE AND AROUND

To visit Vale dos Vinhedos, either rent a car or join an organized tour. From Porto Alegre, Bento Gonçalves is accessible by RS 240 and then RS 470 (exit in São Vendelino). The wineries on Vale dos Vinhedos are on RS 444, which intersects with RS 470 at Km 217.

ESSENTIALS

Make sure you have reais or credit cards when coming to Bento Gonçalves, as currency exchange is not readily available. Most hotels and pousadas have Wi-Fi connections.

6

TOURS

Valle das Vinhas. Based in the heart of the Vale dos Vinhedos, this travel agency can arrange wine tours from one day to one week with an English-speaking winemaker as a guide. Tours can also take in the cultural and natural highlights of the Serra Gaúcha. ✉ *Av. Candido Costa 65, Room 705, Centro, Bento Gonçalves* ☎ *054/3451–4216, 054/3452–0391* ⊕ *valedasvinhastur.com.br* 🖂 *From R$125.*

WINERIES

Casa Valduga. This large winery produces several lines of premium wines; the Cabernets and sparkling wines in particular are highly regarded. In summer you can take a tour of the family-owned vineyards and purchase other house products such as grape juice and fruit jellies. ✉ *Km 6, RS 444, Linha Leopoldina -, Bento Gonçalves* ☎ *054/2105–3122, 054/2015–3154* ⊕ *www.casavalduga.com.br* 🖂 *R$25* ⊙ *Tours Dec.–Feb. by appointment; wine tastings weekdays 9:30–1:30; pairings course 6:15 pm; wine and cheese course twice a month.*

Fodor's Choice ★ **Cave Geisse.** This boutique winery has gathered a cult following for its sparkling wines, made with Pinot Noir and Chardonnay grape varietals using the *méthode champenoise.* What really sets a visit to Cave Geisse apart is the Geisse experience: a bumpy ride for up to five people (R$70 per person) in a 4x4 buggy through parts of the vineyard's 76 hectares of rolling hills, forests, and vines, with a pit stop by a waterfall for an impromptu tasting. Book ahead for a tour in English. ✉ *Linha Jansen s/n, Bento Gonçalves* ☎ *054/3455–7461* ⊕ *cavegeisse.com.br* 🖂 *R$10* ⊙ *Weekdays 9–11:30 and 1–5, weekends 10:15–4:15.*

Don Giovanni. Oozing old-world charm, this family-run winery in the bucolic hills around Pinto Bandeira makes a convenient base camp for a weekend of wine tasting, with a pousada and restaurant on-site. Don Giovanni has reputable sparkling wines, and also produces some Tannat, Merlot, and red blends. Turn up for a tour of the barrel rooms and cellar, or book ahead to arrange a more formal tasting in their tasting lab, or the sunset tasting, from a viewing deck among the vines. ✉ *Linha Amadeo, Km 12, Bento Gonçalves* ☎ *054/3455–6293* ⊕ *dongiovanni.com.br* 🖂 *R$15* ⊙ *Weekdays 9–11:30 and 1–5:30, Sat. 9–4, Sun. 9–1.*

Don Laurindo. Chances are you'll be greeted at this small winery by the affable Ademir Brandelli, the fourth generation of a family of winemakers that dates back to 1887, when his great-grandfather emigrated from Verona. Ademir doesn't speak English, but his son Moisés does, and group visits in English can be booked with him in advance. Wander through the barrel rooms and cellars, learning about the family history and the vines before tasting a selection of Don Laurindo's wines. ✉ *Estrada do Vinho, 8 da Graciema, Vale dos Vinhedos, Bento Gonçalves* ☎ *054/3459–1600* ⊕ *www.donlaurindo.com.br* 🖂 *Wine tasting R$15* ⊙ *Weekdays 8–5:30, Sat. 10–4, Sun. 10–3.*

Vinícola Miolo. The Miolo family made its name in the Brazilian wine industry with Vinícola Miolo. One of Brazil's largest wine exporters, the company produces wines under 100 different labels on seven vineyards

Brazilian Wine

The first grapevines were brought to Brazil in 1532 by early Portuguese colonists, but it was the Jesuits, who settled in the South decades later, who were the first to establish true vineyards and wineries (to produce wine for the Catholic Mass). Viticulture didn't gain importance in Brazil until Italian immigrants arrived, with the blessing of Italian-born empress Teresa Cristina, wife of Dom Pedro II, in 1875. In the next decades at least 150,000 Italians came to settle the Serra Gaúcha. They were the first to produce significant quantities of wine.

Although the South is suitable for growing grapes, the rainfall is often excessive from January to March—when the grapes reach maturity. This has traditionally made local wine-growers true heroes for being able to produce decent wines despite difficult conditions. Traditional grapes such as Merlot and Cabernet were grown to some extent, but most of the wine produced originated from less impressive American stock—Concord and Niagara grapes. These average wines are still produced for local markets.

New agricultural techniques and hybridization of grapes have brought modern viticulture to the area and allowed a dramatic expansion of

higher-quality grapes. This has significantly improved wine quality and attracted such international industry heavyweights as Almadén, Moët et Chandon, and Heublein. In 1992 Almadén broke new ground and established vineyards in the hills near the city of Santana do Livramento—about 480 km (300 miles) southwest of Porto Alegre, on the Uruguay border—where, according to current agricultural knowledge, climate and soils are more apt to produce quality grapes.

Other wineries are following its steps. Today there are more than 300 *cantinas* (winemakers) in Rio Grande do Sul, primarily in the Vale dos Vinhedos (Vineyard Valley) near Bento Gonçalves. The fine wine producers' association of the Vale dos Vinhedos, Aprovale, has 26 members (⊕ www ibravin.com.br) and has registered a government-certified system similar to that used in European countries for controlled-origin wines to promote and warrant the quality of their products.

The Brazilian wine industry promoter IBRAVIN (⊕ www.ibravin.org.br) provides details online about the winemakers in each of Brazil's wine regions.

6

in southern Brazil. A visit to the vineyard gives a glimpse of the Miolo family's wine-making tradition that goes back to the 19th century. Tours of the vineyards and tastings of Chardonnays, Cabernet Sauvignons, Sauvignon Blancs, and sparkling wines are run daily. ⊠ *Km 21, RS 444, Vale dos Vinhedos, Bento Gonçalves* ☎ *054/2102–1500, 0800/9704–165* ⊕ *www.miolo.com.br* ☒ *R$15* ⊙ *Tours daily 9–5.*

WHERE TO EAT AND STAY

$$$ ✕ **Casa Di Paolo.** Be ready for a hearty feast: this highly regarded res-
ITALIAN taurant serves a prix-fixe Italian menu with *galeto al primo canto*
FAMILY (crispy grilled chicken) and a large selection of pasta dishes. Accompaniments include cappelletti soup, polenta, and *radicci* (a green-leaf

salad). $ *Average main: R$59* ⊠ *Km 221.7, RS 470, Centro, Bento Gonçalves* ☎ *054/3463–8505, 054/3463–8505* ⊕ *casadipaolo.com.br* ⊘ *No dinner Sun.*

$$$$
BRAZILIAN
Fodor'sChoice
★

✕ **Valle Rústico.** No restaurant is ever perfect, but Valle Rústico comes pretty close. The chef-owner Rodrigo Bellora—a Slow Food disciple—plucks organic ingredients from the garden and sources local produce to assemble simple but stunning dishes. The Italian-style, four-course set-menu (with three options per course) is a great value (R$78) and can be paired with local wines for an extra R$50. Unpretentious is the watchword here, from the dirt-road entrance to the dining room down in the basement of an old colonial house, where whitewashed walls and exposed wood beams lend a rustic, farmstead touch. $ *Average main: R$78* ⊠ *Linha Marcilio Dias s/n, 15 da Graciema, Vale dos Vinhedos, Bento Gonçalves* ☎ *054/3459–1162* ⊕ *vallerustico.com.br* ⊘ *Closed Mon. and Tues. No dinner Sun.* ⊟ *No credit cards.*

$$$
HOTEL

🏨 **Hotel & Spa do Vinho.** Somewhat incongruous with the small-scale, family-run approach to tourism that gives Vale dos Vinhedos its charm, Hotel & Spa do Vinho is a large hotel that boasts spectacular 360-degree views at one of the highest points in the valley. **Pros:** big enough to host large groups; fantastic views. **Cons:** can get busy on weekends; spa is expensive. $ *Rooms from: R$427* ⊠ *RS 444, Km 21, Vale dos Vinhedos, Bento Gonçalves* ☎ *054/2102–7200* ⊕ *spadovinho. com.br* ⋗ *128 rooms* ¶◎¶ *Breakfast.*

$$$
B&B/INN
FAMILY

🏨 **Pousada Borghetto Sant'Anna.** Hosts Rubens and his wife, Gisele, provide an exuberant welcome at this magical location, which was their weekend home before it became their business. **Pros:** stunning views; close to vineyards; friendly hosts. **Cons:** restaurants are a drive away; no toiletries in the bathroom; some rooms lack privacy. $ *Rooms from: R$430* ⊠ *Via Trento 868, Vale dos Vinhedos, Bento Gonçalves* ☎ *054/3453–2355* ⊕ *borghettosantanna.com.br* ⋗ *3 houses, 4 rooms* ¶◎¶ *Breakfast* ⊟ *No credit cards.*

$$
B&B/INN

🏨 **Villa Valduga.** Casa Valduga winery maintains four redbrick houses with large, comfortable rooms overlooking the vineyards. **Pros:** great services; large and comfortable rooms. **Cons:** few amenities; no children allowed. $ *Rooms from: R$300* ⊠ *Km 6, RS 444, Vale dos Vinhedos, Bento Gonçalves* ☎ *054/2105–3154* ⊕ *www.villavalduga.com.br* ⋗ *24 rooms* ¶◎¶ *Breakfast.*

GRAMADO

115 km (72 miles) northeast of Porto Alegre.

No doubt it was Gramado's mild mountain climate that attracted German settlers to the area in the late 1800s. They left a legacy of German-style architecture and traditions that attract today's travelers. Ample lodging options and a seemingly endless choice of restaurants have given this city a reputation with conventioneers and honeymooners.

Every August the city hosts the Festival de Cinema da Gramado, one of Latin America's most prestigious film festivals. At Christmastime the city is aglow with seasonal decorations and musical performances of the Natal Luz (Christmas lights) festivities. During peak periods around Christmas and in July it can be difficult to find lodgings without a reservation.

GETTING HERE AND AROUND

Gramado is easily reached from Porto Alegre by car. Take BR 116 north for about 40 km (25 miles) to the intersection with RS 115. Then it's 97 km (60 miles) northeast to Gramado. Regular buses run by Citral depart from Porto Alegre every other hour during the day; the trip is 90 minutes and costs R$28. Although you might appreciate the independence of a rental car, most attractions are not too far apart and taxiing about is convenient.

ESSENTIALS

Bus Contacts Citral. ☎ *0800/979–1441* ⊕ *citral.tur.br.* **Estaçao Rodoviária** (*Bus Station*). ✉ *Av. Borges de Medeiros 2100, Centro, Gramado* ☎ *054/3286–1302.*

Taxi Contact Taxi Rodoviária. ☎ *054/3286–1230.*

Visitor Information Centro de Informações Turísticas. ✉ *Praça Major Nicoletti, Av. Borges de Medeiros 1647, Centro, Gramado* ☎ *054/3286–1475* ⊕ *www.gramado.rs.gov.br.*

WHERE TO EAT AND STAY

$$
ITALIAN
✕ **Casa di Pietro.** This Italian cantina-style restaurant has an excellent prix-fixe salad-and-soup buffet at dinner. Surefire soup choices include the cappelletti—best topped with grated Parmesan cheese—and the Serrano (a local vegetable soup). If this light fare doesn't suit you, opt for the grilled beef directly from the grill. $ *Average main: R$42* ✉ *Rua Pedro Benetti 5, Centro, Gramado* ☎ *054/3286–4077, 054/3036–0331* ⊕ *www.dipietro.com.br* ⊘ *Closed Tues.*

$$$$
GERMAN
✕ **Gasthof Edelweiss.** With a veranda that overlooks nearby pine trees and gardens, this German restaurant creates a relaxing ambience that perfectly complements its traditional offerings such as duck *à la viennese* (with an orange-flavor cream sauce)—the house specialty. Some tables are in the wine cellar, which has more than 1,000 bottles. $ *Average main: R$65* ✉ *Rua João Leopoldo Lied 975, Lago Negro, Gramado* ☎ *054/3286–1861* ⊕ *restauranteedelweiss.com.br* ▭ *No credit cards.*

$$$$
FRENCH
✕ **Le Petit Clos.** With fireplaces in the dining rooms and sheepskin rugs on the chairs, the family-run, Alpine-style Le Petit Clos is one for the winter, when families tuck into the house speciality: fondue. The excellent cheese fondue, with chunks of bread and potatoes for dipping, trumps the beef fondue, served with a fussy selection of more than a dozen disappointing sauces. The chocolate fondue, served with fruits, makes for a gluttonous end to the evening. And if that all sounds too heavy, opt for one of the fish dishes instead. $ *Average main: R$78* ✉ *Rua Demétrio Pereira dos Santos 599, Gramado* ☎ *054/3286–1936* ⊕ *lepetitclos.com.br* ⊘ *No lunch.*

$$$$
HOTEL
▦ **Saint Andrews Gramado.** An expensive and luxurious option, Saint Andrews Gramado is set in a grand, former family home in a leafy, residential condominium, with breathtaking views of the forest-covered Quilombo Valley. **Pros:** spectacular views; large sauna, steam room, and

6

heated indoor pool; butler and chauffeur service. **Cons:** only a handful of rooms have a bath; expensive. [$] *Rooms from: R$1,850* ✉ *Rua das Flores 171, Gramado* ☎ *054/3295-7700* 🌐 *www.saintandrews.com.br* 🛏 *10 rooms, 1 suite* 🍴 *Breakfast.*

$$$$ HOTEL FAMILY 🏨 **Serra Azul.** This prestigious downtown hotel is synonymous with fine lodging in the region. **Pros:** downtown location; great service. **Cons:** hectic when hosting business meetings; small bathrooms. [$] *Rooms from: R$1,210* ✉ *Rua Garibaldi 152, Centro, Gramado* ☎ *054/3295–7200* 🌐 *www.serraazul.com.br* 🛏 *152 rooms, 18 suites* 🍴 *Breakfast.*

$$$$ RESORT Fodor's Choice ★ 🏨 **Wish Serrano Resort and Convention Gramado.** Everything at the Serrano is designed to make your stay enjoyable and unforgettable: superb restaurants, plenty of sports and leisure options, and a can't-beat location, just a few blocks from downtown Gramado. **Pros:** excellent facilities; great services; multiple dining options. **Cons:** expensive; hectic when hosting conventions. [$] *Rooms from: R$680* ✉ *Av. das Hortensias 1480, Gramado* ☎ *054/3295–8000, 0800/600–8088* 🌐 *www.wishserrano.com.br* 🛏 *244 rooms, 28 suites* 🍴 *Some meals.*

CANELA

8 km (5 miles) east of Gramado, 137 km (85 miles) north of Porto Alegre.

Gramado's "smaller sister" is quieter and more low-profile. Brazilians immediately associate this city with the beautiful Caracol Waterfall, but it also has great shopping, for cotton and wool-knit apparel, handmade embroidered items, and handicrafts. The impressive views of the forest-clad valleys with meandering rivers also bring many tourists.

Most visitors stay in Gramado, with its abundance of accommodations, and visit the attractions in Canela as a day trip.

GETTING HERE AND AROUND

The route from Porto Alegre to Canela is the same to Gramado; from there drive or a take a taxi via RS 235 east for about 20 minutes to Canela.

EXPLORING

Fodor's Choice ★ **Parque Estadual do Caracol** (*Caracol State Park*). This park is renowned for its breathtaking 400-foot waterfall that cascades straight down into a horseshoe-shape valley carved out of the basaltic plateau. It also includes 50 acres of native forests with several well-marked paths, dominated by Paraná pine and an environmental education center for children. The entrance area is somewhat overcrowded with souvenir shops and snack tents and the river water doesn't smell the best, but the tranquil hikes and stunning waterfall more than make up for this. ✉ *Km 9, Estrada do Caracol, Canela* ☎ *054/3278–3035* 🎫 *Park R$18, elevator to lookout tower R$20* ⏲ *Daily 8:45–5:45.*

Parque da Ferradura. This private nature preserve has three lookouts to the Vale da Ferradura (Horseshoe Valley), formed by Rio Santa Cruz. You can hike across trails in more than 500 acres of pine forests through hilly countryside. A strenuous but rewarding two-hour trek reaches

Rio Caí near its source. Make sure you remain alert while hiking: it's quite common to spot a variety of wildlife here, such as deer, anteaters, and badgers. ⊠ *Km 15, Estrada do Caracol, Canela* ☎ *054/9972–8666* ☒ *R.$8* ⊘ *Daily 8:30–5:30.*

PARQUE NACIONAL DOS APARADOS DA SERRA

47 km (29 miles) north of Gramado, 145 km (91 miles) north of Porto Alegre.

GETTING HERE AND AROUND

Visitors to the park can base themselves in the one-horse town of Cambará do Sul, on the RS 020, up in the Serra Geral plateau. From here it's a 20-km (13-mile) drive on the RS 427 to the Itaimbezinho canyon, where you can park and follow one of two relatively easy paths to the rim of the canyon. For the more adventurous, there are a number of more challenging hikes along the base of of the canyons, and the best hub for these is the town of Praia Grande, accessed from the coast via the SC 494, SC 453 or SC 450, where you can hire a guide, though most pousadas will be able to provide their own associated guide. The drive to the top of the Itaimbezinho canyon from Praia Grande is up a steep, winding dirt road, with stunning mountain scenery.

ESSENTIALS

Visitor Information Centro de Informações Turísiticas (*Tourist Office*). ⊠ *Rua Manoel Justino 331, Praia Grande* ☎ *048/3532–1425* ⊕ *praiagrande. sc.gov.br/turismo.* **Serviço Informação ao Turista** (*Municipal Tourist Information Service*). ⊠ *Avenida Getulio Vargas 1720, Centro, Cambará do Sul* ☎ *054/3251–1320.*

TOURS

Aparados Turismo. The Rio do Boi hike along the river at the base of Itaimbezinho canyon is the most popular day out organized by this adventure company in Praia Grande. Hikes to other canyons, bike tours, and horse riding can also be organized in and around Aparados da Serra National Park. ⊠ *Rua Mário Bordignon 883, Praia Grande* ☎ *048/3532–0513* ⊕ *aparadosturismo.com.br* ☒ *From R$125.*

EXPLORING

Fodor'sChoice **Parque Nacional dos Aparados da Serra.** One of Brazil's first national ★ parks, Aparados da Serra was created to protect Itaimbezinho, one of the most impressive canyons dissecting the plateau in the north of Rio Grande do Sul State. In 1992 the Parque Nacional da Serra Geral was established to protect the other great canyons farther north, including the Malacara, Churriado, and Fortaleza. Winter (June–August) is the best time to take in the spectacular canyon views, as there's less chance of fog. The main entrance to the park, the Portaria Gralha Azul, is 20 km (13 miles) southeast of Cambará do Sul. A visitor center provides information on regional flora and fauna, as well as the region's geology and history. Beyond the entrance you come to grassy meadows that belie the gargantuan depression ahead. A short path (a 45-minute walk, no guide necessary) takes you to the awesome Itaimbezinho canyon rim, cut deep into the basalt bedrock to

6

create the valley 2,379 feet below. A more challenging walk within the park is to follow the Rio do Boi, the river that cuts through the base of Itaimbezinho canyon. You'll need to hire a guide and set aside a whole day to do the 12-km (7-mile) hike, weaving in and out of jungle and along the riverbed. The local tourist office can also make arrangements for other trekking tours in the region.

The best way to visit the park is to join an organized tour in Porto Alegre that includes an overnight stay in one of the region's pousadas. Those visiting Gramado can join a day tour to visit the canyons. ✉ *Parque Nacional dos Aparados da Serra* ✣ *18 km (11 miles) on RS 427 (unpaved road), southeast of Cambará do Sul, and 26 km (16 miles) northwest of Praia Grande* ☎ *054/3251–1277* 🎫 *R$14 per person, R$5 parking ticket* 🕒 *Tues.–Sun. 8–5.*

WHERE TO EAT AND STAY

$ BRAZILIAN 🍴 **Galpão Costaneira.** This churrascaria in a picturesque wooden bungalow is your best bet for experiencing the ubiquitous southern Brazilian *espeto-corrido* (a continuous service of grilled meats). They also serve a fixed-price buffet with less advertised gaúcho dishes such as *arroz de carreteiro* (rice with dried beef), *farofa* (sautéed cassava flour), and cooked cassava. Traditional-music performances take place on Friday and Saturday. [$] *Average main: R$27* ✉ *Rua Dona Úrsula 1069, Centro, Cambará do Sul* ☎ *054/3251–1005* 🕒 *Closed Mon.*

$$$ B&B/INN Fodor's Choice ★ 🏨 **Pedra Afiada Refúgio.** The most comfortable lodging at the end of the canyon valleys, this pousada has established its niche among adventure tourists, who depart from here to explore the Malacara and other canyons beyond. **Pros:** unique location; great for adventure tourism. **Cons:** basic amenities; far from city. [$] *Rooms from: R$400* ✉ *Estrada da Vila Rosa s/n, Parque Nacional dos Aparados da Serra* ☎ *048/532–1059, 051/3338–3323* 🌐 *www.pedraafiada.com.br* 🛏 *19 rooms* 🍽 *Some meals.*

$$ B&B/INN 🏨 **Pousada das Corucacas.** Immerse yourself in the region's rugged landscapes by staying at this inn on a working gaúcho horse-and-cattle farm: the 1,200-acre Fazenda Baio Ruano. **Pros:** great for experiencing local traditions. **Cons:** small bathrooms. [$] *Rooms from: R$260* ✉ *Km 1, RS 020 (Estrada do Ouro Verde), Cambará do Sul* ☎ *054/3251–1123* 🌐 *www.corucacas.com* 🛏 *11 rooms* 🍽 *Some meals.*

SÃO MIGUEL DAS MISSÕES

482 km (300 miles) northwest of Porto Alegre.

Of seven large missions in the area dating from the late 1600s to mid-1700s, São Miguel is the best preserved and the only one that has tourism infrastructure and allows visitors. The 120-acre Parque Histórico de São Miguel was created around the mission, which is a UNESCO World Heritage Site. A nondescript town of about 7,000 has grown around the mission site and shares its name. Joining an organized, Porto Alegre–based tour with an English-speaking guide is the recommended option for visiting the mission.

GETTING HERE AND AROUND

Most of the 482-km (300-mile) route from Porto Alegre to São Miguel das Missões is via toll roads (BR 386 and BR 285), which are single-lane but generally in good condition. Expect heavy truck traffic. São Miguel is 11 km (7 miles) off BR 285, via BR 466.

Ouro e Prata bus lines runs daily service to São Miguel (6 hours; R$101) from Porto Alegre. The closest airport to São Miguel das Missões is 60 km (38 miles) away, in Santo Angelo. It's served daily by NHT, with daily flights from Porto Alegre.

ESSENTIALS

Airport Aeroporto Municipal de Santo Angelo. ⊠ *Km 13, RS 218, Santo Angelo* ☎ *055/3312–9779.*

Bus Contacts Estação Rodoviária *(Bus Station).* ⊠ *Av. Antunes Ribas 1525, Centro, São Miguel das Missões.* **Ouro e Prata.** ⊠ *Rua Frederico Mentz 1419, Anchieta, Porto Alegre* ☎ *0800/051–6216* ⊕ *viacaoouroeprata.com.br.*

EXPLORING

Fodor'sChoice
★

São Miguel das Missões. The best-preserved and best-organized Jesuit mission in Brazil, São Miguel das Missões is an impressive, circa-1745 church built with reddish basalt slabs brought by the Guaranís from quarries miles away. The ruins are now a UNESCO World Heritage Site.

Jesuit missionaries moved into the upper Uruguay River basin around 1700. In the following decades the local Guaraní peoples were converted to Christianity, leading them to abandon their seminomadic lifestyle and congregate around the new missions—locally known as *reduções* (missionary communities). Seven of these existed in what is now Brazil, and several more were in Argentina and Paraguay—all linked by a closely knit trade and communication route. Historians have claimed that at the peak of their influence, the Jesuits actually created the first de facto country in the Americas, complete with a court system and elections. After the Treaty of Madrid granted rights over the lands and native peoples in the area to the Portuguese crown, the Jesuits were under pressure to leave. Recurrent clashes with Portuguese militia precipitated the breakdown of the mission system, but the final blow came with the decree of expulsion of the Jesuit order from Portuguese territory. Most of the Guaranís dispersed back into unexplored country. This important historical period was depicted in the movie *The Mission*, starring Robert DeNiro, with several scenes shot at Iguaçu Falls.

A small museum on the grounds, designed by Lucío Costa (who was instrumental in the development of Brasília), holds religious statues carved by the Guaranís, as well as other pieces recovered from archaeological digs. Guided tours (in Portuguese) are given by appointment. Admission to the site includes a sound-and-light show that tells the mission's story, at 9 pm in summer and 7 pm in winter.

Other mission sites with ruins are **São Lourenço** and **São Nicolau,** about 70 km (43 miles) from São Miguel, but there's much less to be seen at these sites, which are not normally in tours. Across the border in Argentina, there's a larger and better preserved mission site, **San Ignácio Mini.**

6

✉ *Parque Histórico Nacional das Missões, Rua São Luis s/n, Centro, São Miguel das Missões* ☎ *055/3381–1399* 🎟 *R$5.*

WHERE TO STAY

$ HOTEL 🏨 **Tenondé Park Hotel.** Not only the nicest accommodations in the region, the Tenondé Park Hotel is a fine hotel by any standards; the large rooms have colonial-style furnishings and arched doorways that echo the design of the mission a few blocks away. **Pros:** attentive staff; great service; close to the mission. **Cons:** some rooms need updating. [$] *Rooms from: R$220* ✉ *Rua São Miguel 664, Centro, São Miguel das Missões* ☎ *055/3381–2000* 🌐 *tenonde.com.br* 🛏 *78 rooms* 🍴 *Breakfast.*

MINAS GERAIS

Updated By
Angelica Mari

Though it's far from the circuit of Brazil's most visited places, the state of Minas Gerais holds unforgettable historical, architectural, and ecological riches. Minas has more UNESCO World Heritage Sites than any other state in Brazil. This mountainous state's name, which means "general mines," was inspired by the area's great mineral wealth.

Prior to the 18th century, the region was unexplored due to its difficult terrain, but in the late 17th century *bandeirantes*, or adventurers, forged into the interior, eventually discovering vast precious-metal reserves. As a result, the state, and particularly the city of Ouro Preto, became the de facto capital of the Portuguese colony. That period of gold, diamond, and semiprecious-stone trading is memorialized in the historic towns scattered across the jagged blue mountain ridges. It remains a tremendous source of pride for *mineiros* (inhabitants of the state).

Though the Gold Towns—Ouro Preto, Mariana, Tiradentes, and Congonhas—are awe-inspiring, Minas Gerais has other attractions. Roughly six hours south of the state capital of Belo Horizonte, several mineral-spa towns form the Circuito das Águas (Water Circuit). Thought to have healing powers, the natural springs of places such as São Lourenço and Caxambu have attracted the Brazilian elite for more than a century. Close by is the unusual town of São Thomé das Letras—a place where UFOs are said to visit and where mystics and bohemians wait for the dawn of a new world.

ORIENTATION AND PLANNING

GETTING ORIENTED

A landlocked state in southeastern Brazil that encompasses 588,384 square km (227,176 square miles), Minas is approximately the size of France. It shares borders with six other Brazilian states. The Serra da Mantiqueira range creates a natural boundary between Minas and Rio de Janeiro. It encircles to the south the Paraíba Valley, an area between the states of São Paulo, Rio de Janeiro, and Minas Gerais. The Serra da Canastra mountain range is a source of the São Francisco River. The longest river in the country, the São Francisco flows down from the mountains through most of Minas Gerais and Bahia and enters the ocean between the states of Sergipe and Alagoas.

With a population of 19.4 million, Minas is one of Brazil's most populous states, and with approximately 16% of the country's paved roads, it's one of the easiest to navigate. Although Minas is large, its major attractions, including Belo Horizonte, Ouro Preto, and the mineral-spa towns, are in the state's southeastern portion, within driving distance of one another.

TOP REASONS TO GO

Colonial Towns: Walk on the *paralelepípedos* (cobblestones) in Ouro Preto, Diamantina, and Tiradentes, all magnificently preserved baroque towns of white and pastel houses and churches.

Stunning Architecture: See the baroque gems of architect and sculptor Aleijadinho, whom an ex-curator of the Louvre called the "Michelangelo of the Tropics."

Traditional Cuisine: Indulge your taste buds in every Brazilian's favorite culinary state—if only for the *pão de queijo* (cheese bread) and the

doce de leite ("sweet of the milk"), a boiled version of condensed milk.

Shimming Gems: Check out the colored gemstones (Minas Gerais produces the most in the world), including amethysts, aquamarines, tourmalines, and emeralds—and the imperial topaz, which can only be found in Ouro Preto and in the Ural Mountains in Russia.

Parks and Spas: Hike, horseback ride, and swim in and around the beautiful national parks and natural springs tapped by numerous spa towns.

Belo Horizonte. At an elevation of 2,815 feet, Belo Horizonte lies in a valley encircled by a ring of mountains, the Serra do Curral. The City Center was planned for carriages, and the streets crisscross each other at 45-degree angles, hardly efficient for modern-day traffic. Social and cultural activity is concentrated along three main plazas in the center: Praça Sete, Praça da Liberdade, and Praça da Savassi.

The Colonial and Gold Towns. The historic cities of Ouro Preto, Tiradentes, and Diamantina lie in the Serra do Espinhaço range, with Ouro Preto at 4,000 feet. The towns are typically very hilly, with narrow, winding streets that are more easily navigated on foot than in a car.

The Mineral Spa Towns. The Circuito das Águas (Water Circuit) of Minas Gerais is concentrated in the southeastern regions (essentially counties) of Sul de Minas (2.6 million inhabitants) and Mata (population 2.2 million). The small cities of Caxambu and São Lourenço sit at an elevation of about 4,000 feet and have less than 50,000 inhabitants each.

PLANNING

WHEN TO GO

The busiest and most expensive time to travel is during Christmas, Easter, Carnival, and the month of July—because most Brazilians take their vacations at this time. The most exciting time to be in the colonial towns is during the Semana Santa (the Holy Week of Easter), when there are colorful processions of joyous locals in the streets, and everyone celebrates. Temperatures are usually around 24°C (75°F) in summer and 17°C (63°F) in winter. Summer is the rainy season, winter is dry but cooler; sturdy shoes and jackets are highly recommended at all times. To avoid crowds and rain, travel from April to June or August to November.

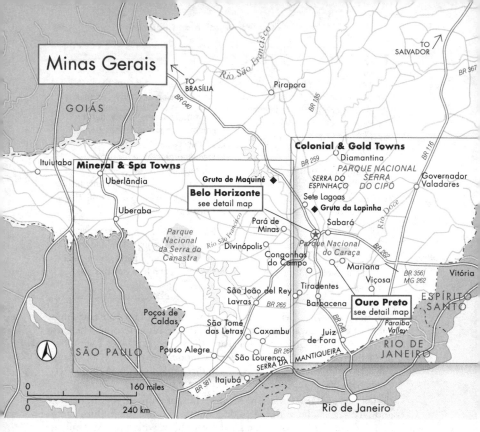

PLANNING YOUR TIME

A week is sufficient to see some of Minas Gerais's highlights, but not enough to cover all the territory the region covers. Not to be missed is Ouro Preto, the gem of the area. Its numerous churches, museums, and cobblestone hills deserve at least two days of exploring. Nearby Belo Horizonte (or BH) is a great place for a long weekend, with its bustling cultural scene, rich museums, and, most important, vibrant nightlife. If you have extra time, choose between the colonial towns of Diamantina or Tiradentes. Just remember that the distances are longer than they appear between towns in Minas Gerais.

GETTING HERE AND AROUND

Aeroporto Internacional Tancredo Neves, near Belo Horizonte, is the main point of entry to Minas Gerais. The domestic airport of Pampulha is more centrally located and closer to Belo Horizonte's main bus station, where connections to other parts of Minas and the country can be made. Bus travel between São Paulo and Rio de Janeiro is feasible, but it is advisable to take *leito* (bed) bus service late at night and arrive early in the morning.

Buses throughout Minas are comfortable and inexpensive, and travel regularly between Belo Horizonte, Diamantina, Ouro Preto, Tiradentes,

A Bit of History

Exploration of Minas began in the 17th century, when *bandeirantes* (bands of adventurers) from the coastal areas came in search of slaves and gold. What they found in the area was a black stone that was later verified to be gold (the coloring came from the iron oxide in the soil). In 1698 the first capital of Minas was founded and called Vila Rica de Ouro Preto (Rich Town of Black Gold), and some 13 years later Brazil's first gold rush began. Along with the fortune seekers came Jesuit priests, who were later exiled by the Portuguese (for fear they would try to manipulate the mineral trade) and replaced by *ordens terceiras* (third, or lay, orders). By the middle of the century the Gold Towns of Minas were gleaming with new churches built first in the baroque-rococo style of Europe and later in a baroque style unique to the region.

By the end of the 18th century the gold had begun to run out, and Ouro Preto's population and importance decreased. The baroque period ended at the start of the 19th century, when the Portuguese royal family, in flight from the conquering army of Napoléon Bonaparte, arrived in Brazil, bringing with them architects and sculptors with different ideas and artistic styles. Ornate twisted columns and walls adorned with lavish carvings gave way to simple straight columns and walls painted with murals or simply washed in white.

Today Minas Gerais is Brazil's second most industrialized state, after São Paulo. The iron that darkened the gold of Ouro Preto remains an important source of state income, along with steel, coffee, and auto manufacturing. The traffic that the mines brought here in the 17th century thrust Brazil into civilization, and now, well into the wake of the gold rush, a steady sense of progress and a compassion for the land remain.

and other historic towns. The only reason to rent a car is to take in some of the national and state parks that are not easily accessed by bus.

RESTAURANTS

Probably the most popular cuisine in the country, *mineiran* food is hearty and mixes Portuguese, Indian, and African flavors. Famous foods include *tutu de feijão*, mashed-up beans mixed with bacon, sausage, and cassava flour; *frango ao molho pardo*, a surprisingly tasty chicken dish with a sauce that is made with its own blood; and *angu*, a vegetarian dish made with polenta. For dessert, you can't go wrong with *goiabada* (guava paste, usually combined with *queijo minas*, a fresh white cheese that has a similar consistency to fresh ricotta). *Pão de queijo*, chewy cheese bread in roll form, is the state's culinary hallmark—mineiran bakeries get the consistency just right. The *cachaça* (sugarcane rum) from the northern region of Salinas is considered the best in the country. Mineiros tend to eat dinner after 8. Many restaurants close on Monday. Reservations may be required, especially on weekends.

HOTELS

In the interior of Minas Gerais, especially in the historic cities and state parks, there are two types of traditional accommodations for tourists: *pousadas* (inns), with simple rooms, and *fazendas* (Texan-ranch-style farms), which can be a fun option. Most hotels outside Belo Horizonte are small, lack English-speaking staff, and have few of the amenities common in American and European chains.

> **YELLOW FEVER VACCINATIONS**
>
> Yellow fever has subsided after a major outbreak in Brazil's interior in 2008. However, Belo Horizonte as well as the rest of Minas Gerais are still in the medium-risk category, so a yellow-fever vaccine, administered at least 10 days before your trip, is advisable.

In Belo Horizonte you can find large hotels and chain hotels equivalent to those found in U.S. cities that cater to the regular and business traveler. When you book, you'll likely be given a choice between an *apartamento standard* (standard room) and an *apartamento de luxo* (luxury room), which may be slightly larger, with air-conditioning and a nicer bathroom. Significant weekend discounts are common in Belo Horizonte. *Hotel reviews have been shortened. For full information, visit Fodors.com.*

WHAT IT COSTS IN REAIS			
	$	$$	$$$	$$$$
Restaurants	under R$31	R$31–R$45	R$46–R$60	over R$60
Hotels	under R$251	R$251–R$375	R$376–R$500	over R$500

Restaurant prices are the average cost of a main course at dinner or, if dinner is not served, at lunch. Hotel prices are the lowest cost of a standard double room in high season, excluding tax.

BELO HORIZONTE

444 km (276 miles) northwest of Rio, 586 km (364 miles) northeast of São Paulo, 741 km (460 miles) southeast of Brasília.

The Cidade de Minas (city of Minas), now Belo Horizonte, was established in 1897, when Ouro Preto, because of its mountainous geography, could no longer afford a population expansion. Since the planned uprising of the Inconfidentes in 1789, however, the residents of Minas Gerais had dreamed of a state capital, free of Portuguese influence, that would open a new historical chapter. The first planned modern city in Brazil (its design was overseen by the engineer Aarão Reis) modeled its streets on the wide avenues of Paris and Washington, and on their circular city centers.

Today Belo Horizonte, the third-largest city in Brazil after Rio and São Paulo, is distinguished by its politics and its contributions to the arts. In the early 20th century, Brazil's political system was referred to as *Café com Leite* ("coffee with milk") because the presidency was alternately held by natives of São Paulo (where much of Brazil's coffee is produced) and natives of Minas Gerais (the milk-producing state). The current system is more diverse, but mineiros are still influential in national politics. Minas Gerais is also home to respected theater and dance companies and some of Brazil's most famous pop bands. The artistic tradition is emphasized by the many festivals dedicated to all forms of art, from comic books to puppet theater and short movies to electronic music. The arts and nightlife scene, along with the stunning modern architecture, are reasons to visit Belo Horizonte before or after traversing Minas Gerais's peaceful countryside.

GETTING HERE AND AROUND

Flights from Rio de Janeiro or São Paulo to Belo Horizonte take less than an hour and can be quite inexpensive. The same trip by bus or car takes approximately six to eight hours. Roads can be bad and truck traffic is constant—flying is by far the easiest option.

AIR TRAVEL Belo Horizonte's main airport—officially Aeroporto Internacional Tancredo Neves, but also called Confins airport (for the town it's in)—receives domestic and international flights. It's a half-hour taxi ride (about R$90) north of the downtown. *Executivo* (air-conditioned) buses leave every 45 minutes and cost R$10–R$15. Aeroporto Pampulha is 9 km (5 miles) northwest of downtown and serves some domestic flights. Taxis from here to downtown cost about R$40.

Airports Aeroporto Internacional Tancredo Neves (*Aeroporto de Confins*). ⊠ *Rodovia MG 10, 38 km (24 miles) north of Belo Horizonte, Confins* 🕾 *031/3689-2700, 031/3689-2700* ⊕ *www.infraero.gov.br.* **Aeroporto Pampulha.** ⊠ *Praça Bagatelle 204, Pampulha, Belo Horizonte* 🕾 *031/3490-2000* ⊕ *www.infraero.gov.br.*

BUS TRAVEL Frequent buses connect Belo Horizonte with Rio (R$80–R$120; 7 hours), São Paulo (R$100–R$190; 8 hours), and Brasília (R$130; 12 hours). Most buses have air-conditioning. It's advisable to use leito services. These buses, with wide, reclinable seats, are the closest to a bed you can get for long journeys. Buy tickets in advance at holiday times. All buses arrive at and depart (punctually) from the Terminal Rodoviário Israel Pinheiro da Silva. Bus companies include Cometa, for Rio and São Paulo; Gontijo, for São Paulo; Itapemirim, for Brasília, Rio, and São Paulo; and Útil, for Rio.

A reliable website for bus timetables and purchasing tickets online is Busca Ônibus (⊕ *www.buscaonibus.com.br/en*). When buying tickets online, make sure you have a confirmation code for your purchase, as you will need it to collect the actual tickets at the bus station. It's best to allow 30 minutes before your departure time.

The central and original section of Belo Horizonte, planned in the 19th century, is surrounded by Avenida do Contorno. The city's main attractions are downtown (the center) and in the southern zone. On a map the center looks easily walkable, but the blocks are a lot larger than they seem and the hills are steep, so sometimes taking a bus is advisable.

City buses in Belo Horizonte are safe and easy to use, though buses are crowded during rush hour. BHTrans, the city's transit authority, has

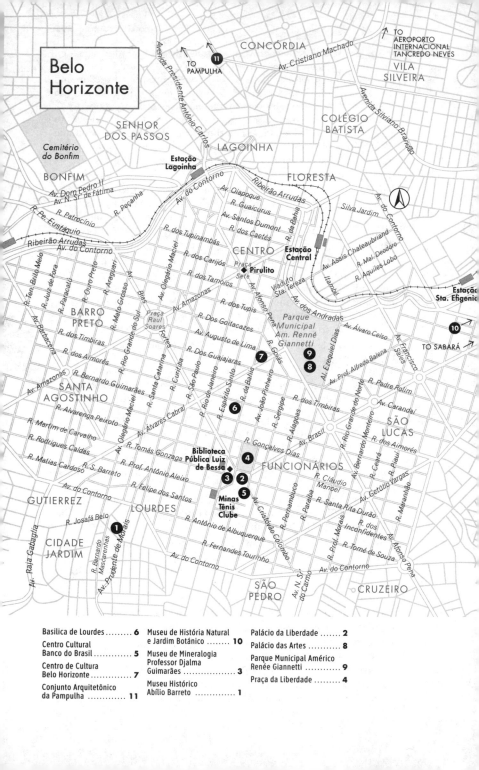

Belo Horizonte

TO PAMPULHA

TO AEROPORTO INTERNACIONAL TANCREDO NEVES

CONCÓRDIA

Av. Cristiano Machado

VILA SILVEIRA

Av. Presidente Antônio Carlos

SENHOR DOS PASSOS

COLÉGIO BATISTA

Avenida Silviano Brandão

Cemitério do Bonfim

LAGOINHA

Estação Lagoinha

BONFIM

Av. Dom Pedro II
Av. N. Sr de Fátima

R. Peçanha

R. Patrocínio

R. Pe. Eustáquio

Ribeirão Arrudas

Av. do Contorno

FLORESTA

Av. do Contorno

Ribeirão Arrudas

Av. Oiapoque

R. Guaicurus

Av. Santos Dumont

R. dos Caetés

da Bahia

Silva Jardim

Av. do Contorno

R. Tien. Brito Melo

R. Luiz de Fora

R. Patacatu

R. Ouro Preto

R. Araguari

Av. Mato Grosso

Blas

R. Rio Grande do Sul

Av. Barbacena

R. Olegário Maciel

R. dos Tupinambás

R. dos Carijós

R. dos Tamoios

R. dos Aimorés

R. dos Timbiras

R. dos Bernardo Guimarães

Praça Raul Soares

Farias

R. Santa Catarina

R. Curitiba

R. São Paulo

Av. Amazonas

CENTRO

Praça Sete

◆ Pirulito

R. dos Tupis

R. Dos Goitacazes

Av. Augusto de Lima

R. Dos Guajajaras

Estação Central

Viaduto Sta. Tereza

Av. Afonso Pena

Av. dos Andradas

Itambé

Av. Assis Chateaubriand

R. Mal. Deodoro

R. Aquiles Lobo

Estação Sta. Efigênia

Parque Municipal Am. Renné Giannetti

R. Goiás

Al. Ezequiel Dias

Av. Álvaro Celso

Av. Prof. Alfredo Balena

R. Padre Rolim

Av. Francisco Sales

TO SABARÁ

BARRO PRETO

SANTA AGOSTINHO

Av. Amazonas

R. Alvarenga Peixoto

R. Martim de Carvalho

R. Rodrigues Caldas

R. Matias Cardoso

Av. do Contorno

GUTIERREZ

R. Josafá Belo

CIDADE JARDIM

R. Raja Gabaglia

Av. Prudente de Morais

R. Bernardo Mascarenhas

R. da Bahia

R. Rio de Janeiro

R. Espírito Santo

R. São Paulo

Av. Álvares Cabral

R. Tomás Gonzaga

R. Prof. Antônio Aleixo

R. Felipe dos Santos

LOURDES

R. Antônio de Albuquerque

R. Fernandes Tourinho

Av. do Contorno

R. João Pinheiro

R. Sergipe

R. Alagoas

Av. Brasil

R. dos Timbiras

R. Gonçalves Dias

SÃO LUCAS

Av. Carandaí

Av. Bernardo Monteiro

R. dos Aimorés

R. Ceará

R. Piauí

FUNCIONÁRIOS

R. Cláudio Manoel

R. Santa Rita Durão

Av. Getúlio Vargas

R. Maranhão

R. Pernambuco

R. Paraíba

R. Prof. Morais

R. dos Inconfidentes

R. Tomé de Souza

Av. Afonso Pena

Biblioteca Pública Luiz de Bessa

Minas Tênis Clube

Av. Cristóvão Colombo

SÃO PEDRO

Av. N. Sr do Carmo

CRUZEIRO

Av. do Contorno

route information. Fares depend on the distance traveled but are always less than R$4.

Bus Contacts BHTrans. ⊠ *Av. Eng. Carlos Goulart 900, Buritis, Belo Horizonte* ☎ *031/3429-0405* ⊕ *www.bhtrans.pbh.gov.br.* **Terminal Rodoviário Governador Israel Pinheiro.** ⊠ *Av. Afonso Pena at Praça Rio Branco s/n, Centro, Belo Horizonte* ☎ *031/3271-3000, 031/3271-8933* ⊕ *www.pbh.gov.br/rodoviaria.* **Viação Cometa.** ☎ *031/3333-0299* ⊕ *www.viacaocometa.com.br.* **Viação Gontijo.** ☎ *031/2104-6039* ⊕ *www.gontijo.com.br.* **Viação Itapemirim.** ☎ *031/3429-2700* ⊕ *www.itapemirim.com.br.* **Viação Útil.** ☎ *031/2105-4646, 031/3907-9000* ⊕ *www.util.com.br.*

BEAUTIFUL HORIZONS

Belo Horizonte assumed its name in 1906. Its name means "beautiful horizons," so called because of the striking panoramic view of the mountains that used to dominate the city when it was just a village. The horizon is not as visible now because of pollution and skyscrapers. Brazilians will be impressed if you refer to the city as BH, (pronounced bei ah- *gah*), its affectionate nickname.

CAR TRAVEL Driving to BH from major cities is safe; the roads are in good condition, although exits aren't always clearly marked. BR 040 connects Belo Horizonte with Rio (6½ hours) to the southeast, and Brasília (10 hours) to the northwest. BR 381 links the city with São Paulo (7½ hours).

Belo Horizonte's rush-hour traffic can be heavy, and parking can be difficult. For on-street parking you must buy a card at a newsstand or bookshop. Taking the bus in Belo Horizonte is recommended over driving because of the traffic and the city's diagonal grid, which is hard to navigate.

TAXI TRAVEL To get to neighborhoods away from downtown, such as Pampulha, taking a bus or a taxi is advisable. When taking taxis, aim for taxi stands or hotels, where taxis can often be found. Most taxis in Belo Horizonte are white (*taxi comum*); there are also special black taxis that can be hailed or called. Both are metered. The meter starts at R$4.10; with R$2.40 added for every kilometer traveled (slightly higher at night and on weekends).

Taxi Contacts Unitaxi. ☎ *031/3418-3020.*

VISITOR INFORMATION
AMO-TE, the Ecotourism Association of Minas Gerais, focuses on adventure and ecotourism. Belotur, Belo Horizonte's official tourism agency, has a website with pages in Portuguese and English and operates several information kiosks throughout the city. The state-run Setur has information about historic cities and attractions.

Visitor Information AMO-TE. ⊠ *Rua Monte Verde 125, São Salvador, Belo Horizonte* ☎ *031/3477-7757.* **BELOTUR.** ⊠ *Mercado das Flores, Av. Afonso Pena 1055, Belo Horizonte* ☎ *031/3277-7666* ⊕ *www.belohorizonte.mg.gov.br/visit/en.* **SETUR.** ⊠ *Rodovia Prefeito Américo Gianetti s/n, Funcionários, Belo Horizonte* ☎ *031/3915-9454* ⊕ *www.turismo.mg.gov.br.*

7

EXPLORING

TOP ATTRACTIONS

FAMILY
Fodor'sChoice
★

Centro Cultural Banco do Brasil. One of the largest cultural centers in Brazil, the Centro Cultural Banco do Brasil (CCBB) hosts a well-curated series of exhibitions, music, theater, and interactive activities for adults and children. It also has a beautiful outdoor area, a café, and a souvenir shop. The CCBB is in a neoclassic mansion originally built in 1930 to house the Social and Security Secretariat. ✉ *Praça da Liberdade 450, Funcionários, Belo Horizonte* ☎ *031/3431–9400* ✆ *Free* ۞ *Wed.– Mon. 9–9.*

Fodor'sChoice
★

Conjunto Arquitetônico da Pampulha. Oscar Niemeyer designed this modern 1940s complex, one of Belo Horizonte's don't-miss sights. On the banks of Lagoa da Pampulha, the Conjunto Arquitetônico da Pampulha encompasses the **Museu de Arte da Pampulha**, the **Casa do Baile**, and the **Igreja de São Francisco de Assis.**

CIRCUITO CULTURAL PRAÇA DA LIBERDADE

The Circuito Cultural Praça da Liberdade is an extensive cultural circuit in the center of Belo Horizonte that encompasses 12 museums and historic venues. It's the best way to take in the city's most interesting sites in one go. The Circuit can be found on maps that are distributed in Belo's tourist offices. For more information on current exhibitions and shows, visit ⊕ *circuitoculturalliberdade.com.br*

The museum, one of Niemeyer's first projects, shows the influence of the European architect Le Corbusier on the young Brazilian. The glass and concrete structure, whose landscape gardens were designed by Richard Burle Marx, served as the city's casino until 1946, when gambling was prohibited in Brazil, and was converted into a museum in 1957.

The Casa do Baile, originally home to a small restaurant and a ballroom, is on a small artificial island connected to the Lagoa's bank by a concrete bridge. After the gambling ban went into effect, the space was used for various commercial activities until 2002, when a renovation project led by Niemeyer allowed for the reopening of the building. It is currently a reference center for architecture and design, and it hosts related exhibitions, workshops, and events. The internal area has a collection of Niemeyer's original sketches.

The glass and stucco 14 exterior mosaic panels of the Igreja de São Francisco de Assis, which describe the life and activities of its namesake, St. Francis of Assisi, are moving riffs off the *azulejos* (decorative blue Portuguese tiles) found in many colonial churches in Brazil. ✉ *Av. Otacílio Negrão de Lima, Pampulha, Belo Horizonte* ☎ *031/3277– 7946 Museum, 031/3427–1644 Church* ✆ *Museum and Casa do Baile free, church R$3* ۞ *Museum Tues.–Sun. 9–9; church Tues.–Sat. 8–5, Sun. 9 (Mass)–2; Casa do Baile Tues.–Sun. 9–6.*

Fodor'sChoice
★

Palácio da Liberdade. Built in 1898, the French-style Liberdade Palace is the former headquarters of the Minas Gerais government. Today, it is the main venue of the Cultural Complex Praça da Liberdade. Of note are the gardens by Paul Villon, the Louis XV–style banquet room, the main staircase brought from Belgium, the paintings in Noble Hall, and a panel by Antônio Pereira. ⊠ *Praça da Liberdade s/n, Funcionários, Belo Horizonte* ☎ *031/3217–9543* 🖾 *Free* ⊘ *Weekends and holidays 10–3.*

Fodor's Choice **Palácio das Artes** (*Palace of the Arts*). Designed by Oscar Niemeyer and
★ built in 1970, the Palace of the Arts is the most important cultural center in Belo Horizonte, comprising three theaters, three art galleries, a movie theater, a bookstore, a coffee shop, and the Centro de Artesanato Mineiro (Mineiro Artisan Center) next door, where contemporary Minas handicrafts—among them wood and soapstone carvings, pottery, and tapestries—are for sale. The main theater, Grande Teatro, stages music concerts, plays, operas, ballets, and other productions by Brazilian and foreign artists. ⊠ *Av. Afonso Pena 1537, Centro, Belo Horizonte* ☎ *031/3236–7400* ⊕ *www.palaciodasartes.com.br* 🖾 *Free* ⊘ *Tues.–Sat. 10–9, Sun. 2–8.*

FAMILY **Parque Municipal Américo Renée Giannetti.** With 45 acres of luscious tropical plants and magical winding walkways, the Parque Municipal (municipal park) was inspired by the landscaping of French belle époque gardens and inaugurated in 1897. It shelters an orchid house, a bandstand, a school, a playground, and the Francisco Nunes Theater, a beautiful modern building designed by the architect Luiz Signorelli in the 1940s that still presents theatrical plays and musical performances. With more than 50 tree species, the Municipal Park is highly recommended for walks. ⊠ *Av. Afonso Pena s/n, Centro, Belo Horizonte* ☎ *031/3273–4161 park, 031/3277–6325 theater* 🖾 *Free* ⊘ *Tues.–Sun. 6–6.*

FAMILY **Praça da Liberdade** (*Liberty Square*). When the city was founded, this square was created to house public administration offices. Today, in addition to centenarian palm trees, fountains, and a bandstand, the square is surrounded by neoclassical, art deco, modern, and postmodern buildings. Take time to linger in the square and wander around the nearby streets. It's the best way to get the pulse of the city. ⊠ *Between Avs. João Pinheiro and Cristóvão Colombo, Funcionários, Belo Horizonte.*

WORTH NOTING

Basílica de Lourdes. Conceived when the capital was founded but only inaugurated in 1923, Our Lady of Lourdes Church was elevated to the category of basilica by Pope Pius XII in 1958. Its Gothic architecture has undergone some adaptations, but it's still a magnificent building, featuring a 400-pipe organ and various towers on the side façade that mix well with Belo's skyscrapers. ⊠ *Rua da Bahia 1596, Lourdes, Belo Horizonte* ☎ *031/3213–4656* ⊕ *www.basilicadelourdes.com.br* 🖾 *Free* ⊘ *Weekdays 7 am–7:30 pm, Sun. and public holidays 7:30 am–8 pm.*

FAMILY **Museu de História Natural e Jardim Botânico** (*Natural History Museum and Botanical Garden*). Although it has an area of nearly 150 acres with Brazilian fauna, flora, archaeology, and mineralogy, the main attraction of this museum run by the Minas Gerais Federal University is the Presépio do Pipiripau (Pipiripau Crèche). This ingenious work of art narrates Christ's life in 45 scenes, with 580 moving figures. It was built by Raimundo Machado de Azevedo, who began assembling it in 1906 and finished in 1984. ⊠ *Rua Gustavo da Silveira 1035, Santa Inês, Belo*

CLOSE UP

Eating Like a Mineiro

Some gastronomic critics say there are only three native Brazilian cuisines: the cuisine from the North (particularly from Pará); the Capixaba cuisine from Espírito Santo; and *comida mineira*, the cuisine from Minas Gerais. Purportedly, all other Brazilian cuisines are originally from outside Brazil. Since Minas Gerais is one of the few states without access to the sea, its cuisine is strongly based on pork and chicken, and legumes and cereals (most notably beans and corn).

The mainstay of comida mineira is *tutu*, a tasty mash of beans that could include anything from roast pork loin and pork sausage to chopped collard greens, manioc meal, and boiled egg. It is served alongside meat dishes. Another favorite is *feijão tropeiro*, a

combination of beans, manioc meal, roast pork loin, fried egg, chopped collard greens, and thick pork sausage. Among meat dishes, pork is the most common, in particular the famed *lingüiça* (Minas pork sausage) and *lombo* (pork tenderloin), which is often served with white rice and/ or corn porridge. The most typical chicken dish is *frango ao molho pardo*, broiled chicken served in a sauce made with its own blood. Another specialty is *frango com quiabo*, chicken cooked in broth with chopped okra. The region's very mild white cheese is known throughout Brazil simply as *queijo Minas* (Minas cheese). Pão de queijo (bread baked with Minas cheese) is irresistible, and popular throughout Brazil. You'll realize very quickly that Minas Gerais isn't the place to start a diet.

Horizonte ☎ 031/3409–7600, 031/3482–9723 ⊕ *www.ufmg.br/museu* 💰 *R$4* ◷ *Tues.–Fri. 8–noon and 1–4, weekends 10–5.*

WHERE TO EAT

$$$$
ECLECTIC
✕ **Casa dos Contos.** A popular gathering place for local journalists, artists, and intellectuals, the old-school House of Tales has an unpretentious and varied menu that includes fish, pasta, and typical mineiro dishes. The filet surprise, a large steak coated in bread crumbs with a cheese and ham filling, is a popular choice. In tune with its bohemian clientele, Casa serves well past midnight. 💲 *Average main: R$75* ⊠ *Rua Rio Grande do Norte 1065, Funcionários, Belo Horizonte* ☎ 031/3261–5853 ⊕ *www. restaurantecasadoscontos.com.br.*

$$$
BRAZILIAN
✕ **Dona Lucinha.** Roughly 32 traditional Minas dishes, like feijão tropeiro, frango com quiabo, and frango ao molho pardo, are available at this reasonably priced buffet restaurant. The food is the only reason to go, as the place—in an old house devoid of taste—lacks charm. Children get significant discounts. 💲 *Average main: R$55* ⊠ *Rua Padre Odorico 38, São Pedro, Belo Horizonte* ☎ 031/3227–0562 ⊕ *www.donalucinha. com.br* ◷ *No dinner on weekends.*

$$$$
ITALIAN
✕ **Memmo Pasta & Pizza.** This casual Italian eatery is popular with Brazilians celebrating the end of the workday with appetizers like the *champignon Recheado* (mushroom stuffed with shrimp and prosciutto), and entrées like *tournedo Amici Miei* (filet mignon wrapped in bacon and

marinated in garlic and olive oil). The pizza is arguably the best in town. The restaurant is often packed both inside and on the large outdoor patio; you may need to wait for the staff to find you a table. [$] *Average main: R$80* ✉ *Rua Tome de Souza 1331, Funcionários, Belo Horizonte* ☎ *031/3282–4992* ⏲ *Closed Mon. No dinner Sun.*

$$$$ ECLECTIC 🍴 **Restaurante Varandão.** On the 25th floor of the Othon Palace hotel, this romantic restaurant has spectacular urban vistas. Start off with a cocktail at one of the outdoor candlelighted tables by the pool before coming inside for dinner. Although à la carte options are available, the feijoada on Saturday, a special meal that centers mainly on pork and beans accompanied by rice and collard greens, is the thing to come here for. On Saturday night, there is often live music. [$] *Average main: R$80* ✉ *Av. Afonso Pena 1050, Centro, Belo Horizonte* ☎ *031/2126–0000, 031/2126–0090* 🌐 *www.othon.com.br.*

$$$$ ITALIAN Fodor's Choice ★ 🍴 **Vecchio Sogno.** What is widely considered Belo Horizonte's best Italian restaurant attracts a well-heeled clientele. Tuxedo-clad waiters serve selections from the extensive wine list as well as steak, seafood, and pasta dishes. Consider the grilled fillet of lamb with saffron risotto in a mushroom-and-garlic sauce; the gnocchi *di mare,* with spinach and potatoes, topped with a white clam and scallop sauce; or the *badejo,* a local white fish baked and dressed in a seafood sauce. The restaurant allows its diners into its kitchen to see the preparation of food. With its beautiful wood paneling and an extensive bar, Vecchio Sogno has the feel of a 1940s jazz club. [$] *Average main: R$100* ✉ *Rua Martim de Carvalho 75, Santo Agostinho, Belo Horizonte* ☎ *031/3292–5251* 🌐 *www.vecchiosogno.com.br* ⏲ *No lunch Sat. No dinner Sun.* ✍ *Reservations essential.*

WHERE TO STAY

Given Belo Horizonte's hills and the long walking distances between key places of interest, the location of your hotel is crucial. To capture a glimpse of everyday life here, the City Center is the best place to be—particularly the region around Avenida Afonso Pena. While the City Center pulses during the day, it's somewhat gritty at night. For an upmarket area with sophisticated evening entertainment, consider the Lourdes and Savassi neighborhoods, around Avenida do Contorno. These are home to top restaurants and bars serving local and international food. The drawback to staying here, though, is the uphill climb from the main tourist destinations in the City Center.

$ HOTEL 🏨 **Ibis Belo Horizonte Liberdade.** A neat and comfortable budget option, the Ibis has spacious rooms with white oak furniture and large beds. **Pros:** in the best part of the city; good choice for disabled visitors. **Cons:** sparse furnishings for a hotel in this price range; basic breakfast. [$] *Rooms from: R$169* ✉ *Rua João Pinheiro 602, Lourdes, Belo Horizonte* ☎ *031/2111–1500* 🌐 *www.accorhotels.com.br* 🛏 *130 rooms* 🍽 *No meals.*

$$ HOTEL Fodor's Choice ★ 🏨 **Mercure Lourdes.** On a main city avenue, close to Savassi and not far from central Belo Horizonte, the Mercure is popular with executives, artists, and athletes. **Pros:** central location near restaurants and bars; rooms on higher floors have wonderful city views; good breakfast.

Cons: small swimming pool. *Rooms from: R$364 ✉ Av. do Contorno 7315, Lourdes, Belo Horizonte ☎ 031/3298–4100 🌐 www.accorhotels.com.br 379 rooms Breakfast.*

$$ HOTEL **Othon Palace.** Across from beautiful and exotic Parque Municipal, the Othon Palace has comfortable rooms with incredible city and park views. **Pros:** superb location; great rooftop pool and bar; good restaurant. **Cons:** dated room decor; slightly far from most good restaurants and bars. *Rooms from: R$280 ✉ Av. Afonso Pena 1050, Centro, Belo Horizonte ☎ 031/2126–0000, 0800/762–1296 266 rooms, 19 suites Breakfast.*

$$ HOTEL Fodor's Choice ★ **Ouro Minas Palace Hotel.** A favorite of well-off Brazilian honeymooners, the palatial Ouro Minas has rooms with large beds and well-appointed bathrooms. **Pros:** great breakfast ; good leisure center, including a well-equipped gym. **Cons:** not centrally located; restaurant lacks ambience. *Rooms from: R$280 ✉ Av. Cristiano Machado 4001, Ipiranga, Belo Horizonte ☎ 031/3429–4001, 031/3429–4000 🌐 www.ourominas.com.br 301 rooms, 45 suites Breakfast.*

NIGHTLIFE AND PERFORMING ARTS

NIGHTLIFE

BARS

Fodor's Choice ★ **Alambique Cachaçaria e Armazém.** For fabulous city views and some of Brazil's best cachaças, head to this bar where musicians perform daily except on Monday. The music is mainly pop-country and *forró*, and the audience is young and hip. You can party all night here: Alambique opens at 10 and closes at dawn. *✉ Av. Raja Gabáglia 3200, Chalé 1D, Estoril, Belo Horizonte ☎ 031/3296–7188 🌐 www.alambique.com.br From R$30 for women and R$40 for men.*

Fodor's Choice ★ **Arrumação.** A traditional bar in a colonial building owned by Brazilian comedian and actor Saulo Laranjeira, Arrumação specializes in cachaças and serves excellent appetizers. It often hosts performances and concerts. *✉ Av. Assis Chateaubriand 524, Floresta, Belo Horizonte ☎ 031/3222–9794.*

Bar do Bolão. Bohemians, musicians, and poets hang out at this large and lively bar and restaurant in Santa Tereza, a neighborhood worth exploring itself. Grab a seat outside and order a cold lager and the *rochedão* (the big rock), a hearty dish of steak, eggs, potatoes, rice, and beans. *✉ Rua Mármore 689, Santa Tereza, Belo Horizonte ☎ 031/3463–0719.*

Cantina do Lucas. Established in 1962, this cantina is a cultural landmark beloved by middle-aged locals, who flock here on weekends for its standard Italian fare. The portions are enormous—and cheap—and the service is efficient and courteous. This could be a good option for the start of your evening: order a *porção* (sharing snack platter) and a glass of cold lager. *✉ Av. Augusto de Lima 233, Loja 18, Centro, Belo Horizonte ☎ 031/3226–7153 🌐 www.cantinadolucas.com.br.*

Mercearia do Lili. One of BH's best bars operates out of a small grocery store in a bohemian enclave. By day the owner sells eggs, cereal, and soap. In the evening, tables are placed on the sidewalk, and he serves iced beer and incomparable appetizers. At the back, there is a great panoramic view of the city. ✉ *Rua São João Evangelista 696, Santo Antônio, Belo Horizonte* ☎ *031/3293–3469.*

CAFÉS

Fodor's Choice
★

Café com Letras. Belo Horizonte's intellectual beau monde collects at this café to eat dainty salads and drink imported wine in a beautiful interior surrounded by books and art. DJs spin music on most nights, and there's sometimes live jazz. ✉ *Rua Antônio de Albuquerque 781, Savassi, Belo Horizonte* ☎ *031/3225–9973* ⊕ *www.cafecomletras.com.br.*

Status Café Cultura e Arte. The Status is a great place to hear live music. The large, warm space houses a café/bar and a bookstore. On Sunday morning, there is a buffet breakfast with music. ✉ *Rua Pernambuco 1150, Funcionários, Belo Horizonte* ☎ *031/3261–6045.*

DANCE CLUBS

Fodor's Choice
★

A Obra. A hip and young crowd ranging in age from 18 to mid-30s gathers at A Obra, a basement-level pub with a dance floor. Music styles vary from indie rock to classic rock and more, but this is always a good place to go for something other than mainstream music. ✉ *Rua Rio Grande do Norte 1168, Funcionários, Belo Horizonte* ☎ *031/3261–9431,* ⊕ *www.aobra.com.br.*

Na Sala Revolution. BH's most modern and well-equipped nightclub is also its premier house-music venue. ✉ *Ponteio Lar Shopping mall, BR 356 no. 2500, Santa Lúcia, Belo Horizonte* ☎ *031/3286–4705* ⊕ *www. nasala.com.br* ☾ *Closed Sun.–Wed.*

LIVE MUSIC

Fodor's Choice
★

Pedacinhos do Céu. Belo Horizonte's best and most authentic live-music venue is Pedacinhos do Céu, literally, "little pieces of heaven." This small bar is known mostly for *choro,* an instrumental version of samba, for which guitars dominate the sound. Groups of musicians gather here with their *cavaquinhos* (small four-string guitars), *violões* (guitars), and flutes for jam sessions that last late into the night. The bar is named after a song by composer Waldir Azevedo (1923–80) and provides access to his archive. ✉ *Rua Belmiro Braga 774, Caiçara Adelaide, Belo Horizonte* ☎ *031/3462–2260* ⊕ *www.pedacinhosdoceu.com.br.*

Fodor's Choice
★

Utópica Marcenaria. By day a furniture store and an architecture office, this space transforms at night into a venue for jazz, blues, and Brazilian and Cuban rhythms. ✉ *Av. Raja Gabáglia 4700, Santa Lúcia, Belo Horizonte* ☎ *031/3296–2868* ⊕ *www.utopica.com.br* ☾ *Closed Sun. and Mon.*

PERFORMING ARTS

CONCERT HALLS

Chevrolet Hall. The 3,700-seat hall presents concerts by famous Brazilian and foreign musical artists. It is also a venue for volleyball and basketball games. ✉ *Av. Nossa Senhora do Carmo 230, Savassi, Belo Horizonte* ☎ *031/4003–5588* ⊕ *www.chevrolethallbh.com.br.*

Palácio das Artes. The center of cultural life in Belo Horizonte, this intimate, centrally located concert hall hosts symphony orchestras; ballet, opera, and theater companies; and famous Brazilian acts. ✉ *Av.*

Afonso Pena 1537, Centro, Belo Horizonte ☎ *031/3236–7400* ⊕ *www. palaciodasartes.com.br.*

SPORTS AND THE OUTDOORS

JOGGING

FAMILY
Fodor'sChoice
★

Parque das Mangabeiras. This 568-acre open space in the mountains surrounding Belo Horizonte is one of Brazil's largest urban parks. Along its jogging paths and hiking trails you might spot monkeys, squirrels, and other local fauna. There are playgrounds, sports courts and fields, and a stage for concerts. ✉ *Av. José do Patrocínio Pontes 580, Mangabeiras, Belo Horizonte* ☎ *031/3277–8277* ⊗ *Closed Mon.*

SOCCER

Estádio Mineirão/Museu Brasileiro de Futebol. Belo Horizonte natives are crazy about football. A running joke is that most could walk blindfolded from their home to 75,000-seat Estádio Mineirão, Brazil's third-largest stadium and the home field of BH's two professional *futebol* (soccer) teams: Atlético Mineiro and Cruzeiro. Expect to pay R$30 and more for tickets to a big game. The on-site Brazilian Football Museum was set up ahead of the 2014 FIFA World Cup as part of the stadium renovations. It offers an interesting collection of memorabilia, as well as the history of mineiro football stars. Guided tours to the stadium take place every hour. ✉ *Av. Antônio Abrahão Caram 1001, Pampulha, Belo Horizonte* ☎ *031/3916–0488* ⊕ *www.minasarena.com.br.*

SPELUNKING

Gruta da Lapinha. This cave is 36 km (22 miles) north of BH, near the city of Lagoa Santa, on the road leading from Tancredo Neves airport. Eight of the various chambers are open for visitation, and the curious limestone formations inside (known as candelabra) are awe-inspiring. It is a medium-level walk into the caves, with a set of stairs and a system of artificial lighting. ☎ *031/3689–8422* 🎟 *R$10* ⊗ *Tues.–Sun. 8:30–4:30.*

Fodor'sChoice
★

Gruta do Maquiné. The most popular cavern around Belo Horizonte, with six large chambers, the Gruta do Maquiné lies 113 km (70 miles) northwest of the capital, near Cordisburgo. Some of the spectacular water-sculpted formations resemble glimmering fairies, bears, and elephants. The large visitation area encompasses a set of sturdy walkways, and there are on-site guides. ✉ *Village Alberto Ramos, Via Alberto Ramos, MG 231, Km 7* ☎ *031/3715–1425* ⊕ *www.grutadomaquine. tur.br* 🎟 *R$16* ⊗ *Daily 8–5.*

MAGICAL REALISM FROM MINAS

João Guimarães Rosa's oeuvre is unlike anything else written in Brazil. It could be compared to Gabriel García Márquez in his use of magic and spiritualism to weave stories in rural settings. Rosa infused readers with the sounds and legends of Minas Gerais, creating a mystical and linguistic landscape not unlike Faulkner's South. During the Second World War, Rosa assumed a diplomatic post in Europe and was instrumental in helping many people fleeing the Holocaust with visas to Brazil.

SHOPPING

The fashionable Savassi and Lourdes neighborhoods have the city's best antiques, handicrafts, and jewelry stores. For clothing, head to one of the major shopping centers such as BH Shopping. On Saturday between 10 am and 6 pm, an antiques fair and food market takes place on the Avenida Bernardo Monteiro between Avenida Brasil and Rua dos Otoni.

Sunday morning the Avenida Afonso Pena is crowded with tents for the Feira de Artesanato (Artisans Fair). This is a meeting point for locals, who come here to grab a few beers and a snack then head off to the neighboring bars along Rua da Bahia to resume drinking and to watch a Sunday football match. Here you can also taste some delicious Brazilian street food, such as *coco gelado,* a large green coconut filled with sweet water, or *acarajé,* a deep-fried pastry stuffed with shrimps, ground cashews, and spices. The artisan market is famous for nice leather shoes and wallets, beautiful knitted shirts and skirts, handmade home accessories, and jewelry made from beads and seashells. It is advisable to get there early, just before 8 am, or after 1 pm, one hour before the vendors start packing up and when you can get the best bargains.

ANTIQUES

Arte Sacra Antiguidades. Fine Minas antiques are the specialty of Arte Sacra Antiguidades. ⊠ *Rua Alagoas 785, Funcionários, Belo Horizonte* ☏ *031/3261–7256.*

CLOTHING

Ronaldo Fraga. Minas Gerais culture influences the work of Ronaldo Fraga, one of Brazil's main fashion designers. Here, you can find unique clothing and accessories for women, men, and children. ⊠ *Rua Fernandes Tourinho 81, Savassi, Belo Horizonte* ☏ *031/3282–5379* ⊕ *www.ronaldofraga.com.*

HANDICRAFTS

Fodor'sChoice
★
Centro de Artesanato Mineiro. The wide range of crafts by regional artisans—including tapestries, embroidery, jewelry, and sculptures—makes this center within the Palácio das Artes complex well worth a visit. ⊠ *Palácio das Artes, Av. Afonso Pena 1537, Centro, Belo Horizonte* ☏ *031/3272–9513.*

Divina Obra. Modern handmade objects, including souvenirs and home decor items made by up-and-coming Brazilian artists, are found in the Divina Obra. ⊠ *Av. Prudente de Morais 1270, Loja 3, Savassi, Belo Horizonte* ☏ *031/2551–9306.*

MALLS AND CENTERS

BH Shopping. Many shops in Belo Horizonte's most exclusive mall sell designer clothes for men and women. It has cinemas and a large and varied food court. ⊠ *BR 356 No. 3049, Belvedere, Belo Horizonte* ☏ *031/4003–4135.*

Shopping Cidade. The shops at this popular downtown mall carry clothes, electronics, and just about everything else you could want. ⊠ *Rua Tupis 337, Centro, Belo Horizonte* ☏ *031/3279–1200* ⊕ *www.shoppingcidade.com.br.*

MARKETS

Mercado Central (*Central Market*). In the more than 400 stores in this beautiful old market dating from 1929 you can find typical products from Minas Gerais such as cheese, guava and milk sweets, arts and crafts, household trinkets, medicinal herbs and roots, and countless varieties of *cachaça*, the Brazilian sugarcane spirit. Everyone from municipal workers to local celebrities stop by the popular bars inside the market to drink beer and sample the notable appetizers, such as liver with onions. The market is particularly crowded on Saturday. ⊠ *Av. Augusto de Lima 744, Centro, Belo Horizonte* ☎ *031/3274–9434* ⊕ *www.mercadocentral.com.br* 🖃 *Free* ⊙ *Mon.–Sat. 7–6, Sun. 7–1.*

SIDE TRIP TO SABARÁ

19 km (12 miles) east of Belo Horizonte.

The grandeur of Sabará's baroque churches, their interiors rich with gold-leaf paneling, makes clear how enormously wealthy Minas Gerais was during the gold-rush days. This former colonial town, now a sprawling Belo Horizonte suburb of 140,000 people, makes for a fun half-day trip. Sabará's historic sites are scattered about, but signs at Praça Santa Rita point to all the major ones. As in most colonial towns, the churches are closed on Monday.

GETTING HERE AND AROUND

Buses for Sabará (Viação Cisne No. 5509) depart from behind the BH bus station (the local part of the station). Buses are frequent, and the ride takes less than 30 minutes. To get here by car, take BR 262 from BH; the drive takes 30 minutes.

EXPLORING

Matriz de Nossa Senhora da Conceição (*Church of Our Lady of the Immaculate Conception*). The ornate Church of Our Lady of the Immaculate Conception, though small, is Sabará's main church and an outstanding example of Portuguese baroque architecture with Asian influences. Its simple exterior gives no indication of the wealth inside, typified by the luxurious gold altar and the lavishly decorated ceiling. ⊠ *Praça Getúlio Vargas 5, Sabará, Belo Horizonte* ☎ *031/3671–1724* 🖃 *R$2* ⊙ *Weekdays 9–noon and 2–5.*

Igreja de Nossa Senhora do Ó. Our Lady of Ó Church, one of Brazil's oldest and smallest churches contains paintings said to have been completed by 23 Chinese artists brought from the former Portuguese colony of Macau. Other signs of Asian influence include the Chinese tower and the gilded arches. ⊠ *Largo de Nossa Senhora do Ó s/n, Sabará, Belo Horizonte* ☎ *031/3671–1724* 🖃 *R$2* ⊙ *Weekends 9–noon and 2–5.*

THE COLONIAL AND GOLD TOWNS

Two hours southeast of Belo Horizonte is Ouro Preto, a UNESCO World Heritage Site. The country's de facto capital during the gold-boom years, it was also the birthplace of Brazil's first independence movement, the Inconfidência Mineira. Today a vibrant student

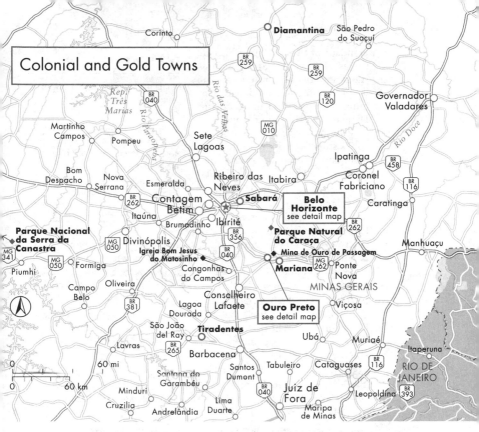

Colonial and Gold Towns

population ensures plenty of year-round activity, and lodging, dining, and shopping options abound.

All the Gold Towns—Ouro Preto, Mariana, Tiradentes, and Congonhas—are characterized by winding cobblestone streets, brilliant baroque churches, impressive mansions and museums, and colorful markets. Tiradentes is smaller than Ouro Preto but no less charming; this town truly seems to have stopped in time about midway through the 18th century. Between Ouro Preto and Tiradentes lies Congonhas, whose Basilica do Bom Jesus de Matosinhos and its famous Prophets, sculpted by Aleijadinho, are UNESCO World Heritage Sites. Diamantina rivals Ouro Preto in its scope and the beautiful scenery of the mountains around it; the rich cultural history here sheds considerable light on colonial Brazil.

DIAMANTINA

290 km (180 miles) northeast of Belo Horizonte.

Diamantina took its name from the diamonds that were extracted in great quantities here in the 18th century. Perhaps because of its remote setting in the barren mountains close to the *sertão* (a remote arid region), Diamantina is extremely well preserved, although its churches lack the grandeur of those in other historic towns. Its white-wall structures stand in pristine contrast to the iron red of the surrounding mountains. The principal attraction in Diamantina is the simple pleasure of walking along the clean-swept cobblestone streets lined with colonial houses—note the overhanging roofs with their elaborate brackets. The city was the home of two legendary figures of the colonial period: diamond contractor João Fernandes de Oliveira and his slave mistress, Chica da Silva, one of Brazilian history's first powerful Afro-Brazilian women. Two area attractions are linked with her; to see them, you should contact the Casa da Cultura to arrange a guided tour. Former Brazilian president Juscelino Kubitschek was also born here.

> **THE SERENADE TOWN**
>
> Diamantina has the distinction of being Brazil's center of serenading. At night, particularly on weekends, romantics gather in a downtown alley called Beco da Mota, the former red-light district and now home to several popular bars. Strolling guitarists also gather on Rua Direita and Rua Quitanda.

GETTING HERE AND AROUND

Twelve daily Pássaro Verde buses leave the rodoviária in Belo Horizonte for Diamantina. The trip takes five hours and costs about R$88. By car, there's no ideal direct route; your best bet is to drive north on BR 040 and then east on BR 259 (4 hours).

ESSENTIALS

Bus Contacts Pássaro Verde. ☎ *038/3531–1471, 0800/724–4400* ⊕ *www. passaroverde.com.br.* **Rodoviária de Diamantina.** ✉ *Largo Dom João 134, Diamantina* ☎ *038/3531–9235.*

Taxi Contacts Ponto de Taxi Largo Dom João. ☎ *038/3531–1413.*

Visitor and Tour Information Secretaria Municipal de Cultura e Turismo. ✉ *Praça Antônio Eulálio 53, Diamantina* ☎ *038/3531–9530,.*

EXPLORING

TOP ATTRACTIONS

Casa de Chica da Silva. One of Brazil's wealthiest and most famous former slaves, Chica da Silva (also spelled Xica da Silva), lived in this colonial house with her partner, João Fernandes de Oliveira, a Portuguese diamond dealer, from 1763 to 1771. Chica da Silva's story is tied to the creation of Diamantina (then known as Arraial do Tijuco) and the heyday of diamond mining in the area. The house, now part of the state's architectural heritage, contains colonial furniture and the façade of Chica's private chapel. A permanent art exhibit shows Chica in torrid poses and tawdry clothes as a personification of the Seven Deadly Sins. ✉ *Praça Lobo de Mesquita 266, Diamantina* ☎ *038/3531–2491* 🎟 *Free* ⊘ *Tues.–Sat. noon–5:30, Sun. 9–noon.*

Fodor's Choice
★

Igreja Nossa Senhora do Carmo (*Church of Our Lady of Mount Carmel*). João Fernandes de Oliveira, one of the wealthiest individuals in colonial Brazil, had the Church of Our Lady of Mount Carmel built as a gift to his mistress, Chica da Silva, a former slave. There are two tales that attempt to explain the bell tower built at the back of the 1751 structure.

The first is that da Silva ordered it to be built there so that the ringing wouldn't disturb her. The other is that the construction would allow her to attend Mass, as a law at the time forbade slaves to go "beyond the towers." The altar has gold-leaf paneling, and the organ has 514 pipes. ✉ *Rua do Carmo s/n, Diamantina* 🎟 *R$2* ⏲ *Tues.–Sat. 8–12 and 2–6, Sun. 8–noon.*

FAMILY **Museu do Diamante.** The city's Diamond Museum, in a building that dates from 1789, displays equipment used in colonial-period mines. The items on exhibit here include instruments made to torture slaves and sacred art from the 16th to the 19th century. There are guided tours of the rooms where diamonds were classified and separated. ✉ *Rua Direita 14, Diamantina* ☎ *038/3531–1382* 🌐 *museudiamante.blogspot.com.br* 🎟 *R$1* ⏲ *Tues.–Sat. 10–5, Sun. 9–1.*

Passadiço da Casa da Glória. On Rua da Glória, there's a covered wooden footbridge that connects the second stories of two buildings that once served as the headquarters of the colonial governors. The houses, originally built around 1876, were initially the residence of young nuns and the idea behind the bridge was to keep the women away from the prying eyes of passing men when they crossed the road. It's now a popular Diamantina postcard. ✉ *Rua da Glória 297/298, Diamantina.*

WORTH NOTING

Casa de Juscelino Kubitschek. The humble childhood home of one of Brazil's most important 20th-century presidents—he was responsible for the construction of Brasília—is now a small museum. ✉ *Rua São Francisco 241, Diamantina* ☎ *038/3531–3607* 🎟 *R$3* ⏲ *Tues.–Thu. 9–5, Fri.–Sat. 9–6, Sun. 9–2.*

WHERE TO EAT AND STAY

$ BRAZILIAN 🍴 **Cantina do Marinho.** This well-respected restaurant specializes in comida mineira. Diners' favorites include pork steak with tutu and pork tenderloin with *feijão tropeiro* (a dish of beans, cooked eggs, and toasted cassava flour). You can order à la carte from the menu or head over to the self-service buffet. [$] *Average main: R$30* ✉ *Rua Direita 113, Diamantina* ☎ *038/3531–1686* ⏲ *No dinner Sun.*

$ HOTEL 🏨 **Hotel Tijuco.** Oscar Niemeyer designed the sleek structure that houses this historic-district inn as a present to former Brazilian president Juscelino Kubitschek. **Pros:** amazing views of the hills from some rooms. **Cons:** few facilities; 1950s-modern structure seems out of place in historic Diamantina. [$] *Rooms from: R$130* ✉ *Rua Macau do Meio 211, Diamantina* ☎ *038/3531–1022* 🌐 *www.hoteltijuco.com.br* 🛏 *27 rooms* 🍽 *Breakfast.*

SHOPPING

Fodor's Choice ★ **Mercado Municipal de Diamantina.** Diamantina's central market takes place on Saturday, and showcases amazing crafts from the region, including ceramic dolls from the Jequitinhonha Valley and colorful tapestries. Live music acts often perform and typical snacks from the north of Minas Gerais are available. ✉ *Praça Baraão de Guaicuí 170, Diamantina* ☎ *038/3531–9548.*

OURO PRETO

97 km (60 miles) southeast of Belo
Horizonte.

Fodor's Choice The former gold-rush capital is
★ the best place to see the legend-
ary sculptor Aleijadinho's artistry.
Now a lively university town, it's
been preserved as a national monument and a World Heritage Site.
The surrounding mountains, geo-
metric rows of whitewashed buildings, cobblestone streets, red-tile
roofs that climb the hillsides, morning mist and evening fog—all give
Ouro Preto a singular beauty.

In its heyday Ouro Preto (also seen
as Ouro Prêto, an archaic spelling)
was one of Brazil's most progressive
cities and the birthplace of the colony's first stirrings of independence.
Toward the end of the 18th century
the mines were running out, with
all the gold and jewels being sent
to Portugal. The residents were
unhappy with the corruption of the

> ### THE PRICE OF BETRAYAL
>
> The Inconfidência Mineira, a 1789 attempt to gain independence from Portugal, was to have been led by Joaquim José da Silva Xavier, better known as Tiradentes, and 11 followers. But Joaquim Silvério dos Reis, a mineiro who was in on the conspiracy, betrayed the movement in exchange for the pardon of his debt to the crown. Tiradentes assumed responsibility for the planned uprising and was sentenced to death. The Empress Dona Maria I documented how he was to be killed: drawn and quartered, with his body parts hung around Ouro Preto. The date of Tiradentes's execution, April 21, is a national holiday.

governor, and the Inconfidência Mineira was organized to overthrow
the Portuguese rulers and establish an independent Brazilian republic.
It was to have been led by a resident of Ouro Preto, Joaquim José da
Silva Xavier, a dentist nicknamed Tiradentes ("tooth-puller").

Walk down the hill from the bus station on the beautiful cobblestone
street and you'll come to the former prison or the Museu de Inconfidência. Praça Tiradentes, the town's central square, teems with gossiping
students, eager merchants, and curious visitors. Ouro Preto has several
museums, as well as 13 colonial *igrejas* (churches) that are highly representative of mineiro baroque architecture. The Minas style is marked
by elaborately carved doorways and curving lines. Most distinctive,
though, are the interiors, richly painted and decorated lavishly with
cedarwood and soapstone sculptures. Many interiors are unabash-
edly rococo, with an ostentatious use of gold leaf, a by-product of the
region's mineral wealth. Note that many museums and churches are
closed on Mondays.

GETTING HERE AND AROUND

Pássaro Verde buses connect Belo Horizonte with Ouro Preto (R$26;
2 hours). Útil serves Ouro Preto from Rio (R$78–R$120; 8 hours). By
car from Belo Horizonte you can take BR 040 south and BR 356 (it
becomes MG 262) east to Ouro Preto (1½–2 hours).

All of the town's sights are within easy walking distance of the central
square, Praça Tiradentes, which is a seven-minute walk from the bus

station. A taxi from the bus station to the center costs R$15. A small bus travels around town every 10 to 15 minutes.

The main streets of Ouro Preto have two names: one from the 18th century, still used by the city's inhabitants, and the other an official name, used on maps but not very popular. Therefore, Rua Conde de Bobadela is better known as Rua Direita, Rua Senador Rocha Lagoa as Rua das Flores, and Rua Cláudio Manoel as Rua do Ouvidor. Street signs sometimes use the official name and sometimes both. We use the official names in this guide.

The steep hills in Ouro Preto are very hard on cars—and legs. And when it rains, cobblestones are very slippery; sturdy footwear and warm clothing are recommended year-round.

VISITOR INFORMATION
The professional tour guides of the Associação de Guias conduct excellent six-hour historic walking tours in English, and the group provides general information about Ouro Preto. Posto de Informações Turísticas dispenses information at the bus station, but its main location is at Praça Tiradentes, where there's an art gallery, a beautiful café, and a bookstore.

ESSENTIALS
Bus Contacts Viação Pássaro Verde. ⊠ *Rua Padre Rolim 661* ☎ *031/3551–1081,* ⊕ *www.passaroverde.com.br.* **Rodoviária Ouro Preto.** ⊠ *Rua Padre Rolim 661, São Cristóvão, Ouro Preto* ☎ *031/3559–3252.* **Viação Útil.** ☎ *031/3551–3160,* ⊕ *www.util.com.br.*

Taxi Contacts Ponto de Táxi. ☎ *031/3551–2675, 031/3551–1977.*

Visitor and Tour Information Associação de Guias de Ouro Preto. ⊠ *Rua Padre Rolim s/n, São Cristóvão, Ouro Preto* ☎ *031/3551–2655.* **Posto de Informações Turísticas.** ⊠ *Praça Tiradentes 4, Centro, Ouro Preto* ☎ *031/3559–3269.*

EXPLORING
TOP ATTRACTIONS
Fodor'sChoice **Igreja de Nossa Senhora do Carmo.** The impressive Our Lady of Carmel
★ Church, completed in 1776, contains the last works of notable Brazilian sculptor Aleijadinho. It was originally designed by Aleijadinho's father, an architect, but was later modified by Aleijadinho, who added additional rococo elements, including the soapstone sculptures of angels above the entrance. Frequented by the high society of Ouro Preto at the time it was inaugurated, the church contains the only examples of *azulejos* (decorative Portuguese tiles) from this period in Minas Gerais. ⊠ *Praça Brigadeiro Musqueira s/n, Centro, Ouro Preto* ☎ *031/3551–2601* ☜ *R$2* ☉ *Tues.–Sun. 9–11 and 1–4:45.*

Fodor'sChoice **Igreja de Nossa Senhora do Pilar.** Local lore has it that 400 pounds of
★ gold and silver leaf were used to cover the interior of Ouro Preto's most richly decorated church, built on the site of an earlier chapel and consecrated in 1733. In addition to gold- and silver-clad sculptures of cherubs, flowers, and saints, highlights of the church's interior include a beautiful series of paintings by Bernardo Pires, as well as two massive angels made in solid silver. The church building also houses the

Museu de Arte Sacra (Museum of Sacred Art), which has a collection of church furnishings and sculptures attributed to Aleijadinho. ⊠ *Praça Monsenhor João Castilho Barbosa s/n, Centro, Ouro Preto* ☎ *031/3551–4736* ⊠ *R$7* ⏱ *Tues.– Sun. 9–10:45 and noon–4:45.*

Igreja de Santa Efigênia. On a hill east of Praça Tiradentes, this interesting slave church was built over the course of 60 years (1730–90) and was funded by Chico-Rei. This African ruler was captured during Brazil's gold rush and sold to a mine owner in Minas Gerais. Chico eventually earned enough money to buy his freedom—in the days before the Portuguese prohibited such acts—and became a hero among slaves.

THE ROYAL ROAD

The *Estrada Real* Royal Road was constructed by slaves, linking the colonial towns with the port of Paraty and the ships waiting to transport the mineral wealth to Portugal. Huge stone slabs are still present in parts of this historical trail. Thousands of slaves died building this road and taking the wealth to the coast. Parts of the road can be traversed by horse, on foot, and by car. Set up trips through the Instituto Estrada Real ☎ *031/3241-7166.*

The clocks on the facade are the city's oldest, and the interior contains cedar sculptures by Francisco Xavier de Brito, the teacher of the noted sculptor Aleijadinho. ⊠ *Rua de Santa Efigênia s/n, Centro, Ouro Preto* ☎ *031/3551–5047* ⊠ *R$2* ⏱ *Tues.–Sun. 8:30–4:30.*

Fodor's Choice ★ **Igreja de São Francisco de Assis** (*Church of Saint Francis of Assisi*). Considered the masterpiece of Brazilian sculptor Aleijadinho, this church was begun in 1766 by the Franciscan Third Order but wasn't completed until 1810. Aleijadinho designed the structure and was responsible for the wood and soapstone sculptures on the portal, high altar, side altars, pulpits, and crossing arch. Manuel da Costa Ataíde, a brilliant artist in his own right, painted the panel on the nave ceiling representing the Virgin's glorification. Cherubic faces, garlands of tropical fruits, and allegorical characters carved into the main altar are still covered with their original paint. ⊠ *Largo de Coimbra s/n, Centro, Ouro Preto* ⊠ *R$6* ⏱ *Tues.–Sun. 8.30–noon and 1:30–5.*

Fodor's Choice ★ **Museu da Inconfidência** (*Museum of Betrayal*). One of the best historical museums in Brazil, this former 18th-century prison and onetime city hall has great interactive computer and television screen displays devoted to the history of the failed uprising of the Inconfidentes, life in colonial Tiradentes, slavery, and a number of other interesting topics. Other displays include period furniture, clothing, slaves' manacles, firearms, books, and gravestones. The museum also holds the remains of revolutionaries, some brought back from exile in Portugal's African colonies, and the document in which Maria I details the fate of Tiradentes's body parts. ⊠ *Praça Tiradentes 139, Centro, Ouro Preto* ☎ *031/3551–1121* ⊕ *www.museudainconfidencia.gov.br* ⊠ *R$6* ⏱ *Tues.–Sun. noon–6.*

Museu de Ciência e Técnica. In the former governor's palace, the Museum of Science and Technology contains an enormous collection of stunning precious and semiprecious gems, along with gold and crystals. Exhibits also survey the geology of Minas Gerais and explain the mining process.

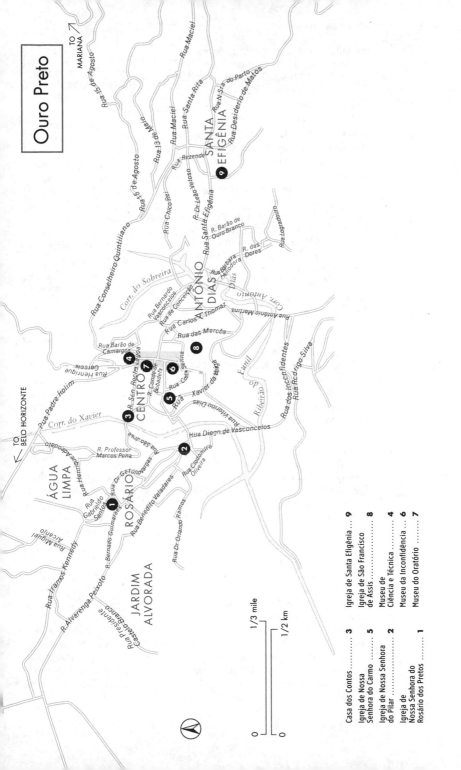

Ouro Preto

TO MARIANA

TO BELO HORIZONTE

SANTA EFIGÊNIA

ANTÔNIO DIAS

CENTRO

ROSÁRIO

ÁGUA LIMPA

JARDIM ALVORADA

Rua Maciel
Rua Santa Rita
Rua N. Sra. do Parto
Rua Maciel
Rua 15 de Agosto
Rua 13 de Maio
Rua Desidério de Matos
Rua Rezende
R. Dr. Leão Veloso
Rua 15 de Agosto
Rua Chico-Rei
Rua Santa Efigênia
R. Barão de Ouro-Branco
Rua Logradouro
Rua Conselheiro Quintiliano
Corr. do Sobreira
R. das Dores
Rua Barbara Heliodora
Rua Bernardo Vasconcelos
Rua de Conceição
Rua Carlos Thomaz
Corr. Antônio Dias
Rua Antônio Marins
Rua das Mercês
Rua Barão de Camargos
Rua Henrique Gorceix
Rua Sen. Rocha Lagoa
R. Conde de Bobadela
Rua Costa Sena
Rua dos Inconfidentes
Rua Rodrigo Silva
Rua Padre Rolim
Corr. do Xavier
Rua São José
Rua Xavier da Veiga
Rua Vitorino Dias
Ribeirão do Funil
Rua Diogn de Vasconcelos
R. Professor Marcos Pena
Rua Henrique Adocado
Rua Dr. Getúlio Vargas
Rua Cláudio Oliveira
Rua Gabriela Santos
R. Bernardo Guimarães
Rua Benedito Valadares
Rua Dr. Orlando Ramos
Rua Miguel Arcanjo
Rua Irmãos Kennedy
R. Alvarenga Peixoto
Casa de Pedra Branco

Casa dos Contos **3**

Igreja de Nossa
Senhora do Carmo **5**

Igreja de Nossa Senhora
do Pilar **2**

Igreja de
Nossa Senhora do
Rosário dos Pretos **1**

Igreja de Santa Efigênia ... **9**

Igreja de São Francisco
de Assis **8**

Museu de
Ciência e Técnica **4**

Museu da Inconfidência ... **6**

Museu do Oratório **7**

1/3 mile

1/2 km

0

An entire floor is devoted to gems organized according to their chemical families. ✉ *Praça Tiradentes 20, Centro, Ouro Preto* ☎ *031/3559–3119* 🌐 *www.museu.em.ufop.br* 🎫 *R$6* 🕒 *Tues.–Sun. noon–5.*

Museu do Oratório. Established in the historic house of the St. Carmel novitiate, once a home to Aleijadinho, this museum celebrates 18th- and 19th-century sacred art. Some of the oratories, which reflect ideas of religious beauty from the period, have been displayed at the Louvre. ✉ *N. Sra. do Carmo 28, Centro, Ouro Preto* ☎ *031/3551–5369* 🌐 *www.museudooratorio.org.br* 🎫 *R$5* 🕒 *Daily 9:30–5:30.*

ALEIJADINHO

Brazil's most famous baroque artist was the son of a Portuguese architect and a former slave. Antônio Francisco Lisboa was born in 1738 in the vicinity of present-day Ouro Preto. In adulthood, a disease left his arms and feet deformed. Unable to hold his instruments Aleijadinho ("little cripple") worked with chisel and hammer strapped to his wrists. His work, primarily in cedarwood and soapstone, is profoundly moving. His sculptures have a singular look, many of his angels have curly hair, and enormous, humble eyes.

WORTH NOTING

Casa dos Contos. This colonial site dating from the 1780s has had many uses: a prison, a tax collection center, and a coinage house, among others. It contains the foundry that minted coins of the gold-rush period and has exhibits of coins and period furniture. The building is considered one of the best examples of Brazilian colonial architecture. The beautiful park at the back of the building snakes past a waterfall and alongside a river to the other side of town. ✉ *Rua São José 12, Centro, Ouro Preto* ☎ *031/3551–1444* 🎫 *R$5* 🕒 *Mon., 2–6, Tues.–Sat. 10–6, Sun. 10–4.*

Igreja de Nossa Senhora do Rosário dos Pretos. The small, intriguing Church of Our Lady of the Rosary of the Blacks was inaugurated by slaves in 1785, some of whom bought their freedom with the gold they found in Ouro Preto. The church's interior is bare, allegedly because the slaves ran out of gold after erecting the building. In the unusual oval interior the baroque church houses sculptures of Santa Helena, Santo Antônio, and São Benedito. ✉ *Largo do Rosário s/n, Centro, Ouro Preto* ☎ *031/3551–4736* 🎫 *Free* 🕒 *Tues.–Sat. noon–4:45.*

WHERE TO EAT

$ CAFÉ FAMILY 🍴 **Café Cultural.** Within the same building as the Tourist Information Office of Praça Tiradentes, Café Cultural is the perfect place to rest a bit and enjoy a cold drink and a quick bite. Quiches, little appetizers, and cakes are served, and the extensive beer list includes local gems such as the Backer beer. Ambient music and comfortable sofas allow you to sit back and watch the world pass by the café's large windows. A small bookstore and a collection of teas and local craft items are also available for purchase. [$] *Average main: R$20* ✉ *Rua Claudio Manoel 15, Centro, Ouro Preto* ☎ *031/3551–1361* 🌐 *cafeculturalop.com.br/en* 💳 *No credit cards* 🕒 *No dinner.*

$$$ BRAZILIAN Fodor's Choice ★ 🍴 **Café Geraes/Escadabaixo.** A Parisian-like café and restaurant in an 18th-century building, this beautiful establishment serves delicious sandwiches, soups, and pastries, as well as full entrées. It's especially appealing on a rainy day to sip a cup of coffee or a glass of wine here to the accompaniment of a good novel. The happy hour bar downstairs, Escadabaixo, is the town's most popular hangout for wealthier *ouro-pretanos* and tourists. Escadacima is a small shop within the restaurant with a good selection of local and imported wine and beer. [$] *Average main: R$50* ✉ *Rua Conde de Bobadela 122, Centro, Ouro Preto* ☎ *031/3551–5097* 🌐 *www.escadabaixo.com.br.*

$$$ BRAZILIAN Fodor's Choice ★ 🍴 **Casa do Ouvidor.** A large and welcoming restaurant above a jewelry store, Casa do Ouvidor has won numerous awards for regional dishes such as tutu, feijão tropeiro, and frango com quiabo. The portions are generous. Since the restaurant's opening in 1972, it has hosted former President of France François Mitterand, actor Richard Dreyfuss, author John Updike, and many other luminaries. Try to sit by the windows, which look out on the street below and save room for the homemade sweets. [$] *Average main: R$50* ✉ *Rua Conde de Bobadela 42, Centro, Ouro Preto* ☎ *031/3551–2141* 🌐 *www.casadoouvidor.com.br.*

$$$ BRAZILIAN 🍴 **Chafariz.** The best place for a mineiran buffet in Ouro Preto is in this vividly decorated eatery near the Casa dos Contos. The large dining room has beautiful furniture designed by Oscar Niemeyer, and the cupboards are decorated with antiques and candles. On the gorgeous balcony in the back, you can sip *jaboticaba* (a purple grape-like fruit) drinks as you peruse the countryside. [$] *Average main: R$50* ✉ *Rua São José 167, Centro, Ouro Preto* ☎ *031/3551–2828* ⏲ *Closed Mon. No dinner.*

7

$$$$ PIZZA FAMILY 🍴 **O Passo Pizza Jazz.** An excellent restaurant just oozing with charm, O Passo serves local meat and pasta dishes in addition to pizza. Large bay windows, subtle colors, and candlelight—as well as jazz and Brazilian popular music (MPB) played live on weekends—create a sophisticated but accessible atmosphere that attracts young couples and families. Among the many tantalizing pizzas worth a try, the *calabresa with azeitona* (wafer-thin slices of cured pork sausage sprinkled with black olives) and the *quatro funghi* (with four types of mushrooms) stand out. An extensive list of artisanal beers is also available. Try to book a table outside with a view of the river. [$] *Average main: R$80* ✉ *Rua São José 56, Centro, Ouro Preto* ☎ *031/3552–5089* 💳 *No credit cards* ✍ *Reservations essential.*

$$$$ ITALIAN 🍴 **Oro Nero Trattoria.** Couples looking for a hearty meal seek out this trattoria in a beautifully decorated house next to the Sanctuary of the Immaculate Conception. The restaurant serves large pasta portions, often flavored with the house's signature and flawless arrabiata sauce; another good choice is the polenta with a sweet-and-spicy pork-sausage ragout. The wine list showcases Italian vintages. Save room for the lush yet light tiramisu. [$] *Average main: R$80* ✉ *Rua Bernardo de Vasconcelos 98, Antônio Dias, Ouro Preto* ☎ *031/3552–2930* 🌐 *www.trattoriaoronero.com.br* 💳 *No credit cards* ⏲ *Closed Mon. and Tues. No dinner Sun.*

$$$$
MODERN FRENCH
Fodor's Choice
★

✕**Senhora do Rosário.** Ouro Preto's finest restaurant is in the Solar Nossa Senhora do Rosário hotel. An elegant atmosphere with formal place settings, attentive service, and soft Brazilian music makes this the ideal spot for a quiet, romantic dinner. The chef, whose menu changes frequently, focuses on Italian and French fare with a mineira accent: you might find intriguing, perfectly prepared dishes such as *carne seca* (beef jerky) risotto with Gorgonzola cheese. The dessert options include *doce de leite* (caramel), a Minas specialty, as well as international options like *petit gâteau* (cake). Argentina, France, Italy, and Brazil itself are among the nations whose wines are represented on the excellent list. $ *Average main: R$100* ✉ *Rua Getúlio Vargas 270, Rosário, Ouro Preto* ☎ *031/3551-5200* ⊕ *www.hotelsolardorosario.com* ⊟ *No credit cards* 🍴 *Reservations essential.*

> **ELIZABETH BISHOP**
>
> One of America's greatest poets, U.S. poet laureate Elizabeth Bishop (1911–79) lived in Ouro Preto for many years with her female partner Lota de Macedo Soares. She bought a house here in 1965 and called it Casa da Mariana, a tribute to the poet Marianne Moore. Ouro Preto is the subject of a number of Bishop's paintings and poems.

WHERE TO STAY

$$
B&B/INN

🏠**Estalagem das Minas Gerais.** Near a nature preserve and perfect for those who love a walk in the woods, this lodging has clean, modern rooms. **Pros:** beautiful setting; rooms in front have wonderful valley views; chalets good for large groups. **Cons:** away from town center. $ *Rooms from: R$260* ✉ *Rodovia dos Inconfidentes, Km 88, Centro, Ouro Preto* ☎ *031/3551-2122* 🛏 *114 rooms, 32 chalets* ⊘ *Breakfast.*

$
HOTEL
FAMILY

🏠**Grande Hotel de Ouro Preto.** Designed by the famous architect Oscar Niemeyer and Ouro Preto's premier modernist structure, the Grande is, as its name suggests, one of the city's largest hotels by overall size. **Pros:** central location; historic building; good restaurant. **Cons:** steep hill from street level to hotel; late-night music from neighboring restaurants can be heard in some rooms; Wi-Fi access is spotty; service can be poor. $ *Rooms from: R$230* ✉ *Rua Senador Rocha Lagoa 162, Centro, Ouro Preto* ☎ *031/3551-1488* ⊕ *www.grandehotelouropreto.com.br* 🛏 *35 rooms* ⊘ *Breakfast.*

$$$
HOTEL
Fodor's Choice
★

🏠**Hotel Solar do Rosário.** In a beautiful 19th-century building, this hotel feels like a bed-and-breakfast, with elegant yet comfortable decor, quiet floors, and well-appointed guest rooms. **Pros:** comfortable rooms; excellent mineiran breakfast. **Cons:** service can be slow and isn't always friendly. $ *Rooms from: R$450* ✉ *Rua Getúlio Vargas 270, Rosário, Ouro Preto* ☎ *031/3551-5200* ⊕ *www.hotelsolardorosario.com.br* 🛏 *41 rooms* ⊘ *Breakfast.*

$
B&B/INN

🏠**Luxor Ouro Preto Pousada.** With dark wooden floors, antique furnishings, and stone walls dating back two centuries, this friendly hotel has the feeling of a rustic 19th-century lodge. **Pros:** comfortable beds; good service; rooms have incredible city views. **Cons:** potentially romantic restaurant often packed with hotel guests. $ *Rooms from: R$190*

✉ *Rua Dr. Alfredo Baeta 16, Antônio Dias, Ouro Preto* ☎ *031/3551–2244* 🌐 *hotelluxor.com.br/pt* 🛏 *19 rooms* 🍴 *Breakfast.*

$$ HOTEL 🏨 **Pousada Clássica.** Near the main churches and museums and the prime shopping area, this pousada occupies an elegant house. **Pros:** spectacular city view from balconies; stylish reception area and breakfast room. **Cons:** boring room decor and furniture; noise from Rua Direita's bars. [$] *Rooms from: R$360* ✉ *Rua Conde de Bobadela 96, Centro, Ouro Preto* ☎ *031/3551–3663* 🌐 *www.pousadaclassica.com.br* 🛏 *25 rooms, 2 suites* 🍴 *Breakfast.*

$$$ HOTEL Fodor's Choice ★ 🏨 **Pousada do Mondego.** This intimate hotel in a 1747 merchant's mansion has period furnishings, gorgeous veranda and dining room (where an exceptional mineiran breakfast is served), and one-hour city tours given in a 1930s minibus. **Pros:** good mix of modern amenities (marble bathrooms, TVs) and 18th-century charm. **Cons:** guests may hear late-night noise in the holiday season. [$] *Rooms from: R$420* ✉ *Largo de Coimbra 38, Centro, Ouro Preto* ☎ *031/3551–2040* 🌐 *www.roteirosdecharme.com.br/pousadamondego* 🛏 *24 rooms* 🍴 *Breakfast.*

$$ HOTEL FAMILY 🏨 **Pousada Minas Gerais.** The wonderful Pousada Minas Gerais occupies a new building that replicates Ouro Preto's colonial exteriors. **Pros:** family-friendly; good business facilities; off-street parking area. **Cons:** no leisure area or swimming pool. [$] *Rooms from: R$290* ✉ *Rua Xavier da Veiga 303, Centro, Ouro Preto* ☎ *031/3551–5506* 🌐 *www.pousadaminasgerais.com.br* 🛏 *18 rooms* 🍴 *Breakfast.*

$ B&B/INN 🏨 **Pouso Café com Arte.** The hospitality at this family-run bed-and-breakfast will make you feel as if you're visiting a friend's house. **Pros:** traditional mineiran decor; great breakfast; central location. **Cons:** few amenities; no room service. [$] *Rooms from: R$200* ✉ *Rua das Mercês 45, Centro, Ouro Preto* ☎ *031/3552–2671* 💳 *No credit cards* 🛏 *5 rooms* 🍴 *Breakfast.*

SHOPPING

HANDICRAFTS

There are numerous handicrafts stores on Praça Tiradentes and its surrounding streets.

Fodor's Choice ★ **Cerâmica Saramenha.** The technique used in the pottery and sculptures at Cerâmica Saramenha has its roots in Portugal. The items were created as a local alternative to the imported goods from Europe in the colonial era. Many local villagers sell plates, pots, pans, and beautiful decorative items in the Saramenha style at the shop in the outskirts of Ouro Preto. ✉ *Rodovia dos Inconfidentes, Km 87, Ouro Preto* ✥ *8 km (5 miles) from Ouro Preto toward Ouro Branco* ☎ *031/99675–0701.*

Fodor's Choice ★ **Gomides.** This shop in the Barra neighborhood carries unique sculptures and opens by appointment only, generally in the evenings. ✉ *Beco da Mãe Chica 37, Barra, Ouro Preto* ☎ *031/3551–4571.*

Maria das Coisas. This shop sells crafts made in Ouro Preto, cosmetics of traditional Brazilian perfumeries, and fine objects and clothes. ✉ *Rua Getúlio Vargas 281, Rosário, Ouro Preto* ☎ *031/3552–2262* ⏲ *Closed Sun.*

Fodor's Choice ★ **Mercado de Pedra Sabão** (*Soapstone Market*). At the daily handicrafts fair in front of the Igreja de São Francisco de Assis, vendors sell various

7

decorative objects carved in soapstone. Paintings and wood carvings can also be found here. ⊠ *Largo de Coimbra s/n, Centro, Ouro Preto.*

Pérola Ouro Preto. Pérola is a cosmetics company run by Fundação Sorria, an NGO that provides dental treatment to children and teenagers of disadvantaged backgrounds. This stall inside Cine Vila Rica sells locally made soaps, shampoos, lotions, and cosmetics. ⊠ *Praça Reinaldo Alves de Brito 47, Centro, Ouro Preto* ☎ *031/8677–2518.*

JEWELRY

Ouro Preto has a reputation for the best selection and prices in Brazil, but keep in mind that gems vary widely in quality and value. Don't buy them on the streets, and be wary about buying them from smaller shops. Gemstones can be fakes—glass colored to look like gemstones—and if real they're apt to be overpriced. Do your research, and get references for a jeweler before you buy. When buying gemstones, check whether the store is affiliated with the Associação de Joalheiros de Ouro Preto, the local jewelers association, which issues a certificate of authenticity for the items.

Imperial Gemas Brasil. Here you can visit a stone-cutting and -setting workshop. Various types of topaz can be found here, as well as green tourmaline and amethyst. You can choose from the available jewelry sets or ask the store to make items to your specifications. ⊠ *Rua Amélia Bernhaus 11, Ouro Preto* ☎ *031/8596–2142.*

Fodor's Choice **Ita Gemas.** This is one of the best gem shops in town, especially for the ★ rare imperial topaz. ⊠ *Rua Conde de Bobadela 40, Centro, Ouro Preto* ☎ *031/3551–4895.*

SIDE TRIP TO MARIANA

11 km (7 miles) east of Ouro Preto, 110 km (68 miles) southeast of Belo Horizonte.

The oldest city in Minas Gerais (founded in 1696) is also the birthplace of Aleijadinho's favorite painter, Manuel da Costa Ataíde. Its three principal churches showcase examples of the art of Ataíde, who intertwined sensual romanticism with religious themes. The faces of his saints and other figures often have mulatto features, reflecting the composition of the area's population at the time. Today Mariana is most visited for the weekly organ concerts at its cathedral.

GETTING HERE AND AROUND

The most enjoyable way to get to Mariana is by train. From Friday to Sunday, vintage trains leave from Ouro Preto train station. Make sure to sit on the right-hand side to get the best views, including one (halfway to Mariana) of a waterfall. One train departs from Ouro Preto in the morning and another in the afternoon, and two trains return from Mariana in the afternoon. The cost for the 30-minute ride is R$40 each way or R$60 for a panoramic carriage. If you are going by train, it is worth buying a one-way ticket and then heading back by bus or taxi so that you don't have to wait for the returning train. Credit cards are accepted at the ticket office, and tickets can be purchased with cash on board. (The credit-card system here has been known to fail, so it's advisable to have sufficient cash just in case.) Buses from Ouro Preto to Mariana depart every 30 minutes (R$3; 30 minutes). If you're driving, take BR 040 south and BR 356 (it becomes MG 262) east to Ouro Preto and continue 11 km (7 miles) to Mariana (30 minutes).

EN ROUTE

Mina de Ouro de Passagem. Between Ouro Preto and Mariana lies Brazil's oldest gold mine. During the gold rush thousands of slaves perished at Mina de Ouro de Passagem because of its dangerous, backbreaking conditions. Although the mine is no longer in operation, you can ride an old mining car through 11 km (7 miles) of tunnels and see exposed quartz, graphite, and black tourmaline. Buses travel here from Ouro Preto (catch them beside the Escola de Minas) and cost about R$3.50; a taxi ride costs about R$40. ✉ *Road to Mariana, 4 km (3 miles) east of Ouro Preto, Mariana* ☎ *031/3557–5001* ⊕ *www.minasdapassagem. com.br* ✑ *R$30* ◷ *Mon. and Tues. 9–5, Wed.–Sun. 9–5:30.*

EXPLORING

Catedral Basílica da Sé. The cathedral, completed in 1760, is best known for its 1701 German organ, built by Arp Schnitger. Transported by mule from Rio de Janeiro in 1720, the instrument was a gift from the Portuguese court to the first diocese in Brazil. This is the only Schnitger organ outside Europe, and one of the best preserved in the world. Concerts take place on Friday at 11 am and Sunday at 12:15 pm. To get a place near the organ, try to arrive at least 30 minutes early.

✉ *Praça Cláudio Manoel s/n, Mariana* ☎ *031/3557–1216* ✑ *R$3 donation, R$30 concerts* ◷ *Tues.–Sat. 8–noon and 2–6:30, Sun. 8–noon and 3–6:30.*

Fodor's Choice
★

Igreja da Nossa Senhora do Carmo (*Our Lady of Carmel Church*). With works by noted artists Ataíde and Aleijadinho, Our Lady of Carmel Church is noteworthy for its impressive facade and sculpted soapstone designs. Ataíde is buried at the rear of the church, built in the late 1700s. A fire in 1999 during renovation nearly destroyed the site, sparing only the rococo-style altar. ✉ *Praça Minas Gerais, Mariana* ☎ *031/3558– 1979* ✑ *R$2* ◷ *Tues.–Sun. 9–noon and 1–4.*

Museu Arquidiocesano de Arte Sacra de Mariana (*Archdiocesan Museum of Sacred Art*). Wood and soapstone carvings by Aleijadinho and paintings by Ataíde are among the noteworthy items on exhibit at the Archdiocesan Museum of Sacred Art, also known as the Aleijadinho Museum. Located behind the Catedral Basílica da Sé in a well-composed rococo structure, the museum claims to have the state's largest collection of baroque painting and sculpture. ✉ *Rua Frei Durão 49, Mariana* ☎ *031/3557–2581* ✑ *R$5* ◷ *Tues.–Sun. 8:30–noon and 1:30–5.*

EN ROUTE

Santuário de Bom Jesus do Matosinho. Dominating the small Gold Town of Congonhas do Campo is the crowning effort of renowned sculptor Aleijadinho: the hilltop pilgrimage church Basílica Bom Jesus do Matosinho. Built in 1757, it's the focus of great processions during Holy Week. At the churchyard entrance are Aleijadinho's 12 life-size Old Testament prophets carved in soapstone, one of the greatest works of art from the baroque period. The prophets appear caught in movement,

7

and every facial expression is unforgettable. Leading up to the church on the sloping hillside are six chapels, each containing a scene of the stations of the cross. The 66 figures in this remarkable procession were carved in cedar by Aleijadinho and painted by Manuel da Costa Ataíde and Francisco Xavier Carneiro.

Congonhas is about 50 km (31 miles) west of Mariana; take BR 356 to MG 440 to MG 030, then go north on BR 040. This is also a fairly easy trip by bus or car from Belo Horizonte (94 km/58 miles) or Tiradentes (130 km/81 miles). ⊠ *Praça da Basílica 180, Congonhas do Campo* ☎ *031/3731–1591* ⊕ *www.santuariodematosinhos. com.br* ⌨ *Free* ☉ *Tues.–Sun. 8–6.*

SMOKING MARY

Maria Fumaça (Smoking Mary), a little red steam train in operation since the 19th century, is a fun way to get from Tiradentes to São João del Rei. The 13-km (8-mile) ride goes up the valley and through the oldest mining area in the state in 35 minutes (round-trip R$56, one-way R$40; twice daily from Friday to Sunday and on holidays). The train leaves from Tiradentes's Estação Ferroviária (Praça da Estação); tickets do not need to be bought in advance. The train leaves Tiradentes at 11 and 2 and returns from São João del Rei at 3.

TIRADENTES

210 km (130 miles) southwest of Belo Horizonte.

Probably the best historic city to visit after Ouro Preto and Diamantina, Tiradentes was the birthplace of a martyr who gave the city its name (it was formerly called São José del Rei) and retains much of its 18th-century charm. Life in this small town—nine streets with eight churches set against the backdrop of the Serra de São José—moves slowly. About two-dozen shops selling excellent handicrafts line Rua Direita in the town center. At the tourist office Secretaria de Turismo de Tiradentes, you can learn about horseback and hiking trips in the area.

GETTING HERE AND AROUND

From Belo Horizonte there are six buses every day. You must first travel to São João del Rei on the Viação Sandra bus line (R$35; 3½ hours), then to Tiradentes on a Vale do Ouro bus. From São João del Rei, buses run every 1½ hours, and the trip costs about R$3.

To reach Tiradentes from Belo by car, take BR 040 south (Congonhas do Campo, with its Igreja Bom Jesus do Matosinho, is on this route) and then BR 265 west. The drive takes approximately 3½ hours.

ESSENTIALS

Bus Contacts Rodoviária (Terminal Turístico). ⊠ *Praça Silva Jardim, near Igreja São Francisco de Paula, Tiradentes* ☎ *032/3355–1100.* **Viação Vale do Ouro.** ☎ *032/3371–5119, 031/3557–9200.* **Viação Sandra.** ☎ *031/3201–2927.*

Visitor and Tour Information Secretaria de Turismo de Tiradentes. ⊠ *Rua Resende Costa 71, Tiradentes* ☎ *032/3355–1212.*

CLOSE UP

Brazilian Baroque

When gold was discovered in Minas Gerais in the 17th century, the Portuguese, to ensure their control of the mining industry, exiled the traditional religious orders, which led to the formation of third orders. Attempts by these lay brothers to build churches based on European models resulted in improvisations (they had little experience with or guidance on such matters) and, hence, a uniquely Brazilian style of baroque that extended into the early 19th century. Many churches from this period have simple exteriors that belie interiors whose gold-leaf-encrusted carvings are so intricate they seem like filigree.

As the gold supply diminished, facades became more elaborate—with more sophisticated lines, elegant curves, and large round towers—and their interiors less so, as murals were used more than carvings and gold leaf. Many sculptures were carved from wood or soapstone. Today Minas Gerais has the largest concentration of baroque architecture and art of any state in Brazil. You can see several outstanding examples of baroque architecture, many of them attributed to the legendary Aleijadinho, in Ouro Preto (where there are 13 such churches) and the other Gold Towns of Minas: Mariana, Tiradentes, and Congonhas.

EXPLORING

Fodor's Choice ★ **Matriz de Santo Antônio.** A celebration of baroque architecture, the Church of Santo Antônio is the one not to miss in Tiradentes. Built in 1710, it contains well-preserved gilded carvings of saints, cherubs, and biblical scenes. The soapstone frontispiece is attributed to Aleijadinho. Organ concerts take place here on Friday evening; if you can time your visit to attend one, by all means do so. ✉ *Rua Padre Toledo s/n, Tiradentes* ☎ *032/3355–1212* 🎫 *R$5; concerts R$30* 🕒 *Daily 9–5, concerts Fri. 8 pm.*

WHERE TO EAT

$$$ BRAZILIAN Fodor's Choice ★ 🍴 **Estalagem do Sabor.** Patrons of the Estalagem rave about the feijão tropeiro and frango ao molho pardo, just two of the Brazilian dishes prepared by friendly chef Beth, who often makes time to come and greet diners. Although the restaurant is small, the atmosphere is elegant. Light music and an attentive staff make this an appealing place to dine. [$] *Average main: R$50* ✉ *Rua Ministro Gabriel Passos 280, Tiradentes* ☎ *032/3355–1144* 🕒 *No dinner Sun.*

$$$ BRAZILIAN 🍴 **Monastério.** Along with its romantic, candlelit settings and smart decor, Monastério's main draw is its variety of fondues. Order the tasty *fondue mineiro,* a mix of pork, sausages, and beef. Risotto and pasta options are also available, and there's a good selection of local and foreign wines. [$] *Average main: R$50* ✉ *Rua Ministro Gabriel Passos, Tiradentes* ☎ *032/3355–2248* 🕒 *Closed Mon. No lunch* 💳 *No credit cards.*

$$$$ ECLECTIC 🍴 **Tragaluz.** This combined store, coffee shop, and restaurant serves unusual dishes such as jaboticaba ice cream. The gnocchi, Argentine meat, *frango de* Angola (marinated chicken), and chorizo beef are all

worth a try, as is, for dessert, the *goiabada frita* (fried goiaba fruit jam). Reservations are essential on weekends. $ *Average main: R$75* ✉ *Rua Direita 52, Tiradentes* ☎ *032/3355–1424, 032/9968–4837* 🌐 *www.tragaluztiradentes.com* 🕒 *Closed Tues. No lunch.*

$$$ BRAZILIAN FAMILY Fodor's Choice ★ 🍴 **Viradas do Largo.** One of Brazil's best restaurants for comida mineira, the Viradas do Largo (also known as Restaurante da Beth) serves dishes such as chicken with *ora pro nobis* (a Brazilian cabbage) and feijão tropeiro with pork chops. Some of the ingredients, such as the *borecole* (kale), are cultivated in the restaurant's backyard. The portions are generous, enough for three or four people, but you can ask for a half order of any dish. The restaurant is also a market, with typical arts and crafts from Minas Gerais. Reservations are essential on weekends. $ *Average main: R$50* ✉ *Rua do Moinho 11, Tiradentes* ☎ *032/3355–1111, 032/3355–1110* 🌐 *www.viradasdolargo.com.br* 🕒 *Closed Tues.*

WHERE TO STAY

$$ B&B/INN 🏨 **Pousada Três Portas.** Locally made furniture and artworks decorate this pousada inside an adapted colonial house in Tiradentes's historic center. **Pros:** central location; clean, modern rooms. **Cons:** prices jump dramatically on weekends. $ *Rooms from: R$330* ✉ *Rua Direita 280A, Tiradentes* ☎ *032/3355–1444* 🌐 *www.pousadatresportas.com.br* 🛏 *8 rooms, 1 suite* 🍽 *Breakfast.*

$$ B&B/INN 🏨 **Pouso Alforria.** The many return guests to Pouso Alforria appreciate its peaceful location and fabulous view of the São José Mountains. **Pros:** light-filled rooms; modern bathrooms; faultless service. **Cons:** with so few rooms, it's necessary to make reservations well ahead of time. $ *Rooms from: R$330* ✉ *Rua Custódio Gomes 286, Tiradentes* ☎ *032/3355–1536* 🌐 *www.pousoalforria.com.br* 🛏 *8 rooms* 🍽 *Breakfast.*

$$$ HOTEL Fodor's Choice ★ 🏨 **Solar da Ponte.** In every respect—from the stunning antiques to the comfortable beds to the elegant place settings—this inn is a faithful example of regional style. **Pros:** breakfast and afternoon tea are included in the rate; beautiful dining room that overlooks well-tended gardens. **Cons:** two-night minimum stay in high season. $ *Rooms from: R$500* ✉ *Praça das Mercês s/n, Tiradentes* ☎ *032/3355–1255* 🌐 *www.solardaponte.com.br* 🛏 *18 rooms* 🍽 *Breakfast.*

PERFORMING ARTS

Centro Cultural Yves Alves. Cultural life in Tiradentes revolves around this arts center, which hosts theatrical performances, films, concerts, and art exhibitions. ✉ *Rua Direita 168, Tiradentes* ☎ *032/3355–1503.*

Fodor's Choice ★ **Theatro da Villa.** A triple-threat bar, restaurant, and late-night entertainment venue, the Theatro da Villa occupies an 1850 theater in the historic center of Tiradentes. On weekends, musical shows accompany dinner inspired by the slow-food movement. The wine list is excellent, and the service is impeccable. ✉ *Rua Padre Toledo 157, Tiradentes* ☎ *032/3355–1275* 🌐 *www.theatrodavilla.com.br.*

SHOPPING

Artstones. Although not as upscale as the stores in Ouro Preto, Artstones carries imperial topazes, emeralds, quartz, and tourmalines, and has some finished jewelry. ⊠ *Rua Ministro Gabriel Passos 22, Tiradentes* ☎ *032/3355–1730.*

Fodor's Choice **Vitoriano Veloso (Bichinho).** The small, quiet village of Vitoriano Veloso, ★ more commonly known as Bichinho, is recognized in the region for the quality of its arts and crafts and reasonable prices. It's a good option for a day trip. All artisans are based on the same road that cuts through the village. If you want to see artisans at work, head to Oficina de Agosto, the workplace of Toti Bech, an artist who created the craft tradition of Bichinho some 15 years ago. ⊠ *8 km (5 miles) northeast of Tiradentes, Tiradentes* ⊕ *www.bichinho.net.*

MINAS'S PARKS

Less than three hours from Belo Horizonte are some wild, wonderful national parks—worth a day or an overnight trip if you have the time. Though it's not a national park, at the Parque Natural do Caraça you can stay at a lovely monastery and have monks cook for you, while during the day you hike the peaks surrounding it.

The parks only take cash, so be sure to bring enough with you.

PARQUE NATURAL DO CARAÇA

123 km (76 miles) southeast of Belo Horizonte.

GETTING HERE AND AROUND

From Belo Horizonte you can either drive or take a bus to Santa Barbara. Pássaro Verde buses (R$30) serve Santa Barbara (2½ hours) a dozen or so times daily; from there it's a 25-minute taxi ride (R$70) to the park. If you're driving from Belo Horizonte, take BR 262 to Santa Barbara (follow signs for Vitória); at Barão de Cocais, continue on BR 262 toward Santa Barbara for 5 km (3 miles) more, until you see a sign on your right for Caraça. The road here leads about 20 km (12 miles) to the park entrance.

ESSENTIALS

Bus Contact **Viação Pássaro Verde.** ⊠ *Rua Itapetinga 200, Parque Nacional do Caraça* ☎ *031/3073-7000* ⊕ *www.passaroverde.com.br.*

EXPLORING

FAMILY **Parque Natural do Caraça.** Waterfalls, natural pools, and caves—among **Fodor's Choice** them Gruta do Centenário, one of the world's largest quartzite caves— ★ fill this rugged park whose name means "big face," in homage to its main mountain. The park's most famous inhabitant is the *lobo guará*, a beautiful orange wolf threatened by extinction. Historic buildings here include an 18th-century convent and the Igreja de Nossa Senhora Mãe dos Homens (Church of Our Lady, Mother of Men), built at the end of the 19th century. The church's French stained-glass windows, rare organ, baroque altars, and painting of the Last Supper by Ataíde make it well worth a stop. There was once a seminary here as well, but it caught fire in 1968. After the accident, the building was transformed into an inn and small museum.

Guided tours—walking, spelunking, and other activities—can be arranged at the administration office, run by priests, once you arrive. You can hike in the lower elevations on your own, but to visit the tallest peaks, some of which rise to about 6,000 feet, you're required to go with a guide. The park's website has information about guides. ✉ *Parque Nacional do Caraça* ☎ *031/3837–2698* 🌐 *www.santuariodocaraca.com.br* 🎫 *R$5 per person, guided tours extra* 🕓 *Daily 8–5; 7 am–9 pm for inn guests.*

THE LEGEND OF CARAÇA

There are many legends about the founder of what's now the Parque Natural do Caraça, Carlos Mendonça. The most famous is that he belonged to a prominent Jesuit family in 18th-century Portugal, at a time when the royal family was persecuting Jesuits. In 1758 there was an assassination attempt against King D. Jose. When suspicion fell on his family, Carlos Mendonça fled to Brazil and joined the Franciscan Order, using the name Father Lourenço. He later founded the sanctuary of Caraça.

WHERE TO STAY

$ B&B/INN Fodor's Choice ★ 🏨 **Pousada do Caraça.** In an old school that was partially destroyed in a 1968 fire, this hotel and restaurant has rooms that are simply furnished and divided between two floors. **Pros:** delicious food; generous breakfasts; some rooms can accommodate five people. **Cons:** tight meal schedule; hotel often books large groups, so reservations need to be made at least three weeks in advance; no frills. $ *Rooms from: R$180* ✉ *Km 25, Parque Natural do Caraça* ☎ *031/3837–2698* 🌐 *www.santuariodocaraca.com.br* 🛏 *51 rooms* 🍴 *All meals.*

PARQUE NACIONAL DA SERRA DA CANASTRA

320 km (199 miles) southwest of Belo Horizonte.

GETTING HERE AND AROUND

From Belo Horizonte take the MG 050 southwest to Piumhi, then take the road to São Roque de Minas. The entrance to the park is 35 km (21 miles) west of São Roque de Minas (320 km from Belo Horizonte). By bus, take the Gardenia line from Belo to Piumhi—there are six buses daily (R$50; 5 hours)—then take the Transunião bus to São Roque de Minas (1½ hours). Canastra Aventura, an adventure-tour company, leads quad bike tours through the park.

ESSENTIALS

Bus Contact Viação Gardênia. ✉ *Rodoviaria de Piumhi, Parque Nacional da Serra da Canastra* ☎ *037/3371–1310* 🌐 *www.expressogardenia.com.br.*

EXPLORING

Parque Nacional da Serra da Canastra. Serra do Canastra National Park was created to preserve the springs of Rio São Francisco, one of the most important rivers in South America, which cuts through five Brazilian states. Its main attractions are its waterfalls, including the 610-foot

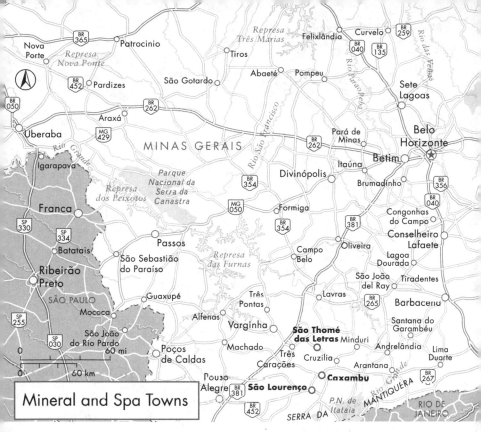

Casca D'Anta. The park is in the city of São Roque de Minas, almost to Minas Gerais's border with São Paulo State. The Brazilian Institute of the Environment (IBAMA) manages the park from its headquarters in São Roque de Minas. ⊠ *Off road to São Roque de Minas, Parque Nacional da Serra da Canastra* ☎ *037/3433–1195 for IBAMA* 🎫 *R$7.50 Brazilians, R$15 foreigners* ☉ *Daily 8–6.*

THE MINERAL SPA TOWNS

Known for the curative properties of their natural springs, a collection of mineral-spa towns in southern Minas Gerais forms the Circuito das Águas (Water Circuit). For more than a century people have flocked to these mystical towns, bathing in the pristine water parks and drinking from the bubbling fountains. Today the towns are especially popular among older, wealthier Brazilians.

■ TIP➔ Despite the purported curative properties of the mineral waters in the spa towns, don't drink too much when you first arrive unless you want to cleanse your system thoroughly.

SÃO LOURENÇO

387 km (240 miles) south of Belo Horizonte.

This most modern of the mineral-spa towns is a good base from which to visit the other Circuito das Águas communities. From here taxis and tour operators happily negotiate a day rate for the circuit, usually around R$50.

GETTING HERE AND AROUND

From Belo Horizonte, there are three buses a day to São Lourenço. The journey takes roughly seven hours and costs about R$100. The bus line is Gardênia. If you're driving, take BR 381 south of Belo Horizonte. You can also take BR 040 south to BR 267 west. For R$80 you can take a taxi from São Lourenço to Caxambu (26 km/16 miles) or São Tomé das Letras R$150 (80 km/50 miles).

ESSENTIALS

Bus Contacts Viação Gardênia. ☎ *0300/313–2020, 031/3495–1010, 035/3423–3272,* ⊕ *www.expressogardenia.com.br.* **Rodoviária-São Lourenço.** ✉ *Rua Manoel Carlos 130, Centro, São Lourenço* ☎ *035/3332–4476.*

EXPLORING

Parque das Águas São Lourenço (*São Lourenço Water Park*). Originally built in 1935, São Lourenço's Water Park includes a picturesque lake with art deco pavilions, fountains, and gorgeous landscaping. The center of activity is its *balneário*, a hydrotherapy spa where you can immerse yourself in bubbling mineral baths and marble surroundings. There are separate bath and sauna facilities for men and women, and you can also get a massage at an extra cost. ✉ *Praça Brasil s/n, São Lourenço* ☎ *035/3332–3066* 🕰 *R$6* ⊙ *Park daily 8–6; Balneário Tues. 8–noon, Wed.–Sat. 8–noon and 2–4:50, Sun. 8:30–noon.*

WHERE TO STAY

$$
RESORT
FAMILY
🏨 **Emboabas Hotel.** This gracious fazenda is more like a private estate than a rural farm. Pros: beautiful farm with nice rooms; occasional performances in the fazenda's theater. Cons: about a half-hour walk from the Parque das Águas. 🟊 *Rooms from: R$350* ✉ *Alameda Jorge Amado 350, Solar dos Lagos, São Lourenço* ☎ *035/3332–4600* ⊕ *www.emboabashotel.com.br* 🛏 *60 rooms* ⦿ *All-inclusive.*

$$
HOTEL
FAMILY
🏨 **Hotel Brasil.** Across from the Parque das Águas, this luxury hotel has its own pools, fountains, and mineral waters, as well as games rooms and tennis courts. Pros: excellent facilities; good prix-fixe regional cuisine. Cons: rooms look dated and lack sophistication and charm. 🟊 *Rooms from: R$265* ✉ *Praça Duque de Caxias, Alameda João Lage 87, São Lourenço* ☎ *035/3332–2000* ⊕ *www.hotelbrasil.com.br* 🛏 *150 rooms* ⦿ *All-inclusive.*

$$
RESORT
FAMILY
🏨 **Hotel Fazenda Vista Alegre.** The many activities at this hotel include boating on the lake, horsback riding, swimming in the thermal and regular pools, and playing tennis. Pros: lots of facilities; good range of rooms. Cons: around 4 km (3 miles) from the town center. 🟊 *Rooms from: R$300* ✉ *Estrada São Lourenço-Soledade, Km 1, São Lourenço* ☎ *035/3331–2920* ⊕ *www.hfvistaalegre.com.br* 🛏 *9 chalets, 35 suites* ⦿ *All meals.*

CAXAMBU

30 km (19 miles) northeast of São Lourenço.

A 19th-century town once frequented by Brazilian royalty, Caxambu remains a favorite getaway for wealthy and retired *cariocas* (residents of Rio). Although most people spend their time here relaxing in bathhouses and drinking curative waters, you can also browse in the markets where local sweets are sold or take a horse-and-buggy ride to a fazenda.

> **TAXI FOR HIRE**
>
> There are plenty of taxis in both Caxambu and São Lourenço waiting to take you around the Circuito das Águas. The taxis line up at the Avenida Getúlio Vargas; for about R$180 drivers will tour the towns of Caxambu, Baependi, Cambuquira, Lambari, and Passa Quatro.

GETTING HERE AND AROUND

Gardênia buses connect Belo Horizonte with Caxambu twice daily (7 hours; R$95). Caxambu is south of BH off BR 381, parts of which are under construction. As an alternative, you can take BR 040 south to BR 267 west. A taxi between São Lourenço and Caxambu runs about R$80.

ESSENTIALS

Bus Contacts **Viação Gardênia.** ☎ *031/3491–3300, 031/3495–1010, 035/3231–3844.* **Rodoviária Caxambu.** ✉ *Praça Cônego José de Castilho Moreira s/n, Caxambu.*

Taxi Contact **Ponto de Táxi.** ☎ *035/3341–1730.*

Visitor and Tour Information **Caxambu Tourist Desk.** ✉ *Rua João Carlos 100, Caxambu* ☎ *035/3341–1298* 🌐 *www.caxambu.mg.gov.br.*

EXPLORING

Cristo Redentor. A chairlift (daily 9–5; R$10) accessed near the bus station heads to the peak of the Cristo Redentor, a smaller version of the Christ the Redeemer statue in Rio. The summit has a small restaurant and an impressive city view. ✉ *Caxambu* ☎ *035/9983–2223.*

Fodor's Choice ★ **Parque das Águas de Caxambu.** Towering trees, shimmering ponds, and fountains containing various minerals—each believed to cure a different ailment—fill the Parque das Águas. Lavish pavilions protect the springs, and the balneário, a beautiful Turkish-style bathhouse, offers saunas and massages. Hundreds of thousands of liters of mineral water are bottled here daily and distributed throughout Brazil. ✉ *Town center, Caxambu* ☎ *035/3341–3266* 🎟 *Park R$5, balneário R$15* 🕒 *Park daily 7–6, balneário Tues.–Sun. 2–5.*

WHERE TO STAY

$$$ RESORT Fodor's Choice ★ 🏨 **Hotel Glória.** Although it's just across from Caxambu's Parque das Águas, this luxury resort has its own rehabilitation pool and sauna as well as numerous sports amenities. **Pros:** gorgeous resort; meals served in an antiques-filled dining room. **Cons:** full-size beds only in luxury rooms. [$] *Rooms from: R$400* ✉ *Av. Camilo Soares 590, Caxambu*

7

☎ *035/3341–9200* ⊕ *www.hotelgloriacaxambu.com.br* ⇗ *145 rooms* ⑩ *All meals.*

SÃO THOMÉ DAS LETRAS

54 km (34 miles) northwest of Caxambu.

With its tales of flying saucers, its eerie stone houses that resemble architecture from outer space, and its 7,500 inhabitants who swear to years of friendship with extraterrestrials, São Thomé das Letras may be one of the oddest towns on Earth. In a stunning mountain setting, it attracts mystics, psychics, and flower children who believe they've been spiritually drawn here to await the founding of a new world. Most visitors make São Thomé a day trip from Caxambu, smartly escaping nightfall's visiting UFOs.

GETTING HERE AND AROUND
To reach São Thomé das Letras by bus from Belo Horizonte (eight buses per day), take the Expresso Gardênia to Três Corações; from there, take the Viação Trectur (five buses daily). The entire journey from Belo Horizonte takes 5½ hours and costs about R$120. São Thomé das Letras can be reached from Belo via BR 381 south or BR 040 south to BR 267 west. A taxi between São Lourenço and São Thomé das Letras costs about R$100.

ESSENTIALS
Bus Contacts Rodoviária. ⊠ *Av. Tomé Mendes Peixoto s/n, São Tomé das Letras* ☎ *035/3237–1530.* **Viação Trectur.** ⊠ *Av. Tomé Mendes Peixoto s/n, São Tomé das Letras* ☎ *035/9901–4889.*

EXPLORING
Caverns and Waterfalls. Just 3 km (2 miles) from São Thomé are a number of caverns, including Carimbado, which is essentially a long and narrow corridor that displays hieroglyphs. There is also the Índio cave, on the road toward Sobradinho, near the Cruzeiro do Cantagalo. Near the caves are the Véu da Noiva and Véu da Eubiose, two powerful waterfalls. ⊠ *São Tomé das Letras.*

Gruta de São Thomé. The Gruta de São Thomé, a small cave that, in addition to its shrine to São Thomé, features some of the mysterious inscriptions for which the town is famous. ⊠ *São Tomé das Letras.*

Igreja Matriz. A center of religious activity and one of the few non-stone buildings in São Thomé, Igreja Matriz is in São Thomé's main square and contains frescoes by Brazilian artist Joaquim José de Natividade, a disciple of the renowned sculptor Aleijadinho. ⊠ *Praca Barao de Alfenas s/n, São Tomé das Letras* ⊕ *Daily 8–5.*

BRASÍLIA AND
THE WEST

Updated
By Mark
Beresford

Once a frontier region that was the preserve of gold explorers and colonial adventurers, the Center-West has been home to the country's political nerve center, the futuristic national capital Brasília, since 1960. This masterpiece of modernist architecture glows in the endless sunshine of the *cerrado*, Brazil's vast savanna region, where wolves and deer still roam among the waterfalls. From Brasília, the cerrado extends hundreds of miles to the west until it meets the waters of the Pantanal, the world's largest wetland and the habitat for an astonishing variety of wildlife, from jaguars to giant otters, from anacondas to toucans.

For many visitors, the Pantanal is the high point of the West, a floodplain the size of Great Britain with ever-present possibilities for spotting wild animals. The cities of Cuiabá and Campo Grande are the gateways to the northern and southern Pantanal respectively. From Campo Grande many visitors also head to swim, snorkel and even scuba dive in the crystal clear rivers around Bonito.

Lúcio Costa, who planned Brasília with architect Oscar Niemeyer, famously said that Brasília's sea is the unending blue sky that stretches all above and around the capital. Here, in Brazil's most affluent and controversial city, modernist structures crawl along the flat landscape and then shoot up in shafts of concrete and glass that capture the sun's rays. Initially the preserve of uprooted bureaucrats, Brasília is now home to a new generation who have grown up in the city and are making it a more lively and interesting place to live and visit.

ORIENTATION AND PLANNING

GETTING ORIENTED

The states that make up the western part of Brazil cover an area larger than Alaska, extending from the heart of the country—where Brasília is located—to the borders of Paraguay and Bolivia. Brasília, Cuiabá, and Campo Grande (the latter two the capitals of Mato Grosso and Mato Grosso do Sul states), form a massive triangle with roughly equal sides of about 700 miles. These large distances through agricultural areas mean that the best way to explore this region is by air.

Brasília. Brasília sits on the flat plateau known as the Planalto Central. The capital is actually part of the *Distrito Federal* (Federal District), a 55,000-square-km (21,000-square-mile) administrative region. Also within this district are the *cidades-satélite* (satellite cities), which

TOP REASONS TO GO

Incredible Architecture: Brasília's remarkable architectural style is unique even among the world's other planned cities.

Eating Out: In Brasília, there are good restaurants for every taste and pocket in the commercial blocks in Asa Sul and Norte. The Italian, *mineiro* (from Minas Gerais State), and *goiana* (from Goiás State) restaurants are some of the country's best.

Amazing Wildlife: The wildlife of the Pantanal, the immense wetlands in the heart of South America, is amazing.

Lovely Parks: The mountains, valleys, and waterfalls of Chapada dos Veadeiros or Chapada dos Guimarães highlands stand out against the plains.

Pantanal Safaris: In the lush Pantanal wetlands it's easy to see birds, monkeys, caimans, capybaras, and the famous piranha. With luck, you might spot elusive jaguars, wild boars, anteaters, and anacondas.

originated as residential areas for Brasília workers but are now communities in their own right.

The Pantanal. Several rivers in the West of Brazil and from neighboring Bolivia and Paraguay run through the sprawling lowlands in the area known as the Pantanal. The region is a vast alluvial plain that covers most of the southwest of the state of Mato Grosso and northwest of Mato Grosso do Sul. The Paraguay River, which runs roughly north–south, is the backbone of the Pantanal, providing the one outlet to the enormous amounts of water that fall during the rainy season. The city of Corumbá, at its southern edge, is about 1,300 km (800 miles) from the Atlantic.

8

PLANNING

WHEN TO GO

In Brasília and much of the West you can count on clear days and comfortable temperatures from March to July (the mean temperature is 22°C/75°F). The rainy season runs from November to February; in August and September the mercury often rises to 38°C (100°F). When congress adjourns (July, January, and February), the city's pulse slows noticeably, and hotel rooms are easier to come by. It's nearly impossible to get a room during major political events. On the other hand, popular holidays such as New Year's and Carnival are much less hectic than in other cities.

The best season to visit the Pantanal depends on what you intend to do. If the plan is to take photos of wildlife, the ideal time is the dry season running from June to October. As the waters dwindle, animals are concentrated in a smaller area, making them easier to spot. For fishing, the best time to visit is from August to October, before the onset of the rainy season, when most fish move upstream to spawn.

CLOSE UP

A Bit of History

The occupation of the Center-West of Brazil did not keep up with the pace of occupation in the other regions. It was not until the discovery of gold in the mid-18th century in the states of Mato Grosso and Goiás that the first prominent urban centers were established in the region: Cuiabá (1727), Vila Boa (1739), and Santíssima Trindade (1752). The roads opened by the first *bandeirantes* (explorers) in the 1820s—probably following the trails of the Indian tribes who lived in the area, the Macro-jê or Tapuias—were used by approximately 6,000 people at the time. The region was an important economic hub 250 years before the construction of Brasília.

Between 1906 and 1910 the government-sponsored Rondon Expedition set out to explore and map an area the size of France. Explorers faced some indigenous Xavantes tribes in the area of the Araguaia River, who attacked to defend their territory. Colonization of the Center-West was intensified in the '50s, with the construction of Brasília and the new integration roads, together with the increase in agricultural practices in the region.

The creation of Brasília began long before its construction in 1956. The idea of moving the capital to the countryside was first voiced in the 18th century, allegedly by the Portuguese Marquis of Pombal. Several sites were proposed, in different central states. A team was commissioned to study the climatic conditions of inland Brazil and demarcate an area for the future capital. The team's final report was submitted in 1894, but it wasn't until 1946 that the plan of moving the capital to the Central Plateau became a reality with the advent of a new Constitution. President Juscelino Kubitschek ordered the construction of Brasília in 1956.

The mystic part of the history of Brasília revolves around Italian priest Dom Bosco and the prophetic dream he had in the 19th century, 75 years before the construction of the city. Dom Bosco dreamed about Brasília being the "promised land, flowing with milk and honey and inconceivable riches" between parallels 15 and 20. Dom Bosco's dream was used as one of the mottos to justify the moving of the capital to the interior of the country.

Brasília was unveiled in 1960. In 1987 UNESCO declared the city a World Heritage Site. Since its founding, Brasília has seen important political and social changes, such as the enactment of the current Brazilian Constitution in 1988 (the first after the military dictatorship stepped down) and rallies against former President Fernando Collor de Mello, the only Brazilian president to be impeached, in 1992.

PLANNING YOUR TIME

For people thinking about visiting the capital, the weekend is the ideal time to come, as premium hotels slash their prices to very reasonable levels and flights can be cheaper. Two or three days is enough time to experience the city's sights and atmosphere. Moving west, whether staying in Cuiabá or Campo Grande, one day should be plenty of time in either city to organize a tour to the Pantanal. Look to spend at least three nights in the Pantanal itself for a real taste of this unique ecosystem. Many travelers combine a visit to the Pantanal from Campo Grande with onward travel to Bolivia and/or a side trip to Bonito.

GETTING HERE AND AROUND

Exploring this region is no small feat and air travel is by far the most practical option. Fortunately, Brasília is well served by airlines and flights are inexpensive, especially if you are flying into the city for the weekend, when politicians leave town for their home states.

Most visitors to the Pantanal arrive at the airports of Cuiabá or Campo Grande, or take the overnight bus from São Paulo to Campo Grande. You can take a bus from Brasília to Cuiabá or Campo Grande, but the journey takes the best part of a day, and you will nearly always be able to fly for the same price, if not less. Having arrived in Cuiabá or Campo Grande, most travelers leave the travel arrangements to their tour operator. To get to the ecotourism destinations of Bonito or Miranda, you will need to take a bus from Campo Grande.

Travelers thinking of exploring the savanna outside Brasília, or visiting the similar landscape of Chapada dos Guimarães north of Cuiabá, should consider renting a car, as the distances are more manageable and buses are infrequent. For the adventurous, it is also possible to hire a car in Cuiabá and drive into the Pantanal along the Transpantaneira road (MT 080) and then back out again, although if it rains you run the risk of being stranded.

RESTAURANTS

As the capital, Brasília attracts citizens from throughout the country as well as dignitaries from around the world. You can find a variety of regional cuisines as well as international fare. Brasília also has plenty of "per kilo" restaurants, usually decently priced cafeteria-like places where you pay according to the weight of your plate. Barring the fish dishes, the food in the Pantanal is neither as interesting nor as flavorful as that found elsewhere in the country. That said, the food is hearty, and the meals are large; affordable all-you-can-eat buffets are everywhere.

HOTELS

Brasília's hotels cater primarily to business executives and government officials. Most hotels, from the upscale resorts to the budget inns, are found in the Hotel Sectors and along Lago Paranoá. For ease in exploring the city, try to stay in Plano Piloto, close to most architectural landmarks, shopping malls, and a number of good restaurants.

West of Brasília, deluxe accommodations are scarcer. In the Pantanal, the *fazendas* (farms) are quite spartan, but there are a few extremely comfortable jungle lodges with nearly everything you could need.

When you book a room, note that a 10% service charge will be added. *Hotel reviews have been shortened. For full information, visit Fodors. com.*

WHAT IT COSTS IN REAIS			
$	**$$**	**$$$**	**$$$$**
Restaurants	under R$31	R$31–R$45	R$46–R$60	over R$60
Hotels	under R$251	R$251–R$375	R$376–R$500	over R$500

Restaurant prices are the average cost of a main course at dinner or, if dinner is not served, at lunch. Hotel prices are the lowest cost of a standard double room in high season, excluding tax.

BRASÍLIA

1,015 km (632 miles) north of São Paulo, 1,200 km (750 miles) northwest of Rio de Janeiro.

The idea of moving Brazil's capital to the interior dates from the early days of the country's independence, but it wasn't until 1955 that the scheme became more than a pipe dream. Many said Brasília couldn't be built; others simply went ahead and did it. The resolute Juscelino Kubitschek made it part of his presidential campaign platform. On taking office, he organized an international contest for the city's master plan. A design submitted by urban planner Lúcio Costa was selected, and he and his contemporaries—including architect Oscar Niemeyer and landscape artist Roberto Burle Marx—went to work. The new capital was built less than five years later, quite literally in the middle of nowhere.

Brasília is a great place for those interested in architecture and in a different city experience from Rio, Salvador, or São Paulo. Everything is divided into sectors (hotels, residences, swimming places, etc.), and the streets were designed without sidewalks—it's said that Brasília is a driver's paradise, but a pedestrian's nightmare. Because of this, Brasília has long been known as "the city without corners."

GETTING HERE AND AROUND

Brasília's international airport, Aeroporto Juscelino Kubitschek (BSB), is one of the busiest in Brazil. To get to the city center, taxis are your only real option. Trips to the hotel sectors along the Eixo Monumental take roughly 15 minutes and cost about R$40. City buses, which cost about R$3, make many stops and don't have space for luggage.

Interstate buses arrive and depart from the Estação Rodoviária. Real makes the 15-hour trip between Brasília and São Paulo. Itapemirim buses run to and from Rio de Janeiro (17 hours). As in most cities in Brazil, the public transportation system is based on commuter buses. Most bus lines depart from Estação Rodoviária, and from there you can go to virtually any part of the city. Rides within the Plano Piloto cost about R$3. Although Brasília does have a subway, it is mainly useful for commuters from suburbs, such as Taguatinga and Samambaia. The regional government has also announced plans to construct a tramway linking the airport with the Eixo Monumental.

The best way to get around is by car—either taxi or rental car. Taxi fares in Brasília are a bit lower than in the rest of the country, and most

The Method to the Madness

Addresses in Brasília's Plano Piloto can make even surveyors scratch their heads. Although the original layout of the city is very logical, it can be hard to get chapter-and-verse addresses, making them seem illogical. Some necessary vocabulary, with abbreviations:

Superquadras (SQ): Supersquares

Setores (S.): Sectors

Quadra (Q.) Block within a Super-square or Sector

Quadra Interna (QI.) Internal block

Bloco (Bl.): A large building within a *superquadra* or *setor*

Lote (Lt.): Lot, subdivision of a block

Conjunto (Cj.): A building subdivision

Loja (Lj.): Part of a larger building.

The Eixo Rodoviário has a line of superquadras made up of two (usually) quadras numbered from 100 to 116, 200 to 216, or 300 to 316 and consisting of six-story blocos. Quadras numbered 400 and above have been added outside the initial plan.

In addresses, compass points are sometimes added: *norte* (north), *sul* (south), *leste* (east), *oeste* (west). So an address might include SQN, meaning "superquadra norte." The *Lago* (Lake) region of the city is divided into the *Lago Sul* and *Lago Norte* districts. The residental areas on the shores of the lake include the *Setores de Habitações Individuais* (SHI) and the *Setores de Mansões* (SM).

Some important neighborhoods are:

Setor Comercial Local (SCL): for commercial areas within the superquadras.

Setor Hoteleiro Norte (SHN): for hotels in the northern part of the city.

Setor Hoteleiro Sul (SHS): for hotels in the southern part of Brasília.

Setor de Diversões Sul (SDS): where the malls are located.

cabs are organized as cooperatives with dispatchers ("radio taxis"). It's best to tackle the Eixo Monumental and then to visit the Praça dos Três Poderes first, and then choose other sights farther away. For this, hire a cab or join an organized tour. Alternatively, combine walking and bus rides with lines 104 and 108, which run by the Eixo Monumental.

ESSENTIALS

Airport Aeroporto Internacional Juscelino Kubitschek (BSB). ⊠ *Aeroporto Internacional de Brasília s/n, Área Especial, Brasília* ☎ *061/3364–9000* ⊕ *www. bsb.aero.*

Bus Contacts Estação Rodoviária. ⊠ *Eixo Monumental, Brasília ✛ at intersection of Asa Norte and Asa Sul* ☎ *061/3327–4631.* **Itapemirim.** ☎ *061/3361– 4505, 0800/723–2121* ⊕ *www.itapemirim.com.br.* **Real Expresso and Rápido Federal.** ☎ *0800/280–7325* ⊕ *www.realexpresso.com.br.* **Rodoviária Interestadual de Brasília.** ⊠ *SMAS, Trecho 4, Cj. 5/6, Asa Sul, Brasília* ☎ *061/3234–2185* ⊕ *www.socicam.com.br/terminais-rodoviarios.php.* **Util.** ☎ *0800/886–1000* ⊕ *www.util.com.br.*

Taxi Contacts Radio Táxi Alvorada. ☎ *061/3321–3030.* **Unitáxi.** ☎ *061/3325–3030* ⊕ *unitaxidf.no.comunidades.net.*

Visitor Information SETUR (*Brasília Tourism Agency*). ⊠ *Eixo Monumental, Centro de Convenções Ulysses Guimarães, Lt. 5, Asa Sul, Brasília* ☎ *061/3214–2744, 061/3429–7600* ⊕ *www.setur.df.gov.br.*

TOURS

Brasília City Tour. Taking in the main sights of the city, these double-decker bus tours in English last 2½ hours with three short stops. They depart from Brasília Shopping three times daily on weekdays, and four times daily on weekends. ⊠ *Brasilia Shopping, side entrance, SCN Q. 05 Bl. A, Asa Sul, Brasília* ☎ *061/9298–9416* ✈ *R$50.*

BSB Tour. This company offers city tours, boat trips on Lago Paranoá, and excursions into the countryside around Brasília. ⊠ *Ed. Garvey Park Hotel, Q. 2, Bl. J, Sala 175, Setor Hoteleiro Norte, Brasília* ☎ *061/3039–2011* ⊕ *www.bsbtour.com.br* ✈ *From R$90.*

e-architect. UK-based e-architect can arrange half-day and full-day architectural tours for groups of up to 20 people. ⊠ *Brasília* ☎ *1620/825722* ⊕ *www.e-architect.co.uk/brazil/brasilia-architecture-tours* ✈ *From $230 per hr.*

SAFETY AND PRECAUTIONS

Brasília, especially the Plano Piloto, is safe. In the residential blocks and their commercial subsectors you can wander in the evening without much concern. One exception is the commercial area around Estação Rodoviária, which can be sketchy at night. Watch out for pickpocketing, counterfeit items, and con artists.

EXPLORING

Shaped like an airplane when seen from above, the Plano Piloto (Pilot Plan) is the name of the original design for the city conceived by Lúcio Costa. The plan had four basic features: well-ventilated housing near green spaces; work spaces that were separate from housing; spaces for cultural activities near residential space; and the separation of vehicle and pedestrian pathways.

The Eixo (pronounced *eye*-shoo) Monumental, the "fuselage" portion of the plan, is lined with government buildings, museums, monuments, banks, hotels, and shops. It runs roughly from the Praça do Cruzeiro to the "cockpit," or the Praça dos Três Poderes. Intersecting the Eixo Monumental to form the Plano Piloto's "wings" is the Eixo Rodoviário. In and around the two main axes are streets and avenues that connect still more residential and commercial areas, parks and gardens, and the Lago Paranoá, formed by a dam built about 16 km (10 miles) southeast of the Plano Piloto. Along the outer shores of this lake, new neighborhoods are sprouting at a fast pace.

EIXO MONUMENTAL

Most of the Plano Piloto's major sights are along or just off the grand 8-km-long (5-mile-long) Eixo Monumental and its multilane boulevards. The distances are quite long, so if you want to explore on your own rather than as part of an organized tour, combine walking with riding the buses or taking taxis.

TOP ATTRACTIONS

Fodor's Choice ★ **Catedral Metropolitana de Nossa Senhora da Aparecida.** The city's cathedral, considered one of Niemeyer's masterpieces, was finished in 1967. From outside, what is visible is a circular structure—a bundle of 16 concrete "fingers" arching skyward. For some, it resembles a crown of thorns. Large panes of stained glass supported by the concrete structure shelter the nave, leaving it awash in natural light. Inside, *Os Anjos* (*The Angels*)—an aluminum sculpture by Brazilian artist Alfredo Ceschiatti—hovers above the altar. The city's first Mass was held at the Praça do Cruzeiro, on May 3, 1957; the *cruz* (cross) used is now here at the cathedral. The building's entrance is guarded by four majestic bronze statues, also by Ceschiatti, *Os Evangelistas* (*The Evangelists*). The outdoor carillon is a gift of the Spanish government. ✉ *Esplanada dos Ministérios s/n, Eixo Monumental, Leste, Zona Cívico-Administrativa, Brasília* ☎ *061/3224–4073* ⌚ *Daily 8–6.*

Memorial JK. This Niemeyer structure is a truncated pyramid and has a function similar to its Egyptian counterpart: it's the final resting place of former president Juscelino Kubitschek, the city's founding father, who died in 1981. The mortuary chamber has a stained-glass roof by local artist Marianne Peretti. JK's office and library from his apartment in Rio have been moved to the memorial's north wing. The bronze statue of JK—his hand raised as if in blessing—surrounded by a half-shell (a trademark of Brasília) looks down upon the Eixo Monumental and makes this one of the capital's most iconic monuments. Permanent and changing exhibits here document the city's construction. The most recent addition is JK's lovingly restored Ford Galaxie. ✉ *Praça do Cruzeiro, at Eixo Monumental Oeste, Zona Cívico-Administrativa, Brasília* ☎ *061/3225–9451* 🌐 *www.memorialjk.com.br* 🎫 *R$10* ⌚ *Tues.–Sun. 9–6.*

Palácio da Justiça. The front and back facades of Niemeyer's Justice Ministry have waterfalls that cascade between its arched columns. Besides the administrative offices, there's a library with more than 80,000 books. On the third floor there's a garden by Burle Marx. The Ministry is closed to visitors, but it's worth a look from the outside. ✉ *Esplanada dos Ministérios, Zona Cívico-Administrativa, Brasília* ☎ *061/3429–3401.*

Fodor's Choice ★ **Palácio do Itamaraty.** For the home of the Foreign Ministry, Niemeyer designed a glass-enclosed rectangular structure with a series of elegant arches on the facade. It's widely considered one of his masterpieces. A reflecting pool augments the sense of spaciousness. The building and the water create a perfect backdrop for the *Meteoro* (*Meteor*), a round, abstract Carrara-marble sculpture by Brazilian-Italian artist Bruno Giorgi. A guided tour shows a collection of art—including paintings by Brazilian artists like Cândido Portinari—and the impressive tropical gardens by Brazilian landscape designer Burle Marx. ✉ *Esplanada dos Ministérios, Zona Cívico-Administrativa, Brasília* ☎ *061/2030–8051* 🌐 *www.itamaraty.gov.br* ⌚ *Daily 9–5* ☞ *Guided tours leave on most hrs, but reserve ahead for tours in English.*

8

Brasília

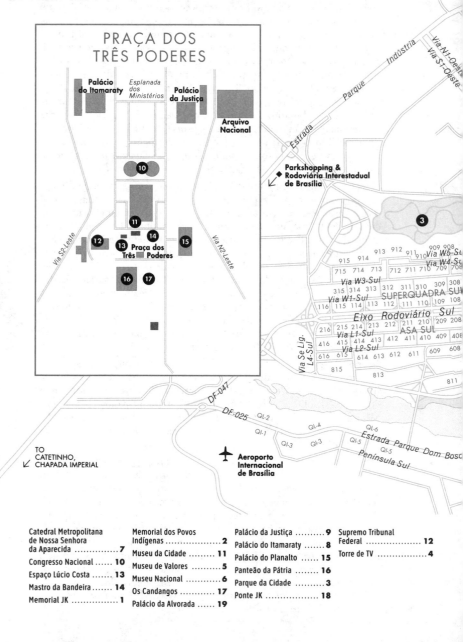

PRAÇA DOS TRÊS PODERES

Palácio do Itamaraty

Esplanada dos Ministérios

Palácio da Justiça

Arquivo Nacional

Parkshopping & Rodoviária Interestadual de Brasília

Praça dos Três Poderes

Via S2-Leste

Via N2-Leste

Via Se Lig. L4-Sul

Parque

Indústria

Via N1-Oeste

Via S1-Oeste

Estrada

Via W6-Su

Via W4-Su

909 908
913 912 911 910
915 914 910 709 708
715 714 713 712 711 710 709 708

Via W3-Sul
315 314 313 312 311 310 309 308
Via W1-Sul SUPERQUADRA SU
116 115 114 113 112 111 110 109 108

Eixo Rodoviário Sul
216 215 214 213 212 211 210 209 208
Via L1-Sul ASA SUL
416 415 414 413 412 411 410 409 40
Via L2-Sul
616 615 614 613 612 611 609 608

815 813 811

DF-047

DF-025 QL-2
QL-1
QI-1 QI-3 QL-4 QL-6
QI-3 QI-3 QI-5 QI-5 *Estrada Parque Dom Bosc*
Península Sul

TO CATETINHO, CHAPADA IMPERIAL

Aeroporto Internacional de Brasília

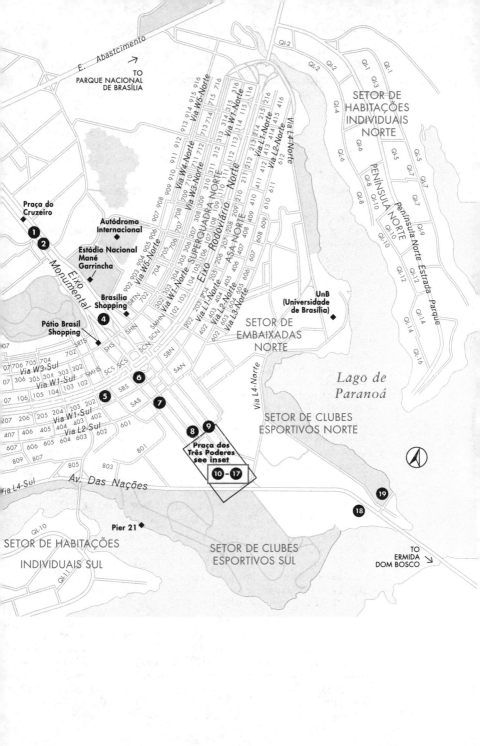

WORTH NOTING

Memorial dos Povos Indígenas. Another Niemeyer project, this cylindrical structure was inspired by the huts built by the Yanomami people. A spiraling ramp leads to a central plaza where collections of indigenous crafts are displayed. Highlights among the main collection include pottery, headdresses, and feather ornaments made by the Kayapó, the Xavante, and other indigenous peoples. The space often houses temporary exhibits from other collections. ⊠ *Palácio do Buriti, Eixo Monumental Oeste, Zona Cívico-Administrativa, Brasília* ☎ *061/3344–1154* ☉ *Tues.–Fri. 9–5, weekends 10–5.*

Museu Nacional. After more than 40 years in the planning stages, the National Museum opened in late 2006, on architect Oscar Niemeyer's 99th birthday. The sweeping, circular design was inspired by the *oca*, the round palm-covered hut of the country's native peoples. The space is mainly used to display frequently changing exhibits, often of works by international artists. ⊠ *Setor Cultural Sul, at Eixo Monumental Leste, Zona Cívico-Administrativa, Brasília* ☎ *061/3225–6410* ☉ *Tues.–Sun. 9–6.*

Fodor's Choice
★ **Museu de Valores.** Located on the second floor of the imposing headquarters of Brazil's central bank, this exhibition explores the often turbulent history of the nation's notes and coins, providing a detailed history of Brazil along the way. Look out for the highest-denomination note ever issued in Brazil. There is also a well designed and informative section devoted to gold and gold mining. On the eighth floor, don't miss the bank's art gallery, home to one of the finest collections of modernist Brazilian art in the country. ⊠ *SBS, Q. 3, Bl. B, Asa Sul, Brasília* ☎ *061/3414–2093* ⊕ *www.bcb.gov.br/?museu* ☉ *Tues.–Fri. 10–6.*

Parque da Cidade. A few blocks from the Instituto Histórico and Geográfico is City Park or Parque da Cidade Dona Sarah Kubitschek, a collaborative effort by Costa, Niemeyer, and Burle Marx. Locals say the park is the largest city park in the world. Bright lights and the reassuring presence of security guards make an evening walk, run, or bike ride along a path more agreeable than ever. There are also playgrounds and fair rides for the young. ⊠ *Entrances at Q. 901 S and Q. 912 S, Asa Sul, Brasília* ☎ *061/3329–0400* ☉ *Daily 5 am–midnight.*

Torre de TV. You'll have a 360-degree view of the city from the Salão Panorâmico (Observation Deck) of this TV tower, which stands over 700-feet high and was designed by Lúcio Costa with the Eiffel Tower as a model. At night the view of the Congress building is spectacular. ⊠ *Eixo Monumental Oeste, Zona Cívico-Administrativa, Brasília* ☎ *061/3325–5735* ☉ *Tues.–Sun. 9–8.*

PRAÇA DOS TRÊS PODERES

The buildings housing the government's three branches symbolically face each other in the Plaza of the Three Powers, the heart of the Brazilian republic. Here both power and architecture have been given balance as well as a view of Brasília and beyond. Indeed, the cityscape combined with the Planalto's endless sky have made the plaza so unusual that Russian cosmonaut Yuri Gagarin once remarked, "I have the impression of landing on a different planet, not on Earth!"

TOP ATTRACTIONS

Congresso Nacional. One of Niemeyer's most daring projects consists of two 28-story office towers for the 500 representatives of the Câmara dos Deputados (House of Representatives) and the 80 members of the Senado (Senate). The convex dome is where the Câmara meets, and the concave bowl-like structure is where the Senado convenes. The main building is connected by tunnels to several *anexos* (annexes) located at the sides of Eixo Monumental. The complex contains

> **WE BUILT THIS CITY**
>
> To build a city in just five years, thousands of laborers were brought here from the country's poor, drought-ridden interior. They often worked in 15-hour shifts, shrouded by red dust in the dry season and sloshing in mud during the rainy season. The nickname *candangos*, once a derisive term, today is proudly used by the workers and their descendants.

works by such Brazilian artists as Di Cavalcanti, Bulcão, and Ceschiatti. A guided tour takes you through major sites within the building. Booking is mandatory on Tuesdays and Wednesdays, and tours in English are available by request. No shorts or sandals allowed. ⊠ *Praça dos Três Poderes, Zona Cívico-Administrativa, Brasília* ☏ *061/3216–1771* ⊕ *www2.congressonacional.leg.br/visite/agendamento-en* ☼ *Daily 9–5*.

Espaço Lúcio Costa. As a tribute to the urban planner who masterminded Brasília, this underground complex was added to the plaza and inaugurated in 1992. It has a 1,500-square-foot display of the city's blueprint, and you can read Costa's original ideas for the project (the text is in Portuguese and English). ⊠ *Praça dos Três Poderes, Zona Cívico-Administrativa, Brasília* ☏ *061/3325–6244* ☼ *Tues.–Sun. 9–6*.

Mastro da Bandeira. This 300-foot steel flagpole supporting a 242-square-foot Brazilian flag is the only element of Praça dos Três Poderes not designed by Niemeyer. In the morning of the first Sunday of the month, members of the armed forces take part in a *troca da bandeira* (flag changing) ceremony, to the sound of the Brazilian Army band. ⊠ *Praça dos Três Poderes, Esplanada dos Ministérios, Zona Cívico-Administrativa, Brasília*.

Os Candangos. This 25-foot-tall bronze sculpture by Giorgi has become the symbol of Brasília. It pays homage to the *candangos*, the workers who built the city from scratch. The statue, depicting two gracefully elongated figures holding poles, is across from the Palácio do Planalto. ⊠ *Praça dos Três Poderes, Esplanada dos Ministérios, Zona Cívico-Administrativa, Brasília*.

Fodor's Choice ★ **Palácio da Alvorada.** Open to the public on Wednesday afternoon, the president's official residence was Niemeyer's first project in the new capital and is located at the edge of Lago Paranoá. Niemeyer used delicate slanting support columns, here clad in white marble. The name of the building translates as Palace of the Dawn, and its design is suitably inspired. Get here by 2 pm to avoid a long wait for a guided tour (Portuguese only). ⊠ *SHTN, Via Presidencial s/n, Zona Cívico-Administrativa, Brasília* ☼ *Wed. 3–5 pm* ☼ *Wed. 3–5:30*.

Palácio do Planalto. Niemeyer gave this highly acclaimed structure, the office of the president, an unusual combination of straight and slanting lines, a variation of the design of Palácio da Alvorada. The access ramp to the main entrance is part of the national political folklore, because it represents the rise to power (presidents go up the ramp when inaugurated). It's only open to the public on Sunday. ✉ *Praça dos Três Poderes, Esplanada dos Ministérios, Zona Cívico-Administrativa, Brasília* ☎ *061/3411–2317* ⊙ *Sun. 9:30–2.*

Panteão da Pátria. Niemeyer designed this building to resemble a dove taking flight. Opened in 1986, the building honors such national heroes as Tancredo Neves, whose untimely death prevented him from being sworn in as Brazil's first democratically elected president after years of military dictatorship. Inside the curved structure are murals and stained-glass panels by Athos Bulcão, Marianne Peretti, and João Camara. One set of panels, *Os Inconfidentes,* depicts the martyrs of the 18th-century republican movement. It's extremely dark inside, so watch your step. An eternal flame burns opposite the memorial. ✉ *Praça dos Três Poderes, Zona Cívico-Administrativa, Brasília* ☎ *061/3325–6244* ⊙ *Tues.–Sun. 9–6.*

> ### THE BRAZILIAN FLAG
>
> The Brazilian flag's green background symbolizes the forests that once spanned much of the country. The yellow diamond represents the gold-mining period that so influenced the nation's history. The blue circle in the center is homage to the great blue skies that dominate the territory; inside it are 27 stars, one for each state and the Federal District. The white band curving across the circle displays the national motto, "Ordem e Progresso" ("Order and Progress").

Supremo Tribunal Federal. The Brazilian Supreme Court building is classic Niemeyer—an otherwise ponderous structure seems lighter than air because of the curving lines of the columns that support the roof. In front of the building is one of the city's best-known monuments, the 10-foot granite statue *Justice,* by Alfredo Ceschiatti. Except on weekends, you have to book ahead for a guided tour. ✉ *Praça dos Três Poderes, Zona Cívico-Administrativa, Brasília* ☎ *061/3217–4066* ⊙ *Weekends 10–3:30.*

WORTH NOTING

Museu da Cidade. Brasília's first museum has a small collection of pictures of the city and writings about it by such luminaries as Pope Pius XII, Kubitschek, and Niemeyer. The statue of Kubitschek on its facade is a 1960 work of Brazilian sculptor José Pedrosa. ✉ *Praça dos Três Poderes, Zona Cívico-Administrativa, Brasília* ☎ *061/3325–5254* ⊙ *Tues.–Sun. 9–6.*

BEYOND THE PLANO PILOTO
TOP ATTRACTIONS

Catetinho. While the new capital was being built, the president's temporary quarters was called the *Catetinho,* meaning a smaller version of the grand Palácio do Catete in Rio. The wooden edifice was built in 10 days during the summer of 1956. A nearby landing strip allowed the

OSCAR NIEMEYER

If you're in Brasília and looking for a monument to Oscar Niemeyer, who died in 2012 at the age of 104, just look around you. The center of the city is a living museum to the legacy of the modernist architect, who has been acclaimed as Brazil's most outstanding figure in any of the arts.

Much of Niemeyer's work molds humble concrete into sweeping lines and graceful, alluring curves, resulting in structures that can appear almost to be visual poems more than just buildings. "What attracts me are free and sensual curves. The curves we find in mountains, in the waves of the sea, in the body of the woman we love," he wrote.

Niemeyer's buildings can be seen all over the world, but Brasília is home to a unique array of celebrated masterpieces, including Congress, the Palácio do Planalto, the Palácio do Itamaraty, and the Cathedral. If you're in the city on a Wednesday afternoon, a visit to the Palácio da Alvorada, the official residence of the president, is a must.

Elsewhere in Brazil, architecture buffs should not miss out on the St. Francis of Assisi church in Belo Horizonte, the Museum of Contemporary Art in Niterói, and the Capanema Palace in Rio.

But it is fitting that Niemeyer's final design, Brasília's striking 560-foot Digital TV tower, is visible on the horizon from all over the city that he shaped.

president to fly in from Rio for his frequent inspections. The recently restored building is a must-see museum for those interested in the city's history. It's surrounded by woods with a small spring where the president and his entourage once bathed. ⊠ *Km 0, BR 040, 16 km (10 miles) southeast of Estação Rodoviária, Brasília* ☎ *061/3338–8803* ⊕ *www. cultura.df.gov.br/nossa-cultura/museus/catetinho* ☉ *Tues.–Sun. 9–5.*

FAMILY **Chapada Imperial.** For a taste of the spectacular landscape of the Planalto Central and the cerrado, drive about an hour northwest along the DF001 and the DF220 until you reach the privately owned Chapada Imperial ranch. Owners Márcio and Marta organize guided tours to a series of stunning waterfalls, on which you'll see an extraordinary range of birds, butterflies, and even deer. ⊠ *Brazlandia, Brasília* ✛ *Drive 9 km (5½ miles) down the DF220 and follow the signs* ☎ *061/9965–2461* ⊕ *chapadaimperial.com.br* ⊠ *R$90 including lunch* ☉ *Weekends only, arrive before 11 am.*

FAMILY **Ermida Dom Bosco.** To view the best sunset in town, head to the Ermida Dom Bosco, in a peaceful setting by the southern shores of Lake Paranoá. There's a small shrine to Dom Bosco, but most people come here to walk, run, swim in the lake, or just watch the sunset with friends. ⊠ *SHIS, Q. 29, Lago Sul, Brasília* ☎ *061/3367–4505* ☉ *Daily 6 am–10 pm.*

Parque Nacional de Brasília. Because of its many springs, locals refer to the 60,000-acre Brasília National Park as Água Mineral (Mineral Water). There are two spring-fed pools where people can cool off, dressing rooms, and picnic areas. Created to protect the water supply of Lago Paranoá, the park also preserves a bit of the region's *cerrado*, or grassy

CLOSE UP

The Making of a Capital

As far back as 1808 Brazilian news-papers ran articles discussing Rio's inadequacies as a capital (Rio became the capital in 1763, following Brazil's first capital, Salvador), the argument being that contact with Pará and other states far from Rio was difficult. Also, Rio was right on the water, and an easy target for enemy invasion. In 1892 Congress authorized an overland expedition to find a central locale where "a city could be constructed next to the headwaters of big rivers" and where "roads could be opened to all seaports." Within three months the expedition leaders had chosen a plateau in the southeastern Goiás region.

But it was not until the mid-1950s that Juscelino Kubitschek made the new capital part of his presiden-tial campaign agenda, which was summarized in the motto "Fifty Years in Five." When he was elected in 1956, he quickly set the wheels in motion. Within a few days the site was selected (in Goiás, as proposed by the 1892 expedition), work committees were set up, and Niemeyer was put in charge of architectural and urban development. The design, called the Plano Piloto (Pilot, or Master, Plan), was the work of Lúcio Costa, chosen from an international contest. The concept was simple and original: "Brasília was conceived by the gesture of those who mark a place on a map: two axes intersecting at a right angle, that is, the sign of a cross mark." The Plano Piloto's most important gardens were to be created by famed land-scape designer Roberto Burle Marx.

Among Costa's objectives were to do away with a central downtown, design highways that were as accident-free as possible, and ensure that the vast horizon would always be visible. Construction officially began in Febru-ary 1957—with 3,000 workers on-site.

Building a modern seat of power for Latin America's largest nation was a monumental undertaking. Before paved roads were built, supplies had to be flown in from the eastern cities. The majority of the workers were immigrants from the Northeast, and unskilled. They learned fast and worked hard, however. Settlements of shacks and tents sprang up around the construction site. The largest, Freetown (now the suburb Nucleo Bandeirante), was home to close to 15,000 workers and their families.

In Rio, opposition to the new capital was heated. Debates in the Senate turned into fistfights. Government employees feared that Rio's business would decline and its real-estate values would drop, and were reluctant to leave Rio's comforts and beaches. Kubitschek's government induced them with 100% salary increases, tax breaks, early retirement options, ridic-ulously low rents, and even discounts on home furnishings.

On April 21, 1960, the city was inau-gurated. The day began with Mass in the uncompleted cathedral and ended with a fireworks display, where the president's name burned in 15-foot-high letters. A new era of pioneering and colonization followed the realiza-tion of Kubitschek's vision of a "nation of the future," looking westward from the coast.

plains interspersed with thickets and woods. An informative trail that runs through mostly flat terrain starts at the visitor center, where you can pick up maps and brochures. ✉ *Rodovia DF 003, Km 8.5, 9 km (6 miles) from Eixo Monumental, Zona Industrial, Brasília* ☎ *061/3233–4553* 🎟 *R$13* 🕐 *Daily 8–4.*

WORTH NOTING

Ponte JK. Opened in late 2002, the third bridge crossing Lake Paranoá is consistent with Brasília's commitment to state-of-the-art architecture and engineering, and has become one of the city's most recognizable landmarks. The award-winning bridge—a project by Alexandre Chan from Rio de Janeiro—is held aloft by three diagonal arcs that crisscross the deck. Its lakeshore location and pleasant promenade attract many people to stroll or bicycle across and enjoy the sunset. ✉ *Via L4, after SCES, south of Eixo Monumental, Asa Sul, Brasília.*

WHERE TO EAT

Brasília enjoys what is generally regarded as one of the best restaurant scenes in Brazil, behind only the much larger cities of São Paulo and Rio de Janeiro. The city has by far the highest per capita income in the country, and in recent years this affluence has been reflected in the rapidly expanding range of dining options. Brasília may be relatively small, but nowhere else in the country can you find such a variety of fine regional and international restaurants and cheerful local bars and eateries all in close proximity to one another.

8

EIXO MONUMENTAL

$ VEGETARIAN 🍴 **A Tribo.** This is one of the city's best options for visiting vegetarians and vegans. Run by South African Natasha Franco, A Tribo operates on a per-weight system, stocked with endless varieties of salads, pulses, and juices. Try the variations on Brazilian themes, such as *acajaré* with a vegan stuffing. There are also fish and chicken dishes, and regular days devoted to Indian cuisine. Get here early for lunch before the buffet runs out—it's popular. [$] *Average main: R$30* ✉ *CLN 105, Bl. B, Lj. 52/59, Asa Norte, Brasília* ☎ *061/ 3039–6430* 🕐 *Closed Mon.* 💳 *No credit cards.*

$ FRENCH Fodor's Choice ★ 🍴 **Café Daniel Briand.** Frenchman Daniel Brand's café has become a Brasília institution since opening in 1995. As well as the croissants and coffee for breakfast, it's the sumptuous cakes and pastries that keep customers coming back for more, year after year, at all times of the day. Try to get a table in the garden. Service can be slow. [$] *Average main: R$30* ✉ *CLN 104, Bl. A, Lj. 26, Asa Norte, Brasília* ☎ *061/3326–1135* 🌐 *www.cafedanielbriand.com* 🕐 *Closed Mon.* 💳 *No credit cards.*

$$$ ECLECTIC 🍴 **Carpe Diem.** If you're a bibliophile or a fan of the arts, you might enjoy the frequent book parties and art exhibits at this restaurant. On weekdays the lunch buffet is very popular with the business crowd. On weekends people flock here for the *feijoada* (meat stew with black beans). Among the regular entrées, the shrimp risotto is one of the most popular. There are five other locations in Brasília, but the original stands out because of its greenery-filled verandas. [$] *Average main:*

R$55 ✉ CLS 104, Bl. D, Lj. 1, Centro, Brasília ☎ 061/3325–5301 🌐 www.carpediem.com.br.

$$ BRAZILIAN 🍴 **Feitiço Mineiro.** Live Brazilian music, from bossa nova to contemporary, is a nightly feature at this restaurant. But the *comida mineira* (food from the state of Minas Gerais) is the best reason to come. One of the most popular dishes is the *costelinha ao Véio Chico* (fried pork ribs with cassava). At lunch, you can help yourself from a large buffet for a set price. The owners run a popular lounge next door, Bar do Feitiço. [$] *Average main: R$37 ✉ CLN 306, Bl. B, Lj. 45 and 51, Asa Norte, Brasília ☎ 061/3272–3032 🌐 feiticomineiro.com.br ⏲ No dinner Sun.*

$$$$ BRAZILIAN STEAKHOUSE Fodor's Choice ★ 🍴 **Fogo de Chão.** One of the most popular fine-dining options in town, this *churrascaria* (steak house) is one of the best of its kind. The sleek ambience of this spacious restaurant adds to the allure. It's famous for its *rodízio* service, in which waiters bring various types of meat on the spit to your table, where they'll carve off as much as you like. The prix-fixe meal includes a large and varied salad bar, but it's the beef that draws the crowds. [$] *Average main: R$116 ✉ SHS Q. 5, Bl. E, Asa Sul, Brasília ☎ 061/3322–4666, 061/3322–4666 🌐 www.fogodechao.com.br.*

$$$ GERMAN 🍴 **Fritz.** This longtime favorite is the place to go for German cuisine. The laid-back atmosphere and no-frills decor draw those looking for authentic food and a great selection of imported beer and wine. Savor the *rollmops* (rolled thinly cut herring fillets) while you wait for your entrée. Good choices include the *Eisbein* (pig's leg with mashed potatoes) or *Ente mit Blaukraut und Apfelpurée* (duck cooked in wine served with red cabbage and applesauce). [$] *Average main: R$60 ✉ CLS, Q. 404, Bl. D, Lj. 35, Asa Sul, Brasília ☎ 061/3223–4622 ⏲ No dinner Sun.*

$$$$ FRENCH 🍴 **La Chaumière.** Since opening in 1966, this small but cozy restaurant has been the mainstay of fine dining *à la française* in the capital, and has numbered Brazilian presidents among its guests. Incredible as it may seem, the friendly owner and chef is a Brazilian who promised the original French owners to keep the original fare and ambience. His resolution still pays off: try the steak au poivre (with a green peppercorn and cream sauce). [$] *Average main: R$110 ✉ SCLS 408, Bl. A, Lj. 13, Asa Sul, Brasília ☎ 061/3242–7599 🌐 www.lachaumiere.com.br ⏲ Closed Mon. No lunch Sat. No dinner Sun.*

$$$$ ECLECTIC 🍴 **Universal Diner.** The kitschy decor is one of the main attractions of this restaurant—bulldog statuettes, miniature porcelain dolls, used vinyl LPs, and other antiques cover the walls and hang from the ceiling. The chef-owner, Mara Alcamim, is always on hand and regularly checks to make sure patrons have enjoyed the food. Favorite dishes include the intriguingly named "sexy shrimp" (they're with a sauce of Brie, champagne, and caviar, accompanied by a strawberry-and-sage risotto). [$] *Average main: R$110 ✉ CLS 210, Bl. B, Lj. 30, Asa Sul, Brasília ☎ 061/3443–2089 ⏲ No lunch Mon. No dinner Sun.*

$$$ ITALIAN 🍴 **Villa Borghese.** The quiet cantina ambience and fantastic cuisine, closely overseen by well-known chef and owner Ana Toscana, make you feel as if you're in Italy. If you're not too concerned about your weight, try the *agnello della nonna* (roasted lamb shank). [$] *Average main: R$60 ✉ SCLS, Q. 201, Bl. A, Lj. 33, Brasília ☎ 61/3226–5650 🌐 www.villaborgheserestaurante.com.br.*

BEYOND THE PLANO PILOTO

$$$$ PIZZA FAMILY 🍴 **Avenida Paulista.** This attractively located pizzeria, situated right by the futuristic Ponte JK on the shores of Paranoá Lake, is a surprisingly good value for such a fashionable spot. Diners can choose from a selection of wood-fired pizzas—try the four-flavor *sinfonia di sapori,* or opt for the buffet of pastas and salads. At lunchtime, take advantage of the set meals with an open salad buffet, reasonably priced by this city's standards. [$] *Average main: R$68* ✉ *SCES Centro de Lazer, Beira Lago, Trecho 2, Lt. 41, Asa Sul, Brasília* ☎ *061/3255–6000* 🌐 *www.restauranteavenidapaulista.com.br* 🕓 *No lunch weekends.*

$$$$ BRAZILIAN FAMILY 🍴 **Mangai.** One of the largest restaurants you may ever eat in, Mangai specializes in cuisine from Brazil's Northeast and has seating for up to 900 people—you still may have to wait for a table. Located near the Ponte JK, Mangai charges R$59.90 for a kilo of food, which you serve up yourself from a vast buffet at the back of the dining hall. Try the *carne de sol com nata* (sun-dried meat in cream) or the tasty shrimp dish *gororoba de camarão.* [$] *Average main: R$120* ✉ *SCE Sul Trecho 2, Cj. 41, Asa Sul, Brasília* ☎ *061/3252–0156* 🌐 *www.mangai.com.br.*

$$$$ MEDITERRANEAN 🍴 **Oliver.** If you're in the vicinity of the Ponte JK or the CCBB cultural center it's well worth dining at Oliver, which specializes in Mediterranean cuisine. It overlooks the golf course, giving it a more open and lighter atmosphere than is usual in the Brasília restaurant scene. Come on weekends for the paella (R$79), or try the signature cod dish Bacalhau Ze do Pipo. Musicians play in the evening. [$] *Average main: R$90* ✉ *Clube de Golfe de Brasília, SCES Trecho 2, Lt. 2, Setor de Clubes Sul, Brasília* ☎ *061/3323–5961* 🌐 *www.restauranteoliver.com.br* 🕓 *No dinner Sun.*

8

WHERE TO STAY

EIXO MONUMENTAL

$$$$ HOTEL 🏨 **Athos Bulcão.** This hotel is a popular choice for visiting business people, politicians, and lobbyists. **Pros:** central location; friendly and efficient staff. **Cons:** underwhelming common areas. [$] *Rooms from: R$570* ✉ *Setor Hoteleiro Norte SHN, Q. 05, Bl. D, Brasília* ☎ *061/3433–3888* 🌐 *www.hplus.com.br/hoteis-athos-bulcao.php* 🛏 *236 rooms* 🍽 *Breakfast.*

$$$ HOTEL 🏨 **Bonaparte Bluepoint.** A sober granite lobby with wood paneling and sophisticated lighting welcomes you to this modern hotel,with spacious, well-appointed suites filled with amenities like plush carpeting, king-size beds, kitchenettes, and oversize bathtubs. **Pros:** perfect for longer stays; stylish furnishings. **Cons:** neighborhood sketchy at night; small common area. [$] *Rooms from: R$493* ✉ *SHS, Q. 02, Bl. J, Asa Sul, Brasília* ☎ *061/2104–6600, 0800/701–9990* 🌐 *www.bonapartehotel.com.br* 🛏 *106 suites* 🍽 *Breakfast.*

$$$$ HOTEL Fodor's Choice ★ 🏨 **Cullinan.** Just off the northern side of the Eixo Monumental, Brasília's latest luxury hotel gives older institutions a run for their money. **Pros:** central location; attentive staff; good pool. **Cons:** lackluster design. [$] *Rooms from: R$670* ✉ *Setor Hoteleiro Norte SHN, Q. 04, Bl. E, Setor Hoteleiro Norte, Brasília* ☎ *061/3433–3888* 🌐 *www.hplus.com.br/hoteis-cullinan.php?lang=en* 🛏 *323 rooms* 🍽 *Breakfast.*

$$$$ HOTEL **Kubitschek Plaza.** Originally owned by descendants of Brasília's founding father, Juscelino Kubistchek, this hotel is decorated with some of his own antiques. **Pros:** attentive, helpful service; top-drawer restaurant; great breakfast. **Cons:** small bathrooms in need of an upgrade; some rooms rather tired looking. [$] *Rooms from: R$816* ✉ *SHN, Q. 02, Bl. E, Asa Norte, Brasília* ☎ *061/3329–3333, 061/3319–3543 reservations* 🌐 *www.kubitschek.com.br* *246 rooms* 🍴 *Breakfast.*

$$$$ HOTEL **Meliá Brasil 21.** This property, with an enviable location on the Eixo Monumental, is adjacent to the Brasil XXI convention center and just steps from the Parque da Cidade, so you often see guests heading out to enjoy the park. **Pros:** near city's main park; attentive staff. **Cons:** neighborhood sketchy at night; can be too busy during conventions. [$] *Rooms from: R$1,569* ✉ *SHS, Q. 6, Cj. A, Bl. D, Asa Sul, Brasília* ☎ *061/3218–4700, 0800/703–3399* 🌐 *www.melia.com/en/hotels/brazil/brasilia/melia-brasil-21/index.html* *237 rooms* 🍴 *Breakfast.*

PRAÇA DOS TRÊS PODERES

$$$$ HOTEL Fodor's Choice ★ **Brasília Palace.** This is your chance to stay in an effortless modernist masterpiece, designed by Oscar Niemeyer, which reopened in 2006 after a top-to-bottom renovation supervised by Niemeyer himself. **Pros:** inspirational, historic building; great oval-shaped swimming pool. **Cons:** a little distance from the City Center. [$] *Rooms from: R$570* ✉ *SHTN, Trecho 01, Lt. 01, Setor Hoteleiro Norte, Brasília* ☎ *061/3306–9000, 061/3306–9000* 🌐 *www.brasiliapalace.com.br* *156 rooms* 🍴 *Breakfast.*

$$$$ HOTEL **Royal Tulip Brasília Alvorada.** President Obama's choice when he came to Brasília in 2011, this swank hotel has a prime location next to the official residence of the president of Brazil, which has made it a firm favorite for visiting politicians and diplomats. **Pros:** quiet location; lovely lake views; postmodern architecture by Ruy Ohtake. **Cons:** hectic during conventions; far from the City Center; impersonal. [$] *Rooms from: R$1,250* ✉ *SHTN Trecho 1, Cj. 1B, Bl. C, Asa Norte, Brasília* ☎ *061/3424–7001, 855/323–2005 For reservations only, in U.S.* 🌐 *www.royaltulipbrasiliaalvorada.com* *395 rooms* 🍴 *Breakfast.*

BEYOND THE PLANO PILOTO

$$ HOTEL **SIA Park Executive Hotel.** If you're looking for a low price and a convenient location near the airport, this hotel is a good option. **Pros:** bargain rates; attentive staff; hearty breakfast. **Cons:** few amenities; far from City Center. [$] *Rooms from: R$339* ✉ *SIA Sul, Q. 2C, Bl. D, Zona Industrial, Brasília* ☎ *061/3403–6655* 🌐 *www.siapark.com.br* *50 rooms* 🍴 *Breakfast.*

NIGHTLIFE AND PERFORMING ARTS

NIGHTLIFE

BARS

Bar Brasília. If you want to experience a typical Brazilian happy hour, go to the traditional Bar Brasília, known for having the best draft beer in town. Traditional appetizers such as *bolinho de bacalhau* (cod cake) round out the offerings. ✉ *506 Sul, Bl. A, Lj. 15, Asa Sul, Brasília* ☎ *061/3443–4323.*

Beirute. An eclectic bar-restaurant with Middle Eastern flair, Beirute has been in business since 1966. During its first decade it drew politicians making deals; today the gay-friendly place attracts a wide range of people. It's known for its ice-cold beer and Lebanese snacks. There's also a branch in the Asa Norte. ⊠ *109 Sul, Bl. A, Lj. 2 e 4, Asa Sul, Brasília* ☎ *061/3244–1717* ⊕ *www.facebook.com/barbeirute.*

Libanus. One of Brasília's less pretentious and more relaxed places for a drink, this bustling bar serves cheap and popular Middle Eastern snacks as well as the all-important ice cold *chopp* (draft beer). ⊠ *206 Sul, Bl. C, Lj. 36, Asa Sul, Brasília* ☎ *061/3244–9795* ⊕ *www.libanus.com.br.*

Loca Como Tu Madre. This cosmopolitan bar and restaurant has become one of the most popular places in town for Brasília's young and alternative set, drawn here by the stylish interior design, international cuisine, imported beers, and DJs who know how to read a crowd. ⊠ *SHC 306, Bl. C, Lj. 36, Asa Sul, Brasília* ☎ *061/3244–5828* ⊕ *www.locacomotumadre.com.br.*

Pinella Bistrô. A popular place for winding down after work, Pinella stocks a large selection of beers. Live music or DJs keep things lively. ⊠ *CLN 408, Bl. B, Lj. 20, Asa Norte, Brasília* ☎ *061/3347–8334* ⊕ *www.pinella.com.br.*

Victrola. A self-styled gastrobar at the heart of an emerging nightlife area in the Asa Norte, Victrola has an outstanding selection of beers for those tired of the average Brazilian offerings. Guests can choose from 4,000 LPs to listen to. ⊠ *CLN 413, Bl. F, Asa Norte, Brasília* ☎ *061/3032–2626.*

NIGHTCLUBS AND LIVE MUSIC

Balaio Café. The action spills into the streets on weekend nights at the city's current hot spot for partying. ⊠ *CLN 201, Bl. B, Lj. 19/31, Brasília* ☎ *061/3327–0732* ⊕ *www.balaiocafe.com.br.*

PERFORMING ARTS

CULTURAL CENTERS

Caixa Cultural Brasília. One of the city's main cultural spaces, Caixa Cultural Brasília puts on exhibitions, concerts, plays, dance, and multimedia events. ⊠ *SBS, Q. 4, Lt. 3/4, Asa Sul, Brasília* ☎ *061/3206–9448* ⊕ *www.caixacultural.com.br* ⊙ *Daily 9–9.*

Fodor'sChoice
★
Centro Cultural Banco do Brasil. Brasília's premier cultural center, aka CCBB, hosts art exhibits, dance shows, and plays. The lunchtime canteen is one of the best dining values in town. There's a regular free bus service to and from the Eixo Monumental. ⊠ *SCES, Trecho 02, Lt. 22, Asa Sul, Brasília* ☎ *061/3108–7600* ⊕ *culturabancodobrasil.com.br/portal/distrito-federal* ⊙ *Wed.–Mon. 9–9.*

MUSIC CENTERS

Clube do Choro. This concert hall in the middle of the Eixo Monumental is where devotees of *chorinho*, a traditional Brazilian music, perform Wednesday to Saturday. ⊠ *SDC, Bl. G, Eixo Monumental, Zona Cívico-Administrativa, Brasília* ☎ *061/3224–0599* ⊕ *www.clubedochoro.com.br.*

SPORTS AND THE OUTDOORS

GOLF

Clube de Golfe de Brasília. At the tip of Eixo Monumental you can play golf on this well-respected course at the Clube de Golfe de Brasília. ⊠ *SCES Trecho 2, Lt. 2, Asa Sul, Brasília* ☎ *061/2191–6500* ⊕ *www. golfebrasilia.com.br* ⬚ *R$150 on weekdays, R$250 on weekends* 🏌 *18 holes, 6788 yards, par 72.*

SOCCER

Estádio Nacional de Brasília Mané Garrincha. This massive stadium seats 70,000 people. It is now used mainly for concerts, other cultural events, and occasional games involving popular Rio-based teams, as Brasília lacks a top-level soccer team. ⊠ *Centro Poliesportivo Ayrton Senna, Centro, Brasília.*

SHOPPING

There are two major shopping districts along the Eixo Monumental: the Setor Comercial Norte (SCN, Northern Commercial Sector) and the Setor Comercial Sul (SCS, Southern Commercial Sector). In addition, almost every *superquadra* has its own commercial district.

EIXO MONUMENTAL
CENTERS AND MALLS

Brasília Shopping. Housed in an odd arch-shape building designed by Ruy Ohtake, Brasília Shopping has several international chain stores as well as movie theaters, restaurants, and snack bars. The mall is close to both hotel sectors and is open until 10 pm daily. ⊠ *SCN, Q. 05, Bl. A, Asa Norte, Brasília* ☎ *061/2109–2122* ⊕ *www.brasiliashopping.com.br.*

Pátio Brasil Shopping. This shopping center often has free concerts and is close to most hotels in SHS. It has a full range of shops and movie theaters. ⊠ *SCS Q. 07, Bl. A, Asa Sul, Brasília* ☎ *061/2107–7400* ⊕ *www. patiobrasil.com.br* ⊗ *Mon.–Sat. 10–10, Sun. noon–8.*

MARKETS

Feira da Torre (*Artisans' Fair*). The foot of the TV tower in the center of the Eixo Monumental is home to a lively art market where you can find semiprecious-stone jewelry, bronze items, wood carvings, wicker crafts, pottery, and dried flowers. ⊠ *Foot of Torre de TV, Eixo Monumental Oeste, Centro, Brasília* ⊕ *www.feiradatorredf.com.br* ⊗ *Tues.–Sun. 8–6.*

BEYOND THE PLANO PILOTO
CENTERS AND MALLS

Iguatemi Shopping. Brasília's newest and most upscale shopping mall, Iguatemi opened in the Lago Norte area in 2010. Posh shops—including branches of Burberry, Gucci, and Louis Vuitton—are open daily, with restaurants open until 10 every night. ⊠ *SHIN CA 4, Lago Norte, Lago Norte, Brasília* ☎ *061/3577–5000* ⊕ *www.iguatemibrasilia.com. br* ⊗ *Mon.–Sat. 10 am–11 pm, Sun. 2–8 pm.*

Parkshopping. Brasília's largest shopping center has more than 300 shops as well as a Burle Marx–designed central garden, the site of many cultural events. Conveniently located by the main bus station. ⊠ *SAI/*

Sudoeste, Área 6580 CCCV, Zona Industrial, Brasília ☎ *061/3362–1300* ⊕ *www.parkshopping.com.br* ۞ *Mon.–Sat. 10–10, Sun. noon–10.*

MARKETS

BSB Mix and Feira da Lua (Moon Fair). These roving retail fairs are good places to find reasonably priced arts and crafts, furniture, jewelry, clothing, homemade food, and much more. The first weekend of the month the Feira da Lua is always in the Gilberto Salomão shopping center. ⊠ *Centro Comercial Gilberto Salomão, Bl. D, Sobreloja 12, Sala 5, Lago Sul, Brasília* ⊕ *luacheiaproducoes.com.br.*

Feira de Antiguidades (*Antiques Fair*). This market takes place in the Gilberto Salomão shopping mall on the last weekend of each month from 10 to 7 and is a good place to buy Brazilian art and antiques. ⊠ *Centro Comercial Gilberto Salomão, Bl. D, Sobreloja 12, Sala 5, Lago Sul, Brasília.*

THE PANTANAL

Fodor'sChoice ★ Smack in the middle of South America, the **Pantanal wetlands** cover a gigantic alluvial plain of the Rio Paraguay and its tributaries. Its area is about 225,000 square km (96,500 square miles), two-thirds of which are in Brazil. Much of the land is still owned by ranching families that have been here for generations. The Portuguese had begun colonizing the area by the late 18th century; today it's home to more than 21 million head of cattle and some 4 million people (most of them living in the capital cities). Yet there's still abundant wildlife in this mosaic of swamp, forest, and savanna. From your base at a *fazenda* (ranch) or lodge—with air-conditioning, swimming pools, and well-cooked meals—you can experience the *pantaneiro* lifestyle, yet another manifestation of the cowboy culture. Folklore has it that pantaneiros can communicate with the Pantanal animals.

It's widely held that the Pantanal is the best place in all of South America to view wildlife. (It's slated to become a UNESCO Biosphere Reserve.) More than 600 species of birds live here during different migratory seasons, including *araras* (hyacinth macaws), fabulous blue-and-yellow birds that can be as long as three feet from head to tail; larger-than-life rheas, which look and walk like aging modern ballerinas; the *tuiuiú*, known as the "lords of the Pantanal" and one of the largest birds known (their wingspan is 5–6 feet), which build an intricate assemblage of nests (*ninhais*) on trees; as well as cormorants, ibis, herons, kingfishers, hawks, falcons, and egrets, to name a few. You're also sure to spot *capivaras* (capybaras; the world's largest rodents—adults are about 60 centimeters/2 feet tall), tapirs, anteaters, marsh and jungle deer, maned wolves, otters, and one of the area's six species of monkeys.

The amphibian family is well represented by *jacarés* (caiman alligators), whose population of 200 per square mile is a large increase from the 1970s, when poaching had left them nearly extinct. (The skin of four animals made just one pair of shoes.) Jacarés are much more tranquil than their North American and African relatives—they don't attack unless threatened. Almost blind and deaf, and lacking a sense of smell,

8

jacarés catch the fish they eat by following vibrations in the water. It's hard to spot jaguars and pumas during the day; a night photographic safari is the best way to try your luck. Native guides (some are actually converted hunters) take you safely to the animals' roaming areas. Sightings are not uncommon in the fazendas that go the extra mile to protect their fauna. Don't let scary tales about *sucuri* (anacondas), which can grow to 30 feet in length, worry you. Sightings of the snakes are extremely rare and instances of them preying on humans are even rarer.

GETTING AROUND THE PANTANAL

The Pantanal is accessible by car and boat, but flights are the most popular—and easiest—way to reach the the gateway cities. The main airports are in Campo Grande (Pantanal South), and Cuiabá (Pantanal North). Cuiabá is also the starting point for trips to Chapada dos Guimarães.

TOURS

When visiting the Pantanal it's essential to have a guide, as you'll be traversing a remote border region. Before you choose a travel agency, ask questions about the planned route, the kind of vehicle that will be used, and the accommodations. Also ask about the guides, especially about their level of experience and their English-language skills. To avoid being overcharged, compare prices at more than one agency.

You can book longer tours—including river trips in luxurious riverboats (locally known as "hotel-boats") equipped with comfortable air-conditioned cabins. There are several kinds of these boat tours. Some are fishing expeditions on the Paraguay River and its tributaries. Others may combine treks into the wetlands by horseback, 4x4 vehicle, or on foot—whatever it takes to get the best animal sightings. The cost is variable, depending on length, type of accommodations, and equipment. Most tours last four to seven days. If you're pressed for time, there are shorter two-day tours.

Fodor's Choice
★ **Ecoverde Tours.** Affable and multilingual Joel Souza pioneered ecological tours of the Pantanal from Cuiabá in the 1980s, and his Ecoverde agency continues to run good-value, high-quality tours into the northern Pantanal. The agency operates out of the simple but friendly Pousada Ecoverde in the City Center. Be sure to bring Joel a T-shirt from your hometown! ⊠ *Rua Pedro Celestino 391, Centro, Cuiabá* ☎ *065/9638–1614, 065/3624–1386,* ⊕ *www.ecoverdetours.com.br* ☜ *From R$550 per day; from R$700 per day for jaguar tours.*

Impacto Turismo. For tours into the south Pantanal, this local agency is a good choice. Established in 1992, Impacto can also organize excursions in Bonito and the Chapada dos Guimarãea, and farther afield to the waterfalls of Foz do Iguaçu. ⊠ *Rua 7 de Setembro 1090, Centro, Campo Grande* ☎ *067/3325–1333* ⊕ *www.impactoturismo.com.br* ☜ *From $R300 per day.*

Pantanal Discovery. A popular choice in Campo Grande, Pantanal Discovery is one of the most experienced tour operators in the southern Pantanal and works regularly with international television companies. Helpful owner Gil and his friendly crew of multilingual guides can arrange transfers and accommodations in Campo Grande and Bonito as well as in the Pantanal itself.

Planning Your Trip to the Pantanal

Nearly all foreign travelers visiting the Pantanal choose to book a tour either from Cuiabá or Campo Grande. Although it is possible to stay in a hotel in the Pantanal itself, a good tour operator will manage all the considerable logistical challenges of coming in and out of the Pantanal, plus your airport transfers. The price of your tour should include full-board accommodations. The only extra you will have to pay for will be drinks. Check that an English-speaking guide will be available before booking any tour.

Tours out of Cuiabá tend to be more expensive than those from Campo Grande. Operators in Cuiabá say they take you deeper into the Pantanal, usually as far as Porto Jofre, where the Transpantaneira road runs out and the jaguars are plentiful. Tours from Campo Grande tend to be of a larger size, and will base you at just one location in the Pantanal, whereas operators in Cuiabá will often put you up at two different sites. Because of the scale of the Pantanal, be prepared for a lot of driving to and from your accommodations, often on dirt tracks.

For travelers planning to enter or leave Brazil via Bolivia, Campo Grande is the obvious choice. Tour operators will organize travel to and from the sweltering border town of Corumbá. They can also arrange trips to and from Bonito.

Your tour operator will pick you up at the airport or bus station and drive you and other guests to the lodge that will be your first or only base. From here, guides will organize walking treks into the savanna, often at sunrise, as well as horse riding, canoeing, boat trips, and piranha fishing, plus night safaris with powerful lights for spotting caiman. Socializing with other guests in the evening is one of the most enjoyable parts of the Pantanal experience. You will need a minimum of three nights to make the most of your trip.

The most popular time to visit the Pantanal is the dry season from April to October, when it is more pleasant to walk through the wilderness, and when jaguars can often be spotted by the water's edge.

You should bring light, preferably cotton, clothes that are quick to dry. Long pants and long-sleeved shirts are a must for keeping off the mosquitos, as are walking shoes, sandals, sunglasses, swimwear, and binoculars. Other essentials include a hat, sunglasses, powerful mosquito repellent, sunscreen, a flashlight, toiletries, batteries, and camera accessories. Malaria is not a problem, but a yellow fever vaccination is recommended.

If you will be in the Pantanal in the rainy season, from November to March, bring a rain jacket and an extra pair of shoes. In the dry season, it can get chilly at night so you will need a sweater and a jacket.

8

⊠ *Nacional Hotel, Dom Aquino 610, Campo Grande* ☎ *067/9163–3518, 067/3383–3518* ⊕ *www.gilspantanaldiscovery.com.br* 🖃 *From R$300 per day.*

Pantanal Nature. Dedicated naturalist and fluent English speaker Ailton Lara is the go-to man for international television companies looking to film in the northern Pantanal, as well as for travelers from around the world. In the dry season, from June to November, the agency runs special jaguar-watching tours. ⊠ *Rua Campo Grande 487, Centro, Cuiabá* ☎ *065/9955–2632, 065/9994–2265* ⊕ *www.pantanalnature.com.br* 🖃 *From US$300 per day; from US$450 per day for jaguar tours.*

Pantanal Viagens e Turismo. This reliable agency has a strong reputation for service. English-speaking sales manager Ronaldo Ribeiro organizes well-reviewed standard and bespoke tours into the southern Pantanal. ⊠ *Rua Joaquim Nabuco 200, shop 9, Campo Grande* ☎ *067/3321–3143* ⊕ *www.pantanalviagens.com.br/english.php* 🖃 *From R$300 per day.*

CUIABÁ

1,130 km (700 miles) west of Brasília, 1,615 km (1,000 miles) northwest of São Paulo.

The northern gateway to the Pantanal wetlands, Cuiabá is also the southernmost gateway to the cerrado and the Amazon beyond. While you're waiting for a tour into the wetlands you can take a jaunt to Chapada dos Guimarães, a mountain range with impressive gorges, waterfalls, and vistas. The capital of Mato Grosso, Cuiabá is well known for being one of the hottest cities in Brazil: mean annual temperature is a sizzling 27°C (81°F). Daily highs surpass 45°C (113°F) several times during the year. The city name comes from the Bororo native people, who lived in the area—it means "place where we fish with spears." It was originally settled in the 18th century, when gold was found in the nearby rivers.

GETTING HERE AND AROUND

Cuiabá is best reached by air from São Paulo, Rio, or Brasília. Cuiabá's Aeroporto Marechal Rondon is about 10 km (6 miles) from downtown. Taxis from the airport cost R$50. Still under construction, a much delayed high-tech tramway will one day link downtown to the airport.

Andorinha buses travel to Cuiabá from Campo Grande (12 hours; R$121). Expresso Rubi buses make the trip from Chapada dos Guimarães (1½ hours; R$14).

ESSENTIALS

Airport Aeroporto Marechal Rondon (*CGB*). ⊠ *Av. João Ponce de Arruda s/n, Cuiabá* ☎ *065/3614–2500.*

Bus Contacts Andorinha. ⊠ *Cuiabá* ☎ *065/3621–3422* ⊕ *www.andorinha.com.* **Expresso Rubi.** ☎ *065/3301–1280.* **Rodoviária de Cuiabá.** ⊠ *Rua Jules Rimet 10, Cuiabá* ☎ *065/3621–3629.*

Taxi Contacts Rádio Táxi Cuiabana. ☎ *065/3322–6664.*

Visitor and Information Centro de Atendimento ao Turista. ⊠ *Praça Rachid Jaudy, Cuiabá* ☎ *065/3617–1225.*

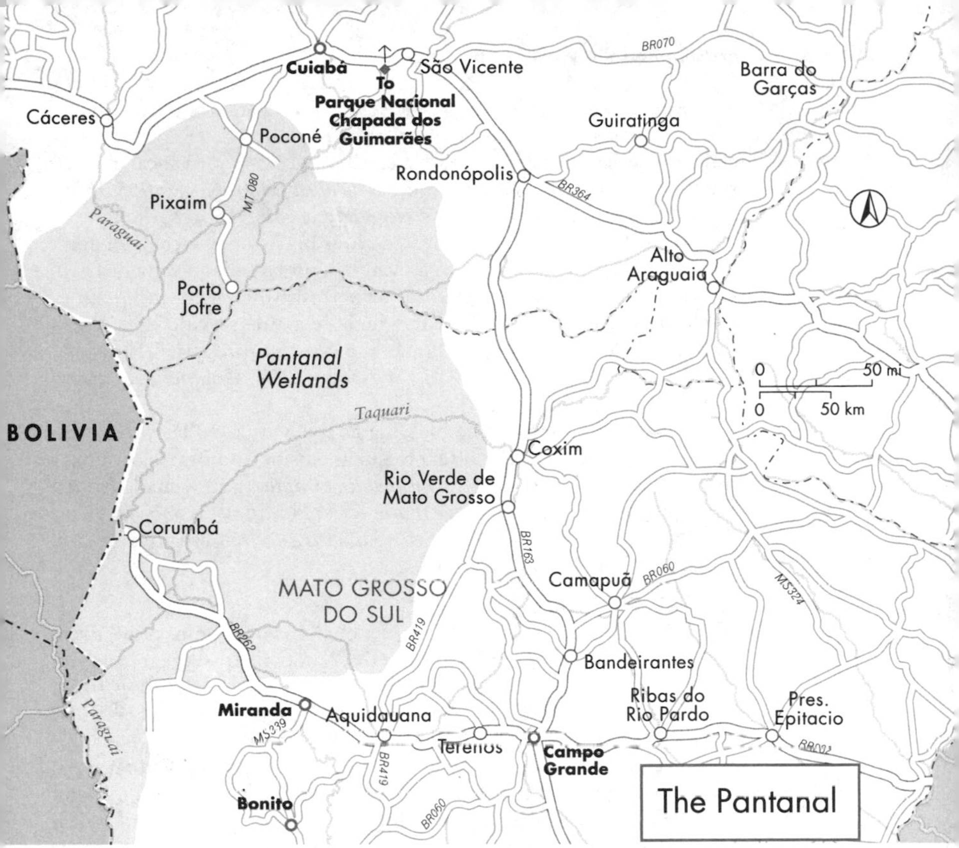

The Pantanal

EXPLORING

Museu do Morro da Caixa d'Agua Velha. One of Cuiabá's most unusual sights, the town's former waterworks is home to a series of permanent and temporary exhibitions about historic and contemporary Cuiabá. ✉ *R. Nossa Senora. de Santana, 1-105, Cuiabá* ☎ *065/3617–1225* 🕑 *Weekdays 8–5:30, weekends 9–5.*

Museu do Rio Cuiabá. On the west bank of Cuiabá River, this museum has maps and models of the river and photos of its history. Information is in Portuguese only. The building, constructed in 1899, was once the public fish market. The **Aquário Municipal** (Municipal Aquarium), with typical fish of the Pantanal, is part of the complex. Some time in 2015 the site will close for a much-needed redesign. ✉ *Av. Beira Rio s/n, Cuiabá* ☎ *065/3617–0928, 065/3617–0929* 🕑 *Tues.–Sun. 8–5.*

WHERE TO EAT

$$$$ STEAKHOUSE 🍴 **Boi Grill.** If you've had your fill of fish, try this churrascaria for as many beef dishes as you can handle. The restaurant uses the all-you-can-eat rodízio system. Two of the most popular cuts are *picanha* (rump) and *costela* (ribs). Another recommended dish is *paleta de cordeiro* (lamb's rib). [$] *Average main: R$70* ✉ *Av. Miguel Sutil 6741, Cuiabá* ☎ *065/3621–4642, 065/3624–9992.*

$ **✕ Choppão.** A Cuiabá institution since 1974, this open-air eatery is always
BRAZILIAN packed and is the best place in town to go for ice-cold beer and local specialties. This is the place to sample *escaldado cuiabano*, a local chicken
soup. $ *Average main: R$20 ⊠ Praça 8 de abril s/n, Cuiabá ☎ 065/3623–
9101 ⊕ www.choppao.com.br ▭ No credit cards ⊙ Closed Tues.*

$$$$ **✕ Peixaria Popular.** This is an unpretentious place to try local fish; don't
SEAFOOD miss the delicious *piraputanga*, a local fish prepared in a stew or fried.
Other options are the *pintado* (a large freshwater fish) and *pacu* (a
small piranha-like fish). All orders include a side serving of *pirão* (a
thick fish gravy with cassava flour) and *banana frita* (fried bananas).
$ *Average main: R$72 ⊠ Av. São Sebastião 2324, Goiabeiras, Cuiabá
☎⊙ No dinner weekends.*

$$$ **✕ Regionalíssimo.** In the same building as the Museu do Rio, this ever-
BRAZILIAN popular self-service eatery offers regional cuisine and Brazilian staples
such as rice and beans. Try the *mojica de pintado*, a stew made from a
local freshwater fish. $ *Average main: R$49 ⊠ Museu do Rio, Av. Beira
Rio s/n, Cuiabá ☎ 065/3623–6881 ⊕ www.restauranteregionalissimo.
com.br ⊙ Closed Mon. No dinner.*

WHERE TO STAY

$$ **☷ Deville.** This hotel has a lot to offer, including large rooms attractively
HOTEL decorated with pictures of birds from the Pantanal. **Pros:** great location;
big breakfast; a new spa. **Cons:** understaffed at times. $ *Rooms from:
R$362 ⊠ Av. Isaac Povoas 1000, Centro, Cuiabá ☎ 065/3319–3000
⊕ www.deville.com.br ⮑ 174 rooms ⦿ Breakfast.*

$$$ **☷ Gran Odara.** Bringing a new level of luxury to the Cuiabá hotel scene
HOTEL since opening in 2011, the Gran Odara is the city's standout top-end
Fodor'sChoice establishment. **Pros:** friendly, multilingual staff; comfortable and stylish
★ rooms. **Cons:** location is not ideal; lobby can get crowded. $ *Rooms
from: R$378 ⊠ Av. Miguel Sutil 8344, Cuiabá ☎ 065/3616–2014
⊕ www.hotelgranodara.com.br ⮑ 136 rooms, 5 suites ⦿ Breakfast.*

$$$$ **☷ InterCity.** This is one of Cuiabá's most popular hotels for both business
HOTEL travelers and tourists, mainly because of its location near the City Center
next to a cluster of restaurants. **Pros:** central location; use of the excel-
lent gym next door. **Cons:** small bathrooms. $ *Rooms from: R$850
⊠ Rua Presidente Arthur Bernardes 64, Centro, Cuiabá ☎ 065/3025–
9900 ⊕ www.intercityhoteis.com.br ⮑ 170 rooms ⦿ Breakfast.*

SHOPPING

Casa do Artesão. Head here for wicker, cotton, and ceramic crafts from
local artists. There's also a small museum in the basement. ⊠ *Rua 13
de Junho 315, Centro Norte, Cuiabá ☎ 065/3611–0500.*

PARQUE NACIONAL CHAPADA DOS GUIMARÃES

74 km (40 miles) north of Cuiabá

The Chapada dos Guimarães is one of the best places to get a taste of the
unique landscape of the cerrado, the endless Brazilian savanna which
covers around a quarter of the country. While much of the cerrado is far
from major cities, this national park is only a short drive from Cuiabá
and a world away from the wetlands of the Pantanal. It is a mainly dry
and rocky terrain dotted with caves, waterfalls, and rock pools and is

perfect for hiking. If you need to wait in Cuiabá for more people to join your tour to the Pantanal or for a flight out, a day or two in the Chapada will be by far the most rewarding way to spend your time.

GETTING HERE AND AROUND

The gateway to the national park is the pretty country town of the same name, Chapada dos Guimarães. Travelers can take the bus from Cuiabá and organize hikes here into the park with a local agency. Alternatively, travel agencies and hotels in Cuiabá can arrange a tour.

ESSENTIALS

Bus Contacts Andorinha. ✉ *Cuiabá* ☎ *065/3621-3422* ⊕ *www.andorinha. com.*

HEALTH CONCERNS IN THE PANTANAL

Malaria is quite rare in tourist areas, but yellow fever has been of greater concern in recent years. If you're traveling to the Pantanal, ask your doctor about getting an inoculation before you leave on your trip. Dengue fever, for which there is no vaccination available, is a worry from November to March. The best way to prevent it is to avoid being bitten by mosquitoes. Lodgings in the Pantanal have screened windows, doors, and verandas. Use strong insect repellent at all times.

TOURS

Chapada Explorer. This friendly and efficient travel agency can arrange tours with English-speaking guides to the main sights of the national park and around. ✉ *Praça Dom Wunibaldo 57, Chapada dos Guimarães* ☎ *065/8106-3612* ⊕ *www.chapadaexplorer.com.br* 💲 *From R$360 for the group* ⊗ *Office open 8–11 am.*

Eco Turismo Cultural. This is a popular agency for arranging a tour guide in the park. ✉ *Av. Cipriano Curvo 655a, Chapada dos Guimarães* ☎ *065/3301-1393, 065/9621-6334* ⊕ *www.chapadadosguimaraes.com. br/ecoturis.htm* 💲 *From R$100 per person, depending on group size.*

EXPLORING

TOP ATTRACTIONS

Parque Nacional Chapada dos Guimarães. Besides the Pantanal, the areas in and around the Parque Nacional Chapada dos Guimarães are the region's most popular attractions. Traveling northeast of Cuiabá, you see the massive sandstone formations from miles away, rising 3,000 feet above the flat cerrado landscape. Since a fatal rock fall in the park in 2008, some attractions and bathing spots have been closed indefinitely, and all visitors must be accompanied by a guide. The **Cachoeira Véu de Noiva** (Bridal Veil Falls), with a spectacular 250-foot freefall, is the most impressive of the falls in the park and is just off the main road. Beyond this point you can take guided treks to hills, caves, more falls, and archaeological sites. The **Circuito das Cachoeiras** (Waterfalls Circuit) is a set of seven waterfalls 3 km (2 miles) from the visitor center.

Walk about 30 minutes beyond the Caverna Aroe Jari to **Gruta da Lagoa Azul** (Grotto of Blue Lagoon), a crystal clear lagoon (bathing is prohibited). You can also walk along the **Vale do Rio Claro** (River Claro Valley) and swim in the river's transparent waters, or climb the **Morro de São Jerônimo** (St. Jerome's Hill), one of the highest points of the Chapada.

8

Entrance to the national park is permitted only with a guide, whom you can hire from an agency in town. ✉ *MT 251 at Km 51, 74 km (40 miles) north of Cuiabá, Chapada dos Guimarães* 🌐 *www.icmbio.gov.br/parnaguimaraes* 🕒 *Daily 8–5.*

Caverna Aroe Jari. If you have time, arrange a guided visit to Caverna Aroe Jari, costing about R$45. The cave's name means "home of souls" in the Bororo language. This mile-long sandstone cave (one of Brazil's largest) can be reached after a 5-km (3-mile) hike through the cerrado, or on the back of a tractor. ✉ *MT 251, 40 km (25 miles) from Guimarães, Chapada dos Guimarães.*

WHERE TO EAT AND STAY

$$$$ BRAZILIAN 🍴 **Morro dos Ventos.** Perched on the edge of a cliff, this restaurant has fantastic views. The palm-shaded building and surrounding gardens add to the atmosphere. This is the place for fantastic regional dishes such as *vaca atolada* (literally "cow stuck in the mud"). The strange-sounding dish is actually beef ribs served in cooked cassava chunks. [$] *Average main: R$105* ✉ *Estrada do Mirante, Km 1, Chapada dos Guimarães* ✥ *Southeast of town* ☎ *065/3301–1030* 🌐 *www.morrodosventos.com.br* 💳 *No credit cards* 🕒 *No dinner.*

$$ PIZZA 🍴 **Pizzaria Margherita.** The pizzas here come with thin crusts, generous servings of mozzarella, and fresh ingredients, but it's the candlelit ambience of the restaurant and garden that have made it one of the most popular eateries in town. [$] *Average main: R$36* ✉ *Rua Fernando Correa, next to Bradesco, Chapada dos Guimarães* ☎ *065/3301–2121* 💳 *No credit cards* 🕒 *Closed Mon. No lunch.*

$ HOTEL 🏨 **Hotel Turismo.** This family-run hotel celebrated its 40th anniversary in 2013 and continues to combine a convenient location with a high caliber of service. **Pros:** central location; large breakfasts. **Cons:** uninspiring rooms. [$] *Rooms from: R$250* ✉ *Rua Fernando Correa 1065, Chapada dos Guimarães* ☎ *065/3301–1176* 🌐 *www.hotelturismo.com.br* 🛏 *31 rooms.*

$$$ RESORT FAMILY 🏨 **Pousada Penhasco.** Clinging to the mesa's edge, this small resort may be far from the Chapada dos Guimarães, but it has tremendous views of the cerrado. **Pros:** many amenities; great sports options. **Cons:** far from town center; popular for company outings. [$] *Rooms from: R$489* ✉ *Av. Penhasco s/n, Bom Clima, Chapada dos Guimarães* ☎ *065/3624–1000 in Cuiabá, 065/3301–1555* 🌐 *www.penhasco.com.br* 🛏 *50 rooms* 🍽 *Breakfast.*

CAMPO GRANDE

1,025 km (638 miles) west of São Paulo, 694 km (430 miles) south of Cuiabá.

Campo Grande is the gateway to the southern Pantanal and to the water sports–rich areas around Bonito. Nicknamed the Cidade Morena (Brunette City) because of the reddish-brown earth on which it sits, this relatively young city (founded in 1899) was made the capital of Mato Grosso do Sul in 1978, when the state separated from Mato Grosso. Campo Grande's economy traditionally relied on ranching, but in the 1970s farmers from the South settled in the region, plowed the plateaus,

The Brazilian Savanna

Brazil's vast *cerrado* (savanna) is the most biologically rich grassland in the world. More than 100,000 species of plants are found in this 500-million-acre (200-million-hectare) territory that covers about 25% of Brazil, and nearly 50% of them are endemic to Brazil. Its small trees, shrubs, and grasses are adapted to the harshness of the dry season, when temperatures in some parts rise well above 38°C (100°F) and humidity drops to a desert low of 13%. Palm species usually stand out among the shrubby vegetation—thick bunches of *buriti* usually grow around springs and

creeks. Cacti and bromeliads are also abundant. Look also for the *pequi*, a shrub that produces berries used in local cuisine, which are called *souari* nuts.

Unfortunately, only about 2% of the cerrado is protected. Since development—mostly in the form of soy and corn farming and cattle ranches—it has become harder to spot such species of cerrado wildlife as deer, jaguars, and giant anteaters. Rheas, however, can be seen wandering through pastures and soybean plantations.

and permanently changed the landscape. Today, ecotourism is gaining on agriculture as the main industry. Campo Grande is all set to open the world's largest freshwater aquarium in 2015.

GETTING HERE AND AROUND

Most tourists coming to the southern part of the Pantanal will fly to Campo Grande. Taxi fare from the Campo Grande airport to the town is about R$25. Andorinha has frequent bus service connecting Campo Grande with Cuiabá (12 hours, R$129), and daily service to and from São Paulo (14 hours, R$205).

A double-decker bus whisks travelers past several points of interest, such as historic buildings and museums. A guide gives details of what's to see, but only in Portuguese. Tours leave at 9 and 2:30 from the Morada dos Baís daily except Monday. Tickets for the 2½-hour tour cost R$33.

ESSENTIALS

Airport Aeroporto Internacional de Campo Grande. ✉ *Av. Duque de Caxias s/n, 7 km (4 miles) west of downtown, Campo Grande* ☎ *067/3368–6000.*

Bus Contacts Andorinha. ☎ *067/3382–3420* ⊕ *www.andorinha.com.* **Terminal Rodoviário de Campo Grande.** ✉ *Av. Guri Marques 1215, Campo Grande* ☎ *067/3026–6789* ⊕ *www.socicam.com.br.*

Taxi Contacts Radio Taxi. ✉ *Campo Grande* ☎ *067/3361–1111.*

Visitor and Tour Information Morada dos Baís. ✉ *Av. Noroeste 5140, Campo Grande* ☎ *067/3324–5830* ⊕ *www.turismo.ms.gov.br.*

EXPLORING

Mercado Municipal. This covered market is a great place to try *sopa paraguaia* (Paraguayan soup), which, despite its name, is a corn pie with cheese, onions, and spices. There are many shops selling handicrafts made by the native peoples of Mato Grosso. ✉ *Rua 7 de Setembro 65, Campo Grande* ⏲ *Mon.–Sat. 6:30–8, Sun. 6:30–noon.*

Museu das Culturas Dom Bosco. This museum contains more than 5,000 indigenous artifacts of the Bororo, Kadiweu, and Carajás tribes. Noteworthy are the taxidermy exhibits of the Pantanal fauna and the formidable seashell collection (with 12,000 pieces). Don't miss the collection of 9,000 butterflies from all over the world, and the bug room, whose walls are covered from floor to ceiling with insects. ✉ *Av. Afonso Pena 7000, Campo Grande* ☎ *067/3326–9788* 🌐 *www.mcdb.org.br* 🎟 *R$5* ⏲ *Tues.–Fri. 8–5, weekends 1–5.*

WHERE TO EAT

$$$$ BRAZILIAN Fodor's Choice ★ 🍴 **Casa do Peixe.** Get your fill of the Pantanal's fish varieties at this restaurant run on a fixed-price *rodízio* system. Couples may want to try the *caldo de piranhã* (piranha stew)—it is reputed to have aphrodisiac properties. [$] *Average main: R$65* ✉ *Rua Dr. João Rosa Pires 1030, Amambaí, Campo Grande* ☎ *067/3382–7121* 🌐 *casadopeixe.com.br* ⏲ *No dinner Sun.*

$$$$ BRAZILIAN Fodor's Choice ★ 🍴 **Fogo Caipira.** This is *the* place for regional cuisine, especially grilled and stewed fish dishes. The standout here is the *picanha na chapa* (grilled rump steak), but the *moqueca de pintado* (a local fish stew) is also recommended. [$] *Average main: R$80* ✉ *Rua José Antônio Pereira 145, Campo Grande* ☎ *067/3324–1641* 🌐 *www.fogocaipira.com.br* ⏲ *Closed Mon. No dinner Sun.*

$$$$ STEAKHOUSE 🍴 **Vermelho Grill.** At Campo Grande's premier steak house, the kitchen takes meat very seriously. All cuts come with certification of origin, and the T-bone steaks are a specialty. The restaurant is right on Campo Grande's swankiest street, but the wooden interior, green spaces, and open barbecue create a relaxing, rustic atmosphere. [$] *Average main: R$180* ✉ *Av. Afonso Pena 6078, Campo Grande* ☎ *067/3326–7813* 🌐 *www.vermelhogrill.com.br* ⏲ *No dinner Sun.*

WHERE TO STAY

$$$ HOTEL Fodor's Choice ★ 🏨 **Grand Park.** Campo Grande's most modern and sophisticated hotel, the Grand Park is helpfully located just across from Shopping Campo Grande. **Pros:** large, bright rooms; sumptuous breakfast; free Wi-Fi. **Cons:** some noise from the main road. [$] *Rooms from: R$405* ✉ *Av. Afonso Pena 5282, Campo Grande* ☎ *067/3044–4444* 🌐 *www.grandparkhotel.com.br* 🛏 *129 rooms* 🍽 *Breakfast.*

$$ HOTEL 🏨 **Jandaia.** Once the leading hotel in town, the Jandaia has lost its former glory and needs some renovation. **Pros:** central location; attentive staff. **Cons:** in need of investment; hectic when conventions are held. [$] *Rooms from: R$290* ✉ *Rua Barão do Rio Branco 1271, Campo Grande* ☎ *067/3316–7700* 🌐 *www.jandaia.com.br* 🛏 *134 rooms, 6 suites* 🍽 *Breakfast.*

$$ HOTEL 🏨 **Novotel.** A red-tile roof gives this hotel a rustic appeal. **Pros:** good location; sleek rooms. **Cons:** small common areas. [$] *Rooms from: R$350* ✉ *Av. Mato Grosso 5555, Campo Grande* ☎ *067/2106–5900* 🌐 *www.accorhotels.com.br* 🛏 *155 rooms* 🍽 *Breakfast.*

$ HOTEL 🏨 **Turis Hotel.** Perhaps the best budget option in Campo Grande, the modern and spacious Turis provides a cool retreat from the Mato Grosso heat. **Pros:** well located; large common areas. **Cons:** breakfast is merely average. [$] *Rooms from: R$141* ✉ *Rua Alan Kardec 200, Campo Grande* ☎ *067/3382–2461 reservations* 🌐 *www.turishotel.com.br* 🛏 *52 rooms* 🍴 *Breakfast.*

NIGHTLIFE

Feira Central. A fun place to go out for an evening, the Feira Central or central fair is home to dozens of friendly snack bars selling local specialty soba noodles, with bands playing and locals drinking in a typically Brazilian atmosphere. ✉ *Rua Quatorze de Julho 3351, Campo Grande* ☎ *067/3317–4671* 🌐 *feiracentralcg.com.br.*

SHOPPING

Casa do Artesão. For baskets of all shapes, beautiful wood handicrafts, and interesting ceramics made by the native peoples of the Pantanal, head to Casa do Artesão. ✉ *Av. Calógeras 2050, Campo Grande* ☎ *067/3383–2633* 🕒 *Weekdays 8–6, Sat. 8–noon.*

Shopping Campo Grande. This massive shopping center has everything you'd expect in an American- or European-style mall, but the many boutiques are what makes it shine. ✉ *Av. Afonso Pena 4909, Campo Grande* ☎ *067/3389–8000* 🌐 *www.shoppingcampogrande.com.br.*

BONITO

277 km (172 miles) southwest of Campo Grande.

The hills around this small town of 15,000, whose name rightly means "beautiful," are on the southern edge of the Pantanal, not too far from the Bodoquena mountain range. The route to the Pantanal is longer than from Campo Grande, but you are well compensated with top-notch hotels that starkly contrast with the rustic Pantanal lodgings. In Bonito you can swim and snorkel among schools of colorful fish in the headwaters of several crystal clear rivers. Fishing, rafting, rappelling, hiking, and spelunking are popular activities in this area. Tour guides can be hired on Bonito's main avenue. Unfortunately, prices for most attractions are steep.

8

GETTING HERE AND AROUND

The paved roads to Bonito follow a circuitous route, but they're better than the more direct route on unpaved roads. Take BR 262 west to the town of Anastacio, then head south on BR 419 for about 100 km (66 miles) to Guia Lopes. From there it's about 56 km (35 miles) northwest to Bonito on MS 178. Viação Cruzeiro do Sul buses run here from Campo Grande (5 hours, R$55). Vanzella runs minivans to and from Campo Grande airport.

ESSENTIALS

Bus Contacts **Estação Rodoviária.** ✉ *Rua Pedro Álvares Cabral s/n, Bonito* ☎ *067/3255–1606.* **Vanzella.** ✉ *Rua 31 de Março, Bonito* ☎ *067/3255–3005* 🌐 *www.vanzellatransportes.com.br.* **Viação Cruzeiro do Sul.** ✉ *Rua Vicente Jacks 1688,* ☎ *067/3312–9700* 🌐 *www.cruzeirodosulms.com.br/passagens.*

Visitor and Tour Information **Centro de Atendimento ao Turista.** ✉ *Rodovia Bonito Guia Lopes, Km 0, Bonito* ☎ *067/3255–1850.*

EXPLORING

TOP ATTRACTIONS

FAMILY **Balneário Municipal.** One of the best-value sights in Bonito this municipal baths complex is just 6 km (4 miles) outside town. You can swim with fish in crystalline waters and get a bite to eat at several simple restaurants full of local people, all at a fraction of the price charged elsewhere in town. ✉ *Rodovia Bonito Guia Lopes, Km 6, Bonito* ☎ *067/3255–1996* 🎟 *R$30* ⏲ *Daily 7:30–6.*

Gruta do Lago Azul (*Blue Lagoon Grotto*). The 160-foot-deep Gruta do Lago Azul has a crystal clear freshwater lake at the bottom and smaller side caves in the calcareous rock. The best time to visit is from mid-November to mid-January at around 8:30 am, when sunlight beams down the entrance, reflecting off the water to create an eerie turquoise glow. See stalagmites and stalactites in various stages of development. ✉ *Rodovia Três Morros, Bonito* ✥ *20 km (12 miles) west of Bonito* 🎟 *R$60* ⏲ *Daily 7–2.*

Parque Ecológico Baía Bonita. At this park just 7 km (4 miles) outside Bonito, you can go snorkeling along in the 1-km-long (½-mile-long) *Aquario Natural,* or "Natural Aquarium." The crystal clear waters reveal an incredible close-up array of colorful fish. Equipment rental is included in the admission price. The park is also home to brightly colored birds and to a handful of captive local mammals. ✉ *Rodovia Bonito/Guia Lopes da Laguna, Km 7, Bonito* ☎ 🌐 *www.aquarionatural.com.br* 🎟 *R$170* ⏲ *Daily 9–5.*

Rio da Prata. One of Bonito's most popular attractions is snorkeling in the crystalline waters of the Rio da Prata (literally, river of silver). No sunscreen is permitted, so as not to pollute waters that are home to a myriad of dazzling tropical fish. Scuba and horseback rides are also available. ✉ *BR 267, Km 512, Zona Rural de Jardim, Bonito* 🌐 *www.riodaprata.com.br/inicio* 🎟 *R$162.*

WORTH NOTING

Parque Ecológico Rio Formoso. The approximately 1½-hour rafting trip on the Rio Formoso takes you through clear waters and some rapids while you observe the fish and the birds of the Pantanal. You might also see and hear bands of *macaco-prego* (capuchin monkeys), the region's largest primates. The tour ends at Ilha do Padre (Priest's Island), where there's a complex of rapids emerging through thick riverine vegetation. There's a snack bar where you can relax after the tour. To best appreciate this attraction, make sure there hasn't been any rain in the previous days—the river gets quite muddy. Horseback riding is also available. ✉ *Fazenda Cachoeira, Rodovia Bonito Guia Lopes, Km 7, Bonito* ☎ *67/3255–2200* 🎟 *R$70.*

WHERE TO EAT

$$$$ BRAZILIAN 🍴 **Cantinho do Peixe.** This establishment is one of your best value choices for enjoying local fish in a very local atmosphere. The highlight is *pintado*, which is prepared in two-dozen different ways. The cheese sauce is a good accompaniment to any of the fish dishes. Musicians play in high season. [$] *Average main: R$65* ✉ *Cel Pilad Rebua 1437, Bonito* ☎ *067/3255–3381* ⏲ *Closed Wed.*

$$$$ BRAZILIAN 🍴 **Casa do João.** One of the best places to try local freshwater fish, this celebrated wood-furnished eating house is just off the town's main square, behind the Banco do Brasil. The specialty of the house is *traira sem espinha* (fried boneless traira fish). Other favorites include grilled pirarara and pacu fish, caiman steaks, and, for dessert, *petit gâteau* (cake) made from guavira, a tasty local fruit. [$] *Average main: R$100* ✉ *Rua Nelson Felicio dos Santos 664-A, Bonito* ☎ *067/3255–1212* 🌐 *www.casadojoao.com.br.*

$$$$ BRAZILIAN 🍴 **Taboá.** Since 1995, this dining and—above all—drinking spot has evolved from a hole in a wall into a Bonito landmark that can seat nearly 300 for dinner. The regional food is respectable, but it's the artisanal cachaça, the music, and the boisterous atmosphere that keep the crowds coming. Customers are encouraged to write on the walls. [$] *Average main: R$65* ✉ *Rua Piad Rebua 1837, Bonito* ☎ *067/3255–3598* 🌐 *www.taboa.com.br* 💳 *No credit cards.*

WHERE TO STAY

$ B&B/INN 🏨 **Catarino's Guest House.** The best budget option in town, this family-run pousada opened in 2012 and has become a favorite with young travelers. **Pros:** attentive, helpful staff; substantial breakfast. **Cons:** basic rooms; can get busy. [$] *Rooms from: R$80* ✉ *Rua 24 de Fevereiro 1640, Bonito* ☎ *067/3255–2823* 🌐 *www.hostelcatarino.com.br* 🛏 *11 rooms* 🍴 *Breakfast.*

$$ HOTEL 🏨 **Marruá.** The modern design of this hotel contrasts with others in town, which lean toward rustic looks. **Pros:** competent staff; soothing atmosphere. **Cons:** few amenities; bland decor. [$] *Rooms from: R$290* ✉ *Rua Joana Sorta 1173, Bonito* ☎ *067/3255–6262, 067/3255–1040* 🌐 *www.marruahotel.com.br* 🛏 *120 rooms* 🍴 *Breakfast.*

8

$ B&B/INN 🏨 **Pousada Rancho Jarinú.** A family-run business, Pousada Rancho Jarinú has friendly owners who go to great lengths to make you feel at home. **Pros:** attentive owners; simple but tastful decor. **Cons:** some rooms are dark; small bathrooms. [$] *Rooms from: R$240* ✉ *Rua 24 de Fevereiro 1895, Bonito* ☎ *067/3255–2094* 🌐 *www.pousadaranchojarinu.com.br* 🛏 *9 rooms* 🍴 *Breakfast.*

$ B&B/INN 🏨 **Pousada Remanso.** Run by the town's former secretary of tourism, this centrally located pousada has bright if small rooms and spacious common areas and a swimming pool, all of which makes for a comfortable stay. **Pros:** central location; knowledgeable staff. **Cons:** few amenities. [$] *Rooms from: R$209* ✉ *Rua Cel. Pilad Rebuá 1515, Bonito* ☎ *067/3255–3469* 🌐 *www.pousadaremanso.com.br* 💳 *No credit cards* 🛏 *21 rooms* 🍴 *Breakfast.*

$$ HOTEL Fodor's Choice ★ 🏨 **Wetiga Hotel.** Large, luxurious, and expertly designed and landscaped, the Wetiga Hotel is the best in downtown Bonito. **Pros:** great amenities; sophisticated decor; excellent service. **Cons:** some bathrooms are small; busy neighborhood. [$] *Rooms from: R$369* ✉ *Rua Pilad Rebuá 679, Bonito* ☎ *067/3255–5100* 🌐 *www.wetigahotel.com.br* 🛏 *64 rooms, 4 suites* 🍴 *No meals.*

$$$$ RESORT FAMILY 🏨 **Zagaia Eco-Resort Hotel.** With decorations inspired by the Kadiweu people's traditional crafts, this eco-lodge has an authentic feel. **Pros:** great amenities for families; unique decor; spacious common areas. **Cons:** hectic during conventions; away from downtown. [$] *Rooms from:*

R$645 ✉ *Km 0, Rodovia Bonito–Três Morros, Bonito* ☎ *067/3255–5500* 🌐 *www.zagaia.com.br* 🛏 *100 rooms, 30 suites* 🍴 *Some meals.*

MIRANDA

205 km (128 miles) west of Campo Grande.

Ecotourism is Miranda's main source of revenue. Comfortable pousadas and farms allow you to get acquainted with the pantaneiro lifestyle. Although Miranda lies just outside the Pantanal proper, the Rio Miranda area has abundant fauna, including a sizable population of jaguars. Here's a great opportunity to practice *focagem,* a local version of a photographic safari: as night falls, guides take you into the Pantanal in 4x4 pickup trucks with powerful searchlights that mesmerize the animals for some time, so you can get a really close look.

GETTING HERE AND AROUND

You must either drive or take a bus to Miranda from Campo Grande. Direct bus lines from Campo Grande are run by Andorinha (four hours, R$48).

WHERE TO EAT AND STAY

$ BRAZILIAN 🍴 **Zero Hora.** This popular buffet-style restaurant on the edge of town serves regional fare by weight, including meat and grilled or stewed local fish. There's a large and varied salad bar. [$] *Average main: R$30* ✉ *Rua Barão do Rio Branco 1146, Miranda* ☎ *067/3242–1330.*

$ B&B/INN 🏨 **Pousada Águas do Pantanal.** A great budget choice, this inn renovated in 2012 occupies a historic house with lots of antiques. **Pros:** good bargain; attentive staff. **Cons:** few amenities; small bathrooms. [$] *Rooms from: R$190* ✉ *Av. Afonso Pena 367, Miranda* ☎ *067/3242–1242* 🌐 *www.aguasdopantanal.com.br* 🛏 *20 rooms* 🍴 *Breakfast.*

$$$$ B&B/INN 🏨 **Refúgio da Ilha.** This pousada is nestled on a 2,000-acre island in the Rio Salobra delta. **Pros:** prime location for wildlife sightings; cozy rooms. **Cons:** extra charge for English-speaking guides; three-night minimum stay. [$] *Rooms from: R$930* ✉ *Miranda* ✥ *31 km (22 miles) west of Miranda, 235 km (146 miles) west of Campo Grande* ☎ *067/3384–3270* 🌐 *www.refugiodailha.com.br* 🛏 *8 rooms* 🍴 *All meals* ☞ *All-inclusive rates exclude drinks.*

SPORTS AND THE OUTDOORS

RANCHES

The last reluctant ranchers are beginning to see tourism as a viable economic alternative in this region, which means you can visit a working ranch or farm for a day.

Fazenda San Francisco. Fazenda San Francisco is a 37,000-acre working ranch where you can go on a photo safari in the morning and a boat tour on Rio Miranda in the afternoon, when you'll have the chance to fish for piranha. The R$165 day fee includes a lunch of rice and beans with beef and vegetables. For overnight stays, the fee is R$448 per person, including a night trip with a good chance of spotting jaguars. ✉ *BR 262, 36 km (22 miles) west of Miranda, Miranda* ☎ *067/3242–1088* 🌐 *www.fazendasanfrancisco.tur.br.*

SALVADOR AND THE BAHIA COAST

Updated By
Lauren Holmes

In "the land of happiness," as the state of Bahia is known, the sun shines almost every day. Its Atlantic Ocean shoreline runs for 900 kilometers (560 miles), creating beautiful white-sand beaches lined with coconut palms. Inland is Parque Nacional da Chapada Diamantina (Chapada Diamantina National Park), with 152,000 hectares (375,000 acres) of mountains, waterfalls, caves, natural swimming pools, and hiking trails. And in Bahia's capital, Salvador, the beat of bongo drums echoing through the narrow cobblestone streets is a rhythmic reminder of Brazil's African heritage.

Bahia's Costa do Coqueiros (Coconut Coast), north of Salvador up to the village of Mangue Seco, on the border of Sergipe State, has 190 kilometers (118 miles) of beautiful beaches. South of Salvador, from Baía de Todos os Santos and its islands (Itaparica and Tinharé) to Itacaré is the Dendê Coast, where you find the African palms that produce the *dendê* oil used in Bahian cooking. The midsection of Bahia's coast is known as the Cocoa Coast, because cocoa plantations dominate the landscape and the economy.

Farther south, the Discovery Coast, from Santa Cruz de Cabrália to Barra do Caí, has many sites linked with the first Portuguese explorers to arrive in Brazil. The last bit of Bahia's coast heading south is the Whale Coast, near the towns of Caravelas and Alcobaça, where humpback whales mate and give birth from June to November.

ORIENTATION AND PLANNING

GETTING ORIENTED

Covering nearly 570,000 square kilometers (220,000 square miles) of eastern Brazil, the state of Bahia is hilly and dry. The vibrant capital of Salvador sits on the Atlantic Ocean about 1,649 km (1,024 miles) north of Rio de Janeiro and 1,962 km (1,219 miles) north of São Paulo. The coastline, with its beautiful beaches, gets most of the attention. The 900 km (560 miles) of coastline is about a third of that in the entire country.

Salvador. On the southern tip of a triangular peninsula, Salvador sits at the mouth of the Bahia de Todos os Santos. The peninsula forms a natural harbor and shelters the city from the open waters of the Atlantic Ocean. Salvador is a hilly city, with the Cidade Alta (Upper City) quite a bit higher than the Cidade Baixa (Lower City).

The Cocoa Coast. The Cocoa Coast, 460 km (286 miles) south of Salvador, combines charismatic surf towns and chic beach resorts with

TOP REASONS TO GO

Soak Up the Sun: Warm waters year-round and a continuous lineup of beautiful beaches from south to north make Bahia one of the premier destinations in Brazil for soaking up the sun.

Unique Cuisine: Bahia's African influence on Portuguese and native Brazilian food has resulted in a distinct regional cuisine.

Carnival: Salvador is one of the top spots in Brazil to celebrate Carnival—its *trios eléctricos*, street parades, and array of big-name entertainers

combine for one long, nonstop party you won't forget.

Afro-Brazilian Culture: Salvador is the capital of Afro-Brazilian culture and its historic center, Pelourinho, is a World Heritage Site with stunning monuments.

Bahian Music: The top names in Brazilian music, Gilberto Gil, Caetano Veloso, Gal Costa, Maria Bethânia, who were some of the musicians nicknamed *Novo Baianos* (New Bahians), are de facto ambassadors of Bahian music.

cocoa plantations and mineral springs, surrounded by one of Brazil's only remaining sections of primary Mata Atlântica rain forest. The faded town of Ilhéus, a famous setting for Jorge Amado's romantic novels of Bahian life, was the bustling heart of Brazil's once-booming *cacao* region.

The Discovery Coast. Located 723 km (450 miles) south of Salvador, Porto Seguro provides the gateway to some of Bahia's best beaches, from happening Trancoso to the more remote Caraíva. As idyllic beach villages absorb development, wandering Robinson Crusoes are traveling ever farther south in search of the ultimate deserted white-sand beach.

PLANNING

WHEN TO GO

Peak seasons for Brazilians to travel are from December to March (South American summer) and the month of July, when schools have winter breaks. Most international visitors come in the months of August and September. Make reservations far in advance for stays during these months, especially if you plan to visit during New Year or Carnival (February or March). As the weather is sunny and warm year-round, consider a trip in the off-season, when prices are lower and the beaches less crowded. Mean temperatures are about 25°C (77°F) in winter (July and August), when there's usually more rainfall, including the occasional tropical downpour. Summer temperatures are a few degrees higher (28°C/82°F), but humidity is somewhat lower.

PLANNING YOUR TIME

Bahia is one of the most versatile and pleasant places to travel in Brazil, with options to suit all manner of budgets and time frames. Distances, as with all of Brazil, are significant, and flights can often be cheaper than bus journeys, so book well in advance or check for last-minute promotions. For a quintessential Bahian experience, plan to spend at

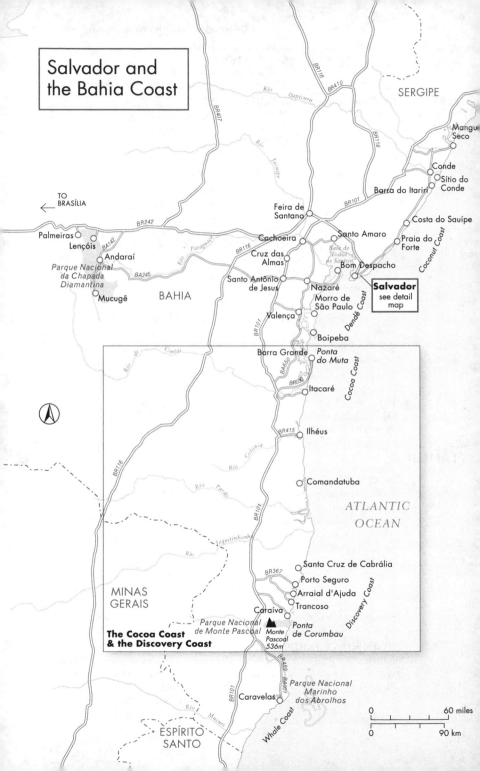

A Bit of History

Portuguese navigator and explorer Pedro Alvares Cabral's first sight of Brazil—on Easter Sunday, April 22, 1500—was an isolated mountain of about 530 meters (1,600 feet) immediately named *Monte Pascoal* (Mount Easter), 750 km (466 miles) south of Salvador. The Portuguese flotilla soon dropped anchor most likely at what is now the fishing village of Curumuxatiba. The explorers were met by the native Tupinambá tribe, who were welcoming and eager to accept gifts and provide food and water. Proceeding up the coast about 130 km (81 miles), the ships landed at what is now Santa Cruz de Cabrália. On a knoll on the Coroa Vermelha Beach, the first mass on this newfound land was held. In his journal, the journey's log keeper, Pero Vaz de Caminha, extolled the future colony "where the land is so fertile that all that is sown will give a bountiful harvest." Within a few years more Portuguese expeditions arrived to comb the coastal forests for highly prized *pau-brasil* (brazilwood) trees, the first of many natural resources to be exploited by the colonial landlords.

In 1549 Tomé de Sousa was appointed Brazil's first governor-general, with orders to establish the colony's capital in Bahia. The deep waters at the mouth of Baía de Todos os Santos (All Saint's Bay) and the nearby hills, which provided a commanding view of the region and protection in case of attack by pirates, indicated a favorable site. Within a few decades the city of Salvador had become one of the most important ports in the Southern Hemisphere, and remained so until the 18th century. In 1763 the capital was moved to Rio de Janeiro, and the city lost part of its economic importance and prestige.

Due to its continental dimensions, Brazil has a diverse culture that is sometimes a mosaic but more often a blend of European, African, and indigenous backgrounds. But in Bahia the historical and cultural influence is predominately African. The large African-Brazilian population (comprising more than 70% of the population), the rhythms with mesmerizing percussion, and the scents on the streets of Salvador immediately evoke the other side of the Atlantic.

Until slavery ended officially in 1888, it's estimated that more than 4 million slaves were brought to Brazil from Africa, and the port of Salvador was a major center of the slave trade. By contrast, only around 600,000 slaves were brought to the United States. The large African slave population here and the generally lenient attitude of Portuguese masters and the Catholic Church led to a greater preservation of African customs in Brazil than in other countries. The indigenous tribes, forced to work with the Portuguese to harvest pau-brasil trees, either fled inland to escape slavery or were integrated into the European and African cultures.

Today Bahia faces several challenges. As Brazil's fourth-largest state, it's struggling to juggle population growth and the economic boom that started 50 years ago when oil was found in its territory. The race is on to preserve its way of life and its landscapes, especially the remaining patches of Mata Atlântica rain forest, coral reefs, mangroves, and interior sierras.

9

least 48 hours in Salvador, getting your bearings and soaking up Bahia's rich history and delicious cuisine before heading off to one of the many beach destinations. First-time visitors should try not to be too ambitious but instead choose one of the three "coasts" to explore (Dendê, Cocoa, or Discovery), using internal flights to the airport hubs of each to save time.

GETTING HERE AND AROUND

Most destinations around Salvador can be easily reached by car. To visit the Discovery Coast, fly to Porto Seguro (723 km [450 miles] south of Salvador), and then rent a car to explore other beaches and attractions. For the Cocoa Coast, you can fly directly to Ilhéus, 460 km (286 miles) south of Salvador.

Distances in Bahia are significant, and the most efficient, comfortable, and often cheapest way to get around is by plane, with internal flights connecting the main hub of Salvador with smaller airports in Ilhéus (the gateway to the Cocoa Coast and Maraú Península) and Porto Seguro (the gateway to the Discovery Coast). There are also direct flights from São Paulo to these destinations. Main carriers in the region include TAM, GOL, Azul, and Avianca.

The bus system in Bahia is extensive and safe, reaching across the state and connecting major and minor towns. The main companies are Aigua Branca for longer journeys and Cidade Sol for shorter ones.

Renting a car is one of the most affordable and enjoyable ways to explore the region, giving you the freedom to hop between beach towns and avoid expensive transfers. Road conditions in Bahia are generally good; roads are often empty and will take you through some incredible scenery. While international companies such as Hertz and Avis do exist, the best options for price, quality, and customer service are local companies Movida and Localiza, which have offices in all of the region's airports. Best rates can be found and compared via ⊕ *www. rentcars.com.br.* ■TIP➜ If you're planning to drive long distances, look to rent a 4x4 or a car with a decent engine in order to be able to overtake trucks safely on the single-lane highways, especially in the rainy season, when unpaved roads can prove a challenge.

RESTAURANTS

The laid-back lifestyle of Bahians is reflected in their food. While breakfast in Brazil is traditionally a minor meal, even the simplest of inns will often provide a buffet spread fit for a king—including tropical fruits, eggs, and endless cakes and pancakes crafted from Tapioca. Lunches are usually casual and not strictly defined by the clock, as the hottest part of the day is not the best for large meals. Dinner is the main meal, and starts late, usually around 9. Bahian cuisine is unique and delicious, and a definite reason to visit. The ever-present *oleo de dendê* (palm oil) is one ingredient that sets it apart from other Brazilian cuisines.

HOTELS

Lodging options in Salvador range from modern high-rises with an international clientele and world-class service to cozy, often family-run *pousadas* (inns). While Costa do Sauipe has a concentration of big resorts, the best ones are scattered along the coast. Pousadas are usually the only option in remote beaches or in fishing villages. Apartment hotels, where guest quarters have kitchens and living rooms as well as bedrooms, are available in some places. Low-end pousadas may not have air-conditioning or hot water; be sure to ask before you book. *Hotel reviews have been shortened. For full information, visit Fodors.com.*

WHAT IT COSTS IN REAIS			
$	**$$**	**$$$**	**$$$$**
Restaurants	under R$31	R$31–R$45	R$46–R$60	over R$60
Hotels	under R$251	R$251–R$375	R$376–R$500	over R$500

Restaurant prices are the average cost of a main course at dinner or, if dinner is not served, at lunch. Hotel prices are the lowest cost of a standard double room in high season, excluding tax.

SALVADOR

According to Salvador's adopted son Jorge Amado, "In Salvador, magic becomes part of the everyday." From the shimmering golden light of sunset over the Baía do Todos os Santos, to the rhythmic beats that race along the streets, Salvador, while no longer Brazil's capital, remains one of its most captivating cities.

A large dose of its exoticism comes down to its African heritage—at least 70% of its 3.5 million population is classified as Afro-Brazilian—and how it has blended into Brazil's different strands, from the native Indians to the Christian colonizers. Salvadorans may tell you that you can visit a different church every day of the year, which is almost true—the city has about 300. Churches whose interiors are covered with gold leaf were financed by the riches of the Portuguese colonial era, when slaves masked their traditional religious beliefs under a thin Catholic veneer. And partly thanks to modern-day acceptance of those beliefs, Salvador has become the fount of Candomblé, a religion based on personal dialogue with the *orixás,* a family of African deities closely linked to nature and the Catholic saints. The influence of Salvador's African heritage on Brazilian music has also turned the city into one of the musical capitals of Brazil, resulting in a myriad of venues to enjoy live music across the city, along with international acclaim for exponents like Gilberto Gil, Caetano Veloso, and Daniela Mercury.

Salvador's economy today is focused on telecommunications and tourism. The still-prevalent African culture draws many tourists—this is the best place in Brazil to hear African music, learn or watch African dance, and see *capoeira,* a martial art developed by slaves. In the district of Pelourinho, many colorful 18th- and 19th-century houses remain, part of the reason why this is the center of the tourist trade.

GETTING HERE AND AROUND
Salvador's Aeroporto Deputado Luís Eduardo Magalhães (SSA) is one of the busiest in Brazil. In the last few years several international carriers have opened direct service from abroad, especially from Europe.

9

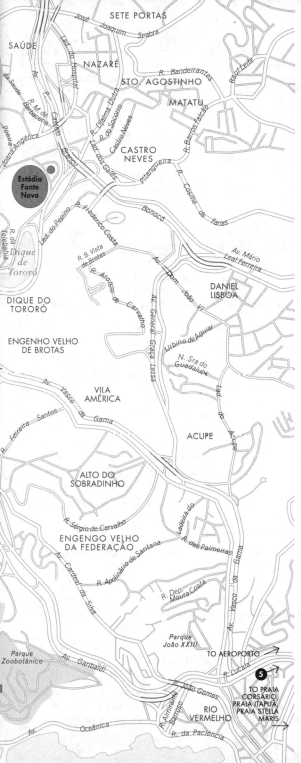

TAM and American Airlines are the only airlines with direct flights from the United States. Most international flights require a change of plane in São Paulo. The airport is quite far from downtown—37 km (23 miles) to the northeast. Taxis to central hotels should cost between R$100 and R$120, with an increase in fare late at night. You can either pay an advanced set fare at the booth inside the terminal, which will be considerably more expensive, or take one of the taxis from the stand outside that run by the meter; if in doubt, ask for a *taxi comum* rather than paying a set fare in advance.

Long-distance buses arrive at Salvador's Terminal Rodoviário. The trips are tortuously long (approximately 32 hours from São Paulo, and 28 hours from Rio de Janeiro) and can be more expensive than flying. Prices start from R$300.

Regular buses (R$2.80) serve most of the city, but they're often crowded and rife with pickpocketing. Fancier *executivo* buses (R$4–R$4.50) are a better option.

Comum taxis (white with a blue stripe) can be hailed on the street or at designated stops near major hotels, or summoned by phone. Taxis are metered, and fares begin at R$3.80. Unscrupulous drivers sometimes "forget" to turn on the meter and jack up the fare. In Salvador tipping isn't expected. A company called Chame Taxi runs taxis that are spacious, air-conditioned, and equipped with modern security devices.

Itaparica and the other harbor islands can be reached by taking a ferry or a *lancha* (a small boat carrying up to five passengers), by hiring a motorized schooner, or by joining a harbor schooner excursion—all departing from two docks. Boats depart from the Terminal Turístico Marítimo or Terminal Marítimo São Joaquim close to the Feira São Joaquim.

ESSENTIALS

Airport Aeroporto Deputado Luís Eduardo Magalhães (SSA). ✉ *Praça Gago Coutinho s/n, São Cristóvão, Salvador* ☎ *071/3204–1010, 071/3204–1444* ⊕ *www.infraero.gov.br.*

Boat Contacts Terminal Marítimo São Joaquim. ✉ *Av. Oscar Ponte 1051, São Joaquim, Salvador* ⊕ *internacionaltravessias.com.br.* **Terminal Turístico Marítimo.** ✉ *Av. da França, Comércio, Salvador.*

Bus Contact Terminal Rodoviário. ✉ *Av. Antônio Carlos Magalhães 4362, Iguatemi, Salvador* ☎ *071/3450–3871.*

Car Rental Contacts Localiza Rent a Car. ✉ *Aeroporto internacional de Salvador, Praça Gago Coutinho, Salvador* ☎ *071/3377–2272* ⊕ *www.localiza. com.* **Movida Rent a Car.** ✉ *Praça Gago Coutinho, Salvador* ☎ *071/3204–1693* ⊕ *www.movida.com.br.*

Taxi Contacts Cometas. ☎ *071/3014–4502.* **Chame Taxi.** ✉ *Salvador* ☎ *071/3241–8888* ⊕ *www.chametaxisalvador.com.br.*

TOURS

Do not hire "independent" guides who approach you on the street, as they are usually not accredited and will likely overcharge you. Also avoid large group tours, which give little information about the sites and are targeted by hordes of street vendors. Private tours with accredited agencies such as Tatur Turismo or the accredited guides that sit at the entrance to specific sites are your best bet. Prices vary depending on the size of the group; most include hotel pickup and drop-off.

Disque Bahia Turismo. A comprehensive and efficient initiative, courtesy of Bahia's secretary of tourism, this central portal provides a 24-hour-a-day service for all tourist information—online, through a real-time chat service, and via a multilingual call center. ✉ *Camino, Salvador* ☎ *071/3103–3103* ⊕ *www.bahia.com.br.*

Salvador Bus. Double-decker tour buses run by Salvador Bus travel around the Upper and Lower Cities and to the beaches. There are two different routes: one that traverses the center of Salvador, and one that connects the beaches of Stella Maris and Itapuã. A R$50 wristband lets you hop off and on as many times as you like. ✉ *Salvador* ☎ *071/3356–6425* ⊕ *www.salvadorbus.com.br/en* 🎟 *From R$50.*

Tatur Tourismo. This outfitter offers fantastic tailor-made city tours, including walking tours of the Pelourinho, programs on the city's African heritage, and experiences with local musicians. They are experts in day trips outside the city and can organize travel throughout Bahia. ✉ *Iguatemi, Salvador* ☎ *071/3114–7900* ⊕ *www.tatur.com.br* 🎟 *From R$110.*

SAFETY AND PRECAUTIONS
In terms of safety, Salvador is no different from most big cities in Brazil: crime is a concern in most neighborhoods, and petty crime is a particular problem. Avoid wearing flashy jewelry or watches, and have a good notion of where you are going in advance. The Centro Histórico area, especially Cidade Alta during daytime, is one of the safest places in Salvador, with tourist police on almost every corner. The buzzy, well-heeled neighborhoods of Rio Vermelho and Barra are also safe for strolling. If in doubt, ask advice from your hotel concierge. At night stick to the main tourist areas and don't walk down deserted streets. It is worth asking at your hotel upon arrival to point out on a map which streets in Pelourinho to avoid. Elsewhere around the city, take a taxi between neighborhoods. Cidade Baixa and the Comércio neighborhood are notorious for petty crime, and pickpocketing is common on buses and ferries and in crowded places.

EXPLORING

Salvador sprawls across a peninsula surrounded by the Baía de Todos os Santos on one side and the Atlantic Ocean on the other. The city has about 50 km (31 miles) of coastline. The original city, referred to as the Centro Histórica (Historical Center), is divided into the Cidade Alta (Upper City), also called Pelourinho, and Cidade Baixa (Lower City).

The Cidade Baixa is a commercial area—known as Comércio—that runs along the port and is the site of Salvador's indoor market, Mercado Modelo. You can move between the Upper and Lower Cities on foot, via the landmark Elevador Lacerda, behind the market, or on the Plano

WALKING THE PELOURINHO

Showcasing the largest collection of colonial buildings in Latin America, the Pelourinho is perfect for exploring by foot. Begin in the Largo do Pelourinho, which was once the whipping post for runaway slaves, where you can now visit the Fundação de Jorge Amado, the Museu da Cidade, and Senac. Head up Rua Maciel de Baixo, the street that runs past the museum, and stroll the cobblestone streets of the colonial district, flanked by houses in pastel shades, until you reach Largo do Cruzeiro de São Francisco, where you can catch your first glimpse of the exuberant São Francisco Church, the most ornate baroque church in Brazil. Continue through Praça da Sé to the Municipal Square towering above the Lower City, which offers wonderful views of the All Saints Bay. Guided tours with a bilingual expert are available through Tatur Turismo.

Inclinado, a funicular lift, which connects Rua Guindaste dos Padres on Comércio with the alley behind Cathedral Basílica.

From the Centro Histórica you can travel north along the bay to the hilltop Igreja de Nosso Senhor do Bonfim. You can also head south to the point, guarded by the Forte Santo Antônio da Barra, where the bay waters meet those of the Atlantic. This area on Salvador's southern tip is home to the trendy neighborhoods of Barra, Ondina, and Rio Vermelho, with many museums, theaters, shops, and restaurants. Beaches along the Atlantic coast and north of Forte Santo Antônio da Barra are among the city's cleanest. Many are illuminated at night and have bars and restaurants that stay open late.

CENTRO HISTÓRICO
TOP ATTRACTIONS

Fodor's Choice ★ **Catedral Basílica.** Recognized as one of the richest examples of baroque architecture in Brazil, this 17th-century masterpiece is a must-visit. The masonry facade is made of Portuguese sandstone, brought as ballast in shipping boats; the 16th-century tiles in the sacristy came from Macau. Inside, the engravings on the altars show the evolution of architectural styles in Bahia. Hints of Asia permeate the decoration, such as the facial features and clothing of the figures in the transept altars and the intricate ivory-and-tortoise shell inlay from Goa on the Japiassu family altar, third on the right as you enter (it is attributed to a Jesuit monk from China). The altars and ceiling are layered with gold—about 10 grams per square meter. ⊠ *Praça 15 de Novembro s/n, Terreiro de Jesus, Salvador* ☎ *071/3321–4573* ✆ *R$3* ☾ *Daily 8–11:30 and 2–5:30.*

Igreja de Nosso Senhor do Bonfim (*Church of Our Lord of Bomfim*). Set atop a hill as the Itapagibe Peninsula extends into the bay, Salvador's iconic Igreja de Nosso Senhor do Bomfim is well worth the 8-km (5-mile) detour from the Centro Histórico and marks a crossroads between the Christian and native African religions. Its patron saint, Oxalá, is the father of all the gods and goddesses in the Candomblé mythology. Built in the 1750s, the church has many ex-votos (votive offerings) of

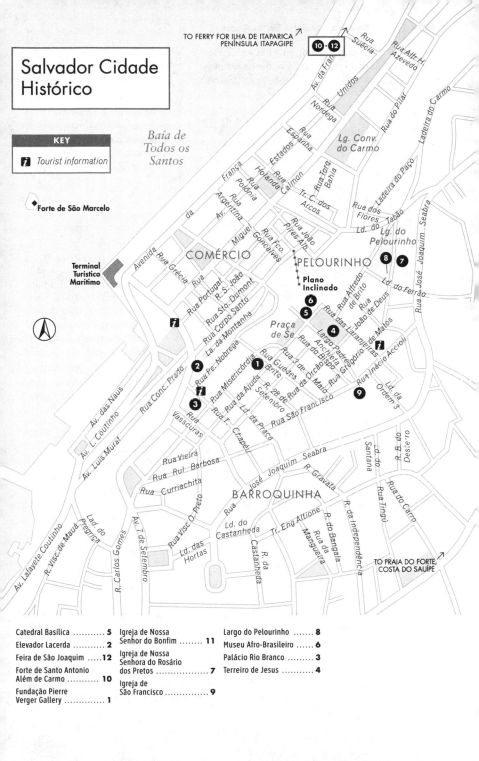

Salvador Cidade Histórico

KEY

i Tourist information

Forte de São Marcelo

Terminal Turístico Maritimo

TO FERRY FOR ILHA DE ITAPARICA
PENÍNSULA ITAPAGIPE

10 - 12

Baía de Todos os Santos

Lg. Conv. do Carmo

COMÉRCIO

PELOURINHO

Plano Inclinado

Lg. do Pelourinho

Praça de Se

BARROQUINHA

TO PRAIA DO FORTE,
COSTA DO SAUÍPE

wax, wooden, and plaster replicas of body parts, left by those praying for miraculous cures. Outside the church, street vendors sell a bizarre mixture of figurines, from St. George and the Dragon to devils and warriors. The morning Mass on the first Friday of the month draws a huge congregation, most wearing white, with practitioners of Candomblé on one side and Catholics on the other. ⊠ *Praça do Senhor do Bonfim, Alto do Bonfim, Salvador* 🕾 *071/3116–2196* 🖃 *Free* ⊙ *Services Wed.–Thurs. 9 am; Fri. 6 am, 9:30 am; Sat. 7 am, 8 am, 5 pm; Sun. 6 am, 7 am, 9 am, 10:30 am, 5 pm.*

> **BAIANAS**
>
> Salvadorian street food is prepared and sold by *baianas*, turbaned women in voluminous lace-trim white dresses who take great pride in preserving their Afro-Brazilian culture. Their outfits, an amalgam of African and Afro-Brazilian designs, symbolize peace in Yoruban culture.

Igreja de Nossa Senhora do Rosário dos Pretos (*Church of Our Lady of the Rosary*). Built by and for slaves between 1704 and 1796, the Igreja de Nossa Senhora do Rosário dos Pretos has finally won acclaim outside the local Afro-Brazilian community. After extensive renovation, it's worth a look at the side altars to see statues of the church's few black saints. African rhythms pervade the services and the Sunday Mass is one not to miss. ⊠ *Largo do Pelourinho s/n, Pelourinho, Salvador* 🕾 *071/3321–6280* 🖃 *Free* ⊙ *Weekdays 8–6, Sat. 9–5, Sun. 10–5.*

Fodor's Choice
★

Igreja de São Francisco. One of the most impressive churches in Salvador, the Church of St. Francis was built in the 18th century on the site of an earlier church that was burned down during the Dutch invasion in the early 1600s. The ceiling was painted in 1774 by José Joaquim da Rocha, who founded Brazil's first art school. The ornate cedar-and-rosewood interior is covered with images of mermaids and other fanciful creatures bathed in gold leaf. Guides say that there's as much as a ton of gold here, but restoration experts maintain there's much less. At the end of Sunday morning Mass, which begins at 8 am, the lights are switched off so you can catch the wondrous subtlety of the gold leaf under natural light. Mass is held Tuesday through Saturday beginning at 7:15 am. ⊠ *Rua da Ordem Terceira s/n, Pelourinho, Salvador* 🕾 *071/3322–6430* 🖃 *R$5* ⊙ *Mon.–Sat. 7–6, Sun. 8–noon.*

Convento de São Francisco. With an interior glittering in gold, the church here is considered one of the country's most impressive. Along with intricately carved woodwork, the convento has an impressive series of 37 white-and-blue tiled panels lining the walls of the cloister that tell the tale of the birth and life of St. Francis of Assisi. It is worth attending Sunday morning Mass for the atmosphere alone. ⊠ *Largo do Cruzeiro de São Francisco s/n, Pelourinho, Salvador* 🕾 *071/3322–6430* 🖃 *R$5, Mass free* ⊙ *Mon. and Wed.–Sat. 9–5:30, Tues. 9–3:30, Sun. 10–3.*

Ordem Terceira de São Francisco. The Ordem Terceira de São Francisco, on the north side of the Igreja de São Francisco complex, has an 18th-century Spanish plateresque sandstone facade—the only one in Brazil—that is carved to resemble Spanish silver altars made by beating the metal into wooden molds. ⊠ *Largo do Cruzeiro de São Francisco, Pelourinho, Salvador* ☎ *071/3321–6968* ▣ *R$3* ۞ *Daily 8–5.*

Largo do Pelourinho (*Pelourinho Square*). Once the "whipping post" for runaway for slaves, this square now serves as the cultural heart of Salvador's Historic Center, with regular live music performed in front of the colorful colonial buildings. The four public stages are named after characters in Jorge Amado novels; a museum on the acclaimed author, who lived from 1912 to 2001, borders the upper end of the square. While summer months see performances nightly, year-around Tuesdays and Sundays are the days not to miss for music in the Pelourinho. The small plaza commemorates the day in 1888 when Princesa Isabel, daughter of Dom Pedro II, signed the decree that officially ended slavery. ⊠ *Intersection of Rua Alfredo de Brito and Ladeira do Ferrão, Pelourinho, Salvador.*

Museu Afro-Brasileiro. Next to the Catedral Basílica, this palatial pink building has a collection of more than 1,100 pieces relating to the city's religious or spiritual history, including pottery, sculpture, tapestry, weavings, paintings, crafts, carvings, and photographs. There's an interesting display on the meanings of Candomblé deities, with huge carved-wood panels portraying each one. The other museum that shares the building is the Museu Arqueologia e Etnologia (Archaeology and Ethnology Museum). Both have information booklets available in multiple languages. ⊠ *Praça 15 de Novembro s/n, Pelourinho, Salvador* ☎ *071/3283–5540* ⊕ *www.mafro.ceao.ufba.br* ▣ *R$6* ۞ *Weekdays 9–5.*

Terreiro de Jesus. This wide plaza lined with 17th-century houses sits in the heart of historic Salvador. Where nobles once strolled under imperial palm trees, there's a crafts fair on weekends. In the afternoons, a group of locals practice *capoeira*—a stylized dance-like fight with African origins—to the sound of the *berimbau,* a bow-shape musical instrument. ⊠ *Intersection of Rua das Laranjeiras and Rua João de Deus, Pelourinho, Salvador.*

9

WORTH NOTING

Elevador Lacerda. For a few centavos, ascend 236 feet in about a minute in the world's first urban elevator, which runs between Praça Visconde de Cayrú in the Lower City and the Paço Municipal in the Upper City. Built in 1872, the elevator originally ran on hydraulics. It was electrified when it was restored in the 1930s. Bahians joke that the elevator is the only way to "go up" in life. Watch out for pickpockets when the elevator's crowded. ⊠ *West side of Praça Visconde de Cayrú, Comércio, Salvador* ▣ *R$0.25* ۞ *Daily 5 am–midnight.*

Forte de Santo Antonio Além do Carmo. While this fort set at the end of Rua Direita de Santo Antonio may not win prizes for its architecture, its real draw is as a center for capoeira, a type of martial art practiced in Brazil. Classes led by different capoeria masters take place in the former cells, each with an individiual schedule, and begin every day at 6 pm. ⊠ *Praça Barão do Triunfo s/n, Santo Antônio, Salvador* ☎ *071/3117–1488.*

Fundação Pierre Verger Gallery. At this gallery dedicated to the works of renowned French photographer Pierre Verger you can catch a rotating

Spiritual Salvador

Evidence that Brazil is officially a Roman Catholic country can be found everywhere. There are beautiful churches and cathedrals across the nation. Most Brazilians wear a religious medal, bus and taxi drivers place pictures of St. Christopher prominently in their vehicles, and two big winter celebrations (in June) honor St. John and St. Peter. For many Brazilians, however, the real church is that of the spirits.

When Africans were forced aboard slave ships, they may have left their families and possessions behind, but they brought an impressive array of gods. Foremost among them were Olorum, the creator; Yemanjá, the goddess of the rivers and water; Oxalá, the god of procreation and the harvest; and Exú, a trickster spirit who could cause mischief or bring about death.

The Catholic Church, whose spiritual seeds were planted in Brazil alongside the rows of sugarcane and cotton, was naturally against such religious beliefs. As a compromise, the slaves took on the rituals of Rome but kept their old gods. Thus, new religions—Candomblé in Bahia, Macumba in Rio, Xangó in Pernambuco, Umbanda in São Paulo—were born.

Yemanjá had her equivalent in the Virgin Mary and was queen of the heavens as well as queen of the seas; the powerful Oxalá became associated with Jesus Christ; and Exú, full of deception to begin with, became Satan. Other gods were likened to saints: Ogun to St. Anthony, Obaluayê to St. Francis, Oxôssi to St. George, Yansan to St. Barbara. On their altars, crosses and statues of the Virgin, Christ, and saints sit beside offerings of sacred white feathers, magical beads, and bowls of cooked rice and cornmeal.

The famous Afro-Brazilian religion called Candomblé, developed in Brazil by enslaved African priests, evolved out of the beliefs and customs of different African tribal religions (primarily from the Yoruba, Fon, and Congo), incorporating elements of the Catholic faith. The basis of the religion is the belief in 13 principal *orixás,* or deities. In addition, each individual is thought to have his or her own orixá to help guide their way.

Salvadorans are eager to share their rituals with visitors, though often for a fee (you can make arrangements through hotels or tour agencies). The Candomblé temple ceremony, in which believers sacrifice animals and become possessed by gods, is performed nightly except during Lent.

Temples, usually in poor neighborhoods at the city's edge, don't allow photographs or video or sound recordings. You shouldn't wear black (white is preferable) or revealing clothing. The ceremony is long and repetitive, and there are often no chairs and there's no air-conditioning; men and women are separated.

A *pãe de santo* or *mãe de santo* (Candomblé priest or priestess) can perform a reading of the *búzios* for you; the small brown shells are thrown like jacks into a circle of beads—the pattern they form tells about your life. Don't select your mãe or pãe de santo through an ad or sign, as many shell readers who advertise are best not at fortune-telling but at saying "100 dollars, please" in every language.

selection of his captivating black-and-white shots of Afro-Brazilian culture from the 1950s–'70s, detailing both daily and religious rituals. A much larger archive is accessible at the foundation, which also hosts workshops and classes and is located on the outskirts of Salvador. ⊠ *Portal da Misericordia 9, Pelourinho, Salvador* ☎ *071/3321–2341* ⊕ *www.pierreverger.org* ⊙ *Mon.–Sat. 9–8, Sun. 9–3.*

Palácio Rio Branco. See where it all began at this neoclassic beauty, constructed on the site of Brazil's first government building. Dating back to 1549, the Palace reopened in 2010 after an extensive, two-year restoration and today stands as a cultural center, housing Salvador's Chamber of Commerce, the Cultural Foundation of the State of Bahia, and the state tourist office. On the first floor there's a small memorial museum depicting the last two centuries of local history. Stop by for one of the guided visits around the Palacio's elaborate chambers, led by local graduates every half hour. Get a great view of Cidade Baixa and the bay from the east balcony. ⊠ *Praça Tomé de Sousa, Pelourinho, Salvador* ☎ *071/3116–6928* 🆓 *Free* ⊙ *Tues.–Fri. 10–6, weekends 9–1.*

GREATER SALVADOR
TOP ATTRACTIONS

FAMILY

Fodor's Choice

★

Casa do Rio Vermelho. Dedicated to the life and work of Salvador's favorite son, author Jorge Amado, this museum is one of the city's star attractions for both literary aficionados and first-time explorers of Amado's poetic world. Expert curation by artist-architect Gringo Cardia and its gorgeous location in the writer's former private home make this a must-see. Through his 32 novels, Amado did much to bring Bahia's rich history to life and preserve its traditions through the most colorful of characters. This state-of-the-art, interactive museum breathes life into the author's residence, where personal objects are coupled with short films and interviews with prominent Brazilian creatives that capture the essence of Amado and his important role in the country's cultural development. Note that credit cards not accepted. ⊠ *Rua Alagoinhas 33, Rio Vermelho, Salvador* ☎ *071/3333–1919* 🆓 *R$20* ⊙ *Tues.–Sun. 10–5.*

Feira de São Joaquim. A visit to this all-encompassing daily market, the largest in the state, is a headfirst dive into Bahian culture. Dress down and wander labyrinthine alleys of exotic fruits, squawking chickens, dried flamingo pink prawns, and household goods crafted from *palha* (straw), before heading into the covered section, where you will find an entire lane dedicated to accessories for *Candomblé* practices. Join early-morning vendors for a break at the *barracas* that line the edges and try the local speciality of *passarinha* (fried cow spleen), if you dare, although a cold beer is probably the safer option. ⊠ *Av. Oscar Pontes, Comércio, Salvador* ⊙ *Mon.–Sat. 5 am–6 pm, Sun. 6–1.*

FAMILY

Forte de Santo Antônio da Barra. A symbol of Salvador, St. Anthony's Fort has stood guard over Salvador since its construction in 1534, and is recognized as Brazil's oldest military structure. The lighthouse atop the fort wasn't built until 1696, after many a ship wrecked on the coral reefs around the Baía de Todos os Santos entrance. Inside, the small Museu Náutico has permanent exhibitions of old maps, navigational equipment, artillery, model vessels, and remnants of shipwrecks found

9

by archaeologists off the Bahian coast. Go in the late afternoon to climb the 22-meter tower before watching the impressive sunset with the crowds who gather on the bank below. Across the road, don't miss stopping by Dinha's barraca for *acarajé*; her version of the typical Bahian speciality is rumored to be the best in town. ⊠ *Praça Farol da Barra, Barra, Salvador* ☎ *071/3264–3296* ⊕ *www.museunauticodabahia.org. br* 🖭 *R$12* ☉ *Museum Tues.–Sun. 8:30–7.*

FAMILY **Museu de Arte Moderna da Bahia (MAM)** (*Bahia Museum of Modern Art*). Fodor'sChoice When Italian-Brazilian modernist architect Lina do Bardi set about ★ transforming this 17th-century private fazenda overlooking the sea, she created one of the world's most picturesque modern art museums. Original white and blue Portuguese tiles lead up to the former *casarão* (mansion), which houses a permanent modernist/contemporary collection, while the former chapel plays host to a rotating schedule of individual shows. Walk through the sculpture garden, with works from artists like Bel Borba and Mario Cravo, before taking a break in the atmospheric basement restaurant, a magic spot for watching the sunset. JAM no MAM, the Saturday evening alfresco jazz shows that kick off at 6 pm, are something not to miss. ⊠ *Av. Contorno, Comércio, Salvador* ☎ *071/3117–6132* ⊕ *bahiamam.org.*

WORTH NOTING

Museu Carlos Costa Pinto. A collection of more than 3,000 objects gathered from around the world by the Costa Pinto family, including furniture, crystal, silver pieces, and paintings, is on display at this museum. Included in the collection are examples of gold and silver *balangandãs*, chains with large silver charms in the shapes of tropical fruits and fish, which were worn by slave women around the waist. ⊠ *Av. 7 de Setembro 2490, Corredor da Vitória, Salvador* ☎ *071/3336–6081* ⊕ *www. museucostapinto.com.br/capa.asp* 🖭 *R$10* ☉ *Mon. and Wed.–Sat. 2:30–7.*

Museu de Arte Sacra (*Museum of Sacred Art*). Housed in a former Carmelite monastery, the museum and the adjoining **Igreja de Santa Teresa** (St. Theresa Church) are among the best in Salvador. An in-house restoration team has worked miracles that bring alive Salvador's golden age as Brazil's capital and main port, told through thoughtfully cared-for collections of religious objects, although lacking in English translations. See the silver altar in the church, recovered from the fire that razed the original Igreja da Sé in 1933, and the blue-and-yellow-tile sacristy replete with a bay view. Access can be tricky to find due to the lack of signs; look for it on Rua Santa Thereza, near the taxi point. ⊠ *Rua do Sodré 276, Centro, Salvador* ☎ *071/3283–5591* 🖭 *R$10* ☉ *Weekdays 11:30–4.*

BEACHES

In general the farther east and north from the mouth of the bay, the better the beaches. To avoid large crowds, don't go on weekends. Regardless of when you go, keep an eye on your belongings and take only what you need to the beach—petty thievery is a problem. There are no public bathrooms. You can rent a beach chair and sun umbrella for about R$1.

Beaches are listed in geographical order, beginning with Praia do Porto da Barra, near the peninsula's tip, and snaking around the coast toward the northeast.

FAMILY **Praia do Porto da Barra.** This popular beach in Barra draws a wide variety of sunseekers from across the city and is a convenient option if you're staying in the hotel districts of Ondina and Rio Vermelho, where rock outcroppings make swimming dangerous and pollution is often a problem. Chairs and umbrellas are available for rent, and you can purchase food from one of the many restaurants lining the promenade. **Amenities:** food and drink; lifeguards; toilets. **Best for:** partiers; surfing; sunset. ⊠ *Av. Oceânica east of Santo Antônio da Barra, Barra, Salvador.*

FAMILY **Praia Stella Maris.** One of the northernmost beaches in the Salvador municipality, Praia Stella Maris's long stretch of sand is ever-popular with families in spite of the strong waves. The myriad of food-and-drink kiosks, serving delicious salty snacks and *água de côco* (coconut water), get busy on the weekends. The airport is located just 10 minutes away. **Amenities:** food and drink; lifeguards; toilets; parking (fee). **Best for:** surfing; walking. ⊠ *20 km (12 miles) north of downtown, after Itapuã, Stella Maris, Salvador.*

FAMILY **Praia do Flamengo.** Clean sand, simple kiosks, and a beautiful view make this long stretch of golden sand a favorite among good-looking locals and surfers drawn to the strong waves. Buses, which run regularly from Barra and the City Center, take just over an hour; the journey is well worth it if you are looking for a serious beach day. **Amenities:** food and drink; lifeguards; parking; toilets. **Best for:** surfing; swimming; walking. ⊠ *Thales de Azevedo s/n, Stella Maris, Salvador.*

Praia Corsário. One of the nicest beaches along Avenida Oceánica is Praia Corsário, a long stretch packed on weekends with a younger crowd. Strong waves make it popular with surfers and bodyboarders, while swimmers should proceed with caution. There are kiosks where you can sit in the shade and enjoy seafood and ice-cold beer. **Amenities:** food and drink; lifeguards; toilets. **Best for:** partiers; surfing. ⊠ *Av. Oceánica, south of Parque Metropolitan de Pituaçu, Pituaçu, Salvador.*

Praia Itapuã. Frequented by the artists who live in the neighborhood, the Itapuã Beach has an eclectic atmosphere. There are food kiosks—including Acarajé da Cira, one of the best places to get *acarajé* (a spicy fried-bean snack). Although the coconut palms and white sands remain idyllic, it is advisable to be watchful of your belongings. Inland from Itapuã, a mystical freshwater lagoon, the **Lagoa de Abaeté**, and surrounding sand dunes are now a municipal park. Itapuã's dark waters are a startling contrast to the fine white sand of its shores, but it's not suitable for swimming. **Amenities:** food and drink; toilets; parking. **Best for:** walking. ⊠ *16 km (10 miles) northeast of downtown, Itapuã, Salvador.*

WHERE TO EAT

You can easily find restaurants serving Bahian specialties in most neighborhoods. Pelourinho and Barra, full of bars and sidewalk cafés, are good places to start. There is also a selection of interesting restaurants in bohemian Rio Vermelho and a slew of places along Orla, the beachfront drive beginning around Jardim de Alah. The regional cuisine leans toward seafood, but some meat dishes should be tried. And, like anywhere else in Brazil, there are *churrascarias* for beef lovers. One main course often serves two; ask about portions when you order. Beware that regional food is normally spicy and hot.

> **FAST FOOD**
>
> Baianas typically make *acarajé*, a delicious street food made of bean dough fried with palm oil and filled with bean paste and shrimp. *Moqueca* is another specialty made with palm oil, coconut milk, and fish or shrimp cooked slowly over a low fire.

CENTRO HISTÓRICO

$$$ ITALIAN FAMILY 🍴 **L'Arcangelo.** Tucked away on a quiet cobbled street, this lively cantina combines good-value Italian classics with a cozy atmosphere. Owner Rafaele makes the most of fresh local seafood for signature dishes such as *spaghetti ai frutti di mare* and grilled seafood platter to share. Homemade pastas, tasty meat dishes, and endless indulgent desserts have turned this into a local favorite. Come Sunday, regulars spill out onto tables on the street between watching international football on the large TV and sipping limoncello. The wine list is one of the most varied in town and is well priced, and the fixed-price lunch menu is an excellent value. [$] *Average main: R$50* ✉ *Rua das Laranjeiras 17, Pelourinho, Salvador* ☎ *071/3322–0066* 🕒 *Closed Wed.*

$$$ BRAZILIAN FAMILY 🍴 **Senac.** The delicious 30-dish buffet served in the wood-paneled dining room of this restored town house set right on the Pelourinho provides a comprehensive A to Z of Bahian cuisine for the uninitiated at a set price. Start at the small museum on the ground floor, where English-speaking staff will guide you through Bahian food's African roots, before heading up to the breezy dining room to experience it in action. Superbly run by the hospitality school SENAC, the students are responsible for the golden moquecas and impossibly sweet desserts—as well as excellent service. Everything is executed under the watchful eye of professors in suits. Vegetarians should make for the Kilo restaurant below. [$] *Average main: R$48* ✉ *Praça José de Alencar 13/19, Pelourinho, Salvador* ☎ *071/3324–4550* 🌐 *www.ba.senac.br* 🕒 *No dinner Sun.*

$$$ BRAZILIAN FAMILY 🍴 **Uauá.** Tucked away above a busy street in the Pelourinho, Uauá's tasty, typically Brazilian dishes and reliable service make it one of the most popular restaurants in Salvador—and therefore one of the most crowded. Come early to avoid the rush. Don't skip the Northeastern specialities, like *guisado de carneiro* (minced mutton), moqueca, or *carne do sol com purê de macaxeira* (salted beef with *mandioca* (cassava) purée). Portions are big enough to share. [$] *Average main: R$50* ✉ *Rua Gregório de Matos 36, Pelourinho, Salvador* ☎ *071/3321–3089* 🕒 *Closed Sun.*

GREATER SALVADOR

$$$$ SEAFOOD FAMILY 🍴 **Bargaço.** Delicious Bahian dishes of fresh seafood are served at this longtime favorite, where the ample portions are great for sharing and the alfresco setting provides a convivial vibe for a family celebration. *Pata de caranguejo* (vinegary crab claws) is hearty and may do more than

Afro-Brazilian Heritage

Of all of Brazil's states, Bahia has the strongest links with its African heritage. There are few other countries with such a symphony of skin tones grouped under one nationality. This rich Brazilian identity began when the first Portuguese sailors were left to manage the new land. From the beginning, Portuguese migration to Brazil was predominantly male, a fact that led to unbridled sexual license with Indian and African women.

The first Africans arrived in 1532, along with the Portuguese colonizers, who continued to buy slaves from English, Spanish, and Portuguese traders until 1855. All records pertaining to slave trading were destroyed in 1890, making it impossible to know exactly how many people were brought to Brazil. It's estimated that from 3 million to 4.5 million Africans were captured and transported from Gambia, Guinea, Sierra Leone, Senegal, Liberia, Nigeria, Benin, Angola, and Mozambique. Many were literate Muslims who were better educated than their white overseers and owners.

It was common in the main houses of sugar plantations, which relied on slave labor, for the master to have a white wife and slave mistresses. In fact interracial relationships and even marriages were openly accepted. It was also fairly common for the master to free the mother of his mixed-race offspring and allow a son of color to learn a trade or inherit a share of the plantation.

When the sugar boom came to an end, it became too expensive for slave owners to support their "free" labor force. Abolition occurred gradually, however. It began around 1871, with the passage of the Law of the Free Womb, which liberated all Brazilians born of slave mothers. In 1885 another law was passed, freeing slaves older than 60. Finally, on May 13, 1888, Princess Isabel, while Emperor Dom Pedro II was away on a trip, signed a law freeing all slaves in the Brazilian empire.

The former slaves, often unskilled, became Brazil's unemployed and underprivileged. Although the country has long been praised for its lack of discrimination, this veneer of racial equality is deceptive. Afro-Brazilians still don't receive education on par with that of whites, nor do they always receive equal pay for equal work. There are far fewer black or mixed-race professionals, politicians, and ranking military officers than white ones, although this is changing gradually.

Subtle activism to bring about racial equality and educate all races about the rich African legacy continues. For many people the most important holiday is November 20 (National Black Consciousness Day). It honors the anniversary of the death of Zumbi, the leader of the famous *Quilombo* (community of escaped slaves) de Palmares, which lasted more than 100 years and was destroyed by *bandeirantes* (slave traders) in one final great battle for freedom.

9

take the edge off your appetite for the requisite moqueca *de camarão* (with shrimp) or moqueca *de siri mole* (with soft-shell crab); try the *cocada* (coconut confections) for dessert, if you have room. [$] *Average main: R$75* ✉ *Rua Antonio da Silva Coelho s/n, Jardim Armação, Salvador* ☎ *071/3231–1000* 🌐 *www.restaurantebargaco.com.br.*

$$$$ BRAZILIAN FAMILY 🍴 **Boi Preto.** For a set price this top-quality, all-you-can-eat Brazilian *churrascaria* serves a selection of meat cooked to perfection and a generous choice of sides. A flurry of white-coated waiters appear at your table to carve different options of meat straight onto your plate *rodizio* style, so try not to fill up on the steaming *pao de quiejo* (cheese balls), salads, sushi, and seafood from the accompanying buffet—and also know that the best cuts are usually brought toward the end of the meal. Drinks and dessert are charged separately. [$] *Average main: R$110* ✉ *Av. Otávio Mangabeira s/n, Jardim Armação, Salvador* ☎ *071/3362–8844* 🌐 *www.boipretogrill.com.br.*

$$$ SPANISH Fodor's Choice ★ 🍴 **La Taperia.** You'll be hard-pressed to find a Spanish restaurant in Brazil that matches the outstanding food and cocktails served at this vibrant bar-restaurant overlooking the bay in Rio Vermelho and packed with locals every night of the week. Located in a converted town house, tables are scattered through a series of small rooms, styled with vintage Spanish prints on exposed-brick walls. While the most sought-after spot is out on the terrace, if you are in a hurry, opt for one of the stools along the bar and tuck into the delectable menu, featuring inventive salads, fresh seafood, and world-class paella. While the extensive wine list offers Spanish classics, don't miss the expertly prepared cocktails, such as the *jabuticaba caipiroska* (a vodka caipirinha made with native jabuticaba fruit). [$] *Average main: R$50* ✉ *Rua da Paciencia 251, Rio Vermelho, Salvador* ☎ *071/3334–6871* 🕒 *Closed Sun. and Mon. No lunch.* 💳 *No credit cards.*

$$$$ BRAZILIAN FAMILY Fodor's Choice ★ 🍴 **Paraíso Tropical.** Ask locals and longtime expats alike what not to miss in Salvador and the response you get will be unanimous: Paraíso Tropical. In a tropical garden in the suburb of Cabula, a 20-minute taxi ride from the Historic Center, this relaxed, gourmet spot treats patrons to Bahian classics with a twist. Chef Beto reinvents heavy dishes like *moqueca* and *bobo* using natural dendê fruit rather than oil, combined with rare tropical fruits sourced from more than 6,000 square meters of native Mata Atlântica forest. Everything is cooked in *agua de coco*instead of water to increase the nutritional value of the dishes. Go with friends and go hungry, for while the *siri catado* (Bahia soft-shell crab), *salada duca* (mango, baby coconut, and cashew salad), and Beto's special moqueca stand out, you'll want to try everything. [$] *Average main: R$70* ✉ *Rua Edgar Loureiro 98-B, Cabula, Salvador* ☎ *071/3384–7464* 🌐 *www.restauranteparaisotropical.com.br* 🕒 *No dinner Sun. Closed Mon.*

WHERE TO STAY

The Centro Histórico and the nearby neighborhood of Santo Antonio offer a good selection of places to stay, many of which combine a unique atmosphere with immediate access to the colonial charms of the Pelourinho. Heading south into the Vitória neighborhood along

Avenida 7 de Setembro are a number of inexpensive establishments convenient to beaches and sights. In the fashionable Barra neighborhood, many hotels are within walking distance of the beach, while Rio Vermelho is the favored choice of most Brazilians and where the city's best bars, restaurants, and nightclubs can be found, although it is a 20-minute taxi ride from downtown. High seasons are from December to March and the month of July. For Carnival, reservations must be made months in advance, and prices are substantially higher.

CENTRO HISTÓRICO

$$$$ HOTEL
Aram Yami Hotel. This intimate boutique hotel on the outskirts of the Pelourinho—featuring personalized service, beautiful rooms, and a unique design—is a favorite among couples celebrating something special. **Pros:** multilingual staff; privacy. **Cons:** pricey; street-facing rooms can be noisy. [$] *Rooms from: R$670* ✉ *Rua Direita de Santo Antonio 132, Santo Antônio, Salvador* ☎ *071/3242–9412* 🌐 *www.hotelaramyami.com* 🛏 *6 rooms* 🍴 *Breakfast.*

$$$ B&B/INN
Casa do Amarelindo. While the bright Aztec-inspired colors may not be to everyone's taste, this small, centrally located boutique hotel ticks all the boxes, with king-size beds, in-room Nespresso machines, delicious food, and a rooftop bar that's one of the city's best spots to watch the sunset over Bahia dos Santos. **Pros:** rooftop bar; attentive service; free high-speed Wi-Fi. **Cons:** bright design not for everyone; noisy air-conditioning; kids must be over 14. [$] *Rooms from: R$379* ✉ *Rua das Portas do Carmo 6, Pelourinho, Salvador* ☎ *071/3266–8550* 🌐 *www.casadoamarelindo.com* 🛏 *10 rooms* 🍴 *Breakfast.*

$ B&B/INN FAMILY
Pousada do Boqueirão. From Brazilian actresses to professors, the list of returning customers to this charming, Italian-style pensione is as varied as the legendary breakfast, served amongst tropical plants on the sun-drenched veranda to spectacular views over the bay. **Pros:** great value; fabulous breakfasts; family-run and full of character. **Cons:** Wi-Fi only in communal areas; few amenities; uncomfortable mattresses in some rooms. [$] *Rooms from: R$240* ✉ *Rua Direita de Santo Antonio 48, Santo Antônio, Salvador* ☎ *071/3241–2262* 🌐 *www.pousadaboqueirao.com.br* ⏲ *Closed June–July* 🛏 *11 rooms* 🍴 *Breakfast.*

$$$$ HOTEL Fodor's Choice ★
Villa Bahia. The most evocative place to stay in town, this boutique hotel combines beautiful design inspired by Salvador's colorful history and a fabulous restaurant with a privileged location in the heart of the Pelourinho. **Pros:** inspirational experience; fantastic food; personalized service. **Cons:** can be noisy; small pool. [$] *Rooms from: R$674* ✉ *Largo do Cruzeiro de São Francisco 16/18, Pelourinho, Salvador* ☎ *071/3322–4271* 🌐 *en.lavillabahia.com/pousada-bahia* 🛏 *17 rooms* 🍴 *Breakfast.*

GREATER SALVADOR

$$ B&B/INN FAMILY
Casa da Vitoria. This excellent value option on a tranquil side street of residential Campo Grande offers an intimate B&B experience, with owner Augusta going out of her way to ensure guests feel right at home. **Pros:** value for money; family environment; immaculate. **Cons:** no 24-hour reception; some rooms can be dark. [$] *Rooms from: R$279* ✉ *Aloísio De Carvalho 95, Vitória, Salvador* ☎ *071/3013–2016* 🌐 *www.casadavitoria.com* 🛏 *8 rooms* 🍴 *Breakfast.*

$$ ⌖ **Catussaba Resort Hotel.** A longtime favorite among business travel-
RESORT ers and families due to its close proximity to the airport and extensive
FAMILY facilities—including direct access onto the beautiful Itapuã Beach—this
resort hotel could do with an overhaul. **Pros:** direct access to the beach;
ocean views; plenty of amenities. **Cons:** parts of the hotel are tired; ser-
vice can be patchy; far from tourist attractions. $ Rooms from: R$352
⊠ *Alameda da Praia, Itapuã, Salvador* ☎ *071/3374–8000* ⊕ *www.*
catussaba.com.br ⇨ *253 rooms, 6 suites* |❍| *Breakfast.*

$ ⌖ **Hotel Catharina Paraguaçu.** A long-standing favorite in the Rio Ver-
B&B/INN melho district, this quirky 19th-century mansion is full of character,
FAMILY offering friendly service, delicious breakfasts, and small but comfortable
rooms. **Pros:** family-friendly environment; near dining and nightlife.
Cons: can be noisy on weekends; amenities, such as Wi-Fi and AC, could
be updated. $ Rooms from: R$199 ⊠ *Rua João Gomes 128, Rio Ver-*
melho, Salvador ☎ *071/3334–0089* ⊕ *www.hotelcatharinaparaguacu.*
com.br ⇨ *30 rooms, 2 suites* |❍| *Breakfast.*

$ ⌖ **Hotel Mercure Salvador.** In the bohemian district of Rio Vermelho,
HOTEL this reliable hotel combines sleek, modern design, quality service, and
FAMILY a stunning rooftop infinity pool a short distance from some of the city's
most happening bars and restaurants. **Pros:** excellent views; good ame-
nities for business travelers; helpful staff. **Cons:** breakfast is not included
in the rate; impersonal feel. $ Rooms from: R$215 ⊠ *Rua Fonte de Boi*
215, Rio Vermelho, Salvador ☎ *071/3172–9200* ⊕ *www.accorhotels.*
com.br ⇨ *174 rooms* |❍| *Breakfast.*

$ ⌖ **Pousada Estrela do Mar.** This pleasant B&B a few steps from Barra
B&B/INN Beach wins over independent travelers, couples, and families alike with
FAMILY its competitive prices and Mediterranean-style design. **Pros:** near the
beach; good value; free Wi-Fi. **Cons:** rooms can be noisy. $ *Rooms*
from: R$165 ⊠ *Rua Afonso Celso 119, Barra, Salvador* ☎ *071/3022–*
4882 ⊕ *www.estreladomarsalvador.com* ☾ *Closed June* ⇨ *9 rooms*
|❍| *Breakfast.*

$$ ⌖ **Sheraton da Bahia.** One of the most sophisticated choices for business
HOTEL travelers and families alike, this modern hotel in well-heeled Campo
Grande offers sleek, spacious rooms, a large swimming pool, and internationally recognized bilingual service. **Pros:** trusted service; sophisticated, modern design; fabulous buffet breakfast. **Cons:** no extra beds
for small children; few notable bars or restaurants nearby. $ *Rooms*
from: R$334 ⊠ *Av. Sete de Setembro 1537, Campo Grande, Salva-*
dor ☎ *071/3021–6700* ⊕ *www.sheratondabahia.com* ⇨ *284 rooms*
|❍| *Breakfast.*

$$$ ⌖ **Zank by Toque Hotel.** It's the combination of elegant design, sophisti-
HOTEL cated service, and location overlooking the curved beach of bohemian
Fodor's Choice neighborhood Rio Vermelho that makes this converted colonial man-
★ sion such a winner. **Pros:** great location; beautiful rooftop pool and
spa; chic bar and terrace. **Cons:** rooms can be compact; no ceiling
fans. $ *Rooms from: R$400* ⊠ *Rua Almirante Barroso 161, Rio Ver-*
melho, Salvador ☎ *071/3083–4000* ⊕ *www.zankhotel.com.br* ⇨ *16*
rooms |❍| *Breakfast.*

NIGHTLIFE AND PERFORMING ARTS

Pelourinho is the place to catch live music, particularly on Tuesday and Saturday, when musicians perform at stages dotted across the various squares, from Largo do Terreiro de Jesus to Largo do Pelourinho and up the Ladeiro do Carmo. Saturday's sunset jazz sessions held at the MAM (Museum of Modern Art) are also a must for music lovers. For action any night of the week, head to the trendy, bohemian neighborhood of Rio Vermelho, where locals catch up over acarajé in squares like Largo da Santana before heading on to experimental performance spaces such as Lálá.

> **THE SAMBA MAN**
>
> Dorival Caymmi, one of the greatest Brazilian composers, was born in Salvador in 1914. With his beautiful Bahian sambas, Caymmi brought the sights, smells, and sounds of his native state into the popular imagination. One of his most beautiful compositions is called "Minha Jangada Vai Sair Pro Mar" ("My Boat Will Go Out to Sea").

NIGHTLIFE

BARS

FAMILY **Cafelier.** While this laid-back spot is also recommended for coffee, crepes, and great-value lunches, it is the lime caipirinhas made from artisanal cachaça that draw the crowds who want to enjoy cocktails while watching the sunset over the Bahia de Todos os Santos. ⊠ *Rua do Carmo 50, Santo Antônio, Salvador* ☎ *071/3241–5095* ⊗ *Closed Wed.*

Fodor's Choice ★ **Lálá.** Since it opened in 2014, this vibrant experimental art space in a beautiful town house on Rio Vermelho's bay has turned into the hot spot for the city's creatives to meet. Expect regular exhibitions from local artists, theater performances, a wine bar, and a rooftop cocktail bar, which also plays host to live music and DJs on the weekends. ⊠ *Rua da Paciência 329, Rio Vermelho, Salvador* ☎ *071/9974–4248* ⊗ *Closed. Mon.–Wed.*

O Cravinho. This wood-paneled local drinking spot serves up more than 50 types of flavored cachaça infused in giant barrels, including house specialties like cinnamon, clove, and jambu fruit, as well as traditional caipirinhas and tasty snacks. ⊠ *Terreiro de Jesus 3, Pelourinho, Salvador* ☎ *071/3322–6759* ⊕ *www.ocravinho.com.br.*

DANCE SHOWS

FAMILY **Balé Folclórico de Bahia.** Cited as one of the best dance experiences in Brazil, and at a great value, too, this show lasts just an hour and provides an exhilarating window into the Afro-Brazilian culture. Shows begin daily at 8 pm and tickets cost R$45 per person. ⊠ *Rua Gregório de Matos 49, Pelourinho, Salvador* ☎ *071/3322–1962* ⊕ *www.balefolcloricodabahia.com.br.*

PERFORMING ARTS

CARNIVAL REHEARSALS

Associação Cultural Bloco Carnavalesco Ilê Aiyê. This group, which started out as a Carnival bloco and is renowned as the oldest Afro bloco in Brazil, has turned itself into a dynamic cultural hub. It now has its

9

Carnival in Salvador: Brazil's Wildest Party

Jostling for first place beside Rio and Recife, Salvador is one of Brazil's Carnival kings. While it may have a reputation for being the country's wildest Carnival, it is also the most accessible and authentic large-scale Carnival in Brazil—an explosion of more than 2 million revelers, all dancing in frenzied marching crews, called *blocos,*or hopping parade-side as *pipoca,* or popcorn. At the center of each bloco is the *trio elétrico,* a colossal, creeping stage whose towering speakers blare walls of energetic, ribcage-rattling *axé*music—a danceable and distinctly Bahian mix of African rhythms, rock, and reggae. Top pop stars like Daniela Mercury or Ivete Sangalo perform their party-stoking Carnival favorites, while the Brazilian glitterati enjoy the show from *camarotes* (boxes often sponsored by big name brands), where guests are plied with endless lavish food and champagne.

To be part of the action, and to avoid the hordes of pickpockets that are unfortunately part of the "excitement," join a bloco, which is roped off from the general public. Each bloco has its own all-purpose beer, first-aid, and toilet truck—and you'll have instant camaraderie with your crewmates. (A warning: it's not unusual for women to be kissed by strangers. It might sound feeble, but having a male friend close may deter unwanted groping.)

Favorite bloco themes include Egyptian-garbed percussion band Olodum, and axé acts Are Ketu and Timbalada. Alternatively, there's the peaceful Filhos de Ghandy (Children of Ghandi), a white sea of robes and jeweled turbans. Once you've chosen your bloco, all you have to do is lay down upward of US$100 to buy a crew-specific T-shirt, called an *abadá,*purchased at Central do Carnival kiosks, or at markets from scalpers.

Blocos travel along specific *circuitos* (routes) through the city. Seaside Dodô (about 1 mile, 5 hours) is the route of choice for Carnival's biggest stars and begins at Farol da Barra. Osmar (about 2 miles, 6 hours), beginning near Campo Grande, is large and traditional. The less-populated and calmer Batatinha, which clings to historic Pelourinho, allows an intimate look at smaller percussionist groups and is popular with families. Prepare by checking the official schedule at ⊕ *www.carnaval.salvador.ba.gov.br* (click on "Programação").

Add to all these fine reasons to patronize Salvador's Carnival the more than 20 pre-Carnival warm-up celebrations and it's hard to argue that Brazil's most exuberant street party can be anywhere but Salvador.

own school and promotes the study and practice of African heritage, religion, and history. To take part, call ahead to schedule a visit to the school. Contributions are appreciated. Its Carnival *camarote*is considered one of the best. ⊠ *Rua do Curuzu 288, Liberdade, Salvador* ☏ *071/2103–3400* ⊕ *www.ileaiyeoficial.com.*

Casa do Olodum. Salvador's best-known percussion group, Olodum, gained international fame when it participated in Paul Simon's "Rhythm of the Saints" tour and recordings. Its vibrant samba-reggae vibe makes it one of Salvador's most popular Carnival schools. Olodum has its own venue, the Casa do Olodum, and performs live shows around town, often on Tuesday or Sunday. ✉ *Rua Gregorio de Matos 5, Pelourinho, Salvador* ☎ *071/3321–5010* ⊕ *www.olodum.com.br.*

MUSIC, THEATER, AND DANCE

FAMILY
Fodor's Choice
★

Jam no Mam. The cobblestone outcropping that runs alongside Salvador's picturesque Museum de Arte Moderna (MAM) is the place to watch Jam no Mam's live jazz sessions, every Saturday beginning at sunset. Once inside, stands sell fresh-fruit caipirinhas, pancakes, and snacks, and plastic chairs are available to pull up close to the band. ✉ *Av. Contorno s/n, Comércio, Salvador* ☎ *071/3241–2983* ⊕ *www.jamnomam.com.br* 🎫 *R$10.*

Teatro Castro Alves. Salvador's largest theater holds classical and popular music performances, operas, and plays. ✉ *Praça 2 de Julho s/n, Campo Grande, Salvador* ☎ *071/3535–0600* ⊕ *www.tca.ba.gov.br.*

Teatro Vila Velha. Founded in 1969, this is one of the most important cultural venues in Salvador, with workshops, music, dance, and theater. Although plays are almost always staged in Portuguese, the production is top quality. It is also the stage for Bando de Teatro Olodum. ✉ *Av. Sete de Setembro s/n, Campo Grande, Salvador* ☎ *071/3083–4600* ⊕ *www.teatrovilavelha.com.br.*

SPORTS AND THE OUTDOORS

CAPOEIRA

You can see *capoeira*, a type of martial art popular in Brazil, in almost any beach or park in Salvador and Bahia. Some places are traditional gathering points for practitioners. One such place is the parking lot of Forte de Santo Antônio on Tuesday, Thursday, and Saturday early evenings. Two schools practice here, of which the Grupo de Capoeira Angola is the best known.

Bimba's Academy. There are several capoeira schools in Salvador for anyone who wants to learn the art that trains both the mind and body for combat. Mestre Bamba (Rubens Costa Silva) teaches at Bimba's Academy, located in the heart of the Pelourinho. ✉ *Rua das Laranjeiras 01, Pelourinho, Salvador* ☎ *071/3322–0639* ⊕ *www.capoeiramestrebimba.com.br.*

SOCCER

Arena Fonte Nova. This sparkling soccer-only stadium was created as the replacement for the original Estádio Fonte Nova in order to host the 2014 World Cup and to act as first division team for Bahia's home turf. ✉ *Rua Lions Club 217–547, Nazar, Salvador* ⊕ *www.arenafontenova.com.br.*

Estádio Manuel Barradas. Bahia and Vitória are the two local teams that play in the first division of the Brazilian soccer federation. There are games year-round in the Estádio Manuel Barradas, which is also used for other sporting events and concerts. Advance tickets sales are available, but games hardly ever sell out. The best seats are in the

Capoeira: The Fight Dance

Dance and martial arts in one, *capoeira* is purely Brazilian. The early days of slavery often saw fights between Africans from rival tribes who were thrust together on one plantation. When an owner caught slaves fighting, both sides were punished. To create a smoke screen, the Africans incorporated music and song into the fights. They brought a traditional *berimbau* string-drum instrument (a bow-shape piece of wood with a metal wire running from one end to the other, where there's a hollow gourd containing seeds) to the battles. Tapped with a stick or a coin, the berimbau's taut wire produces a throbbing, twanging sound whose rhythm is enhanced by the rattling seeds. Its mesmerizing reverberations were accompanied by singing and chanting, and when the master appeared, the fighters punched only the air and kicked so as to miss their opponents.

The fights have been refined into a sport that was once practiced primarily in Bahia and Pernambuco but has now spread throughout Brazil and around the world. Today's practitioners, called *capoeristas*, swing and kick—keeping their movements tightly controlled, with only hands and feet touching the ground—to the beat of the berimbau without touching their opponents. The goal is to cause one's opponent to lose concentration or balance. Capoeira is traditionally performed in a *roda* (wheel), which refers both to an event of continuous capoeira and to the circle formed by players and instrumentalists. Strength, control, flexibility, artistry, and grace are the tenets of capoeira. In any exhibition the *jogadores*, or players, as they are called—with their backs bending all the way to the floor and their agile foot movements (to avoid an imaginary knife)—as well as the compelling music, make this a fascinating sport to watch.

higher-priced *arquibancada superior* (upper-level section). ⊠ *Av. Artêmio Valente s/n, Tancredo Neves, Salvador* ⊕ *www.ecvitoria.com.br.*

SHOPPING

ANTIQUES

Nino Nogueira Decor. This exquisite, pricey antiques and furniture shop is a design buff's dream, combining Bahia antiques and classic Brazilian modernist pieces with local artwork, reclaimed wood furniture, and treasures sourced from owner Nino Nogueira's travels around the globe. It's well worth a look for pure design inspiration as you explore Rio Vermelho, although they do ship internationally. ⊠ *Rua da Paciencia 229, Rio Vermelho, Salvador* ☎ *071/3334–6760* ⊕ *www. ninonogueira.com.*

AREAS AND MALLS

Largo do Pelourinho. To pick up contemporary local art, art naïf, and gemstones, visit the many galleries in the Cidade Alta and around the Largo do Pelourinho: Rua do Carmo and Direito do Santo Antonio have some particularly good options. ✉ *Rua Alfredo de Brito at Ladeira do Taboão, Salvador.*

Shopping Barra. One of the best shopping malls in Salvador, Shopping Barra isn't far from the historic center and has cinemas, restaurants, and local boutiques, as well as branches of the major Rio, São Paulo, and Minas Gerais retailers. Many hotels provide transportation to the mall, but you can also take the Rodoviária bus line. ✉ *Av. Centenário 2992, Chame Chame, Salvador* ⊕ *shoppingbarra.com.*

ART GALLERIES

Atelier Bel Borba. Bahia's answer to Dalí, Bel Borba is one of the region's most famous living artists. He picked up a bit of international prestige as well, due to his 2012 installations in New York City and a documentary about his work released the same year. A visit to his little atelier, where you can also pick up a piece of his work, is a must. ✉ *Ladeira do Carmo 14, Pelourinho, Salvador* ☎ *071/3243–9370.*

FAMILY **Urban Arts.** For affordable gifts with a modern twist, this art gallery-cum–printer offers a wide range of images and prints by Brazilian artists that can be customized to size, finish, and frame. ✉ *Rua Bartholomeu de Gusmão 754, Rio Vermelho, Salvador* ☎ *071/3037–3144* ⊕ *urbanarts.com.br.*

BOOKS

Livraria Siciliano. The local branch of a major Brazilian chain, Livraria Siciliano has lots of foreign-language books and international magazines. ✉ *Shopping da Bahia, Av. Tancredo Neves 148, Camino dos Árvores, Salvador* ☎ *071/3450–7737* ⊕ *www.livrariasaraiva.com.br.*

HANDICRAFTS

Instituto de Artesanato Visconde de Mauá. Of Salvador's state-run handicrafts stores, the best is the Instituto de Artesanato Visconde de Mauá. Look for exquisite lace, musical instruments of African origin, weavings, and wood carvings.

✉ *Rua Gregorio de Matos 27, Pelourinho, Salvador* ☎ *071/3116–6700* ⊕ *www.maua.ba.gov.br.*

Mercado Modelo. Set on the bay in Cidade Baixa, this crafts market was once the holding pen for slaves between the 17th and 19th century as they arrived off the boat from Africa. Today it's a convenient place to buy handicrafts, although don't expect a great deal of variety or innovation—this is a market for tourists rather than locals. Bargaining is expected here for goods like *cachaça* (sugarcane liquor), cashews, pepper sauce, cigars, leather goods, hammocks, musical instruments, and semiprecious stones. Head up to the the the alfresco terrace on the

---

MEET DONA FLOR

Prepare yourself for Bahia by reading *Dona Flor and Her Two Husbands,* a Jorge Amado novel steeped in the history and culture of Bahia. At the center of the story is a passionate young widow who finds love and propriety with her well-respected second husband, only to face a dilemma when her rogue first husband comes back from the dead and tries to claim her back. Sonia Braga starred in a film that was shot in the streets of Salvador.

9

top-floor restaurant to enjoy a cold beer while watching the boats set off for Morro do Sao Paulo. ☒ *Praça Visconde de Cayrú 250, Cidade Baixa, Salvador* ☎ *071/3241–0242* ⊕ *www.mercadomodelobahia.com. br* ▣ *Mon.–Sat. 9–7, Sun. 9–2.*

JEWELRY AND GEMSTONES

Bahia is one of Brazil's main sources of gems, with amethysts, aquamarines, emeralds, and tourmalines being the most abundant. Prices for these stones are usually cheaper here than elsewhere in Brazil, but you should have an idea of what stones are worth before you enter a shop.

Bahia Preciosa. The city's most famous jeweler, Bahia Preciosa allows you to peer through a window into the room where goldsmiths work. ☒ *Rua Terceira Ordem 1, Pelourinho, Salvador* ☎ *071/3242–5218.*

H.Stern. The well-known, reputable H.Stern has several branches in Salvador, most of them in malls and major hotels. ☒ *Av. Centenario 2992, Chame Chame, Salvador* ☎ *071/3264–3599* ⊕ *www.hstern.net.*

SIDE TRIPS FROM SALVADOR

Although attractions in Salvador can keep you entertained for more than a week, there are a number of easily accessible places for a one- or two-day break in more relaxing environs. Plan a day trip to Praia do Forte or the other northern beaches, less crowded and more beautiful than those in and near Salvador; or head out to the charming colonial town of Cachoeira. While two to three days is the minimum you will need to explore the near-pristine beaches and tropical forests of Morro de São Paulo and Boipeba, chances are you will wish you were staying a week.

CACHOEIRA

109 km (67 miles) northwest of Salvador.

This riverside colonial town dates from the 16th and 17th centuries, when sugarcane was the economy's mainstay. It has been designated a national monument and is the site of some of Brazil's most authentic Afro-Brazilian rituals. After Salvador it has the largest collection of baroque architecture in Bahia, with the interior of baroque church Ordem Terceiro do Carmo rivaling São Francisco's in Salvador. A major restoration of public monuments and private buildings includes revitalized streets and plazas in town. On an excursion to Cachoeira you can walk through the colorful country market and see architecture preserved from an age when Cachoeira shipped tons of tobacco and sugar downriver to Salvador.

GETTING HERE AND AROUND

To drive from Salvador, take BR 324 north for about 55 km (34 miles), then head west on BR 420 through the town of Santo Amaro. The trip takes 1½ hours. Santana has daily bus service from Salvador to Cachoeira that leaves hourly from 5:30 am to 9:30 pm from the Rodoviaria and costs R$21.10 one way.

Bus Contacts Santana. ☎ *071/3450–4951.*

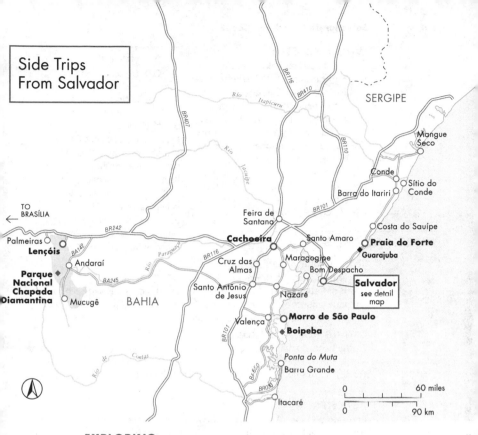

EXPLORING

FAMILY **Centro Cultural Dannemann.** Cross over the rustic wooden bridge to the small town of São Félix set across the water to pay a visit to Centro Cultural Dannemann. This cultural center is housed in a stunning colonial building that acts as both a working vintage-cigar factory and a contemporary-art space. ⊠ *Av. Salvador Pinto 29, São Félix* ☎ *075/3438–2500* ⊕ *www.centrodannemann.com* ⊙ *Tues.–Sun. 8–noon and 1–5.*

Centro Cultural da Irmandade da Boa Morte. Restored in 2014 after a R$900,000 investment, this small museum located inside the Sisterhood of Good Death's headquarters displays photos and ceremonial dresses worn during their rituals and festivals. You can also meet some of the elderly, energetic women whose ancestors protested slavery. The best time of year to visit is in August, during the monthlong festival that celebrates Bahia's black heritage. ⊠ *Rua 13 de Maio, Cachoeira* ☎ *075/9965–6195* ⊠ *By donation* ⊙ *Daily 10–6.*

Igreja da Ordem de Terceiro do Carmo (*Church of the Third Order of Carmo*). This gilded baroque splendor from 1702 rivals the interior of Salvador's São Francisco; watch, too, for the white and blue Portuguese tiles and sculptures of Christ, dripping in cow's blood and imported from Macau. ⊠ *Praça de Aclamação s/n, Cachoeira* ☎.

WHERE TO STAY

$ ⛅ **Pousada do Convento.** You can stay
B&B/INN   overnight in one of the large rooms
at this onetime Carmelite monastery
that dates back to the 17th century.
Pros: good food; beautiful colonial
furniture; swimming pool. **Cons:**
simple accommodations; few amenities; rooms can be musty. $ *Rooms
from: R$105* ✉ *Praça da Aclamação s/n, Cachoeira* ☎ *075/3425–
1716* ⊕ *www.pousadadoconvento.
com.br* ⇝ *26 rooms* ⏍ *Breakfast.*

> **OUR LADY OF
> GOOD DEATH**
>
> Devotion to Nossa Senhora da
> Boa Morte (Our Lady of Good
> Death) began in the slave quar-
> ters, where discussions on aboli-
> tion of slavery took place. The
> slaves implored Our Lady of Good
> Death to end slavery and prom-
> ised to hold an annual celebration
> in her honor should their prayers
> be answered. Brazil was the last
> country in the Western Hemi-
> sphere to abolish slavery, in 1888.

NORTH COAST BEACHES

To reach some of Bahia's more pristine and less crowded beaches, head
north of Salvador on the Estrada do Coco (Coconut Road), leaving the
baroque churches and colonial dwellings behind in favor of miles of
quiet road lined with coconut palms.

GETTING HERE AND AROUND

At the fishing village and turtle haven of Praia do Forte, take the Linha
Verde (Green Line) up the coast. Buses to this string of beaches are
readily available, but the convenience of having your own car is justi-
fied here.

BEACHES

Barra do Jacuípe. A river runs down to the ocean at this long, wide,
pristine beach lined with coconut palms, where the beachfront snack
bars provide the perfect turf for watching the surfers and kitesurfers,
although swimmers should be wary of strong tides. The Santa Maria/
Catuense bus company operates six buses here daily. **Amenities:** food
and drink; parking (fee); toilets. **Best for:** surfing; walking. ✉ *41 km
(25 miles) north of Salvador, Barra do Jacuipe, Arembepe, Salvador.*

Guarajuba. With palm trees and calm waters banked by a reef, this is
the nicest beach of them all, preferable to the bustle of Praia do Forte's
main beach, even though it's lined with condos. The bus to Barra do
Jacuípe continues on to Guarajuba, which has snack kiosks, fishing
boats, surfing, dune buggies, and a playground. **Amenities:** food and
drink; parking (fee); toilets. **Best for:** sunrise; swimming; walking. ✉ *60
km (38 miles) north of Salvador, Praia de Guarajuba, Camaçari* ⊕ *www.
guarajuba.com.*

PRAIA DO FORTE

72 km (45 miles) northeast of Salvador.

On a relaxing day-trip from Salvador you can visit Praia do Forte's
village, get to know the sea-turtle research station, swim, or snorkel.
The town also has a beautiful coconut-lined beach. If you decide to
stay longer, there are many lodging options, and the nightlife, although

toned down a few decibels from that in Salvador, is still lively. Almost everything in town is on the main street, Alameda do Sol. You can book a trip here through any Salvador tour operator or travel agent, or simply take a bus directly on a day trip.

GETTING HERE AND AROUND

To reach Praia do Forte by car from Salvador, take the Estrada do Coco (BA 099) north and follow the signs. From there on, it's called Linha Verde (Green Line), to Costa do Sauípe and the northern beaches all the way to the Sergipe border. Linha Verde operates a bus service from Salvador to Praia do Forte that runs four to six times a day. The two-hour trip on the un-air-conditioned bus costs R$10.

ESSENTIALS

Visitor and Tour Information Porto Mar. ⊠ *Rua da Aurora 1, Praia do Forte* ☎ *071/367–6010* ⊕ *www.portomar.com.br.*

EXPLORING

FAMILY **Projeto Tamar.** The headquarters of this nationwide turtle preservation project, established in 1980, has turned what was once a small, struggling fishing village into a tourist destination with a mission—to save Brazil's giant sea turtles and their hatchlings. Five of the seven surviving sea-turtle species in the world roam and reproduce on Brazil's Atlantic coast, primarily in Bahia. During the hatching season (September through March), workers patrol the shore at night to locate nests and move eggs or hatchlings at risk of being trampled or run over to safer areas or to the open-air hatchery at the base station. It is here that you can watch adult turtles in the small swimming pools and see the baby turtles that are housed in tanks until they can be released to the sea, something you can take part in between December and February. The headquarters also has educational videos, lectures, and a gift shop. Thirty-three other Tamar stations on beaches across Brazil protect about 15 million hatchlings born each year. If you are looking for a more intimate experience, seek out one of the smaller bases, as this project is certainly the most commercial. ⊠ *Av. Farol Garcia D'Ávila s/n, Praia do Forte* ☎ *071/3676–0321* ⊕ *www.tamar.org.br* ⊠ *R$18* ⊙ *Daily 9–5:30.*

Reserva de Sapiranga. If you have a couple of days to visit Praia do Forte, spend one of them exploring the Reserva de Sapiranga, spread over 600 hectares (1,482 acres) of Atlantic Forest that contains rare orchids and bromeliads. The reserve is a sanctuary for endangered animals. Kayaking is possible on the Rio Pojuca, which flows through the park, and Lago Timeantube, where more than 180 species of native birds have been sighted. Whether you explore by foot, bike, or Jeep, going with an agency, such as PortoMar, is recommended. This local operator also oraganizes zip-lining experiences. ⊠ *5 km (3 miles) south of Praia do Forte on BA-099, Praia do Forte* ☎ *071/9600–7503* ⊕ *www. florestasustentavel.org.br/contato.html.*

BEACHES

FAMILY **Papa Gente.** Swim or snorkel in the crystal clear (and safe) waters of the Papa Gente, a 3-meter- (10-foot-) deep natural pool formed by reefs at the ocean's edge. Located 1½ km (1 mile) from Projecto Tamar, walk

9

north along the beach when the tide is low and look out for a coconut vendor, who sits in front of the path that leads to the pools and has masks and snorkels for rent. **Amenities:** none. **Best for:** solitude; snorkeling; swimming; walking. ✉ *1½ km (1 mile) north of the center of Praia do Forte, Praia do Forte.*

WHERE TO EAT AND STAY

$$$ BRAZILIAN SEAFOOD 🍴 **Sabor da Vila.** It isn't surprising that seafood fresh from the ocean is the specialty at this simple yet ever-popular Bahian restaurant on Praia do Forte's main street. Choose between eight different varieties of seafood moqueca, or opt for the lighter option of *ensopado.* [$] *Average main: R$60* ✉ *Av. Acm. 159, Praia do Forte* ☎ *071/3676–1156* 🌐 *www.sabordavila.com.*

$$ B&B/INN FAMILY 🏨 **Pousada Rosa dos Ventos.** Centrally located between Praia do Forte's main beach and the center of town, this intimate, family-friendly pousada offers six comfortable rooms, personalized service, and a small pool. **Pros:** good location; clean, comfy rooms; friendly staff. **Cons:** can be noisy; no bar or restaurant service during the day. [$] *Rooms from: R$270* ✉ *Alameda da Lua s/n, Praia do Forte* ☎ *071/3676–1271* 🌐 *www.pousadarosadosventos.com.br* 🛏 *6 rooms* 🍽 *Breakfast.*

$$$$ RESORT FAMILY 🏨 **Tivoli Eco Resort Praia do Forte.** Relax in a hammock and contemplate the sea from your private veranda at this chic five-star beachfront resort and wellness center. **Pros:** plenty of amenities; relaxing spa therapies. **Cons:** pricey; some rooms are far from the central facilities. [$] *Rooms from: R$1,015* ✉ *Av. do Farol s/n, Praia do Forte, Mata de São João* ☎ *071/3676–4000* 🌐 *www.tivolihotels.com* 🛏 *287 rooms* 🍽 *Some meals.*

MORRO DE SÃO PAULO

Eternally popular among travelers seeking fun in the sun, Morro de São Paulo is the largest village on the Ilha de Tinharé, where thick Atlantic Forest protected by a state park helps it remain predominantly car-free. Step off the direct catamarã from Salvador to find wheelbarrows and donkeys waiting to help heavy packers reach the beaches, identified by number. Tourism's footprint can certainly be felt, with beaches lined with accommodations options and restaurants. While Praia Primeria is the most family-friendly, Praia Segunda is party-central, with fresh-fruit *caipi* carts parked directly on the sand and live music every night during high season. Praia Terceira and Praia Quarta provide more peaceful options.

GETTING HERE AND AROUND

To get here from Salvador, take either a *lancha* (small boat carrying up to five passengers) or larger *catamarã* (catamaran) from Salvador's Terminal Maritimo. Lanchas and catamarãs leave daily from 8 am to 2 pm on the two-hour journey and return from Morro de São Paulo from 9 am and 2 pm. Fares range from R$50 to R$75 and are worth booking in advance during high season. Those prone to sea-sickness should opt for the more comfortable catamarã, for the crossing can be rocky.

A handful of small flight operators, including Bahia Terra Turismo, have service to Morro de São Paulo from Salvador. The 20-minute flight costs about R$395 one-way. There's only a landing strip at Morro de São Paulo.

ESSENTIALS

Airline Contacts **Bahia Terra Turismo.** ✉ *Praia Boca da Barra, Boipepa* ☎ *075/3653–6017* 🌐 *www.boipebatur.com.br.*

BEACHES

Popular beaches dot the 40-km (25-mile) Atlantic side of Tinharé. Starting at the village of Morro de São Paulo, beaches begin with Primeira (First) and go on to Segunda, Terceira, and so forth. Local boats offer the best way to explore the island, while horses are also available for hire. Waters are calm thanks to the coral reef just off the surf, whose abundant marine life (mostly in the form of small fish) makes scuba diving or snorkeling worthwhile. The number of tourists nearly triples from December to February, when Brazilians on their summer vacation fill the pousadas for festival and Carnival season. The southernmost beaches near Boca da Barra are usually quieter even during peak season. The government has begun to charge an environmental tourism tax of R$15 per person.

WHERE TO STAY

$$ B&B/INN FAMILY 🏨 **Anima Hotel.** Set on the island's secluded fifth beach, Praia do Encanto, this intimate hotel has nine stand-alone bungalows scattered through 6 hectares (15 acres) of tropical forest—a favorite among couples and those on the hunt for some serious downtime. **Pros:** excellent staff; proximity to the beach; good in-house restaurant. **Cons:** slow Wi-Fi; far from town. [$] *Rooms from: R$300* ✉ *Praia do Encanto s/n, Morro de São Paulo* ☎ *075/3652–2077* 🌐 *www.animahotel.com* 🛏 *9 bungalows* 🍴 *Breakfast.*

BOIPEBA

5 hours south of Salvador.

With few direct transport links, Boipeba's pristine white sand, turquoise waters, and virgin forests have remained something of a Robinson Crusoe's dream. Surrounded by the Atlantic Ocean on one side, and Rio do Inferno (Hell's River) on the other, access to the island from Salvador can be time-consuming and requires a little more effort and planning than most places—allow at least three days in Boibepa—but it is well worth it. As yet, no big hotels have found their foothold on the island, and the pousadas here range from the simple to increasingly rustic-chic. Many serve lunch and dinner as well as breakfast. Wi-Fi access is often patchy, so workaholics should come expecting to switch off.

GETTING HERE AND AROUND

From Salvador, there are a number of different options depending on time and budget. Ferries for Bom Despacho (1 hour for R$3.95) depart regularly from São Joaquim terminal in Salvador. From there you can take a bus (2 hours for R$15) or taxi (1 hour for R$150) to Valença or Gracioso, where small speedboats await to transfer you to the final section (1½ hours for R$35). The last speedboat departs at 5 pm, so be sure to leave enough time. The entire journey takes approximately

5 hours. Bahia Terra Turismo also offers airplane taxis that depart 3 times a day from Salvador's international airport; flights cost R$485 each way and take 25 minutes.

TOURS

Boipebatur. This efficient agency has an office in Velha Boipeba and can solve all your transfer solutions, working with reliable small aircraft, speedboats, and taxis to connect the dots. They also organize day trips around the island by speedboat, from R$100 per person for a group experience or R$200 per person for a private boat. ⊠ *Praia Boca da Barra, Boipepa* ☎ *075/3653–6017* ⊕ *www.boipebatur.com.br.*

EXPLORING

The pace on Boipeba is syrupy slow, but if you manage to make it out of your hammock, there is much to explore on and around the 7-km- (4-mile-) wide island. Hire a boat through the local guides' association or via one of the pousadas and spend the day exploring the natural swimming pools that lie before the Ponta dos Castelhanos. After lunch, head to Vila de Moreré, a small beach community of 250 people; some accommodations are available here. Other activities include sunset canoe rides through the mangrove and a visit to Velha Boipeba (the commercial heart of the island). Some pousadas, like Pousada Santa Clara, offer the chance to take part in local environmental and community projects.

Moreré. Those looking to fall even farther off the grid should head straight for Moreré, Boipeba's second village, set on the beach and accessible only by boat ride or a 45-minute tractor trip through the jungle from the main town square of Velha Boipeba. Moreré's insular fishing community of 250 inhabitants is now balanced by an interesting mix of expats, who run many of the pousadas and simple restaurants and have injected a welcome level of sophistication into the area. The real draw of Moreré is the beauty of the surrounding nature and the island's spectacular beaches—so remote that even during high season, you won't have to share them with more than a few other souls. The beach here varies dramatically with the tide—at high tide, its crystal- line waters make for great swimming and form natural pools among the rocks. ⊠ *Praia do Moreré, 6½ km (4 miles) SE of Velha Boipeba, Boipepa.*

BEACHES

Boca da Barra. The closest beach to Boipeba's small town, Velha Boipeba, is also the island's busiest, dotted with pousadas and beachfront restau- rants serving Bahian seafood and ice-cold beer. Although the turquoise waters are calm enough for swimming, they get rougher when the tide comes in, swallowing most of the sand and making sunbathing a chal- lenge. Where the sea joins with the Rio do Inferno is one of the island's best spots for watching the sunset. **Amenities** : food and drink. **Best for:** sunset; walking. ⊠ *¾ km (½ mile) south of Velha Boipeba along the beach, Boipepa.*

Fodor's Choice **Ponta dos Castelhanos.** Named in honor of a Spanish galleon that sank
★ off the coast in 1535, this postcard-perfect deserted beach fringed in coconut palms offers good snorkeling (take your own masks) in calm

crystalline waters framed in coral reefs. Access is by boat from Velha Boipeba, Boca da Barra, or nearby Moreré. Bring your own water as there are no beach vendors. **Amenities:** none.e **Best for:** snorkeling; swimming; walking. ✉ *Ilha de Boipeba, Boipepa.*

Praia da Cueira. A 40-minute walk along the sand from Boca da Barra, following the jungle track after Praia Tassimirim, is the immense curved Bay of Cueira, a favorite for local soccer matches and for families to spend the day. A smattering of restaurants, including Guido's lobster shack, serve lunch and ice-cold coconuts. **Amenities:** food and drink; toilets. **Best for:** swimming; walking. ✉ *2½ km (1½ miles) south of Velha Boibepa, Boipepa.*

FAMILY **Praia de Bainema.** A 20-minute walk along a lovely trail that winds between the forest and the beach from Moreré, this deserted beach's long stretch of golden sand is a favorite with families due to the calm waters and natural pools that form at midtide. Make sure you bring your own water and seek shade beneath a coconut palm. **Amenities:** none. **Best for:** surfing; swimming; walking. ✉ *3 km (2 miles) southeast of Moreré, Boipepa.*

WHERE TO EAT AND STAY

$$ SEAFOOD FAMILY 🍴 **Guido's.** Local lobster man Guido has grown into something of a Brazilian legend over the past 15 years, since he first began serving up succulent whole lobsters fished right out of the rocks in front of his beachside café on the curved bay of Praia da Cueira, a 30- to 40-minute walk during low tide from Velha Boibepa. It's a laid back family affair, with plastic tables and chairs set in the sand and sizeable portions of lobster cooked in spices and honey, served up with traditional rice, beans, and salad. [$] *Average main: R$45* ✉ *Praia da Cueira, Boipepa* ☎ *075/9907–7049* ⏲ *No dinner.*

$ B&B/INN Fodor's Choice ★ 🏨 **Eco-Pousada Casa Bobó.** Perched atop a hill in the the Mata Atlântica rain forest, with a 360-degree view across the beaches of Moreré and Bainema, this bohemian eco-pousada is the ultimate into-the-jungle retreat. **Pros:** romantic; healthy, homemade food. **Cons:** remote; not suitable for the less active. [$] *Rooms from: R$250* ✉ *Vila Monte Alegre s/n, Boipepa* ☎ *075/9930–5757* 🌐 *www.pousadacasabobo.com* 🛏 *3 bungalows* 🍽 *Breakfast* 💳 *No credit cards.*

$$ B&B/INN FAMILY Fodor's Choice ★ 🏨 **Pousada A Mangueira.** Providing a surprising level of sophistication in the midst of such remote natural beauty, this pousada's chic chalets come with private verandas and double hammocks, set among a tropical garden blooming in mango trees and hibiscus just 50 meters from Moreré Beach. **Pros:** excellent location; fabulous food; charming bilingual owners. **Cons:** no TVs. [$] *Rooms from: R$205* ✉ *Praia de Moreré, Boipepa* ☎ *075/3653–8915* 🌐 *pousadamangueira.com* ⏲ *Closed May–July* 🛏 *7 bungalows* 🍽 *Breakfast.*

$ B&B/INN 🏨 **Pousada Luar das Águas.** Right on the shore of Boca da Barra beach, these simple, stylish bungalows are well suited for gourmands on a budget, combining competitive pricing with charming, laid-back service and a tasty beachfront restaurant. **Pros:** good value; beachfront location. **Cons:** few amenities; standard apartments are musty; no TVs. [$] *Rooms from: R$240* ✉ *Rua da Praia s/n, Boipepa* ☎ *075/3653–6015* 🌐 *www.luardasaguas.com* 🛏 *10 bungalows* 🍽 *Breakfast.*

$$$ 🖭 **Pousada Mangabeiras.** Set amid native forest with views that stretch
B&B/INN over the island and out to sea, the colorful bungalows at this pousada
are some of Boipeba's more upmarket options. **Pros:** generous buf-
fet breakfast; 360-degree views. **Cons:** brightly colored rooms not to
everyone's taste; tricky access; often requires a minimum two-night
stay. Ⓢ *Rooms from: R$425* ✉ *Praia Boca Da Barra, Rua Da Praia
s/n, Boipepa* 🕾 *075/3653–6153* ⊕ *www.pousadamangabeiras.com.br*
Ⓧ *Closed June* ⇥ *9 rooms* ⊙l *Breakfast.*

$ 🖭 **Pousada Santa Clara.** This well-run pousada 50 meters back from
B&B/INN Boca da Barra Beach ticks all the boxes for those looking to kick back
FAMILY in paradise on a budget: simple, spacious rooms, a tropical garden
complete with giant hammocks, and a lavish, homemade breakfast
that changes daily. **Pros:** great food; bilingual service; good value.
Cons: patchy Wi-Fi; air-conditioning not in all rooms; simple rooms.
Ⓢ *Rooms from: R$240* ✉ *Trv. da Praia No. 5, Boipeba* 🕾 *075/3653–
6085* ⊕ *www.santaclaraboipeba.com* Ⓧ *Closed mid May–early June*
⇥ *12 rooms* ⊙l *Breakfast.*

LENÇÓIS

*427 km (265 miles) west of Salvador; 1,133 km (704 miles) northeast
of Brasília.*

In a region of outstanding natural beauty, the small town of Lençóis
was once known as the Diamond Capital thanks to the frenzy that
took hold in 1822 after the discovery of the precious gems in riverbeds
around the town of Mucugê. Hordes of people hoping to make their
fortune flooded the region, and the town earned its name—Lençóis
means "bedsheet" in Portuguese—thanks to the hundreds of makeshift
tents of white cotton fabric built by *garimperos* (gold and precious-
stoneseekers). While the heady golden age of quick fortunes came to a
halt toward the end of the 19th century, diamond prospecting by local
garimperos continued right up until 1993, when it was deemed illegal
due to environmental concerns. Some say that only 40% of the area's
diamonds have actually been recovered.

What could have spelled the rapid decline of this historic town, as was
the case with Ilhéus and the end of the cacao industry, turned out to be
its savior: in 1985 Lençóis and the surrounding area was designated a
national park, now known as the Parque Nacional de Chapada Dia-
mantina. Tourism really took off in 1992 when the area was used as
the location for filming the Brazilian soap opera *Pedra por Pedra*. Cha-
pada Diamantina's stunning natural splendor captivated the nation and
visitors flocked to explore the nascent adventure capital's verdant hills
and waterfalls, while former miners found work building new hotels,
restoring historic buildings, and training as local guides. While far from
perfect, Lençóis has evolved into one of Brazil's most charming small
towns, where nature-lovers from across the world settle and locals still
tell tales of those heady diamond days.

GETTING HERE AND AROUND

Driving from Salvador to Chapada Diamantina is both straightforward and a beautiful way to explore the surrounding countryside: take BR 342 west to Feira de Santana, then BR 242 to Lençóis. Both roads are in good condition. Real Expresso/Rapido Federal buses make the six-hour trip from Salvador to Lençóis for R$64–R$75. Departures are from the Estação Rodoviária at 7 am, 1 pm, 5 pm, and 11:30 pm daily, with the return running at 7:30 am, 1:15 pm, and 11:30 pm daily. Local airline Azul operates return flights from Salvador to Lençóis on Thursday and Sunday.

ESSENTIALS

Bus Contacts Estação Rodoviária. ⊠ *Av. Senhor dos Passos s/n, Lençóis* ☎ *075/3334–1112, 075/3334–1595.* **Real Expresso.** ☎ *011/2142–7100 Central Office in São Paulo* ⊕ *www.realexpresso.com.br.*

TOURS

Fora da Trilha. This adventure outfitter offers a range of "off the beaten track" experiences across Chapada Diamantina, specializing in rappeling and climbing, as well as longer hikes of 2–8 days, including a highly recommended 4-day trek through the Vale do Pati. Groups are arranged on level of expertise and fitness. The company can also organize lodging and transfers for you. ⊠ *Rua das Pedras 202, Lençóis* ☎ *075/3334–1326* ⊕ *www.foradatrilha.com.br* ☝ *From R$120.*

FAMILY
Fodor'sChoice
★
Nas Alturas. This professional, friendly agency offers a range of expert, multilingual guides specializing in Chapada Diamantina tours and experiences. Drop by for a chat when you arrive and they will advise on how to make the most of your time, with a variety of different tours departing daily, as well as private guiding for groups. Among the more alternative options is a gourmet coffee tour of the region. ⊠ *Praça Horacio de Matos 130, Lençóis* ☎ *075/3334–0054* ⊕ *www.nasalturas.net* ☝ *From R$120.*

EXPLORING

Igatú. A steep 6-km (4-mile) cobblestone road connects the BA 142 highway with the village of Igatú, a former boomtown of the 19th century where the faded ruins of abandoned mansions surround contemporary pastel cottages. The open-air museum Galeria Arte e Memoria celebrates the life and customs of the *garimperos,* combining former stone houses with a sculpture garden and café, while at the Mina Brejo-Veruga, you can venture into what was once the area's largest diamond mine. For those looking for an alternative to hiking, this provides an interesting half-day experience into the history of the region and can be done alone or as part of a tour. ⊠ *96 km (60 miles) south of Lençóis, Lençóis.*

FAMILY
Lapa Doce Cave. A 15-minute hike takes you down to the mouth of the Lapa Doce cave, where you will see a stunning collection of large stalagmites, stalactites, and columns. Access is only possible with a local guide, included in the price of admission along with a flashlight for navigating in the dark and exploring the unique frescoe-like coloring and natural sculptures. Local guides only speak Portuguese, so if you are looking for greater insight, plan to go with your own guide as part

9

CLOSE UP

Making the Most of your Time

There is such a wealth of breathtaking spots to explore in and around Lençóis and Chapada Diamantina that it is worth doing some advance research and planning your trip with the help of a local guide or agency. If you have only a few days, do the classic one-day experience, which combines a visit to Poço de Diablo, the stunning stalagmite and stalactite caves of Lapa Doce, and the tabletop mountain of Pai Inácio. The rest of your time can be happily spent between the waterfall and refreshing natural pools of Ribeirão do Meio (a 40-minute walk from town through the forest) or Rio Serrano (a 10-minute walk from town), both of which can be visited without a guide. Those with the time and inclination to delve deeper should consider the four-day hike through the Tupi pilgrim trail of Vale do Pati, or plan to visit the spectacular Cachoeira de Buracão, around 195 km (120 miles) from Lençóis.

of a longer day experience. Because it's so accessible, Lapa Doce is especially recommended for children. ✉ *67 km (42 miles) northwest of Lençóis, Lençóis* ✣ *From Lençóis, take BR 141 on to the main road, and then BR 242 west 25 km (16 miles), then take BA 122, the road to Iraquara, for about 18 km (11 miles)* ☎ *075/3625–1084* 🎟 *R$15* ⏲ *Daily 9–6.*

FAMILY Fodor's Choice ★ **Ribeirão do Meio Waterfall.** A visit to this waterfall, set within a verdant valley 3½ km (2 miles) from the center of Lençóis, is one of the most pleasant ways to spend half a day. The trail is accessible from the west of town, next to Pousada Canto das Aguas, and winds through the forest, with a number of small *barracas*set up along the way selling water and *agua de coco.*This is a local favorite for basking in the sun, swimming in the pools, and playing around on the waterfall's naturally crafted slide. The easy hike takes approximately 40 minutes each way and can be done without a guide. ✉ *Lençóis.*

FAMILY **Rio Serrano.** One of the region's most popular hiking trails runs along a section of Rio Lençóis called Rio Serrano. It's surrounded by exuberant forest, now protected as municipal park. The reddish-color water is due to organic matter from the forest floor. You can bathe and relax in several natural pools—they look a bit like hot tubs—formed on the rock-strewn riverbed. There are also three waterfalls scattered around the surrounding hills, best accessed with a local guide. To reach the easily accessible trailhead to the river, head up the hill after Hotel de Lençóis. ✉ *End of Rua Altina Alves, Lençóis.*

WHERE TO EAT AND STAY

$ CAFÉ 🍴 **Café Ba-Cana.** Regular live music and excellent cocktails make this a popular hangout with visitors and locals come nightfall. During the day it's a hot spot for caffeine aficionados, with a range of organic locally produced coffees complementing delicious homemade cakes and a simple menu of salads, sandwiches, and pasta dishes. [$] *Average main: R$30* ✉ *Rua Boa Vista 60, Lençóis* ☎ *075/9979–2387* 🌐 *www.cafebacana.wix.com/cafebacana.*

$$$$ BRAZILIAN 🍴 **Cozinha Aberta.** You'll be forgiven for wanting to order everything on the menu at Brazilian chef Deborah Doitschinoff's Slow Food spot set right on the river, where passionate staff talk diners through the rare local ingredients (such as *batata da serra*) that inspire the menu. Highlights include cacao spaghetti with shrimp, cashew-filled eggplant rolls, and cinnamon and tamarind caipirinhas. And while the flavors could be more inventive for the price, the experience itself—dining alfresco overlooking Lencois's rushing waterway with excellent service—makes for one of the most pleasant meals in town. [$] *Average main: R$70* ✉ *Av. Rua Barbosa 42, Lençóis* ☎ *075/3334–1321* 🌐 *cozinhaaberta.com.br.*

$ PIZZA FAMILY 🍴 **Pizzeria da Gente.** Arguably the best-value dining experience in town, this hole-in-the-wall spot is a local favorite for its tasty thin-crust wood-oven pizzas and ice-cold beer, which can be ordered to take away or enjoyed at one of the metal tables set out in the street. Still hungry? Stop off next door for a sugar high at Pavê e Comê, a dessert-only café run by charismatic granny Sonia, who specializes in classic Brazilian treats such as *pavê de chocolate com caldo quente e sorvete de maracujá* (chocolate cake with hot sauce and passion-fruit ice cream). [$] *Average main: R$20* ✉ *Rua das Pedras s/n, Lençóis* ☎ *075/3334–1963* 🕓 *No lunch.*

$ B&B/INN 🏨 **Estalagem de Alcino.** Guests rave about the endless gourmet breakfasts at this beautiful restored colonial house a few minutes stroll from the center of town. **Pros:** charming host; fantastic homemade breakfast; interesting local experience. **Cons:** not suited for couples looking for privacy; few amenities; some rooms can be noisy. [$] *Rooms from: R$190* ✉ *139 General Vivieros, Lençóis* ☎ *075/3334–1171* 🌐 *www.alcinoestalagem.com* 🛏 *7 rooms (3 with shared bath), 4 suites* 🍽 *Breakfast.*

$$$ B&B/INN FAMILY 🏨 **Hotel Canto das Águas.** One of the first hotels to open after the creation of the national park, Canto das Águas remains one of the most comfortable places to stay in Lençóis, with spacious rooms overlooking the river and stone archways opening to a garden and large swimming pool that frames the main building. **Pros:** superb location near the main plaza; lots of amenities, including a sauna, games room, and pool; good for families. **Cons:** noisy during festivals; design can be a little dated. [$] *Rooms from: R$388* ✉ *Av. Sr. dos Passos 1, Lençóis* ☎ *075/3334–1154* 🌐 *www.lencois.com.br* 🛏 *36 rooms, 8 suites* 🍽 *Breakfast.*

$ B&B/INN FAMILY 🏨 **Pousada Casa da Geléia.** If you're seeking a home away from home, look no further than this simple pousada's clean, spacious, white-walled rooms, where the English-speaking owners will entertain you with tales of the history of the Chapada. **Pros:** fantastic breakfast; friendly owners; spacious grounds. **Cons:** no in-room TVs; design lacks charm. [$] *Rooms from: R$190* ✉ *Rua General Viveiros 187, Lençóis* ☎ *075/3334–1151* 🌐 *www.casadageleia.com.br* 🛏 *6 rooms* 🍽 *Breakfast.*

$ B&B/INN FAMILY Fodor's Choice ★ 🏨 **Vila Serrano.** A short stroll from Lençóis's charming cobbled center, this relaxed hotel's rustic rooms fan out around a beautiful garden and combine privacy (each has its own hammock hung on a private terrace) with friendly staff. **Pros:** great value; relaxed environment; comfortable rooms. **Cons:** rooms on ground floor can be noisy; verdant gardens mean mosquitos. [$] *Rooms from: R$230* ✉ *Rua Alto do Bonfim 8, Lençóis* ☎ *075/3334–1486* 🌐 *vilaserrano.com.br/chapada_diamantina* 🛏 *13 rooms* 🍴 *Breakfast.*

PARQUE NACIONAL CHAPADA DIAMANTINA

60 km (37 miles) west of Lençóis.

GETTING HERE AND AROUND

The town of Lençóis is by far the best gateway to the park.

SAFETY AND PRECAUTIONS

Traversing the roads and especially the trails within the park definitely requires experienced guides, as trails are not well marked.

EXPLORING

FAMILY **Parque Nacional Chapada Diamantina.** Established in 1985, the 1,520-square-km (593-square-mile) national park is one of the most scenic places in Brazil. Here you can find crystal clear creeks, rivers with abundant rapids and waterfalls, and more than 70 grottos and caverns. There are also the tall peaks of the Sincorá Range; the highest point is Barbados Peak (2,080 meters/7,000 feet). The flora and fauna of the area, which include many varieties of cactus, orchids, and bromeliads, and more than 200 bird species, have been the subject of two extensive studies by the Royal Botanical Gardens at Kew in England. The best time to visit the park is in the dry season, from March to October, but expect high temperatures during the day (rarely above 36°C/100°F). From May to July, temperatures might drop to near 10°C (45°F). The park does not have a visitor center, but there's a small ranger headquarters in the town of Palmeiras. ✉ *Lençóis* 🌐 *www.guiachapadadiamantina.com.br.*

FAMILY **Cachoeira da Fumaça.** One of the most popular hikes in the national park leads to the country's tallest waterfall, 1,312-foot Cachoeira da Fumaça (Smoke Waterfall). Most of the falling water evaporates before reaching the ground, hence the odd name. A 6-kilometer (3-mile) path from the village of Caeté-Açú takes you to the canyon's rim, where you can marvel at the smoke rising from above. Visiting the waterfall from Lençóis takes the best part of the day and should be done with a guide. ✉ *90 km (55 miles) west of Lençóis, Lençóis.*

Fodor's Choice ★ **Cachoeira de Buracão.** Considered by many to be one of the most stunning waterfalls in Brazil, Buracão may not be easy to get to, but it is defintitely worth the effort. Located 195 km (120 miles) south of Lençóis, it is recommended that you stay overnight in the nearby town of Mucugê before undertaking the one-hour trek from the start of the trail through verdant forest. The final stretch of the journey involves passing through a canyon and swimming to reach the entrance to the waterfall. Life jackets are obligatory and will be provided by your local guide. It is impossible to enter the park without a local guide. Most tours that originate in Lençóis also include a visit to the brilliant-blue pools of Poço Encantando (141 km [88 miles] south of Lençóis) and Poço Azul (81 km [50 miles] south of Lençóis), formed by a combination of minerals and reflections in the water from the surrounding caves. Between

August and November, beams of sunshine light up the water, maximizing the brilliant color and enhancing visibility. ⊠ *78 km (48 miles) south of Mucûge, 210 km (130 miles) south of Lençóis, Ibicoara, .*

FAMILY
Fodor's Choice
★

Morro de Pai Inácio. The icon of Chapada Diamantina, this tabletop mountain sits at 1,120 meters (3,675 feet) above sea level and provides a spectacular 360-degree view across the Vale do Capão and Morro do Camelo. Access up a steep, short path is easy and can be undertaken without a guide. Orchids, bromelias, and cacti flourish on top of the rocky plateau. Local legend goes that the mountain was named after a black slave and local hero, Pai Inácio, who fell in love with the ruling colonel's daughter. In order to escape the colonel's men, he ran up the mountain and jumped off, breaking his fall with an umbrella and disappearing into the valley, where he was reunited with his true love. ⊠ *Lençóis ✛ 26 km (16 miles) north of Lençóis, along the BR242* ⊠ *R$5.*

SPORTS AND THE OUTDOORS

Vale do Pati. One of the country's most scenic treks, this onetime pilgrim trail of the Tupi Indians takes you between towering sierras, through caves, and past waterfalls. The 70-km (43-mile) trail starts in Bomba, climbs to Candombá Hills, follows a plateau at Gerais de Vieira, then goes alongside the steep Rio Paty toward Andaraí. Along the way, you can either camp or sleep in simple, clean wood huts provided by locals. Although the trek itself is not challenging, it does cover a considerable distance spread over four days and requires a general level of fitness and good walking shoes. A six-day trek is also available. ⊠ *20 km (12 miles) west of Lençóis, Lençóis.*

THE COCOA COAST

180 kilometers (112 miles) of golden beaches, flanked by coconut groves, dense Mata Atlântica rain forest, and exotic cocoa plantations, stretch between the hip surf town of Itacaré and sleepy Canavieras, making the Cocoa Coast one of Bahia's best driving routes. Along the way are fishing villages, fresh seafood, and luxurious beach resorts, where you could happily get lost for weeks. Regional bus service to towns on the Cocoa Coast departs from Salvador's Terminal Rodoviário.

9

ILHÉUS

460 km (286 miles) south of Salvador.

In Brazil, Ilhéus (literally meaning "islanders") is synonymous with cocoa and Jorge Amado, one of Brazil's best-known 20th-century writers. Amado spent his childhood here, and the house he lived in is now a cultural center. Many of his world-famous novels are set in places in and around Ilhéus and bring to life the golden age of the region, when cocoa production was so prosperous that it was nicknamed "black gold." Catedral de São Sebastião (San Sebastian Cathedral) is the heart of the central area—a plaza surrounded by colonial-period buildings akin to those in Pelourinho.

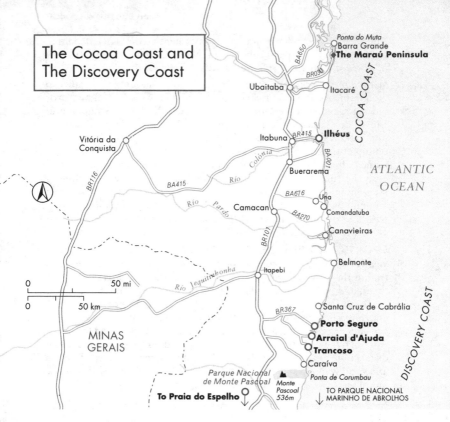

The Cocoa Coast and
The Discovery Coast

Ponta do Muta
Barra Grande
The Maraú Peninsula

Ubaitaba
Itacaré

COCOA COAST

Vitória da
Conquista

Itabuna
BR415
Ilhéus

Colônia

Buerarema

ATLANTIC
OCEAN

BA415
Rio

Rio Pardo
Camacan

BA676
Una

BA270
Comandatuba

Canavieiras

Itapebi
Belmonte

0   50 mi
0   50 km

MINAS
GERAIS

Rio Jequitinhonha

BR367
Santa Cruz de Cabrália

Porto Seguro
Arraial d'Ajuda
Trancoso

DISCOVERY COAST

Caraíva

Parque Nacional
de Monte Pascoal   Monte
Pascoal
To Praia do Espelho   536m

Ponta de Corumbau

TO PARQUE NACIONAL
MARINHO DE ABROLHOS

GETTING HERE AND AROUND

There are daily flights to Ilhéus from Rio de Janeiro, Saõ Paulo, and
Salvador. Águia Branca buses travel from Salvador to Ilhéus in about
eight hours. The cost is R$105 for a regular bus and R$170 for an
executive bus. By car take Rodovia BR 101 south.

ESSENTIALS

Airport Aeroporto de Ilhéus Jorge Amado. ⊠ *Rua Brigadeir o Eduardo
Gomes s/n, Pontal, Ilhéus* ☎ *073/3234-4000* ⊕ *www.infraero.gov.br.*

Bus Contact Águia Branca. ☎ *073/3288–1039, 073/4004–1010* ⊕ *www.
aguiabranca.com.br.*

Car Rental Contacts Movida Rent a Car. ⊠ *Aeroporto de Ilhéus—Jorge
Amado, Rua Brigadeiro Eduardo Gomes s/n, Ilhéus* ☎ *073/9119–8156* ⊕ *www.
movida.com.br.*

Taxi Contacts Ilhéus Taxi. ☎ *073/3634–4213.*

WHERE TO STAY

$$$$
RESORT
FAMILY
🏝 **Transamérica Ilha de Comandatuba.** On an island with a giant coconut
grove, this grande dame of Brazilian beach resorts remains a favorite choice for families with kids, golf lovers, and water-sport fanat-
ics. **Pros:** all-inclusive activities for families; nicely furnished rooms;

CLOSE UP

Beach Savvy

■ As a rule, the farther away from the downtown area, the better the beach in terms of water cleanliness and number of people, especially on weekends.

■ Beaches in Bahia, as in most of Brazil, tend not to have facilities like bathrooms or showers.

■ Pickpocketing and minor theft can be a problem. Bring as few items to the beach as possible, and just enough money for the day. Be cautious about leaving anything unattended.

■ Vendors, especially in Salvador, had a reputation for being overly persistent, but this is something that has changed considerably, and you should now find that you can shop in peace.

■ Larger cities such as Salvador, Ilhéus, and Porto Seguro have quick and comfortable public transportation to beaches, like the *ônibus executivo* (executive bus; a minibus or van, usually labeled "roteiro das praias").

■ Be careful when entering the water for the first time—a few steps in can put you in deep waters.

■ Be aware of rock outcroppings and coral reefs that can cut your feet.

■ If you plan to snorkel, bring your own gear. Rentals are not always available.

■ Food and drink are available at almost every beach, except those you have to hike to. However, if you're squeamish about eating food from a beach vendor, bring your own.

lovely beach. **Cons:** remote; can get very busy. $ *Rooms from: R$888* ✉ *Ilha de Comandatuba s/n, Una* ☎ *073/3686–1122, 0800/012–6060* ⊕ *www.transamerica.com.br* ↪ *231 rooms, 115 bungalows, 16 suites* ❑ *Some meals.*

$$$$ ⊡ **Txai Resorts.** This sprawling, luxury ecoresort sits among 100 hect-
RESORT ares (250 acres) of coconut groves on one of the region's most beautiful
FAMILY beaches and has delightful facilities, including a hilltop spa with views
over the ocean and virgin Mata Atlântica rain forest. **Pros:** beautiful
beach location; great for families; good service. **Cons:** can feel isloated;
rustic bathrooms. $ *Rooms from: R$1,300* ✉ *Rodovia Ilhéus Itacare,
Km 48, Ilhéus* ☎ *073/2101–5000* ⊕ *www.txai.com.br* ↪ *38 bungalows*
❑ *Breakfast.*

THE MARAÚ PENINSULA

276 km (171 miles) south of Salvador

In the native Indian Tupi Guarani language, Maraú means the "sun's light at daybreak," likely an homage to the dazzling light that governs the peninsula, from spectacular sunrises and sunsets to the chance to watch the full moon rise red out of the ocean. One of Bahia's best-kept secrets, the Maraú Peninsula is little known by international tourists yet increasingly popular with hip Brazilians looking to escape to more than 40 km (25 miles) of deserted beaches, some of which have crystalline, natural swimming pools and other surf breaks. On the inside of the peninsula, an extensive waterway connects an archipelago of uninhabited islands of virgin rain forest, mineral-enriched lagoons, and waterfalls.

GETTING HERE AND AROUND

The best way to access the peninsula is from the small port town of Camamu, where regular speedboats await to transport passengers across the bay to the pier at Barra Grande, Campinho, or Porto do Jobel. Or by car, take the BA 001 from Camamu or the BR 030 from Itacaré. If your point of departure is Salvador, you can opt for a private taxi transfer (which takes 6–7 hours and costs R$700) or take the adventurer's route, which combines ferry, bus, and speedboat. Take a ferry from Salvador's Terminal Marítimo de São Joaquim across the bay to Bom Despacho on the island of Itaparica (60 min, R$1.95, departures every hour). Buses run 3 or 4 times a day from Bom Despacho to Camamu (4 hours, R$27) and are operated by Aguía Branca and Cidade Sol. At Camamu, there are a variety of different companies that offer the 20-minute speedboat crossing to Barra Grande (R$30). Camamu Aventures is one of the most regular and reliable.

The nearest airport to the peninsula is at Ilhéus, 62 km (39 miles) away, and offers the easiest way to access the area. While there is no bus service from Ilhéus to Barra Grande, there is once-daily service with Cidade Sol from Ilhéus to the town of Maraú, which sits halfway up the peninsula. The best option is to take a private taxi, which costs R$200–R$300, depending on the season, or rent a car. If driving, renting a 4x4 is recommended, although not essential. Roads, while unpaved, are safe and easy to navigate, and having your own car is a great way to explore the peninsula without having to pay for expensive local taxis.

ESSENTIALS

Bus Contacts Aguia Branca. ☎ *073/2102–5353* ⊕ *www.aguiabranca.com.br.* **Cidade Sol.** ☎ *077/3423–1839* ⊕ *www.viacaocidadesol.com.br.*

Taxi Contacts Taxi Maraú. ✉ *Barra Grande* ☎ *073/8117–1730.*

TOURS

Camamu Adventures. One of the largest and most experienced operators on the island, with locations at the start of Barra Grande's pier as well as in Camamu, this tour company can arrange day trips to places like the Cachoeira Tremembé; boat transfers to Camamu, Boipeba, Itacaré, and Valença; as well as quad bike rental. ✉ *Av. Beira Mar 1* ☎ *073/3255–2138* ⊕ *www.camamuadventure.com.br.*

EXPLORING

FAMILY **Cachoeira de Tremembé.** One of the best ways to explore the peninsula is to join a boat trip or hire a private boat to explore the tropical islands, verdant coastline, and mangroves that line Camamu Bay down to the Tremembé Waterfall—one of the only freshwater waterfalls in Brazil that falls into saltwater, it's an impressive sight. Local kids act as guides to help the adventurous traverse it, and there are small pools for bathing at the top. Don't miss lunch at Ilha de Venezia, a little restaurant set in the forest to the left-hand side of the waterfall, where you can feast on locally grown *palmito* (palm heart) roasted in butter, *pitu* (crayfish), pitu moqueca, and *pitanga*cherry caiprinhas. It's pricey but well worth it. ✉ *BA 001, Km 25, Maraú.*

BEACHES

FAMILY Fodor's Choice ★ **Ponta de Mutá.** Make for one of the beach bars that line the sand to watch Barra Grande's legendary sunset. The calm waters also make this a good choice for families to spend the day. **Amenities:** food and drink; toilets . **Best for:** partiers; swimming; walking. ✉ *500 meters north of the Barra Grande Pier, Ponta de Mutá, Barra Grande.*

FAMILY Fodor's Choice ★ **Praia de Algodões.** This breathtaking beach is said to earn its name from the cresting waves that look like balls of cotton—*algodão* means cotton in Portuguese. Aside from a handful of sophisticated beachfront restaurants, you'll find the long curved bay all but deserted. **Amenities:** food and drink; parking (free); toilets. **Best for:** surfing; swimming; walking. ✉ *20 km (12 miles) south of Barra Grande, Praia de Algodões, Barra Grande.*

Taipu de Fora. On a clear day, the natural swimming pools that form in the turquoise waters just off the coast of Taipu de Fora beach make for great snorkeling. They are best explored when the tide is halfway out and masks can be rented from coconut vendors that line the shores. Taipu de Fora is also considered one of the area's best spots for surfing, and one of the liveliest places to spend the day relaxing at one of the beach bars. **Amenities:** food and drink; parking (free); toilets. **Best for:** partiers; snorkeling; surfing. ✉ *6 km (4 miles) south of Barra Grande, Praia Taipu de Fora, Barra Grande.*

WHERE TO EAT

$$ SEAFOOD FAMILY Fodor's Choice ★ 🍴 **Bar do Raúl.** The freshest of such Bahian delicacies as *mariscada* (seafood stew), *casquinha de siri* (shredded crab), and *arroz de polvo* (octopus rice) at great-value prices and served right on the beach are what make Raúl's a longtime local favorite. The service is friendly and slick and the portions so generous that one main course can be shared among three or four people. Set on the beach of Saquaira, Raúl's is a lot more laid-back than the beach bars in Barra Grande and a good opportunity to catch a slice of local life. [$] *Average main: R$40* ✉ *18 km (11 miles) south of Barra Grande, Praia da Saquaíra s/n, Barra Grande* ☎ *073/3258–4019* 🕒 *No dinner.*

$$ ECLECTIC FAMILY 🍴 **Lá em Casa.** This Praia de Algodoes restaurant–beach bar is run by Helena and Fernando, a charming couple from Rio, whose tapas-style menu and specials evolve daily around fresh local ingredients and create one of the most pleasant dining experiences in Maraú. Tables are set on a first-floor terrace, so diners have views of the bright green coconut palms framing the ocean. *Lá em casa* translates as "at home," and there is a relaxed feeling of being guests in a friend's house as Helena bustles in and out of the kitchen while her partner Fernando shakes up mango margaritas. They also offer two comfortable bungalows for rent. [$] *Average main: R$40* ✉ *23 km (14 miles) south of Barra Grande, Rua Praia de Algodões s/n, Barra Grande* ☎ *073/9900–9919.*

$$$ ✕ **Macunaíma Beach Lounge.** This hippie-chic beach bar is loved as much
BRAZILIAN for its signature cocktail, the Anti-Stress (vodka muddled with lemongrass, mint, and ginger), as for its extensive, tasty menu (try the tuna tartare and teriyaki salmon) and position on the beach at Ponto do Mutá. During high season, it's best to book ahead if you want one of the tables in the sand, perfect for whiling away the day until it's time to watch the sunset. Service can be alternately brilliant and patchy, but when everything clicks, it's one of the more sophisticated options on the peninsula. $ *Average main: R$50* ⊠ *Ponta da Mutá* ☎ *073/3258–6263* ⊗ *No dinner.*

WHERE TO STAY

$ ⊡ **Caiçara Bangalôs.** Beautifully designed, spacious wood bungalows
B&B/INN complete with private kitchens, set in a tropical garden off Praia de
FAMILY Bombaça, provide an ideal option for couples or friends looking to
Fodor's Choice relax in tranquil surroundings a 15-minute walk along the beach from
★ the Barra Grande. **Pros:** beautiful design details; great guest experience; own kitchen. **Cons:** not directly on the beach; better with own transportation. $ *Rooms from: R$215* ⊠ *Rua Dos Flamboyants, Praia de Bombaça, Barra Grande* ☎ *073/9975–1109* ⊕ *www.caicarabangalos. com.br* ⌫ *5 bungalows* ⦿ *Breakfast.*

$$ ⊡ **Dreamlands Bungalows.** Couples and families flock to the deliciously
B&B/INN laid-back Dreamlands, where 10 simple, stylish Scandinavian-esque
FAMILY bungalows sit overlooking a great surf break on Taipu de Fora Beach, and the hotel's beach bar is one of the best. **Pros:** lovely bilingual owners; trendy beach bar; access to surf beach and natural pools. **Cons:** food is pricey; small bathrooms. $ *Rooms from: R$330* ⊠ *1½ km (1 mile) north of Taipu de Fora, 4½ km (3 miles) south of Barra Grande, Barra Grande* ☎ *073/3258–6087* ⊕ *www.dreamlandbungalows.com* ⌫ *10 rooms* ⦿ *Breakfast.*

$$ ⊡ **Nirvana Beach Hotel.** While superbly located on the tip of hip Mutá
B&B/INN Point, a five-minute stroll down the beach from Barra Grande's bustling
FAMILY pier, Nirvana Beach Hotel's expansive 6-hectare (15-acre) grounds give
Fodor's Choice guests the sense of being marooned in the tropical rain forest. **Pros:** inti-
★ mate, homey atmosphere; charming bilingual service; beautiful rooms. **Cons:** no pool (until 2016); no a/c; no TV in the rooms. $ *Rooms from: R$295* ⊠ *Ponta de Mutá, Barra Grande* ☎ *073/3258 6357* ⊕ *www. nirvanabeachhotel.com* ⌫ *5 rooms* ⦿ *Breakfast.*

THE DISCOVERY COAST

The Discovery Coast is where Portuguese explorer Pedro Alvares Cabral first sighted the jungle-covered mountain of Monte Pascoal, 35 km (22 miles) south of Trancoso, claiming the country for the Portuguese. The birthplace of Brazil, the area remains one of the country's most outstanding areas of natural beauty, encompassing a series of national reserves that make up the largest section of Brazil's primary Mata Atlântica rain forest, destroyed across most of the rest of Brazil and replanted as secondary Mata Atlântica. Considered to be the world's richest rain forest in number of trees per square hectare, it was designated a UNESCO World Heritage Site in 1999. Dense emerald forests

Eating Bahian

When African slaves arrived in Bahia, they added coconut milk, palm oil, and hot spices into Portuguese and Indian dishes, transforming them into something quite new. Additional basic raw materials are lemon, coriander, tomato, onions, dried shrimp, salt, and hot chili peppers. Seafood is the thing in Bahia, and most regional seafood dishes are well seasoned, if not fiery hot. Bahia's most famous dish is *moqueca*, a seafood stew made with fish and/or shellfish, dendê oil, coconut milk, onions, and tomatoes, cooked quickly in a clay pot over a high flame. *Bobó* is an equally tasty but creamier version of moqueca due to the addition of cassava flour. Other classics include *vatapá*, a thick purée-like stew made with fish, shrimp, cashews, peanuts, and a variety of seasonings; *caruru*, okra mashed with ginger, dried shrimp, and palm oil;

ximxim de galinha, chicken marinated in lemon or lime juice, garlic, and salt and pepper, then cooked with dendê and peanut oil, coconut milk, tomatoes, and seasonings; and *efo*, a bitter chicory-like vegetable cooked with dried shrimp. *Sarapatel* is a Portuguese dish, a stew of pig meat and inner organs that has been incorporated seamlessly into Bahian cuisine.

A popular snack is *acarajé*, a pastry of *feijão fradinho* (black-eyed beans) flour deep-fried in dendê oil and filled with *camarão* (sun-dried shrimp) and *pimenta* (hot-pepper sauce). A variation is *abará*, peas or beans boiled in a banana leaf instead of fried. Note that palm oil is high in saturated fat and hard to digest; you can order these dishes without it. Restaurants in Bahia usually serve hot pepper sauce on the side of all dishes, which is unusual elsewhere in Brazil.

and golden beaches dominate the landscape that surrounds chic beach towns such as Trancoso and Arraial d'Ajuda, while farther south lie deserted beaches and communities of fishermen that were off the grid until a few years ago

9

ARRAIAL D'AJUDA

10-minute ferry ride from Porto Seguro.

This town was founded by Jesuits that arrived in 1549 with the Portuguese official Tomé de Souza, the first governor-general of Brazil. Its name is a tribute to Our Lady of Help, a much-revered saint in Portugal. The church and parish were the center of the Catholic Church in Brazil for more than a century.

In the 1970s, laid-back Arraial d'Ajuda attracted Brazilian hippies; and then a slew of foreign adventurers moved here, giving the place an eclectic atmosphere and the nickname "Corner of the World." Nowadays, its popularity has spawned hundreds of pousadas and restaurants catering to all budgets. During high season, the small town is overrun with vacationers and a young Brazilian crowd drawn to the regular roster of beach parties, concentrated around Praia Parracho.

GETTING HERE AND AROUND

Take one of the ferries that depart from Porto Seguro's small ferry terminal every half hour. The five- to 10-minute trip costs R$3 per person and R$13.50 for cars. During high season, ferries depart as soon as they fill up, and those driving should be prepared to wait up to an hour. If you are in a hurry, look to do the trip by foot or taxi—local taxis are exempt from queuing.

BEACHES

FAMILY **Praia de Pitanga.** While often busy, the calm, warm waters at this long beach framed in multicolored cliffs make it a winner with families, while the many beach bars that line the shore make it a good option to spend the day, relaxing with friends and enjoying the music; beach bar Flor do Sal is recommended. **Amenities:** food and drink; parking (free); toilets. **Best for:** swimming; walking. ✉ *2 km (1 mile) south of Arraial D'Ajuda, Arraial d'Ajuda.*

Praia de Taípe. A two-hour walk along the sand from the center of town (or 20 minutes by car) takes you to Arraial's most deserted beach, framed in dusky pink cliffs. Stop for lunch in one of the few beachfront restaurants. **Amenities:** food and drink; toilets. **Best for:** swimming; walking. ✉ *15 km (9 miles) south of Arraial D'Ajuda, Arraial d'Ajuda.*

Praia do Mucugê. Arraial d'Ajuda's main beach is best avoided by those looking for a peaceful escape into nature: always crowded and sometimes dirty, this is the place to come if you are looking for loud music, a cold beer, and traditional Brazilian deep-fried snacks. During high season, the beach hosts full-moon parties and electronic raves. **Amenities:** food and drink; lifeguards; parking (free); toilets. **Best for:** partiers. ✉ *Arraial d'Ajuda town center, Arraial d'Ajuda* ✣ *Access at the end of Rua do Mucugê.*

WHERE TO EAT AND STAY

$ BRAZILIAN ECLECTIC 🍴 **A Portinha.** This good-value, lunch-only, buffet-style restaurant attracts both locals and foreign visitors with its generous salad bar and variety of "slow-cooked" options. The restaurant serves a different type of cuisine daily, so the fare for any given day might include Brazilian, Italian, or Asian specialties. Price is charged per weight of the food on your plate. [$] *Average main: R$30* ✉ *Shopping d´Ajuda, Rua do Mucugê 333, Arraial d'Ajuda* ☎ *073/3575–1289* 🌐 *www.portinha.com.br* 🕓 *No dinner.*

$$$$ RESORT FAMILY 🏨 **Arraial d'Ajuda Eco Resort.** This resort should be your choice if you're looking for a beachfront hotel offering ample activities for kids, plus a gorgeous beach complete with natural pools. **Pros:** water park admission included in rates; comfortable rooms; great for kids. **Cons:** can be crowded with day-trippers; some rooms are musty; buffet food could be improved. [$] *Rooms from: R$605* ✉ *Ponta do Apaga Fogo, Arraial d'Ajuda* ☎ *073/3575–8500* 🌐 *www.arraialresort.com.br* 🛏 *164 rooms* 🍽 *Some meals.*

$$$$ B&B/INN 🏨 **La Residence.** Set right on the idyllic Praia do Pescador, this intimate boutique hotel combines highly personalized service from French owner Giovanna with peaceful, elegant rooms, far from the bustle of the town center. **Pros:** peaceful location; elegant design; first-class service. **Cons:**

far from the center of town. [$] *Rooms from: R$600* ✉ *Estrada da Balsa 940, Arraial d'Ajuda* ☎ *073/3575–1572* 🛏 *4 rooms* 🍴 *Breakfast.*

$ B&B/INN 🏨 **Manacá Pousada Parque.** The main draw at this charming pousada are the rooms, which are large, comfortable, well-decorated, and appointed with king-size beds, balconies, and hammocks. **Pros:** pleasant rooms; great-value rates; pool with ocean view. **Cons:** not on the beach. [$] *Rooms from: R$170* ✉ *Estrada Arraial 500, Arraial d'Ajuda* ☎ *073/3575–1442* 🌐 *www.pousadamanaca.com.br* 🛏 *29 rooms* 🍴 *Breakfast.*

TRANCOSO

725 km (450 miles) from Salvador.

One of Bahia's most picturesque beach towns, Trancoso was founded by Jesuit missionaries in 1586 and orginally named St. John Baptist of the Indians. Life here circles around a grassy central plaza, the *Quadrado* (the Square), where no cars mean kids and wild horses roam free and the long stretch of grass plays host to local football matches and capoiera displays. This is where everybody goes for shopping, dining, and people-watching.

GETTING HERE AND AROUND

Take a ferry to from Porto Seguro to Arraial d'Ajuda and catch one of the buses that leaves from the ferry terminal there. If you're driving, take BA 101 from Arraial d'Ajuda to Trancoso. The journey takes 30–40 minutes. Taxis in and around Trancoso are expensive, with fixed rates controlled by the local taxi association.

ESSENTIALS

Taxi Contacts **Associação de Taxistas Trancoso.** ✉ *Praça S João s/n, Centro, Trancoso* ☎ *073/3668–1260.*

TOURS

Brazilian Beach House. This bilingual travel specialist rents some of Brazil's most beautiful private houses, from intimate fisherman's cottages to fully staffed beachfront mansions for groups of 20. Many options are available in and around Trancoso. ☎ *203/287–4345* 🌐 *www.brazilianbeachhouse.com.*

Natural Eco Bike Trancoso. This professional agency organizes mountain-biking treks through the local buffalo farm and eco-biking along the beach. ✉ *Av. Presidente Tancredo Neves, Trancoso* ☎ *073/3668–1855* 🌐 *www.naturalecobike.com* 🎫 *From R$150 per person for three hours, with transport and equipment included.*

EXPLORING

OFF THE BEATEN PATH

Parque Nacional Marinho de Abrolhos. One of the best scuba-diving spots in Brazil, Marinho de Abrolhos marine reserve, 856 km (532 miles) south of Salvador, was created to protect these remote gigantic coral reefs teeming with marine wildlife. Charles Darwin's expedition made a stop here in 1832, and noted the abundant bird, whale, turtle, and fish populations. The archipelago, 36 km (23 miles) off the coast of southern Bahia, is made up of five islands, four of which are within the park. Ilha Santa Barbara is a naval base with a lighthouse run by the Brazilian

Navy. The shallow waters on the continental shelf are the Abrolhos Banks, containing one of the major coral formations in the Atlantic. Water visibility for scuba diving is best from December to March, while whale-watching season runs July to November. Only accredited boats are allowed inside the park, so look to hire a catamaran from one of the agencies in Caravelas. Excursions normally last 1–3 days. ✉ *Praia do Quitongo (Park Administration), Caravelas* ☎ *073/3297–2258* 🌐 *www.icmbio.gov.br/parnaabrolhos* 🎟 *R$360 for a day's catamaran hire* 🕒 *By guided tour only.*

WHERE TO EAT

$$$ SEAFOOD FAMILY 🍴 **Capim Santo.** Located in the heart of the Quadrado, Capim Santo — which means lemongrass in Portuguese—is one of the best restaurants in town. Open since 1985, the family-run business retains an essence of informality and coziness, even though service is super sharp and the healthy, seafood-based menu sophisticated enough to warrant a second branch in São Paulo. Highlights include fresh fish cooked in lemongrass and lobster served in a whole pineapple. Reservations in high season are a must, where regular live music, the flickering candlelight, and jabuticaba caipirinhas make this one of the hottest, and most romantic, spots in Trancoso. [$] *Average main: R$60* ✉ *Rua do Beco 55, Trancoso* ☎ *073/3668–1122* 🌐 *www.capimsanto.com.br* 🕒 *Closed Sun. No lunch.*

$$$ ITALIAN 🍴 **Pizzeria Maritaca.** Fabulous thin-crust pizza, homemade pasta, and a happening scene keep this lively local spot ever popular, even if the prices may make your eyes water. [$] *Average main: R$50* ✉ *Rua Carlos Alberto Parracho s/n, Trancoso* ☎ *073/3668–1702* 🕒 *Closed Mon. No lunch.*

$$$$ BRAZILIAN Fodor's Choice ★ 🍴 **São João Batista.** Three chefs from São Paulo are behind the innovative, sophisticated dishes at this recently opened fine-dining spot sandwiched between two furniture shops on the Quadrado. Classic Brazilian dishes are reinvented with state-of-the-art techniques, and the chefs prioritize fresh local ingredients and working directly with local producers. Starters, such as the tapioca with foie gras and fresh whole crab, are particularly good. [$] *Average main: R$70* ✉ *Quadrado de Trancoso s/n, Trancoso* ☎ *011/9856–33610.*

$$ THAI Fodor's Choice ★ 🍴 **Thaicoso.** A compact menu of delicious, fresh-flavored Thai dishes changes daily at this affordable, alfresco spot, with a handful of candlelit tables set out in front of the vibrant pink facade of ecelctic design shop Quadrado 13. The green papaya salad and sweet-and-sour slow-roasted pork make a particularly welcome change from endless moqueca. A great spot for cocktails, too. [$] *Average main: R$35* ✉ *Praça são João 13, Trancoso* ☎ *073/9905-8405* 🕒 *No lunch.*

WHERE TO STAY

Trancoso offers some of the most sophisticated accommodations options in Bahia, from beach-shack chic pousadas to high-end resorts. Between December and March, make sure you book well in advance.

$$$$ HOTEL 🏨 **Etnia.** While just a few minutes' stroll from Trancoso's happening square, this elegant, spacious hotel feels like a world of its own: the seven individually styled bungalows (try Morocco or Mediterranean)

are scattered through 7,000 square meters of native forest, so you may not glimpse another guest except during dips in the gorgeous semi-Olympic-size pool or over breakfast, where a delicious homemade buffet changes daily. **Pros:** good for families; charismatic, efficient staff; fantastic pool. **Cons:** leafy grounds mean mosquitos; a short walk to the beach. $ *Rooms from: R$540* ⊠ *Av. Principal 25, Trancoso* ☎ *073/3668–1137* ⊕ *www.etniabrasil.com.br* ☉ *Closed May–June* ⇱ *9 bungalows, 2 villas* ⦿ *Breakfast.*

$$ ⏢ **Pousada Capim Santo.** This delightful, family-run pousada set right on
B&B/INN the Quadrado is one of the oldest in town, dating back to the '80s when
FAMILY owner Sonia arrived from São Paulo with the first wave of hippies and
Fodor's Choice began cooking up delicious food in her kitchen. **Pros:** vibrant hospital-
★ ity; excellent value; location. **Cons:** Wi-Fi doesn't always reach rooms; mezzanine rooms should be avoided by anyone with mobility issues. $ *Rooms from: R$330* ⊠ *Rua do Beco 55, Trancoso* ☎ *073/3668–1122* ⊕ *capimsanto.com.br* ⇱ *20 rooms* ⦿ *Breakfast.*

$$$$ ⏢ **Uxua Casa Hotel & Spa.** Wilbert Das, creative director of the clothing
HOTEL brand Diesel, found his calling designing this property: the 12 private
Fodor's Choice bungalows encapsulate the original, quirky character of former fish-
★ ermen's abodes, while remaining impeccably furnished with products from local designers. **Pros:** inspirational and locally themed design; sophisticated facilities; friendly local staff; indigenous spa products and treatments. **Cons:** expensive restaurant; very expensive. $ *Rooms from: $1,680* ⊠ *Quadrado, Trancoso* ☎ *073/3668–2277* ⊕ *uxua.com* ⇱ *12 rooms* ⦿ *Breakfast.*

PRAIA DO ESPELHO

40 minutes south of Trancoso.

One of the region's most idolized spots and a regular winner of Brazil's best beach, Praia do Espelho is reached from Trancoso through fields of buffalo and communities of Pataxó Indians. During sunny days, the giraffe-like coconut palms provide shade for bathers, while a smattering of simple-chic restaurants serve cold agua de coco and fresh seafood. Come during the week and you will have the perfect horseshoe bay all to yourself. Beach strollers will want to head right, where more deserted coves of golden sand await. *Espelho* means "mirror" in Portuguese and alludes to the shimmering layer of water that reflects the sky during low tide. The more adventurous can continue on to the small town of Caraíva, accessible only by wooden boat.

WHERE TO EAT AND STAY

$$$$ ✕ **Restaurante da Sylvinha.** This colorful cottage with some of the most
ECLECTIC innovative food in Bahia, set right on Praia do Espelho, draws Tran-
Fodor's Choice coso's jet set, who get here via a bumpy 40-minute drive on dirt roads.
★ Sylvinha serves a generous set menu that blends Brazilian and Asian flavors (think ginger-infused fish and tropical fruit chutneys) to diners who gather around a few big tables on the terrace of her house. Daybeds are set under the coconut palms for post-lunch snoozing. Reservations are essential at this lunch-only spot. $ *Average main:*

9

R$120 ✉ *Praia do Espelho s/n, Praia do Espelho* ☎ *075/9985–4157* 💳 *No credit cards* 🕒 *Closed Sun. No dinner* ✍ *Reservations essential.*

$$$$ B&B/INN 🏨 **Cala e Divino.** One of the only options for staying overnight on Praia do Espelho, this former artist's residence offers 10 Santorini-esque private chalets scattered up the bluff overlooking the beach. **Pros:** access to one of Brazil's most beautiful beaches; great food; tranquillity. **Cons:** can feel isloated; poor Wi-Fi. [$] *Rooms from: R$600* ✉ *Estrada Trancoso/Caraíva, Km 22, Trancoso* ☎ *073/3668–1380* 🌐 *www.divinoespelho.com.br* 🛏 *10 rooms* 🍴 *Breakfast.*

THE NORTHEAST

Updated By
Lauren Holmes

Like the whole of Brazil, the Northeast is a place of contrasts. Churches, villas, and fortresses in Recife, Natal, and Fortaleza tell the tale of Portuguese settlers who fought Dutch invaders and amassed fortunes from sugar. The beaches in and around these cities evoke Brazil's playful side and its love affair with sun, sand, and sea. West of the cities, the rugged, often drought-stricken *sertão* (bush) shows Brazil's darker side—one where many people struggle for survival. This warp and weave of history and topography is laced with threads of culture: indigenous, European, African, and a unique blend of all three that is essentially Brazilian.

Brazil's northeastern cities are experiencing a renaissance whose changes strike a balance between preservation and progress. Recife remains a bubbling hub of northeastern creativity, while nearby Olinda is still a charming enclave of colonial architecture—though bohemians have long since replaced sugar barons. On Ceará State's 570-km-long (354-mile-long) coast, Fortaleza continues to thrive against a backdrop of fantastic beaches and timeless white dunes. Although smaller and with less-storied pasts, Natal and surrounding beach towns like Praia da Pipa have cemented their status as some of the country's most beautiful and popular tourist destinations. Meanwhile little-known Alagoas, Brazil's smallest state, is gaining recognition as the place where white-sand beaches and fisherman villages still remain gloriously underexplored.

ORIENTATION AND PLANNING

GETTING ORIENTED

The Northeast of Brazil includes the coastal states of Bahia, Sergipe, Alagoas, Pernambuco, Rio Grande do Norte, Paraiba, Ceará, Maranhão, and the landlocked state of Piauí. In the middle of this region are two large and vibrant cities, Recife and Fortaleza. The region, which covers an area of 1,554,257 square km (600,102 square miles), is home to a little less than a third of the population of the entire country.

Recife. In the state of Pernambuco, the sprawling city of Recife is bounded by the Beberibe and the Capibaribe Rivers, which flow into the Atlantic. The city is known for the dozens of bridges linking its many boroughs. It is 2,392 km (1,486 miles) from Rio de Janeiro and 2716 km (1,688 miles) from São Paulo.

Natal. The capital of Rio Grande do Norte, Natal has a population of 1,234,819. The city is surrounded by dunes on both sides, which gives

TOP REASONS TO GO

Idyllic Beaches: Relax on some of Brazil's most beautiful beaches, with warm water all year and sand dunes high enough to ski down.

Gorgeous Olinda: Wander along the winding streets of Olinda as you gaze up at the beautiful colonial-era architecture.

Stargaze: Stargaze and watch the full moon rise in some of the world's clearest skies.

Carnival: The energetic Carnival in Olinda is considered to be among the best in Brazil, rivaling those in Rio and Salvador.

Northeastern Eats: Try the amazing *carne de sol,* or sun-dried beef, as well as the other unique northeastern dishes using lobster, shrimp, and crabs.

it a unique appearance. It's 2,680 km (1,665 miles) from Rio de Janeiro and 3,011 km (1,871 miles) from São Paulo.

Fortaleza. A thriving economic center, Fortaleza is the entry point for the state of Ceará. The population is 2,416,920, and is growing at a rapid pace. On the Atlantic Ocean, it's 2,808 km (1,744 miles) from Rio de Janeiro and 3,109 km (1,932 miles) from São Paulo.

Fernando de Noronha. An archipelago in the state of Pernambuco, the national marine park of Fernando de Noranha consists of 21 sparsely populated islands. About 354 km (219 miles) from the coast of Brazil, these islands have a population of roughly 2,000.

PLANNING

WHEN TO GO

High season corresponds to school vacations (July) and the period between Christmas and Carnival (late December–mid-March). Prices are better off-season, but if you've come to partake in festivities, Olinda has one of the best Carnival celebrations in the country. Also, the region has two of the most popular out-of-season Carnival celebrations: Carnatal in Natal, on the first weekend in December; and Fortal in Fortaleza, on the last weekend in July. Temperatures hover between about 20°C and 35°C (70°F and 95°F) year-round—temperatures get hotter the farther north you go. Rain is heaviest from May to August in Recife. In Fortaleza, March and April are the rainiest months. Natal sits at about 25°C (75°F) year-round; it sees much less rain than Fortaleza or Recife, but May through July are the wettest months and best avoided if you are looking for sunny beach days.

PLANNING YOUR TIME

With three main airports, Brazil's Northeast is one of the most accessible regions to navigate. Most visitors start by choosing one of the hubs (Recife, Natal, or Fortaleza) and branching out from there. Of the three cities, Recife is the most dynamic and warrants at least a few

10

days. Fortaleza is best as a jumping-off point to explore the spectacular dunes and nearby beach towns, such as Jericoacoara. Natal, the smallest of the three, is used by many as an airport access to the idyllic surf town of Praia da Pipa, 84 km (52 miles) to the south.

GETTING HERE AND AROUND
The distances between the cities in Northeast Brazil make flying the best way to get around. Even then, the times involved are not small. Flying to Fortaleza from Salvador, for example, takes 2½ hours. That's nothing compared to the 24 hours you'd spend on a bus. Once you've reached your destination, there's often no reason to rent a car. In Natal or Fortaleza you can easily get around by taxi or bus. Renting a car to explore the coast around Recife is highly recommended. As you head farther north, however, the growing number of sand dunes and dirt roads means it's better to leave it to the professionals and explore by beach buggy.

RESTAURANTS
The Northeast has little of the hustle and bustle you'll find in the southern cities of Rio de Janeiro and São Paulo. Residents enjoy a relaxed lifestyle, so in restaurants you'll find that casual attire is the norm. The many *batidas* (tropical fruit cocktails) are the highlights of the local cuisine, but many restaurants serve foods from other parts of Brazil. You'll also have many other options, including Italian, Dutch, and French restaurants set up by expats who never left. Dinner begins around 8 pm. Most hotels include breakfast in the cost of your room. Restaurants not in hotels are usually not open for breakfast.

HOTELS
Hotels are plentiful throughout the Northeast. Prices range from moderate to pricey, depending on season. Many hotels are sleek and modern, comparable to those you'd find in tourist destinations around the world. Pousadas tend to have a bit more charm and personalized service. Making reservations is advisable during high seasons. Keep in mind that prices listed at the hotel reception are often considerably higher than those that can be found online. Many business hotels will also drop their rates on the weekends. *Hotel reviews have been shortened. For full information, visit Fodors.com.*

WHAT IT COSTS IN REAIS			
$	**$$**	**$$$**	**$$$$**
Restaurants	under R$31	R$31–R$45	R$46–R$60	over R$60
Hotels	under R$251	R$251–R$375	R$376–R$500	over R$500

Restaurant prices are the average cost of a main course at dinner or, if dinner is not served, at lunch. Hotel prices are the lowest cost of a standard double room in high season, excluding tax.

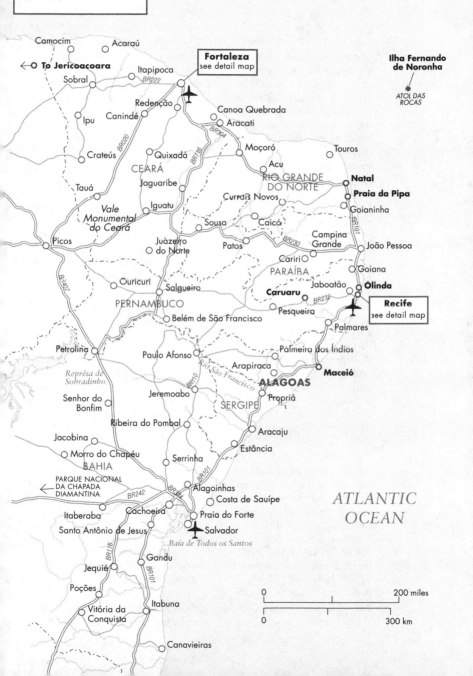

The Northeast Coast

Camocim

Acaraú

← To Jericoacoara

Itapipoca
BR222

Sobral

Fortaleza
see detail map

**Ilha Fernando
de Noronha**

*ATOL DAS
ROCAS*

Redenção

Canoa Quebrada

Ipu

Canindé

Aracati

Crateús

Quixadá

Moçoró

Touros

CEARÁ

Acu

Natal

RIO GRANDE
DO NORTE

Tauá

Jaguaribe

Currais Novos

Praia da Pipa

*Vale
Monumental
do Ceará*

Iguatu

Caicó

Goianinha

Sousa

Campina
Grande

BR101

Picos

Juàzeiro
do Norte

Patos

BR230

João Pessoa

Cariri

Goiana

Ouricuri

Salgueiro

PARAÍBA

Jaboatão

Olinda

PERNAMBUCO

Caruaru

BR232

Recife
see detail map

Belém de São Francisco

Pesqueira

Petrolina

Paulo Afonso

Palmares

*Reprêsa de
Sobradinho*

Rio São Francisco

Palmeira dos Índios

Arapiraca

Maceió

Senhor do
Bonfim

Jeremoabo

BR10

ALAGOAS

Propriá

Ribeira do Pombal

SERGIPE

Jacobina

Aracaju

Morro do Chapéu

Serrinha

Estância

BAHIA

PARQUE NACIONAL
← DA CHAPADA
DIAMANTINA

BR242

BR101

Alagoinhas

**ATLANTIC
OCEAN**

Itaberaba

Cachoeira

Costa de Sauípe

Santo Antônio de Jesus

Praia do Forte

BR116

Salvador

Baía de Todos os Santos

Jequié

Gandu

BR101

Poções

Itabuna

Vitória da
Conquista

0		200 miles
0		300 km

Canavieiras

RECIFE

829 km (515 miles) north of Salvador; 522 km (324 miles) south of Natal.

This vibrant metropolis has a spirit that's halfway between that of the modern cities of Brazil's South and of the traditional northeastern centers. It offers both insight on the past and a window to the future. The city has beautiful buildings alongside the rivers that remind many visitors of Europe. Unfortunately, huge swathes of 19th-century buildings were razed to make way for modern structures. As a result, the center of the city has pockets of neocolonial splendor surrounded by gap-toothed modern giants. Today Recife is a leader in health care and has benefited from significant government investment in recent years, resulting in a boom in infrastructure and construction industries. It's also Brazil's third-largest gastronomic center—it's almost impossible to get a bad meal here.

Recife is built around three rivers and connected by 49 bridges. Its name comes from the *recifes* (reefs) that line the coast. Because of this unique location, water and light often lend the city interesting textures. In the morning, when the tide recedes from Boa Viagem Beach, the rocks of the reefs slowly reappear. Pools of water are formed, fish flap around beachgoers, and the rock formations dry into odd colors. And if the light is just right on the Rio Capibaribe, the ancient buildings of Recife Antigo (Old Recife) are reflected off the river's surface in a watercolor display.

GETTING HERE AND AROUND

The Aeroporto Internacional Guararapes is 10 km (6 miles) south of Recife, just five minutes from Boa Viagem, and 15 minutes from the City Center. There are numerous daily flights from São Paulo and Rio de Janeiro to Recife on GOL, TAM, Avianca, and Azul. Recife has also developed into one of the northeastern hubs for international flights, with a weekly flight to Miami with TAM, and daily flights to Lisbon with Tap. In the airport lobby, on the right just before the exit door, is a tourist-information booth, and next to that is a taxi stand. You can pay at the counter; the cost is about R$25 to Boa Viagem and R$40 to downtown. There are also regular buses and microbuses (more expensive). The bus labeled "aeroporto" runs to Avenida Dantas Barreto in the center of the city, stopping in Boa Viagem on the way.

The Terminal Integrado de Passageiros (TIP), a metro terminal and bus station 14 km (9 miles) from the Recife City Center, handles all interstate bus departures and some connections to local destinations. To reach it via metro, a 30-minute ride, enter through the Museu do Trem, opposite the Casa da Cultura, and take the train marked "rodoviária." Expresso Guanabara has several buses a day to Fortaleza (13 hours, R$75), while Viação Progresso provides a frequent service to Natal (two hours, R$69) and Caruaru (two hours, R$12). São Geraldo has buses to Rio de Janeiro (36 hours, R$412) and Penha runs a daily service to Salvador (14 hours, R$155).

Driving in Recife is relatively straightforward, and renting a car is often the best option when it comes to exploring some of the area's better

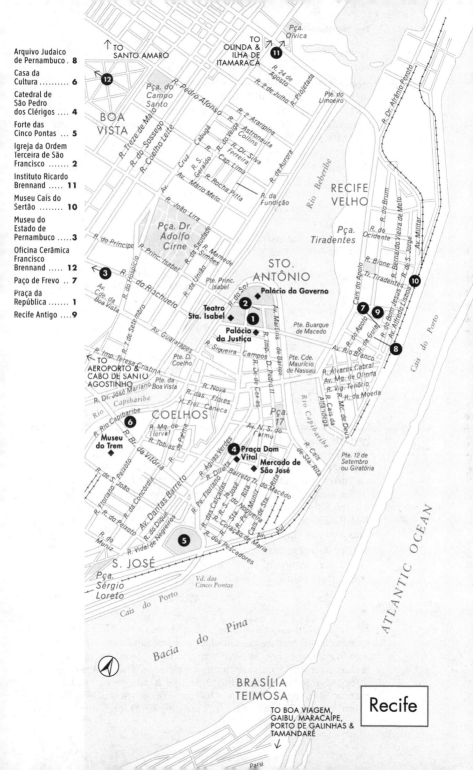

Recife

beaches. If you rent a car, make sure that your hotel has parking facilities, as finding parking on the street can be tricky.

Recife is the only northeastern city with a subway system. A single ride on the metro is R$1.60. Transfer tickets and city bus tickets cost about R$1.75. Buses are clearly labeled and run frequently. Many stops have signs indicating the routes. To reach Boa Viagem via the metro, get off at the Joana Bezerra stop (a 20-minute ride) and take a bus or taxi (R$20) from here. Buses are free when using the metro and vice versa.

Taxis are cheap (fares are higher on Sunday and at night), but drivers seldom speak English. All use meters. You can either hail a cab on the street or call for one. Taxis are the recommended form a transport to get around after dark.

ESSENTIALS

Airport Aeroporto Internacional Guararapes (REC). ⊠ Praça Ministro Salgado Filho s/n, Recife ☎ 081/3322–4188, 081/3322–4188.

Bus Contacts Expresso Guanabara. ⊠ Rua Min Mário Andreazza 30, Recife ☎ 085/4005–1992 ⊕ www.expressoguanabara.com.br. **São Geraldo.** ☎ 0800/728–0044 ⊕ www.saogeraldo.com.br. **Terminal Integrado de Passageiros.** ⊠ Av. Prefeito Antônio Pereira s/n, Recife ☎ 081/3452–1211. **Viação Progresso.** ☎ 024/2251–5050 ⊕ www.viacaoprogresso.com.br.

Car Rental Contacts Movida Car Rental. ⊠ Aeroporto Internacional do Recife, Praça Ministro Salgado Filho, Recife ☎ 081/3322–4895 ⊕ www.movida.com.br.

Taxi Contacts Coopertáxi. ☎ 081/3424–8944. **Ouro Táxi Recife.** ☎ 081/3423–7777.

TOURS

Catamaran Tours. Catamaran cruises along the Rio Capibaribe take you past Recife's grand houses, bridges, and mangrove forests. Catamaran Tours offers two such excursions: an hour-long afternoon trip goes through the old rotating bridge and passes Recife Antigo and São José, the customs quay, the Santa Isabel Bridge, and the Rua da Aurora quays to the area near the Casa da Cultura. A two-hour-long night tour is aboard a slower—but more lively—vessel. It passes the quays of São José Estelita. ⊠ Praça Marco Zero, Recife ☎ 081/3424–2845 ⊕ www.catamarantours.com.br ≦ From R$40.

SAFETY AND PRECAUTIONS

With the exception of Recife Antigo, Recife's downtown area is dead at night and should be avoided as a safety precaution.

EXPLORING

Recife is spread out and somewhat hard to navigate. The Centro—with its mixture of high-rises, colonial churches, and markets—is always busy during the day. The crowds and the narrow streets can make finding your way around even more confusing. The Centro consists of three areas: Recife Antigo (the Old City); Recife proper, with the districts of Santo Antônio and São José; and the districts of Boa Vista and Santo Amaro. The first two areas are on islands formed by the rivers

Capibaribe, Beberibe, and Pina; the third is on an island created by the Canal Tacaruna.

Six kilometers (4 miles) south of Centro is the upscale residential and beach district of Boa Viagem, reached by bridge across the Bacia do Pina. Praia da Boa Viagem (Boa Viagem Beach), the Copacabana of Recife, is chockablock with trendy clubs and restaurants as well as many moderately priced and expensive hotels.

TOP ATTRACTIONS

Catedral de São Pedro dos Clérigos. The facade of this cathedral, which was built in 1728, showcases fine wooden sculptures and a splendid trompe-l'oeil ceiling. The square surrounding the cathedral is lined with many restaurants, shops, and bars, and is a hangout for local artists, who often read their poetry or perform music, particularly on Tuesday evening. The square is a focal point during Carnival and the Festa Junina, a lively pagan festival that takes place nationwide through the month of June. ⊠ *Rua Patio de São Pedro, São José, Recife* ☎ *081/3224–2954* ⊕ *www.patiodesaopedro.ceci-br.org/saopedro/en* ⬚ *Free* ☉ *Tues.–Fri. 8–11 and 2–4, Sat. 8–10:30.*

Igreja da Ordem Terceira de São Francisco. Built in 1606, this church has beautiful Portuguese tile work, while the adjoining Capela Dourada (Golden Chapel), constructed in 1697, is an outstanding example of Brazilian baroque architecture. The complex also contains a convent— the Convento Franciscano de Santo Antônio—and a museum displaying sacred art. ⊠ *Rua Imperador Dom Pedro II s/n, Santo Antônio, Recife* ☎ *081/3224–0530* ⬚ *R$2* ☉ *Weekdays 8–11:30 and 2–5, Sat. 8–11:30.*

FAMILY
Fodor'sChoice
★
Instituto Ricardo Brennand. The impressive private archive of Pernambucan collector Ricardo Brennand is displayed in a fairy-tale castle approximately 15 km (9 miles) north of Boa Viagem and surrounded by 77 hectares of forest. While the paintings and artifacts range in origin from the 15th and 21st centuries and hail from all corners of the globe, the focus is on pieces that illuminate what life was like in Recife during the Dutch imperial rule (1600–1700). ⊠ *Alameda Antônio Brennand, Recife* ☎ *081/2121–0352* ⊕ *www.institutoricardobrennand.org. br* ⬚ *R$20* ☉ *Tues.–Sat. 1–5.*

FAMILY
Fodor'sChoice
★
Museu Cais do Sertão. This modern, interactive musuem is one of the new hot spots on Recife's cultural map. Regular live shows and cultural workshops add extra flavor to the top-class permanent exhibition that explores the key pillars of northeastern culture. Highlights include a film that portrays the challenges of life in the Sertão (interior drylands), interactive interviews with famous *nordestino*figures, and exhibitions on Recife's vibrant culture and artisan traditions. The building itself is beautifully designed and guides speak English. Check the website for their cultural agenda. ⊠ *Porto de Recife, Av. Alfredo Lisboa s/n, Recife* ☎ *081/3089–2974* ⊕ *www.caisdosertao.com.br* ⬚ *R$8* ☉ *Tues. 9–9, Wed.–Fri. 9–5, Sat. 1–7, Sun. 11–7.*

Museu do Estado de Pernambuco. The state historical museum, in a mansion once owned by a baron, seems more like a home filled with beautiful antiques than a museum, providing visitors with a taste of how life was lived in Recife 200 years ago. Among the 14,000 objects on display,

10

there is a grand piano, a dining-room table set with 18th-century china, an ornate 19th-century crib, and many beautiful paintings. ⊠ *Av. Rui Barbosa 960, Graça, Recife* ☎ *081/3184–3174* ✉ *R$5* ☺ *Tues.–Fri. 9–5, weekends 2–5.*

FAMILY **Oficina Cerâmica Francisco Brennand.** In the old São José sugar refinery, this museum houses more than 2,000 ceramic pieces by the great (and prolific) Brazilian artist Francisco Brennand. Having studied in France, he was influenced by Pablo Picasso and Joan Miró, among others, and his works also include paintings, drawings, and engravings. About 15 km (9 miles) from Recife Antigo, the museum's location amid forests and fountains is almost as appealing as its displays. ⊠ *Propriedade Santo Cosme e Damião s/n, Km 16, Recife* ☎ *081/3271–2466* ⊕ *www. brennand.com.br* ✉ *R$8* ☺ *Weekdays 8–5, weekends 10–6.*

FAMILY **Paço de Frevo.** This new cultural space celebrates and showcases all
Fodor's Choice things related to *Frevo*, the infectious music and dance that governs
★ Pernambucan culture and Carnival. Information in this small museum is in English, and the displays and videos full of color. Regular shows take place on the third floor of the reformed townhouse, where you can also sign up for dance classes. ⊠ *Praça Do Arsenal Da Marinha, Recife* ☎ *081/3355–9527* ⊕ *www.pacodofrevo.org.br* ✉ *R$6* ☺ *Tues.–Wed. and Fri 9–6, Thurs. 9–9, weekends noon–7.*

FAMILY **Praça da República.** In the heart of Rio Antigo, the city's original cultural and political meeting point of the 17th century was given a new lease on life by landscape architect Burle Marx in the 1930s, and now features rows of Imperial palms and a hundred-year-old Baobab tree among the elaborate 19th- and 20th-century architecture. Highlights include the Teatro Santa Isabel (St. Isabel Theater, 1850); the Palácio do Campo das Princesas, also known as the Palácio do Governo (Government House, 1841); and the Palácio da Justiça (Court House, 1930). ⊠ *Praça da República, Recife Antigo, Recife.*

Fodor's Choice **Recife Antigo.** Most of Old Recife's colonial-era public buildings and
★ houses have been restored. The area between Rua do Bom Jesus and Rua do Apolo is full of shops, cafés, and bars, making it the hub of downtown life both day and night. On weekends there's live *maracatu* music and dancing, and a handicrafts fair is held Sunday from 2 to 8 on Rua do Bom Jesus. ⊠ *Recife Antigo, Recife.*

WORTH NOTING

Arquivo Judaico de Pernambuco. In Recife Antigo, on the site of the America's first synagogue, this excellent museum offers insight into the history and culture of the city, told through the experience of the Jewish population during the 1600s. All that remains of the original sanctuary, built in 1641, are the walls and the ground, which can be viewed through glass floor panels. Some guides speak English, and the informative signs are bilingual. ⊠ *Projeto Sinagoga Kahal Zur Israel, Rua do Bom Jesus 197, Recife Antigo, Recife* ☎ *081/3224–8351* ⊕ *www.arquivojudaicope.org. br* ✉ *R$10* ☺ *Weekdays 9–4:30, Sun. 2–5:30.*

Casa da Cultura. The old cells of this former 19th-century prison have been transformed into shops that sell works from Pernambuco's artisans, including clay figurines, wood sculptures, carpets, leather goods, and items made from woven straw. One of the cells has been kept in its original form to give visitors an idea of how the prisoners there lived. ⊠ *Rua Floriano Peixoto, Recife* ☎ *081/3224–0557* ⊕ *www. casadaculturape.com.br* ▨ *Free* ☉ *Mon.–Sat. 9–7, Sun. 9–2.*

Forte das Cinco Pontas. Originally constructed from mud in 1630, the "Fort of Five Points" was rebuilt in 1677 with stone and mortar; even though it now has only four sides, the fort has retained its original name. One of the last buildings built duing the era of Dutch dominance, this military fort now houses the **Museu da Cidade,** where an array of maps and photos illustrates Recife's history. ⊠ *Praça das Cinco Pontas, São José, Recife* ☎ *081/3224–8492* ☉ *Tues.–Fri. 9–6, weekends 1–5.*

BEACHES

Boa Viagem. Coconut palms line Recife's most popular beach, the 9-km-long (4-mile-long) Praia da Boa Viagem. A steady Atlantic breeze tames the hot sun, and reef formations create pools of warm water, although surfing and swimming are limited to designated areas because of the sharks beyond the reef. Sailors and fishermen beach their *jangadas* (handcrafted log rafts with beautiful sails), and vendors sell coconut drinks from kiosks. Avenida Boa Viagem separates a row of hotels and apartments from the beach, which is lined by a wide blue *calçadão* (sidewalk) that's perfect for running, bike rides, or evening promenades. On weekend afternoons there's a handicrafts fair in Praça da Boa Viagem. **Amenities:** food and drink; lifeguards, parking (fee). **Best for:** partiers; sunrises; walking. ⊠ *Boa Viagem, Recife.*

Cabo de Santo Agostinho. Some of Pernambuco's finest beaches are clustered around the small town of Cabo de Santo Agostinho, 35 km (22 miles) south of the city. The town's eponymous beach is better for soaking up the view of the cliffs and surrounding colonial houses rather than sunbathing, as there is little sand to sit on. Buses to and from Recife depart regularly and cost R$2. **Amenities:** food and drink; toilets. **Best for:** sunsets.

Gaibu. Surrounded by palm trees and favored by local surfers, beautiful Gaibu has become one of the area's most happening hangout spots. Volleyball competitions, fishing, and surfing are all practiced along the shore, while at the end of the beach, you can visit the ruins of the Fort of San Francisco Xavier. Some parts of the beach are not recommended for swimming. Its popularity means the beach can sometimes get crowded, noisy, and dirty **Amenities:** food and drink; lifeguards. **Best for:** partiers; surfing; sunset. ⊠ *Recife* ✛ *30 km (19 miles) south of Recife.*

FAMILY **Ilha de Itamaracá.** This island is set off the coast of the historic city of Igarassu and has a number of beautiful beaches with calm waters for swimming, as well as a protected area for manatees. The best beach is Coroa do Avião. To get to its secluded golden sands and handful of pricey beach restaurants, you need to take a boat or canoe from Forte Orange (R$10 per person). Buses to Igarassu and Ilha de Itamaracá leave from the center of Recife, at the Cais de Santa Rita in front of the Fórum Thomas de Aquino. **Amenities:** food and drink; toilets. **Best for:** swimming; walking. ⊠ *Recife* ✛ *39 km (24 miles) north of Recife.*

10

Maracaípe. South of Recife on the road past Porto das Galinha lies serene Maracaípe Beach. The excellent waves and happening *Quiosques* (beach bars) have made this a popular weekend spot with younger crowds, although the rough waters and strong currents make it more suited to surfers than swimming. **Amenities:** food and drink; lifeguards; parking; toilets; water sports. **Best for:** partiers; surfers; windsurfing. ✉ *Recife* ✣ *73 km (46 miles) southwest of Recife.*

Porto de Galinhas. Once considered one of the most beautiful beaches in Brazil, this historic port has lost a considerable dose of its original charm because of the increasingly heavy influx of tourists drawn to the beach's transparent natural swimming pools. If you don't mind sharing the beauty, there is a good variety of hotels and restaurants, as well as *jangadas* (small boats) for hire. The beach, which follows the curve of a bay lined with coconut palms and cashew trees, gets crowded on weekends year-round. **Amenities:** food and drink; lifeguards; parking (fee); showers; toilets; water sports. **Best for:** partiers; snorkeling; sunrise; surfing. ✉ *Recife* ✣ *70 km (43 miles) south of Recife.*

FAMILY
Fodor's Choice ★
Praia da Paiva. One of the secret refuges of Recife, this long stretch of golden shore has the feel of a private beach, yet is open to the public via the pay-toll and small bridge on the road to Barra de Jangada-Gaibu (cars cost R$3.50 on weekdays and R$5.50 at weekends). The only refreshments available come from passing beach vendors, but you can stop for lunch at Marina Pôr do Sol, a decent restaurant on the water to the right of the pay-toll. From Boa Viagem, you can access Praia da Paiva by several connecting buses, although the easiest way to get there is by taxi or rental car. **Amenities:** parking (free). **Best for:** solitude; surfing; walking. ✉ *Jaboatão dos Guararapes* ✣ *45 km (27 miles) south of Recife on the road to Cabo Santo Agostinho.*

FAMILY
Fodor's Choice ★
Tamandaré. Situated 109 km (68 miles) south of Recife, this beach region shares the same calm, warm waters and natural pools as Porto das Galinhas, yet lacks the crowds. The postcard-perfect **Praia dos Carneiros** has brilliantly clear emerald waters that are home to shoals of tropical fish. The beach huts there serve fresh coconut water and seafood snacks. **Amenities:** food and drink; lifeguards; parking (fee); toilets. **Best for:** snorkeling; solitude; sunrise; swimming. ✉ *Recife* ✣ *109 km (68 miles) south of Recife.*

WHERE TO EAT

$$$$
SEAFOOD
🍴 **Bargaço.** For those looking for an authentic taste of Bahia, this pleasant restaurant serves up golden *moquecas baianas* (fish cooked with onion, tomatoes, peppers, parsley, and coconut milk) and flavorful *caju caipirinhas* (cocktails made with cashew fruit). Service can be slow and the prices are high, so make sure you aren't in a hurry or on a budget when you come here. [$] *Average main: R$80* ✉ *Av. Antonio de Góes 62, Pina, Recife* ☎ *081/3465–1847* 🌐 *www.restaurantebargaco.com.br.*

$$$$
PORTUGUESE
FAMILY
🍴 **Leite.** For a memorable lunch, look no further than Leite. Since 1882, this Recife institution has served expertly prepared Portuguese classics in a refined setting, where white-coated waiters serve delectable dishes such as *bacalão com nata* (cod in buttermilk) amid live piano music.

Even though its downtown location requires something of a detour, it's well worth the effort. $ *Average main: R$96* ✉ *Praca Joaquim Nabuco 147, Recife* ☎ *081/3224–7977* ⊕ *www.restauranteleite.com. br* ⊗ *Closed Sat. No dinner* ⊟ *No credit cards.*

$ ✕ **Parraxaxá.** Waiters at this popular restaurant wear the bent orange
BRAZILIAN hats of Lampião, a Jesse James–like folk hero who made his way
FAMILY through the interior of northeastern Brazil during the early 20th cen-
tury. The buffet has a wide selection of the regional specialties that Lampião might have encountered back then. The food is priced per kilogram, so the cost will depend on how hungry you are. Try the amazing *escondinho* (a wonderful meat and cheese dish), *charque* (dried beef), and *carne sol* (brisket). $ *Average main: R$28* ✉ *Av. Fernando Simoes Barbosa 1200, Boa Viagem, Recife* ☎ *081/3463–7874* ⊕ *www. parraxaxa.com.br.*

$$$ ✕ **Tio Pepe.** Specializing in innovative yet traditional dishes, this lively
BRAZILIAN restaurant has loyal locals queuing out the door for juicy portions of
Fodor's Choice *carne de sol* (sun-dried beef) and *porco vulcanico* (pork fillet served
★ with a special house sauce, beans, and manioc). The menu revolves around the grill, with a wide variety of fish as well as meat dishes gener- ous enough to be shared. Opt for a table among the tropical plants on the breezy terrace, where colorful tablecloths and eclectic design add to the character. $ *Average main: R$60* ✉ *Rua Almirante Tamandare 170, Boa Viagem, Recife* ☎ *081/3341–7153* ⊕ *www.tiopepe.com.br* ⊗ *Closed Mon. No dinner Sun.*

WHERE TO STAY

$$ 🛏 **Atlante Plaza Hotel.** The city's smartest business hotel, this glimmering
HOTEL high-rise looks directly over Recife's most popular beach. **Pros:** helpful service; rooftop pool; extensive facilities. **Cons:** can be overrun by busi- ness folk and flight crews; overall design feels dated. $ *Rooms from: R$345* ✉ *Av. Boa Viagem 5426, Boa Viagem, Recife* ☎ *081/3302–3333* ⊕ *www.atlanteplaza.com.br* ⇆ *214 rooms, 27 suites* ⦿ *Breakfast.*

$$ 🛏 **Beach Class Suites.** In one of the trendiest parts of Boa Viagem and
HOTEL right across from the beach, this modern hotel has elegantly designed rooms and the sort of smiling, efficient service you would expect from one of Brazil's largest hotel groups. **Pros:** hip design; trendy location; free Wi-Fi and free parking. **Cons:** small swimming pool faces directly on to busy traffic; pricey. $ *Rooms from: R$313* ✉ *Av. Boa Viagem 1906, Boa Viagem, Recife* ☎ *081/2121–2626* ⊕ *www.atlanticahotels. com.br* ⊟ *No credit cards* ⇆ *158 rooms, 12 suites* ⦿ *Breakfast.*

$$ 🛏 **Courtyard Recife Boa Viagem.** Down a cobbled street three blocks from
HOTEL the beach in Boa Viagem, this hotel from the Marriott group com-
FAMILY bines exceptional service with a gorgeous rooftop pool. **Pros:** friendly staff; fast Wi-Fi. **Cons:** no service by the pool; can be tricky to find. $ *Rooms from: R$299* ✉ *Av. Engenheiro Domingos Ferreira 4661, Recife* ☎ *081/3256–7700* ⊕ *www.marriott.com/hotels/travel/reccy-courtyard-recife-boa-viagem* ⇆ *169 rooms* ⦿ *Breakfast.*

$$$$ 🛏 **Transamérica Prestige.** This spacious, modern hotel is a favorite among
HOTEL both businesspeople and families for its comfortable facilities and pro- fessional service. **Pros:** large rooms; clean and modern decor; 24-hour

10

room service. Cons: restaurant lacks atmosphere; no pool bar; pricey. [$] *Rooms from: R$520* ✉ *Av. Boa Viagem 420, Boa Viagem, Recife* ☎ *081/3039–9000* 🌐 *www.transamericagroup.com.br* 💳 *No credit cards* 🛏 *191 rooms, 4 suites* 🍴 *Breakfast.*

NIGHTLIFE AND PERFORMING ARTS

NIGHTLIFE

BARS

Boteco. Chilled draft beer, tasty snacks, and a view of the beach make Boteco one of the most popular bars in town. ✉ *Av. Boa Viagem 1660, Boa Viagem, Recife* ☎ *081/3325–1428.*

Galeria Joana D'Arc. A popular hangout spot that attracts an electic, artsy crowd, Galeria Joana D'Arc is a cluster of small cafés and bars, among them Café Poire, Anjo Solto, Barnabé, and Oriente Médio. ✉ *Rua Herculano Bandeira 513, Pina, Recife* ☎ *081/9162–3742.*

UNDER THE SEA

More than a dozen shipwrecks make good destinations for underwater explorers of all experience levels. The *Vapor de Baixo* is one such dive site. Bombed by the Germans during World War II, it's 20 meters (65 feet) down and is crawling with lobsters and turtles.

O Biruta. Repeatedly selected as Recife's best beach bar, O Biruta is a great spot to watch the moon rise over the beach while enjoying a refreshing cocktail and seafood snacks. There's live samba music every Saturday. ✉ *Rua Bem-te-vi 15, Brasília Teimosa, Recife* ☎ *081/3326–5151* 🌐 *www.birutabar.com.br.*

PERFORMING ARTS

Caixa Cultural. In a beautifully restored belle epoque mansion in Recife Antigo, this huge arts space includes three exhibitions rooms, a theater, a coffee shop, dance studios, and a roof-terrace with wonderful views over the city. ✉ *Av. Alfredo Lisboa no. 505, Recife Antigo, Recife* ☎ *081/3425–1900* 🌐 *www.caixacultural.com.br* 🕒 *Closed on Mon.*

Teatro Santa Isabel. Built in 1850, lovely Teatro Santa Isabel looks splendid after a major restoration. The neoclassical theater is the setting for operas, plays, and classical concerts, as well as the home of the Recife Symphony Orchestra. ✉ *Praça da República s/n, Santo Antônio, Recife* ☎ *081/3355–3323, 081/3355–3322* 🌐 *www.teatrosantaisabel.com.br.*

SPORTS AND THE OUTDOORS

SCUBA DIVING

For centuries the treacherous offshore reefs that gave Recife its name have struck fear into the hearts of sailors. Many a vessel has failed to navigate the natural harbor successfully, resulting in Recife earning the nickname of "Shipwreck Capital." There is a wide range of fascinating wrecks to be explored by divers, capitalizing on optimum conditions thanks to warm waters and superior visibility. Though diving is practiced year-round, visibility is best between October and May, when the wind and water are at their calmest.

Aquáticos. Recife's largest and most structured dive center, this professional operator caters to all levels of divers, offering both day cruises and dive excursions to a wide selection of underwater wrecks. ⊠ *Cais de Cinco Pontas s/n, Recife* ☎ *081/3424–5470* ⊕ *www.aquaticos.com.br.*

SHOPPING

Centro de Artesenato de Pernambuco. This shop occupies an entire warehouse and contains the work of more than 15,000 regional artisans. It is a wonderful place to pick up local souvenirs, from ceramics to original prints. Prices are reasonable and there is a nice buffet restaurant and auditorium in the adjoining warehouses. ⊠ *Av. Alfredo Lisboa 11, Recife Antigo, Recife* ☎ *081/3181–3450* ⊕ *www.artesanatodepernambuco. pe.gov.br.*

Mercado de São José. In the city's most traditional market, vendors sell handicrafts, clothing, produce, and herbs. It's housed in a beautiful cast-iron structure that was imported from France in the 19th century. ⊠ *Praça Dom Vital s/n, São José, Recife* ☎ *081/3424–4681.*

Shopping Center Recife. The enormous Shopping Center Recife is the place to go if you are looking for a shopping fix. There are more than 450 stores, along with a 10-screen cinema and a food court. The center is not far from Boa Viagem Beach. ⊠ *Rua Padre Carapuceiro 777, Boa Viagem, Recife* ☎ *081/3464–6000* ⊕ *www.shoppingrecife.com.br.*

SIDE TRIP TO OLINDA

7 km (4 miles) north of Recife.

The name of Pernambuco State's original capital means "beautiful," and this must have been what came to mind when the first Europeans stood atop the forested hills and gazed down at the ocean and beach spread out before them. Today the town's natural beauty is complemented by colonial buildings painted in a rainbow of colors, making it a stunning slice of the old Northeast.

Founded by the Portuguese in 1535, Olinda was developed further by the Dutch during their brief turn at running Pernambuco in the 1600s. The narrow cobblestone streets of this UNESCO World Heritage Site curve up and down hills that, at every turn, offer spectacular views of both Recife and the Atlantic. The scenery is just as nice up close: many houses have latticed balconies, heavy doors, and stucco walls. The zoning laws are strict, resulting in a beautiful, compact city that artists, musicians, and intellectuals have made their own.

The City Center is hilly but fairly easy to explore by foot. You may want to hire a guide to help provide some historical background on the city and its principal sites. Look for the official guides (they have ID cards and bright orange or blue T-shirts) who congregate in the Praça do Carmo. They are former street children, and half the R$45 fee for a full city tour goes to a home for kids from the streets.

10

OLINDA'S CARNIVAL

Many rate Carnival in Olinda as one of the best in Brazil, rivaling those in Rio de Janeiro and Salvador. It's considered Brazil's most traditional Carnival—meaning there's noticeably less skin exposed. Music is generally the slower-paced *forró* or the frenetic *frevo*, in contrast to Rio's *samba* and Salvador's *axé*.

Carnival here lasts a full 11 days. Highlights include the opening events—led by a *bloco* of more than 400 "virgins" (men in drag)—and a parade of *bonecos de pano* (huge dolls) and *mamulengos* (marionettes) in the likenesses of famous northeasterners. The dolls and puppets are made of Styrofoam, fabric, and papier-mâché, and are often so elaborate that they take neighborhood artists most of the year to make.

GETTING HERE AND AROUND

A cab from the airport in Recife costs between R$50 and R$65. Alternatively, you can take the "aeroporto" bus to Avenida Nossa Senhora do Carmo in Recife and transfer to the "casa caiada" bus bound for Olinda.

Visitor Information Casa Da Turista. ⊠ *Rua Prudente de Morais 472, Carmo Olinda, Olinda* ☎ *081/3305–1060.*

EXPLORING
TOP ATTRACTIONS

FAMILY
Fodor's Choice
★

Alto da Sé. This is the most scenic spot for soaking up Olinda's views of Recife and the ocean, particularly during sunset. It's also a good place to see some historic churches as well as to sample Bahia-style *acarajé* (black-eyed pea fritters served with dried prawns) and Pernambuco's famous tapioca cakes. Make sure you try the *cartola*, a heavenly combination of fried cheese, banana, cinammon, and condensed milk. Have a seat at one of the outdoor tables here, or browse in the shops that sell handicrafts—including lace—and paintings. Don't miss a trip up the restored elevator inside the renovated *Caixa d'Água* (Water Tower) for stunning 360-degree vistas. To get here, just walk up on Ladeira da Sé. ⊠ *Ladeira da Sé, Carmo Olinda, Olinda.*

Fodor's Choice
★

Basílica de São Bento. The main chapel of the Basílica de São Bento, a Benedictine monastery, is Olinda's richest church and considered to be one of Brazil's most beautiful. Brilliant gold covers the elaborately carved wooden altar and frames the sumptously furnished private balconies that overlook it, providing a dramatic contrast with the white walls and frescoed ceilings. Sunday's 10 am Mass features Gregorian chants. ⊠ *Rua de São Bento s/n, Varadouro, Olinda* ☎ *081/3316–3290* ☒ *Free* ☉ *Daily 8:30–11:45 and 2–6:30.*

Igreja da Sé. Built in 1537, the Igreja da Sé has been restored as much as possible to its original appearance. From its side terrace you can capture a postcard-perfect view of the Old City and the ocean. ⊠ *Alto da*

Sé, Carmo, Olinda 🎫 *Free* ⊙ *Daily 8–noon and 2–4:30.*

WORTH NOTING

Convento de São Francisco. Built in 1577, the Convento de São Francisco was the first Franciscan convent in Brazil. The floors are Portuguese tile work, ceilings are frescoed, and walls are made of ground-up local coral. ✉ *Rua São Francisco 280, Carmo Olinda, Olinda* 📞 *081/3429–0517* 🎫 *R$3* ⊙ *Mon.–Sat. 9–12:30 and 2–5:30.*

TAPIOCA STANDS

While in Olinda, try the food at stands selling *tapioca*, gluten-free pancakes made from manioc flour, a by-product of the cassava root. Many claim that the tapioca here is the best in the country. Try the savory chicken and Catupiry cheese tapioca, then follow it up with a *cartola* (grilled cheese, banana, and cinnamon) tapioca for dessert.

WHERE TO EAT AND STAY

$$$
BRAZILIAN

✕ **Oficina do Sabor.** Setlle down in the leafy dining room of this regional restaurant, and take in the views of the coconut palms of Olinda while sampling the house speciality of stuffed pumpkin for two. While there are 15 different fillings, it is the *abóbora com camarão* (pumpkin stuffed with shrimp and served with a *pitanga* cherry sauce) that really stands out. 💲 *Average main: R$55* ✉ *Rua do Amparo 335, Olinda* 📞 *081/3429–3331* ⊕ *www. oficinadosabor.com* ⊙ *Closed Mon.*

$
BRAZILIAN
FAMILY

✕ **Olinda Art and Grill.** Good-value hearty meals, such as whole roast chicken with rice, beans, and salad, are served at this popular restaurant on a lovely terrace, which has spectacular views over Olinda. Because of its popularity, service can be on the slow side. 💲 *Average main: R$30* ✉ *Rua Bispo Coutinho 35, Olinda* 📞 *081/3429–9406* ⊙ *No dinner Sun.* 🚫 *No credit cards.*

$$
HOTEL
FAMILY
Fodor's Choice
★

🏨 **Hotel 7 Colinas.** Named after the seven hills that surround the hotel, 7 Colinas is a sprawling oasis that sits amid the trees and flowers of a tropical estate that once belonged to the São Francisco religious order. **Pros:** cozy rooms; nice atmosphere; fantastic swimming pool. **Cons:** Wi-Fi can be slow; food could be improved. 💲 *Rooms from: R$345* ✉ *Ladeira de São Francisco 307, Olinda* 📞 *081/3493–7766* ⊕ *www. hotel7colinas.com.br* 🛏 *44 rooms* 🍽 *Breakfast.*

$$
B&B/INN

🏨 **Hotel Pousada Quatro Cantos.** In a converted mansion, this pousada has rooms that vary considerably in size, quality, and price; the suites, with hardwood floors, rival those at the best hotels, but the standard rooms are just average. **Pros:** wonderful suites; English-speaking staff. **Cons:** not all rooms are equal; decorations can be dated. 💲 *Rooms from: R$255* ✉ *Rua Prudente de Morais 441, Olinda* 📞 *081/3429–0220* ⊕ *www.pousada4cantos.com.br* 🛏 *16 rooms, 2 suites* 🍽 *Breakfast.*

$
B&B/INN
FAMILY
Fodor's Choice
★

🏨 **Pousada Cama e Café Olinda.** At this intimate, family-run bed-and-breakfast, guests rave about the personalized service, spacious rooms, and fabulous homemade breakfast. **Pros:** great value; family atmosphere. **Cons:** books up quickly. 💲 *Rooms from: R$140* ✉ *Rua da Bertioga 93, Olinda* 📞 *081/8822–9083* ⊕ *www.camaecafeolinda.com* 🛏 *2 rooms* 🍽 *Breakfast* 🚫 *No credit cards.*

$$$
HOTEL

🏨 **Pousada do Amparo.** This eclectic pousada is made up of two colonial houses with soaring ceilings; wood and brick details, original artwork,

10

and an indoor garden lend considerable warmth to the cavernous spaces. **Pros:** atmospheric buildings; helpful staff. **Cons:** poor Wi-Fi connection; dated design. [$] *Rooms from: R$460* ✉ *Rua do Amparo 199, Varadouro, Olinda* ☎ *081/3439–1749* 🌐 *www.pousadadoamparo.com.br* 🛏 *18 rooms* 🍴 *No meals.*

SHOPPING

Casa do Artesão. For regional crafts, head to the Casa do Artesão. It's open weekdays 9–6 and Saturday 9–2. ✉ *Rua Prudente de Morais 458, Carmo, Olinda* ☎ *081/3061–1292* 🌐 *casadoartesaoolinda.blogspot.com.br.*

Rua do Amparo. Along Rua do Amparo, one of the cultural hubs of Olinda, you will find an eclectic collection of artists' workshops. The artists themselves will happily welcome you inside and let you browse through their work. ✉ *Rua do Amparo, Varadouro, Olinda.*

SIDE TRIP TO CARUARU

134 km (83 miles) west of Recife.

Caruaru and its crafts center, Alto do Moura (6 km/4 miles south of Caruaru), became famous in the 1960s and '70s for clay figurines made by local artisan Mestre Vitalino. There are now more than 500 craftspeople working in Alto do Moura, with numerous ateliers dotted along the main street of Rua Mestre Vitalino. At the crafts center you can buy not only figurines, which depict northeasterners doing everyday things, but also watch the artisans work.

GETTING HERE AND AROUND

A shuttle bus runs between Recife and Caruaru every hour. Caruaruense buses cost R$23. To reach Caruaru from Recife by car, take BR 232 west; the trip takes two hours.

ESSENTIALS

Bus Contacts **Caruaruense.** ☎ *081/3722-1611.*

WHERE TO STAY

$ B&B/INN 🏨 **Caruaru Park Hotel.** On the outskirts of town, the Caruaru Park's colorful rooms and chalets are sparsely decorated but neat and clean. **Pros:** pleasant rooms; good breakfast. **Cons:** basic decor; not within walking distance of town. [$] *Rooms from: R$132* ✉ *Rodovia BR-232, Km 128, Caruaru* ☎ *081/3727–9494* 🌐 *www.caruaruparkhotel.com.br* 🛏 *76 rooms* 🍴 *Breakfast.*

SHOPPING

Feira de Caruaru. This fantastic open-air market, the largest in Northeast Brazil, takes place daily. Here, as the songwriter Luis Gonzaga put it, "it is possible to find a little of everything that exists in the world." Look for pottery, leather goods, ceramics, hammocks, and baskets. On Saturday, roving musicians provide a soundtrack to shopping with violins and folk music. ✉ *Parque 18 de Maio, Caruaru.*

SIDE TRIP TO ALAGOAS

For a long time, Brazil's smallest state was known for little else than sugar production and as the breeding ground (and favored retreat) of some of the country's most corrupt politicians. However, in the last five years, the state has begun to gain ground as one of the country's emerging tourist destinations, particularly for Brazilians who have tired of the increasing commercialization of Bahia's beach towns.

From Barra de São Miguel south of the capital Maceió up through the *rota ecológica* toward Recife, the coast is lined with coconut palms and remarkably free, thus far, of large resorts. Instead, you will find small communities of fisherman's villages, boutique pousadas, and deserted beaches. The *rota ecológica,* also known as the Costa dos Corais after the coral reef that runs along its shore, is one of the area's highlights: 20 km (12½ miles) of road that veer off from the main highway and pass through villages such as São Miguel de los Milagres. The predominantly calm warm waters here make it a great choice for families with small children.

GETTING HERE AND AROUND

There are numerous daily flights from Brasília, Recife, São Paulo, and Rio de Janeiro to Maceió, the capital of Alagoas, on GOL, TAM, Avianca, and Azul. Buses run regularly between Recife and Maceió, with the "conventional" class stopping off at beach towns along the way. Prices start from R$35, and it takes approximately 4 hours. If you want to hop between beaches, renting a car in either Recife or Maceió is recommended. A taxi from São Miguel dos Milagres to Recife costs around R$250 and takes between 2–3 hours.

ESSENTIALS

Airport Maceió Airport. ⊠ *Rodovia BR 104, Km 91, Tabuleiro do Pinto Maceió, Alagoas* ☎ *082/3036-5200.*

Bus Contacts Real Alagoas. ☎ *081/3452-9400* ⊕ *www.realalagoas.com.br.*

Rental Car Contacts Movida Car Rental. ⊠ *Aeroporto de Maceió, Aeroporto de Maceió, Rodovia BR 104 s/n, Km 91* ☎ *082/3261-4903* ⊕ *www.movida. com.br.*

TOURS

Gato do Mato. This agency specializes in a wide range of ecotours and adventure activities throughout the region, from kayaking trips, jungle hikes, canoe trips through the mangroves. They can also arrange transfers. ⊠ *Alagoas* ☎ *082/9992-6111* ⊕ *www.gatodomato.com* 🖼 *From R$100.*

EXPLORING

FAMILY
Fodor'sChoice
★

Saõ Miguel dos Milagres. This fisherman's village is surrounded by some of the region's most charming independent pousadas, most of which face directly onto the sand and are focused on preserving the natural surroundings. The beaches along this part of the coast form one long trail of coconut palms, perfect for long walks and soaking up the natural beauty, while the sea itself is protected by a fringe of coral that keeps conditions continuously calm. One thing not to miss is the Sea-Cow

10

Sanctuary, which rehabilitates wounded manatees and is one of the best places in Brazil to get close to these endangered animals. Look for signs on the main road that point toward the workshops of local artisans, where you can find furniture and handicrafts carved from local materials. ✉ *Access via BR101 South of Recife, Km 233, Alagoas.*

BEACHES

FAMILY Fodor's Choice ★ **Praia do Patacho.** Almost always deserted, this long stretch of white sand is the Coral Coast's most beautiful beach, with warm waters calm enough for even small kids to feel like they are taking a bath. The landscape changes signficantly between high and low tide, when the water retreats from the coconut-lined shore up to 500 meters, leaving an iridescent layer of water that reflects the sunlight. **Amenities:** none. **Best for:** snorkeling; solitude; sunrise; swimming; walking. ✉ *Porto das Pedra, Alagoas* ✥ *140 km (87 miles) from Recife via BR 101 south.*

WHERE TO STAY

$$$$ RESORT Fodor's Choice ★ 🏨 **Kenoa.** Brazil's first eco-design resort, this remarkable property provides high-end luxury while maintaining its dedication to the preservation of nature and the local culture. **Pros:** stunning design; five-star service; excellent spa; well-priced restaurant. **Cons:** far from the nearest town. [$] *Rooms from: R$1,337* ✉ *Rua Escritor Jorge de Lima nº 58, Barra de São Miguel, Alagoas* ☎ *082/3272–1285* 🌐 *www.kenoaresort.com* 💳 *No credit cards* 🛏 *23 rooms* 🍴 *Breakfast.*

$$$$ B&B/INN FAMILY 🏨 **Pousada Amendoeira.** Perched on a deserted white-sand beach, this pousada is a contender for Brazil's most tranquil place to unwind. **Pros:** romantic atmosphere; excellent location; stellar service. **Cons:** rooms can be a little small; no pool. [$] *Rooms from: R$540* ✉ *Praia do Toque, São Miguel dos Milagres, Alagoas* ☎ *082/3295–1213* 🌐 *www.pdamendoeira.com.br* 🛏 *9 rooms* 🍴 *Some meals.*

$$$ B&B/INN FAMILY Fodor's Choice ★ 🏨 **Pousada Xuê.** This beach-chic pousada stands out for its exceptional food and bungalows that open directly onto beautiful beaches. **Pros:** excellent service; fantastic food; great for families. **Cons:** far from the nearest town; Internet only in communal areas. [$] *Rooms from: 450* ✉ *Praia do Patacho, Porta das Pedra, Alagoas* ☎ *082/3298–1197* 🌐 *www.pousadaxue.com.br/site* 💳 *No credit cards* 🛏 *5 bungalows* 🍴 *Some meals.*

NATAL

287 km (178 miles) north of Recife; 522 km (324 miles) southeast of Fortaleza.

Natal has been growing by leaps and bounds over the past decade. The capital of Rio Grande do Norte has become an important industrial center, yet no industry has had more effect on the economy than tourism. The past few administrations have invested heavily in the infrastructure and promotion, effectively placing it on the map as one of the prime tourism destinations for Brazilians traveling within Brazil.

Although it has little in the way of historical or cultural attractions, the city's main asset is its location along one of the most beautiful stretches of coast in Brazil. In fact, Natal's foundation and much of its history have been all about location. In 1598 the Portuguese began construction of the Fortaleza dos Reis Magos in present-day Natal. Its location was strategic for two reasons. First, it was at the mouth of the Rio Potengi. Second, it was near the easternmost point of the continent and therefore was closest to Europe and Africa. On December 25, 1599, the city was founded and named Natal, Portuguese for "Christmas."

GETTING HERE AND AROUND

Aeroporto Internacional Governador Aluízio Alves is 27 km (9 miles) west of the town center. Taxis to Ponta Negra or downtown Natal cost around R$115. Vans from the airport to downtown costs R$2.50

Natal's bus station, the Rodoviário de Natal, is 5 km (3 miles) from Ponta Negra. It's often referred to as the *terminal nova* (new terminal). Several buses daily go to Praia da Pipa (three hours; R$15), Recife (four hours; R$48–R$69), Fortaleza (eight hours; R$91–R$110), and Rio de Janeiro (40 hours; R$449).

Natal lies at the northern end of BR 101, making it an easy trip by car from Recife, which is due south on BR 101. To reach Praia da Pipa, head south on BR 101 and then take RN 003 to the east. To Fortaleza, take BR 304 northwest and then head north on BR 116.

Natal's few museums and historic buildings are mostly clustered in the Cidade Alta (Upper City), within easy walking distance of each other. Ponta Negra is still small enough that it can easily be explored on foot—most hotels and restaurants are very close to the beach. All taxis have meters and are easy to locate in Ponta Negra and downtown.

ESSENTIALS

Airport Aeroporto Internacional Governador Aluízio Alves *(NAT).* ⊠ *Av. Ruy Pereira dos Santos 3100, Natal* ☎ *084/3343-6060.*

Bus Contacts Terminal Rodoviário de Natal. ⊠ *Av. Capitão Mor. Gouveia 1237, Cidade de Esperança, Natal* ☎ *084/3205-2931, 084/3232-7312.*

Taxi Contacts Rádio Cooptáxi. ⊠ *Natal* ☎ *084/3205-4455.* **Rádio Táxi.** ⊠ *Natal* ☎ *084/3221-5666* ⊕ *www.radiotaxinatal.com.br.*

Visitor Information SETUR. ⊠ *Rua Mossoró 359, Tirol, Natal* ☎ *084/3232-2785, 084/3232-2500.*

10

TOURS

Cariri Ecotours. This bilingual ecotourism operator arranges trips throughout the Northeast, including to Praia da Pipa and the deserted beaches en route to Sagi and Fernando do Noronha. ⊠ *Av. Prudente de Morais 4262, Loja 3B, sala 1, Lagoa Nova, Natal* ☎ *084/9993-0027* ⊕ *www.caririecotours.com.br* ✆ *From R$70.*

Marazul. This agency specializes in buggy tours to Genipabu and along both coasts, boat trips to Galinhos, and van transfers to Praia da Pipa. ⊠ *Rua Vereador Manoel Sátiro 75, Loja 1, Natal* ☎ *084/3219-2221* ⊕ *marazulreceptivo.com.br* ✆ *From R$60.*

EXPLORING

WORTH NOTING

FAMILY **Forte dos Reis Magos.** Natal owes its existence to this impressive five-sided fort, which juts out into the sea on an artificial spit. It was built by the Portuguese in 1598, one year before the founding of Natal, and controlled by the Dutch between 1633 and 1654. Visitors can see the old quarters, the chapel, and rusted cannons; there is an impressive viewing point of the sea, especially when the tide is coming in. ⊠ *Northern end of Av. Praia do Forte, continuation of Via Costeira that extends to Ponta Negra, Praia do Meio, Natal* ☎ *084/3202–9006* 🖼 *Free* ◷ *Daily 8–4.*

Maracajaú. The principal draw at Maracajaú is the large coral reef 6 km (4 miles) off the coast. Teeming with marine life, the sizable reef offers the best snorkeling in the Natal area, and the natural pools are some of Brazil's most beautiful. Visitors can catch a minivan from Natal, followed by a small boat or catamaran across to the reefs. A day trip starts from R$130 per person. ⊠ *Take BR 101 north to Maracajaú access road; 54 km (34 miles) north of Natal (Ma-noa Aquatic Park), Enseada Pontas dos Anéis, Maracajaú, Natal* ⊕ *www.maracajaureservas.com. br/maracajau.*

BEACHES

Búzios Beach. This beach is endowed with great natural beauty yet does not usually draw many visitors. On the left side of the beach, the barrier reef creates an area of clear, calm waters ideal for bathing, snorkeling, and scuba diving. In the background are some impressive dunes, covered with palm trees and other vegetation. The modest infrastructure consists of just a few small pousadas and restaurants. While the right side of the beach is best for surfing, parents with children should avoid swimming here due to unpredictable currents. **Amenities:** food and drink; lifeguards; parking; toilets. **Best for:** snorkeling; solitude; swimming. ⊠ *RN 063 (Rota do Sol), Natal* ✛ *35 km (21 miles) south of Natal.*

Fodor's Choice **Genipabu.** Massive dunes have made this one of the best-known beaches
★ in the country. The area is most commonly explored on thrilling day-trips across the dune by buggy, stopping off at three lakes and two parks along the way. You have two choices: *com emocão* (literally, "with emotion"), which rivals any roller coaster, or *sem emocão* (without emotion), a little calmer but still fairly hair-raising. Buggy operators, who usually find you before you find them, charge around R$100 per person, although it is recommended to book in advance through a reputable operator. You can also explore the dunes on camels imported from southern Spain. Other activities include half-hour boat rides and skyboarding (also called skysurfing)—which is basically snowboarding down the dunes. The beach is attractive, although it gets crowded during high season. Because Genipabu is close to Natal, it's primarily a day-trip destination. There are a few small pousadas and restaurants near the beach, but the town shuts down at night. Buses leave from the Rodoviário Velho every half hour or so for the 45-minute trip. **Amenities:**

food and drink; toilets. **Best for:** walking. ✉ *Natal* ✥ *Take BR 101 north to Pitanguí access road; 10 km (6 miles) north of Natal.*

Pirangi do Norte. This long white-sand beach is an extremely popular summer vacation destination for residents of Natal. Boat rides to nearby coral reefs and beaches run frequently. Near the beach is the world's largest cashew tree, according to the *Guinness Book of World Records.* Its circumference measures 500 meters (1,650 feet), and it's as big as roughly 70 normal cashew trees. The entrance fee is R$4, and includes free cashew nuts and cashew juice. There is a small market nearby for souvenirs. **Amenities:** food and drink; parking; toilets; water sports. **Best for:** walking. ✉ *RN 063, 28 km (17 miles) south of Natal, Natal.*

Ponta Negra. Nearly all tourism development has focused on or around this beach in the past decade, with both negative and positive repercussions. It has a multitude of pousadas, restaurants, and shops, and even a few large resorts at the northern end. The beach itself, around 2½ km (1½ miles) long, can no longer be called pristine, but is still attractive and reasonably clean. If you seek a connection with nature, you would be best advised to head to one of the city's outer beaches during the day and venture to Ponta Negra for the nightlife, which ranges from buzzy to seedy. Ponta Negra's distinguishing feature is the *Morro da Careca* (Bald Man's Hill), a 120-meter (390-foot) dune at the southern end. You can catch a taxi or a bus (look for buses marked "Ponta Negra") at various stops along the Via Costeira south of Natal. From Ponta Negra to downtown Natal, look for buses marked "Centro" or "Cidade Alta." **Amenities:** food and drink; lifeguards; parking (fee); toilets. **Best for:** partiers. ✉ *Via Costeira, Natal* ✥ *10 km (6 miles) south of Natal.*

WHERE TO EAT

$$$ SEAFOOD

🍴 **Camarões Potiguar.** Locals and visitors alike rate this classic seafood restaurant as one of the best dining options in town. The house specialty is seafood, with fresh shrimps prepared in an impressive number of ways (try the shrimp cooked in pumpkin or shrimp fondue) and served in portions big enough for two. Be prepared to wait for a table if you haven't made a reservation, or head for happy hour of fresh fruit caipirinhas and tasty *pasteis de camarão* (shrimp pasties). Although there are now four branches of this family institution, this converted house is the chicest. [$] *Average main: R$50* ✉ *Rua Pedro Fonseca Filho 8887, Natal* ☎ *084/3209–2424* 🌐 *www.camaroes.com.br* 💳 *No credit cards.*

$ BRAZILIAN Fodor's Choice ★

🍴 **Mangai.** Choose from more than 40 delicious regional specialties at this immensely popular buffet restaurant. Tourists and town residents eat together at communal wood tables, which fit the typical rustic decor of the sertão. To top off your meal, consider ordering the *cartola,* a popular dessert made of caramelized banana, cheese, and cinnamon. [$] *Average main: R$28* ✉ *Av. Amintas Barros 3300, Lagoa Nova, Natal* ☎ *084/3206–3344* 🌐 *www.mangai.com.br* 🕒 *Daily 11–11.*

$$$ ITALIAN FAMILY

🍴 **Piazzale Itália.** During the high season (July and December–mid-March), it's necessary to make a reservation at this popular joint, or you'll be among the many waiting outside, salivating from smells of fresh tomato sauce and garlic. The restaurant's popularity is a result of reasonable prices, a romantic atmosphere, proximity to the Ponta Negra Beach, and skillful preparation of pasta, meat, and seafood dishes. Particularly recommended is the *tagliolini allo scoglio* (pasta with lobster, shrimp, and mussels). $ *Average main: R$50* ⊠ *Av. Deputado Antônio Florêncio de Queiroz 12, Ponta Negra, Natal* ☎ *084/3236–2697* ⊕ *www.piazzaleitalia.com.br* ☉ *Closed Mon. No lunch Tues.–Thurs.*

WHERE TO STAY

$$

HOTEL

FAMILY

Fodor'sChoice

★

Best Western Hotel Majestic Natal. This hotel from the reputable international chain Best Western provides one of the best options for both families and business travelers alike, with superior beds, modern amenities, and efficient, bilingual service. **Pros:** fantastic breakfast; fast Wi-Fi. **Cons:** small pool; limited gym. $ *Rooms from: R$288* ⊠ *Av. Engenheiro Roberto Freire 3800, Natal* ☎ *084/3642–7011* ⊕ *www. majesticnatal.com.br* ⇆ *136 rooms, 14 suites* ⦿ *Breakfast.*

$$$$

B&B/INN

Fodor'sChoice

★

Kaná Pousada do Charme. In Pirangi do Norte, this chic-boutique pousada offers fabulous service in a priviledged, yet secluded, location. **Pros:** romantic atmosphere; total escape; great massages. **Cons:** far from nightlife options. $ *Rooms from: R$675* ⊠ *Rua Nivea Madruga 1, Pirangi do Norte, Natal* ⊹ *26 km (16 miles) south of Natal* ☎ *084/ 3238–2137* ⊕ *www.kanapousadadecharme.com.br* ⇆ *10 rooms, 2 suites* ⦿ *Breakfast.*

$$

HOTEL

Fodor'sChoice

★

Manary Praia Hotel. Both the service and decor at this small hotel reflect tremendous attention to detail. **Pros:** good location; beautiful building; lovely swimming pool. **Cons:** not all rooms have great views. $ *Rooms from: R$359* ⊠ *Rua Francisco Gurgel 9067, Ponta Negra, Natal* ☎ *084/3204–2900* ⊕ *www.manary.com.br* ⇆ *23 rooms* ⦿ *Breakfast.*

$$

RESORT

FAMILY

Rifóles. At the end of Ponta Negra Beach, this resort offers extensive facilities, family-oriented entertainment, and the chance to unwind in the blazing northeastern sun in one of the six swimming pools. **Pros:** on the beach; friendly atmosphere. **Cons:** lacks personal service; in need of an update. $ *Rooms from: R$306* ⊠ *Rua Coronel Inácio Vale 8847, Ponta Negra, Natal* ☎ *084/3646–5000* ⊕ *www.rifoles.com.br* ⇆ *204 rooms* ⦿ *Breakfast.*

NIGHTLIFE

BARS

Taverna Pub. A bar with character, Taverna Pub is in the basement of a stylized medieval castle. It's popular with locals in their twenties and tourists who stay in the partnering hostel upstairs (Lua Cheia). ⊠ *Rua Dr. Manuel Augusto Bezerra de Araújo 500, Ponta Negra, Natal* ☎ *084/3236–3696* ⊕ *www.tavernapub.com.br.*

DANCE CLUBS

Downtown. Inspired by London's rock-and-roll scene, Downtown has live rock and blues music Thursday through Saturday. ⊠ *Rua Chile 11, Bairro da Ribeira, Natal* ☎ *084/3424–6317* ⊕ *www.downtownpub. com.br.*

Old Five. At this charming beachfront bar, tables are lit by candles and overlook the water. Cocktails include the cashew nut and tangerine caiprinha, and there is a varied menu of snacks for sharing. There is live music Thursday to Sunday. ⊠ *Rua Erivan França 230, Natal* ☎ *084/3025–7005.*

SIDE TRIP TO PRAIA DA PIPA

85 km (51 miles) south of Natal.

Praia da Pipa was a small fishing village until it was "discovered" by surfers in the '70s. Word of its beauty spread, and it's now one of the most famous and fashionable beach towns in the Northeast. It's also rapidly gaining a reputation for having an extremely active nightlife. Praia da Pipa receives a truly eclectic mix of people: hippies, surfers, foreign backpackers, Brazilian youth, and, most recently, high-end visitors attracted by the increasingly upscale restaurants and pousadas.

On either side of the town is a string of beaches with amazingly varied landscapes created by stunning combinations of pink cliffs, black volcanic rocks, palm trees, and natural pools. You can spend hours exploring the various beaches, most of which are deserted because they fall within environmentally protected areas. Another recommended activity is the boat ride to see dolphins, which often frequent the surrounding waters, although if you wait till low tide, you can walk along the shore to the breathtaking Baía dos Golfinhos and swim with them for free.

> ### COUNTRY MUSIC
>
> Forró is the name of what was considered Northeast country music. It became a national favorite in the 1950s, and is still played and danced to up and down the coast. It features *zarumba* (African drum), accordion, and triangle accompaniments. As the story goes, U.S soldiers or British engineers stationed in the Northeast during World War II always invited the townsfolk to their dances, saying they were "for all." This term, when pronounced with a Brazilian accent, became "forró." But music historians trace the origin of the term to an abbreviation of an Indian word *forróbodo*, or craziness.

GETTING HERE AND AROUND

Take BR 101 south from Natal. Buses leave from the Rodoviário de Natal several times daily (2 hours; R$15).

ESSENTIALS

Bus Contacts Oceano. ⊠ *Natal* ☎ *084/3311–3333* ⊕ *www.expresso-oceano. com.br.*

EXPLORING

FAMILY **Santuário Ecológico de Pipa** (*Pipa Ecological Sanctuary*). Nature lovers will enjoy the Santuário Ecológico de Pipa, a 120-hectare (300-acre) protected area. Sixteen short, well-maintained trails pass through Atlantic Forest vegetation and allow for some great views of the ocean. Between January and June, visitors can take part in baby-turtle conservation effort organized by Projecto Tamar. Call ahead for details and availability. ⊠ *Estrada para Tibau do Sul, 2 km (1 mile) northwest of town, Praia da Pipa* ☎ *084/3201–2007* 🎫 *R$10* ⊙ *Daily 8–4.*

BEACHES

Barra de Cunhaú. An idyllic paradise off the beaten track, this beach is blessed with white sands, turquoise waters, and a handful of small bars and restaurants. Even though there is an access road, the best option is to take a buggy trip from Praia da Pipa and spend the day. Steady winds also make it a favorite with kitesurfers. **Amenities:** food and drink; toilets. **Best for:** kitesurfing; solitude; swimming. ⊠ *Praia da Pipa* ⊕ *14 km (8½ miles) south of Praia da Pipa.*

Fodor's Choice
★
Praia das Minas. Walk 30 minutes north of Pipa's main street via a terra-cotta dirt road or along the beach (depending on the tide) and you will arrive at the deserted, rugged beauty of Praia das Minas. Luxury eco-hotel Toca da Coruja now runs the sole beach bar and restaurant, serving delicious fresh fish and caipirinhas as a reward for your efforts. Big waves and strong currents make the water best for paddling. **Amenities:** food and drink; shower; toilets. **Best for:** solitude; sunrise; walking. ⊠ *Praia da Pipa.*

Praia do Amor. The reliably strong waves at Praia do Amor are what makes Pipa such a surfer's town. Surf schools offer boards and lessons, as well as lounge chairs, umbrellas, and waiter service for avid spectators. At the right-hand side of the beach, the water is calmer and offers great swimming, particularly in the natural pools that are formed during low tide. Stand atop the dusky red cliffs and look down over Praia do Amor and you will see that the shoreline curves in the shape of a heart. **Amenities:** food and drink; lifeguards; parking; showers; toilets. **Best for:** partiers; sunrise; surfers; swimming; walking. ⊠ *Praia da Pipa.*

FAMILY
Praia do Madeiro. The soft, white sand and calm, warm waters of Praia do Madeiro make it a favorite for long days swimming and soaking up the sun. The steep path that winds through the trees down from the road offers glimpses of the glistening sea through the forest and keeps the masses at bay. Beginner surf schools and beach barracas serving coconut water and crispy shrimp are clustered at the right-hand side of the beach; if you head left along the long curve of sand, you'll have the coconut plams all to yourself. To get there, catch one of the minivans that run between Praia da Pipa and Tibau do Sul and request to stop at Madeiro. **Amenities:** food and drink. **Best for:** solitude; surfing; swimming; walking. ⊠ *Av. Antonio Florencio 2695, Praia da Pipa.*

Fodor's Choice
★
Praia dos Golfinhos. One of the Northeast's most magical spots, this local favorite is accessible only during low tide and the most likely place to swim with wild dolphins outside Fernando do Noronha. There is no access point down from the salmon-pink cliffs that frame the long slip of sand, which means that aside from a lone water seller who makes the trek daily, the beach's pristine beauty is preserved. To get there, consult the tide chart and head northwest from Pipa's central beach. **Amenities:** food and drink. **Best for:** solitude; swimming; walking. ⊠ *Praia da Pipa.*

WHERE TO EAT AND STAY

$ ITALIAN FAMILY 🍴 **Pizzeria dall'Italiano.** The thin-crust pizza at this lively spot is a serious contender for the best in Brazil. Originally from Italy, owners Paulo and Michela designed and built their own wood-fire oven to ensure that their secret recipe for pizza dough turned out just like at home. Regulars stop by for caiprinhas, making it a great spot to chat with the locals. [$] *Average main: R$30* ✉ *Av. Baia Dos Golfinhos 731, Praia da Pipa* ☎ *084/9152–8651* 💳 *No credit cards* ⏲ *Closed Tues.*

$ SEAFOOD FAMILY Fodor's Choice ★ 🍴 **Rola Peixe.** Fantastic seafood and tapas are the specialties at this family-run, laid-back spot. While the decor may be unpretentious, the Basque owners ensure that the service and the quality of dishes, like octopus carpaccio, tuna tartare, and grilled robalo, are flawless. For non–fish eaters, the daily changing menu offers several options of meat, pasta, and salad. [$] *Average main: R$30* ✉ *Av. Baia dos Golfinho, Praia da Pipa* ☎ *084/9157–7354* ⏲ *Closed Wed. No lunch.*

$$$ ECLECTIC Fodor's Choice ★ 🍴 **Tapas.** There are several good reasons why this hole-in-the-wall restaurant has an almost religious following: their tapas dishes fuse Spanish and Asian flavors and make the most of local seafood, and the wine list is one of Pipa's most varied and reasonably priced. Choose from favorites like sesame-crusted seared tuna alongside daily specials written on a blackboard menu hanging from the crimson walls. The relaxed yet sophisticated design creates the perfect spot for sharing food with friends—two to three plates per person should do it. [$] *Average main: R$55* ✉ *Rua dos Bem te Vis s/n, Praia da Pipa* ☎ *084/9414–4675* ⏲ *Closed Mon. No lunch.*

$ B&B/INN Fodor's Choice ★ 🏨 **Pousada Xamã.** A calm oasis tucked away near Praia do Amor, this well-run pousada offers friendly service, charming rooms, and a beautiful swimming pool surrounded by tropical trees. **Pros:** beautiful garden and swimming pool; excellent value; great breakfast. **Cons:** 10-minute walk into town; rooms on the ground floor can be dark. [$] *Rooms from: R$140* ✉ *Rua dos Cajueiros 12, Praia da Pipa* ☎ *084/3246–2267* 🌐 *www.pousadaxama.com.br* 🛏 *16 rooms* 🍽 *Breakfast.*

$$$$ HOTEL Fodor's Choice ★ 🏨 **Toca da Coruja.** One of the first properties to open in Praia da Pipa and a pioneer of the eco-hotel movement in Brazil, this luxury retreat remains the best in the area. **Pros:** beautiful, colonial-style bungalows; eco-friendly; superb service. **Cons:** slow Internet in the rooms; not the best place for families with small children. [$] *Rooms from: R$702* ✉ *Av. Baía dos Golfinhos 464, Praia da Pipa* ☎ *084/3246–2226* 🌐 *www.tocadacoruja.com.br* 🛏 *28 bungalows* 🍽 *Breakfast.*

FORTALEZA

523 km (324 miles) northwest of Natal

Called the "City of Light," Fortaleza claims that the sun shines on it 2,800 hours a year. And it's a good thing, too, as the coastline stretches far beyond the city. To the east, along the Litoral Leste or the Costa Sol Nascente (Sunrise Coast) are many fishing villages. To the west, along the Litoral Oeste or the Costa Sol Poente (Sunset Coast), there are pristine stretches of sand. The shores here are cooled by constant breezes and lapped by waters with an average temperature of 24°C (72°F).

Today Fortaleza, a large, modern state capital with more than 2 million inhabitants, is Brazil's fifth-largest city. It's also on the move, with one of the country's newest airports, a modern convention center, a huge cultural center with a planetarium, large shopping malls, several museums and theaters, and an abundance of sophisticated restaurants. At Praia de Iracema there's a revitalized beachfront area of sidewalk cafés, bars, and dance clubs. But if you wander along the shore, you're still bound to encounter fishermen unloading their catch from traditional jangadas—just as they've done for hundreds of years.

GETTING HERE AND AROUND

Tap is the only international airline that flies directly to Fortaleza from Europe (Lisbon); all flights to the United States connect in São Paulo or Rio de Janeiro. Aeroporto Internacional Pinto Martins is 6 km (4 miles) south of downtown. After clearing customs, those headed downtown can prepay for an *especial* (special) taxi that costs around $60, or opt for one of the licensed *taxi común* outside the airport. These are charged on a meter and a trip to Iracema costs around R$45.

City buses run frequently from the airport to the main bus station, Terminal Rodoviário João Tomé, 6 km (4 miles) south of the Centro, and Praça José de Alencar in the Centro. In low season you can buy tickets at the station right before leaving. Expresso Guanabara has four daily buses to Recife (14 hours; R$68–R$156). Between Itapemerim and Penha, there is one daily bus to Salvador (29 hours; R$231) and São Paulo (R$56 hours; R$422). Itapemerim runs daily buses to Rio de Janeiro (45 hours; R$440).

The easiest way to get around the city is by bus and taxi. All taxis have meters, so make sure they have been restarted and are turned on before you set off. Fares from Beira Mar to Fortaleza Centre and Praia do Futuro will be between R$18 and R$25. Rides to Das Dunas cost around R$90. The fare on city buses is R$2.40.

ESSENTIALS

Airport Aeroporto Internacional Pinto Martins (*FOR*). ⊠ *Av. Senador Carlos Jereissati 3000, Serrinha, Fortaleza* ☎ *085/3392-1200.*

Bus Contacts Expresso Guanabara. ⊠ *Fortaleza* ☎ *085/4005-1992.* **Itapemirim.** ⊠ *Fortaleza* ☎ *085/3235-2678* ⊕ *www.itapemirim.com.br.* **Penha.** ⊠ *Fortaleza* ☎ *085/3256-3308* ⊕ *vendas.nspenha.com.br.* **São Benedito.** ⊠ *Fortaleza* ☎ *085/3444-9999.* **Terminal Rodoviário Engenheiro João Tomé.** ⊠ *Av. Borges de Melo 1630, Fátima, Fortaleza* ☎ *085/3256-2200.*

Taxi Contacts Disquetáxi. ☎ *085/3287-7222.* **Radio Táxi Fortaleza.** ⊠ *Fortaleza* ☎ *085/3254-5744* ⊕ *www.radiotaxifortaleza.com.br.*

Visitor Information SETUR. ⊠ *Aeroporto Internacional Pinto Martins, Av. Senador Carlos Jereissati, Serrinha, Fortaleza* ☎ *085/3392-1667.* **SETUR.** ⊠ *Terminal Rodoviário João Tomé, Av. Borges de Melo 1630, Fátima, Fortaleza* ☎ *085/3230-1111.*

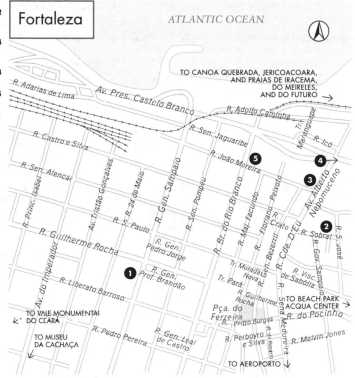

TOURS

OceanView Tours and Travel. This professional tour company offers guides in English, day trips to beaches such as Flexeiras and Canoa Quebrada, and private transfers to Jericoacoara. It also organizes city tours and transfers. ⊠ *Av. Monsenhor Tabosa 1165, Meireles, Fortaleza* ☎ *085/3219–1300* ⊕ *www.oceanviewturismo.com.br* ✉ *From R$45.*

Vitorino Turismo. This knowledgable tour operator offers day trips and private transfers to all the main beaches along Fortaleza's coasts. It can also advise on how best to enjoy and travel through the region. ⊠ *Av. Monsenhor Tabosa 1067, Fortaleza* ☎ *085/3047–1047* ⊕ *www. vitorinotur.com.br* ✉ *From R$40.*

EXPLORING

TOP ATTRACTIONS

Catedral Metropolitana. Inspired by the famous cathedral in Cologne, the Catedral Metropolitana was built between 1937 and 1963 and has a dominant Gothic look. Its two spires are 75 meters (250 feet) high, and it can accommodate 5,000 worshipers, who no doubt draw inspiration from its beautiful stained-glass windows. Don't be put off by the grimy exterior—the interiors gleam brilliant white. ⊠ *Rua Sobral 1, Centro,*

10

Fortaleza ☎ *085/3388–8702* ⊕ *www.arquidiocesedefortaleza.org.br* ✉ *Free* ⊙ *Weekdays 8–5, weekends 8–11.*

Fodor's Choice **Centro Dragão do Mar de Arte e Cultura.** Not far from the Mercado Cen-
★   tral, this majestic cultural complex is an eccentric mix of curves, straight lines, and angular and flat roofs. What's inside is as diverse as the exterior. There's a planetarium and contemporary theater, as well as art museums with permanent exhibitions of Ceará's two most famous artists, Raimundo Cela and Antônio Bandeira. Another museum presents Ceará's cultural history, with exhibits of embroidery, paintings, prints, pottery, puppets, and musical instruments. When you need a break, head for the center's romantic Santa Clara Café Orgânico, which serves a variety of cocktails made with coffee as well as little meat or vegetarian pies. There are also some great bars installed in the converted colonial houses that surround the complex. The center's bookstore has English-language titles as well as souvenirs and cards. ⊠ *Rua Dragão do Mar 81, Praia de Iracema, Fortaleza* ☎ *085/3488–8600* ⊕ *www. dragaodomar.org.br* ✉ *Museums R$2, planetarium R$8* ⊙ *Tues.–Fri. 8 am–9:30 pm, weekends 2–9:30.*

FAMILY **Museu da Cachaça** (*Cachaça Museum*). An interesting day-trip from Fortaleza, this museum offers tours of a cachaça plant, where you learn about the history of how the sugarcane juice is fermented and distilled. Most notably, cachaça is the primary ingredient for the *caipirinha*, widely considered Brazil's national cocktail. Afterward, there are tasting sessions. The 98,736-gallon wooden barrel in the tavern is the largest in the world. The museum is located inside the I-Park, which has a variety of fun activities well suited to kids of all ages, from paddleboats and archery to a climbing wall and a decent restaurant ⊠ *Fortaleza* ✛ *50 km (31 miles) southwest of Fortaleza, turn left off CE 65 just before small town of Maranguape* ☎ *085/3341–0407* ✉ *R$28* ⊙ *Wed.–Sun. 9–5.*

FAMILY **Passeio Público.** Also called the Praça dos Mártires, this landmark square
Fodor's Choice dates from the 19th century. In 1824 many soldiers were executed here
★   in the war for independence from the Portuguese crown. It has a central fountain and is full of century-old trees and statues of Greek deities. Look for the ancient baobab tree. Small stalls sell snacks and handicrafts and there is occasional live music. ⊠ *Fortaleza.*

Theatro José de Alencar. This theater is a rather shocking example (especially if you come upon it suddenly) of the eclectic phase of Brazilian architecture, showcasing a mixture of neoclassical and art nouveau styles. The top of the theater, which looks as if it was designed by the makers of Tiffany lamps, really stands out against Fortaleza's perpetually blue sky. It was built in 1910 of steel and iron (many of its cast-iron sections were imported from Scotland) and was restored in 1989. It's still used for cultural events—including concerts, plays, and dance performances—and houses a library and an art gallery. Some of the tour guides speak English; call ahead for reservations. ⊠ *Praça do José Alencar s/n, Centro, Fortaleza* ☎ *085/3101–2583* ⊕ *www.secult.ce.gov. br* ✉ *R$4* ⊙ *Wed.–Fri. 9–noon, 2–5, weekends 2–5.*

WORTH NOTING

FAMILY **Forte de Nossa Senhora da Assunção.** Built by the Dutch in 1649, this fort was originally baptized Forte Schoonemborch. In 1655 it was seized by the Portuguese and renamed after the city's patron saint, Nossa Senhora da Assunção. It was rebuilt in 1817 and is now a military headquarters. The city took its name from this fortress (*fortaleza*), which still has the cell where the mother of one of Ceará's most famous writers, José de Alencar, was jailed. Guided tours are led by the soldiers themselves, although few speak English. ⊠ *Av. Alberto Nepomuceno s/n, Centro, Fortaleza* ☎ *085/3255–1600* ⊕ *www.10rm.eb.mil.br* 🎫 *Free* ⊙ *Daily 8–11 and 2–5.*

BEACHES

Fortaleza's enchanting coast runs 22 km (14 miles) along the Atlantic between the Rio Ceará, to the west, and the Rio Pacoti, to the east. The feel of this great urban stretch of sand along with its scenery varies as often as its names: Barra do Ceará, Pirambu, Formosa, Iracema, Beira-Mar, Meireles, Mucuripe, Mansa, Titanzinho, Praia do Futuro, and Sabiazuaba.

In the City Center and its immediate environs, feel free to soak up the sun and the ambience of the beaches, but stay out of the water. Even though you might see locals swimming, the pollution levels are too high, with the exception of Praia do Futuro. For swimming, it's best to take a day trip to the beaches outside the city that have cleaner waters.

Canoa Quebrada. Hidden behind dunes, the stunning Canoa Quebrada Beach was "discovered" in the 1970s by French doctors working in the area. The spectacular scenery includes not only dunes but red cliffs and groves of palm trees. Carved into a cliff is the symbol of Canoa: a crescent moon with a star in the middle. The village now has good roads and an endless choice of comfortable pousadas, bars, and restaurants. The most efficient and economical way to get here is on a trip offered by one of Fortaleza's many tour operators, with prices from R$45 per person. **Amenities:** food and drink; parking; toilets; water sports. **Best for:** partiers; surfing; swimming; walking; windsurfing. ⊠ *Fortaleza* ✈ *Take BR 116 to BR 304; 164 km (101 miles) east of Fortaleza.*

FAMILY

Fodor's Choice
★

Flecheiras. The ocean is always calm at this beach, which is surrounded by coconut trees, lagoons, and sand dunes. During low tide the reefs surface, and you can see small fish and shells in the rocks. When the tide comes in and the natural pools form, you can grab your mask and go snorkeling. In a 5-km (3-mile) stretch between Flexeiras and Mundaú—another almost-deserted beach—there are several fishing villages and a working lighthouse. A river joins the ocean at Mundaú, forming a large S on the sand; on one side is a line of coconut trees and on the other, fishermen with their jangadas—the scene conveys the very essence of Ceará. Flexeiras is about a 90-minute drive from Fortaleza. You can take the Rendenção bus or arrange a trip here with a tour operator. As yet there are no luxury resorts here, but there are several simple, clean pousadas. **Amenities:** food and drink; parking; toilets. **Best for:**

10

snorkeling; solitude; swimming. ✉ *CE 085, Fortaleza* ⊕ *177 km (110 miles) northwest of Fortaleza.*

Iguape. Surrounded by white-sand dunes, this laid-back beach in the nearby village of Aquiraz has calm and clean water. There are both fishermen and lace makers (lace is sold at the Centro de Rendeiras). There's also a lookout at Morro do Enxerga Tudo. Buses depart from Fortaleza for this beach several times daily on the route to Aquiraz. **Amenities:** food and drink; parking; toilets. **Best for:** solitude; surfing; swimming. ✉ *CE 040, Aquiraz, Fortaleza* ⊕ *50 km (31 miles) east of Fortaleza* 🌐 *www.iguapece.com.br.*

Porto das Dunas. Tourists and locals alike flock to this beach to enjoy the many water sports (including surfing) and gawk at the lovely sand dunes. Porto das Dunas is south of Fortaleza in the municipality of Aquiraz. It also has a golf course overlooking the beach. São Benedito operates the Jardineira bus that runs from Centro to Porto das Dunas; you can catch it along Avenida Beira-Mar. **Amenities:** food and drink; lifeguards; parking; toilets; water sports. **Best for:** surfing; windsurfing. ✉ *Aquiraz, Fortaleza* ⊕ *Take Av. Washington Soares, then follow signs to Estrada da Cofeco and Beach Park; 22 km (14 miles) southeast of Fortaleza.*

FAMILY
Fodor's Choice ★
Praia de Cumbuco. Thirty-seven km (23 miles) west of Fortaleza, this former fisherman's colony is one of the best options for a relaxing day-trip from Fortaleza. The long stretch of tranquil golden sands is framed in immense dunes and coconut palms. The reliable winds make it a favorite among kitesurfers, while adventure lovers can bounce around the dunes by buggy, ride horses along the beach, or take a trip out to sea in one of the traditional *jangadas*. **Amenities:** food and drink; parking; toilets. **Best for:** solitude; swimming; walking; windsurfing. ✉ *Fortaleza* ⊕ *37 km (23 miles) west of Fortaleza on the CE-090 or CE-085.*

FAMILY
Praia do Futuro. Hands-down the city's best beach for swimming, this long curve of golden sand lines the only part of Fortaleza's sea regularly clean enough to take a dip. Framing the beach are *mega-barracas*, sophisticated beach clubs that have restaurants, bathrooms, bars, and even swimming pools with slides for kids. The regular waves attract local surfers. If returning after dark, it is best to take a taxi (approximately R$25 to Praia dos Mereilles). **Amenities:** food and drink; lifeguards; parking (fee); showers; toilets. **Best for:** partiers; surfing; swimming; walking. ✉ *Praia do Futuro, Fortaleza.*

WHERE TO EAT

$$$$
SEAFOOD
FAMILY
Fodor's Choice ★
🍴 **Coco Bambu Frutos do Mar.** Lovers of seafood should look no further than this elegant spot overlooking the beach, which serves prawns in all imaginable forms. Its popularity has reached such heights that there are now 12 Coco Bambus across Brazil. Start with the giant king prawns encrusted in coconut and served with mango chutney, and then follow that up with grilled lobster with Sicilian lemon risotto. Portions are often big enough for two. The spacious restaurant has a number of different areas for dining, from the ample open-air terrace to an air-conditioned salon [$] *Average main: R$65*

✉ *Av. Beira-Mar 3698, Meireles, Fortaleza* ☎ *085/3198–6000* 🌐 *www.restaurantecocobambu.com.br* 💳 *No credit cards.*

$$ BRAZILIAN 🍴 **Colher de Pau.** Ana Maria Vilmar and her mother opened Colher de Pau more than a decade ago in a small rented house in the Varjota district. The regional cuisine here has become so popular that there is now a sister spot in São Paulo. The sun-dried meat is served not only with *paçoca* but also with banana and *baião-de-dois* (rice and beans). The shellfish dishes, many prepared with regional recipes, are also standouts. Generous portions serve two or three people, and live music is performed nightly in the alfresco courtyard. [$] *Average main: R$40* ✉ *Rua Ana Bilhar 1178, Varjota, Fortaleza* ☎ *085/3267–6680* 🌐 *www.colherdepaufortaleza.com.br* ⏲ *No lunch weekdays.*

> **LOCAL SPECIALTIES**
>
> When in Fortaleza, be sure to try *lagosta ao natural* (lobster served with homemade butter), sun-dried meat with *paçoca* (manioc flour seasoned with herbs and red onions), and *caldeirada* (shrimp and vegetable soup with strong spices).

$$$$ FUSION 🍴 **L'Ô Restaurante.** This elegant restaurant serves sophisticated Mediterranean-Brazilian fusion dishes. The surrounding area may be a little run-down, but inside the decor is art deco–inspired and there is a beautiful alfresco bar in the garden. Highlights include slow-roasted lamb served with cashew nuts and an extensive wine list. While pricey, the experience is classier than most of its Fortaleza competitors. [$] *Average main: R$68* ✉ *Av. Pessoa 217, Fortaleza* ☎ *085/3265–2288* 🌐 *www.lorestaurante.com.br* ⏲ *No lunch Mon.–Thurs. and Sat. No dinner Fri. and Sun.* 💳 *No credit cards.*

$$$$ STEAKHOUSE FAMILY 🍴 **Santa Grelha.** In a restored colonial house, Santa Grelha is off the tourist path and specializes in exceptional grilled meat and fish, served with legendary home-made *farofa* (roasted manioc flour). Black-suited waiters and a climatized wine cellar of more than 600 options add to the air of elegance. [$] *Average main: R$76* ✉ *Rua Tibúrcio Cavalcante 790, Meireles, Fortaleza* ☎ *085/3224–0249* 🌐 *www.socialclube.com.br.*

$$ MEDITERRANEAN Fodor's Choice ★ 🍴 **Vojnilô Praia.** An excellent option for lunch on the beach is this chic spot that combines Mediterranean dishes with good music, beautiful people, and reliable service. Freshness and quality are guaranteed. Specialties include whole roasted fish and ceviche. On Thursday, stop by for whole crab and live music; on Saturday, a DJ spins tunes at sunset. Reservations are recommended on the weekends. [$] *Average main: R$44* ✉ *Av. Zezé Diogo 2771, Barraca D, Fortaleza* ☎ *085/3267–3081* ⏲ *No dinner* 💳 *No credit cards.*

10

WHERE TO STAY

$ B&B/INN FAMILY Fodor's Choice ★ 🏨 **0031 Boutique Hotel.** Near some beautiful beaches, this well-run pousada has comfortable rooms with private verandas that line the lovely pool. **Pros:** intimate, family environment; great value; multilingual service. **Cons:** can be too informal for some; slow Wi-Fi. [$] *Rooms from: R$195* ✉ *Av. Das Dunas 2249, Cumbuco, Fortaleza* ☎ *085/9214–5238* 🌐 *www.0031.com* 🛏 *15 rooms* 🍴 *Breakfast.*

$ B&B/INN

Hotel Casa de Praia. On a small side street three blocks from the beach, this laid-back hotel offers some of the best value for money in town, with friendly service and a charming rooftop terrace. **Pros:** near the beach; affordable price. **Cons:** small bathrooms; dated design; rooms can be noisy. [$] *Rooms from: R$135* ✉ *Rua Joaquim Alves 169, Praia de Iracema, Fortaleza* ☎ *085/3219–1022* 🌐 *www.hotelcasadepraia.com.br* 🛏 *40 rooms* 🍴 *Breakfast.*

$$$ HOTEL Fodor's Choice ★

Hotel Gran Marquise. Overlooking the beach, this luxury hotel has beautiful rooms; friendly, five-star service; and a prime location that makes it a wonderful base for exploring Fortaleza. **Pros:** great location; fantastic service. **Cons:** not all rooms have views; lobby is a little dated. [$] *Rooms from: R$380* ✉ *Av. Beira-Mar 3980, Mucuripe, Fortaleza* ☎ *085/4006–5000* 🌐 *www.granmarquise.com.br* 🛏 *230 rooms, 26 suites* 🍴 *Breakfast.*

$$ HOTEL

Hotel Luzeiros. With modern rooms, a rooftop pool, two restaurants, and a bar, this stylish hotel is one of the best options in town. **Pros:** great views; professional staff. **Cons:** slow Wi-Fi connection; lower rooms can be noisy. [$] *Rooms from: R$293* ✉ *Av. Beira Mar 2600, Meireles, Fortaleza* ☎ *085/4006–8585* 🌐 *www.hotelluzeiros.com.br* 💳 *No credit cards* 🛏 *202 rooms, 2 suites* 🍴 *Breakfast.*

NIGHTLIFE AND PERFORMING ARTS

NIGHTLIFE

BARS AND CLUBS

Arre Égua. This popular restaurant and bar has live local bands playing *forró*and *sertanejo* almost every night of the week. It serves a well-priced buffet of northeastern classics. ✉ *Rua Delmiro Gouveia 420, Fortaleza* ☎ *085/3267–2325* 🌐 *www.arreegua.com.br* 🎟 *R$20.*

Boteco Praia. In a light blue mansion overlooking Iracema Beach, this lively boteco bar is a great spot for an afternoon beer. The *choppe* (Brazilian draft beer) is always extra cold and the waiters bring deep-fried snacks directly to your table. ✉ *Av. Beira Mar 1680, Fortaleza* ☎ *085/3248–4773* 🌐 *www.botecofortaleza.com.br.*

FAMILY **Pirata Bar.** This pirate-inspired bar is packed every Monday night with what they describe as the "happiest party in South America." Excellent live bands play sertenejo and forró as the crowd takes to the dance floor. Drinks and snacks are available. ✉ *Rua dos Tabajaras 325, Fortaleza* ☎ *085/4011–6161* 🌐 *www.pirata.com.br* 🎟 *R$50.*

PERFORMING ARTS

Centro Cultural Banco do Nordeste. The Centro Cultural Banco do Nordeste hosts plays, concerts, and art exhibitions. ✉ *Rua Conde d'Eu 560, Centro, Fortaleza* ☎ *085/3464–3108* 🌐 *www.bnb.gov.br/cultura.*

Centro Dragão do Mar de Arte e Cultura. The large Centro Dragão do Mar de Arte e Cultura, near the Mercado Central, has several theaters and an open-air amphitheater that host live performances. There are also classrooms for courses in cinema, theater, design, and dance. ✉ *Rua Dragão do Mar 81, Praia de Iracema, Fortaleza* ☎ *085/3488–8600* 🌐 *www.dragaodomar.org.br.*

SHOPPING

Fortaleza is one of the most important centers for crafts—especially bobbin lace—in the Northeast. Shops sell a good variety of handicrafts, and others have clothing, shoes, and jewelry along Avenida Monsenhor Tabosa in Praia de Iracema. Shopping centers both large and small house branches of the best Brazilian stores.

Fodor's Choice
★
Aquiraz. For lace aficionados, a trip to the town of Aquiraz is a must. Ceará's first capital (1713–99) is today a hub for artisans who create the famous *bilro* (bobbin) lace. On the beach called Prainha (6½ km [4 miles] east of Aquiraz) is the Centro de Rendeiras Luiza Távora. Here, seated on little stools, dedicated and patient lace makers explain how they create such items as bedspreads and tablecloths using the bilro technique. ⊠ *30 km (19 miles) east of Fortaleza, Fortaleza.*

Ceart. First-class artisan work from across the region is featured at this upmarket workshop, where you can often catch the craftspeople at work. Even though the prices for wood, straw, and ceramic work may be steeper than at the Mercardo Central, the high quality more than makes up for this. ⊠ *Av. Santos Dumont, Aldeota, Fortaleza.*

Feirinha Noturna. More than 600 artisans sell their work at this nightly fair. ⊠ *Av. Beira-Mar, Meireles, Fortaleza.*

Mercado Central. With four floors and more than 600 stores, this central market stocks a varied selection of northeastern handicrafts and local products, such as *castanha de caju* (caju nuts). It has elevators to take you from one floor to the next, but since it's built with an open style and has ramps that curve from one floor to the next, it's just as easy to walk up. The place itself is fairly scruffy and it's worth keeping a close eye on your belongings. ⊠ *Av. Alberto Nepomuceno 199, Centro, Fortaleza* ☎ *085/3454–8586* ⊕ *www.mercadocentraldefortaleza.com.br* ⊙ *Weekdays 8–6, Sat. 8–4, Sun. 8–noon.*

SIDE TRIP TO JERICOACOARA

300 km (186 miles) northwest of Fortaleza.

10

Fodor's Choice
★
In Jericoacoara, or Jerí, time seems endless. It's the ultimate relaxing vacation, and not because there isn't anything to do. You can surf down sand dunes or ride up and down them in a dune buggy. You can take an easy hike to the nearby Pedra Furada, or Arched Rock, a gorgeous formation sculpted by the waves. Jerí is also Brazil's premier destination for kitesurfing and windsurfing.

GETTING HERE AND AROUND

From Fortaleza, Fretcar buses depart six times a day and arrive in Jijoca around five hours later. From there an open-air bus drives you the rest of the way to Jericocoara. The journey costs between R$43 and R$70. Buy your return ticket as soon as you arrive in Jericocoara, as they sell out quickly. Another good option is to arrange your transfer with one of the travel agencies in Fortaleza. Unless you plan on hiring a 4x4 and are familiar with the road, driving to Jericoacoara is not recommended.

ESSENTIALS

Bus Contacts Fretcar. ☎ *085/3402–2222* 🌐 *www.fretcar.com.br.*

> **SAY BONGIORNO!**
>
> If you make it to Jericoacoara, you might feel you're in the heart of Italy. It's a great place to practice your Italian, as it's spoken far more widely than Portuguese as a result of the multitude of expats who have made it their home.

TOURS

Fodor's Choice ★ **Hard Tour Ecotourismo.** This English-speaking tour operator specializes in a variety of off-road experiences with quality vehicles. Highlights include a one- to three-day off-road trip between Fortaleza and Jericoacoara, stopping at beaches along the way, and a four-day experience from Jericoacoara to São Luis, via the spectacular dunes of the Lençóis Maranhenses National Park. ✉ *Rua Francisco Holanda 843, Fortaleza* ☎ *085/9925–6262* 🌐 *www.hardtour.com.br* 🎟 *From R$180.*

BEACHES

FAMILY **Lagoa do Paraíso.** The fine white sand and crystalline, calm turquoise waters at idllyic Lagoa do Paraíso are excellent for sunbathing. Take the shuttle from the center of town (approximately 40 minutes) through the dunes and spend the day. There are restaurants lining the shore, paddle-boards for rent, and hammocks suspended in the water for snoozing. **Amenities:** food and drink; water sports. **Best for:** swimming; walking. ✉ *13 km (8 miles) south of Jericoacoara, Jericoacoara.*

FAMILY Fodor's Choice ★ **Praia de Jericoacoara.** Jericoacoara's main beach encircles the small village of this former fisherman's colony and is the heart of the action, from sunrise horseback riding to sunset capoiera displays. Waters are usually calm and clean, good for surfing and swimming, but conditions can vary depending on the wind. It can get busy with beach buggies and fishing boats. Don't miss watching the legendary sunset from the dunes that frame the sands. **Amenities:** food and drink; toilets. **Best for:** partiers; solitude; sunset; surfing; walking. ✉ *Jericoacoara.*

WHERE TO EAT AND STAY

$$$ ITALIAN 🍴 **Na Casa Dela.** Slip off your flip-flops and tuck into pizza, pasta, and regional specialities in the charming garden of this friendly restaurant. Even though some dishes can be hit-or-miss, the wood-fire oven and romantic atmosphere keep locals and tourists alike coming back for more. Most of the tables are outside, so the restaurant doesn't open when it rains. [$] *Average main: R$50* ✉ *Rua Principal 20, Jericoacoara* ☎ *088/9717–8649* 💳 *No credit cards* 🕒 *Closed Sat.*

$$ B&B/INN 🏨 **Casa na Praia.** True to its name, which translates as "house on the beach," this intimate pousada opens right onto the sand and has one of the best views in town over the dune. **Pros:** personalized service; delicious breakfast. **Cons:** rooms lack TVs; small rooms; no rooms have views. [$] *Rooms from: R$320* ✉ *Av. Beira Mar s/n, Jericoacoara* ☎ *088/3669–2374* 🌐 *www.casanapraiajeri.com* 🛏 *9 rooms* 🍽 *Breakfast.*

$ B&B/INN 🏨 **Pousada Ibirapuera.** Wind chimes, candles, a verdant garden, and swimming pool help create a sense of peace and tranquillity at this well-priced, no-frills pousada. **Pros:** pleasant rooms; quiet location. **Cons:**

few amenities; a 10-minute walk to the beach. $ *Rooms from: R$160* ⊠ *Rua S da Duna 06, Jericoacoara* ☎ *088/9977–5747, 088/9602–2020* ⊕ *www.pousadaibirapuera.com.br* ➬ *8 apartments* ⦿ *Breakfast.*

$$$$
HOTEL
FAMILY
⊡ Pousada Jeribá. You need to book well in advance to stay at this chic, eco-friendly pousada, where stylish ocean-view rooms, superior service, and a great restaurant set it above the rest. **Pros:** romantic ambience; spacious rooms; great breakfast. **Cons:** 10% service charge added on to bill; small pool. $ *Rooms from: R$860* ⊠ *Rua do Ibama s/n, Jericoacoara* ☎ *088/3669–2206* ⊕ *www.jeriba.com.br* ➬ *14 rooms* ⦿ *Breakfast.*

$$$$
HOTEL
FAMILY
⊡ Pousada Vila Kalango. Out of the many upmarket pousadas that have opened in Jericoacoara in the last five years, Vila Kalango stands above the crowd with its private bungalows propped on stilts. **Pros:** complimentary transfers for kitesurfers; connection with nature; excellent service. **Cons:** can be noisy due to passing beach buggies; slow Wi-Fi. $ *Rooms from: R$504* ⊠ *Rua das Dunas 30, Jericoacoara* ☎ *088/3669–2289* ⊕ *www.vilakalango.com.br* ➬ *24 bungalows* ⦿ *Breakfast.*

SPORTS AND THE OUTDOORS
BUGGY RIDES
Buggy Tours. One of the highlights of Jericoacoara is exploring the dunes by beach buggy. There are various possible routes depending on the amount of time you have. First-timers should journey to the village of Tatajuba, passing through mangroves and stopping off at the Rio Camboa to spot sea horses. On arrival at Tatajuba, lunch is served while you relax in hammocks suspended on the edges of the Lagoa da Torta. Other itineraries include a trip to the Lagoa Azul (Blue Lake) to bathe in the cystalline waters, or across the dunes at Praia do Préa. Ask for a recommendation from your pousada for the best *bugueiro.* ⊠ *Jericoacoara* ⧆ *From R$250 for 4 people.*

KITESURFING
Rancho do Kite. Windy all year-round, Jericoacoara is considered one of the world's premier destinations for kitesurfing, especially between July and January, when conditions are the most consistent. Regular wind and a glut of good teachers also make Jericoacoara a great place for beginners to get started. Rancho do Kite, the best kite school, offers equipment and various levels of training (from beginning to advanced) in over five languages. Courses take place on Praia do Préa and last between one and three days. ⊠ *Rua da Praia s/n, Preá Beach, Jericoacoara* ☎ *088/3669–2080* ⊕ *www.ranchodokite.com.br* ⧆ *From R$308.*

10

FERNANDO DE NORONHA

322 km (200 miles) off the coast of Recife.

This stunning archipelago is widely recognized as one of Brazil's crown jewels. The 16 beaches are incomparably beautiful, and the brilliant turquoise waters make for some of the best diving in the Southern Hemisphere. It's little wonder that Fernando de Noronha ranks among the world's most romantic spots.

This group of 21 islands is part of the Mid-Atlantic Ridge, an underwater volcanic mountain chain more than 15,000 km (9,315 miles) long.

First discovered in 1503 by the Italian explorer Amérigo Vespucci, the archipelago was soon taken over by Fernando de Noronha of Portugal. While Brazil originally used these islands as a prison and a military training ground, growing appreciation of its natural beauty and underwater wonders led to its designation as a protected marine park in 1988. Today, stringent regulations protect the archipelago's ecology.

The mountainous, volcanic main—and only inhabited—island of Fernando de Noronha is ringed by beaches with crystal clear warm waters that are perfect for swimming, snorkeling, and diving. In summer surfers show up to tame the waves. There are shipwrecks to explore and huge turtles, stingrays, and sharks (14 species of them) with which to swim. Diving is good all year, but prime time is from December to March on the windward side (facing Africa) and from July to October on the leeward side (facing Brazil).

GETTING HERE AND AROUND

A one-hour flight connects Fernando de Noronha with either Natal (one flight daily) or Recife (three flights daily). Flights on Azul and Gol can cost around R$500 when booked in advance, or up to R$2,500 during peak season. Taxis from the airport cost about R$30.

A maximum of 1,000 visitors are allowed here each day. There's a daily tourist tax of R$51.40, including the day you arrive and the day you leave. Divers pay an additional R$20 a day.

In 2012, a new tax was introduced for visitors to access the National Park and the most popular beaches: R$130 for foreigners and R$65 for Brazilians. The money is to improve infrastructure and increase preservation. Payment can be made at the Projecto Tamar in the village of Boldró.

Bring enough reais to last the trip, as credit cards are not widely accepted and changing money can be difficult.

ESSENTIALS

Airport Aeroporto de Fernando de Noronha. ⊠ *Fernando de Noronha.*

TOURS

Ilha de Noronha. This tour operator can organize complete package visits (often the cheapest option), as well as various other excursions around the island. ⊠ *Alameda das Acácias 566, Fernando de Noronha* ☎ *081/3076-9777* ⊕ *www.ilhadenoronha.com.br* ⊠ *From R$125.*

BEACHES

Fodor's Choice **Baía dos Porcos** (*Bay of Pigs*). The best showcase for the island's stunning natural beauty, the "Bay of Pigs" is a literal paradise tucked away on the north ridge of the island. Strict conservation laws ensure that its crystalline waters are rarely crowded. Grab a mask and dive into the natural swimming pools here to glimpse starfish, sea urchins, and even the occasional turtle or stingray. The view over the rugged rocks in the bay is awe-inspiring. Buggy drivers (*bugueiros*) are the local means of transportation for accessing the different beaches here. **Amenities:** none. **Best for:** solitude; snorkeling; swimming. ⊠ *Fernando de Noronha.*

Fodor'sChoice ★ **Baía do Sancho.** Surrounded by cliffs draped in lush green vegetation, Baía do Sancho is breathtakingly beautiful. Its crystal clear waters shift in tonality from sparkling blue to emerald green, while the coral reefs make it a prime spot for snorkeling. Be prepared for a lengthy descent down a natural stairway to reach the shore, although those with mobility problems can access the beach by boat trip. **Amenities:** none. **Best for:** solitude; snorkeling; swimming. ✉ *Fernando de Noronha.*

AN ISLAND PRISON

Brazil took advantage of Fernando de Noronha's isolated location and built a prison on one of the islands. The vegetation on the island was cut down so that prisoners wouldn't be able to build rafts on which to escape. In the 1930s and 1940s the prison was used to house political prisoners, specifically communists and anarchists.

FAMILY **Praia da Conceição.** This beach is one of the island's best spots for watching the sunset. From April to November, calm, transparent waters make this a good beach for walking; during the summer months, the tall waves draw surfers from across the country. **Amenities:** food and drink; lifeguards; toilets. **Best for:** sunsets; surfing; walking. ✉ *Fernando de Noronha.*

WHERE TO EAT AND STAY

$$$$ SEAFOOD 🍴 **Ecologiku's.** This small restaurant is known for its seafood, especially lobster. If you can't decide what to order, the *sinfonia ecologiku* is a sampling of every type of seafood on the menu. Ask your pousada to call ahead and the restaurant will send a transfer to collect you, since finding this tucked-away establishment can be a challenge. [$] *Average main: R$84* ✉ *Estrada Velha do Sueste, near the airport, Fernando de Noronha* ☎ *081/3619–0031.*

$$$$ SEAFOOD 🍴 **Mergulhão.** This contemporary restaurant serves fresh seafood with attentive service. With deck chairs, a breezy terrace, and beautiful views over the port during sunset, this is a great spot for a romantic date. [$] *Average main: R$85* ✉ *Porto Santo Antonio s/n, Fernando de Noronha* ☎ *081/3619–0215* 🌐 *www.mergulhaonoronha.com.br.*

$$$$ ECLECTIC Fodor'sChoice ★ 🍴 **Mesa da Ana.** The most unique dining experience on the island, this closed-door restaurant cooks up four high-quality dishes for a maximum of 10 guests per evening, served at the long table in a lovely garden. During high season, reservations need to be made up to a month in advance. [$] *Average main: R$150* ✉ *Estrada da Atalaia 230, Fortaleza* ☎ *081/3619–0178* 🕓 *No lunch. Closed weekdays. Closed May–June* ✍ *Reservations essential* 💳 *No credit cards.*

$$$$ HOTEL 🏨 **Pousada Teju-Acu.** Resembling tropical tree houses constructed from reclaimed wood, this eco-pousada's comfortable bungalows were designed with couples in mind. **Pros:** great ambience; excellent service. **Cons:** small pool; slow Wi-Fi. [$] *Rooms from: R$1,389* ✉ *Estrada da Alamoa s/n, Fernando de Noronha* ☎ *081/3619–1277* 🌐 *www.pousadateju.com.br* 🛏 *12 bungalows* 🍽 *Breakfast.*

$$$$ B&B/INN FAMILY [Fodor's Choice icon] **Pousada do Vale.** Near Praia do Cachorro amid verdant forest, this picturesque pousada offers 12 well-equipped, comfortable rooms and fantastic home-cooking, including a complimentary afternoon tea. **Pros:** hospitable staff; lovely ambience. **Cons:** slow Wi-Fi; no swimming pool. [$] *Rooms from: R$615* ✉ *Rua Pescador Sérgio Lino 18, Fortaleza* ☎ *084/4042–1793* 🌐 *www.pousadadovale.com* 🛏 *12 rooms* 🍴 *Breakfast.*

SPORTS AND THE OUTDOORS

Well-maintained trails and well-trained guides make for enjoyable hikes. You can also enjoy the landscape on a horseback trek to the fortress ruins and isolated beaches where hundreds of seabirds alight. In addition, Projeto Tamar has an island base for its work involving sea turtles. One of the most fascinating exploring experiences, however, is an afternoon boat trip to the outer fringes of the Baía dos Golfinhos (Bay of the Dolphins), where dozens of spinner dolphins swim south each day to hunt in deep water. If you enjoy independence, look to rent a buggy from your pousada and explore the island's beaches at your own pace.

SCUBA DIVING

Diving is excellent year-round, but prime time is from December to March on the windward side and from July to October on the leeward side. If you're an experienced diver, be sure to visit the Ipiranga, a small Brazilian destroyer that sank in 1987. It sits upright in 60 meters (200 feet) of water and is swarming with fish. You can see the sailors' personal effects, including uniforms still hanging in closets. Another good site is the Sapata Cave, which has an antechamber so large that it has been used for marriage ceremonies (attended by giant rays, no doubt).

Atlantis Divers. For dive trips, Atlantis Divers has excellent English-speaking staffers and good boats. ✉ *Praça do Cruzeiro s/n, Fernando de Noronha* ☎ *084/3206–8840* 🌐 *www.atlantisdivers.com.br* 🎫 *From R$420 for a beginner session of three hours, with 30 minutes in the water.*

THE AMAZON

Updated By
Lauren Holmes

Aerial photographs, films, and documentaries can give a sense of the Amazon's magnificence, but there is nothing like experiencing its majesty, and fragility, in person. Traveling in the Amazon may seem daunting at first, not least because of its size: the region covers more than 10 million square km (4 million square miles) and makes up roughly 40% of Brazil, divided between the states of Acre, Rondônia, Amazonas, Roraima, Pará, Amapá, and Tocantins. But don't let its size deter you. With some advanced planning, you'll be able to plan your once-in-a-lifetime trip with minimal hassle.

The most practical way to explore the Amazon is by internal flights, which are efficient and often cost-effective if booked in advance. For those with more time and a keen sense of adventure, there is also an extensive boat network, which is the area's primary mode of transportation. River travel offers the opportunity to experience the region like a local and gain closer insight into Amazonian culture and nature.

In the vibrant city of Belém, you can marvel over an array of exotic goods at the Ver-O-Peso market, dine on Amazonian delicacies, and explore the spectacular white-sand beaches nearby, such as Alter do Chão. From Manaus, you can marvel at the Meeting of the Waters, and then set out for a jungle lodge. No matter what you choose to do, you'll be awed by the unique landscapes and magnificent wildlife.

ORIENTATION AND PLANNING

GETTING ORIENTED

A trip along the Amazon itself is a singular experience. From its source in southern Peru it runs 6,300 km (3,900 miles) to its Atlantic outflow and averages more than 3 km (2 miles) in width, but reaching up to 48 km (30 miles) across in the rainy season. Of its hundreds of tributaries, 17 are more than 1,600 km (1,000 miles) long. The Amazon is so large it could hold the Congo, Nile, Orinoco, Mississippi, and Yangtze Rivers with room to spare. In places it is so wide you can't see the opposite shore, earning it the appellation Rio Mar (River Sea).

Although there has been increasing urbanization in the Amazon region, between one-third and one-half of the Amazon's residents live in rural settlements, many of which are along the riverbanks, where transportation, water, fish, and good soil for planting are readily available.

TOP REASONS TO GO

The Rain Forest: Experience the largest tropical forest in the world and its abundant wildlife in one of the wildest places on the planet.

The River: Explore the largest river in the world (by volume) and the second-longest, spanning more distance than the continental United States; the Amazon is also the earth's biggest freshwater ecosystem, and home to more fish than the Atlantic Ocean.

Exotic Foods: Dig into water-buffalo steak, duck in manioc sauce (*pato no tucupi*), fried piranha, and other exotic river fish.

The Beaches: Kick back on the golden sands and swim in the crystal clear waters in and around the town of Alter do Chão.

Handicrafts: Shop for traditional indigenous crafts, such as wood-crafted and woven items, bows, arrows, blowguns, and jewelry and headdresses of seeds and feathers.

Manaus. This city is the Amazon's largest city as well as its main entrance. It was built largely on the good fortune of a couple of economic booms. The first was rubber. The second was the creation of a tax-free zone. Getting around the city or heading north to Venezuela is done by car or bus. To go anywhere else, you must use a boat or plane. Don't plan to drive south to Porto Velho or Bolivia. The road will be gone in a number of places.

Between Manaus and Belém. As one would expect, distances between the major cities are huge. Traveling from one to another is done mostly by internal flights, since there are no roads connecting them. Boats commonly run from Belém to Manaus and back, though the 1,150-mile journey takes four or five days and the cost can often be similar to flying. Large planes connect cities and larger towns. Small planes reach some smaller towns, though they can be costly. While the Transamazônica Highway is intended to connect the eastern and western regions, nature is still in control.

Belém. Belém lies 60 miles upstream from the ocean at the confluence of several rivers. It was one of the first areas to be settled by the Portuguese. Its blend of river, ocean, and tropical forest makes for interesting geography and traveling. Buses run to landlocked villages northeast and southwest of the city, while boats run elsewhere. Boats are slow, so add extra time to your travel plans.

PLANNING

WHEN TO GO

While the Amazon is a destination that can be visited year-round, the time of year can significantly alter the experience you have and wildlife you see. The dry season (low water) between Belém and Manaus runs roughly from mid-June into December, and it's often brutally hot. Shortly before the new year, rains come more often and the climate cools a bit. The average annual temperature is 80°F (27°C) with high humidity. The early morning and the evening are always cooler and are the best times for walking around. The rainy season (high water) runs from December to June. "High water" means flooded forests and better boat access to lakes and wetlands for wildlife spotting. It also means flooded river beaches. Fishing is prime during low water, when fish move from the forest back into rivers and lakes, making them more accessible. Keep in mind that even the driest month has an average rainfall of 2 inches (compared with up to 13 inches during the wet season), so some kind of raingear is always recommended. Depending on where you are in the Amazon, during the rainy season it may rain every day, or three out of every four days, whereas during the dry season it may rain only one out of four days or less.

PLANNING YOUR TIME

With daily international flights to Miami and an extensive web of internal flights across Brazil, Manaus is the gateway to the Amazon. While the city itself is practical and continually modernizing, it lacks much of the charm of Belém and warrants little more than a day's exploring before heading off to a jungle lodge or departing on a river cruise. In contrast, plan to spend a few days soaking up Belém's vibrant parks, museums, and culinary and music scene.

Travelers should allow a minimum of 4–5 days in the Amazon to visit a single destination, using the Manaus or Belém airport as a hub for connecting flights to smaller airports like Santarém or Tefe, or as a jumping-off point to one of the lodges accessible by boat or car. If you have more time, consider combining a jungle lodge or boat trip with a few days of city exploration, and then head to one of the Amazon's famed white-sand beaches, such as Alter do Chão, to unwind.

WHAT TO BRING

Amazon essentials include a high-quality rain poncho, comfortable shoes, a sun hat, swimwear, and lightweight long shirts, and cotton or linen trousers to keep off mosquitos. Extras include mosquito repellent, sunscreen, earplugs (the Amazon can be noisy at night!), a flashlight, matches, sunglasses, and a waterproof camera case. Plan for drenching downpours by bringing sufficient plastic bags, especially for important items. Regular suitcases are fine for jungle lodges and river cruises, but for remote travel in the Amazon, a small backpack is the most efficient way to carry your gear. Specific things to consider packing for an off-the-grid Amazon vacation are: a water bottle, filter, purification tablets, sunscreen, a good medical kit, knife, a lightweight hammock (*rede de garimpeiro*), mosquito netting, sheets, 3 yards of ¼-inch rope, and a tent (if you're planning to camp).

GETTING HERE AND AROUND

Given the enormous size of the region and the difficulty of traveling large distances, most visitors travel through only one region. For example, you can visit Manaus and its surrounding area or choose the Belém region. If you fly into Manaus, see the Meeting of the Waters, walk through the Adolfo Lisboa Market, and take a tour in Teatro Amazonas. Then take a boat to a jungle lodge for a few days for trekking, swimming, and wildlife viewing. Conversely, fly into Belém and

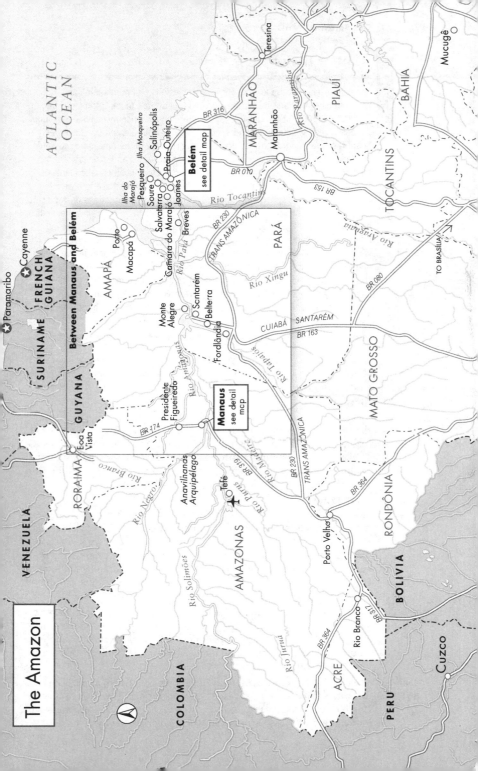

A Bit of History

Spaniard Vicente Pinzón is credited with being the first to sail the Amazon, in 1500. But the most famous voyage was undertaken by Spanish conquistador Francisco de Orellano, who set out from Ecuador on a short mission to search for food in 1541. Instead of gold or a lost kingdom, however, Orellano ran into natives, heat, and disease. When he emerged from the jungle a year later, his crew told a tale of women warriors they called the Amazons (a nod to classical mythology), and the story lent the region its name. In the late 19th century, rubber production transformed Belém and Manaus into cities. Rubber barons constructed mansions and monuments and brought life's modern trappings into the jungle. Since the rubber era, huge reserves of gold and iron have been discovered in the Amazon. Land-settlement schemes and development projects, such as hydroelectric plants and major roadworks, have followed. In the process, vast portions of tropical forest have been indiscriminately cut; tribal lands have been encroached upon; and industrial by-products, such as mercury used in gold mining, have poisoned wildlife and people. The Brazilian government has established reserves and made some efforts to preserve the territory, but there is much more to be done.

explore historic sites for a couple of days and then take a boat and van to a ranch on Marajó Island for a cultural experience and some wildlife spotting.

AIR TRAVEL

Increasing frequency and new destinations have made hopping around the Amazon by plane considerably easier and cheaper, opening up the region like never before. Azul is the main carrier, operating flights to 18 destinations within the Amazon. Tam and Gol also operate on the major routes. There are five flights daily between Manaus and Belém; to guarantee the best prices, book well in advance.

BOAT TRAVEL

Sleep in a hammock on the middle deck of a thatch-roof riverboat or in the air-conditioned suite of an upscale tour operator's private ship. Keep in mind that wildlife viewing is not good on boats far from shore. Near shore, however, the birding can be excellent. Binoculars and a bird guide can help, and shorebirds, raptors, and parrots can be abundant. Common in many parts of the river system are *boto* (pink dolphins) and *tucuxi* (gray dolphins).

ADVENTURE CRUISES Adventure cruises combine the luxury of cruising with exploration. Their goal is to get you close to wildlife and local inhabitants without sacrificing comforts and amenities. Near daily excursions include wildlife viewing in smaller boats with naturalists, village visits with naturalists, and city tours.

OCEANGO-ING SHIPS Some cruise ships call at Manaus, Belém, and Santarém as part of their itineraries. Most trips take place October through May. They range in length from 10 to 29 days, and costs vary. Two major lines making such journeys are Princess Cruises and Royal Olympic Cruises.

TOURIST BOATS Private groups can hire tourist boats that are more comfortable than standard riverboats. They generally travel close to the riverbank and have open upper decks from which you can observe the river and forest. The better tour operators have an English-speaking regional expert on board—usually an ecologist or botanist. You can either sleep out on the deck in a hammock or in a cabin, which usually has air-conditioning or a fan. Meals are generally provided.

SPEEDBOATS You can take a speedboat to just about anywhere the rivers flow. Faster than most options, speedboats can be ideal for traveling between smaller towns, a morning of wildlife viewing, or visiting a place that doesn't have regular transportation, such as a secluded beach or waterfall. You design the itinerary, including departure and return times. Prices and availability vary with distance and locale. Contact tour agencies, talk with locals, or head down to the docks to find a boat willing to take you where you want to go. Work out the price, destination, and travel time before leaving. You may have to pay for the gas up front, but don't pay the rest until you arrive. For trips longer than an hour, bring water, snacks, and sunscreen.

MACAMAZON BOATS Longer boat routes on the lower Amazon are covered by MACAMAZON. Regular departures run between Belém, Santarém, Macapá, Manaus, and several other destinations. The boats are not luxurious but are a step above regional boats. You can get a suite for two from Belém to Manaus with air-conditioning and bath. *Camarote* (cabin) class gets you a tiny room for two with air-conditioning and a shared bath. *Rede* (hammock) class is the cheapest and most intimate way to travel, since you'll be hanging tight with the locals on the main decks. Hammocks are hung in two layers very close together, promoting neighborly chats. Arrive early for the best spots, away from the bar, engine, and bathrooms. Keep your valuables with you at all times and sleep with them. Conceal new sneakers in a plastic bag. In addition to a hammock (easy and cheap to buy in Belém or Manaus), bring two 4-foot lengths of 3/8-inch rope to tie it up. Also bring a sheet, since nights get chilly. Prices between Belém and Manuas start from R$250 per person.

REGIONAL BOATS To travel to towns and villages or to meander slowly between cities, go by *barco regional* (regional boat). A trip from Belém to Manaus takes about five days; Belém to Santarém is two days. The double- or triple-deck boats carry freight and passengers. They make frequent stops at small towns, allowing for interaction and observation. You might be able to get a cabin with two bunks (around R$400 for a two-day trip), but expect it to be claustrophobic. Most passengers sleep in hammocks with little or no space between them. Bring your own hammock, sheet, and two 4-foot sections of rope. Travel lightly and inconspicuously.

Booths sell tickets at the docks, and even if you don't speak Portuguese, there are often signs alongside the booths that list prices, destinations, and departure times. Sanitary conditions in bathrooms vary from boat to boat. Bring your own toilet paper, sunscreen, and insect repellent. Food is sometimes served, but the quality ranges from so-so to deplorable. Consider bringing your own water and a *marmita* (carry-out meal) if you'll be on the boat overnight. Many boats have a small store at the stern where you can buy drinks, snacks, and grilled *mixto quente* (ham-and-cheese) sandwiches. Fresh fruit and snacks are available at stops along the way. Be sure to peel or wash fruit thoroughly with bottled water before eating it.

BUS TRAVEL
Long-distance buses arrive from various locales around the country. The Transbrazilian Highway has daily bus service to Belém from Rio de Janeiro and São Paulo, as well as from a number of other locations. Bus travel is recommended in Brazil because it's inexpensive and comfortable, although flights are increasingly competitive and sometimes cheaper; it's well worth comparing in advance, as you could save considerable travel time for little extra cash. The downside of buses is that schedules are not often convenient for travelers and it often takes longer than by car.

CAR TRAVEL
A lot of the roads in this region are unpaved and more often than not flooded. Driving conditions in the cities are good, although renting a car is rarely worth it. In the smaller towns and villages we recommend using taxis or motorcycles. Driving from state to state is not advisable and often impossible.

TAXI TRAVEL
There are plenty of taxis in Amazon cities, and they're easy to flag down. All have meters, and tips aren't necessary. If there isn't a meter, you have to bargain for the price. Smaller towns also have motorcycle taxis called *mototaxis.* They're much cheaper but only carry one passenger.

RESTAURANTS
Dining in the Amazon is often an adventure in itself, with an abundance of ingredients that are rarely found outside the region. This is particularly true of giant Amazonian river fish, such as *pirarucú, tambaqui,* and *tanadré,* traditionally served with white rice and *farofa de tucumã* (palm fruit fried flour), or *baio de dois* (a bean salad from the Northeast). Where possible, sample freshly caught fish from the river, rather than the farmed variety; you'll notice a big difference in flavor. Other highlights include *caldinho de tucupi, jambu, e camarão,* a regional delicacy made from manioc extract and mixed with a white glutonous gum and served with the spinach-like *jambu* leaf (which can turn the mouth numb). Exotic fruits, such as *cupuaçu* and *tucumã,* are ubiquitous in desserts and juices, as are excellent quality *castanha de pará* (cashew nuts), cultivated in the state of Pará.

Reservations and dressy attire are rarely needed in the Amazon (indeed, reservations are rarely taken). Tipping isn't customary except in finer restaurants. Call ahead on Monday night, when many establishments are closed.

HOTELS
Amazon hotel prices tend to be reasonable and include breakfast. Services and amenities such as laundry, however, may cost quite a bit extra. Don't expect to be pampered. When checking in, ask about discounts (*descontos*). During the slow season and midweek, you may get a break.

CLOSE UP

Health in the Amazon

11

Several months before you go to the Amazon, visit a tropical medicine specialist to find out what vaccinations you need. Describe your planned adventure, and get tips on how to prepare.

BITES AND STINGS

Tropical forests are home to several biting and stinging insects and other creatures. Most are harmless and many, such as snakes, are rarely seen. Mosquitoes can carry malaria and dengue, so it's important to protect yourself. To avoid snake bites, wear boots and pants in the forest and watch closely where you step. Some anti-itch ointment will help you sleep at night and offer relief from any little bug bites you might receive.

FOOD AND WATER

In rural areas, avoid drinking tap water and using ice made from it. In the cities most restaurants buy ice made from purified water. Beware of where you eat. Many street stands are not very clean. Over-the-counter remedies can ease discomfort. For loose bowels, Floratil can be purchased without a doctor's prescription. Estomazil and Sorrisal (which may contain aspirin) are remedies for upset stomach.

INFECTIONS AND DISEASES

Dehydration and infections from insect bites and cuts are hazards. Get plenty of (bottled or purified) water and treat infections quickly. Rabies, Chagas' disease, malaria, yellow fever, meningitis, hepatitis, and dengue fever are present in the Amazon. Research tropical diseases in the Amazon so you know the symptoms and how to treat them should you fall ill. You shouldn't have problems if you take precautions.

HEALTH TIPS

■ If you're allergic to stings, carry an adrenaline kit.

■ Use screens on windows and doors, and sleep in rooms with air-conditioning, if possible.

■ Apply strong repellents containing picaridin or DEET (diethyl toluamide) when hiking in rural or forested areas.

■ A *mosquiteiro* (netting for hammock or bed) helps tremendously at night—to be effective it must reach the floor and not touch your skin.

■ Cover up with long pants and a shirt at night indoors, and wear pants, a long-sleeved shirt, and boots in the forest.

■ Check inside your shoes every morning for small guests.

■ Do not leave water in sinks, tubs, or discarded bottles. Dengue mosquitoes thrive in urban areas and lay their eggs in clean water.

■ If you have dengue symptoms, *do not* take aspirin, which can impair blood clotting.

■ If you find a tick on your skin, carefully remove it, treat the site with disinfectant, and see a doctor as soon as possible.

■ To avoid hard-to-see chiggers, which inhabit grassy areas, spray repellent or sprinkle powdered sulfur on shoes, socks, and pants.

■ Don't bathe in lakes or rivers without knowing the quality of water and the risks involved.

Cry a little, as the Brazilians say, and you may get a larger discount. Paying with cash may lower the price. Rooms have air-conditioning, TVs, phones, and bathrooms unless we indicate otherwise, but showers don't always have hot water. Jungle lodges and smaller hotels in outlying areas often lack basic amenities. *Hotel reviews have been shortened. For full information, visit Fodors.com.*

WHAT IT COSTS IN REAIS			
$	**$$**	**$$$**	**$$$$**
Restaurants	under R$31	R$31–R$45	R$46–R$60	over R$60
Hotels	under R$251	R$251–R$375	R$376–R$500	over R$500

Restaurant prices are the average cost of a main course at dinner or, if dinner is not served, at lunch. Hotel prices are the lowest cost of a standard double room in high season, excluding tax.

MANAUS

766 km (475 miles) west of Santarém; 1,602 km (993 miles) west of Belém.

The capital of Amazonas State, Manaus is the Amazon's most popular tourist destination, largely because of the many jungle lodges in the surrounding area. The city's principal attractions are its lavish, brightly colored houses and civic buildings—vestiges of an opulent time when the wealthy sent their laundry to be done in Europe and sent for Old World artisans and engineers to build their New World monuments.

Founded in 1669, Manaus took its name, which means "mother of the Gods," from the Manaó tribe. The city has long flirted with prosperity. Of all the Amazon cities and towns, Manaus is most identified with the rubber boom. In the late 19th and early 20th centuries, it supplied 90% of the world's rubber. The industry was monopolized by rubber barons, whose number never exceeded 100 and who lived in the city and spent enormous sums on ostentatious lifestyles. They dominated the region like feudal lords, and their footprints are still present through the city.

GETTING HERE AND AROUND

Brigadeiro Eduardo Gomes Airport is 17 km (10 miles) north of downtown. Most flights connect in São Paulo. Azul, TAM and GOL have regular flights to and from Brasília, Rio, and São Paulo. The trip to Manaus Centro from the airport by taxi takes 25 minutes and is a fixed rate of R$65. A trip on one of the city buses, which depart regularly during the day and early evening, costs R$3 for a normal bus and R$4.75 for an air-conditioned one.

If you're looking for a boat from Manaus to another town, a lodge, or a beach, go to the Hidroviária Regional Terminal. At the ticket or tourist information booths you can get information about prices and departure times and days to all the locations. You can also walk down to Porto Flutuante via the bridge behind the terminal to take a look at the regional boats. Their destinations and departure times are listed on plaques.

MACAMAZON boats run from Manaus to Santarém daily (Monday to Saturday) and Amazon Star has departures on Wednesday and Friday from the Porto São Raimundo (west of downtown) or the Porto Flutuante. The journey takes two days and costs around R$147 for a hammock and R$700 for a two-person cabin. Boats from Manaus to Belém follow the same route and run twice a week; the trip takes five days and costs R$326 for a hammock, and R$1,000 for a two-person cabin.

The bus station in Manaus, Terminal Rodoviário Huascar Angelim, is 7 km (4 miles) north of the city center. From Manaus, BR 174 runs north (471 miles) to Boa Vista in Roraima State. BR 319 travels south to Porto Velho in Rondônia State but involves a ferry crossing and is only paved for about 100 km (63 miles); the road is eventually invaded by rivers and lakes. Even if you're after adventure, don't think about driving to Porto Velho.

The city bus system is extensive, easy to use, and inexpensive (R$3). Most of the useful buses run along Avenida Floriano Peixoto, including Bus 120, which goes to Ponta Negra and stops near the Hotel Tropical. From the airport a taxi to Hotel Tropical costs R$65; a trip from the Tropical to the center of town also costs R$65. Manaus has its share of traffic and parking problems, but the driving is calmer than in Belém.

ESSENTIALS

Airport Information Aeroporto Brigadeiro Eduardo Gomes. ⊠ *Av. Santos Dumont 1350, Iarumã, Manaus* ☎ *092/3652-1210, 092/3652-1210.*

Boat Contacts MACAMAZON. ☎ *091/3031-5899, 091/3222-5604* ⊕ *www. macamazon.com.br.*

Bus Contacts Terminal Rodoviário Huascar Angelim. ⊠ *Av. Mário Ypiranga Monteiro 2833, Flores, Manaus* ☎ *092/3642-5805.*

Taxi Contacts Recife Rádio Táxi. ☎ *092/3238-7301.* **Tucuxi Taxi.** ☎ *092/2123-9090, 092/3622-4040* ⊕ *www.tucuxitaxi.com.br.*

Visitor Information Centro de Atendimento ao Turista (CAT). ⊠ *Av. Eduardo Ribeiro 666, Centro, Manaus* ☎ *092/3182-6250.*

TOURS

Fontur. This trusted operator offers a range of boat and city tours, as well as river cruises and airplane tickets to various locations. Fontur can also arrange trips to jungle lodges. ⊠ *Hotel Tropical, Av. Coronel Teixeira 1320, Ponta Negra, Manaus* ☎ *092/3658-3052, 092/8114-8136* ⊕ *www.fontur.com.br* ☉ *Daily 7–5* ⊠ *From R$150.*

Gero Tours. At Gero's offices in Manaus, bilingual specialists can talk you through their wide range of day trips, riverboat cruises, and jungle lodges. One of the most reliable agencies in town, Gero also offers a superior experience of the quintessential Meeting of the Waters day trip, with their own speedboat and guaranteed English-speaking guide. ⊠ *Rua 10 de Julho 679, Sala 2, Manaus* ☎ *092/9983-6273* ⊕ *www. amazongerotours.com* ⊠ *From R$200.*

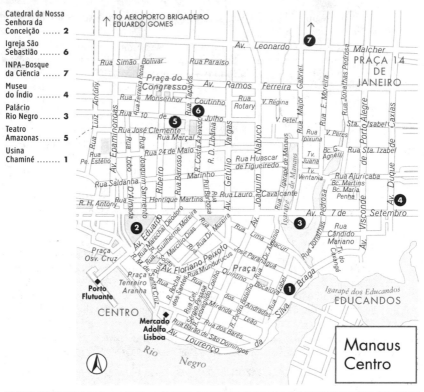

Manaus
Centro

EXPLORING

CENTRO

Manaus's downtown area has a lot going on. The floating docks are here, with tourist shops nearby. Open markets sell fish, meats, and all sorts of produce, while general stores ply machetes, hoes, hardtack, cassava flour, and boat motor parts to those pursuing a livelihood outside the city. The Centro is also the most important historic section of the city. The Teatro Amazonas and the Adolfo Lisboa Market are here, along with old churches, government buildings, and mansions. The result is a mix of neoclassical, Renaissance, colonial, and modern architecture.

TOP ATTRACTIONS

Palácio Rio Negro. The extravagant Rio Negro Palace was built at the end of the 19th century as the home of a German rubber baron and was later used as the official governor's residence. Today it houses some of the city's finest art exhibits and a cultural center. The Centro Cultuak Rio Negro, on the same property, has three daily screenings of art films and documentaries Tuesday through Friday and four screenings daily on weekends. Don't miss the cultural exhibits out back, which include a *caboclo* home (an indigenous home) and a cassava-processing house.

✉ *Av. 7 de Setembro 1546, Centro, Manaus* ☎ *092/3232–4450* ⛶ *Free* ⊙ *Tues.–Fri. 10–4, Sun. 5–8.*

FAMILY
Fodor's Choice
★

Teatro Amazonas. Built during the rubber boom of the late 1800s, the grandiose Teatro Amazonas was financed by wealthy Brazilian rubber barons who wanted a cultural gem rivaling those in Europe. All the bricks for the building were brought over in ships as ballast from England, and the crystal chandeliers and mirrors were imported from France and Italy. Don't miss the impressive ceiling murals in the main hall, painted by renowned European artists of the time. ✉ *Av. Eduardo Ribeiro 659, Centro, Manaus* ☎ *092/3622–1880* ⛶ *Tours R$10* ⊙ *Mon.–Sat. 9–5.*

FAMILY

Usina Chaminé. In an early-20th-century sewage-treatment plant that never functioned, this cultural center on the banks of the Rio Negro features interesting permanent exhibitions that explore Amazonian tribes, the illegal exploitation of the Amazon's flora and fauna, and the essence of famous fragrances such as Chanel No. 5. English-speaking guides are available and there are interactive sections for kids. Its elegant neo-Renaissance–style interior, with hardwood floors and massive wood beams, is reason enough to visit. ✉ *Av. Lourenço da Silva Braga, Centro, Manaus* ☎ *092/3633–3026* ⛶ *Free* ⊙ *Tues.–Fri. 9–6, Sat. 5–8.*

WORTH NOTING

Catedral da Nossa Senhora da Conceição. Built originally in 1695 by Carmelite missionaries, the Cathedral of Our Lady of Immaculate Conception (also called Igreja Matriz) burned down in 1850 and was reconstructed in 1878. It's a simple, predominantly neoclassical structure with a bright, colorful interior. ✉ *Praça Osvaldo Cruz 1, Centro, Manaus* ☎ *092/3234–7821* ⊕ *catedralnsconceicao.org* ⛶ *Free* ⊙ *Mon.–Sat. 9–5. Hours sometimes vary.*

Igreja São Sebastião. With its charcoal-gray exterior and medieval style, this neoclassical church (circa 1888) seems foreboding. Its interior, however, is luminous and uplifting, with white Italian marble, stained-glass windows, and beautiful ceiling paintings. The church has a tower on only one side. No one is sure why this is so, but if you ask, you may get one of several explanations: the second tower wasn't built because of lack of funds; it was omitted as a symbolic gesture to the poor; or the ship with materials for its construction sank. As you stroll through the church plaza, note the black-and-white Portuguese granite patterns at your feet. They are said to represent Manaus's meeting of the waters. ✉ *Rua Tapajós 54, Centro, Manaus* ☎ *092/3232–4572* ⛶ *Free* ⊙ *Mon.–Sat. 9–5. Hours sometimes vary.*

Museu do Índio. The Indian Museum is maintained by Salesian Sisters, an order of nuns with eight missions in the upper Amazon. It displays handicrafts, weapons, ceramics, ritual masks, and clothing from the region's tribes. Although small, it is well-organized, and English-speaking guides are available. The gift shop sells traditional crafts such as necklaces made from seeds and feathers and baskets. ✉ *Rua Duque de Caxias 356, Centro, Manaus* ☎ *092/3635–1922* ⛶ *R$10* ⊙ *Weekdays 8:30–11:30 and 2–4:30, Sat. 8:30–11:30.*

ELSEWHERE IN MANAUS

Most of the area surrounding downtown Manaus is not very attractive to visit. The few places of interest include the Natural History Museum and INPA's Bosque da Ciência in Aleixo. The Bosque and nearby Parque Municipal do Mindu in Parque 10 are both forested and good for walks. A taxi will cost around R$30 one-way from downtown to these sites. Ponta Negra along the Rio Negro has several restaurants and is super for evening strolls. Also, Hotel Tropical is on its upstream end. Taxis charge R$65 from downtown.

TOP ATTRACTIONS

FAMILY
Fodor's Choice
★
INPA–Bosque da Ciência. Used as a research station for the INPA (Instituto Nacional de Pesquisa da Amazônia), the 13 hectares of tropical forest here are home to a great diversity of flora and fauna. Highlights include manatee tanks, caiman ponds, turtles, a museum, a botanical garden with an orchidarium, and nature trails where you can spot monkeys. It's a great place for a walk in the shade and as an Amazonian introduction for kids. ⊠ *Rua Otávio Cabral s/n, Petropolis, Manaus* ☎ *092/3643–3192* ⊕ *www.inpa.gov.br* ✉ *R$5* ☉ *Weekdays 9–noon and 2–5, weekends 9–4.*

FAMILY
Fodor's Choice
★
Meeting of the Waters. Outside Manaus, the slow-moving, muddy Amazon and the darker, quicker Rio Negro flow side by side for 6 km (4 miles) without mixing. If you run your foot in the water at the meeting place, you can feel the difference in temperature—the Amazon is warm and the Negro is cold, the consistencies of the rivers are different, and the experience is magical. The most comfortable way to experience this phenomenen is to book a day trip organized by a recommended tour operator, departing from Porto de Manaus. However, if you are short on time or want to skip the additional activities, head to the CEASA port, where you can rent a boat, or go with a tour company. It takes about an hour to go from CEASA to the Meeting of the Waters, spend some time there, and return. A taxi to CEASA from downtown is about R$30. ⊠ *Manaus.*

Fodor's Choice
★
Museu do Seringal Vila Paraiso. Originally constructed as part of a film set, this rubber museum is in a 19th-century mansion on the banks of the Rio Negro, a 25-minute boat trip from Ponta Negra. Here, visitors can witness the extraction of latex from the rubber trees that surround the house, as well as learn about what life was like for the rubber gatherers. Elaborate European antiques and a grand piano allude to the owners' wealth. To visit the museum, head to the Marina do David in Ponta Negra and give the name of museum to the boatmen (round-trip approximately R$15), or have a tour operator in town take you there. ⊠ *Manaus* ☎ *092/3631–3632* ⊕ *www.cultura.am.gov. br/museu-do-seringal-vila-paraiso.*

BEACHES

To reach most Manaus-area beaches, catch a boat from Porto Flutuante in downtown or from Ponta Negra. Boats are available throughout the week—just make sure to inquire about return trips, especially on weekdays when there are fewer departures. Look for people wearing the

A Vanishing People

11

In 1500, when the Portuguese arrived in Brazil, the indigenous population was 4.5 million, with an estimated 1,400 tribes. From the beginning the Portuguese divided into two camps regarding the native people: the missionaries, who wanted to "tame" them and convert them to Catholicism, and the colonizers, who wished to enslave and exploit them. The missionaries lost, and when it became apparent that the indigenous people couldn't be enslaved, the infamous *bandeirantes* (assault forces) relentlessly persecuted them so as to "liberate" tribal lands. Many lost their lives defending their land and their way of life, but the greatest killers were smallpox and influenza—European diseases against which they had no immunity. Slow but steady integration into Portuguese society caused the native population to dwindle.

Today, of Brazil's 328,000 remaining indigenous people, about 197,000 live in the Amazon. Each of the 220 societies has its own religious beliefs, social customs, and economic activities. The larger groups include the Manaó, Yanomami, Marajó, Juma, Caixana, Korubo, and Miranha. Each speaks one of the 170 distinct languages spoken by the indigenous peoples of Brazil; Tupi (with seven in-use derivations, including Tupi-Guarani) is the most widely spoken, followed by Macro Jê, Aruák, Karíb, and Arawá.

Throughout Brazil's history sporadic efforts were made to protect indigenous people, but it was only in 1910 that the government established an official advocacy agency, the Service for the Protection of the Indians (SPI), to support Indian autonomy, ensure respect for traditional practices, and help indigenous peoples to acquire Brazilian citizenship. In 1930 the SPI was abolished due to corruption and lack of funds. It was replaced in 1967 by the current governmental advocacy group, FUNAI (Fundação Nacional do Indio, or the National Indian Foundation). Although it has been highly criticized, FUNAI helped to get the first (and, thus far, only) indigenous person elected into office: Mario Juruna, an Indian chief, served as federal deputy from 1983 to 1987. The foundation has also defended the rights of indigenous people to protect their lands (it allows only legitimate researchers to visit reservations), which are increasingly targeted for logging, rubber extraction, mining, ranching, or the building of industrial pipelines and hydroelectric plants.

The indigenous people of the Amazon have always respected and understood their environment; their plight and that of the rain forest are closely linked. Conservation efforts to preserve the rain forest have called attention to some of FUNAI's issues, but for the Brazilian government the issue is complicated: rain-forest conservation is often overshadowed by economic development. Further, the indigenous people still lack many basic human rights, and violence (such as the 1998 murder of prominent activist Francisco de Assis Araujó) still sporadically occurs, as the indigenous people continue to defend their way of life against outsiders.

green vests of the Associação dos Canoeiros Motorizados de Manaus near the Porto Flutuante or at the Marina de David. They can set you up with local boat trips at reasonable prices. Beaches are best visited during the dry season (September–April), when there is more sand.

THE RAREST BEER

Amazonian tribes have been making manioc and corn beers for about 2,000 years. The most popular of these is a hearty dark beer used during social and religious festivals. All types of celebrations are accompanied with beer drinking in the Amazon. The Tapajó tribe used to add the unique ingredient of cremated human bones to ensure that their ancestors would carry on in them. Try the Xingu beer that is sold all over.

Praia da Lua. Named after its crescent-shaped beach, Praia da Lua is on the Rio Negro, and is located 10 minutes away from Ponta Negra in Manaus. Avoid this beach on the weekends when the warm waters are overcrowded and noisy. Don't expect any frills here, just wooden tables and benches to eat your food at, and small restaurants selling pricey food and drinks from tents. Catch boats from the Marina do David at the end of Coronel Teixeira Avenue in Ponta Negra near the Tropical Hotel and expect to pay R$10 round-trip, per person. **Amenities:** food and drink. **Best for:** sunsets; swimming. ✉ *Manaus.*

Praia da Ponta Negra. Known as the Copacabana of the Amazon, this beach is next to the Hotel Tropical and has restaurants, bars, sports, and nightlife facilities. The water is not always clean, so it's not great for swimming. But it's a good place to soak up a bit of the city's bustle. **Amenities:** food and drink; parking; toilets. **Best for:** partiers; sunset. ✉ *Manaus.*

FAMILY **Praia do Tupé.** This lovely, clean beach on the Rio Negro is popular with locals and tends to fill up on Sunday and holidays. Calm waters make it a good choice for children. Visitors will sometimes be greeted by members of a local tribe dancing, but beware that you will be charged for taking part in the festivities (around R$10 per person). A selection of simple beach kiosks serves fresh grilled fish, rice, and salad for lunch. Expect to pay around R$25–30 per person round-trip to get here from Manaus (30 minutes each way). You can hire boats either from the main port in Manaus or from Ponta Negra. **Amenities:** food and drink; toilets. **Best for:** swimming. ✉ *Manaus* ✣ *34 km (20 miles) northwest of Manaus.*

WHERE TO EAT

$ ECLECTIC 🍴 **Abaré SUP and Food.** This floating restaurant has an innovative menu (detox juices and exotic tapioca pancakes), trendy vibe, and complimentary stand-up paddleboards for diners to paddle out on the Rio Negro. It can get busy, especially around sunset, when good tunes enliven the bar with a party atmosphere. To avoid the crowds and sun's strongest rays, head for a morning coffee. Access is from Praia Dourada, where a small boat will transport you to the middle of the river. [$] *Average main:*

R$30 ✉ Rio Tarumã, acess from Praia Dourada, Manaus ☎ 092/9624–6940 ⏲ Closed Mon.–Thurs. No dinner.

$$$$ BRAZILIAN FAMILY Fodor's Choice ★ 🍴 **Banzeiro.** Run by the brothers Felipe and Thiago Schaedler, this restaurant specializes in top-notch regional Amazon cuisine. Fresh fish from the Amazon rivers reigns supreme here—you can't go wrong with the grilled tambaqui fish ribs served with *tucupi farofa* (palm heart fruit manioc flour). For dessert, try the banana cake drizzled with molasses. Popular with locals, the place fills up on weekends. Check the restaurant's website before going for English descriptions of their main dishes, as no menus in English are available in the restaurant, and most staff speak only Portuguese. [$] *Average main: R$75 ✉ Rua Libertador 102, Vieralves, Manaus ☎ 092/3234–1621 🌐 www.restaurantebanzeiro.com.br.*

$$$ LATIN AMERICAN SEAFOOD 🍴 **Canto da Peixada.** Although the decor is clean and simple, the quality of the fish dishes speak for themselves—testament to which, it was chosen as the restaurant to host Pope John Paul II when he came to Manaus in 1981. Don't miss the house speciality *caldeirada de tambaqui* (tambaqui fish stew) and be sure to come hungry, as one platter comes with enough food for two people. [$] *Average main: R$50 ✉ Rua Emilio Moreira 1677, Praça 14, Manaus ☎ 092/3234–1066 🌐 www.cantodapeixada.com ⏲ No dinner Sun.*

$$$$ STEAKHOUSE Fodor's Choice ★ 🍴 **Churrascaria Búfalo.** Twelve waiters, each with a different cut of beef, chicken, or goat, scurry around this large, sparkling clean restaurant. As if the delectable meats weren't enough, tables are also stocked with side dishes, including manioc root, pickled vegetables, and caramelized bananas. You can eat as much as you like for a fixed price of R$90 per person. [$] *Average main: R$90 ✉ Rua Pará 490, Vieralves, Manaus ☎ 092/9219–7243 🌐 www.churrascariabufalo.com.br ⏲ No dinner Sun.*

$$$ BRAZILIAN 🍴 **Fiorentina.** The green awning and red-and-white-check tablecloths are hints that this restaurant serves authentic Italian cuisine. Pasta dishes are delicious, especially the lasagna *fiorentina* (with a marinara and ground-beef sauce). A buffet is also available every day for lunch. [$] *Average main: R$50 ✉ Praça Heliodoro Balbi, Rua José Paranguá 44, Centro, Manaus ☎ 092/3215–2233.*

WHERE TO STAY

Manaus has several decent in-town hotels. Consider staying in the Centro if you have limited time in the city and explore the key sights by foot. If you're interested in Amazon adventures, then the jungle lodges outside town are where you should base yourself. Most jungle lodges have naturalist guides, swimming, caiman searches, piranha fishing, and canoe trips. Many jungle lodges are near the Rio Negro, where mosquitoes are less of a problem because they can't breed in its acidic black water.

$ B&B/INN FAMILY Fodor's Choice ★ 🏨 **Boutique Hotel Casa Teatro.** While the rooms at this charming, eclectic hotel are compact, its central location—a block from the Teatro Amazonas—and helpful staff make it one of Manaus's top choices. **Pros:** central location; cozy atmosphere; excellent customer service. **Cons:** can feel cramped; basement dining room. [$] *Rooms from: R$165 ✉ Rua*

Dez de Julho 632, Manaus ☎ *092/69010–060* 🌐 *www.casateatro.com.br* 🛏 *23 rooms* 🍴 *Breakfast.*

$ HOTEL FAMILY 🏨 **Caesar Business Manaus.** While primarily aimed at business travelers, this superior hotel's slick service, extensive amenities, and outdoor pool also provide a haven for returning jungle travelers in need of civilization. **Pros:** reliable Internet; extensive amenities. **Cons:** breakfast not included; few points of interest within walking distance. [$] *Rooms from: R$243* ✉ *Av. Darcy Vargas 654, Manaus* ☎ *092/3306–4700* 🌐 *www.accorhotels.com/gb/hotel-8945-caesar-business-manaus/index.shtml* 🛏 *229 rooms, 16 executive suites, 1 presidential suite* 🍴 *Breakfast.*

$ B&B/INN FAMILY 🏨 **Chez les Rois.** Although rooms are simply decorated, you'll feel like you're staying in a friend's house at this popular and cozy bed-and-breakfast, set in a lemon-yellow house in a quiet residential area. **Pros:** friendly, laid-back staff; homely atmosphere; swimming pool. **Cons:** a bit out of the way. [$] *Rooms from: R$165* ✉ *Trv. Dos Cristais 01, Conjunto Manauense off Rua Acre, Vieralves, Manaus* ☎ *092/3584–3549* 🌐 *www.chezlesrois.com.br* 💳 *No credit cards* 🛏 *10 rooms* 🍴 *Breakfast.*

$ B&B/INN FAMILY Fodor's Choice ★ 🏨 **Hotel Seringal.** This friendly hotel has some of the most spacious rooms in Manaus. **Pros:** good rooms; central location; full of character; great service. **Cons:** weak Wi-Fi in the rooms. [$] *Rooms from: R$185* ✉ *Rua Monsenhor Coutinho 758, Manaus* ☎ *092/3307–9303* 🌐 *www.seringalhotel.com* 🛏 *16 rooms* 🍴 *Breakfast.*

$$ HOTEL 🏨 **Tropical Manaus Ecoresort.** Nothing in Manaus can match the majesty of this grand, if dated, resort hotel, located 20 km (12 miles) northwest of downtown. **Pros:** beautifully appointed rooms; lovely location; all the amenities of a high-class resort. **Cons:** far from all points of interest; much of the hotel is in need of refurbishment. [$] *Rooms from: R$353* ✉ *Av. Coronel Teixeira 1320, Ponta Negra, Manaus* ☎ *092/2123–5000* 🌐 *www.tropicalhotel.com.br* 🛏 *611 rooms* 🍴 *Breakfast.*

NIGHTLIFE AND PERFORMING ARTS

NIGHTLIFE

For information on concerts and events in town, access the official cultural website for Manaus: 🌐 *www.cultura.am.gov.br. Boi bumbá* (ox legend) music and dance—native to the central Amazon region—tells stories with tightly choreographed steps and strong rhythms. The amphitheater at Praia da Ponta Negra holds regular boi-bumbá performances.

BARS

Botequim. Near the Teatro Amazonas, Botequim is a great place for a drink and features live bands that play a mix of MPB (*música popular brasileira,* or Brazilian pop music), samba, bossa nova, and other Brazilian styles on Thursday, Friday, and Saturday. ✉ *Rua Barroso 279, Centro, Manaus* ☎ *092/3232–1030.*

PERFORMING ARTS

Fodor's Choice ★ **Teatro Amazonas.** Teatro Amazonas draws some of the biggest names in theater, opera, and classical music. Monday-evening performances are free, and the Amazonas Philharmonic Orchestra plays every Thursday

Chico Mendes: Environmental Pioneer

11

Born in 1944 in the northwestern state of Acre, Chico Mendes was the son of a *seringueiro* (rubber-tree tapper) who had moved across the country in the early 20th century to follow the rubber boom. Chico followed in his father's footsteps as a seringuero in Xapuri, close to the Bolivian border. In the 1960s rubber prices dropped dramatically, and tappers began to sell forests to cattle ranchers who cut them for pastures. In the '70s, to protect forests and the tappers' way of life, Mendes joined a group of nonviolent activists who managed to prevent many ranch workers and loggers from clearing the rubber trees. On the local council of Xapuri, he promoted the creation of forest reserves for rubber and Brazil-nut production. He founded the Xapuri Rural Workers Union and the National Council of Rubber Tappers to educate tappers on forest issues.

In 1987 Mendes was invited to Washington, D.C., to help convince the Inter-American Development Bank to rescind its financial support of a planned 1,200-km (750-mile) road to be constructed through the forest. That same year, Mendes was awarded the Global 500 environmental achievement award from the United Nations, making him an international celebrity.

In 1988 Mendes stopped rancher Darly Alves da Silva from extending his ranch into a reserve. On December 22, 1988, da Silva and son Darcy murdered Mendes outside his home. Upon his death, Chico Mendes made the front page of the *New York Times* and numerous other publications worldwide. Subsequently, Brazil created the Chico Mendes Extractive Reserve near Xapuri, along with 20 other reserves covering more than 8 million acres.

night. The Teatro holds an opera festival every year in April and May. ⊠ *Rua Tapajos 5, Centro, Manaus* ☎ *092/3232-1768* ☎ *R$10–R$40.*

SHOPPING

INDIGENOUS CRAFTS

Ecoshop. Ecoshop sells regional art and a variety of indigenous crafts made from wood, seeds, and straw. ⊠ *Amazonas Shopping, Chapada, Manaus* ☎ *092/3642-2026* ⊕ *www.ecoshop.com.br.*

Galeria Amazônica. This contemporary gallery sells a good selection of high-quality artisan pieces sourced from tribes across the Amazon by the Waimiri Atoari tribe. Highlights include tribal jewelry, hammocks, and baskets—each piece is labeled with its tribal origin. Across the square from the Teatro Amazonas, it's well worth a visit. ⊠ *Rua Costa Azevdeo 272, Largo do Teatro, Manaus* ☎ *092/3302-3633* ⊕ *www. galeriamazonica.org.br.*

MALLS

Amazonas Shopping. With more than 300 stores and restaurants, Amazonas Shopping is one of the city's top shopping malls. ⊠ *Av. Djalma Batista 482, Chapada, Manaus* ☎ *092/3303-9000* ⊕ *www. amazonasshopping.com.br.*

Manauara Shopping. This is the chicest mall in Manaus, with an excellent range of shops, a cinema, and a great caçhaca bar, Cachaçaria do Dedé, in the food court. ⊠ *Av. Mário Ypiranga 1300, Manaus* ☎ *092/3236–8820* ⊕ *www.manauarashopping.com.br.*

MARKETS

Fodor'sChoice **Mercado Municipal Adolfo Lisboa.** One of the best places to buy all kinds
★ of things, from fresh fish to hammocks and souvenirs, is Mercado Adolfo Lisboa, down along the river. Built between 1880 and 1883, the building was based on Les Halles in Paris and has intricate ironwork that was made in France and shipped over by boat. It was made an historical landmark in 1987. ⊠ *Rua Dos Barés 46, Centro, Manaus* ☎ *092/3663–8342.*

AMAZON EXCURSIONS FROM MANAUS

PLANNING YOUR AMAZON JUNGLE EXCURSION

The Amazon, home to more than 200 species of mammals and 1,800 species of birds, and providing 20% of the earth's oxygen, is the world's largest and densest rain forest. Stretching 6,300 km (3,900 miles), the Amazon River is the world's longest river. From its source in the Peruvian Andes, the river and its tributaries snake through parts of Bolivia, Ecuador, Colombia, and Brazil before emptying into the Atlantic.

Though Belém, Santarém, and their surrounding areas offer some of the more interesting jungle and river excursions, they don't have nearly the selection or number of visitors that Manaus has. The most common excursion is a half- or full-day tourist-boat trip that travels 15 km (9 miles) east of Manaus to where the coffee-colored water of the Rio Negro flows beside and gradually joins the coffee-with-cream-color water of the Rio Solimões. According to Brazilians, this is where the Amazon River begins. The waters flow alongside one another for 6 km (4 miles) before merging. Many of these Meeting-of-the-Waters treks include motorboat side trips along narrow streams or through bayous. Some also stop at the Parque Ecológico do Lago Janauari, where you can see birds and a lake filled with the world's largest water lily, the *vitória régia.*

Nighttime boat trips into the forest explore flooded woodlands and narrow waterways. Some stop for trail hikes. Some companies take you by canoe on a caiman "hunt," where caimans are caught and released. Trips to the Rio Negro's upper reaches, where wildlife is a little wilder, are also offered. Such trips usually stop at river settlements to visit with local families. They may include jungle treks, fishing (they supply the gear and boat), and a trip to Anavilhanas, the world's largest freshwater archipelago. It contains some 400 islands with amazing Amazon flora, birds, and monkeys.

Whatever your style of travel, there's a boat plying the river to suit your needs. Sleep in a hammock on the deck of a thatch-roof riverboat or in the air-conditioned suite of an upscale vessel. A typical river program includes exploring tributaries in small boats; village visits, perhaps with

CLOSE UP

What to Expect at a Jungle Lodge

11

Most of the jungle lodges near Manaus are around 200 km (125 miles) northwest of the city, in the district known as Novo Airão. Whether luxurious or rustic, they offer similar activities that revolve around boat rides along the Rio Negro. Here's what you can expect from a stay in a jungle lodge:

Night sighting of animals and caimans: Although the Amazon jungle is full of wildlife, some visitors may be disappointed at how few animals they actually encounter. Your best bet at spotting wildlife comes from night tours of riverbank areas, where you might find large snakes in the treetops, sloths, and small owls. Caimans, a smaller type of alligator, are also usually sighted at night.

Spotting pink dolphins: Tours to see Amazon river dolphins, also called pink dolphins or *botos* in Portuguese, are popular. Some lodges include such excursions in their packages, others charge extra. Some lodges will allow you to feed the dolphins, but be careful not to move your hands or legs suddenly, as they might bite. Their long beaks have sharp rows of teeth on each side of the jaws.

Hiking through the jungle: Led by knowledgeable local guides, often of indigenous origin, these hikes offer

visitors the chance to learn about various Amazonian plants and insects. The massive ant hills and ground-level homes of tarantulas are impressive. Be sure to wear long pants and long-sleeved shirts, and bring along insect repellent and bottled drinking water.

Fishing for piranha: Although there are more than 30 varieties of piranhas, you will probably be fishing for the smaller variety of these carnivorous fish. Some lodges will gladly cook any fish you catch, most likely in a fish stew since their bodies have little flesh and are full of spiky bones.

Watching the sunrise: Expect a wake-up knock at your cabin at 5 am in order to glimpse the spectacular colors of the sunrise over the Rio Negro.

Visiting riverside communities: At these communities, visitors often learn how to make manioc flour, a staple of the Amazonian diet, and sample fruit from Amazonian trees such as the tucuman, which has round fruit with a fleshy, orange-colored inside. Riverside communities carve the pits of these fruit to make black-colored bracelets and rings. There is usually the opportunity to buy handcrafted artisanal pieces, so make sure to bring money in small change.

a blowgun demonstration; piranha fishing; nocturnal wildlife searches; and rain-forest walks with a naturalist or indigenous guide to help you learn about plants, wildlife, and traditional medicines. River journeys along the Brazilian Amazon typically begin in Manaus and feature three to 10 days on the water, plus time in Manaus and, sometimes, Rio de Janeiro.

TOUR OPERATORS

Though most tour companies will pick you up at the airport and drop you off following your adventure, airport pickup should not be assumed in all situations. It's often included in tour packages, but ask while making arrangements. Local naturalist guides are often available at lodges. Though knowledgeable, they're neither biologists nor teachers and may not always impart accurate information.

Amazon Jungle Tours. This Manaus-based tour operator offers a variety of jungle excursions for those on a budget: four- to six-night riverboat cruises, four-night stays at jungle lodges, and seven-day jungle survival trips. Trips include airport pickup, English-speaking guides, three meals a day and mineral water, activities, and accommodations at basic, no-frills lodges. ⊠ *10 de Julho St. 708, Centro, Manaus* ☎ *092/3087–0689, 092/9184–8452* ⊕ *www.amazonjungletours.com.br* ⊠ *From R$200.*

Amazon Tours Brazil. Specializing in private boat cruises that take you far from traditonal tourist spots, this tour operator is run out of Manaus by Carlos Damasceno. Bilingual Carlos was born in the Amazon jungle and personally leads many of the tours. Amazon Tours Brazil has cruises ranging from three to five days, with prices starting at US$1,000 per person for a three-day cruise sleeping in a hammock on a regular riverboat, to US$1,800 per person for a four-day cruise on a luxury boat with special air-conditioned cabins. Prices vary depending on the number of people and days. Credit cards are not accepted, so payment needs to be done by wire transfer or in cash. ⊠ *Manaus* ☎ *092/915–67185* ⊕ *www.amazontoursbrazil.com* ⊠ *From US$1,000.*

Katerre. One of the more luxurious options for exploring the Amazon by boat, this quality specialist runs three of its own boats (sleeping up to 16 people) on six different routes across the western Amazon, ranging from 3–10 days. Some are geared toward wildlife spotting, while others are focused on adventure, including a 10-day cruise to the Aracá mountain range, one of the most unexplored corners of the Amazon, where the El Dorado Waterfall can be found. Boats are usually booked privately, but they also run group excursions. ⊠ *Rua São Domingos 03, Nsa Sra Auxiliadora Novo Airão, Manaus* ☎ *092/6973–0000* ⊠ *From R$2,975.*

Maia Expeditions. This expert tour operator creates personalized itineraries through the Amazon for a range of different budgets. Alongside traditional day-trips from Manaus and excursions to luxury jungle lodges, owner Max Maia also owns the excellent Turtle Lodge, a sustainable eco-pousada run by the local community, with fantastic guides and a reforestation program. The adventurous should consider Maia's Amazon Survival Expedition, which includes sleeping overnight in hammocks or *caboclo* homes, canoeing, hunting for food, and constructing shelters. ⊠ *Rua Badajo 62, Parque Shangrila, Flores, Manaus* ☎ *092/99983–7141* ⊕ *www.maiaexpeditions.com* ⊠ *From R$920.*

River Cruises vs. Jungle Lodges

11

While planning your trip into the Amazon, the first question to ask is whether you want to stay at a jungle lodge or take a river cruise. There are advantages to both.

River cruises allow you to visit more remote spots of the jungle, where vegetation and wildlife are abundant. They also tend to be more intimate experiences, offering extended contact with the guides and the chance to explore at your own pace. Journey times range from 3–10 nights, with longer trips venturing into places, like El Dorado, that are impossible to reach any other way. While Manaus is the most obvious starting point, you can also embark from the beach town of Alter do Chão along the Rio Tabajós. Make sure you have an English-speaking guide on board.

Although some boats match the best of the jungle lodges, expect to sacrifice comfort and variety in food for the uniqueness and intimacy of the experience.

Jungle lodges tend to afford an additional degree of comfort and flexibility. Most are located 3–4 hours outside Manaus, scattered between the Rio Negro, the Anavilhanas Archipelago, and Juma Lake. With packages ranging from 2–8 nights, daily itineraries are planned so that you can tick off the most quintessential experiences: swimming or visiting pink river dolphins, spotting caimans at night, visiting a local community, fishing for piranhas, canoeing down *igarapés*. Nearly all come with comfortable living conditions, English-speaking guides, and all meals included.

JUNGLE LODGES NEAR MANAUS

Because the Amazon and its tributaries provide easy access to remote parts of the jungle, river transport often serves as the starting point for camping and lodge excursions. Many lodges and camps are within or near national parks or reserves. Accommodations range from hammocks to comfortable rooms with private, hot-water bathrooms. Nature walks, canoe trips, piranha fishing, and visits to indigenous villages are typically part of rain-forest programs led by naturalists or indigenous guides. Most lodges will collect you from your hotel or the airport as part of the package.

$$$$
RESORT
FAMILY
Amazon Eco Lodge. Twenty rustic floating cabins make up this remote lodge, one of the oldest in the Amazon, located within 337 hectares of its own reserve on Juma Lake. **Pros:** proximity to nature; great guiding. **Cons:** steeply priced; some rooms have shared bathrooms. $ *Rooms from:* ⊠ *74 km (50 miles) south of Manaus, Lago Juma, Manaus* ☎ *092/3308–8393, 092/99604–5724* ⊕ *www.amazonlodgeamazonas. com.br* ⤴ *20 rooms, 2 wedding suites* ¶⊙ *All meals.*

$$
HOTEL
Amazon Ecopark Lodge. Proximity to Manaus (45 minutes) and decent rooms (complete wiith air-conditioning and hot water) make this a good option for travelers short on time or seeking a certain level of creature comforts. **Pros:** accessibility; good food; comfortable rooms. **Cons:** limited contact with the native Amazon; not for wildlife lovers. $ *Rooms from: R$299* ⊠ *Rio Tarumã, Manaus* ☎ *021/2547–7742 Reservations,*

CLOSE UP

How to Choose a Jungle Lodge

The level of comfort is often related to budget you have. The general rule is that the farther away the lodges are from human settlements, the better your connection with nature will be. Pricey expensive lodges provide an additional level of comfort (including TVs, air-conditioning, cocktail bars, hot water, and good food), but the level of guiding and the experiences offered in cheaper options can be just as good. While a few lodges offer private guides, excursions at most lodges often include 5–15 other guests per guide, depending on the season.

Travel outside the peak season and big groups shouldn't be a problem, or look for a lodge with few rooms. Another factor to consider is the lodges environmental concerns and its connection with the local communities. It pays to research all the options online in advance and not to book spontaneously through a local operator selling a package, so you can make sure you are getting the experience most suited to you.

092/9146–0594 Lodge 🌐 www.amazonecopark.com.br 🛏 64 rooms 🍴 Some meals.

$$$$ RESORT FAMILY Fodor's Choice ★ 🏨 **Anavilhanas Jungle Lodge.** Tucked away among the islands of the Ananvilhanas Archipelago on the Rio Negro, this luxury resort is unparalleled in its sophistication, combining beautiful cabins with superior guiding and expectional food. **Pros:** excellent service; gourmet food; spacious rooms; beautiful swimming pool. **Cons:** expensive. *[$] Rooms from: R$2,100 ✉ Around 180 km (112 miles) northwest of Manaus, Rodovia Am 352, Km 1, Igarapé do Monteiro, Novo Airão, Manaus ☎ 092/3622–8996 🌐 www.anavilhanaslodge.com 🛏 16 rooms, 4 bungalows 🍴 All meals.*

$$$$ HOTEL 🏨 **Juma Lodge.** The luxurious Juma Lodge has atmospheric bungalows built on stilts, with private terraces and hammocks overlooking the lake. **Pros:** fantastic guiding; varied activities; great rooms. **Cons:** limited wildlife spotting; few guides during high season. *[$] Rooms from: R$1,777 ✉ Lago do Juma, Lado esquerdo s/n, Autazes, Manaus ☎ 092/3232–2707 🌐 www.jumalodge.com.br 🛏 20 rooms 🍴 All meals.*

$$$$ RESORT Fodor's Choice ★ 🏨 **Tariri Amazon Lodge.** On the shores of Lake Acajatuba, this family-owned resort consists of charming wooden rooms built on stilts above the jungle floor. **Pros:** personal attention from the owners; delicious food; good value. **Cons:** no air-conditioning, hot water, Internet, or television. *[$] Rooms from: R$950 ✉ Around 180 km (112 miles) northwest of Manaus, Lago de Acajatuba, Municipio de Iranduba, Manaus ☎ 092/99137–1925 🌐 www.taririamazonlodge.com.br 💳 No credit cards ⏲ Closed Oct. 15–Nov. 15 🛏 6 cabins for couples, 4 cabins for families 🍴 All meals.*

$$$$ RESORT FAMILY Fodor's Choice ★ 🏨 **Uakari Lodge/Pousada Uacari.** This sustainable floating lodge, set in the middle of a tributary, offers the only way for visitors to explore the Mamirauá Reserve, led by biologists in tandem with local guides from the communities. **Pros:** beautiful location; unparalleled connection with nature; fantastic guiding; great food. **Cons:** few amenities;

sporadic hot water. $ *Rooms from:
R$1,620* ✉ *One hour by boat
from Tefé, Manaus* ☎ *097/3343–
4160, 097/8123–1800* ⊕ *www.
mamiraua.org.br and www.uakari
lodge.com.br* ➪ *10 rooms* ⦿ *All
meals* ✉ *R$1,620 per person dou-
ble occupancy, 4 days and 3 nights.*
**Mamirauá Sustainable Development
Reserve.** The largest freshwater tropical reserve in the world,
Mamirauá is about 1,050 km (650

> **THE AMAZON CANOPY**
>
> Trees in the Amazon are not
> only connected at the roots, but
> they're linked at the branches as
> well. This creates an enormous
> ecosystem far above the ground.
> The canopy holds more species of
> insects than any other part of the
> rain forest.

miles) west of Manaus on the Rio Solimões. The reserve is known for
its abundant wildlife, including the endangered red-faced uakari monkey. It is also a pioneer at successfully integrating sustainable tourism
into a protected nature area. The reserve and its associated projects are
managed by the renowned Mamirauá Institute, which is dedicated to
furthering biodiversity preservation and monitoring humans' impact on
the Amazon. Research stations are set up throughout the reserve. For
visitors, a trip to Mamirauá is a rare opportunity to participate firsthand
in an organization that is making a difference in the preservation of
the world's greatest natural resource. To get to the reserve, you'll need
to fly to Tefé (a one-hour flight from Manaus) and take Mamirauá's
boat one hour up the river to Pousada Uacari. It's a bit of an effort, but
well worth it. ✉ *Manaus* ☎ *097/3343-4160* ⊕ *www.mamiraua.org.br.*

BETWEEN MANAUS AND BELÉM

The smaller communities between the Amazon's two major cities give
the best picture of pure Amazonian culture. Life tends to be even more
intertwined with the river, and the center of activity is the dock area in
village after village. Even a brief stop in one of these towns provides an
interesting window into the region's day-to-day life.

SANTARÉM

836 km (518 miles) west of Belém; 766 km (475 miles) east of Manaus.

Since its founding in 1661, Santarém has ridden the crest of many an
economic wave. First wood, then rubber, and more recently minerals
have lured thousands of would-be magnates hoping to carve their fortunes from the jungle. The most noteworthy of these may have been
Henry Ford. Although he never actually came to Brazil, Ford left his
mark on this country in the form of two rubber plantations southwest
of Santarém—Fordlândia and Belterra.

Santarém-based trips can take you into a little-known part of the Amazon to places where the ecosystem is greatly different from those around
Belém and Manaus. The area receives much less rain than upstream or
downstream, and has rocky hills, enormous wetlands, and the Amazon's
largest clear-water tributary, the Rio Tapajós. While Santarém itself can

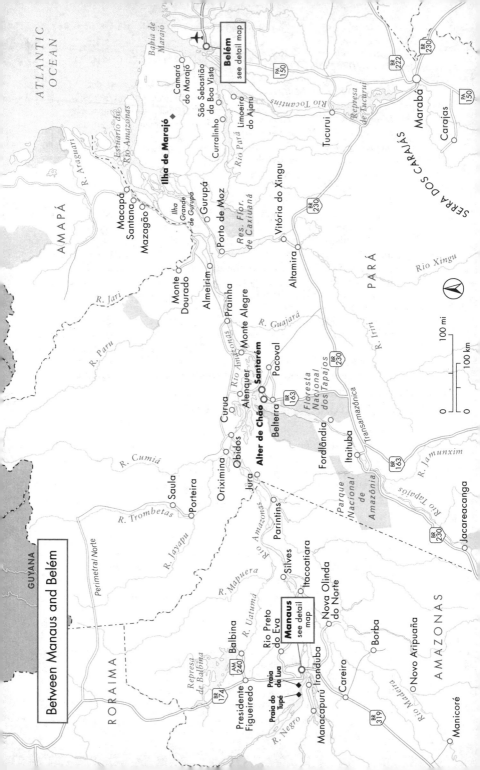

11

feel built-up and lacking in charm, it is the gateway to one of Brazil's emerging hot spots, Alter do Chão.

GETTING HERE AND AROUND

Domestic carriers GOL and Azul have flights to Santarém, and Santarém is easily accessible by air via Belém or Manaus. Aeroporto Maestro Wilson Fonseca is 14 km (23 miles) west of town, and buses and taxis from the airport are plentiful; a taxi ride costs around R$43.

MACAMAZON runs from Belém to Santarém. The three-day journey costs R$160 for a hammock, R$500 for a two-person cabin. Taxis are always at the docks in Santarém. The cost to any of the nearby hotels in town is less than R$10.

ESSENTIALS

Airport Aeroporto Maestro Wilson Fonseca. ⊠ *Rodovia Fernando Guilhon, Praça Eduardo Gomes s/n, Santarém* ☎ *093/3522–4328, 093/3522–4328.*

Boat Contacts MACAMAZON. ☎ *091/3222–5604, 091/3031–5899.*

EXPLORING

Centro Cultural João Fona (*João Fona Cultural Center*). To learn more about Santarém's culture and history, head for the Centro Cultural João Fona. This small museum has a hodgepodge of ancient ceramics, indigenous art, and colonial-period paintings and a library for more in-depth studies. It also houses the Secretary of Tourism. ⊠ *Praça Barão de Santarém, Santarém* ☎ *093/3523–2934* 🎟 *Free* ⏱ *Weekdays 8–5.*

Meeting of the Waters. In Santarém, for about 5½ miles, the beautiful, aquamarine Rio Tapajós floats next to the murkier waters of the Amazon, until the larger river finally absorbs it. Seeing the Meeting of the Waters here is breathtaking. It's best viewed from the **Praça Mirante do Tapajós**, on the hill in the center of town and just a few blocks from the waterfront. ⊠ *Santarém.*

WHERE TO EAT

$ ✕ **Mascote.** Since 1934 this has been one of the most popular and famous
ECLECTIC restaurants in town. The indoor dining area is enchanting, but the palm-lined patio is well lighted and inviting and has a good view of the river and the plaza. An extremely varied menu includes pizzas, sandwiches, steaks, and seafood. $ *Average main: R$20* ⊠ *Praça do Pescador s/n, Santarém* ☎ *093/3072–1700.*

$ ✕ **Mistura Brasileira.** Excellent sandwiches and a self-service buffet
BRAZILIAN keep the Mistura Brasileira hopping. Try the beef fillet sandwich or the lasagna. The restaurant is housed in a hotel of the same name. $ *Average main: R$18* ⊠ *Trv. Quinze de Novembro, Central, Santarém* ☎ *093/3522–4819* ⏱ *No dinner.*

ALTER DO CHÃO

About 30 km (about 20 miles) west of Santarém.

Fodor's Choice Dubbed the "Carribean of the Amazon" because of its crystalline
★ waters, white-sand beaches, and laid-back vibe, Alter do Chão is a relaxing place to spend a few days in the Amazon. The village itself is simple, with only a handful of pousadas and restaurants, but Alter's

Ford's Impossible Dream

Henry Ford spent millions of dollars to create two utopian company towns and plantations to supply his Model T cars with rubber tires. In 1927 he chose an area 15 hours southwest of Santarém. A year later all the materials necessary to build a small town and its infrastructure were transported by boat from Michigan to the Amazon. Small Midwestern-style houses were built row after row. *Seringueiros* (rubber tappers) were recruited with promises of good wages, health care, and schools for their children. Fordlândia was born. Despite all the planning, the scheme failed. The region's climate, horticulture, and customs weren't taken into account. Malaria and parasites troubled the workers; erosion and disease plagued the trees.

Convinced that he had learned valuable lessons from his mistakes, Ford refused to give up. In 1934 he established another community in Belterra, 48 km (30 miles) outside Santarém. Although some rubber was extracted from the plantation, production fell far short of original estimates. World War II caused further disruptions as German boats cruised the Brazilian coast and prevented food and supplies from arriving. Advances in synthetic rubber struck the final blow. Today some rusted trucks and electric generators, a few industrial structures, and many empty bungalows are all that remain of Ford's impossible dream.

cosmopolitan community unites hippies, herbalists, and healers with nature lovers and off-duty entrepreneurs drawn to the area's natural beauty.

During the dry season (August–February), white-sand islands and beaches emerge from the green waters of the Rio Tabajós, the only clear river in the Amazon. During high tide, you can explore jungle trails or take canoe trips through the extensive network of *igarapés* and *igapós* (small flooded waterways). During the wet season (May–July), the rainfall limits many activities. Year-round, one of the best ways to explore is by boat trip, which allows you to visit the culturally dynamic communities within a few hours of Alter do Chão. There is an abundance of wildlife nearby, from monkeys to *botos*, the famous pink river dolphins.

GETTING HERE AND AROUND
Buses from Santarém to Alter do Chão depart from Praça Tiradentes in the City Center or from Avenida Cuiabá (near the Amazon Park Hotel). They make the journey back and forth five or six times a day and hourly on Sunday (32 km/20 miles, 45 minutes). The one-way ride costs R$2.40. A taxi to Alter do Chão costs R$70. It's best to take sufficient cash with you to Alter do Chão.

ESSENTIALS
Taxi Contacts Taxi Teo. ☎ *093/99182–5180.*

TOURS

AMZ. AMZ can organize great day trips in and around Alter do Chão, and book hotels and transfers. But their specialty is private river cruises, exploring the Tabajós, Arapiuns, and Amazonas Rivers. Itineraries skirt between deserted beaches, secluded communities, and virgin forest; and include bilingual guides, private chefs, a bar, speedboat, paddleboards, and biodegradable beauty kits made from Amazonian miracle plants. Sleeping options range from hammocks to luxury cabins. Prices for a five-day trip start at R$5,000 per person, all-inclusive. There are also excursions around Alter do Chão and a three-day visit to a community by boat. ⊠ *Alter do Chão* 📞 *011/99703–0906, 011/98220–6962* ⊕ *amzprojects.com* 🖂 *From R$60.*

EXPLORING

Lago Verde. A local favorite for escaping the crowds during high season, Lago Verde can be accessed by a short boat ride from Alter do Chao. There are secluded sandbanks that separate this lake from Rio Tabajós. Due to the sediment, the water takes on a translucent green color at times. When the waters are high, the surrounding forest is all but submerged, with the treetops forming a fantastical landscape that earned it the name of "floresta encantanda" (enchanted forest). Plan a day trip through a tour agency or speak to one of the boatmen at the main pier below the square. ⊠ *Alter do Chão.*

Ponto do Cururú. The best place to watch the sunset, surrounded by *botos* (pink dolphins), this sandy headland is a 15-minute speedboat trip from the pier. You can negotiate directly with the boatmen. There are no vendors, so take your own refreshements. ⊠ *Alter do Chão.*

Serra Piroca. The small mountain that towers over Ilha do Amor is accessible by a single trail that starts at the end of the island and snakes up through the forest. A grueling 45-minute hike rewards you with spectacular views over Alter do Chão. A magical spot for sunset, go with a local guide and flashlight to help you on the return journey. ⊠ *Alter do Chão.*

Jamaraquá. A 40-minute speedboat trip south of Alter do Chão is the community of Jamaraquá, which has developed a strong cultural identity. Here you can head into the forest for a three-hour hike to see a 500-year-old Samuama tree, or visit the rubber factory, where local artisans will explain how they extract rubber from the *seringuero* tree. Around the community there are numerous streams to explore by canoe and paddleboard. Many travelers end up spending a night or two in the community's small pousada, where both hammocks and private rooms are available. Prices start at R$20 per night. Jamaraquá is also accessible by road (R$15 one-way, three hours) ⊠ *52 km (32 miles) south of Alter do Chão, Alter do Chão.*

BEACHES

Ilha do Amor. Jutting out into the river across from the main square, this fat finger of golden sand is one of Alter's picture-perfect postcard shots and a great place to spend a day basking in the sun, swimming, and paddleboarding. Rowboats transfer you across (R$10 return), as you will only be able to walk when the waters are at their lowest. Straw cabanas serving fresh grilled fish set out chairs and sun-loungers on the edge of the water. Paddleboards are available for rent for R$50 an hour. **Amenities:** food and drinks; toilets; water sports. **Best for:** sunset; swimming. ✉ *Alter do Chão.*

WHERE TO EAT AND STAY

$ ECLECTIC

🍴 **Arco-Iris.** With tables set outside on the main square, this is a great spot to watch the world go by over a varied menu that includes salads, vegetarian dishes, sandwiches, and excellent steak fillet. Inside, a shop sells semiprecious gems and artisan pieces from local tribes. [$] *Average main: R$25* ✉ *Praça 7 de Setembro, Alter do Chão* ☎ *093/3527–1182.*

$ VEGETARIAN FAMILY Fodor's Choice ★

🍴 **Siria.** This cheerful vegetarian spot serves some of the tastiest food in town. Settle into one of the few tables set out on the porch as chef and owner Bêtania whisks up fresh salads, soups, and excellent-value set-menus in her kitchen. A three-course lunch menu, including coffee and fresh juice, costs R$25. [$] *Average main: R$25* ✉ *Rua Antonio Agostinho Lobato s/n, Alter do Chão* ☎ *093/9124–0224.*

$ HOTEL FAMILY Fodor's Choice ★

🏨 **Beloalter.** A short walk from town directly on a white-sand beach, Beloalter has spacious rooms and swimming pool, making it one of the more sophisticated places to stay. **Pros:** large and pleasantly decorated rooms; beachfront location; lovely staff. **Cons:** lesser views in lower-priced rooms; few amenities; a bit shabby. [$] *Rooms from: R$196* ✉ *Rua Pedro Texeira 500, Alter do Chão* ☎ *093/3527–1247, 093/3527–1230* 🌐 *www.beloalter.com.br* 🛏 *26 rooms* 🍽 *Breakfast.*

SHOPPING

Fodor's Choice ★

Araribá Arte e Artes. Part shop, part museum, Araribá Arte e Artes has one of the best selections of authentic native artisanal items in Brazil. Owner Marcelo spends half the year traveling to hard-to-reach tribes for the pieces. Highlights include hand-woven wall-hangings, baskets, and jewelry. ✉ *Rua Dom Macedo Costa s/n, Alter do Chão* ☎ *093/3527–1251* 🌐 *www.araribah.com.br.*

Semente. For soaps, face creams, and healing remedies handcrafted from the most powerful Amazonian fruits and plants, head to Semente. Don't miss picking up some healing *androibe* oil (an antioxidant oil used for massage and to treat skin infections) and antiwrinkle cream crafted from cashew nuts and Cupaçu. ✉ *Rua Copacabana, Canto da Orla, Alter do Chão* ☎ *093/9164–5033* 🌐 *ekilibrenatura.wordpress.com.*

ILHA DO MARAJÓ

Soure (the island's largest town) is 82 km (49 miles) northwest of Belém.

With an area of roughly 49,600 square km (18,900 square miles), Ilha do Marajó is reputedly the world's largest river island. Its relatively unspoiled environment and abundant wildlife make it one of the few accessible places in the Amazon that feel isolated.

Ilha do Marajó's western half is dominated by dense forest and its eastern half by expansive plains, wetlands, and savannas. The island is ideal for raising cattle and water buffalo and has a half-million water buffalo and more than a million head of cattle; the human head count is about 250,000. According to local lore, the arrival of the water buffalo was an accident, the result of the wreck of a ship traveling from India to the Guianas.

On the island, you may see caiman, toco toucans, monkeys, and capybara, the world's largest rodent. Hiking is better in the dry season and boating in the rainy season. Warm, freshwater rivers are great for swimming, and there are numerous white-sand beaches to explore, making Marajó a good option for a few days of relaxation after a more intense jungle trek.

VAMPIRES IN THE RIVER

A new species of fish was recently discovered in the Amazon. Related to the candiru (which is attracted to urine and lodges itself in the urinal tract of a swimmer) this little catfish clamps onto the host and sucks its blood. Always wear snug swimming trunks and bikinis to keep the little critter from going any farther.

Local cuisine invariably involves the water buffalo, whether in the form of a succulent steak or in cheeses and desserts made with buffalo milk. There's also an array of local fish to try. Bring cash in small bills, as breaking large ones can be a challenge and credit cards are rarely accepted. In a pinch, beer vendors can usually make change.

GETTING HERE AND AROUND
Arapari operates boats between Belém and Camará, on Ilha do Marajó, twice daily Monday through Saturday. A one-way trip from Belém to Ilha de Marajó takes two hours and costs about R$21 in economy class, and R$34 in the VIP section. Departures leave from the Termi nal Hidroviário in Belém. Those traveling by car will need to take the ferry from Icoaraci, 25 km (15½ miles) from Belém, with departures every morning (R$70 for the car, R$13 for additional passengers). Buy your return ticket at the same time as the outward journey; during high season, car spaces can get booked up quickly.

On Ilha do Marajó one of the best ways to reach the beaches or to explore towns is to use a bike. Rates are R$2 an hour. You can find motorcycles to rent for R$60–R$70, though you'll have to ask around, since they're not advertised. The locals usually know who has equipment for rent.

ESSENTIALS
Boat Contacts Arapari. ⊠ *Rua Siqueira Mendes 120, Cidade Velha, Belém* ☎ *091/3242–1870.*

TOURS
Rumo Norte Expedições. This upmarket tour operator in Belém offers two-day packages to Marajó from Belém that include pickup from your hotel, return boat trip, and a two-night stay in Paracuary Eco-Pousada with breakfast and all activities included. ⊠ *Av. Serzedelo Correa 895, casa 59, Belém* ☎ *091/3225–5915* ⊕ *www.rumonorte.tur.br* ✉ *From R$957.*

EXPLORING
Marajó is a huge island, but most human activity is clustered on its eastern coast, due to proximity to Belém. The western side of the island is beachless and floods during the rainy season.

Caju Una. Tricky access has ensured that this breathtaking beach and its associated self-sustaining fishing village have remained remote. The village and its neighbor, Vila do Céu, are about a 45-minute drive (19 km/11 miles) north of Soure. You can also access both communities by boat, crossing the river that rounds Praia Pesqueiro by canoe and then walking the remaining distance.

Camará. One of the island's most important ports, Camará is where many boats from Belém dock. Buses to Camará pass by the riverside in Soure regularly.

Joanes. Roughly 23 km (14 miles) southwest of Soure, the small beach-village of Joanes was the island's first settlement. Poke around the ruins of a 16th-century Jesuit mission blown up by the Portuguese when they expelled the order from the area, bask on a beach, and have a meal in one of the town's seafood restaurants. A taxi from Soure costs about R$60 round-trip.

Salvaterra. A half-km (quarter-mile) boat ride across the narrow Rio Paracauari, the village of Salvaterra is smaller than Soure but equally charming. Boats called *rabetas* cost R$1. Don't miss the idyllic beach, and be sure to try an extra-sweet, locally grown pineapple.

Soure. With almost 20,000 people, Soure is Ilha do Marajó's largest town. Its many palm and mango trees, simple but brightly painted houses, and shore full of fishing boats make it seem more Caribbean than Amazonian. Make sure to try the local white cheese, called *queijo de Marajó*, made from buffalo's milk.

BEACHES

Praia do Araruna. Coconut trees line the 8-km (5-mile) length of this beach, about 20-minutes (a 4-km/2-mile taxi ride) northeast of Soure. Here you may see flocks of scarlet ibis that appear out of nowhere. This beach tends to be much emptier than the nearby Praia da Barra, and you can swim in the small tributaries away from the main river. **Amenities:** none. **Best for:** solitude; sunset; swimming; walking.

FAMILY Fodor's Choice ★ **Praia do Pesqueiro.** Thirteen km (8 miles) north of Soure, Praia do Pesqueiro is the island's most popular beach. When you stand on the white-sand expanse looking out at the watery horizon, the waves lapping at your feet, it's hard to believe you're not on the ocean. The beach has several thatch-roof restaurant-bars, making this an ideal place to spend an afternoon. You can travel here from Soure by taxi, by moto-taxi (for one passenger), or by bike. Ask locals or hotel staff about bike rentals when you arrive in Soure. **Amenities:** food and drink. **Best for:** swimming; walking.

WHERE TO STAY

$$$ B&B/INN FAMILY Fodor's Choice ★ 🏨 **Fazenda Carmo.** As a guest in this small, antiques-filled farmhouse, you're privy to wonderful hospitality in a simple and rustic setting, and homestyle meals prepared with farm-fresh ingredients. **Pros:** a bed-and-breakfast experience; fresh food; uniquely decorated rooms. **Cons:** lacks basic creature comforts like hot water, private bathrooms, and sometimes electricity; no English spoken. [$] *Rooms from:*

R$390 ✉ Salvaterra ☎ 091/ 3015–1019, 091/99112–6875 🌐 www.carmocamara.com.br 🛏 8 rooms 🍴 All meals.

$ B&B/INN 🏨 **Pousada & Camping Boto.** This pousada offers lovely gardens, clean, simple rooms, friendly staff, and good food for a reasonable price. **Pros:** pleasant surroundings; well-kept rooms. **Cons:** the restaurant is open only on the weekend; the rooms are small. [$] *Rooms from: R$100 ✉ Av. Alcindo Cacela, Salvaterra ☎ 091/3765–1539 🌐 www.pousadaboto.com.br 🛏 9 rooms 🍴 Breakfast.*

SHOPPING

Curtume Marajó. For sandals, belts, and other leather goods, head to Curtume Marajó, a five-minute walk from downtown Soure and next to the slaughterhouse. The workers here can give you a tour of the tannery. *✉ Rua Primeira 450, Bairro Novo, Soure ☎ 091/8156–6818, 091/8870–3804 🌐 www.curtumeartcouromarajo.com.br.*

Socieddade Marajara Das Artes. This artisan collective has stalls with everything from Marajoara pottery and woven items to T-shirts and liquor. In theory, the hours are daily 8–7, and Sunday 8–12; the reality may be something else entirely. *✉ Rua 3, between Trvs. 18 and 19, Soure ☎ 091/8175–5712.*

BELÉM

1,602 km (993 miles) east of Manaus; 2,933 km (1,760 miles) north of Rio de Janeiro.

The capital of Pará State, Belém is a river port of around 1.4 million people on the south bank of the Rio Guamá. The Portuguese settled here in 1616, using it as a gateway to the interior and an outpost to protect the area from invasion by sea. Because of its ocean access, Belém became a major trade center. Like the upriver city of Manaus, it rode the ups and downs of the Amazon booms and busts. The first taste of prosperity was during the rubber era. Architects from Europe were brought in to build churches, civic palaces, theaters, and mansions, often using fine, imported materials. When Malaysia's rubber supplanted that of Brazil in the 1920s, wood and, later, minerals provided the impetus for growth.

Belém is more than just a jumping-off point for the Amazon. It has several good museums and restaurants and lots of extraordinary architecture. Restored historic sites along the waterfront provide areas to walk, eat, and explore. Several distinctive buildings—some with Portuguese *azulejos* (tiles) and ornate iron gates—survive along the downtown streets and around the Praça Frei Caetano Brandão, in the Cidade Velha (Old City). East of here, in the Nazaré neighborhood, colorful colonial structures mingle with new ones housing trendy shops.

GETTING HERE AND AROUND

There are several daily flights to Belém from Rio and São Paulo. Azul-Trip flies to Belém from Campinas. All airlines arrive at the Aeroporto Internacional Val-de-Cans, 11 km (7 miles) northwest of the city. Varig and TAM sometimes offer direct flights from Miami. TAM and GOL fly regularly from Rio, São Paulo, Brasília, and Manaus.

During the Brazilian summer flights to Belém can be cheap since this is the rainy season and most flock to the beaches instead. If time is not an issue, there are daily buses from Rio and São Paulo on Transbrasilia (45 hours).

Most long-distance ships arrive and depart from the Terminal Hidroviário (Avenida Marechal Hermes). MACAMAZON and Bom Jesus (based in Macapá) have ships and standard riverboats to Macapá, Santarém, Manaus, and other places. The Belém-to-Santarém boat on MACAMAZON takes three days and costs R$160 for a hammock, and R$500 for a two-person cabin. The Belém-to-Manaus boat on MACAMAZON takes five days and costs R$250 for a hammock and R$1,000 for a two-person cabin. A trip to Ilha de Marajo from Belém takes two hours and costs R$21.72. From Belém to Macapá the boat takes 24 hours and the hammock costs R$130, and R$400 for a two-person cabin.

Belém's local bus service is safe (though you should keep an eye on your belongings) and comprehensive, but a little confusing. Ask a resident for guidance. The bus costs R$2.20.

ESSENTIALS

Airport Information **Aeroporto Internacional Val-de-Cans.** ⊠ *Av. Julio Cesár s/n, Belém* ☏ *091/3210–6000, 091/3257–3780.*

Boat Contacts **MACAMAZON.** ⊠ *Boul Castilhos França 744, Campina, Belém* ☏ *091/3031–5899, 091/3228–0774.*

Bus Contacts **Rodoviário de Belém.** ⊠ *Praça do Operário, São Brás, Belém* ☏ *091/3266–2625, 091/3266–2625* ⊕ *www.rodoviariadebelem.com.br.*

Taxi Contacts **Coopertáxi.** ☏ *091/3257–1041, 091/3257–1720.* **Taxi Nazaré.** ☏ *091/3242–7867.*

TOURS

Sightseeing boats leave from Estação das Docas Avenida Marechal Hermes, and from behind Hotel Beira Rio on Rua Bernardo Saião, 20 minutes southeast of town near the Federal University.

Amazon Star. This reputable tour agency offers a wide range of tours in and around Belém (including Ilha de Marajó), and will book boat tickets to destinations across the Amazon. ⊠ *Rua Henrique Gurjão 210, Reduto, Belém* ☏ *091/3241–8624, 091/3212–6244* ⊕ *www.amazonstar.com.br* ☉ *Weekdays 8–6, Sat. 8–noon* ☑ *From R$150.*

Valeverde Turismo. One of the largest tour specialists, Valeverde Turismo offers city tours in Belém (three hours), trips to Ilha de Marajó, tours to Salinas (12 hours), and tours to Mosquiero. ⊠ *Av. Alcindo Cacela 104, Cremação, Belém* ☏ *091/3218–7333* ⊕ *www.valeverdeturismo.com.br* ☑ *From R$170.*

SAFETY AND PRECAUTIONS

In Belém watch out for pickpockets everywhere, but especially at Vero-Peso, on Avenida President Vargas, and in Comércio. Avoid walking alone at night or on poorly lighted streets, and don't wear jewelry, especially gold.

EXPLORING

CIDADE VELHA

Cidade Velha (Old City) is the oldest residential part of Belém. Stunning colonial mansions are part of the city's treasured legacy, remnants of a time when it was the region's primary port for rubber exportation and great wealth that flowed through the cobbled streets found its way into the architecture. Many of the houses are protected, and have been transformed into hotels, bars, and restaurants. Most of the city's key sites are within walking distance of one another in the Cidade Velha. Take off watches and jewelry and only take necessary cash in order to avoid unwanted attention.

TOP ATTRACTIONS

Fodor's Choice ★ **Casa das Onze Janelas.** At the end of the 18th century, sugar baron Domingos da Costa Barcelar built the neoclassical House of Eleven Windows as his private mansion. Today Barcelar's mansion is a gallery for contemporary arts, including photography and visiting expositions. The view from the balcony is impressive. Take a walk through the courtyard and imagine scenes of the past. This is where the aristocracy took tea and watched over the docks as slaves unloaded ships from Europe and filled them with sugar and rum. ⊠ *Praça Frei Caetana Brandão, Cidade Velha, Belém* ☎ *091/4009–8821* 🖰 *R$2, free Tues.* ☉ *Tues.–Fri. 10–6, weekends 9–1.*

Estação das Docas. Next to Ver-o-Peso market on the river, three former warehouses have been artfully converted into a commercial–tourist area. All have one wall of floor-to-ceiling glass that provides a full river view when dining or shopping. The first is a convention center with a cinema and art exhibits. The second has shops and kiosks selling crafts and snacks, and the third has a variety of restaurants and bars. Live-music performances take place regularly. The buildings are air-conditioned and connected by glass-covered walkways and contain photos and artifacts from the port's heyday. A stroll outside along the docks provides a grand view of the bay. Tourist boats arrive and depart at the dock, making it a good place to relax both day and night. ⊠ *Av. Boulevard Castilho França s/n, Cidade Velha, Belém* ☎ *091/3212–5660* 🖰 *Free.*

FAMILY **Forte do Presépio** (*Fort of the Crèche*). Founded January 12, 1616, this fort is considered Belém's birthplace. From here the Portuguese launched conquests of the Amazon and watched over the bay. The fort's role in the region's defense is evidenced by massive English- and Portuguese-made cannons pointing out over the water. They are poised atop fort walls that are three yards thick in places. Recent renovations unearthed more than two-dozen cannons, extensive military middens from the moat, and native Tupi artifacts. A small museum of prefort indigenous cultures is at the entrance. Just outside the fort, cobblestone walkways hug the breezy waterfront. ⊠ *Praça Frei Caetano Brandão, Cidade Velha, Belém* ☎ *091/4009–8828* 🖰 *R$2, Tues. free* ☉ *Tues.–Fri. 10–6, weekends 9–1.*

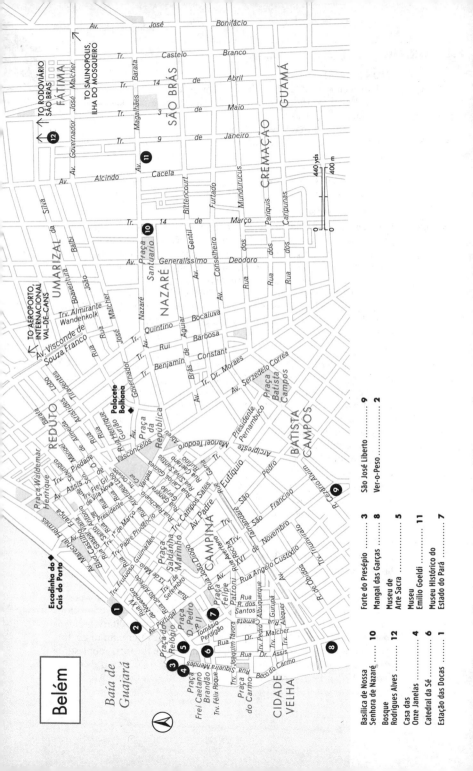

Belém

Baía de Guajará

Escadinho do Cais do Porto

Palacete Bolhona

SÃO BRÁS

UMARIZAL

REDUTO

NAZARÉ

CREMAÇÃO

GUAMÁ

CAMPINA

BATISTA CAMPOS

CIDADE VELHA

TO AEROPORTO, INTERNACIONAL VAL-DE-CANS

TO RODOVIÁRIO SÃO BRÁS

FÁTIMA

TO SALINÓPOLIS, ILHA DO MOSQUEIRO

0   440 yds
0   400 m

FAMILY
Fodor'sChoice
★

Mangal das Garças. City beautification efforts to increase tourism and encourage environmental conservation led to the creation of the Mangrove of the Egrets, a verdant park that lines the Rio Guamá. It's a great place for a short stroll. There is an aviary, a lookout tower with a view of Belém, a navigation museum, a boardwalk leading to a lookout over the Rio Guamá, a live butterfly museum, ponds with aquatic plants, food vendors, a gift shop, and an excellent restaurant. Entrance to the park is free, although each attraction costs R$3. ⊠ *Praça Carneiro da Rocha, Cidade Velha, Belém* ☏ *091/3242–5052* ⊕ *www.mangalpa.com.br* ⧠ *R$3 each or R$9 for all, Tues. free* ☾ *Weekdays 9–6.*

> ### DANCE THE LAMBADA
>
> This musical form, popular among Brazilians in the '80s and early '90s, originated in the state of Pará in the 1970s. The first *lambada* was composed by the Pinduca, who had written a number of *carimbós*. The music swept the North and Northeast, and even became popular outside the country. Two American movies popularized the genre but were made only after the craze began to wane—*Lambada* (1990) and *The Forbidden Dance* (1990).

Museu de Arte Sacra. A guided tour (call 48 hours in advance to reserve an English-speaking docent) begins in the early-18th-century baroque Igreja de Santo Alexandre (St. Alexander's Church), which is distinguished by intricate woodwork on its altar and pews. The church was abandoned for 40 years, resulting in much of the wood ceiling being lost to termites and water damage, but the areas that were restored are spectacular. On the second half of the tour, you see the museum's collection of religious sculptures and paintings. ⊠ *Praça Frei Caetano Brandão, Cidade Velha, Belém* ☏ *091/4009–8805* ⧠ *R$4, Tues. free* ☾ *Tues.–Fri. 10–6, weekends 9–1.*

Fodor'sChoice
★

Ver-o-Peso. Its name literally meaning "see the weight" (a throwback to the time when the Portuguese weighed everything entering or leaving the region), this market is a hypnotic confusion of colors and voices. Vendors hawk tropical fruits, regional wares, and an assortment of tourist kitsch. Most interesting are the *mandingueiras,* women who claim they can solve any problem with "miracle" jungle roots and charms for the body and soul. They sell jars filled with animal eyes, tails, and even heads, as well as herbs, each with its own legendary power. The sex organs of the pink river dolphin are a supposedly unrivaled cure for romantic problems. In the fish market you get an up-close look at pirarucu, the Amazon's most colorful fish and the world's second-largest freshwater species. Look for bizarre armored catfish species, such as the *tamuatá* and the huge *piraiba.* Across the street is a small arched entrance to the municipal meat market. Duck in and glance at the French-style pink-and-green-painted ironwork, imported from Britain. Be sure to visit Ver-o-Peso before noon, when most vendors leave. It opens around 6 am. Leave your jewelry at home and beware of pickpockets. ⊠ *Av. Castilhos França s/n, Comércio, Belém.*

WORTH NOTING

Catedral da Sé. In 1755 Bolognese architect Antônio José Landi, whose work can be seen throughout the city, completed this cathedral's construction on the foundations of an older church. Carrara marble adorns the rich interior, which is an interesting mix of baroque, colonial, and neoclassical styles. The high altar was a gift from Pope Pius IX. ⊠ *Praça Dom Frei Caetano Brandão s/n, Cidade Velha, Belém* ☎ *091/3223–2362, 091/3223–2362* ⊠ *Free* ⊙ *Mon. 2–8:30, Tues.–Fri. 8–noon and 2–8:30, Sat. 7–10 am and 4–8, Sun. 6:30-noon and 4–8.*

Museu Histórico do Estado do Pará. The Pará State Museum is in the sumptuous Palácio Lauro Sodré (circa 1771), an Antônio Landi creation with Venetian and Portuguese elements. Consistently outstanding visiting exhibits are on the first floor; the second floor contains the permanent collection of furniture and paintings. ⊠ *Praça Dom Pedro II, Cidade Velha, Belém* ☎ *091/4009–8805* ⊠ *R$2, Tues. free* ⊙ *Tues.–Fri. 10–6, weekends 10–2.*

São José Liberto. Belém's old prison began as a monastery, became a brewery, then an armory, a nunnery, and eventually the final stop for many criminals. Today, it is one of the best places to pick up traditional Marajoara ceramics and local handcrafts and jewelry. There is also a small precious-gem museum and a tranquil central courtyard. ⊠ *Praça Amazonas, Jurunas, Belém* ☎ *091/3344–3500* ⊕ *www.saojoseliberto. com.br* ⊙ *Tues.–Sat. 9–7, Sun. 10–6.*

NAZARÉ

TOP ATTRACTIONS

Fodor'sChoice **Basílica de Nossa Senhora de Nazaré.** It's hard to miss this opulent Roman-
★ style basilica—not only does it stand out visually, but there's an enormous *samauma* tree (kapok variety) filled with screeching white-winged parakeets in the plaza out front. The basilica was built in 1908 as an addition to a 1774 chapel, on the site where a *caboclo* (rural, riverside dweller) named Placido is said to have seen a vision of the Virgin in the early 1700s. The basilica's ornate interior is constructed entirely of European marble and contains elaborate mosaics, detailed stained-glass windows, and intricate bronze doors. ⊠ *Praça Justo Chermont, Nazaré, Belém* ☎ *091/4009–8436, 091/4009–8407 museum* ⊠ *Free* ⊙ *Weekdays 6 am–8 pm, weekends 6–noon and 3–9.*

FAMILY **Museu Emílio Goeldi.** Founded by a naturalist and a group of intellectuals in 1866, this complex contains one of the Amazon's most important research facilities. Its museum has an extensive collection of indigenous artifacts, including the distinctive and beautiful pottery of the Marajó tribes, known as *marajoara*. A small forest has reflecting pools with giant water lilies. But the highlight is the botanical zoo, where you can visit a variety of Amazon wildlife, including jaguars, panthers, manatees, anacondas, macaws, sloths, and monkeys. As of this writing, the aquarium is closed for renovation. ⊠ *Av. Magalhães Barata 376, São Braz, Belém* ☎ *091/3219–3342* ⊕ *www.museu-goeldi.br* ⊠ *Park R$2 or R$4,50 for the park, aquarium, and museum together* ⊙ *Park: Tues.– Sun. 9–5. Museum and aquarium: Tues.–Sun. 9–noon and 2–5.*

CLOSE UP

Tales from the Mist

11

The immense Amazon region is fertile ground not only for flora and fauna but also for legends, which are an integral part of local culture and are remarkably consistent throughout the region.

One particularly creepy legend is that of Curupira, who appears as a nude and savage indigenous child whose feet are turned backward. He is said to lure people into the jungle, causing them to become irreversibly lost. As the story goes, white men cut off his feet before killing him; a god sewed Curupira's feet on backward and returned him to the forest to exact revenge. Some people claim you can solicit Curupira's help for hunting and crop failures. As payment, you must bring him tobacco, matches, and a bottle of liquor—the latter of which he will down in one swig to seal the pact. If you ever tell anyone about the agreement, Curupira will hunt you down and stab you to death with his long, sharp fingernails.

Several tales explain the origins of important fruits and vegetables. Guaraná, for example, was the name of a young child beloved by all. As the story goes, he was killed by the jealous god Jurupari, who disguised himself as a snake. Lightning struck as the village gathered around Guaraná's body and wept. At that moment the lightning god, Tupã, ordered the villagers to bury the child's eyes. The *guaraná* fruit (which actually resembles eyes) sprouted from the burial spot.

In a legend explaining the origins of the *açaí* fruit (a rich, dark-purple fruit endemic to the Amazon), the chief of a starving tribe ordered all babies to be sacrificed to end the famine. The chief's daughter, Iaçá, had a beautiful baby. Before its sacrifice, she found the child holding a palm tree, and then he suddenly vanished. The tree then became full of açaí (which is Iaçá spelled backward), from which a wine was made that saved the tribe and ended the sacrifices. To this day, Amazonians call the cold soup made from the fruit *vinho* (wine).

The legend of the native water flower *vitória régia* begins with a beautiful girl who wished to become a star in the heavens. She trekked to the highest point in the land and tried in vain to touch the moon. Iaci—the god of the moon—was awed by the girl's beauty. He knew that a mortal could never join the astral kingdom, so he decided to use his powers to immortalize the girl on earth instead. He transformed her into a stunning flower with an alluring scent. Realizing that he needed something fitting to help display this "star," he stretched a palm leaf and created a lily pad, and thus the vitória régia came to be.

WORTH NOTING

FAMILY **Bosque Rodrigues Alves.** In 1883 this 40-acre plot of rain forest was designated an ecological reserve. Nowadays it has an aquarium and two amusement parks as well as natural caverns, a variety of animals (some in the wild), and mammoth trees. ✉ *Av. Almirante Barroso 2453, Marco, Belém* ☎ *091/3277–1112* 🎫 *R$2 for adults, R$1 for students and children* ⏱ *Tues.–Sun. 8–5.*

WHERE TO EAT

$$ BRAZILIAN 🍴 **Boteco das Onze.** In the Casa das Onze Janelas, the Boteca das Onze has thick stone-and-mortar walls stylishly adorned with antique instruments. The full bar has a complete drink menu with one of the largest selections of wines in the city. The patio has a view of the garden and river. A house favorite is the seafood platter for two. The all-you-can-eat lunch buffet is a good deal, and includes dessert but not drinks. The sunset happy hour is one of the most happening in town, usually with live music. [$] *Average main: R$45* ✉ *Praça Frei Caetano Brandão, Cidade Velha, Belém* ☎ *091/3224–8599, 091/3241–8255* 🌐 *botecodasonze.com.br* 🕒 *No lunch Mon.*

> **BIBLICAL NAMES**
>
> Belém is the Portuguese name for Bethlehem. One of its main neighborhoods, Nazaré, is Portuguese for Nazareth. The city was renamed three times before it assumed its current name: Feliz Lusitânia, Santa Maria do Grão Pará, Santa Maria de Belé do Grão Para.

$$ ITALIAN 🍴 **Famiglia Sicilia.** From gnocchi to ravioli, flawless preparation of the basics distinguishes this Italian eatery from others. Everyone in town knows this, so reservations are a good idea—particularly on weekends. Be sure to try one of their 600 varieties of wine on offer. Don't leave without ordering a scrumptious *dolce Paula* (ice cream–and–brownie dessert). [$] *Average main: R$35* ✉ *Av. Conselheiro Furtado 1420, Batista Campos, Belém* ☎ *091/4008–0001* 🌐 *www.famigliasicilia.com* 🕒 *No lunch Mon.–Sat. No dinner Sun.* ✍ *Reservations essential.*

$$ BRAZILIAN Fodor's Choice ★ 🍴 **Lá em Casa.** Regional cuisine, prepared to exacting specifications, has earned Lá em Casa its stellar reputation and made it a favorite of the locals. Consider trying Belém's premier dish, *pato no tucupi* (duck in a yellow manioc–herb sauce served with the mildly intoxicating *jambu* leaf). Crabs on the half-shell covered with *farofa* (finely ground manioc fried in margarine) is another good choice, as is *açaí* sorbet for dessert. Sitting on the patio overlooking the river and fringed by tropical vines and bromeliads, you feel as if you're dining in the middle of the forest. [$] *Average main: R$45* ✉ *Estação das Docas, Boul Castilhos França 707, Belém* ☎ *091/3212–5588* 🌐 *www.laemcasa.com.*

$ BRAZILIAN 🍴 **Palafita.** Ice-cold beers served in buckets, fruit caipirinhas, and *pastéis de pato* (deep-fried duck pastries) served with postcard-perfect views of the bay are why locals love Palafita. Palafita has music on weekend evenings. During the sunset happy hour, it is a great spot to mingle with locals. [$] *Average main: R$25* ✉ *Praça da Sé, Rua Siquiera Mendes 264, Cidade Velha, Belém* ☎ *091/3212–6302.*

WHERE TO STAY

$$$ HOTEL 🏨 **Golden Tulip Belém.** This four-star hotel has sleek but understated rooms, with all the amenities one would want. **Pros:** great furnishings; friendly staff; free parking and Wi-Fi. **Cons:** tiny lobby; small bathrooms. [$] *Rooms from: R$483* ✉ *Trv. Dom Romualdo de Seixas 1560,*

Umarizal, Belém ☎ *091/3366–7575* 🌐 *www.goldentulipbelem.com* 🛏 *127 rooms* 🍴 *Breakfast.*

$ HOTEL 🏨 **Hotel Regente.** This hotel is well suited to business travelers thanks to its reasonable rates and downtown location. **Pros:** lovely views; great location. **Cons:** Internet isn't free; lacks charm. [$] *Rooms from: R$242* ✉ *Av. Governador José Malcher 485, Nazaré, Belém* ☎ *091/3181–5000* 🌐 *www.hotelregente.com.br* 🛏 *219 rooms* 🍴 *Breakfast.*

$$$ HOTEL FAMILY Fodor's Choice ★ 🏨 **Radisson Hotel Maiorana Belém.** This smart hotel combines an excellent central location with a great breakfast, extensive amenities, and sleek, spacious rooms. **Pros:** rooftop pool; well-equipped rooms; fast, free Wi-Fi. **Cons:** parking is an additional cost; pool can get crowded. [$] *Rooms from: R$426* ✉ *Av. Comandante Bras de Aguiar 321, Belém* ☎ *091/3205–1399* 🌐 *atlanticahotels.com.br/hotel/belem/radisson-hotel-belem* 🛏 *153 rooms* 🍴 *Breakfast.*

CARIMBÓ

The *carimbó* is an indigenous dance and music form, originating in Belém and the island of Marajó that later gave way to the rhythms of the lambada. This music is steeped in the sounds of the Amazon and its folklore, but has also been influenced by African culture. It's accompanied by wooden tambourines. During the dance the woman passes her skirt over the man.

NIGHTLIFE AND PERFORMING ARTS

NIGHTLIFE

BARS

Bar Casa do Gilson. This bar has excellent live choro and samba on Friday from 8 pm to midnight and also on weekends from midday to midnight. Lunch is served on both days as well. ✉ *Trv. Padre Eutíquio 3172, Condor, Belém* ☎ *091/3272–7306.*

Cosanostra Caffé. If you prefer music in a relaxed environment, head to Cosanostra Caffé, which has live MPB (*música popular brasileira)* and jazz. Catering to locals and expatriate foreigners alike, it serves food from an extensive menu, including tasty pizzas, until late in the night. ✉ *Trv. Benjamin Constant 1499, Nazaré, Belém* ☎ *091/3241–1068.*

Roxy Bar. This bar tops nearly everyone's list of hip places to sip a drink, listen to great tunes, and people-watch. ✉ *Av. Senador Lemos 231, Umarizal, Belém* ☎ *091/3224–4514* 🌐 *www.roxybar.com.br.*

PERFORMING ARTS

Estação das Docas. Live music is played nightly at the Estação das Docas. Weekday shows usually consist of acoustic singers and/or guitarists. On weekends, rock, jazz, and MPB bands play on a suspended stage that moves back and forth on tracks about 8 meters (25 feet) above patrons of the microbrewery and surrounding restaurants. ✉ *Av. Boulevard Castilho França s/n, Campina, Belém* ☎ *091/3212–5525* 🌐 *www.estacaodasdocas.com.br.*

Teatro da Paz. Greek-style pillars line the front and sides of this 1878 neoclassical theater, modeled on Milan's La Scala opera house; inside, note the imported details such as Italian marble pillars and French chandeliers. Classical-music performances are also held in the theater, which seats more than 800 people. The Teatro often hosts plays, philharmonic concerts, and dance recitals. ⊠ *Praça da República, Rua da Paz s/n, Campina, Belém* ☎ *091/4009–8756, 091/4009–8750* ⊕ *www. theatrodapaz.com.br* ۞ *Tours on the hr, weekdays 9–5, weekends 9–1.*

SHOPPING

The main shopping street in Belém is Avenida Presidente Vargas, especially along the Praca da Republica. In addition, there are many boutiques and specialty shops in Nazaré.

INDIGENOUS CRAFTS
São José Liberto. São José Liberto is a combination museum and high-price jewelry and craft shops with Amazonian wares of gold, amethyst, and wood; pottery; and seeds and plant fibers. ⊠ *Praça Amazonas, Jurunas, Nazaré* ⊕ *www.saojoseliberto.com.br.*

MARKETS
Praça da República. This town square is busy only on Sunday, when *barracas* (small shops) pop up to sell paintings, snacks, artisanal items, and regional foods. You can watch the action from a park bench while sipping a cold coconut or eating a slice of *cupuaçú* cake. It's a local favorite for morning family strolls. ⊠ *Bounded by Av. Presidente Vargas, Trv. Osvaldo Cruz, and Av. Assis de Vasconcelos, Nazaré, Belém.*

SHOPPING AREAS AND MALLS
Icoaraci. A riverside town 18 km (11 miles) northeast of Belém, Icoaraci is a good place to buy marajoara pottery. ⊠ *Belém* ⊕ *www. anisioartesanato.com.br.*

Shopping Patio Belém. To shop in air-conditioning, head for the upscale Shopping Patio Belém, a mall in the truest sense of the word. There are 198 stores, including four department stores with a bit of everything. The mall also includes a multiscreen cinema, banks, a food court, and currency-exchange shops. ⊠ *Trv. Padre Eutíquio 1078, Batista Campos, Nazaré* ☎ *091/4008–5800* ⊕ *www.patiobelem.com.br.*

UNDERSTANDING BRAZIL

Brazilian Portuguese
Vocabulary

BRAZILIAN PORTUGUESE VOCABULARY

	ENGLISH	PORTUGUESE	PRONUNCIATION
BASICS			
	Yes/no	Sim/Não	**see** ing/nown
	Please	Por favor	pohr fah- **vohr**
	May I?	Posso?	**poh**-sso
	Thank you (very much)	(Muito) obrigado	(**moo** yn-too) o-bree- **gah**-doh
	You're welcome	De nada	day **nah**-dah
	Excuse me	Com licença	con lee- **ssehn**-ssah
	Pardon me/what did you say?	Desculpe/O que disse?	des- **kool**-peh/o.k. **dih**-say
	Could you tell me?	Poderia me dizer?	po-day- **ree**-ah mee dee- **zehrr**
	I'm sorry	Sinto muito	**seen**-too **moo** yn-too
	Good morning!	Bom dia!	bohn **dee**-ah
	Good afternoon!	Boa tarde!	**boh**-ah tahr-dee
	Good evening!	Boa noite!	**boh**-ah nohee-tee
	Goodbye!	Adeus!/Até logo!	ah- **deh** oos/ah- **teh** **loh**-go
	Mr./Mrs.	Senhor/Senhora	sen- **yor** /sen- **yohr**-ah
	Miss	Senhorita	sen-yo- **ri**-tah
	Pleased to meet you	Muito prazer	**moo** yn-too prah- **zehr**
	How are you?	Como vai?	**koh**-mo **vah**-ee
	Very well, thank you	Muito bem, obrigado	**moo** yn-too **beh**-in, o-bree- **gah**-doh
	And you?	E o(a) Senhor(a)?	eh oh sen- **yor** (**yohr**-ah)
	Hello (on the telephone)	Alô	ah- **low**
NUMBERS			
	1	um/uma	oom/ **oom**-ah
	2	dois	**doh** ees
	3	três	**treh** ys
	4	quatro	**kwa**-troh

ENGLISH	PORTUGUESE	PRONUNCIATION
5	cinco	**seen**-koh
6	seis	**seh** ys
7	sete	**seh**-tee
8	oito	**oh** ee-too
9	nove	**noh**-vee
10	dez	**deh**-ees
11	onze	**ohn**-zee
12	doze	**doh**-zee
13	treze	**treh**-zee
14	quatorze	kwa- **tohr**-zee
15	quinze	**keen**-zee
16	dezesseis	deh-zeh- **seh** ys
17	dezessete	deh-zeh- **seh**-tee
18	dezoito	deh- **zoh** ee-toh
19	dezenove	deh-zeh- **noh**-vee
20	vinte	**veen**-tee
21	vinte e um	**veen**-tee eh **oom**
30	trinta	**treen**-tah
32	trinta e dois	**treen**-ta eh **doh** ees
40	quarenta	kwa- **rehn**-ta
43	quarenta e três	kwa- **rehn**-ta e **treh** ys
50	cinquenta	seen- **kwehn**-tah
54	cinquenta e quatro	seen- **kwehn**-tah e **kwa**-troh
60	sessenta	seh- **sehn**-tah
65	sessenta e cinco	seh- **sehn**-tah e **seen**-ko
70	setenta	seh- **tehn**-tah
76	setenta e seis	seh- **tehn**-ta e **seh** ys
80	oitenta	ohee- **tehn**-ta
87	oitenta e sete	ohee- **tehn**-ta e **seh**-tee
90	noventa	noh- **vehn**-ta

ENGLISH	PORTUGUESE	PRONUNCIATION
98	noventa e oito	noh- **vehn**-ta e **oh** ee-too
100	cem	**seh**-ing
101	cento e um	**sehn**-too e **oom**
200	duzentos	doo- **zehn**-tohss
500	quinhentos	key- **nyehn**-tohss
700	setecentos	seh-teh- **sehn**-tohss
900	novecentos	noh-veh- **sehn**-tohss
1,000	mil	meel
2,000	dois mil	**doh** ees meel
1,000,000	um milhão	oom mee-lee- **ahon**

COLORS

black	preto	**preh**-toh
blue	azul	a- **zool**
brown	marrom	mah- **hohm**
green	verde	**vehr**-deh
pink	rosa	**roh**-zah
purple	roxo	**roh**-choh
orange	laranja	lah- **rahn**-jah
red	vermelho	vehr- **meh**-lyoh
white	branco	**brahn**-coh
yellow	amarelo	ah-mah- **reh**-loh

DAYS OF THE WEEK

Sunday	Domingo	doh- **meehn**-goh
Monday	Segunda-feira	seh- **goon**-dah **fey**-rah
Tuesday	Terça-feira	**tehr**-sah **fey**-rah
Wednesday	Quarta-feira	**kwahr**-tah **fey**-rah
Thursday	Quinta-feira	**keen**-tah fey-rah
Friday	Sexta-feira	**sehss**-tah fey-rah
Saturday	Sábado	**sah**-bah-doh

	ENGLISH	PORTUGUESE	PRONUNCIATION
MONTHS			
	January	Janeiro	jah- **ney**-roh
	February	Fevereiro	feh-veh- **rey**-roh
	March	Março	**mahr**-soh
	April	Abril	ah- **breel**
	May	Maio	**my**-oh
	June	Junho	jy **oo**-nyoh
	July	Julho	jy **oo**-lyoh
	August	Agosto	ah- **ghost**-toh
	September	Setembro	seh- **tehm**-broh
	October	Outubro	owe- **too**-broh
	November	Novembro	noh- **vehm**-broh
	December	Dezembro	deh- **zehm**-broh
USEFUL PHRASES			
	Do you speak English?	O Senhor fala inglês?	oh sen- **yor fah**-lah een- **glehs**
	I don't speak Portuguese.	Não falo português.	nown **fah**-loh pohr-too- **ghehs**
	I don't understand (you)	Não lhe entendo	nown ly **eh** ehn- **tehn**-doh
	I understand	Eu entendo	**eh**-oo ehn- **tehn**-doh
	I don't know	Não sei	nown say
	I am American/British	Sou americano (americana)/inglês (inglêsa)	sow a-meh-ree- **cah**-noh (a-meh-ree- **cah**-nah)/een- **glehs** (een- **gleh**-sa)
	What's your name?	Como se chama?	**koh**-moh seh **shah**-mah
	My name is . . .	Meu nome é . . .	mehw **noh**-meh eh
	What time is it?	Que horas são?	keh **oh**-rahss **sa**-ohn
	It is one, two, three . . . o'clock	É uma/São duas, três . . . hora/horas	eh **oom**-ah/ **sa**- ohn **doo**-ahss, **treh** ys **oh**-rah/ **oh**-rahs
	Yes, please/No, thank you	Sim por favor/Não obrigado	seing pohr fah- **vohr** / nown o-bree- **gah**-doh

ENGLISH	PORTUGUESE	PRONUNCIATION
How?	Como?	**koh**-moh
When?	Quando?	**kwahn**-doh
This/Next week	Esta/Próxima semana	**ehss**-tah/ **proh**-see-mah seh- **mah**-nah
This/Next month	Este/Próximo mêz	**ehss**-teh/ **proh** see-moh mehz
This/Next year	Este/Próximo ano	**ehss**-teh/ **proh**-see-moh **ah**-noh
Yesterday/today/ tomorrow	Ontem/hoje/amanhã	**ohn**-tehn/ **oh**-jeh/ ah-mah- **nyan**
This morning/ afternoon	Esta manhã/tarde	**ehss**-tah mah- **nyan** / **tahr**-deh
Tonight	Hoje a noite	**oh**-jeh ah **noh** ee-tee
What?	O que?	oh **keh**
What is it?	O que é isso?	oh **keh** eh **ee**-soh
Why?	Por quê?	pohr- **keh**
Who?	Quem?	**keh**-in
Where is . . . ?	Onde é . . . ?	**ohn**-deh **eh**
the train station?	a estação de trem?	ah es-tah- **sah**-on deh train
the subway station?	a estação de metrô?	ah es-tah- **sah**-on deh meh- **tro**
the bus stop?	a parada do ônibus?	ah pah- **rah**-dah doh **oh**-nee-boos
the post office?	o correio?	oh coh- **hay**-yoh
the bank?	o banco?	oh **bahn**-koh
the hotel?	o hotel . . . ?	oh oh- **tell**
the cashier?	o caixa?	oh **kah** y-shah
the museum?	o museo . . . ?	oh moo- **zeh**-oh
the hospital?	o hospital?	oh ohss-pee- **tal**
the elevator?	o elevador?	oh eh-leh-vah- **dohr**
the bathroom?	o banheiro?	oh bahn-yey-roh
the beach?	a praia de . . . ?	ah prahy-yah deh
Here/there	Aqui/ali	ah- **kee** /ah- **lee**

ENGLISH	PORTUGUESE	PRONUNCIATION
Open/closed	Aberto/fechado	ah- **behr**-toh/ feh- **shah**-doh
Left/right	Esquerda/direita	ehs- **kehr**-dah/ dee- **ray**-tah
Straight ahead	Em frente	ehyn **frehn**-teh
Is it near/far?	É perto/longe?	eh **pehr**-toh/ **lohn**-jeh
I'd like to buy . . .	Gostaria de comprar . . .	gohs-tah- **ree**-ah deh cohm- **prahr**
a bathing suit	um maiô	oom mahy- **owe**
a dictionary	um dicionário	oom dee-seeoh- **nah**-reeoh
a hat	um chapéu	oom shah- **peh** oo
a magazine	uma revista	oomah heh- **vees**-tah
a map	um mapa	oom **mah**-pah
a postcard	cartão postal	kahr- **town** pohs- **tahl**
sunglasses	óculos escuros	ah-koo-loss ehs- **koo**-rohs
suntan lotion	um óleo de bronzear	oom **oh**-lyoh deh brohn-zeh- **ahr**
a ticket	um bilhete	oom hee-lyeh-teh
cigarettes	cigarros	see- **gah**-hose
envelopes	envelopes	eyn-veh- **loh**-pehs
matches	fósforos	**fohs**-foh-rohss
paper	papel	pah- **pehl**
sandals	sandália	sahn- **dah**-leeah
soap	sabonete	sah-bow- **neh**-teh
How much is it?	Quanto custa?	**kwahn**-too **koos**-tah
It's expensive/cheap	Está caro/barato	**ehss**-tah **kah**-roh/ bah- **rah**-toh
A little/a lot	Um pouco/muito	oom **pohw**-koh/ **moo** yn-too
More/less	Mais/menos	**mah**-ees / **meh**-nohss
Enough/too much/ too little	Suficiente/demais/ muito pouco	soo-fee-see- **ehn**-teh/ deh- **mah**-ees/ **moo** yn-toh pohw-koh

ENGLISH	PORTUGUESE	PRONUNCIATION
Telephone	Telefone	teh-leh- **foh**-neh
Telegram	Telegrama	teh-leh- **grah**-mah
I am ill.	Estou doente.	**ehss**-tow doh- **ehn**-teh
Please call a doctor.	Por favor chame um médico.	pohr fah- **vohr** shah-meh oom **meh**-dee-koh
Help!	Socorro!	soh- **koh**-ho
Help me!	Me ajude!	mee ah- **jyew**-deh
Fire!	Incêndio!	een- **sehn**-deeoh
Caution!/Look out!/ Be careful!	Cuidado!	kooy- **dah**-doh

ON THE ROAD

Avenue	Avenida	ah-veh- **nee**-dah
Highway	Estrada	ehss- **trah**-dah
Port	Porto	**pohr**-toh
Service station	Posto de gasolina	**pohs**-toh deh gah-zoh- **lee**-nah
Street	Rua	**who**-ah
Toll	Pedagio	peh- **dah**-jyoh
Waterfront promenade	Beiramar/orla	behy-rah- **mahrr** / **ohr**-lah
Wharf	Cais	**kah**-ees

IN TOWN

Block	Quarteirão	kwahr-tehy- **rah**-on
Cathedral	Catedral	kah-teh- **drahl**
Church/temple	Igreja	ee- **greh**-jyah
City hall	Prefeitura	preh-fehy- **too**-rah
Door/gate	Porta/portão	**pohr**-tah/porh- **tah**-on
Entrance/exit	Entrada/saída	ehn- **trah**-dah/ sah- **ee**-dah
Market	Mercado/feira	mehr- **kah**-doh/ **fey**-rah
Neighborhood	Bairro	**buy**-ho
Rustic bar	Lanchonete	lahn-shoh- **neh**-teh

ENGLISH	PORTUGUESE	PRONUNCIATION
Shop	Loja	**loh**-jyah
Square	Praça	**prah**-ssah

DINING OUT

ENGLISH	PORTUGUESE	PRONUNCIATION
A bottle of...	Uma garrafa de...	**oo** mah gah- **hah**-fah deh
A cup of...	Uma xícara de...	**oo** mah **shee**-kah-rah deh
A glass of...	Um copo de...	oom **koh**-poh deh
Ashtray	Um cinzeiro	oom seen- **zeh** y-roh
Bill/check	A conta	ah **kohn**-tah
Bread	Pão	**pah**-on
Breakfast	Café da manhã	kah- **feh** dah mah- **nyan**
Butter	A manteiga	ah mahn-tehy-gah
Cheers!	Saúde!	sah- **oo**-deh
Cocktail	Um aperitivo	oom ah-peh-ree- **tee**-voh
Dinner	O jantar	oh **jyahn**-tahr
Dish	Um prato	oom **prah**-toh
Enjoy!	Bom apetite!	bohm ah-peh- **tee**-teh
Fork	Um garfo	**gahr**-foh
Fruit	Fruta	**froo**-tah
Is the tip included?	A gorjeta esta incluída?	ah gohr- **jyeh**-tah ehss-**tah** een-clue- **ee**-dah
Juice	Um suco	oom **soo**-koh
Knife	Uma faca	**oo** mah **fah**-kah
Lunch	O almoço	oh ahl- **moh**-ssoh
Menu	Menu/cardápio	me- **noo** / kahr-dah-peeoh
Mineral water	Água mineral	**ah**-gooah mee-neh- **rahl**
Napkin	Guardanapo	gooahr-dah- **nah**-poh
No smoking	Não fumante	nown foo- **mahn**-teh

ENGLISH	PORTUGUESE	PRONUNCIATION
Pepper	Pimenta	pee- **mehn**-tah
Please give me	Por favor me dê	pohr fah- **vohr** mee **deh**
Salt	Sal	sahl
Smoking	Fumante	foo- **mahn**-teh
Spoon	Uma colher	**oo** mah koh- **lyehr**
Sugar	Açúcar	ah- **soo**-kahr
Waiter!	Garçon!	gahr- **sohn**
Water	Água	**ah**-gooah
Wine	Vinho	**vee**-nyoh

PRONOUNCING PLACE NAMES

NAME	PRONUNCIATION
Amazônia	ah-mah- **zoh**-knee-ah
Bahia	bah- **ee**-ah
Belém	beh- **lein**
Belo Horizonte	**beh**-loh ho-rih- **zon**-teh
Brasília	brah- **zee**-lee-ah
Fortaleza	for-tah- **leh**-zah
Manaus	mah- **nah**-oos
Minas Gerais	**mee**-nahs jyeh- **rah**-ees
Paraná	pah-rah-nah
Porto Alegre	**pohr**-toh ah- **leh**-greh
Recife	heh- **see**-fee
Rio de Janeiro	**hee**-oh day jah- **ne**-roh
Rio Grande do Sul	**hee**-oh **gran**-deh doh sool
Salvador	sahl-vah- **dohr**
Santa Catarina	sahn- **tah** kah-tah-reeh-nah
São Paulo	saohn **pow**-low

TRAVEL SMART
BRAZIL

GETTING HERE AND AROUND

Brazil is one of the biggest countries in the world, and larger than the continental United States. In fact, the Amazon jungle alone is slightly larger than India. This means that you'll be hard-pressed to see the Amazon, Bahia, Rio de Janeiro, and São Paulo during a weeklong vacation. You can, however, cover a lot of territory if your trip is well planned. If you want to start from the North and Northeast and then later on go southward, go ahead. We just recommend spending a little time gaining a clear idea of the often-vast distances between destinations.

Road conditions in Brazil vary widely throughout the country, and passenger train travel is almost nonexistent. Private cars and public buses are the main modes of intercity road travel. Buses can range (depending on the route and the price) from luxurious and well maintained to basic and mechanically unsound. Traveling by plane is a good option, especially considering the large distances between cities. It's fast, safe, and you can get good prices on tickets.

TRAVEL TIMES FROM SÃO PAULO TO	BY AIR	BY BUS
Rio de Janeiro	1 hour	6 hours
Salvador	2 hours, 30 minutes	27 hours
Manaus	4 hours	54 hours
Florianópolis	1 hour, 15 minutes	9 hours
Brasília	1 hour, 45 minutes	13 hours

■ AIR TRAVEL

Within a country as big as Brazil, it's especially important to plan your itinerary with care. Book as far in advance as possible, particularly for weekend travel. Planes tend to fill up on Friday, especially to or from popular destinations like Rio, São Paulo, Brasília, or Manaus. For more booking tips and to check prices and make online flight reservations, see individual airline sites listed at ⊕ *www. infraero.gov.br.*

The majority of direct flights to Brazil fly to São Paulo's Guarhulhos International Airport, although with the increased demand created by the 2016 Olympics, many more direct flights run from New York to Rio than in the past. It's still the case though that most flights to Rio stop in Miami. Most flights from Los Angeles go through Miami as well, save a few nonstops to São Paulo, and flight times are about 13 hours, not including layover in Miami. For flights to Brasília, Manaus, and Salvador, you can fly nonstop from Miami. The flying time from New York is 10½ hours to Rio and 10 hours to São Paulo. From Miami it's just under 8 hours to Brasília (the nation's capital), just under 9 hours to Rio de Janeiro, 8½ hours to São Paulo, and 8 hours to Salvador. Usually the connection time in São Paulo is an hour to 90 minutes.

■ TIP➜ Reconfirm flights within Brazil, even if you have a ticket and a reservation, as flights tend to operate at full capacity.

When you leave Brazil, be prepared to pay a hefty departure tax, which runs about R$82 ($30) for international flights. A departure tax also applies to flights within Brazil; amounts run as high as R$22 ($8). Although some airports accept credit cards to pay departure taxes, it's wise to have the appropriate amount in reais.

Airline Security Issues Transportation Security Administration. ⊕ *www.tsa.gov.*

Air Travel Resources in Brazil National Civil Aviation Agency (ANAC). ☎ *61/3905–2645 in Brasília, 0800/725–4445 toll-free within Brazil* ⊕ *www.anac.gov.br.*

TRANSFERS BETWEEN AIRPORTS

In the major hubs, airport transfers are offered between airports: in São Paulo between Guarulhos and Congonhas, and in Rio de Janeiro between Galeão and Santos Dumond. This type of service is not common outside of Rio and São Paulo; most other Brazilian cities have only one commercial airport.

FLIGHTS
TO BRAZIL

Miami, New York, and Toronto are the major North American gateways for flights to Brazil—typically to São Paulo and Rio, and sometimes Brasília as well.

United Airlines flies nonstop from Houston, Newark, and Chicago; American Airlines has direct service from Dallas, Miami, and New York; and Delta offers nonstop service from Atlanta and New York. Air Canada has nonstop service between Toronto and São Paulo.

LATAM Airlines (still known as TAM within Brazil) flies nonstop from Miami to Rio and São Paulo, and from New York to São Paulo with onward service to Rio and many other cities. TAM also offers nonstop service between Miami and Manaus. GOL Linhas Aéreas Intelligentes covers several American cities, including New York, Miami, Atlanta, Los Angeles, Las Vegas, Detroit, Austin, and Chicago. The Colombian airline Avianca flies from Washington, D.C., to São Paulo, with a brief stopover in Bogotá.

Airline Contacts Air Canada. *☎ 888/247-2262 in North America, 11/3254-6630 in Brazil ⊕ www.aircanada.com.* **American Airlines.** *☎ 800/433-7300 in North America, 0300/789-7778 in Brazil ⊕ www.aa.com.* **Avianca Airlines.** *☎ 800/284-2622 in North America, 0800/891-8668 in Brazil ⊕ www. avianca.com.* **Delta Airlines.** *☎ 800/241-4141 in North America, 0800/881-2121 in Brazil ⊕ www.delta.com.* **GOL Linhas Aéreas Intelligentes.** *☎ 855/862-9190 in North America, 0800/704-0465 in Brazil ⊕ www.voegol.com. br.* **TAM.** *☎ 888/235-9826 in North America, 21/3212-9400 in Rio, 11/3274-1313 in São Paulo ⊕ www.tam.com.br.* **United Airlines.**

☎ 800/864-8331 in North America, 011/3145-4200 in São Paulo, 0800/16-2323 in Rio de Janeiro and other cities within Brazil ⊕ www. united.com.

WITHIN BRAZIL

There's regular jet service within the country between all major and most medium-size cities. Remote areas are also accessible—as long as you don't mind small planes. Flights can be long, lasting several hours for trips to the Amazon, with stops en route. Domestic airlines include TAM and GOL, a reliable low-cost airline with routes covering most major and medium-size Brazilian cities. Another option is Azul Linhas Aéreas, with service to about 100 domestic destinations.

The flight from Rio to São Paulo or Belo Horizonte is 1 hour; Rio to Brasília is 1½ hours; Rio to Salvador is 2 hours; Rio to Belém is 3½ hours; and Rio to Curitiba is 1½ hours. From São Paulo it's 4 hours to Manaus, 1½ hours to Iguaçu Falls, 2½ hours to Salvador, and just over an hour to Belo Horizonte or Florianópolis.

Domestic Airlines Azul Linhas Aéreas. *☎ 11/4003-1118 in São Paulo, 0800/884-4040 toll-free from other cities within Brazil ⊕ www.voeazul.com.br.* **GOL Linhas Aéreas Intelligentes.** *☎ 855/862-9190 in North America, 0800/704-0465 in Brazil ⊕ www. voegol.com.br.* **TAM.** *☎ 888/235-9826 in North America, 0800/570-5700 in Brazil ⊕ www.tam. com.br.*

AIR PASSES

If you reside outside Brazil, you're eligible to purchase air passes from TAM or GOL. If you're planning four or more flights within the country within 30 days, these passes—available online through Miami-based travel agency and tour operator Brol—can save you hundreds of dollars. Prices start around $530 (plus tax), and you must purchase your pass before you enter Brazil. Passes that include flights between Brazil and other South American countries are also available.

Air Pass Information Brol. ☎ 888/527–2745 in North America, 21/3500–6704 in Rio ⊕ www.brol.com.

▌BUS TRAVEL

The nation's *ônibus* (bus) network is affordable, comprehensive, and efficient—compensating for the lack of trains and the high cost of air travel. Every major city can be reached by bus, as can most small to medium-size communities.

The quality of buses in Brazil is good; in many cases better than in the United States. The number of stops at roadside cafés depends on the length of the journey. A trip from São Paulo to Curitiba, for example, which takes about six hours, has only one 20-minute stop. Usually buses stop at large outlets with food services, and souvenir and magazine stalls.

Lengthy bus trips can involve travel over some poorly maintained highways, a fact of life in Brazil. Trips to northern, northeastern, and central Brazil tend to be especially trying; the best paved highways are in the Southeast and the South. When traveling by bus, bring water, toilet paper or tissues, and an additional top layer of clothing (handy if it gets cold or as a pillow). Travel light, dress comfortably, and keep a close watch on your belongings—especially in bus stations. If your bus stops at a roadside café, take your belongings with you.

When buying a ticket, you'll be asked whether you want the *ônibus convencional,* the simplest option; the *ônibus executivo,* which gets you a/c, coffee, water, a sandwich, more space between seats, and a pillow and blanket; or the *ônibus-leito,* where you have all facilities of an executive bus plus a seat that reclines completely. If you're over 5 ft. 10 in., it's prudent to buy the most expensive ticket and try for front-row seats, which usually provide more space.

Most buses used for long trips are modern and comfortable, usually with bathrooms and a/c. Note that regular buses used for shorter hauls may be labeled "ar condicionado" ("air-conditioned") but often are not.

Bus fares are substantially cheaper than in North America or Europe. Between Rio and São Paulo (6½–7 hours), for example, a bus departs every half hour and costs about $28; a night sleeper will run about $60. Sometimes competing companies serve the same routes, so it can pay to shop around.

Tickets are sold at bus-company offices, at city bus terminals, in some travel agencies, and online. Larger cities may have different terminals for buses to different destinations, and some small towns may not have a terminal at all (you're usually picked up and dropped off at the line's office, invariably in a central location). Expect to pay with cash, as credit cards aren't accepted everywhere. Reservations or advance-ticket purchases generally aren't necessary except for trips to resort areas during high season—particularly on weekends—or during major holidays (Christmas, Carnival, etc.) and school-break periods (July and December/January). In general, arrive at bus stations early, particularly for peak-season travel.

Traveling between Argentina and Brazil by bus is also a good idea if time is not an issue. The same can be said for Uruguay, Chile, Peru, and other neighboring countries. It's inexpensive and you can enjoy the landscapes. Expect to pay $200 for the 14-hour trip between São Paulo and Buenos Aires.

▌**TIP→ To ensure that your destination is understood, write it down on a piece of paper and present it to bus or taxi drivers, most of whom don't speak English.**

Bus Information Expresso Brasileiro.
☎ 0300/700–9000 ⊕ www.expressobrasileiro. com. **Itapemirim.** ☎ 0800/723–2121 ⊕ www. itapemirim.com.br. **Pluma International.** ☎ 41/3212–2689 long distance from North America, 0800/646–0300 toll-free within Brazil ⊕ www.pluma.com.br.

CAR TRAVEL

Traveling by car is recommended if you meet the following criteria: you're not pressed for time, you enjoy driving even in places you do not know well, and you do not want to be limited by airline or bus schedules. Traveling by car is, especially if you avoid driving at night, reasonably safe in most areas and is a wonderful way to see the country and access lesser-known areas.

Driving can be chaotic in cities like São Paulo, but much easier in cities like Curitiba and Brasília. In the countryside the usually rough roads, lack of clearly marked signs, and language difference can make driving a challenge. Further, the cost of renting can be steep. All that said, certain areas are most enjoyable when explored on your own in a car: the beach areas of Búzios and the Costa Verde (near Rio), and the Belo Horizonte region; the North Shore beaches outside São Paulo; and many of the inland and coastal towns of the South, a region with many good roads.

ROAD CONDITIONS

Brazil has more than 1.7 million km (1.05 million miles) of highway, about 12% of it paved. While roads in the South are often excellent, the country's highway department estimates that 40% of the federal highways (those with either the designation *BR* or a state abbreviation such as *RJ* or *SP*), which constitute 70% of Brazil's total road system, are in a dangerous state of disrepair. Evidence of this is everywhere: potholes, lack of signage, inadequate shoulders. Landslides and flooding after heavy rains are frequent and at times shut down entire stretches of key highways. Recent construction has improved the situation, but independent land travel in Brazil definitely has its liabilities.

The Brazilian federal government maintains a (Portuguese-language) website with up-to-date information on road conditions throughout the country (⊕ *www.dnit.gov.br*); the site also has

downloadable state road maps. A private Brazilian company, Quatro Rodas (⊕ *www.guia4rodas.com.br*), publishes road maps that list local phone numbers for obtaining current road conditions; these cost about R$36 ($14).

FROM	TO	DISTANCE
São Paulo	Rio de Janeiro	430 km (267 miles)
Rio de Janeiro	Búzios	168 km (104 miles)
Rio de Janeiro	Salvador	1,560 km (970 miles)
São Paulo	Belo Horizonte	596 km (370 miles)
São Paulo	Florianópolis	691 km (430 miles)
São Paulo	Foz do Iguaçu	1,037 km (644 miles)

ROADSIDE EMERGENCIES

Apart from toll roads, which generally have their own services, roadside assistance is available only sporadically and informally through local private mechanics. However, the Automóvel Clube do Brasil (Automobile Club of Brazil) provides emergency assistance to foreign motorists who are members of an automobile club in their own nation. If you're not a member of an automobile club, you can call 193 from anywhere in the country. This is a universal number staffed by local fire departments. The service is in Portuguese only. In case of emergency, the fastest way to summon assistance is to call one of the following services: Fire Brigade (193); Police (190); Federal Highway Patrol (191); Ambulance (192); Civil Defense (199).

RULES OF THE ROAD

Brazilians drive on the right, and in general traffic laws are the same as those in the United States. The use of seat belts is mandatory. The minimum driving age is 18 and children should always sit in the backseat. Do not use your cell phone while driving.

The national speed limit ranges from 50 to 90 kph (31 to 56 mph), although vehicles considered light can often travel at higher speeds on freeways. Pay close attention to signs. Some sections of highway have pedestrian crossings and the speed limit drops as you approach them. In large cities like São Paulo, Curitiba and Brasília there are now cameras to detect and fine speeding and aggressive drivers. This has decreased traffic accidents significantly, but you should be careful anyway. Some drivers slow down only when close to these cameras. The worst offenders are bus and truck drivers. In cities be very careful around motorcycles, as their drivers are notorious for flouting traffic rules.

If you get a ticket for some sort of violation, be polite with the police officer and try to solve the issue either by accepting the ticket (if you committed the violation) or by explaining your position (if you did not commit a violation). Even though it's common to see scams in cases like this, the best option is to solve the problem as honestly as possible, especially if you're a foreigner.

TRAFFIC AND PARKING

In major cities, traffic jams are common in rush hours (8 am, 6 pm); the problem is especially bad in São Paulo and Rio de Janeiro. In Brasília there are special roads for those driving faster (the so-called Eixão, where the limit is 80 kph/49 mph). At rush hour you may find the local driving style more aggressive.

Finding a space in most cities—particularly Rio, São Paulo, Brasília, Belo Horizonte, and Salvador—is a major task. It's best to head for a garage or a lot and leave your car with the attendant. The cost of parking depends on the city and the neighborhood: downtown garages, close to stores, will certainly be more expensive than those in residential areas. There are no meters; instead you must post a coupon in your car's window, which allows you to park for a certain time period (one or two hours). You can buy them from uniformed street-parking attendants or at newsstands. Should you find a space on the street, you'll probably have to pay a fee for parking services.

■TIP➜ **No-parking zones are marked by a crossed-out capital letter** *E* **(which means** *estacionamento,* **Portuguese for "parking").**

TOLL ROADS

Tollbooths, better known as *pedagio* in Portuguese, are common in Brazil. These are located along many highways, especially in the Southeast and around São Paulo. Fees depend on the type of vehicle you're driving. Make sure you carry cash, including some small change.

GASOLINE

In Brazil gasoline costs around R$2.80 per liter, ($1.05 or about $4 per gallon). Unleaded gas, called *especial,* costs about the same. Brazil also has an extensive fleet of ethanol-powered cars, *carro a álcool,* and you might end up with one from a rental agency. Ethanol fuel is sold at all gas stations and is a little cheaper than gasoline. However, these cars get lower mileage, so they offer little advantage over gas-powered cars. Stations are plentiful within cities and on major highways, and many are open 24/7. In smaller towns few stations take credit cards, and their hours are more limited. If you want a receipt, ask for a *recibo.*

DRIVER'S LICENSES

Visitors to Brazil can drive with their home-country driver's license for the first 180 days they are in the country, as long as they also carry a copy of it translated into Portuguese and another piece of ID. You can also drive with an international driver's license. International driving permits (IDPs) are available from the American and Canadian automobile associations. These international permits, valid only in conjunction with your regular driver's license, are universally recognized.

CAR RENTAL

Rates are sometimes—but not always—better if you book in advance or reserve through a rental agency's website. Although international car-rental agencies have better service and maintenance track records than local firms (they also provide better breakdown assistance), your best bet at getting a good rate is to rent on arrival, particularly from local companies. But reserve ahead if you plan to rent during a holiday period or at a particularly popular destination, or need a specific type of car (an SUV or a van). You can contact local agencies through their websites in advance. At many airports, agencies are open 24 hours.

When you reserve a car, ask about cancellation penalties, taxes, drop-off charges (if you're planning to pick up the car in one city and leave it in another), and surcharges (for being under or over a certain age, for additional drivers, or for driving across state or country borders or beyond a specific distance from your point of rental). All these things can add substantially to your costs. Request car seats and extras such as a GPS when you book.

■ TIP➔ **Make sure that a confirmed reservation guarantees you a car. Agencies sometimes overbook, particularly for busy weekends and holiday periods.**

CAR-RENTAL INSURANCE

Car insurance is not compulsory when renting a car, but if you have plans to drive in more than one city we strongly recommend buying car insurance, given the bad conditions of Brazilian roads in some states and the risk of accidents. Most car-rental companies offer an optional insurance against robbery and accidents. Minimum age for renting a car is 21, but some companies require foreign clients to be at least 25 or charge extra for those under 26.

If you own a car, your personal auto insurance may cover a rental to some degree, though not all policies protect you abroad; always read your policy's fine print. If you don't have auto insurance, then seriously consider buying the collision- or loss-damage waiver (CDW or LDW) from the car-rental company, which eliminates your liability for damage to the car.

Some credit cards offer CDW coverage, but it's usually supplemental to your own insurance and rarely covers SUVs, minivans, luxury models, and the like. If your coverage is secondary, you may still be liable for loss-of-use costs from the car-rental company. But no credit-card insurance is valid unless you use that card for *all* transactions, from reserving to paying the final bill. All companies exclude car rental in some countries, so be sure to find out about the destination to which you are traveling.

Some rental agencies require you to purchase CDW coverage; many will even include it in quoted rates. All will strongly encourage you to buy CDW—possibly implying that it's required—so be sure to ask about such things before renting. In most cases it's cheaper to add a supplemental CDW plan to your comprehensive travel-insurance policy than to purchase it from a rental company. That said, you don't want to pay for a supplement if you're required to buy insurance from the rental company. Another possibility is to purchase insurance through a third-party provider such as Travel Guard (⊕ *www.travelguide.com*), which can cost significantly less than coverage offered by car-rental companies.

ESSENTIALS

■ ACCOMMODATIONS

All hotels in Brazil have bathrooms in their rooms. The simplest type of accommodations usually consists of a bed, TV, table, a little fridge, a telephone, and a bathroom with a shower. (Budget hotels in the Amazon or Northeast don't always have hot water.) In luxury hotels you'll also generally have Internet, cable TV, and a bathroom with a bathtub and shower. Hotels listed with EMBRATUR, Brazil's national tourism board, are rated using stars. Staff training is a big part of the rating, but it's not a perfect system, since stars are awarded based on the number of amenities rather than their quality.

If you ask for a double room, you'll get a room for two people, but you're not guaranteed a double mattress. If you'd like to avoid twin beds, ask for a *cama de casal* ("couple's bed").

■**TIP**➜ **For top hotels in Rio, Salvador, and Recife during Carnival you must make reservations a year in advance.**

Carnival, the year's principal festival, takes place during the four days preceding Ash Wednesday. Hotel rates rise by at least 30% for Carnival. Not as well known outside Brazil but equally impressive is Rio's New Year's Eve celebration. More than a million people gather along Copacabana Beach for a massive fireworks display and to honor the sea goddess Iemanjá. To ensure a room, book at least six months in advance.

In the hinterlands it's good to look at any room before accepting it; expense is no guarantee of charm or cleanliness, and accommodations can vary dramatically within a single hotel. Also, be sure to check the shower: some hotels have electric-powered showerheads rather than central water heaters. In theory, you can adjust both the water's heat and its pressure. In practice, if you want hot water you have to turn the water pressure down; if you want pressure, expect a cool rinse. Note that in the Amazon and other remote areas what's billed as "hot" water may be lukewarm at best, even in higher-end hotels.

■**TIP**➜ **Don't adjust the pressure while you're under the water—you might get a little electric shock.**

Most hotels and other lodgings require you to give your credit-card details before they will confirm your reservation. However you book, get confirmation in writing and have a copy of it handy when you check in.

Be sure you understand the hotel's cancellation policy. Some places allow you to cancel without any kind of penalty—even if you prepaid to secure a discounted rate—if you cancel at least 24 hours in advance. Others require you to cancel a week in advance or penalize you the cost of one night. Small inns and B&Bs are most likely to require you to cancel far in advance. Most hotels allow children under a certain age to stay in their parents' room at no extra charge, but others charge for them as extra adults; find out the cutoff age for discounts.

BED AND BREAKFASTS

B&Bs in Brazil are comfortable, friendly, and offer a modicum of privacy. They're a nice option if you're looking for something a little more intimate than a hotel.

AirBnB is another option that has become a popular choice in Brazil. You can look up listings of short-term lets and small B&Bs that locals post on the site. Often you will be staying in someone's home while they are away. Usually the rates are a fraction of other accommodations.

Contacts AirBnB. ⊕ *www.airbnb.com.* **Bed & Breakfast.com.** ☎ *844/271–6829, 512/322–2710* ⊕ *www.bedandbreakfast.com.* **BnB Finder.com.** ☎ *888/469–6663* ⊕ *www. bnbfinder.com.*

FAZENDAS

Another accommodations option is to stay on a *fazenda* (farm), or *hotel fazenda*, where you can experience a rural environment. They are ideal for families with kids, as most have adventure sports and programs for children. Some farms in the state of São Paulo date back to colonial times, when they were famous Brazilian coffee farms. Prices range from around $70 to $150 per day for adults, but the actual cost depends a lot on which facilities and activities you choose. The prices we give usually include all meals (but be sure to check this beforehand) and are valid for the months of January, February, July, and December (high season). You can get discounts of up to 30% during the low season.

POUSADAS

If you want the facilities of a hotel plus the family environment of an apartment, but at a lower cost, a *pousada* is a good option. Cheaper than hotels and farms, pousadas are simple inns, often in historic houses. They usually offer breakfast and have swimming pools, parking lots, air-conditioning and/or fans, TVs, refrigerators, and common areas such as bars, laundry, and living rooms. Some have a common kitchen for guests who prefer to cook their own meals. Hidden Pousadas Brazil is a helpful website for locating pousadas.

Contacts Hidden Pousadas Brazil. ☎ *219/8122–2000* ⊕ *www.hiddenpousadasbrazil.com.*

▋ ADDRESSES

Finding addresses in Brazil can be frustrating, as streets often have more than one name, and numbers are sometimes assigned haphazardly. In some places street numbering doesn't enjoy the wide popularity it has achieved elsewhere; hence, you may find the notation "s/n," meaning *sem número* (without number). In rural areas and small towns there may only be directions to a place rather than a formal address (i.e., street and number). Often such areas do not have official addresses.

In Portuguese *avenida* (avenue), *rua,* (street) and *travessa* (lane) are abbreviated (as *Av., R.,* and *Trv.* or *Tr.*), while *estrada* (highway) often isn't abbreviated, and *alameda* (alley) is abbreviated (Al.). Street numbers follow street names. Eight-digit postal codes (CEP) are widely used.

In some written addresses you might see other abbreviations. For example, an address might read, "R. Presidente Faria 221-4°, s. 413, 90160-091 Porto Alegre, RS," which translates to 221 Rua Presidente Faria, 4th floor, Room 413 ("s." is short for *sala*), postal code 90160-091, in the city of Porto Alegre, in the state of Rio Grande do Sul. You might also see *andar* (floor) or *edifício* (building).

The abbreviations for Brazilian states are: Acre (AC); Alagoas (AL); Amapá (AP); Amazonas (AM); Bahia (BA); Ceará (CE); Distrito Federal (Federal District, aka Brasília; DF); Espírito Santo (ES); Goiás (GO); Maranhão (MA); Minas Gerais (MG); Mato Grosso do Sul (MS); Mato Grosso (MT); Pará (PA); Paraíba (PB); Paraná (PR); Pernambuco (PE); Piauí (PI); Rio de Janeiro (RJ); Rio Grande do Norte (RN); Rio Grande do Sul (RS); Rondonia (RO); Roraima (RR); Santa Catarina (SC); São Paulo (SP); Sergipe (SE), Tocantins (TO).

▋ COMMUNICATIONS

INTERNET

Internet access is widespread, and Wi-Fi is often available, especially in the big cities. Many hotels have in-room access to Wi-Fi, but some charge $5 to $10 per day for the privilege. In big cities like São Paulo and Rio, 3G access is common, but check with your local provider to find a plan that mitigates the often-steep roaming charges. Switching your device from cellular data to Wi-Fi whenever it is available should save you money.

Be discreet about carrying laptops, smartphones, and other obvious displays of wealth, which can make you a target of thieves. Conceal your laptop in a generic bag and keep it close to you at all times.

PHONES

The good news is that you can now make a direct-dial telephone call from virtually any point on earth. The bad news? You can't always do so cheaply. Calling from a hotel is almost always the most expensive option; hotels usually add huge surcharges to all calls, particularly international ones. In remote areas you can phone from call centers or sometimes even the post office, but in big cities these call centers don't exist anymore. Calling cards usually keep costs to a minimum, but only if you purchase them locally. And then there are mobile phones, which are sometimes more prevalent—particularly in the developing world—than landlines; as expensive as mobile phone calls can be, they are still usually a much cheaper option than calling from your hotel.

Because of the recent increase in demand for mobile phones in Brazil, an extra digit has been added to mobile phone numbers to make more numbers available. If calling a mobile phone in the states of São Paulo, Rio, Espírito Santo, Amapá, Amazonas, Maranhão, Pará, and Roraima, make sure to add a 9 in front of the usual eight digits of the number. The rest of the country will be included in this change by the end of 2016.

The country code for Brazil is 55. When dialing a Brazilian number from abroad, dial the international access code of your home country, the Brazilian country code, the two-digit area code (drop the initial 0 if there is one), and the local number.

Public phones are everywhere and are called *orelhões* (big ears) because of their shape. The phones take phone cards only.

CALLING WITHIN BRAZIL

Local calls can be made most easily from pay phones, which take phone cards only. A bar or restaurant may allow you to use its private phone for a local call if you're a customer.

If you want to call from your hotel, remember long-distance calls within Brazil are expensive, and hotels add a surcharge.

With the privatization of the Brazilian telecommunications network, there's a wide choice of long-distance companies. Hence, to make direct-dial long-distance calls, you must find out which companies serve the area from which you're calling and then get their access codes—the staff at your hotel can help. (Some hotels have already made the choice for you, so you may not need an access code when calling from the hotel itself.) For long-distance calls within Brazil, dial 0 + the access code + the area code and number. To call Rio, for example, dial 0, then 21 (for Embratel, a major long-distance and international provider), then 21 (Rio's area code), and then the number.

CALLING OUTSIDE BRAZIL

International calls from Brazil are extremely expensive. Hotels also add a surcharge, increasing this cost even more. Calls can be made from public phone booths with a prepaid phone card. You can also try going to a phone office, although with the rise of mobile phones, very few of these still exist. The staff at your hotel may know whether there is one nearby.

For international calls, dial 00 + 23 (for Intelig, a long-distance company) or 21 (for Embratel, another long-distance company) + the country code + the area code and number. For operator-assisted international calls, dial 00–0111. For international information, dial 00–0333. To make a collect long-distance call (which will cost 40% more than a normal call), dial 9 + the area code and the number.

The country code for United States and Canada is 1.

AT&T and Sprint operators are also accessible from Brazil; get the local access codes before you leave home.

Access Codes **AT&T Direct.** ☎ *0800/703–6335 for individuals* ⊕ *www.att.com/esupport/traveler.jsp.* **Sprint International Access.** ☎ *866/866–7509* ⊕ *mysprint.sprint.com.*

CALLING CARDS

All pay phones in Brazil take phone cards only. Buy a phone card, a *cartão telefônico*, at a newsstand, drugstore, or post office. Cards come with a varying number of units (each unit is usually worth a couple of minutes), which will determine the price. Buy a couple of cards if you don't think you'll have the chance again soon. These phone cards can be used for international, local, and long-distance calls within Brazil. Be aware that calling internationally using these cards is extremely expensive and your units will expire pretty quickly. It's advisable to buy several cards with the maximum number of units (75 minutes). A 20-minute card costs about $1.25, a 50-minute card about $3.25, and a 75-minute about $5.

In big cities like São Paulo and Rio de Janeiro you can buy an international phone card, which is around the same price as the 75-minute local card.

MOBILE PHONES

Big cities in Brazil often have 4G Internet available to anyone with a smartphone, although 3G usually works much better and is more readily available. Roaming charges can be extremely high, however, so make sure to check rates with your provider before arriving in Brazil. Your provider may offer international data plans and should be able to provide details on connectivity. It's a good idea to use local Wi-Fi when available and to make international calls with services like Skype, Viber, or WhatsApp.

If you will be making many local calls and will be in the country for a few weeks, consider buying a new SIM card (note that your provider may have to unlock your phone for you), and signing up for a pay-as-you-go plan. You'll then have a local number and can make calls at local rates. Be aware that as a non-Brazilian

you must show proof of citizenship (such as a passport) to buy a SIM card, which costs around $10. Note that you'll use up the credit on your SIM card more quickly when calling numbers in a Brazilian state other than the one in which you purchased the card. Many travelers buy a new SIM card in each state they visit. If you plan on visiting rural areas, find out from locals which mobile phone provider works best in the area before buying your SIM card. There are often several available, but one or two providers tend to get better coverage because of tower locations, especially in Amazonas.

▍ EATING OUT

Food in Brazil is delicious, inexpensive (especially compared with North America and Europe), and bountiful. Portions are huge and presentation is tasteful. A lot of restaurants prepare plates for two people; when you order, be sure to ask if one plate will suffice—or even better, glance around to see the size of portions at other tables.

In major cities the variety of eateries is staggering: restaurants of all sizes and categories, snack bars, and fast-food outlets line downtown streets and fight for space in shopping malls. Pricing systems vary from open menus to buffets where you weigh your plate. In São Paulo, for example, Italian eateries—whose risottos rival those of Bologna—sit beside pan-Asian restaurants, which, like the chicest spots in North America and Europe, serve everything from Thai *satay* to sushi. In addition, there are excellent Portuguese, Chinese, Japanese, Lebanese, and Spanish restaurants.

Outside the cities you find primarily typical, low-cost Brazilian meals that consist simply of *feijão preto* (black beans) and *arroz* (rice) served with beef, chicken, or fish. Manioc, a root vegetable that's used in a variety of ways, and beef are adored everywhere.

Many Brazilian dishes are adaptations of Portuguese specialties. Fish stews called *caldeiradas* and beef stews called *cozidos* (a wide variety of vegetables boiled with different cuts of beef and pork) are popular, as is *bacalhau,* salt cod cooked in sauce or grilled. *Salgados* (literally, "salteds") are appetizers or snacks served in sit-down restaurants as well as at stand-up *lanchonetes* (luncheonettes). Dried salted meats form the basis of many dishes from the interior and Northeast of Brazil, and pork is used heavily in dishes from Minas Gerais. Brazil's national dish is *feijoada* (a stew of black beans, sausage, pork, and beef), which is often served with rice, shredded kale, orange slices, and manioc flour or meal—called *farofa* if it's coarsely ground, *farinha* if finely ground—that has been fried with onions, oil, and egg.

One of the most avid national passions is the *churrascaria,* where meats are roasted on spits over an open fire, usually *rodízio* style. *Rodízio* means "going around," and waiters circulate nonstop carrying skewers laden with charbroiled hunks of beef, pork, and chicken, which are sliced onto your plate with ritualistic ardor. For a set price you get all the meat and side dishes you can eat. Starve yourself a little before going to a rodízio place. Then you can sample everything on offer.

At the other end of the spectrum, vegetarians can sometimes find Brazil's meat-centric culture challenging, especially outside larger cities. Increasingly, though, salads and vegetarian options are offered at nicer restaurants in areas catering to foodies, tourists, and those with more international tastes. You'll also find salads at buffet restaurants, called *quilos,* found throughout Brazil.

Brazilian *doces* (desserts), particularly those of Bahia, are very sweet, and many are descendants of the egg-based custards and puddings of Portugal and France. *Cocada* is shredded coconut caked with sugar; *quindim* is a small tart made from egg yolks and coconut; *doce de banana* (or any other fruit) is banana cooked in sugar; *ambrosia* is a lumpy milk-and-sugar pudding.

Coffee is served black and strong with sugar in demitasse cups and is called *cafezinho.* (Requests for *descafeinado* [decaf] are met with a firm shake of the head "no," a blank stare, or outright amusement.) Coffee is taken with milk—called *café com leite*—only at breakfast. Bottled water (*agua mineral*) is sold carbonated or plain (*com gás* and *sem gás,* respectively).

MEALS AND MEALTIMES

Between the extremes of sophistication and austere simplicity, each region has its own cuisine. You find exotic fish dishes in the Amazon, African-spiced dishes in Bahia, and well-seasoned bean mashes in Minas Gerais.

It's hard to find breakfast (*café da manhã*) outside a hotel restaurant, but in bakeries (*padarias*) you can always find something breakfast-like. At lunch (*almoço*) and dinner (*jantar*) portions are large. Often a single dish will easily feed two people; no one will be the least bit surprised if you order one entrée and ask for two plates. In addition some restaurants automatically bring a *couvert* (an appetizer course of such items as bread, cheese, or pâté, olives, quail eggs, and the like). You'll be charged extra for this, and you're perfectly within your rights to send it back if you don't want it.

Mealtimes vary according to locale. In Rio and São Paulo, lunch and dinner are served later than in the United States. In restaurants lunch usually starts around noon and can last until 3. Dinner is always eaten after 7 and in many cases not until 10. In Minas Gerais, the Northeast, and smaller towns in general, dinner and lunch are taken at roughly the same time as in the States.

Unless otherwise noted, the restaurants listed in this guide are open daily for lunch and dinner.

PAYING

Credit cards are widely accepted at restaurants in the major cities. In the countryside all but the smallest establishments generally accept credit cards as well, but check before you order. Smaller, family-run restaurants are sometimes cash-only. Gratuity is 10% of the total sum, and it's usually included in the bill. The tip is always optional; if you weren't happy with the service, you can ask for it to be removed from your bill.

For more tip guidelines, see Tipping.

RESERVATIONS AND DRESS
Appropriate dress for dinner in Brazil can vary dramatically. As a general rule, dress more formally for expensive restaurants. In most restaurants dress is casual.

Regardless of where you are, it's a good idea to make a reservation if you can. We only mention them specifically when reservations are essential (there's no other way you'll ever get a table) or when they're not accepted. For popular restaurants, book as far ahead as you can (often 30 days), and reconfirm as soon as you arrive. (Large parties should always call ahead to check the reservations policy.) We mention dress only when men are required to wear a jacket or a jacket and tie.

WINES, BEER, AND SPIRITS
The national drink is the *caipirinha*, made of crushed lime, sugar, and *pinga* or *cachaça* (sugarcane liquor). When whipped with crushed ice, fruit juices, and condensed milk, the pinga/cachaça becomes a *batida*. A *caipivodka*, or *caipiroska*, is the same cocktail with vodka instead of cachaça. Most bars also make both drinks using a fruit other than lime, such as kiwi and *maracujá* (passion fruit). Brazil has many brands of bottled beer. In general, though, Brazilians prefer tap beer, called *chopp*, which is sold in bars and restaurants. Be sure to try the carbonated soft drink *guaraná*, made using the Amazonian fruit of the same name. It's extremely popular in Brazil.

▌ ELECTRICITY
The current in Brazil isn't regulated: in São Paulo and Rio it's 110 or 120 volts (the same as in the United States and Canada); in Recife and Brasília it's 220 volts (the same as in Europe); and in Manaus and Salvador it's 127 volts. Electricity is AC (alternating current) at 60 Hz, similar to that in Europe. To use electric-powered equipment purchased in the United States or Canada, it's wise to bring a converter and adapter, although these days, increasingly, most electronics are designed to convert themselves—if your device specifies a range of 100 to 240 volts, you won't have any problem using it in Brazil. Wall outlets take Continental-type plugs, with two or three round prongs, although you may come across older outlets that take two-pronged flat plugs. Consider buying a universal adapter, which has several types of plugs in one handy unit. Some hotels are equipped to handle various types of plugs and electrical devices.

▌ EMERGENCIES
In case of emergency, call one of the services below. Calling the fire brigade is a good option, since they're considered one of the most efficient and trustworthy institutions in Brazil. If you need urgent and immediate support, talk to the people around you. Brazilians are friendly and willing to help. They'll go out of their way to speak your language and find help.

If you've been robbed or assaulted, report it to the police. Unfortunately, you shouldn't expect huge results for your trouble. Call your embassy if your passport has been stolen or if you need help dealing with the police.

General Emergency Contacts
Federal Highway Patrol. ☎ *191.* **Fire Brigade (Bombeiros).** ☎ *193* ⊕ *www. bombeirosemergencia.com.br.* **Police.** ☎ *190.* **Ambulance.** ☎ *192.* **Civil Defence.** ☎ *199.*

■ HEALTH

The most common types of illnesses are caused by contaminated food and water. Especially in developing countries, drink only bottled, boiled, or purified water and drinks; don't drink from public fountains or use ice. It's even prudent to use bottled water to brush your teeth. Make sure food has been thoroughly cooked and is served to you fresh and hot; avoid vegetables and fruits that you haven't washed (in bottled or purified water) or peeled yourself. If you have problems, mild cases of traveler's diarrhea may respond to over-the-counter medications. Be sure to drink plenty of fluids; if you can't keep fluids down, seek medical help immediately.

Infectious diseases can be airborne or passed via mosquitoes and ticks and through direct or indirect physical contact with animals or people. Some, including Norwalk-like viruses that affect your digestive tract, can be passed along through contaminated food. If you're traveling in an area where malaria is prevalent, use a repellent containing DEET and take malaria-prevention medication before, during, and after your trip as directed by your physician. Speak with your physician and/or check the CDC or World Health Organization websites for health alerts, particularly if you're pregnant, traveling with children, or have a chronic illness.

English-speaking medical assistance in Brazil is rare. It's best to contact your consulate or embassy if you need medical help. Seek private clinics or hospitals, since getting an appointment in the government's health-care system is a slow process.

■ TIP➔ If you're traveling to the Amazon, extra precautions are necessary.

DIVERS' ALERT

Do not fly within 24 hours of scuba diving. Neophyte divers should have a complete physical exam before undertaking a dive. If you have travel insurance that covers evacuations, make sure your policy applies to scuba-related injuries, as not all companies provide this coverage.

FOOD AND DRINK

The major health risk in Brazil is traveler's diarrhea, caused by eating contaminated fruit or vegetables or drinking contaminated water. So watch what you eat—on and off the beaten path. Avoid ice, uncooked food, and unpasteurized milk and milk products, and drink only bottled water or water that has been boiled for at least 20 minutes, even when brushing your teeth. The use of bottled water for brushing your teeth is not necessary in large cities, where water is treated. Don't use ice unless you know it's made from purified water. (Ice in city restaurants is usually safe.) Peel or thoroughly wash fresh fruits and vegetables. Avoid eating food from street vendors.

Choose industrially packaged beverages when you can. Order tropical juices only from places that appear clean and reliable.

INFECTIOUS DISEASES AND VIRUSES

The Amazon and a few other remote areas are the only places in Brazil where you really need worry about infectious diseases. Most travelers to Brazil return home unscathed. However, you should visit a doctor at least six weeks prior to traveling to discuss recommended vaccinations, some of which require multiple shots over a period of weeks. If you get sick weeks, months, or in rare cases, years after your trip, make sure your doctor administers blood tests for tropical diseases.

Meningococcal meningitis and typhoid fever are common in certain areas of Brazil—and not only in remote areas like the Amazon. Meningitis has been a problem around São Paulo in recent years. Dengue fever and malaria—both caused by mosquito bites—are common in Brazil or in certain areas of Brazil, like Rio de Janeiro. Both are usually only a problem in the Amazon, but dengue can affect urban areas and malaria is sometimes found in urban peripheries. Talk with your doctor about what precautions to take.

PESTS AND OTHER HAZARDS

You'll likely encounter more insects than you're used to in Brazil, but they generally only present health problems in the Amazon.

Heatstroke and heat prostration are common though easily preventable maladies throughout Brazil. The symptoms for either can vary but always start with headaches, nausea, and dizziness. If ignored, these symptoms can worsen until you require medical attention. In hot weather be sure to rehydrate regularly, wear loose lightweight clothing, and avoid overexerting yourself.

OVER-THE-COUNTER REMEDIES

Mild cases of diarrhea may respond to Imodium (known generically as loperamide) or Pepto-Bismol (not as strong), both of which can be purchased over the counter at a *farmácia* (pharmacy). Drink plenty of purified water or *chá* (tea)—*camomila* (chamomile) is a good folk remedy, as is dissolving a tablespoon of cornstarch in a mix of lime juice and water. In severe cases rehydrate yourself with a salt–sugar solution: ½ teaspoon *sal* (salt) and 4 tablespoons *açúcar* (sugar) per quart of *agua* (water).

An effective home remedy for diarrhea is the same as the rehydrating concoction: a teaspoon of sugar plus a quarter teaspoon of salt in a liter of water.

Aspirin is *aspirina*; Tylenol (acetaminophen; paracetamol) is pronounced *tee-luh-nawl*. Advil (ibuprofen) is ah-jee-viu.

SHOTS AND MEDICATIONS

■ TIP➜ If you travel a lot internationally—particularly to developing nations—refer to the CDC's Health Information for International Travel (aka Traveler's Health Yellow Book). Info from it is posted on the CDC website (wwwnc.cdc.gov/travel).

The best recommendation to avoid health problems is to see a doctor before and after traveling, just to be on the safe side. Some vaccines must be applied long before traveling so that their protective effect is guaranteed, and some prophylactic medicines must be taken also in advance so that the doctor and the patient are aware of possible side effects.

Vaccinations against hepatitis A and B, meningitis, typhoid, and yellow fever are highly recommended. Consult your doctor about whether to get a rabies vaccination. Check with the CDC's International Travelers' Hotline if you plan to visit remote regions or stay for more than six weeks.

Discuss the option of taking antimalarial drugs with your doctor. Note that in parts of northern Brazil a particularly aggressive strain of malaria has become resistant to one antimalarial drug—chloroquine. Some antimalarial drugs have rather unpleasant side effects—from headaches, nausea, and dizziness to psychosis, convulsions, and hallucinations.

For travel anywhere in Brazil, it's recommended that you have updated vaccines for diphtheria, tetanus, and polio. Children must additionally have current inoculations against measles, mumps, and rubella.

Yellow fever immunization is compulsory to enter Brazil if you're traveling directly from one of the following countries in South America (or from one of several African countries): Bolivia; Colombia; Ecuador; French Guiana; Peru; or Venezuela. You must have an International Certificate of Immunization proving that you've been vaccinated.

Health Warnings National Centers for Disease Control & Prevention (*CDC*). ☎ *800/232–4636* ⊕ *www.cdc.gov.* World Health Organization (*WHO*). ⊕ *www.who.int.*

■ MONEY

Brazil's unit of currency is the *real* (R$; plural: *reais*). One real is 100 *centavos* (cents). There are notes worth 2, 5, 10, 20, 50, and 100 reais, together with coins worth 5, 10, 25, and 50 centavos and 1 real.

ATMS AND BANKS

Your own bank will probably charge a fee for using ATMs abroad; the foreign bank you use may also charge a fee. Nevertheless, you'll usually get a better rate of exchange at an ATM than you will at a currency-exchange office. And extracting funds as you need them is a safer option than carrying around a large amount of cash.

■ TIP➜ **PINs with more than four digits are not recognized at ATMs in many countries. If yours has five or more, remember to change it before you leave.**

Nearly all the nation's major banks have ATMs, known in Brazil as *caixas eletrônicos,* for which you must use a card with a credit-card logo. MasterCard/Cirrus holders can withdraw at Banco Itau, Banco do Brasil, HSBC, and Banco24horas ATMs; Visa holders can use Bradesco ATMs and those at Banco do Brasil. American Express cardholders can make withdrawals at most Bradesco ATMs marked "24 horas." To be on the safe side, carry a variety of cards. For your card to function in some ATMs, you may need to hit a screen command (perhaps, *estrangeiro* or *inglês*) if you are a foreign client.

Banks are, with a few exceptions, open weekdays 10 to 4. Avoid using ATM machines alone and at night, and use ATMs in busy, highly visible locations whenever possible.

CREDIT CARDS

It's a good idea to inform your credit-card company before you travel, especially if you're going abroad and don't travel internationally very often. Otherwise, the credit-card company might put a hold on your card owing to unusual activity—not a good thing halfway through your trip. Record all your credit-card numbers— as well as the phone numbers to call if your cards are lost or stolen—in a safe place, so you're prepared should something go wrong. Both MasterCard and Visa have general numbers you can call (collect if you're abroad) if your card is lost, but you're better off calling the number of your issuing bank, since Master-Card and Visa usually just transfer you to your bank; your bank's number is usually printed on your card.

If you plan to use your credit card for cash advances, you'll need to apply for a PIN at least two weeks before your trip. Although it's usually cheaper (and safer) to use a credit card abroad for large purchases (so you can cancel payments or be reimbursed if there's a problem), note that some credit-card companies *and* the banks that issue them add substantial percentages to all foreign transactions, whether they're in a foreign currency or not. Check on these fees before leaving home, so there won't be any surprises when you get the bill. Credit-card fraud does happen in Brazil, so always conceal PIN numbers and keep your receipts.

■ TIP➜ **Before you charge something, ask the merchant whether he or she plans to do a dynamic currency conversion (DCC). In such a transaction the credit-card processor (shop, restaurant, or hotel, not Visa or MasterCard) converts the currency and charges you in dollars. In most cases you'll pay the merchant a 3% fee for this service in addition to any credit-card company and issuing-bank foreign-transaction surcharges.**

Dynamic currency conversion programs are becoming increasingly widespread. Merchants who participate in them are supposed to ask whether you want to be charged in dollars or the local currency, but they don't always do so. And even if they do offer you a choice, they may well avoid mentioning the additional surcharges. The good news is that you *do* have a choice. And if this practice really gets your goat, you can avoid it entirely thanks to American Express; with its cards, DCC simply isn't an option.

In Brazil's largest cities and leading tourist centers, restaurants, hotels, and shops accept major international credit cards.

Off the beaten track, you may have more difficulty using them. Many gas stations in rural Brazil don't take credit cards.

For costly items use your credit card whenever possible—you'll come out ahead, whether the exchange rate at which your purchase is calculated is the one in effect the day the vendor's bank abroad processes the charge or the one prevailing on the day the charge company's service center processes it at home.

Reporting Lost Cards American Express.
☎ *800/528–4800 in U.S., 336/393–1111 collect from abroad* ⊕ *www.americanexpress. com.* **Diners Club.** ☎ *800/234–6377 in U.S., 514/881–3735 collect from abroad* ⊕ *www. dinersclub.com.* **MasterCard.** ☎ *800/627–8372 in U.S., 636/722–7111 collect from abroad, 0800/891–3294 in Brazil* ⊕ *www.mastercard. com.* **Visa.** ☎ *800/847–2911 in U.S., 410/581– 9994 collect from abroad, 0800/891–3679 in Brazil* ⊕ *www.visa.com.*

CURRENCY AND EXCHANGE

At this writing, the real is at about 2.87 to the U.S. dollar and 2.30 to the Canadian dollar.

For the most favorable rates, change money through banks. Although ATM transaction fees may be higher abroad than at home, ATM rates are excellent because they're based on wholesale rates offered only by major banks. You won't do as well at *casas de câmbio* (exchange houses), in airports or bus stations, in hotels, in restaurants, or in stores. ATMs also allow you to avoid the often long lines at airport exchange booths.

Outside larger cities, changing money in Brazil becomes more of a challenge. When leaving a large city for a smaller town, bring enough cash for your trip.

■ **TIP→ Even if a currency-exchange booth has a sign promising no commission, rest assured that there's some kind of huge, hidden fee. And as for rates, you're almost always better off getting foreign currency at an ATM or exchanging money at a bank.**

■ PACKING

For sightseeing, casual clothing and good walking shoes are appropriate; most restaurants don't require formal attire. For beach vacations, bring lightweight sportswear, a bathing suit, a beach cover-up, a sun hat, and waterproof sunscreen that is at least SPF 30. A sarong or a light cotton blanket makes a handy beach towel, picnic blanket, and cushion for hard seats, among other things.

If you're going to coastal cities like Rio, Florianópolis, and Salvador in summer (December, January, and February), dress more informally and feel free to wear flip-flops (thongs) all day—and don't forget your sunglasses. Southeastern cities like São Paulo, Curitiba, and Porto Alegre, which have lower temperatures, tend to be more formal and more conservative when it comes to clothing (sometimes even Brazilians are shocked by the way people in Rio dress). In urban areas it's always a good idea to have some nice outfits for going out at night.

Travel in rain-forest areas requires long-sleeved shirts, long pants, socks, waterproof hiking boots (sneakers are less desirable, but work in a pinch), a hat, a light waterproof jacket, a bathing suit, and plenty of strong insect repellent. (Amazonian bugs tend to be oblivious to non-DEET or non-picaridin repellents.) Other useful items include a screw-top water container that you can fill with bottled water, a money pouch, a travel flashlight and extra batteries, a Swiss Army knife with a bottle opener, a medical kit, binoculars, a pocket calculator, spare camera batteries, and a high-capacity memory card.

■ PASSPORTS AND VISAS

At this writing, passports and visas are required for citizens—even infants—of the United States and Canada for entry to Brazil. Business travelers may need a special business visa. It has all the same requirements as a tourist visa, but you'll also need a letter on company letterhead addressed to the embassy or consulate and signed by an authorized representative (other than you), stating the nature of your business in Brazil, itinerary, business contacts, dates of arrival and departure, and that the company assumes all financial and moral responsibility while you're in Brazil.

PASSPORTS

When in Brazil, carry your passport or a copy with you at all times. Make two photocopies of the data page (one for someone at home and another for you, carried separately from your passport). If you lose your passport, promptly call the nearest embassy or consulate and the local police.

If your passport is lost or stolen, first call the police—having the police report can make replacement easier—and then call your embassy. You'll get a temporary Emergency Travel Document that will need to be replaced once you return home. Fees vary according to how fast you need the passport; in some cases the fee covers your permanent replacement as well. The new document will not have your entry stamps; ask if your embassy takes care of this, or whether it's your responsibility to get the necessary immigration authorization.

Contacts Brazilian Embassy. ☎ *202/238–2700* ⊕ *washington.itamaraty.gov.br/en-us.* **Brazilian Embassy.** ☎ *613/237–1090* ⊕ *ottawa.itamaraty.gov.br/pt-br.*

VISAS

A visa is essentially formal permission to enter a country. Visas allow countries to keep track of you and other visitors—and generate revenue (from application fees).

Go to the website for the Brazilian embassy or consulate nearest you for the most up-to-date visa information. At this writing, tourist visa fees are US$160 for Americans and C$81.25 for Canadians. Additional fees may be levied if you apply by mail. Obtaining a visa can be a slow process, and you must have every bit of paperwork in order when you visit the consulate, so read instructions carefully. (For example, in the United States, the fee can only be paid by a U.S. Postal Service money order.)

To get the location of the Brazilian consulate to which you must apply, contact the Brazilian embassy. Note that some consulates don't allow you to apply for a visa by mail. If you don't live near a city with a consulate, consider hiring a concierge-type service to do your legwork. Many cities have these companies, which not only help with the paperwork, but also send someone to wait in line for you.

When you apply by mail, you send your passport to a designated consulate, where your passport will be examined and the visa issued. Expediters—usually the same ones who handle expedited passport applications—can do all the work of obtaining your visa for you; however, there's always an additional cost (often at least $50 per visa).

Most visas limit you to a single trip—basically during the actual dates of your planned vacation. Other visas allow you to visit as many times as you wish for a specific period of time. Remember that requirements change, sometimes at the drop of a hat, and the burden is on you to make sure that you have the appropriate visas. Otherwise, you'll be turned away at the airport or, worse, deported after you arrive in the country. No company or travel insurer gives refunds if your travel plans are disrupted because you didn't have the correct visa.

U.S. Passport Information U.S. Department of State. ☎ *877/487–2778* ⊕ *travel.state.gov.*

U.S. Passport and Visa Expediters A. Briggs Passport & Visa Expeditors. ☎ *800/806–0581, 202/338–0111* ⊕ *www.abriggs.com.* **American Passport Express.** ☎ *800/455–5166,* ⊕ *www.americanpassport.com.* **Passport Express.** ☎ *800/362–8196* ⊕ *www. passportexpress.com.* **Travel Document Systems.** ☎ *800/874–5100, 202/638–3800* ⊕ *www.traveldocs.com.* **Travel the World**

Visas. ☎ *866/886–8472, 202/223–8822* ⊕ *www.world-visa.com.*

GENERAL REQUIREMENTS FOR BRAZIL	
Passport	Must be valid for 6 months after date of arrival.
Visa	Required for Americans (US$160) and Canadians (C$81.25)
Vaccinations	Needed in some areas: yellow fever and diphtheria. Recommended for all travelers but not mandatory: hepatitis A and B, typhoid, meningitis, tetanus, polio.
Driving	Driver's license with Portuguese translation or international driver's license required; CDW is compulsory on car rentals and will be included in the quoted price.
Departure Tax	Approximately R$82 ($30), payable in cash only

▮ RESTROOMS

The word for "bathroom" is *banheiro,* though the term *sanitários* (toilets) is also used. *Homens* means "men" and *mulheres* means "women." Around major tourist attractions and along the main beaches in big cities, you can find public restrooms, which aren't necessarily clean. In some smaller beach cities, there are no facilities at the beach, so be prepared to walk a bit to find a bathroom. In other areas you may have to rely on the kindness of local restaurant and shop owners. If a smile and polite request (*"Por favor, posso usar o banheiro?"*) doesn't work, become a customer—the purchase of a drink or a knickknack might just buy you a trip to the bathroom. Rest areas with relatively clean, well-equipped bathrooms are plentiful along major highways. Still, carry a pocket-size package of tissues in case there's no toilet paper. Tip bathroom attendants with a few spare centavos.

▮ TAXES

Sales tax is included in the prices shown on goods in stores but listed separately on the bottom of your receipt. Hotel, meal, and car-rental taxes are usually tacked on in addition to the costs shown on menus and brochures. At this writing, hotel taxes are roughly 5%, meal taxes 10%, and car-rental taxes 12%.

Departure taxes on international flights from Brazil aren't always included in your ticket and can run as high as R$82 ($30); domestic flights may incur a R$22 ($8) tax. Although U.S. dollars are accepted in some airports, be prepared to pay departure taxes in reais.

▮ TIME

Brazil covers four time zones. Most of the country—including Rio, São Paulo, Porto Alegre, Salvador, Brasília, and Belo Horizonte—is three hours behind GMT (Greenwich mean time). Manaus and Pantanal are an hour behind those cities, and the far western Amazon is an hour behind Manaus. Fernando de Noronha, an archipelago off Brazil's northeast coast, is two hours behind GMT. From October to March (exact days vary), Brazil observes daylight saving time in most of the country, so in many areas it stays light until 8:30 pm.

▮ TIPPING

Wages can be paltry in Brazil, so a little generosity in tipping can go a long way. Tipping in dollars is not recommended—at best it's insulting; at worst, you might be targeted for a robbery. Large hotels that receive lots of international guests are the exception. Some restaurants add a 10% service charge onto the check. If there's no service charge, you can leave as much as you want, but 15% is a good amount. In deluxe hotels tip porters R$2 per bag, chambermaids R$2 per day, and bellhops R$4–R$6 for room and valet service. Tips for doormen and concierges vary, depending on the services provided. A good tip is around R$30, with the average at about R$15. For moderate and inexpensive hotels, tips tend to be minimal (salaries are so low that virtually anything is well received). If a taxi driver helps you with your luggage, a per-bag charge of about R$1 is levied in addition to the fare. In general, you don't tip taxi drivers. If a service station attendant does anything beyond filling up the gas tank, leave him a small tip of some spare change. Tipping in bars and cafés follows the rules of restaurants, although at outdoor bars Brazilians rarely leave a gratuity if they have had only a soft drink or a beer. At airports and at train and bus stations, tip the last porter who puts your bags into the cab (R$1 a bag at airports, 50 centavos a bag at bus and train stations).

▌ VISITOR INFORMATION

EMBRATUR, Brazil's national tourism organization, doesn't have offices overseas, though its website is helpful. For information in your home country, contact the Brazilian embassy or the closest consulate, some of which have websites and staff dedicated to promoting tourism. The official consular website in New York, ⊕ *novayork.itamaraty.gov.br/en-us*, has details about other consulates and the embassy as well as travel information and links to other sites. Cities and towns throughout Brazil have local tourist boards, and some state capitals also have state tourism offices.

Contacts Brazilian Consulate–New York. ☎ *917/777–7777* ⊕ *www.brazilny.org.* **EMBRA-TUR.** ☎ *61/2023–7146 in Brazil* ⊕ *www. visitbrasil.com.*

ONLINE RESOURCES

The like-minded travelers on Fodors.com are eager to answer questions and swap travel tales. For further information you may have to search by region, state, or city—and hope that at least one of them has a comprehensive official site of its own.

The online magazine *Brazzil* and Internet newspaper the Rio Times Online have interesting English-language articles on culture and politics. Brazil's biggest national newspaper, *Folha de S.Paulo*, also publishes its content in English and Spanish on the international version of its site. Gringoes.com is an online forum for foreigners living in or traveling to Brazil, where you'll find info about everything from security to getting a driver's license. And VivaBrazil.com provides background and travel info on Brazil's different regions as well as links that will help you arrange your trip.

All About Brazil Brazzil Magazine. ⊕ *www. brazzil.com.* **Folha de S.Paulo.** ⊕ *www1.folha. uol.com.br/internacional/en.* **Gringoes.com.** ⊕ *www.gringoes.com.* **Rio Times Online.** ⊕ *www.riotimesonline.com.* **VivaBrazil.com.** ⊕ *www.vivabrazil.com.*

INDEX

PHOTO CREDITS

Front cover: SNEHIT / Shutterstock [Description: Rio De Janeiro, Brazil]. 1, Alexandre Fagundes De Fagundes I Dreamstime.com. 2, Tony1 I Dreamstime.com. 4, Ekaterinabelova I Dreamstime.com. 5 (top), Celso Pupo/Shutterstock. 5 (bottom), Alexandre Fagundes De Fagundes I Dreamstime.com. 6 (top left), Gianluca Curti/Shutterstock. 6 (bottom left), HandmadePictures/Shutterstock. 6 (top right), Mircea BEZERGHEANU/Shutterstock. 6 (bottom right), LAND/Shutterstock. 7 (top), Sfmthd I Dreamstime.com. 7 (bottom), Paura I Dreamstime.com. 8 (top left), Maxisport/Shutterstock. 8 (top right), Yadid Levy / age fotostock. 8 (bottom), Travel Pix / Alamy. Chapter 1: Experience Brazil: 13, travelstock44 / Alamy. 14, Halaska/Mauritius/age fotostock. 15 (left), Ken Ross/viestiphoto.com. 15 (right), giulio andreini/Marka/age fotostock. 20, Blaine Harrington/age fotostock. 21, giulio andreini/Marka/age fotostock. 23, Jeffrey Dunn/viestiphoto.com. 25 (left), giulio andreini/Marka/age fotostock. 25 (right), vittorio sciosia/age fotostock. 26, Rechitan Sorin/age fotostock. 27, Jeremy Reddington/age fotostock. 28, PCL / Alamy. 29 (left), Ken Welsh/age fotostock. 29 (right), Bruno Perousse/age fotostock. Chapter 2: Rio de Janeiro: 35, Celsodiniz I Dreamstime.com. Chapter 3: Side Trips from Rio: 117, Icon72 I Dreamstime.com. Chapter 4: Sao Paulo: 149, cifotart/Shutterstock. Chapter 5: Side Trips from Sao Paulo: 213, Katoton I Dreamstime.com. Chapter 6: The South: 237, Afagundes I Dreamstime. com. 256, Fritz Poelking/ age fotostock. Chapter 7: Minas Gerais: 289, Pixattitude I Dreamstime.com. Chapter 8: Brasilia and the West: 329, ostill/Shutterstock. Chapter 9: Salvador and the Bahia Coast: 367, Alfredo Borba/Shutterstock. Chapter 10: The Northeast: 421, sohadiszno/Shutterstock. Chapter 10: The Amazon: 461, Dirk Ercken/Shutterstock. Back cover, from left to right: JM-Design / Shutterstock; Damian Palus / Shutterstock; Gigi Peis / Shutterstock. Spine: Mark Schwettmann/Shutterstock.

Welcome To The Rio Olympics insert: 1 (top), Stephen Frink Collection / Alamy. 1 (bottom), Courtesy of Rio 2016™ Committee. 2, Fernando Maia I Rio Tur. 3, John Biever/Sports Illustrated/Getty Images. 4, J.P. Engelbrecht I Rio Tur. 5, Ian Trower/ AWL Images Ltd. 6, Epa European Pressphoto Agency b.v. / Alamy. 7, T photography / Shutterstock. 8, Filipe Frazao / Shutterstock.

About Our Writers: All photos are courtesy of the writers except for the following: Catherine Balston, courtesy of Harry Balston; Mark Beresford, courtesy of Ludmilla Diniz; Lucy Bryson, courtesy of Ademar Ribiero.

NOTES

NOTES

NOTES

NOTES

NOTES

NOTES

Fodor's BRAZIL

Publisher: Amanda D'Acierno, *Senior Vice President*

Editorial: Arabella Bowen, *Editor in Chief*; Linda Cabasin, *Editorial Director*

Design: Tina Malaney, *Associate Art Director*; Chie Ushio, *Senior Designer*

Photography: Jennifer Arnow, *Senior Photo Editor*; Mary Robnett, *Photo Researcher*

Production: Linda Schmidt, *Managing Editor*; Evangelos Vasilakis, *Associate Managing Editor*; Angela L. McLean, *Senior Production Manager*

Maps: Rebecca Baer, *Senior Map Editor*; Mark Stroud, Moonstreet Cartography, *Cartographers*

Sales: Jacqueline Lebow, *Sales Director*

Marketing & Publicity: Heather Dalton, *Marketing Director*; Katherine Punia, *Publicity Director*

Business & Operations: Susan Livingston, *Vice President, Strategic Business Planning*; Sue Daulton, *Vice President, Operations*

Fodors.com: Megan Bell, *Executive Director, Revenue & Business Development*; Yasmin Marinaro, *Senior Director, Marketing & Partnerships*

Writers: Catherine Balston, Mark Beresford, Lucy Bryson, Lauren Holmes, Jill Langlois, Angelica Mari, Claire Rigby

Editors: Luke Epplin, Kathryn Lane, Denise M. Leto

Production Editor: Evangelos Vasilakis

7th Edition

ISBN 978-1-101-87832-3

ISSN 0163-0628

SPECIAL SALES

This book is available at special discounts for bulk purchases for sales promotions or premiums. For more information, e-mail specialmarkets@penguinrandomhouse.com.

PRINTED IN THE UNITED STATES OF AMERICA

10 9 8 7 6 5 4 3 2 1

ABOUT OUR WRITERS

Catherine Balston moved to São Paulo from London in 2009, just for a year or two, and six years on she can't imagine living anywhere else. After three years editing the Food and Drink section of *Time Out São Paulo,* she has become something of an expert on Brazilian cuisine, and now writes about food and travel for the British press, including *the Guardian, the Independent,*and *Monocle.* For this edition, Catherine updated the South chapter.

Born in Scotland, **Mark Beresford** has been a resident of the warmer climes of Rio de Janeiro since 2007. He regularly writes about Brazil and Latin America for supplements of the *Wall Street Journal, Barron's,* and other publications. When not cycling along the beaches of the Zona Sul, Mark likes to escape to the hills and old towns of Goiás, his home-away-from-home in Brazil. For this edition, Mark updated the Brasília and the West chapter.

Lucy Bryson is a freelance British writer based in Rio de Janeiro since 2007. She writes for a range of print and web publications and is Rio Local Expert for *USA TODAY 10 Best.* Lucy is author and editor of a Horizon Travel Press ebook about Rio Carnival, and editor of Horizon's upcoming guide to travel in the Amazon. Lucy lives in the beautiful historic neighborhood of Santa Teresa with her Brazilian partner, their British-Brazilian daughter, and their lively carioca dog. For this edition, Lucy updated the Experience Brazil, Rio de Janeiro, and Side Trips from Rio chapters and the Olympics anchor.

Growing up in London, long-time Rio resident **Lauren Holmes** couldn't resist the lure of Brazilian beach life. Working as a freelance journalist for publications like *Monocle, Condé Nast Traveler,* and the *South China Morning Post,* Lauren loves traveling through Brazil, tracking down the best botecos and emerging beach hot spots. For this edition, Lauren updated the Salvador and the Bahia Coast, the Northeast, and the Amazon chapters.

Jill Langlois is a Canadian freelance journalist who has been living in São Paulo since 2010. She has covered Brazil for publications like the *New York Times,*the *Los Angeles Times, USA Today, Fortune,* and *Foreign Policy.* Jill loves searching for hidden gems and new hot spots across the country with her Brazilian husband by her side. For this edition, Jill updated Travel Smart Brazil.

Angelica Mari is a Brazilian journalist based between the city of São Paulo and the mountain resort of Serra Negra. She is a Brazil correspondent for international technology and business titles and also contributes to several travel and lifestyle magazines, mostly on off-the-beaten-track destinations in the states in the southeast of Brazil. For this edition, she updated the Minas Gerais and Side Trips from São Paulo chapters.

Claire Rigby moved to Brazil in 2010 to launch and run *Time Out São Paulo* as its editor in chief, having previously been editor of Time Out's Buenos Aires magazine, and before that, its Mexico City guide. In 2014, she became a freelance journalist, and now reports from Brazil for publications including the *Guardian, New York Times, Monocle,* and *VICE News,* as well as a range of art and travel titles. For this edition, Claire updated the São Paulo chapter.

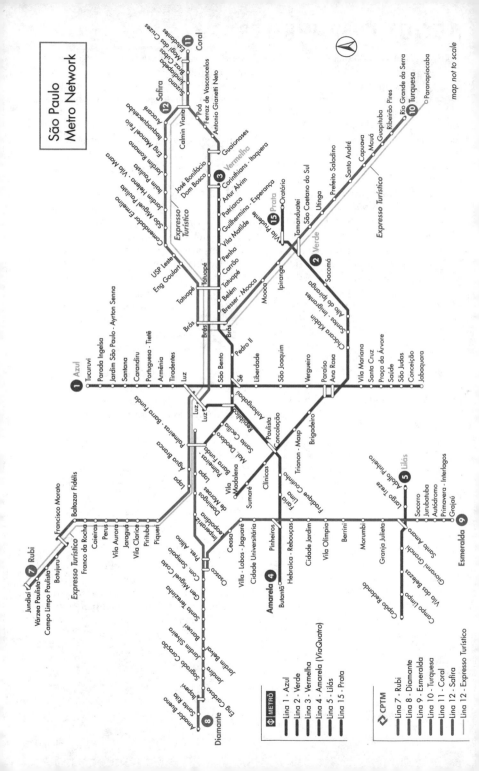